D1289148

Dictionary of Literary Biography • Volume Forty-one

Afro-American Poets Since 1955

Dictionary of Literary Biography

1: *The American Renaissance in New England,* edited by Joel Myerson (1978)

2: *American Novelists Since World War II,* edited by Jeffrey Helterman and Richard Layman (1978)

3: *Antebellum Writers in New York and the South,* edited by Joel Myerson (1979)

4: *American Writers in Paris, 1920-1939,* edited by Karen Lane Rood (1980)

5: *American Poets Since World War II,* 2 parts, edited by Donald J. Greiner (1980)

6: *American Novelists Since World War II,* Second Series, edited by James E. Kibler, Jr. (1980)

7: *Twentieth-Century American Dramatists,* 2 parts, edited by John MacNicholas (1981)

8: *Twentieth-Century American Science-Fiction Writers,* 2 parts, edited by David Cowart and Thomas L. Wymer (1981)

9: *American Novelists, 1910-1945,* 3 parts, edited by James J. Martine (1981)

10: *Modern British Dramatists, 1900-1945,* 2 parts, edited by Stanley Weintraub (1982)

11: *American Humorists, 1800-1950,* 2 parts, edited by Stanley Trachtenberg (1982)

12: *American Realists and Naturalists,* edited by Donald Pizer and Earl N. Harbert (1982)

13: *British Dramatists Since World War II,* 2 parts, edited by Stanley Weintraub (1982)

14: *British Novelists Since 1960,* 2 parts, edited by Jay L. Halio (1983)

15: *British Novelists, 1930-1959,* 2 parts, edited by Bernard Oldsey (1983)

16: *The Beats: Literary Bohemians in Postwar America,* 2 parts, edited by Ann Charters (1983)

17: *Twentieth-Century American Historians,* edited by Clyde N. Wilson (1983)

18: *Victorian Novelists After 1885,* edited by Ira B. Nadel and William E. Fredeman (1983)

19: *British Poets, 1880-1914,* edited by Donald E. Stanford (1983)

20: *British Poets, 1914-1945,* edited by Donald E. Stanford (1983)

21: *Victorian Novelists Before 1885,* edited by Ira B. Nadel and William E. Fredeman (1983)

22: *American Writers for Children, 1900-1960,* edited by John Cech (1983)

23: *American Newspaper Journalists, 1873-1900,* edited by Perry J. Ashley (1983)

24: *American Colonial Writers, 1606-1734,* edited by Emory Elliott (1984)

25: *American Newspaper Journalists, 1901-1925,* edited by Perry J. Ashley (1984)

26: *American Screenwriters,* edited by Robert E. Morsberger, Stephen O. Lesser, and Randall Clark (1984)

27: *Poets of Great Britain and Ireland, 1945-1960,* edited by Vincent B. Sherry, Jr. (1984)

28: *Twentieth-Century American-Jewish Fiction Writers,* edited by Daniel Walden (1984)

29: *American Newspaper Journalists, 1926-1950,* edited by Perry J. Ashley (1984)

30: *American Historians, 1607-1865,* edited by Clyde N. Wilson (1984)

31: *American Colonial Writers, 1735-1781,* edited by Emory Elliott (1984)

32: *Victorian Poets Before 1850,* edited by William E. Fredeman and Ira B. Nadel (1984)

33: *Afro-American Fiction Writers After 1955,* edited by Thadious M. Davis and Trudier Harris (1984)

34: *British Novelists, 1890-1929: Traditionalists,* edited by Thomas F. Staley (1985)

35: *Victorian Poets After 1850,* edited by William E. Fredeman and Ira B. Nadel (1985)

36: *British Novelists, 1890-1929: Modernists,* edited by Thomas F. Staley (1985)

37: *American Writers of the Early Republic,* edited by Emory Elliott (1985)

38: *Afro-American Writers After 1955: Dramatists and Prose Writers,* edited by Thadious M. Davis and Trudier Harris (1985)

39: *British Novelists, 1660-1800,* 2 parts, edited by Martin C. Battestin (1985)

40: *Poets of Great Britain and Ireland Since 1960,* 2 parts, edited by Vincent B. Sherry, Jr. (1985)

41: *Afro-American Poets Since 1955,* edited by Trudier Harris and Thadious M. Davis (1985)

Documentary Series

1: *Sherwood Anderson, Willa Cather, John Dos Passos, Theodore Dreiser, F. Scott Fitzgerald, Ernest Hemingway, Sinclair Lewis,* edited by Margaret A. Van Antwerp (1982)

2: *James Gould Cozzens, James T. Farrell, William Faulkner, John O'Hara, John Steinbeck, Thomas Wolfe, Richard Wright,* edited by Margaret A. Van Antwerp (1982)

3: *Saul Bellow, Jack Kerouac, Norman Mailer, Vladimir Nabokov, John Updike, Kurt Vonnegut,* edited by Mary Bruccoli (1983)

4: *Tennessee Williams,* edited by Margaret A. Van Antwerp and Sally Johns (1984)

Yearbooks

1980, edited by Karen L. Rood, Jean W. Ross, and Richard Ziegfeld (1981)

1981, edited by Karen L. Rood, Jean W. Ross, and Richard Ziegfeld (1982)

1982, edited by Richard Ziegfeld; associate editors: Jean W. Ross and Lynne C. Zeigler (1983)

1983, edited by Mary Bruccoli and Jean W. Ross; associate editor: Richard Ziegfeld (1984)

1984, edited by Jean W. Ross (1985)

Dictionary of Literary Biography • Volume Forty-one

Afro-American Poets Since 1955

Edited by
Trudier Harris and Thadious M. Davis
University of North Carolina at Chapel Hill

A Bruccoli Clark Book
Gale Research Company • Book Tower • Detroit, Michigan 48226

Matthew J. Bruccoli and Richard Layman, *Editorial Directors*
C. E. Frazer Clark, Jr., *Managing Editor*

Printed in the United States of America

Published simultaneously in the United Kingdom
by Gale Research International Limited
(An affiliated company of Gale Research Inc.)

The paper used in this publication meets the minimum requirements of American National Standard for Information Sciences—Permanence Paper for Printed Library Materials, ANSI Z39.48-1984. ™

Library of Congress Cataloging-in-Publication Data
Main entry under title:

Afro-American poets since 1955.

(Dictionary of literary biography; v. 41)
"A Bruccoli Clark book."
Includes index.
1. American poetry—Afro-American authors—History and criticism. 2. American poetry—20th century—History and criticism. 3. American poetry—Afro-American authors—Bio-bibliography. 4. American poetry—20th century—Bio-bibliography. 5. Afro-American poets—Biography—Dictionaries. 6. Poets, American—20th century—Biography—Dictionaries. I. Davis, Thadious M., 1944- II. Harris, Trudier. III. Series
PS153.N5A38 1985 811'.54'09896 85-16093

ISBN 0-8103-1719-2

For
Sam Allen

For
Unareed Harris

Contents

Plan of the Series

. . . Almost the most prodigious asset of a country, and perhaps its most precious possession, is its native literary product—when that product is fine and noble and enduring.

Mark Twain*

The advisory board, the editors, and the publisher of the *Dictionary of Literary Biography* are joined in endorsing Mark Twain's declaration. The literature of a nation provides an inexhaustible resource of permanent worth. It is our expectation that this endeavor will make literature and its creators better understood and more accessible to students and the literate public, while satisfying the standards of teachers and scholars.

To meet these requirements, *literary biography* has been construed in terms of the author's achievement. The most important thing about a writer is his writing. Accordingly, the entries in *DLB* are career biographies, tracing the development of the author's canon and the evolution of his reputation.

The publication plan for *DLB* resulted from two years of preparation. The project was proposed to Bruccoli Clark by Frederick G. Ruffner, president of the Gale Research Company, in November 1975. After specimen entries were prepared and typeset, an advisory board was formed to refine the entry format and develop the series rationale. In meetings held during 1976, the publisher, series editors, and advisory board approved the scheme for a comprehensive biographical dictionary of persons who contributed to North American literature. Editorial work on the first volume began in January 1977, and it was published in 1978.

In order to make *DLB* more than a reference tool and to compile volumes that individually have claim to status as literary history, it was decided to organize volumes by topic or period or genre. Each of these freestanding volumes provides a biographical-bibliographical guide and overview for a particular area of literature. We are convinced that this organization—as opposed to a single alphabet method—constitutes a valuable innovation in the presentation of reference material. The volume plan necessarily requires many decisions for the placement and treatment of authors who might properly be included in two or three volumes. In some instances a major figure will be included in separate volumes, but with different entries emphasizing the aspect of his career appropriate to each volume. Ernest Hemingway, for example, is represented in *American Writers in Paris, 1920-1939* by an entry focusing on his expatriate apprenticeship; he is also in *American Novelists, 1910-1945* with an entry surveying his entire career. Each volume includes a cumulative index of subject authors. The final *DLB* volume will be a comprehensive index to the entire series.

With volume ten in 1982 it was decided to enlarge the scope of *DLB* beyond the literature of the United States. By the end of 1984 fourteen volumes treating British literature had been published, and volumes for Commonwealth and Modern European literature were in progress. The series has been further augmented by the *DLB Yearbooks* (since 1981) which update published entries and add new entries to keep the *DLB* current with contemporary activity. There have also been occasional *DLB Documentary Series* volumes which provide biographical and critical background source materials for figures whose work is judged to have particular interest for students. One of these companion volumes is entirely devoted to Tennessee Williams.

The purpose of *DLB* is not only to provide reliable information in a convenient format but also to place the figures in the larger perspective of literary history and to offer appraisals of their accomplishments by qualified scholars.

We define literature as the *intellectual commerce of a nation:* not merely as belles lettres, but as that ample and complex process by which ideas are generated, shaped, and transmitted. *DLB* entries are not limited to "creative writers" but extend to other figures who in this time and in this way influenced the mind of a people. Thus the series encompasses historians, journalists, publishers, and screenwriters. By this means readers of *DLB* may be aided to perceive literature not as cult scripture in the keeping of cultural high priests, but as at the center of a nation's life.

DLB includes the major writers appropriate to each volume and those standing in the ranks immediately behind them. Scholarly and critical counsel has been sought in deciding which minor figures to include and how full their entries should be. Wherever possible, useful references will be made to figures who do not warrant separate entries.

Each *DLB* volume has a volume editor responsible for planning the volume, selecting the figures for inclusion, and assigning the entries. Volume editors are also responsible for preparing, where appropriate, appendices surveying the major periodicals and literary and intellectual movements for their volumes, as well as lists of further readings. Work on the series as a whole is coordinated at the Bruccoli Clark editorial center in Columbia, South Carolina, where the editorial staff is responsible for the accuracy of the published volumes.

One feature that distinguishes *DLB* is the illustration policy—its concern with the iconography of literature. Just as an author is influenced by his surroundings, so is the reader's understanding of the author enhanced by a knowledge of his environment. Therefore *DLB* volumes include not only drawings, paintings, and photographs of authors, often depicting them at various stages in their careers, but also illustrations of their families and places where they lived. Title pages are regularly reproduced in facsimile along with dust jackets for modern authors. The dust jackets are a special feature of *DLB* because they often document better than anything else the way in which an author's work was launched in its own time. Specimens of the writers' manuscripts are included when feasible.

A supplement to *DLB*—tentatively titled *A Guide, Chronology, and Glossary for American Literature*—will outline the history of literature in North America and trace the influences that shaped it. This volume will provide a framework for the study of American literature by means of chronological tables, literary affiliation charts, glossarial entries, and concise surveys of the major movements. It has been planned to stand on its own as a vade mecum, providing a ready-reference guide to the study of American literature as well as a companion to the *DLB* volumes for American literature.

Samuel Johnson rightly decreed that "The chief glory of every people arises from its authors." The purpose of the *Dictionary of Literary Biography* is to compile literary history in the surest way available to us—by accurate and comprehensive treatment of the lives and work of those who contributed to it.

The *DLB* Advisory Board

*From an unpublished section of Mark Twain's autobiography, copyright © by the Mark Twain Company.

Foreword

In Afro-American literary history, one of the most striking phenomena has been the tremendous outpouring of poetry since the mid-1950s. A large and diverse group of writers born during the 1930s and 1940s, along with a smaller, but equally diverse, contingent of writers born between the two World Wars, has created a new black poetry. Writers such as Amiri Baraka (LeRoi Jones), Larry Neal, Etheridge Knight, Sonia Sanchez, A. B. Spellman, in conjunction with Haki R. Madhubuti (Don L. Lee), Johari Amini (Jewel C. Latimore), Nikki Giovanni, David Henderson, and Tom Dent were fresh voices that complemented those of already established writers such as Gwendolyn Brooks, May Miller, Margaret Walker Alexander, Dudley Randall, Robert Hayden, and Samuel Allen. Flourishing together in the 1960s, these generations of Afro-American poets achieved a new black renaissance that outdistanced the Harlem or New Negro Renaissance of the 1920s in terms of productivity and impact.

The convergence of political activity, social consciousness, and creative expression is one way to explain the burgeoning of Afro-American poetry. From the first successful bus boycott and lunch counter sit-in to voter registration drives and freedom rides, young black artists were in the forefront of political activism and social commitment. They joined their elders in the struggle for justice and equality to chart strategies and work for change in the condition of all Afro-Americans. Their energy and determination helped to fuel and sustain the civil rights movement, and their racial consciousness and social solidarity were sounded especially clearly in Afro-American poetry. Cultural messages to and for the people expressed black pride, strength, power, and beauty; based upon a shared heritage, these messages conveyed the reality of oppression along with the call for freedom for all Afro-Americans no matter what their social class or economic condition might be.

Poetry became the genre that could immediately connect the familiar oral tradition (the sermons, oratory, and spirituals of the black church as well as the folk rhymes, ballads, and blues of the secular world) with both the dynamic sociopolitical activity and the written literary heritage of blacks. In new freedom songs and resurrected folk forms, the new black poetry became dynamic, immediate, accessible, and relevant because its authors were visionary, articulate individuals who knew how to draw upon cultural resources to create a viable art for a people. As Larry Neal pointed out, "Afro-American life and history is full of creative possibilities."

More than any other genre, then, poetry acquired expanded significance among writers and among audiences. "Let the world be a Black Poem," Amiri Baraka proclaimed, "And let All Black People Speak This Poem / Silently or LOUD." In theme, image, and form, the new poetry functioned as a creative forum for transmitting ideas and shaping awareness. The poets rejected a white-oriented system of values and insisted upon "taking care of business," upon reaffirming a racial consciousness, and utilizing black life as a model for their art. Drawing upon a history that includes the legacies of Africa and the American South, they recognized their literary antecedents not only in the racially defined twentieth-century Harlem Renaissance poets—Claude McKay, Countee Cullen, and Langston Hughes in particular—but also in black poets of the eighteenth century—Phillis Wheatley and Lucy Terry—in the nineteenth century—George Moses Horton, Frances Watkins Harper—and those "black and unknown bards" who composed spirituals, folk, and sorrow songs. With these resources, poets as different as Carolyn Rodgers and Margaret Burroughs, Ted Joans and Lance Jeffers were free, in the words of Haki Madhubuti, to "walk the way of the new world," and to bring that world to the people in poems.

Of the many black poets who actively published their works after 1955, a small group of young poets took center stage. In their nationalistic, frequently militant stance, poets such as Nikki Giovanni, Sonia Sanchez, Haki R. Madhubuti, and Etheridge Knight sometimes seemed to overshadow the quieter strains of older poets contemporary with them—Robert Hayden, Margaret Danner, Samuel Allen, and May Miller for instance. These two groups of poets, many of them published by Dudley Randall's Broadside Press, began to coalesce with the publication of Madhubuti's *Think Black* in 1967, and from that point on, carved out a place for themselves in print and in popular media. They captured the imagination of the masses of black people in addition to inspiring literary creation among their own ranks.

Frequently acting as trumpeters rather than warriors, the new black poets aroused feelings of nationhood in black people throughout the United States and encouraged them to shed traces of whiteness from their lifestyles as well as from their minds.

They viewed themselves as teachers who provided instruction on various subjects: how to be black, how to establish a black nation, how to fight for black people, how to lead a revolution, how to love black people. Poets such as Baraka, Madhubuti, Giovanni, Neal, Henderson, Donald L. Graham (Dante), and Sanchez gave directions to black people for bringing about the social, political, and moral revolution that cultural theorists like Maulana Ron Karenga espoused as an essential part of a black aesthetic. They taught their readers how to feel proud of their race and culture. "Nigger can you kill," Giovanni asked, "Can you kill your nigger mind . . . Learn to kill niggers/Learn to be Black men." Sanchez, in her poem "nigger," reveals "that word ain't shit to me. . . . i know i am/black./ beautiful./with meaning." Madhubuti also encouraged blacks to "change change your change change change./your mind nigger," and while he gave special directives to black men to set models of revolutionary behavior for black women, Conrad Kent Rivers asked black women to teach black men how to live. In their admonitions to black people to "get the white out" of everything in their lives, the new black poets, whether of the younger or older generation, attempted to reclaim the beauty in blackness that few previous generations of black people had been able to achieve across such a wide spectrum of the society.

When Etheridge Knight penned "The Idea of Ancestry," he introduced another theme for black poets—the effect of the drug culture upon black lives and the prison debts black men frequently had to pay. In prison for a robbery related to his drug abuse Knight could begin to see what it meant to have relatives who cared about him, and he could see the value of Madhubuti's comments that black poets should not ride the "white horses that the white poets ride"; black poets had a mission to black people that precluded such senseless self-destruction. Indeed, the poets became priests of sorts, whose responsibility it was to keep the people healthy and sane, and to lead them in the paths that were most appropriate to communal survival.

Dedicated to the education of black people and to constructing positive images, poets such as Eugene Perkins, Lorenzo Thomas, Jayne Cortez, and Sonia Sanchez worked to establish black self-worth and identity. In repeating "I'm Black and I'm proud," or "Black is Beautiful," and evoking "Soul," these writers seized an opportunity for "heavy raps," serious messages delivered in meaningful language. Ron Karenga insisted that black art must be "functional," "collective," and "committed," and the majority of the poets agreed, so that little "art for art's sake" is evident in their poems, whether they are written in a popular idiom (as in the work of Sarah Webster Fabio, Angela Jackson, Gerald Barrax, or Eugene Redmond), or in jazz rhythms (as in Sanchez, Tom Weatherly, Gil Scott-Heron, or Bob Kaufman), in blues forms (as in Alvin Aubert, Calvin Forbes, Henry Dumas, or A. B. Spellman), or conventional patterns (as in Everett Hoagland, Pinkie Gordon Lane, Julia Fields, or Naomi Long Madgett).

The poets used a variety of methods to get their messages to the people. Following the pattern of Baraka, Ted Joans, Russell Atkins, Spellman, and Kaufman, who were associated with the avant-garde Beat movement, many of the contemporary black poets gave performances of their poems, and took their innovations to audiences on sidewalks, in coffee houses, and bars, as well as in schools, churches, and community centers. Poets such as Ebon, Victor Hernández Cruz, Weatherly, Askia Muhammad Touré, Sanchez, Giovanni, and Cortez were as adept at performing their works as they were at writing them. Their techniques appropriated in many instances the chanting of the folk preacher at the height of his sermon; in other instances, they consciously adopted musical rhythms and tried to accomplish, with scatlike renditions of their poetry, the liveliness they felt was missing from the static conventional structures used in the composition of traditional poetry. Jayne Cortez has been especially effective in wedding improvisational black music with improvisational style in black poetry. Several other poets, Atkins, Young, and Joans, are also musicians, and a number of others are music critics—Spellman, Baraka, and Neal. Nikki Giovanni was in the forefront of exploring the use of music when she recorded her poetry in studios to the thunderous backup of the New York Tabernacle Choir, after which she sold the forty-fives across the country and became as popular as some of the black singers of the period. Other poets, too, including Eugene Redmond, Gil Scott-Heron, Johari Amini, and Baraka, made recordings of their poetry. Calvin Hernton, David Henderson, Ishmael Reed, Norman Pritchard, and Ronald Stone came together to record *The New Jazz Poets,* but they were not as commercially successful as The Last Poets, whose several albums combining music and poetry enjoyed a wide appeal. In many ways, the poets of the 1960s were what Jean Toomer and *Cane* were to the 1920s. The lyrical rhythms Toomer adopted were echoed, for example, in the works of Henderson and Dumas and Madhubuti's adaptation of jazz rhythms from musicians such as John Coltrane; Madhubuti's interest in jazz also tied him to Langston Hughes, whose *Ask Your Mama: 12 Moods for Jazz* (1961) was a virtuoso performance in the incorporation of musical rhythms into black poetry.

The poetic experimentation included exploring the limits of language through dialect and typography. Some forms of experimentation were bold nationalistic statements. For example, capitalization at the beginning of sentences was usually disallowed, and words universally capitalized, such as "America," "I," and "English," were denied that distinction. Dialect forms from black folk speech were incorporated, and symbols and letters were often used in place of writing out words. Some words were shortened and some were combined for effect. Poems such as Amini's "Upon Being Black One Friday Night in July" and Madhubuti's "Don't Cry, Scream" are well-known examples of experimental technique, and even Sonia Sanchez's titles alone reflect her political poetics: "a chant for young/brothas sistuhas"; "to CHucK"; "to Blk/record/buyers." A few lines from Mari Evans's "Viva Noir!" illustrate the use of dialect as well as typography:

i
am going to rise
en masse
from Inner City
sick
of newyork ghettos
chicago tenements
l a's slums
weary
of exhausted lands
sagging privies
saying yessuh yessuh
yes SIR
in an assortment
of geographical dialects . . .
. . . .
. . . i'm
gonna make black bunnies black
fairies black santas black
nursery rhymes and
black
ice cream
i'm
gonna make it a
crime
to be anything BUT black. . . .

The emphasis on a functional, communal art motivated the formation of writing collectives and cultural organizations, which helped in educating the community and, not incidentally, in inspiring new commitments to "nationbuilding," which would bring a vital black future. Across the country myriad groups sprang up. In Chicago, the Organization of Black American Culture (OBAC), guided by Haki Madhubuti, brought together Gwendolyn Brooks, Ebon, Carolyn Rodgers, Johari Amini, Sterling Plumpp, and a variety of other poets, and became one of the major collective efforts. In New York, the Umbra Workshop evolved in 1961 with David Henderson, Calvin Hernton, Tom Dent, Charles Patterson, Lorenzo Thomas, and Raymond Patterson; within a short time, the workshop had attracted Norman Pritchard, Ishmael Reed, and Oliver Pitcher, and it energetically arranged public poetry readings. Such groups from the early 1960s were joined later by those in numerous places, particularly on the West Coast, where the Watts Writers' Workshop provided stimulation for poets like Quincy Troupe, and in the South, where BLKARTSOUTH with Kalamu ya Salaam (Val Ferdinand) as a guiding spirit grew out of New Orleans's Free Southern Theater. Not all of the groups were nationalistic in ideology, but many were founded by nationalists, as was Baraka's Spirit House in Newark, and they were committed to fostering black poetry, shaping black poets, and building black audiences for their work.

The communal spirit encouraged the creation of little magazines and small publishing houses that were dedicated to getting the word to the people. Many of these were founded in the 1960s: *NOMMO,* the journal of the OBAC Writers' Workshop and edited by Hoyt Fuller (who also edited *Negro Digest, Black World,* and *First World*); *Umbra* and the Umbra writers' *Blackworks,* edited by Henderson, Dent, and Hernton; *Rhythm,* the journal of the Atlanta Center for Black Art founded by A. B. Spellman and edited by Donald Stone; *NKOMBO,* the journal of BLKARTSOUTH, edited by Dent and ya Salaam; the *Journal of Black Poetry,* founded on the West Cost by Joe Goncalves; and *The Black Scholar,* founded in San Francisco by Robert Chrisman. These periodicals represent only a few examples of the major journal outlets for poetry that by the 1970s were joined by other magazines like Ahmos Zu Bolton's *HooDoo,* published in Washington, D.C., and later Louisiana and Texas. Journals such as *Callaloo,* founded in 1974 by Charles H. Rowell, Tom Dent, and Jerry Ward, and *Obsidian,* founded by Alvin Aubert in 1975, have been central to allowing new voices in the 1970s and 1980s to be heard, and they indicate the shift to academic settings that has marked both journals and poets since the 1970s.

Small presses established in the 1960s included Madhubuti's Third World Press in Chicago and Dudley Randall's Broadside Press in Detroit, which, along with London publisher Paul Breman, whose Heritage series began to publish books by black poets in 1962, became the first to publish black poets on a continuing basis. These and other small presses made it possible for works by black poets to reach larger audiences. For example, Lotus Press of Detroit was founded by poet Naomi Long Madgett, who performed a function similar to that of Gwendolyn Brooks in encouraging younger black poets, such as Gayl Jones and Houston A. Baker, Jr., to publish their works.

Not to be overlooked in significance are the anthologies that made the works of the poets available to teachers and students. Among the most important of the early collections were: *Black Fire* (1968), edited by LeRoi Jones (Baraka) and Larry Neal; *Kaleidoscope* (1968), edited by Robert Hayden; *The New Black Poetry* (1968), edited by Clarence Major; *Dices or Black Bones* (1970), edited by Adam David Miller; *A Broadside Treasury* (1971), edited by Gwendolyn Brooks; *The Black Poets* (1971), edited by Dudley Randall; *three hundred and sixty degrees of blackness* (1971), edited by Sonia Sanchez; and *Understanding the New Black Poetry* (1972), edited by Stephen Henderson. Although there were numerous other works from small and large publishers, and several by major trade houses, these anthologies in particular gave concrete evidence of the extent to which black poetry had become a dominant and enriched cultural and racial art by the end of the 1960s.

Like many of the writers of the Harlem Renaissance, the poets of the 1960s and 1970s were intent not only upon bringing their own work to the public eye, but in sounding forth their notions of heroes and heritage. They sang praises to the black leaders of the civil rights movement, especially those who were martyred for the cause of black revolution; however, they never lost sight of the contributions made by the little known or unnamed laborers in the struggle. Troupe, Giovanni, Allen, Madhubuti, and Evans all wrote poems on the assassination of Dr. Martin Luther King, Jr., in 1968. David Henderson, Robert Hayden, James A. Emanuel, Neal, Baraka, and a host of others paid tribute to Malcolm X in poems after his death in 1965; *For Malcolm: Poems on the Life and Death of Malcolm X* (1967), edited by Dudley Randall and Margaret Burroughs, reflects the range of poets affected by Malcolm, especially the Malcolm who was the Islamic El-Hajj Malik El Shabazz. Many of the poets adopted his political philosophies and his interest in Africa and an African heritage. The process of name changing, as exemplified by Baraka, Amini, Ebon, Marvin X (El Muhajir), Madhubuti, Askia Touré, and ya Salaam, reflected a desire to reclaim a heritage, to return to African roots unspoiled by a slave heritage.

The idea of ancestry has been central to the poetry of June Jordan, Lucille Clifton, Lance Jeffers, Gerald Barrax, Cruz, Aubert, and Harper who, though beginning to publish in the 1960s, won more appreciation after the appearance of more of their poems in the 1970s. Their quieter celebratory strains would be picked up by other poets in the 1980s, for instance Jodi Braxton, as she celebrates the influence of her familial and racial ancestors. Jordan, Clifton, Burroughs, Walker, Giovanni, and Sanchez made a special commitment to preserving a strong sense of racial heritage by writing books for black children.

Stimulated in part by the First World Festival of Negro Arts (1965) held in Dakar, Senegal, and by the Pan African Cultural Festival (1969) in Algiers, contemporary Afro-American poetry has also evidenced an international and Pan-Africanist perspective, which has been nurtured by the poets' own travel outside of the United States and by their interaction with third-world writers who immigrated to this country. One of the most influential of the Pan-Africans was the South African poet and nationalist Keorapetse (Willie) Kgositsile, who was a master of idioms and musicality in English. Poets such as Margaret Danner in the "Far From Africa" sequence, Sam Allen in *Paul Vesey's Ledger,* Audre Lorde in *Black Unicorn,* Ebon in *Revolution,* and Lance Jeffers in *O Africa Where I Baked My Bread,* all draw upon the connections that Afro-Americans have with Africans and the African continent.

A perspective that moves beyond that of Western values and ideologies is especially important in the poetry inspired by the Muslim faith; the works of Marvin X, Askia Touré, and Sanchez (Sister Sonia), especially in her *Blues Book for Blue Black Magical Women* (1974), all reveal this rich and cosmic view of people and the world. In addition, an Islamic influence inspired in part by Malcolm X's religious beliefs and in part by the strong presence of the Nation of Islam in urban areas and among prison populations is clearly discernible in the works of other poets, such as Knight, Neal, Baraka, and Madhubuti. This non-Western perspective may, in fact, stem from a variety of sources and models, but it unites many of the contemporary black poets in "sing[ing] new songs," as Knight puts it, and in "purify[ing] old ones by fire."

The writers represented in this volume reflect one of the strongest literary movements in the history of Afro-American creativity. These poets not only helped to shape a contemporary literature, but they also helped to reclaim, recapture, and reshape a culture. For their efforts—their inventiveness and their wisdom—the black poets of the post-1955 era deserve attention. Their poetry, in language and style, in form and substance, in message and image, has invigorated Afro-American and American literature.

—*Trudier Harris and Thadious M. Davis*

Acknowledgments

This book was produced by BC Research. Karen L. Rood is senior editor for the *Dictionary of Literary Biography* series. Ellen Rosenberg Kovner was the in-house editor.

Art supervisors are Claudia Ericson and Patricia M. Flanagan. Copyediting supervisor is Joycelyn R. Smith. Typesetting supervisor is Laura Ingram. The production staff includes Rowena Betts, Kimberly Casey, Patricia Coate, Tara P. Deal, Kathleen M. Flanagan, Joyce Fowler, Pamela Haynes, Judith K. Ingle, Victoria Jakes, Vickie Lowers, Judith McCray, and Jane McPherson. Jean W. Ross is permissions editor. Joseph Caldwell, photography editor, did photographic copy work for the volume.

Walter W. Ross did the library research with the assistance of the staff at the Thomas Cooper Library of the University of South Carolina: Lynn Barron, Daniel Boice, Sue Collins, Michael Freeman, Gary Geer, Alexander M. Gilchrist, David L. Haggard, Jens Holley, David Lincove, Marcia Martin, Jean Rhyne, Karen Rissling, Paula Swope, and Ellen Tillett.

We would like to acknowledge the invaluable help given by E. Ethelbert Miller, who shared information and materials.

Serendipity Books in Berkeley, California, and University Book Place in New York City assisted in providing illustrations.

Dictionary of Literary Biography • Volume Forty-one

Afro-American Poets Since 1955

Dictionary of Literary Biography

Nanina Alba

(21 November 1915-24 June 1968)

Enid Bogle
Howard University

BOOKS: *The Parchments: A Book of Verse* (N.p.: Merchants Press, 1962);

The Parchments II: A Book of Verse (N.p.: Privately printed, 1967).

OTHER: *Omnibus: A Journal of Creative Writing*, cofounded by Alba (Alabama State College: Writers Guild, 1957).

PERIODICAL PUBLICATIONS:

FICTION

"So Quaint," *Negro Digest,* 13 (February 1964): 76-79;

"The Satin-back Crepe Dress," *Negro Digest,* 14 (May 1965): 36-38;

"A Scary Story," *Negro Digest,* 15 (July 1966): 65-68.

NONFICTION

"The Negro and the American Colloquy," *Negro Digest,* 14 (June 1965): 33-36;

"The Negro and the American Colloquy-revisited," *Negro Digest,* 16 (January 1967): 37-39.

Nanina Alba, born in Montgomery, Alabama, received her early education at the Haines Institute in Augusta, Georgia. Her father, the Reverend I. C. Champney, a Presbyterian minister, exposed her at an early age to the doctrine and principles of the church. Nannie Williemenia Champney (who later blended Nannie and Williemenia to Nanina) was an avid reader of European and American writers and turned frequently to the poets for relaxation and meditation. She began writing poetry at the age of nine; her earliest published poem, "My Muvver's Pies," was written in 1926 when she was eleven.

Upon her graduation from Knoxville College with a B.A. in 1935, Alba accepted a teaching position at Alcorn State College. There she met Reuben Andres Alba, whom she married on 27 November 1937. Their union produced two daughters, Panchita and Andrea, and Alba's devotion to her career was surpassed only by her devotion to her family. In fact, while she commuted to Alabama State College for graduate work, she complained about the time her traveling robbed from her family. She was determined, however, to pursue a program that would enhance her career as a teacher. In 1955 she graduated from Alabama State College with an M.A. in education, and her thesis on listening was the first of its kind to be done in Alabama.

Alba taught at several public schools in Alabama and at Alcorn State College, Alabama State College, and Tuskegee Institute. Her students attest to the vigilance with which she promoted academic excellence. Despite the rigor of being a conscientious teacher and devoted mother, Alba found time to pursue further graduate studies at Indiana University during the summers and returned intermittently to the writing of poetry. An examination of her writings reveals the influences that her life experiences had in shaping her artistic inventions. She dedicates her first collection of poems, *The Parchments: A Book of Verse* (1962), to her father, who taught her to understand life; to her mother, who taught her to understand beauty; and to the Reverend William Lloyd Imes, whose sermon gave the title for the volume. Reverend Imes likened St. Paul's "parchments" to the apostle's creative work. This reference inspired Alba to consider her creative works as parchments.

Many of the poems published in this collection

appeared previously in journals, magazines, and newspapers, such as *Phylon, Crisis,* and *Montgomery Advertiser.* (More recently, two of her poems have been reprinted in several anthologies and *Negro Digest.*) Her well-ordered notebook gives a record of each poem: the name of the publisher to which it was sent, the date it was sent, and the response of the publisher. The poems represent Alba's understanding of life with its trials and its heroes, with its despair but with its beauty.

Alba was a talented piano player who taught music in the public schools in Alabama. Many of the poems in *The Parchments* use music or musicians as a device through which an underlying theme is orchestrated. In the opening poem, "The Holy Blues," or in "Songs My Mother Taught Me," Alba presents the inescapable hardships that afflict yet do not destroy the characters. In "The Holy Blues" a troubled man twists his hungry mouth across a cheap harmonica: "And close/his eyes/And slowly pat his feet/And make his sorrows moan/until his worldly blues went holy/circling his head in a halo of relief." Alba finds beauty and strength in this man's ability to transform his sorrow and despair into a positive and sustaining note. She uses lines from the spiritual "Nobody Knows the Trouble I See" as a refrain and as counterpoint to a society that is obsessed with space exploration while it neglects the immediate concerns of the poor and needy. Music, too, is the dominant image in the poem "To One at the Chancel," dedicated to Mrs. Lillian Sims, the organist at the Tuskegee Institute chapel. The musical tones produced by Sims are like raindrops in spring, "sparkling silently and gleaming," yet powerful enough to enchant the congregation and ease their sorrow.

Alba uses the blues form in "Black Minstrel and Banjo" to ridicule the blind acceptance of values held in high esteem in Western tradition. According to Ole Tom "de truf it sho do hurt" and with due reverence to the "Word," turning the other cheek is contrary to human nature, which has a penchant for striking back—"he jes cain' help a-strakin' back." In "Black Minstrel and Banjo" Alba uses dialect to present the musings of her persona. Although she taught English composition at Tuskegee Institute, she did not allow her knowledge of standard English to interfere with the credibility of her characters. In fact, she published two articles on the dialect of the Negro and was influenced by the extent to which Langston Hughes had used dialect in his writings.

Alba often remarked that Langston Hughes and Countee Cullen had a significant influence on

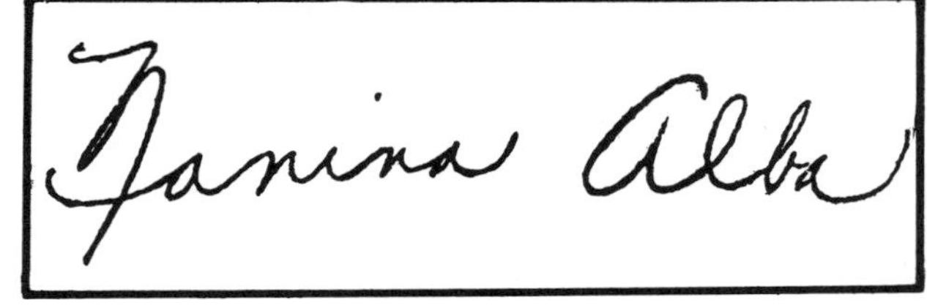

her early writings. She corresponded with Hughes, who encouraged her, and she kept among her possessions an autographed copy of *The Sweet Flypaper of Life* (1955), which he had presented to her. In "Largesse Unlimited" Alba celebrates the versatility of Hughes as a writer. She speaks of the immortality of Hughes, whose scope captured the spirit of his people "from the depths to the steeple." "For Countee Cullen" was written as a lament upon Cullen's death, which dealt a savage blow to her; she had hoped that their spirits, through the "mystic doctrine of affinity," might have shared in the "shaping of their consummate goals" and might have salvaged "life's laments."

The dominant theme throughout *The Parchments* is celebration—celebration of people who left an indelible impression on the young artist. But her commemoration is not limited to local music makers and nationally acclaimed writers. Alba commemorates noteworthy contributions of Afro-Americans in a variety of professions and emphasizes the modesty of these giants. "For Ralph Bunche" is an exquisite rendition of the pioneer work of Bunche as a statesman and the honor which he bestows on his people. "Carver" focuses not so much on George Washington Carver as a botanist and chemist, but on his unpretentious demeanor. In spite of his exemplary achievement, "Here was a man of modesty, restraint/A man who gave his honors back to God." "For Isaac Scott Hathaway" praises the genius of the sculptor, whom Alba met at Tuskegee. She observes: "Here in this crowd/of faces, those not knowing/might pass you by for some lesser spark showing/its glinting light . . . in those fragile hands and in that fertile mind/Rest grandeur."

Alba participated in the boycott of the Montgomery, Alabama, bus system sparked by Mrs. Rosa Parks's refusal to sit in the back of a city bus. The poet later remarked that her feet grew two sizes from walking. The pivotal events surrounding the boycott, particularly the role of women who were compelled to seek employment in the homes of whites, form the background for the fable "So Quaint." Taken from this story and included in *The Parchments* is the poem "But my Soul's A-Restin'!" The poem catalogs the experiences of the colored woman who devotes her time to seeking employment or "cookin' and washin' " and taking care of her employers' children while hers remain unattended. It speaks too of her foibles, of her disappointments, and of her endurance, but also of the ultimate reward obtained through active participation and group effort. The poem ends with the proclamation: "My feets is tired, but my Soul's A-Restin'!"

Alba's concern for her people is summed up in her most intense poem. "Be Daedalus," for which she received critical acclaim, is dedicated to the "struggle that the Negro has always had to make in adjusting to the myriad and complex problems of his living." The title is an allusion to Daedalus, in Greek mythology. With his son, Icarus, Daedalus escaped the confines of the Cretan Labyrinth by using wings made of wax. However, freedom for them was short-lived because Icarus, disregarding the warnings of his father, flew too close to the sun. Alba exhorts the Negro to be like Daedalus, ingenious and rational in the struggle toward his salvation, always mindful of illusions of grandeur or temporary euphoria which do irreparable harm. With Icarus it is the "parching sun that brings/ Death as its tax/Suns can be brutal things," she warns.

For *The Parchments II: A Book of Verse* (1967), Alba collaborated with her daughter Panchita Alba Crawford, who served as the illustrator. Some of these poems also had appeared previously in magazines, anthologies, and newspapers. The collection reflects the scope of the poet's readings and meditations and her attempt to forge and refine her craft. She focuses on global issues and experiments with different styles, which result in a medley of rhythms.

The opening trilogy, "Tria Juncta" ("Resartus," "A World Envenomed," "Future Imperfect?"), presents an indictment of a world that embraces worn-out creeds. The emptiness of this world is manifested in two types of people: those who "stare/at empty idols/they wish they had" and those who "are glad, so very glad at what they possess." The patched-clothes image in "Resartus" gives way to decay in "A World Envenomed," which portrays a world that is withering, decaying, dying: indeed, a wasteland. The malaise in "Future Imperfect?" is that man-made inventions ("insects") explore space and the "Stars/Now trafficked as the solemn ocean/ their secrets bared and bleeding to the soulless sound."

Alba's preoccupation with global concerns emerges in other poems. Whether it is the world portrayed as a nervous woman lacking direction ("Psychosis") or the tragedy of war ("Shades of the Ardennes, et al."), the message is the same: gloom and despair. And these are expressed in different forms. In "Commentary" it is expressed in the dreamlike quality of the woman who fondles items she cannot buy; the cripple who looks at shoes he cannot wear; the blind man who searches for what he cannot see. In "Petition," it is expressed through derangement and in "Lines" through stark horror.

The poet turns periodically to the theme of religion. "For All Who Blow the Bitter Horn" pays homage to Christ; "After Mardi Gras" depicts the sacrifice and repentance practiced during the Lenten season that follows the revelry of Mardi Gras; and "Prayer," written for her second daughter, Andrea, gives thanks for having conceived Andrea and implores divine attention and inspiration for the child.

The poet twists and turns in *The Parchments II;* it is not all lament or religion. She pays tribute to John Donne and Ernest Hemingway; she speaks of the power of words in "Est modus in rebus," and she alludes to other authors. For instance, "Lines" is subtitled "The horror!" "The horror!" after Joseph Conrad's *Heart of Darkness;* "On a Darkling Plain" alludes to Matthew Arnold's "Dover Beach"; and "Lines found in a Victorian Reticule" has the signature of a poet named Coatsworth, suggestive of William Wordsworth.

Throughout *The Parchments II,* Alba experiments with different forms. She breaks from the confinement of the traditional modes that pervade *The Parchments* and adds haiku and free verse to her repertoire. It is in "Ratamacue! Paradiddle!" that her style takes a crystallized form: the rhythm of the drum beating out the meaning and the movement is inextricably entwined in the evolution of the message.

The satirical fable "So Quaint" introduces the Miss Lucy series, a set of prose works by Alba. The central character is a white woman, and the setting is the South in the 1950s. The narrator is Miss Lucy's Negro helper who is intrigued and sometimes baffled by her employer's patronizing attitude to Negroes, whose behavior is excused by Miss Lucy because "They are so quaint." In the story Miss Lucy protests the harrassment of Negroes by whites and leaves her home when she is threatened for not cooperating with her race. Later, she returns to celebrate the President's proclamation against segregation laws concerning public transportation. After making a speech condemning the actions of the whites, Miss Lucy is shot. She dies

Poem (Work)	Sent to	Date Sent	Reply (11-63)
Quaint Future Imperfect	Negro Digest " "	10-14-63	Accepted [illegible] See letter in file! Not replied to up 8-1
For John Donne	Peninsula Poets	10-15-63	Favorable; accepted for Winter, 1964, Peninsula Poets 64.
Sonnet For the Poet	South & West Miss Sue Abbott Boyd	10-15-63 for Special Anthology	Ret'd
"Largesse Unlimited"	Negro History Bulletin	10-22-63	Ret'd ([illegible])
Capitulation"	Phylon	10-23-63	Published - Fall quarter, 1963
"The Specialist"	[illegible]	10-15-63	Ret'd: 10-24-63
"With How Sad Steps"	International Poetry Review Henry Picola, Editor	1-9-64	Ret'd ?
"Listening"	Words of Cheer Mennonite Pub. co.	1-9-64	

		Sent	
"The Cliche"	The CEA Critic	1-12-64	Answered - to reply later after decision is made [illegible] 12-26
"Listening"	Optical Journal & Review of Optometry	" "	Ret'd
Listening "Selected Short Subjects"	Doorway: Comment from the Co-op	" "	Ret'd
Listening	Progress	" "	
Listening	Accent on Living	" "	Ret'd - between 12-2[illegible]
Selected Short Subjects"	For Laughing Out Loud	" "	Ret'd - between 12-26
			" "
"Listening"	Listenings (See Market)	3-9-64	
"The Holy Blues" "Largesse Unlimited"	Umbra	3-9-64	No reply (7-29-64)

Alba kept meticulous records of her submissions in a ledger (courtesy of the estate of Nanina Alba).

"Listening"	Farm Journal, Manitoba	?	Ret'd - 8-13-64
"The Cliché" "Selected Short Subjects"	Etc.	3-9-64	Ret'd
"It Is a Gap We Have in Greene" The Prophecy, Ring Rapidly the Bell	College English	3-9-64	Ret'd
"Into This Scarlet Wrapped in Early Spring"	Message Magazine	3-9-64	Ret'd
Petition (July, 1964) " " "	Negro Digest The Nation	7-29-64 " " "	See letter in file, to be published in Sept. issue 8-1-64 (Negro Digest)
"Cinquains"	Presbyterian Survey	" " "	Letter about article on [illegible] but no return of poems. 8-4-64
The Parchments	Miss Jean Blackwell Hutson, Curator 103 West 135 th St. N.Y. 30, N.Y. Schomburg Collection	No reply 9-2-64 7-29-64	
"Bird-talk"	Mr. Harry Smith, Ed. The Smith, 15 Park Row N.Y., N.Y.	7-29-64	
"Recantus" "Capitulation" "And If We Must Have Sex"	The U. of Tampa Poetry Review U. of Tampa Tampa, Fla.	7-29-64	Ret'd See file Aug. 1, 1964
"Candid Summary" "Listening"	Mr. Thorpe Menn, Lit. Ed. The Kansas City Star Kansas City, Mo.	8-3-64	Ret'd (8-64)

		Sent	Ret'd
"And If We Must Have Sex"	The Evergreen Review	8-~~4~~9-64	8-14-64
"Capitulation" "Recantus"	Renascence Poetry	8-9-64	acknowledged by letter (see file) "Capitulation" - accepted - Autumn issue, possibly. "Recantus" already [illegible]
"It Is a Gap We Have in Greene" "The Prophecy"	Four Quarters	" " "	Acknowledged receipt - 8-12-64 Ret'd 8-64
"Listening"	Language Learning	" " "	
"	The Nation's Schools	" " "	Returned, with note 8-13-64
"Transfiguration"	The Christian Science Monitor	" " "	Ret'd (8-64)
"~~[illegible]~~"	December		
"Xmas, 1961"	Christianity Today	8-3-64	Ret'd with letter (8-64)
"Psychosis" "Listening" "The Holy Blues"	Phylon	8-8-64 No reply (9-4-64)	[illegible]
	Burning Deck, p. 142	8-8-64	
Future Imperfect	"The Carolina Quarterly	8-8-64	8-12-64

mumbling to the narrator "Your people, they're so qu—!"

Although "So Quaint" was Alba's first published work in prose, chronologically it is last in the Miss Lucy series. Both "The Satin-back Crepe Dress" and "A Scary Story" precede the action of "So Quaint." In the first of these stories, crazy Lee Roy, whose mother had just died, steals Miss Lucy's satin-back crepe dress that the narrator had taken home to shorten. Lee Roy claims that he needs the dress for his mother who "didn't have no pretty dress to be buried in." The sympathetic Miss Lucy not only allows him to keep the dress, which she had planned to wear to a banquet, but buys him a suit and pays the "fun'al" expenses. "A Scary Story" depicts the attitude of Southerners to interracial marriage. Miss Lucy's brother Victor, knowing he could not marry a dark girl in Georgia, takes her to Chicago where he marries her. Victor's family informs him he "couldn't come back no mo' and they was goin' to leave him out of the will." However, at the news of his father's death, Victor and his wife return secretly. Miss Lucy hides them in her home until the day of the funeral when Victor ventures out. At the gathering for the reading of the will, Mr. Sam, Miss Lucy's other brother, shoots Victor before he knows that Victor has been left only one dollar, because "that's all he need to take care of hisself and his black wife."

Throughout the series Alba is consistent in her portrayal of Miss Lucy: she refuses to sign a petition to rid the Negroes of their land ("So Quaint"); she is accommodating to Lee Roy and leaves $10,000 in her will for the narrator and her husband, Bill ("The Satin-back Crepe Dress"); and she hides Victor's wife in her home having planned to give the couple her portion of the inheritance ("A Scary Story"). For these acts, the nameless narrator considers Miss Lucy a good woman, but "quaint."

Alba uses the Negro's "gift of tongues" extensively in her short stories. Her astute use of folk expressions and dialect, impeccable attention to detail, significant diversion, and subtle humor elevates the simple plot of each story. The range of her writing (prose and poetry) reflects a convergence of her experiences. With dexterity she meshes Christian imagery, Greek mythology, black folkways, global and local concerns into a tapestry with images meant to "capture/The Mystic recurrent hum/ Of Afric drum/Or hurricane wind/Singing songs to keep the world Kin'd." Her poems and short stories remain a testimony to her creative talent and her insight into the lives of and concern for her people. Nanina Alba died of cancer in June 1968, leaving behind a number of personal, unpublished pieces.

Reference:

Eugene B. Redmond, *Drumvoices: The Mission of Afro-American Poetry, A Critical History* (Garden City: Anchor/Doubleday, 1976), pp. 319, 332, 333.

Samuel W. Allen

(9 December 1917-)

Ruth L. Brittin
Auburn University

BOOKS: *Elfenbein Zähne (Ivory Tusks),* as Paul Vesey; bilingual, edited and translated by Janheinz Jahn (Heidelberg: Wolfgang Rothe, 1956);

Ivory Tusks and Other Poems (New York: Poets Press, 1968);

Paul Vesey's Ledger (London: Paul Breman, 1975).

OTHER: "Negritude and Its Relevance to the American Negro Writer," in *The American Negro Writer and His Roots* (New York: American Society of African Culture, 1960);

Pan-Africanism Reconsidered, general introduction and introductions to four individual sections by Allen (Berkeley: University of California Press, 1962);

"Tendencies in African Poetry," in *Africa Seen by American Negro Scholars* (New York: American Society of African Culture, 1963), pp. 175-198;

Samuel Allen (photograph by Chester Higgins, Jr.)

Arna Bontemps, ed., *American Negro Poetry,* includes poems by Allen (New York: Hill & Wang, 1963);

Langston Hughes, ed., *New Negro Poets: USA,* includes poems by Allen (Bloomington: Indiana University Press, 1964);

N. Aruri and E. Ghareeb, eds., *Enemy of the Sun,* introduction by Allen (Washington: Drum & Spear Press, 1970);

"The Civil Rights Struggle," in *What Black Educators Are Saying,* edited by Nathan Wright, Jr. (New York: Hawthorn, 1970);

Poems from Africa, edited by Allen (New York: Crowell, 1973);

Stephen Henderson, ed., *Understanding the New Black Poetry: Black Speech & Black Music as Poetic References,* includes poems by Allen (New York: Morrow, 1973);

Woodie King, Jr., ed., *The Forerunners: Black Poets in America,* includes poems by Allen (Washington, D.C.: Howard University Press, 1981).

PERIODICAL PUBLICATIONS: Jean-Paul Sartre, "Black Orpheus," translated by Allen, *Présence Africaine,* first series nos. 10-11 (1960);

"Two Writers: Senghor and Soyinka," *Negro Digest,* 16 (June 1967): 54-67;

"The African Heritage," *Black World,* 20 (January 1971): 14-18.

With poems reprinted in more than one hundred anthologies, including Stephen Henderson's *Understanding the New Black Poetry* (1973) and Woodie King, Jr.'s *The Forerunners: Black Poets in America* (1981), Samuel W. Allen today holds a distinguished place among Afro-American poets. Living in Europe, primarily in France and Germany after World War II, he became steeped in the literature of the negritude movement and inspired to write a poetry grounded in the fusion of African and Afro-American culture. He has played a significant role in African and Afro-American criticism as a scholar, reviewer, translator, editor, and lecturer. He has lectured on Afro-American and African literature and extensively on Frantz Fanon; he has participated in major national and international conferences on black affairs both literary and political; he has been a professor and writer-in-residence at several universities; and he has read his poetry at institutions throughout the United States and abroad. Allen has had a strong influence on younger writers, not only because of his published works but also because of his accessibility as a teacher and critic. In addition to his literary accomplishments, by 1971 Allen had completed an impressive legal career in public service. When Leroy Collins announced Allen's appointment as legal counsel for the Community Relations Service, he paid tribute to Allen's "rare combination of lawyer and poet."

Allen's family roots are in the South, specifically Alabama, the birthplace of his paternal grandparents and the adopted home of his maternal grandparents. His paternal grandfather, a slave until the age of nine, became a member of the Alabama legislature during Reconstruction and later was the editor of the *Southern Christian Recorder,* an A.M.E. church paper. His maternal grandparents, graduates of Howard University, went South after the Civil War to help the recently freed blacks. His maternal grandfather, a physician, practiced in Mobile and Birmingham and was for several years the school physician at Tuskegee Institute. His grandmother, Josephine Washington, formerly a "copygirl" for Frederick Douglass in Washington, D.C., served as Booker T. Washington's secretary. She was as well a poet, who published her work in magazines and achieved some recognition as a writer at the turn of the century. His mother, Jewett Washington Allen, also wrote poetry and was "class poetess" at Clark College. Both of Allen's parents graduated from Clark College; his father, Alexander Joseph Allen, went on to pastor A.M.E. churches in New England, Pennsylvania, and Ohio and was later elected a bishop of the A.M.E. Church.

The second of four sons, Sam Allen was born in Columbus, Ohio, and reared in a home where he felt "a family atmosphere of established goals and expectations," he says. Being a minister's family, the Allens always lived "in the heart of the black community" and were never "insulated from its problems or deprived of its energies or resources." Allen depicts the social concern of his family in "View from the Corner," where he, the child, listens to his father and uncle discuss what "the Negro has got to do."

At Fisk University Allen majored in sociology, was a member of James Weldon Johnson's creative writing workshop, and contributed to the literary magazine. He says that Johnson served as a role model for him. He became "enthralled" by the Harlem Renaissance poets: Claude McKay, "for his forthright condemnation of the intense racism he found in this country"; Countee Cullen, for his "erudition, sophistication, . . . and his extraordinary felicity of expression" (Allen also identified "with much of the confessional vein of his poetry in its exploration of the interior meaning of the black experience"); Langston Hughes and Sterling Brown, whom he grew to appreciate for their use of folk heritage. He notes that in their use of folk tradition they were probably closest to "an authentic black experience." Among English poets, he says that he was "fascinated by the angular rhythms of John Donne" and "attracted by the mystical strain in Blake." He recalls writing his second poem during the summer following his freshman year after reading Goethe's *Faust*.

Having received his B.A. (magna cum laude) from Fisk in 1938, Allen entered the Harvard Law School and received his J.D. in 1941. Drafted into the U.S. Army, he served in the Armed Forces from 1942 to 1946 and was commissioned in the Adjutant General's office. Afterward he was Deputy Assistant District Attorney of New York City (1946-1947). On the G.I. Bill he completed additional studies in the humanities at the New School for Social Research (1947-1948). He then went to Paris, where he enrolled in the Alliance Francaise (1948) and studied at the Sorbonne (1949-1950).

After World War II he lived in France as a student and later in Germany (1951-1955) as civilian attorney with the U.S. Armed Forces. Although Allen was a lawyer, he was also actively composing poetry. Upon returning from Europe to the United States, he went into private practice in New York City from 1956 to 1958. For two years (1958-1960) he taught law at Texas Southern University in Houston, but he returned to government service as assistant general counsel in the United States Information Agency, Washington, D.C. (1961-1965), and as chief counsel in the Community Relations Service, Washington, D.C. (1965-1968). In 1968 he left the law permanently to pursue his interests in literature. He became the Avalon Professor of Humanities at Tuskegee Institute, Alabama (1968-1970), and taught for a year at Wesleyan University (1970-1971) and at Boston University from 1971 until his retirement in 1981. Although retired from his duties as professor of English, Allen has since served as writer-in-residence at Tuskegee and at Rutgers University, Newark. In recent years he has devoted full time to his writing.

Allen's first publications appeared during his years in France, when two groups of people made profound impressions on him: the American expatriates, the best-known of whom were Richard Wright and James Baldwin, and the negritude poets, a Paris group made up of Africans and West Indians who were writing in French. From Africa were Léopold Senghor, whom Allen calls "foremost articulator of Negritude," David Diop, and Birago Diop; and from the Caribbean, Aimé Césaire, Jacques Roumain, Réné Depestre, Léon Damas, Léon Laleau, and Paul Niger. Allen recalls that his encounter with the work of the negritude poets, especially "the surrealistic strain manifest notably in the poetry of Césaire," had an important influence on him. In 1949, Richard Wright arranged to publish Allen's poems in *Présence Africaine,* the magazine established as "a vehicle for the dialogue between whites and blacks; for defense of the black man's cultural values, negritude, African personality, unity, and independence." Wright also introduced him to the *Présence Africaine* circle. Thus Allen became part of an exciting literary endeavor and for some time recruited materials in English for *Présence Africaine* and helped with editing and translating.

Allen's work on *Présence Africaine* complemented his writing of poetry, because the explorations of Pan-African culture, identity, and literature by Wright, Alioune Diop, Jean-Paul Sartre, Léon Damas, and others were intrinsic to Allen's own creative work. The perspective in his poetry was, from the beginning, grounded in the heritage of black people, a heritage evident in "A Moment Please" and "The Staircase." The awareness central to his poetic vision was of a shared history that transcended geographic and chronological boundaries, as "Ivory Tusks" and "The Mules of Caesar" illustrate. Already these poems and others, such as "There Are No Tears," drew upon cross-cultural kinships and traditions. Allen's poems were rooted in a folk heritage of thought, feeling, and perception apparent in the oral tradition, the African survivals, and the black church of the American South, which he claimed as a seminal influence on his poetry. The church, especially, with its emphases on communal spirit, verbal expression, and sacred music, guided his sense of the possibilities for poetry; as he has since stated on reflection, "the eloquence, the pageantry, and the music" of the black church were some of the strongest influences on his work, so that he became fond of quoting in regard to his own poems James Baldwin's apt statement: "There is no music like the music of the saints rejoicing." Because Allen believed that the black writer needed to be cognizant of his roots and to go back to those roots in order "to achieve his full stature in a racist, exploitative society," he felt an immediate empathy with the negritude movement, which added a global dimension to his perspective.

The seeds for Allen's work as a critic were sown during his Paris period, particularly in 1951 when he translated Sartre's "Black Orpheus," the introduction to Senghor's *Anthologie de la Nouvelle Poésie Nègre* (1948), thus making the essay available to non-French-speaking readers. By the end of the 1950s, Allen's own criticism had taken shape; it is largely Pan-African with a special concern for the relationship between creative work and cultural conditions. Essays such as "Tendencies in African Poetry" (*Présence Africaine,* 1958) and "Negritude and Its Relevance to the American Negro Writer" (New York Black Writers' Conference, 1959) make clear his assessment of the African and Afro-American as "bound fast in the culture prison of the Western World," but also as recognizing that "his poetic concern has been his liberation from that prison, with the creation of a truer sense of identity, with the establishment of his dignity as a man." In these and other cogent essays since the 1960s, Allen has maintained a vision of the interrelatedness of the African and the Afro-American, and has consistently advised the Afro-American writer to utilize his American experience and history as well as his African heritage for creative, artistic endeavors. His 1971 essay, "The African Heritage," is a primary example of Allen's critical concerns with cultural contexts for art and with African carryovers in the Afro-American church, literary forms, and secular life.

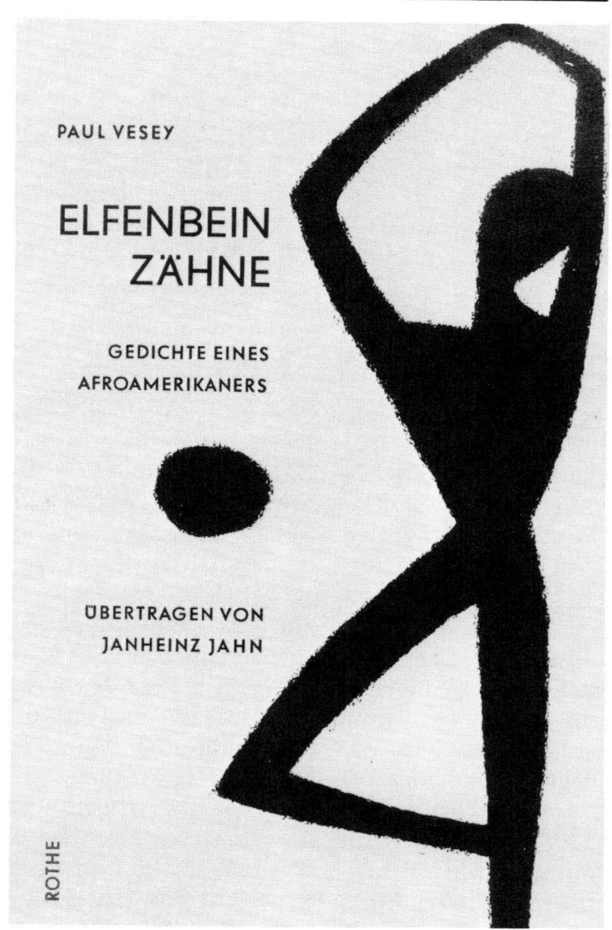

Dust jacket for Allen's first poetry collection, printed in English with German translations on facing pages

His statement in *The Forerunners: Black Poets in America* summarizes core aspects of his critical vision: "black poets are continuing with an increasingly sharpened sense of direction both to define and to vivify the black experience, drawing upon and utilizing a more profoundly explored heritage. They listen with new awareness to black music, to the wisdom of the folklore, to the rhythms of the varied speech, and, like the sorcerer, conjure up from the wellsprings of the creative consciousness an identity both old and new, a vision whole and sufficient." Important, then, for Allen, the black poet has "the task of striking from the disparate elements of the alienated African presence in the West the coin of new awareness," which is "a fusion" emphasizing "the denied, but essential, sources of the black experience." Both this task and this fusion, as Allen identifies them in his statement, are evident in his poetry from the first collection *Elfenbein Zähne* (1956) to the more recent *Paul Vesey's Ledger* (1975).

After the initial publication of his poems in *Présence Africaine,* Allen's work appeared in other magazines, but his first volume of poetry, *Elfenbein Zähne* (*Ivory Tusks*), did not appear until 1956. The bilingual (German-English) edition, with translations and an epilogue by German critic Janheinz Jahn, was published under the pseudonym Paul Vesey. Allen had used this pseudonym earlier, he says, because he had "another vocational identity" as a lawyer and the use of a pseudonym afforded him a "greater sense of freedom." Jahn, who had published an article in a German journal on the young poet in 1952, requested that Allen stick with the pseudonym signed to the book, for Jahn did not wish to " 'discover' an ephemeral, disappearing poet." And the name has stuck.

Elfenbein Zähne comprises twenty of Allen's most complex poems, which Jahn contrasts with earlier Afro-American poetry. Allen, while retaining, according to Jahn, "the sad bass voice and the biblical parallel[s]" of the traditional American black poets, goes beyond them to include "the knowledge of the coexistence of the African heritage." The poems reveal Allen's consciousness of multiple cultural forces at work on the individual struggling to comprehend both his world and himself.

In "There Are No Tears" the poet contrasts the inhuman, pitiless, mechanical skyscraper (representative of urban life and modern civilization) with man and his human values—the former also representing the culture of America and the latter the culture of Africa, pulling the Afro-American in opposite directions. Against the "irrefractible steel" solidly anchored "in the deep earth," "tall and cold," "a stranger to regret" and tears, he presents the human doubts, "the dark incertainties," "the lonely cry for the lost old gods," the "cries for the ancient moorings." With "the lonely cry for the lost old gods," he juxtaposes "the frenetic night of your pursuit of the bright new gods." Alienated from the old spiritual culture, but ambivalent toward the new materialistic culture, the individual suffers psychically. Similarly, in "The Dog Stalks Forth," "the great dog" (the American beast) strikes terror as "assassin, fiend," dangerous and powerful destroyer, yet he is "stupendous . . . resplendent." "Caress me," the narrator says to the "brute," as he is attracted to, yet at the same time frightened and repulsed by, the beast. In both "There Are No Tears" and "The Dog Stalks Forth," there is the conflict between what America represents—"the great dog," the foreign land, the cold skyscraper—and what Africa represents, as the homeland of "the ancient moorings," "the lost old gods," "the ancient component" from which blacks have been wrenched. And also present is the violence inflicted on the African brought to America against his will.

Allen's imagery of physical violence assaulting the human spirit is most dramatic when he combines lynching imagery with the portrayal of the black man as a Christ figure. Two of the finest poems in the volume, totally uncompromising in their starkness, are "Willie McGee," an account of a legal lynching—an execution—and "They Have Anointed Him," in which the lynching ritual is represented fully but economically by only a few suggestive details. Both poems are ironic: in the former, the Christian God approves of the efficient, cruel executioner's act; in the latter, "he" is anointed with tar and gasoline by the mob of "thick-necked countrymen/raging to kill/their muscles massive/for a bit of murder." After the bloodhounds and the manhunt,

Their sacrificial rites begin
They have anointed him
but first the gouging knife to take the fingers
eyes, the tongue
The twitching mass is ready for the last flowing
expiation
and so it is done,
the cooling flames are welcome now
his tongueless shriek is higher than the flames can
writhe
into death's numbing kingdom.

Evocative, yet precise, the poem relies upon religious imagery to heighten the contrast between the public spectacle and its human implications. As Ezekial Mphahlele has observed, "the dramatic method is Samuel Allen's forte."

Allen fuses historical, classical, and biblical allusions into a rich metaphorical language, not merely in order to depict the violence and oppression blacks suffer but also to portray their survival and transcendence. For example, at the end of "Jason Who Was Rent," the title character, "rent, nailed on the northern cross of the rack," manages to rise: "On the peak of the cross of the reigning north/Jason stands who was rent." And in "The Mules of Caesar," while a black youth reports that "Poppa always say bow down bow *down*/when the caravan passes" and that "Poppa live a long time look like forever/till a police broke his back with a chair," the mules of Caesar, pulling a caravan of the

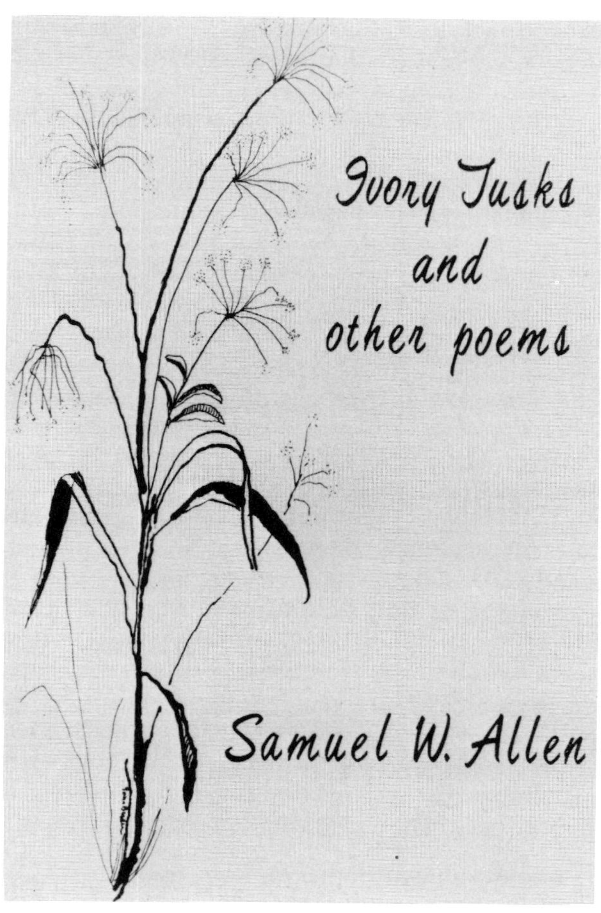

Most of the poems in Allen's 1968 volume address the black American experience.

dead, confront "the great black face, glistening ebony against the span of sand" and scream, trembling in the shame of their servitude.

The contrapuntal structure of "The Mules of Caesar" is characteristic of a number of Allen's poems, including one of his most effective, "A Moment Please." In that poem, a meditation on the nature and fate of the universe is interspersed with the narration of a more immediate reality:

When I gaze at the sun
    I walk to the subway booth
    for change for a dime.
and know that this great earth
    Two adolescent girls stood there
    alive with eagerness to know
is but a fragment from it thrown. . . .

The girls ask, "Are you Arabian? Egyptian? Or Nigger?" The racial epithet causes the narrator to pause, while the philosophical reflection provides a larger backdrop against which the small, but momentous incident can be measured:

    A moment, please
What is it that to fury I am roused?
    for still it takes a moment
What meaning for me
    and now
in this homeless clan
    I'll turn
the dupe of space
    and smile
the toy of time?
    and nod my head.

Although reminiscent of Countee Cullen's brief poem "Incident," Allen's poem is more encompassing in its understanding of the human condition and more positive in its vision of a black individual in a limited environment.

The insight illuminated by counterpoint in "A Moment Please" is expanded in "The Staircase," which renders clearly the general plight of blacks by means of an individual, along with his twin, for whom "stairs mount to eternity." Surrounded by decay and disrepair (a rotten floor, "cracked ceiling," and "dripping faucet"), the individual faces an "unending" climb and cannot reach his full potential, or reconciliation with the other half of his self. The poem is surrealistic in its images of destruction in Western civilization and disturbing in its messages about the experiences of blacks.

Although *Elfenbein Zähne* was well received by European and African audiences, it was not widely circulated in the United States. American audiences did not have ready access to Allen's poetry until the late 1960s, when, some twelve years after *Elfenbein Zähne,* Allen published *Ivory Tusks and Other Poems* (1968). Because of the title, it is often assumed that this book is simply the English edition of the earlier volume. It is not: actually, only four of the *Elfenbein Zähne* poems appear in *Ivory Tusks;* eighteen of the twenty-two poems are new. Evident in the four republished poems is Allen's inclination toward revision—he is constantly changing his poems, attempting to strengthen them. More than *Elfenbein Zähne, Ivory Tusks* reveals the diversity of Allen's poetry in form, tone, voice, and subject. The poems, while continuing to evidence a consciousness of the modern experience of blacks in a broad historical spectrum, depend upon more familiar, and thus accessible, analogies and allusions. However, as in the first volume, much of the imagery in *Ivory Tusks* assumes the interconnection of African heritage and Afro-American experience, as in the title poem and "Deliberate Speed (1)," and asserts, as well, the poet's own commitment to articulating that connection, as in "I Heard the Sirens Sound" and "I Promise."

The manipulation of language through specified voices and their appropriate idioms is perhaps the most striking feature of *Ivory Tusks.* In this regard, the "Deliberate Speed" poems are especially effective. "Deliberate Speed (1)," set in the African desert, satirizes America's failure to implement the Civil Rights Act. After using terms such as "timeless chant," "for hours approached," "at last," "Right back—in a thousand years," "destined for eternity," Allen neatly telescopes the important words within the response to a desert woman's question:

"Tell him El Hassanaubusarnettallace said. . . ."
he paused a brief half hour
regarding her silently
weighing his word
"Wait."

Allen also uses the dramatic monologue as a vehicle for giving voice to characters drawn from public life who represent facets of the racial concerns shared by blacks. In several of the monologues, he adopts a bemused or humorous tone that is edged with irony. "I Say, Mr. Armstrong" and "To Satch (American Gothic)," for example, illustrate the poet's capacity to project his ideas by means of dramatic personae whose modern experiences—those of the famous jazz musician Louis Armstrong and of the legendary baseball player Satchell Paige—expose the reality of American racism. "To Satch" is one of Allen's most anthologized poems, one which Eugene Redmond calls a praise poem to suggest its link to African praise songs. Satchell Paige, the speaker, "will *never* stop/Just go on forever":

Till one fine mornin
I'm gonna reach up and grab me a handful of stars
Swing out my long lean leg
And whip three hot strikes burnin down the heavens
And look over at God and say
How about that!

Although good-humored in presenting Satch's accomplishments and a humanistic deity similar to the god of James Weldon Johnson's *God's Trombones,* "To Satch," with its subtitle, "American Gothic," underscores an ironical, tragic situation: one of the greatest pitchers of all times being denied major league play because of his race.

The poems, then, are celebratory, even as they evoke painful racial memories. "Nat Turner," for instance, celebrates the historical figure while recreating the pain of enslavement. The poem invites the reader to see clearly the rebel-giant from the past and to join him: "From the obscurity of the past, we saw/the dark now flaming face of a giant Nathaniel/call whosoever will let him come." At the same time, it humanizes the man: "Turner's face softened . . ./and he mourned for the lost years/the eternity of grief/the thousands, millions of his people/torn from the soil of their fathers/for a living death in a strange land." And the reader empathizes with Turner, whose loss and grief become the reader's, so that the necessity of his "face harden[ing]" for the task of recruiting for the rebellion is clear.

The pain of loss and separation and the pain of recovering racial memory coalesce both the personal and political realities dominating the volume and characterizing the imagery. The title poem, "Ivory Tusks," and "In My Father's House: A Reverie," two of the most effective works in the collection and among all of Allen's poems, illustrate this point. Racial identity based on cultural artifacts unappreciated by the larger society produces the pain of "all that matters lost" and precludes the integration of personality in "Ivory Tusks":

Pale and uncertain
lost in the distance
the ivory tusks they do not want.
The bleached sands sweep my eyelids,
heavy with revolving doors
I turn and reeling, turn again
but I am not yet comforted.

"In My Father's House" places the speaker back in the time period of "panther night" and "earthen floor," in the moment formed out of historical fact and racial memory, when the child is snatched from his father's house, from the familiar and the secure, by an unnamed "someone some power":

It came on me out of the night and I rushed to the yard
If I could throw the ball the stone the spear in my hand
Against the wall my father would be warned but now
Their hands had fallen on me and they had taken me
and I tried
To cry out but O I could not cry out and the cold gray
waves
Came over me O stifling me and drowning me. . . .

The poem is simultaneously evocative of both the capture of an African child by slavers and the entrapment of the Afro-American child by Western

Samuel Allen

pb

was born in 1917, at Columbus in Ohio. He was a student in James Weldon Johnson's creative writing class at Fisk University, but afterwards went through Harvard Law School. These dual interests have largely determined the course of his life.

After his war service he went to the New School for Social Research, then attended the Sorbonne in Paris under the G. I. Bill. Richard Wright introduced him to the Présence Africaine circle; his first published poems appeared in their magazine in 1949.

Allen's varied legal career has included employment and general practice in New York City, a two year stint in the teaching of law at Texas Southern University and service with the federal govenment in Washington during the Kennedy and Johnson years. In the summer of 1968 Allen left the law for literature. He was professor of humanities at Tuskegee for two years, teaching literature and conducting a writers' workshop. Since 1971 he has been teaching at Boston University. His subject is African, Afro-American and Third-World literature.

An early awareness of what Senghor dubbed 'négritude' had made him translate Sartre's 'Orphée noir' essay in 1951; it also led to an article on 'Tendencies in African poetry' (Présence Africaine 1958) and the 'Pan-Africanism reconsidered' volume which he co-edited, with an introduction, in 1962. 'Négritude and its relevance to the American Negro writer', a paper delivered at the 1959 New York Black writers' conference, has become the frequently-reprinted classic text on the subject. Allen has read his poetry at universities throughout the States, at the Library of Congress, and at Ile Ife in Nigeria. His anthology 'Poems from Africa' was published in 1973.

Sam Allen's first published book of poems appeared in Germany. Called 'Elfenbeinzähne – Ivory tusks', it was a bilingual edition with translations by Janheinz Jahn. It was published in 1956 under the pseudonym Paul Vesey (used in most of his early work). The next book of poems was published by Diane DiPrima in 1968 under his real name. Although it had almost the same title as the first (Ivory tusks) it was a new book with few old poems. The present collection of verse is indeed a wholly new book. It was selected out of a larger body of work which resulted from the first two or three years of Allen's life 'outside the law'. The title is borrowed from an earlier unpublished set bearing the subtitle 'An Afro-American Experience' – the eighteen poems which make up 'Paul Vesey's Ledger' reflect only the American phase of this experience. In style, they pay tribute to several of the poet's great precursors, including the famous with the anonymous, with casual nods in some surprisingly eclectic directions.

Covers for the 1975 collection of poems about black cultural heritage

culture. The result in either case is separation, isolation, and alienation, a symbolic death that is at once individual, familial, and racial.

In 1975 Allen published a collection of totally new poems, *Paul Vesey's Ledger*. The volume is tightly organized by chronology and theme, which broadly is black cultural heritage. The first of the eighteen untitled poems sets the tone and theme for the book: "the enormity/of these four hundred years." *Paul Vesey's Ledger* is very much a volume of the civil rights era (the 1960s and early 1970s), but it also stresses the disgraceful history of American oppression as far back as the original decimation of native Americans. Allen skillfully handles his motif, a consideration of the United States, this "strange and ferocious land," with understatement throughout. For example, in "Out on that ancient seascape," the whites' treatment of native Americans is explained away by the speaker who identifies with the manifest destiny of American colonists and pioneers; he concludes that "in those glorious days/everything was permitted," and justifies "Genocide": "Of course, it's true/the natives were rebellious."

A number of poems draw upon the period of slavery: for example, "I did not climb the apple trees in Sussex," which uses the Mississippi of slavery time for setting, plays on a phrase from the folksong "Roll the Cotton Down"—to bring the cotton down. The poem, which distinguishes its speaker's heritage from that of Anglo-Americans who "wait[ed] upon the queen in London town," is one of Allen's finest works in its rendering of the middle passage, enslavement "in the blistering hell of Mississippi," and the loss of African gods—Shango and Damballah. Allen's narrative ability comes out in the forceful poem depicting Harriet Tubman, the small, brave "Moses" who brought so many of her people out of slavery via the Underground Railroad. One of the escaping slaves chased by patterrollers and bloodhounds falters; Moses, his savior, holds her revolver to his head and gives him a choice: "Move or die." Allen also uses a folk hero in "John Henry was a steel drivin man," again making use of narrative technique and folksong.

In many poems Allen plays on the aspects of the American dream denied blacks. In "We scrounged in the alleys of those shabby days," he says "how quaint the sound" is of "due process," "a fair share," "an equal opportunity" compared to the reality of injustice in this "strange and ferocious land." His images of the degradation of Afro-Americans are vividly cast against the African scene, pointing up the defeat of the African kings by "power." But he concludes: "We work for the coming of the day/of justice."

In "Are they safe?" Allen strikes a satiric note by asking the question about well-to-do white women and children and then about black women and children on the auction block and black men in the face of the Klan. Again he uses two contrapuntal voices to dramatize the situation. The ironic reversal is very effective, but has even greater effect in the poem "The lingering doubt," where the doubt is that perhaps "the races are hierarchical," and the hope is that "they may yet be raised." However, the typical or expected situation is reversed, and the race needing lifting from "moral unfitness" is the *white* race.

"We were in the 'sylum, see" is a dramatic and humorous presentation of black insistence on civil rights: the black man in an insane asylum stands up to "White, Mr. Ruler of the Whole Damn Universe" and concludes about whites: "Man, I mean those people are *crazy*." "This blood was puttin down some fine never no mind" uses the same idiom in another dramatic presentation of a major black problem: the white encouragement of black-on-black violence.

The final poem, "As the names of the martyrs mount," rounds out the volume; the martyrs of the poem are heroes in the struggle for rights. It is an assurance that there still are those who will carry on the fight exemplified by Nat Turner, Harriet Tubman, John Henry, Martin Luther King, and Malcolm X. The remaining unnamed heroes will justify the sacrifices that have been made by "those/who dared to dream."

Because Allen is a perfectionist who never rushes his poems into print—he is his own severest critic—his output has been relatively small, but his patient and skillful craftsmanship has assured superior poetry and impeccable scholarship. Recognition of his stature as a poet is reflected in Allen's having had his poetry widely anthologized and his having been invited to read his poems at universities throughout the United States, at the Shrine of the Black Madonna in Detroit, and in Canada, Senegal, and Nigeria. In 1972 he gave a poetry reading at the Library of Congress, which was recorded for the permanent collection. During the same year the Nigerian Broadcasting Corporation of Lagos taped a dramatization of his poetry. He has been awarded two fellowships by the Wurlitzer Foundation of Taos, New Mexico (1979 and 1980-1981); an NEA Creative Writing Fellowship Award in poetry (1979); and a Rockefeller Foundation Grant at the Bellagio Conference and Study Center, Bellagio, Italy (1981).

In the introduction to his anthology, *Poems from Africa* (1973), Allen maintains: "To enter into another culture is to risk misunderstanding. The danger is lessened, however, if we are introduced through the creative arts. As we approach another community of men, we become aware that poetry is one of the best roads to understanding." His statement might well be applied to his own work, his poems, which, as he said of those he collected from Africa, "are of interest not only for their beauty, but also for the insights they offer into societies of great cultural wealth whose image has been dominated by the popular distortions. . . ."

Illustrated by Romare Bearden, Allen's anthology is representative in terms of African geography, historical periods, and poetic types, but it is also perhaps representative of his cross-cultural artistic and critical concerns and of his faith in the transforming power of the creative arts, of poetry in particular, as he suggests in *The Forerunners:* "Black poetry will be . . . a poetry of self-discovery, of self-realization, enabling us to know and to touch the wonder and the beauty, as well as the pain, of our common lot in this time and place. It is, ultimately, in its best expression, the task of the discovery of man, not in the sense of two thousand years of a xenophobic Western culture or of some universal abstraction, but in a more humanistic celebration of our own denied and particular experience." It is precisely for such "humanistic celebration," perhaps Allen's greatest achievement, that we continue to read his published poems and to anticipate his poetry in progress.

References:

Wilfred Cartey, "Dark Voices," *Présence Africaine* (n.d.): 94-97;

George Dickenberger, "Paul Vesey," *Black Orpheus*, 4 (October 1958): 5-8;
Ezekial Mphahlele, "Roots," in *The African Image* (New York: Praeger, 1962), pp. 49-55;
Mphahlele, *Voices in the Whirlwind and Other Essays* (New York: Hill & Wang, 1972);
Eugene Redmond, ed., *Drumvoices: The Mission of Afro-American Poetry, A Critical History* (Garden City: Anchor/Doubleday, 1976);
Frederick C. Stern, "Black Lit., White Crit?," *College English*, 35 (March 1974): 637-658.

Johari M. Amini
(Jewel Christine McLawler Latimore/Johari M. Kunjufu)

(13 February 1935-)

Fahamisha Patricia Brown
Boston College

BOOKS: *Images in Black*, as Jewel C. Latimore (Chicago: Third World Press, 1967);
Black Essence, as Jewel C. Latimore (Chicago: Third World Press, 1968);
A Folk Fabel [sic] (For My People), [broadside] (Chicago: Third World Press, 1969);
Let's Go Some Where (Chicago: Third World Press, 1970);
An African Frame of Reference (Chicago: Institute of Positive Education, 1972);
A Hip Tale in the Death Style [broadside] (Detroit: Broadside Press, 1972);
Commonsense Approach to Eating (Chicago: Institute of Positive Education, 1975).

Johari M. Amini

RECORDINGS: *Spectrum in Black*, includes Amini's poetry (Scott Foresman, 1971);
Black Spirits, includes Amini's poetry (Motown/Black Forum Records, 1972).

OTHER: Darwin T. Turner, ed., *Black American Literature*, includes poems by Amini (Columbus, Ohio: Charles E. Merrill, 1969);
Nikki Giovanni, ed., *Night Comes Softly: Anthology of Black Female Voices*, includes poems by Amini (New York: NikTom, 1970);
"Cromlech," [fiction] in *Jump Bad: A New Chicago Anthology*, edited by Gwendolyn Brooks (Detroit: Broadside Press, 1971);
Dudley Randall, ed., *The Black Poets*, includes poems by Amini (New York: Bantam, 1971);
Arnold Adoff, ed., *The Poetry of Black America*, includes poems by Amini (New York: Harper & Row, 1972);
Woodie King, Jr., ed., *Blackspirits: A Festival of New Black Poets in America*, includes poems by Amini (New York: Random House, 1972);
Adoff, ed., *Celebrations: A New Anthology of Black American Poetry*, includes poems by Amini (Chicago: Follett, 1977);
Erlene Stetson, ed., *Black Sister: Poetry by Black American Women, 1746-1980*, includes poems by

Johari M. Kunjufu (Bloomington: Indiana University Press, 1981);

Amiri Baraka and Amina Baraka, eds., *Confirmation: An Anthology of African-American Women,* includes poems by Amini (New York: Quill Books, 1983).

PERIODICAL PUBLICATIONS:

FICTION

"Wednesday," *Black World* (June 1970).

NONFICTION

"Redefinition: Concept as Being," *Black World* (May 1972)—later published separately as *An African Frame of Reference*;

"Statement on the Black Arts," *Black World* (February 1975).

Although born in Philadelphia, Johari Amini, who began her writing career as Jewel C. Latimore, must be defined as a Chicago poet. Her writing career coincides with the growth and development of several of that city's literary and cultural institutions. A founding member of Third World Press, the Writers Workshop of the Organization of Black American Culture (OBAC), the Kuumba Theater, and the Institute of Positive Education, Johari Amini has combined the careers of poet, educator, and health worker in an effort to restore wholeness to her people.

The first of six children of clergyman Vol William and songwriter Alma Bazel McLawler (composer of well-known gospel works, such as "If I Can Help Somebody"), Jewel Christine McLawler was something of a child prodigy. Under the nurturant guidance of her maternal grandmother, Frances Theresa Smith (herself a graduate from Knoxville College, teacher, elocutionist, missionary, and religious poet), young Amini could read by the age of three and could perform basic arithmetic functions by five. She had an excellent memory for poems. The *Pittsburgh Courier* ran two articles about Amini who started school in the second grade in 1941 (she was six years old), spent one term in the third grade and one term in the fourth. She graduated from the eighth grade in 1947 from Chicago's McCosh Elementary School. She then attended Englewood High School. She was sixteen years old when she wed for the first time. After high school and marriage, she found her life filled by her two children, daughter Marcianna (Marci) and son Kim Allan. They were teenagers when she was widowed and decided to return to school. She enrolled in Chicago's Wilson Junior College (now Kennedy-King City College). During her first year at Wilson, she met poet Haki Madhubuti (Don L. Lee). She had already discovered that she enjoyed writing essays for her classes, but it was Madhubuti who encouraged her to write poetry. When asked how she became interested in writing poetry, Amini responded, "It was a part of that time. I don't know if it would have happened [at any other time] . . . but that was a time of recognition . . . of coming around 360 degrees. . . . It was a time of foment and discovery." Amini's early work reflects that sense of self-discovery, and it was during this period that Jewel C. McLawler Latimore changed her name to "Johari Amini," which means in Swahili "Faithful Jewel."

In the summer of 1967, Amini, together with poets Madhubuti and Carolyn Rodgers, cofounded Third World Press. Modeled on Dudley Randall's Broadside Press of Detroit (then Madhubuti's publisher), Third World Press originally limited itself to the publishing of new black poetry, but later expanded to include prose, both nonfiction and fiction, as well as children's literature. Carolyn Rodgers's *Paper Soul* (1967) and Amini's *Images in Black* (1967) were the new press's first publications.

Images in Black demonstrated Amini's literary promise. Despite its limitations—forced diction, conventional images, and typography more faddish than poetic—the poetry contains jewels of language and imagery and addresses the issues of love, especially as a transforming power, and of identity, specifically in social terms, that have remained primary concerns of the writer. The short poem "Reservation" signals the poet's concern with precise definition and demonstrates her use of witty epigrams and apostrophe in her poetry. The volume's eleven poems include sensuous love lyrics, praise poetry, narrative, fable, and preachment. One of Amini's early concerns is the question of identity, particularly black female identity, but also the identity of the poet. Who am I? What is my task? How do I achieve my goal? Such questions are at the core of much of the poet's work. In the poem "Identity (For Don L. Lee)," she envisions the poet as "wearing a crown/of nature/a prophet/creator of change/showing identity/to Negroes (the/whiteminded ones)" and as asking the "—what are you—" question that leads the persona to ponder her own identity:

> the pain
>   stopped
> I took a breath of
>   life
> birth was   completed
>   growth was   begun

I was sister
I was Black
Proud Identity

In this poem and others on the question of identity, Amini frequently uses the radical rhetoric of the 1960s, but she attempts to make it personal and immediate, particularly in poems such as "Upon Being Black One Friday Night in July" that combines a specific incident with a reflection on its meaning for revolutionary nationalism.

Her first volume also reveals her concern with the future of black Americans, a concern that has become increasingly dominant in her work. The futuristic fable "And Then" is built upon a belief often voiced in the late 1960s: in a state of emergency the United States government would resort to containing its rebellious black population in urban concentration camps. Amini returns to this possible future in later poems. Ultimately, though, the central themes of *Images in Black* and most of Amini's later work are the centrality of love as a basis for racial unity and of unity as a precondition for power.

Summer 1967 saw the establishment of another major Chicago cultural institution. The Writers Workshop of the Organization of Black American Culture (commonly referred to as OBAC, pronounced ohBAHsee) included mentor Hoyt W. Fuller (editor of *Negro Digest,* later *Black World*), Cecil Brown, Sam Greenlee, Haki Madhubuti, and Carolyn Rodgers. Amini served as the group's treasurer until 1974. OBAC provided an atmosphere for supportive criticism and mutual growth. Workshop members collaborated on public readings and on their publication, *NOMMO,* a Bantu expression for the actualizing or empowering word. Popular themes shared by workshop members included black power and unity, black male/female love, and pan-Africanism. Because of the OBAC emphasis on public readings, the poets in the group became known for their highly charged style of reading. The community of poets who shared the OBAC experience have been criticized for being overly doctrinaire in matters of style and subject. However, unique voices did emerge, and Amini's was one of them.

Increasingly, while Amini's poetry reflected her membership in OBAC and her association with Madhubuti, it demonstrated a growing confidence in her technical skill and her own voice. In 1968, Third World Press published Amini's second book, *Black Essence.* In the book's preface, Madhubuti wrote, "Her growth is not exaggerated—it's noticeable and solid. . . ." And indeed it was. Three poems, "(For Nigareens)," "Masque," and "Sisters," resume Amini's explorations into the souls of black women. The poems call for black women to love themselves, their sisters, and their men, for as "Masque" makes clear, "a sister false is/cause/to make one bleed." The poem "Utopia" is reminiscent of "Reservation" of the first book in its epigrammatic definition laced with irony:

brothers

brothers

everywhere—

and

not a one

for sale

Lavish in their imagery, her "4 Poems of blk/love" are sensuous explorations of the physical joys of love: "making their love/was dessert/lush/rich/topped fullness/seeped black pleasure/joyously consumed" and elsewhere, "night was wool/dark-covered nappy flesh/our reaching bodies moved:/combined." There are fewer typographical games in this volume than in the previous one, and most often the typography reinforces imagery, vocabulary, or rhythm. For example, the first stanza of "Saint Malcolm" employs typography effectively:

The prophet speaks
his images disseminate
stripping facade
and the Dream stands naked
visibly before creation
as the Nightmare
in a truth of beasts grasping men. . . .

In 1968, Amini began her association with the founders of the Kuumba Performing Arts Company of Chicago, actor/director Val Gray-Ward and her husband Francis Ward, a journalist. Gray-Ward had incorporated some of Amini's poetry into her programs of dramatic readings and had invited Amini to become writer-in-residence of the new company. Amini admits learning a great deal from Francis Ward, who served first as adviser and later as coordinator of Kuumba's writing component. That same year, some of the OBAC writers and others began meeting with Illinois poet laureate

Gwendolyn Brooks in what became the Gwendolyn Brooks Writers' Workshop. This workshop, too, was an enriching experience for Amini. The older poet often joined the younger ones on public platforms, gave them the benefit of her experiences writing poetry, and won their affection and respect for her shared commitment to poetry as an instrument for change. From Brooks, the younger poets learned more of the art and discipline of their chosen craft and made connection with their literary history. In that community, there was no generation gap. For instance, Brooks would later write about Amini's poetry in words stemming from the OBAC writers' own critical, revolutionary vocabulary:

> [Johari Amini] is armed with understanding and with assistance for her people. She is diligent revolt. A salted frenzy. A freedom.
>
> Even the most exquisite freedom needs an anonymous spine of discipline, and this may be found in Johari's poetry. . . .
>
> Music is here. But it is music relevant to Johari's blacktime. . . .

A summer 1969 performance by the Kuumba players was the occasion for the first public reading of Amini's *A Folk Fabel [sic] (For My People)*. This cautionary fable later was published in broadside form in 1969. The tale of rebellion on earth, colonization of the moon, and the re-enslavement of black people to work in the moon mines is exemplary of Amini's maturing style. Equal parts sermon and fable, the long poem's chantlike rhythms enhance its subtext of the Africanity of black America. The poem's concluding vision, "the cosmos was whole/again &/the worlds had become new," repeats the poet's message of self-love and unity as preconditions for power. "A Folk Fabel" reveals that by the end of the 1960s Amini had defined a main function of her poetry: to preach the reality and the possibility of African-American existence.

Amini's third book, *Let's Go Some Where* (1970), was introduced by Gwendolyn Brooks, who remarked upon the poet's spirit, but especially upon her beauty without "beauty-tantrums" and her music with "honeying smoothing—which explodes." Brooks concluded that the poems are "About freedom. There *is* such freedom in what the 'new' black poets are doing now. . . . They feel free to run words together, or pull them impudently and unprecedentedly away from each other. To make a squalling harmony. Johari's poems are of this constructive impudence, this endorsement of chainlessness, this singular blend of confidence and awe." The first poem in the volume reciprocates; it is a praise-poem "For Gwendolyn Brooks—A Whole & Beautiful Spirit," which takes its text from David Llorens: "an act of living is an act of love. . . ." Brooks is equated to the "sight" and "seed" of blackness in the beginning:

Front cover for Amini's 1970 poetry book. Sonia Sanchez wrote in Negro Digest, *"right on: sister amini. Keep yr/bullet words coming . . . blow our minds with terrible images till we know/ realize a change had BETTER come. soon."*

> (for she is sure direction/voice
> (which makes us brittle in ourselves
> moving selfhate moving dross
> changing moving toward the cite
> of blackness beginning from the seed
> beginning from her sight which is
> an act of love which is an act of
> life

The poems in this collection again sing of love and unity. Of the book's eighteen poems and one prose poem, "Letter to a Blkwoman's Daughter," seven poems explore varying aspects of male/female relations. These poems combine sensuous images of physical love with introspective reflections on the nature of relationships. At times they are celebratory lovesongs, as in "A Celebration" in which "love is/life./velvet as/it grows. . . . man/woman/one/being/ascending/living/creating a/velvet celebration." At other times, they are blues lyrics, as in "21 Lines" when the poet asks "will u comfort/my womb . . . /will u cover/me in the darkness/will you comfort/me with the silence of nightnoises. . . ." Amini's love poetry, Gwendolyn Brooks has observed, "is remarkable. It is a penetrating sensuousness, with the frankness unfolding as the lines gather, until there it all is, perfectly open and deliberate before you: the *womancommitment.*"

Two other poems in the volume, "Untitled" and "A Revolutionary Requiem in Five Parts (With Prelude)," find Amini once more in the sermonic mode. Yoking images of the Nigerian civil war with images of gang warfare in Chicago, "Untitled (in commemoration of the blk/family)" urges the listener/reader on to the poem's terrifying conclusion, "we will be no mor. . . ." "A Revolutionary Requiem" is another cautionary fable, a strong reminder that "we blk/can move two ways as a/nation—toward survival/or toward death." How can a people win a revolutionary struggle if its warriors are high on drugs? While "tanks rumbled off th eisenhow/er & dan ryan frum racine/to cicero & 95th to 22nd/the task forse surrounded evree thang/blk . . . " the young "bruh" high on drugs "wuz still/out/there. yea./(spacin/didnt know th sewers/had backed/up." The poem is also a tour de force in Amini's experiments in black language. Part five, for example, shows her use of a black idiom and linguistic style:

yea. bruh wuz still
out
there
inthway
when th tank
rolled
o
ver hm maauled
hs
hed
bruh wuz
reeeeeallleespaced
dusted
yea.bruh
Died

In most instances, the spelling, typography, and punctuation enhance the poem's rhythms and images.

In contrast to the cautionary visions of "Untitled" and "A Revolutionary Requiem," "Hear Our Silence" offers the more hopeful "remembrance/of our ancient selves/ancient as we were/selves echoed from the burned/gold prebeginnings/of this now age." The vision here is optimistic; there will be a future:

listen through the sun
through essence sprung
from what we once have been
the once sun of our blackness
propelled into a million midnight stars
we will come
we will come
we will come
once more.

Amini's use of consonance, repetition, and off-rhyme produces a sonorous and moving poem.

After the publication of *Let's Go Some Where*, Amini published poetry infrequently (a new broadside, *A Hip Tale in the Death Style* in 1972, several new poems in *Black World*, and appearances of works from her books in anthologies). She continued her education and received a bachelors degree (1970) from Chicago State University as well as a masters degree (1972) from the University of Chicago, for which she wrote the thesis "Some Effects of Acculturation on the Ashanti Nation." More recently she completed professional training, earning a bachelor of science degree and a doctorate in chiropractic from the National College of Chiropractic. In addition, during the early 1970s, she taught Afro-American literature and psychology (her major field of study) at Kennedy-King College (1970 to 1972) and then at the University of Illinois at Chicago Circle (1972 to 1976). She also continued to work as an editor of Third World Press, as an officer of the Institute of Positive Education and OBAC. Although her work for the Institute's educational and cultural center occupied much of her time, during this same period Amini reviewed books for *Negro Digest*, *Black World*, and *Black Books Bulletin*, a publication of the Institute of Positive Education. She also published a pamphlet, *An African Frame of Reference* (1972), an expansion of her article "Redefinition: Concept as Being" (originally published earlier that same year in *Black*

World). The essay includes a discussion of the concepts of "universal art" and "protest literature."

In 1975, Amini's "Statement on the Black Arts" appeared in *Black World* and expanded on the aesthetic standards she had introduced in the earlier work. "I am an Afrikan woman who is also a writer—in that order," wrote Amini. "[T]he responsibility of those of us who deal in images is a very heavy one. . . . Nothing we create is neutral." Elsewhere in the same article she writes, "we create from the urgency of the ways we live here in this place, and urgency of our children." And in "Redefinition" she affirms, "the artist creates the We Are." These aesthetic principles inform her poetry. It is, Amini believes, the responsibility of the artist to provide her community with positive identity, purpose, and direction. Her most recent poetry publications in the anthologies *Black Sister: Poetry by Black American Women, 1746-1980* (1981) and *Confirmation: An Anthology of African-American Women* (1983) reflect her continued adherence to these beliefs.

"There Is No Title: Only Echoes," "The Promise," and "Story for the Remainder" appear in Amiri and Amina Baraka's *Confirmation: An Anthology of African-American Women.* Of the three, only "There Is No Title," previously published in *Black World* (1970), is a love poem; the other two are poems for the black family and community. "The Promise" presents a mother, awaiting her sons, who is filled with a sense of life, future, and growth. "Story for the Remainder" exhorts the black community to move away from the negative aspects of drugs, materialism, and decay toward the positive values of love, responsibility, and children as investments in a wholesome, fertile future. "Ceremony," "Return," and "The Promise" appear in Erlene Stetson's *Black Sister: Poetry by Black American Women, 1746-1980;* "Ceremony," addressed to "sisters," contains the refrain "libation," which the persona offers to the spirits "to cleanse us up in this place/ and drive out the non sense from our minds/and the crap from our dreams." The poem stresses the essential role of black women in nation building, raising children, and supporting men, so that the black family, and by extension the entire race, "will not keep screamin and dyin in confusion/lost to ourselves and what we need to do." Black women are not only "the color of our Men like the sun in the soil/we the Mothers of the earth/the Mothers of the Generations of Life/we the/libation."

Amini's poetry has not been the object of much critical discussion even though it has appeared in over fifteen anthologies, including Stephen Henderson's *Understanding the New Black Poetry: Black Speech and Black Music as Poetic References* (1973). Reviews of her books appeared in *Negro Digest* (April 1969) and *Black World* (December 1970); Sonia Sanchez favorably reviewed *Black Essence* for *Negro Digest,* while Sarah Webster Fabio enthusiastically reviewed *Let's Go Some Where* for *Black World.* Aside from reviews, Amini's work receives brief mention in Eugene Redmond's *Drumvoices: The Mission of Afro-American Poetry* (1976). Redmond only states that Amini "relies heavily upon black colloquialisms, usually achieving success. But she has other ranges, as can be seen in 'Brother,' which longs for the 'soil' of black people, where they can feel the ['] universe shudder . . . [']." However, there is little significant criticism yet available on the majority of the "new black poets" of the 1960s, much less on groups such as the OBAC or Chicago poets.

Nonetheless, Amini remains one of the significant voices to emerge from among the Chicago writers. She has extended her range of language, imagery, and rhythm while remaining constant in her choice of themes. She is a poet/preacher whose poems are sermons of love and unity. She is also a storyteller whose fables teach lessons of self-love for

Amini and Woodie King, Jr., at the 1972 DuSable Museum party honoring the publication of his Blackspirits: A Festival of New Black Poets in America *(photograph by Hoyt W. Fuller, courtesy of Johari Amini)*

her daughter and her sisters. She is a lyricist singing praise songs, lovesongs, and blues. Finally, she is a black woman with urgent messages of survival and self-love for her daughter and her sisters. Some readers may argue with Amini's images of female submission to males; a few of her statements may even be read as homophobic. But much of Amini's work can probably be defined as feminist; her preachments on self-love and sisterly solidarity affirm women. Nonetheless, Amini's primary messages concern the love and unity necessary for the race as a whole, undivided by gender. Her prophetic visions of what can be, her clear-eyed examinations of what is, and her reflections on the past place her solidly in the context of the nationalist, pan-African poets who emerged during the 1960s.

For Amini, the personal not only *is* political, but is as well a paradigm for the communal. Healthy personal relationships are prerequisites for a healthy and whole community. Thus, the writer's careers merge. Her concern with physical health, represented by her studies and work in nutrition and chiropractic intersect her work as a poet/educator writing prescriptions for mental and spiritual health. In 1975, she published *Commonsense Approach to Eating*, which is a collection of her nutrition and health articles, "Living Well," first published in *Black Books Bulletin*. Single again, she lives with her younger son Shikamana in Atlanta, Georgia, where she works as a chiropractor. In a recent interview, she indicated that now that she is out of school, there will be more poetry forthcoming, and her poem, "The Promise," included in both of her latest appearances in anthologies, augurs for its maturity and wisdom:

i am warm
great
i am undulating life

my sons are coming home

and they will not remember the cold tribes
the years
far away within the snow
and dying trees

they will not remember
the stripes and the lashes
whip stroking across
the sunless days

they will only know me

A grandmother of six, Amini continues to look to the future, a healthy future not only for herself and her children but for the entire black community, as she indicates in "Story for the Remainder": "our children are wanted treasures/growing in the richness of our own/Creator's sun/alerted with wisdom from our mouths and ways/ . . . When we dance now we celebrate/and not decay."

References:

Sarah Webster Fabio, Review of *Let's Go Some Where*, *Black World*, 20 (December 1970): 68;

Eugene Redmond, *Drumvoices: The Mission of Afro-American Poetry, A Critical History* (Garden City: Anchor/Doubleday, 1976);

Sonia Sanchez, Review of *Black Essence*, *Negro Digest*, 18 (April 1969): 91-92.

Russell Atkins

(25 February 1926-)

Ronald Henry High

BOOKS: *A Podium Presentation* (Cleveland: Free Lance Press, 1960?);

Phenomena (Wilberforce: Free Lance Poets and Prose Workshop, 1961);

Objects (Eureka, Cal.: Hearse Press, 1963);

Two by Atkins: The Abortionist and The Corpse (Cleveland: Free Lance Press, 1963);

Objects 2 (Cleveland: Renegade Press, 1964);

Heretofore (London: Breman Publishers, 1968);

The Nail, to be Set to Music (Cleveland: Free Lance Press, 1970);

Maleficium (Cleveland: Free Lance Press, 1971);

Here in The (Cleveland: Poetry Center of Cleveland State University, 1976);

Whichever (Cleveland: Free Lance Press, 1978).

PERIODICAL PUBLICATIONS: "A Psychovisual Perspective for 'Musical' Composition," *Free Lance*, 3 (Winter 1955-1956): 2-16; 5 (November 1958): 7-47;

"The Hypothetical Arbitrary-Constant of Inhibition," *Free Lance*, 8 (November 1964): 33-61;

"Of," *Free Lance*, 18, nos. 1-2 (1976-1977): 16-24.

Russell Atkins, author, composer, lecturer, commentator, theorist, and artist, is one of the leading experimental figures of the past three decades. One of the earliest concrete poets in this country, Atkins is an innovator in poetic drama who has a high regard for craftsmanship. Better known abroad than in America, he brought a "new sweep, a complex of relationships to poetry and music" that did not exist prior to the appearance of his works.

Atkins was born on 25 February 1926 in Cleveland, Ohio, to Perry Kelly and Mamie Bell Atkins. He studied piano with his mother at the age of seven and showed evidence of drawing and painting skills in the early grades at Giddings Elementary School. By the time he was thirteen, Atkins had won several poetry contests and had written short plays for puppets which he had created himself.

Atkins attended Central High School and exceeded the limits of the curriculum by becoming acquainted with the major classics in literature and philosophy and by publishing his first poem in the 1944 graduates' yearbook. He remarked, "I was avant-garde before I knew there was one." He admits that Ezra Pound and Marianne Moore were influences on him, in that they were the first contemporary poets whom he encountered in high school. From them Atkins received an additional feeling of freedom from traditional poetry; he had already developed his own style, which was to stretch or distort in exaggerated ways the denotations and connotations of words.

The publication of several of his poems followed introductions through correspondence to Carl Van Vechten, Charles Henri Ford, Parker Tyler, Edith Sitwell, and the editors of *View* (1947). Atkins's early works appeared in *Experiment* (1947-1951), *Beloit Poetry Journal* (1951, 1952, 1955, 1957), *New York Times* (1951), *Four Winds* (1952), *Western Review* (1953-1954), and *Botteghe Oscure* (1955).

Atkins received additional education at the Cleveland School of Art, the Karamu Theatre, the Cleveland Music School Settlement, and the Cleveland Institute of Music. Military complications precluded Atkins from completing his work at Cleveland College, but he later studied composition from 1950 to 1954 with J. Harold Brown. All of these experiences were important because one of Atkins's salient features is his versatility as a writer and as a musician.

From 1950 on, Atkins devoted his time to composing, writing, and the founding of *Free Lance* magazine with Caspar L. Jordan. This publication of poetry and prose is probably the oldest black-owned literary magazine, although white writers were included in its pages. *Free Lance*, which was established as Cleveland's avant-garde periodical, was significant in that it played a major part in the development of ideas and techniques of the New American poetry. The first issues of the magazine were put together by hand, but the later ones took on a more professional look. The magazine was printed by Villiers in England, and contributors to the first edition included Russell Atkins, Rose Greene, Helen Collins, Beatrice Augustus, Vera

Photograph by Louis T. Milic

Steckler. Langston Hughes provided an introduction in which he commented: "Skilled or unskilled, wise or foolish, nobody can write a poem without revealing something of himself. Here are people. Here are poems. Here is revolution." *Free Lance*'s popularity was evident through its widespread distribution in Scotland, Ireland, France, Denmark, Sweden, and Australia.

As far as Atkins's own writing is concerned, he states: "Originality is not necessarily what has never been done before. More often it is doing what has been done before differently." His early stylistic period occurred at the time when conservatism was prevalent in American poetry—the day of the academic poets. Even where Atkins seems eclectic in the academic sense, there is a consolidation of direction, aesthetic, and imagination that goes beyond the prevailing work of that period. His starkly dramatic handling of such subjects in poetry as dope addiction, sexual aberration, necrophilia, and abortion went beyond the academic reserve of the early 1950s, and these themes recur many times. Atkins himself in a poem, "There She Sits," for the Walt Whitman issue of *Beloit Poetry Journal* (1955) implies that American poetry had forgotten the uninhibited spirit of Whitman in pursuit of the formalism of Eliot:

"For Heaven's sake. O Muse!
It pains me. Hers once
The ear into which I
Said everything hugely.
She was fearless!"

No more. We must whisper.
She has professor's ears.
Not so loud, Walt, will you?
Walt! Wait!

"Listen, dear Muse, to me!
I'm Walt Whitman!"—

An example of Atkins's early style can be seen in the poem "Tempest" in which he uses the contraction for the first time:

's nightly subterfuge
someone is sitting restlessly
. . . .
out) night's a-fledge
. . . .
when 'ts HARSHLY—

After Atkins submitted this poem to *View Magazine,* he was commended on his "experimental style and good ear" by editor Parker Tyler.

With another stylistic feature, the apostrophe, Atkins managed to wrench the words so violently that their connotations seemed to make them "three-dimensional." Atkins exaggerated grammatical structures by shifting parts of speech while converting them into past participles or weak verbs. Examples of this technique may be seen in the poem "Rehabilitation Building Entrance":

to sight, drastic'd its
lo and behold alack'd:
where were both should be legs?
nor for grasp his hands
of these and one grisly'd
as in a kind—but who might know
the kind—of plastercast'd
skin came no to a living look.
. . . .
how, to a view, sudden mishap
crooked. Cruel'd sharp. Ax'd
as of monstrous'd vex.

Atkins was said to have told a friend that he wanted a verbal technique so complex and weighted that it would be almost incomprehensible to the casual reader.

A second phase of Atkins's style was his involvement with concrete poetry, in which the visual pattern or arrangement of words and letters is predominant. If not exactly the first, certainly Atkins's work was among the earliest examples of what was to be called "concrete." He comments on this in a letter to editor Paul Breman: "Saw an article on concrete poetry in Times Supplement. Many do not know that I was, possibly, the first to write it over here in the U.S.A."

Atkins's first "concrete-like" poem was "Night and a Distant Church" which appeared in *Free Lance* (1950). The poem contains "darkened insinuation of religious alarm, sinister wind and suppressed omen":

Forward abrupt up
the mmm mm
wind mmm m
mmm
upon
the mm mm
wind mmm m
mmm
into the mm wind
rain now and again
the mm wind
ells
b
ells
b

One can hear the sound of the wind and rain just by looking at the poem on the printed page.

Every conceivable example of "concrete" can be found in "Nocturne and Prelude," which was published by *Beloit Poetry Journal* in 1951:

By N x x x x x
x x x O x
x .
x
x .
(ight rE
o
from the ((((((((((((((Sh///
you may very reverently
begin /// wa lk // Ing
com mmm mmmmmmm mmmmmm mmm

Robert H. Glauber of *Beloit Poetry Journal* wrote to Atkins that there was a great deal of his work that interested them, and he also complimented Atkins on the clarity and excitement of "Nocturne and Prelude."

A poem which is less controversial than those which employ the concrete method is Atkins's "Trainyard at Night." This poem, which effectively uses onomatopoeia to describe the sound of thunder, was introduced to the public in 1951 by Marianne Moore over radio station WEVD in New York:

then huge bold blasts black
hiss, insists, upon hissing insists
on insisting on hissing hiss
hiss s ss sss ssss s

Marianne Moore liked the poem very much and felt that it should be heard by the public.

Another device which Atkins used during this stylistic period was the continuous embedding of words within words. This technique is apparent in

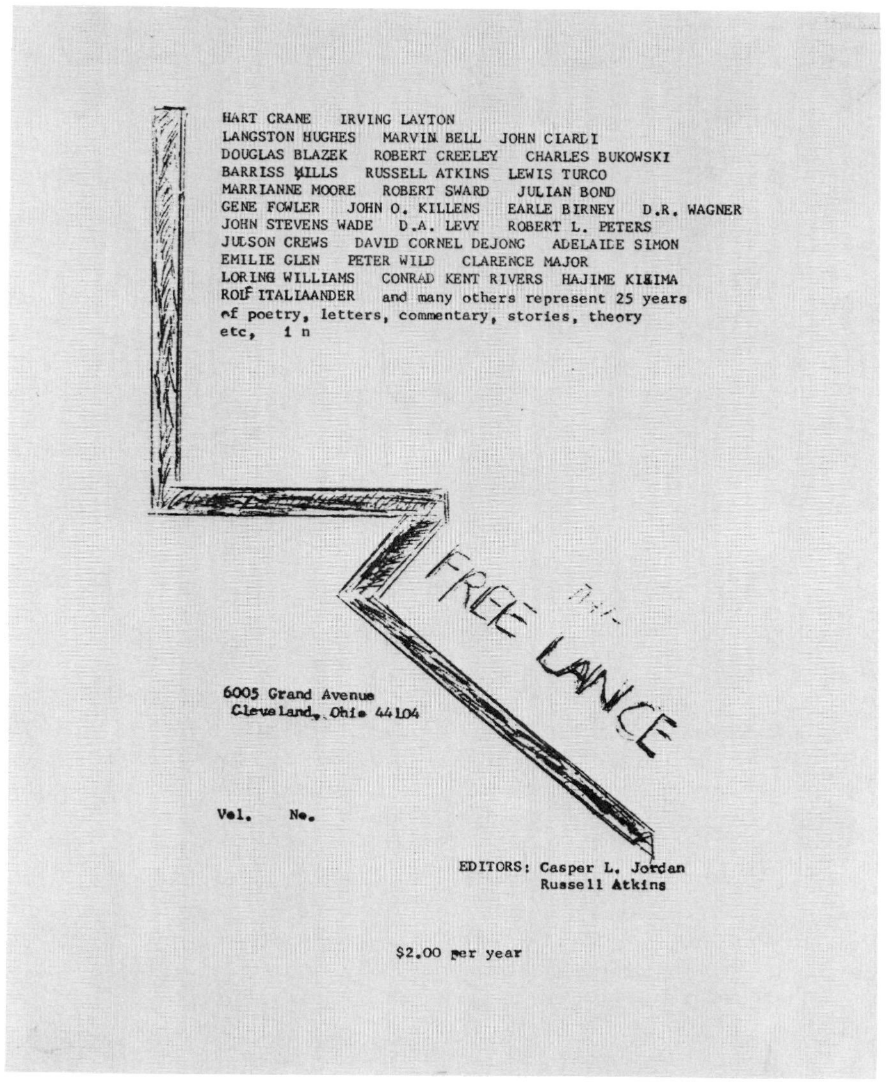

Early flyer for the literary magazine founded by Atkins and Caspar L. Jordan (courtesy of Russell Atkins)

the poem "Lisbon," which was published in *Free Lance* (1953):

> oneE very huGe To W'erE dged
> C On vent s an' K/ill'd
> multituDes per at En
> trance of horror
> o theR ush

Continuous words are also used in Atkins's 'NIGH)TH CRY, PT:

> Then lis Ten! O c Lock ed in I
> Found mysel F or bade on
> By the strange in fluences I
> Am on g St ones of lost . . .

All of these poems were among the precursors of the concrete movement in American poetry.

Through the 1950s, Atkins continued to write poetry and music and remained involved with activities in those areas. He became affiliated with the Iowa Workshop of the University of Iowa from 1953 to 1954. In 1954 two plays, *The Abortionist* and *The Corpse,* were published and were later reissued in 1963 as *Two by Atkins. The Abortionist,* which neither condones nor condemns abortion, tells of a Dr. Drassakar who avenges himself by giving Miss Harrington, the daughter of a hated colleague, a violent abortion. *The Corpse* is the story of a deranged widow who visits her husband's tomb each year to watch his body decay. With the production of these works, Atkins began experimenting with "poems in play form." The simplest, though not the most complete, explanation of this phrase is that instead of a regular play written in verse, poems would be arranged as plays.

American theater has been largely realistic and representational and even middle-class in its taste. Because poetics on the stage conflicts with this sense of realism, it is not surprising that Atkins's poems in play form elicited such comments as "outré" in 1954. With the exceptions of Archibald MacLeish, Maxwell Anderson, and T. S. Eliot, modern poetic drama of any kind has been rare. Until the "theatre of the absurd," which was imported from Europe, established itself in the 1960s, Atkins's little poem-plays were avant-garde and unique on the American scene. A nude woman being given an abortion on the stage was not commonplace in the 1950s; neither was a widow kneeling in a mausoleum fondling her husband's bones and skull ordinary American playfare.

Adelaide Simon described *The Abortionist* and *The Corpse* as "two brief hysterically ghoulish shadow plays which would guarantee a stunning production of some liberated Grand Guignol." In the editor's notes to the works, Casper L. Jordon stated that with the production of these works, Atkins began a series of original experiments for poems as dramas.

When the works were reissued later, Tina Morris of *Poetmeat* stated: "*The Abortionist* reminded me of one of those wonderful melodramatic silent films, reaching a wonderful climax with the 'villain' Dr. Drassakar, crying (in subtitles) 'You can't save her' as help comes at last for the unfortunate heroine." She went on to say, "*The Corpse* isn't quite as funny . . . I mean it isn't quite as experimental . . . it was far too reminiscent of Shakespeare, complete with weather forecasts to create the appropriate atmosphere for each scene." Morris assessed Atkins's work as interesting at times but usually lacking in depth and emotion.

One of the most significant contributions to avant-garde musical thought during the 1950s was Atkins's theory of psychovisualism, which was published by *Free Lance* (1955-1956; 1958). Based on Gestalt theory which studies the forming of patterns, it explains how we perceive the nonverbal "high and low" in music. His work added considerably to the use of graphs to organize notes by recognizing that the brain, not the ear, is the right instrument for understanding composition in music. The ear merely receives the stimuli. Atkins draws a sharp line between "music" and composition and claims that the two are contradictory.

The theory attracted the attention of composers like Stefan Wolpe, who introduced the work at the Darnstadt Festival of Contemporary Music in 1956. European avant-garde music critic H. H. Stückenschmidt also mentioned Atkins's theory in his book *Twentieth Century Music* (1969). The significance of the theory lies in the fact that the ideas continue to influence avant-garde centers in Europe, as well as to add to Atkins's reputation as an avant-garde poet.

In 1956 Atkins was invited to Middlebury College's Bread Loaf Writers Conference, conducted that year by Robert Frost and John Ciardi. The following year Atkins was made assistant to the director of the Sutphen School of Music of the National Guild of Community Music Schools.

In the mid-1950s, Atkins's writing began to move in a different direction as he became less satisfied with one course. He felt that the path of concretism was not flexible enough to serve the narrative technique he had in mind. His abstractive technique, which he called "phenomenalism," implies that each work functions autonomously. There is a juxtaposition of familiar and unfamiliar elements and the apostrophe becomes more prevalent.

With the advent of the 1960s, Atkins published some of his better known collections of poems. *A Podium Presentation,* which was published by *Free Lance* in 1960, consists of four poems. The first, "Lines in Recollection," is a mixture of Atkins's early and middle style. However, the first part of the poem uses the apostrophe to a lesser degree than found in his earlier poems:

> I had just arrived on the advanced slope and I
> did think of Grant Wood and some others:
> . . . .
> th' uproarious trees of startlingly beautious flowers.

In the second part of the poem, Atkins places the words so that one has to visualize the "long place" which is referred to in the passage. At the word "moving," there is a diagram which gives visual meaning to the reader. This portion of the poem is representative of the continuous word device, as well as Atkins's phenomenalist abstractive technique.

```
L    L      L      L
  On) G ONg) ON G L oNg
    e              e

place           that          PLACE
```

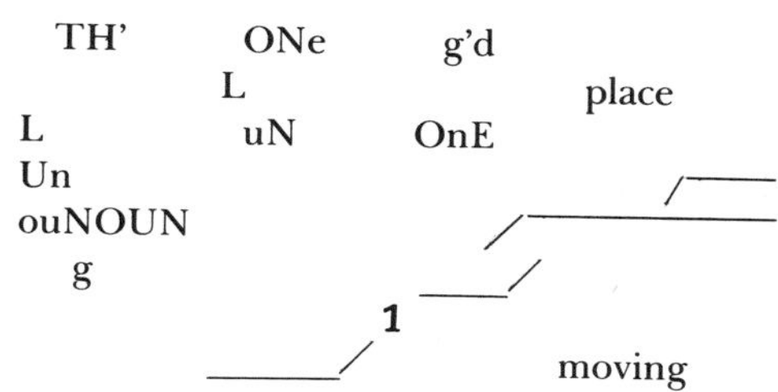

TH'
ONe
g'd
L
place
L
uN
OnE
Un
ouNOUN
g
1
moving

Another poem in *Podium Presentation,* "Three O' Clock (afternoon)," uses the early apostrophe device and relies upon the play on important words:

LONE of a car
Passes below
In the street's around
Gas station, bank,
And barbershop
Murmur'd MURMUR
murmurs, passes

Finally, however, the poems in this collection seem to be less experimental than those in some of the subsequent volumes.

Phenomena, a book of avant-garde poems and plays, was published in 1961 by Wilberforce University Press. The work opens with "The Prelude," which aptly describes the earth's birth in terms of violence. Its premise is anything might follow from so violent a beginning. The themes and techniques of the entire book reflect that premise.

The second work in the book is a poem in play form entitled "The Drop of Blood," which is a derivative of "The Corpse" in that they both are written in loosely rhymed tercets and quatrains. The story tells of an older woman who is married to a young man and is driven to a state of hallucination by her lack of trust in him. The woman converses with a drop of blood which insists that her husband is unfaithful. The wife kills the husband after she learns this accusation is true.

"Of Angela" relates the story of an intellectual, Laird, who is rejected by Angela, a sexually promiscuous woman. Out of anger and humiliation, Laird begins to function as a deviate, and he seeks revenge on Angela by stealing her male prostitute lover. The poem ends with Angela confronting the two with her unwanted pregnancy. The prostitute kills her, beats up Laird, and flees. Adelaide Simon referred to "Of Angela" as a saga of lust.

Phenomena ends with "The Exoneration," which was performed in 1973 by the Karamu Theater in Cleveland. The play is the story of a false arrest of a black suspect. The detective constantly uses abusive language, and the play ends with a four-letter word. This aggressive use of language further substantiates the fact that Atkins's writing during the 1950s and 1960s was daring.

Phenomena, and especially "Of Angela," struck some readers as "explicitly crude." The entire book has an unsettling mood which overtakes the reader, even when the meaning escapes one. Strangely enough, the book was a remarkable forecast of the 1960s' themes: nudity, four-letter words, police brutality, and sexual aberration.

In 1963 Atkins's *Objects* was printed by Hearse Press; the next year *Objects 2* by Renegade Press appeared. These collections of poems were reprinted from various magazines and contain some of Atkins's better-known poems: "Tempest," "Elegy to Hurt Bird That Died," "Trainyard at Night," and "Night and a Distant Church," among others. Although the *Smith* described *Objects* as a "galaxy of unpredictable fascinating phenomena," Tina Morris of *Poetmeat* found the book just left her cold.

Heretofore, which became one of Atkins's better known books, was published by Breman of London in 1968. In a letter to the editor, Atkins remarked: "The title of the book might be *Erst* by Russell Atkins. Since the book, as I told you, was to trace my former work up to now, technically at least, and to publish several pieces (Fantasie, Seventh Circle) which were written years ago but never published." Atkins felt strongly about *Heretofore,* and he admits that the subject matter varies violently from the controversial to the respectable.

Heretofore opens with "Fantasie," a poem that portrays man's current and past hurts. It was written at the tail end of the surrealist movement and was originally submitted to *View* in 1946, but after consideration the editors rejected "Fantasie." Some passages are almost free association, while others only loosely maintain a kind of narrative which may seem incomprehensible to many readers:

Now as I went walking
the swollen deep
reared higher—
a sudden dismissal of obstructed view

Another poem in *Heretofore* uses a similar technique. "Christophe" is about a black hero for whose glory the flag waved:

Up Up
Christophe
appeared in th'imminent

an' th' passion overjoying the hour
unfolded
flaming
Highly th'imperial sign
shone in his glory.

The poem does not contain the complexity of meaning which is so typical of Atkins. However, Langston Hughes wrote to Atkins on 15 June 1949 remarking how much the students in his survey of American poetry classes in Chicago were "intrigued" by this poem.

The Seventh Circle, a radio play written in 1957 and originally intended for *Experiment Magazine* (which folded before the play's publication) also appears in *Heretofore.* It tells of a day in the life of a man who does not want to get involved with trivialities, but who cannot control the sensitivity of his feelings. Perhaps the play would win wide acceptance if it were performed on radio because, although the technique is complex, it is not beyond the scope of the average listener.

Free Lance published two more important works by Atkins, *The Nail* (1970) and *Maleficium* (1971). The former work, adapted from the short story by Pedro Antonio de Alarcón, is a poetic libretto which was suggested for an opera by composer Hale Smith. The story tells of an official, Judge Zarco, who loves a married woman who calls herself Mercedes. After murdering her husband by driving a nail through his skull, she disappears for a while and becomes known as a fugitive under her married name, Dona Gabriela Zahara. The judge does not know that he is hunting down the woman he loves until she appears before him to be sentenced after giving herself up. *The Nail* is filled with suspense and intensity as the reader tries to discover the woman's true identity.

Maleficium is a series of twenty short stories, many of which portray their characters as having an

According to Atkins, the subject matter in this 1968 volume varies sharply from the respectable to the controversial.

underlying viciousness. For example, in "Story No. 2" a young man writes to his mother telling her that he is doing very well and that his many activities include car theft, murder, and rape. The man closes the letter by telling his mother that one of his friends who is an expert murderer is coming to visit. The collection contains four-letter words and is filled with the candor which is so representative of Atkins.

Since *Maleficium* two books of poetry have been published: *Here in The* (1976) and *Whichever* (1978). The former consists of thirty-nine poems, three of which had appeared previously. In the poem "Shipwreck," Atkins makes no apologies for the direction his writing has taken:

With today's sympathetics who can be
 dare?
in the old days when sailed struck,
sank, who knew? few, comparatively
(-no speaking cabinets),
much less "typographical" compassion)
But these days terroring,
the grim fashion's that the speaking cabinet
and the typographical
leave what sympathetics more than fear?

Unfortunately, there has been no critical review of the book; however, the poems are written in a refined, mellower style, yet within the experimental framework which so characteristically flavors Atkins's writing.

Whichever (1978), published with support of the Ohio Arts Council, is a booklet of fourteen poems which contain elements of Atkins's earlier style—image as action coupled with the rhythmic flow of avant-garde jazz music. This may be seen in "Stepmothers: Grimm Bros. RE-VISITED":

"Ha, ha." he flung
his lunchpail down "Honey, baby,
honey, come to daddy."

The poems in the volume are on a wide range of subjects (including the weather, dope, crime, apparitions, and disco dancing) but seem to be less complex than poems in previous collections; however, there is no doubt that the works flow from Atkins's pen. There is freshness and excitement to each one of them.

Aside from writing, Atkins was involved with other activities during the 1970s. In 1971 he was consultant for Cleveland's WVIZ television and for the Karamu Writers Conference (the Karamu House presented an evening called "A Tribute to Russell Atkins" in the same year). In 1973 he was selected as writer in residence at Cuyahoga Community College, and in 1976 Cleveland State University bestowed an honorary doctorate upon Atkins. A recipient of a $5,000 Creative Fellowship from the Ohio Arts Council, Atkins has been awarded numerous other grants for literary writing. Since *Free Lance* ceased publication (1979-1980) after having thrived for nearly thirty years, Atkins has been writing several pieces for piano, as well as operas. He now resides in Cleveland, Ohio.

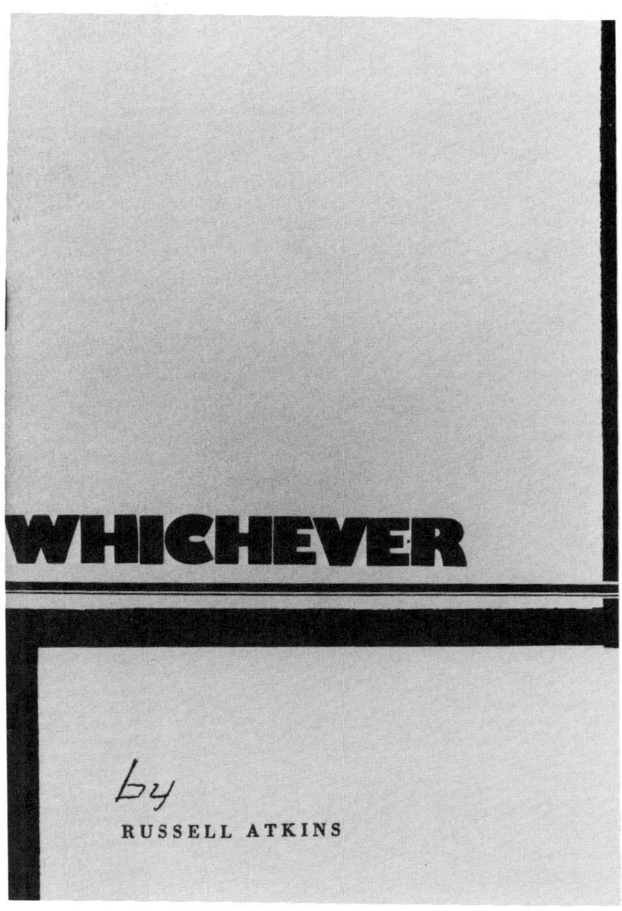

The poems in Atkins's 1978 collection are characterized by the juxtaposition of disparate elements.

Unfortunately, there has been little critical comment on Atkins's works, which could be due in part to their daring nature. Also, his works are disparate and perhaps need to be collected in order for readers to recognize him as one of the most innovative forces in poetry of the past thirty years. Casper L. Jordan had the following to say in accounting for the lack of critical reception of Atkins's works: "For many, accustomed to prosaic reticence, so-called 'evenness' of line as 'a good ear' (too often a dull ear) Mr. Atkins's poetry may hold little interest. . . . Mr. Atkins raises 'a good ear' into an *artistic one*. . . ."

Furthermore, Eugene Redmond in *Drum Voices* (1976) feels that Atkins's aesthetic ideas are as complex as the poetry itself. Adelaide Simon states in *Input* (1964) that there is a great deal of sadness in the lack of acclaim for Atkins's work in the very avant-garde itself. She commends him on his constant experimentation with words and sounds alone. And although Kirby Congdon replied to Simon's comments by wishing Atkins would write in a language the average reader understands, he also expressed admiration for Atkins's ideas.

Finally, as more people get familiar with Atkins, his approach to literary expression will be better appreciated and more fully understood. As his work is more performed and more read, as it garners more critical attention and documentation, his genius will come to be recognized in the United States as it is in Europe.

References:

Paul Breman, *You Better Believe It* (Baltimore: Penguin, 1973), pp. 206-208;

Free Lance, Russell Atkins Issue, 14 (Second Half 1970-1971): 1-30;

Eugene Redmond, *Drum Voices* (Garden City: Anchor/Doubleday, 1976), pp. 292-293.

Papers:

Trevor Arnett Archives of Atlanta University, Atlanta, Georgia, holds a large amount of information on Atkins and his works. Vivian Harsh Collection of the Chicago Public Library has two boxes of Atkins's letters and corrected copies of *Heretofore* (Heritage Archive Series).

Alvin Aubert

(12 March 1930-)

Norman Harris
Wayne State University

BOOKS: *Against the Blues* (Detroit: Broadside Press, 1972);

Feeling Through (Greenfield Center, N.Y.: Greenfield Press, 1975).

OTHER: J. W. Corrington and Miller Williams, eds., *Southern Writing in the Sixties: Poetry,* includes poems by Aubert, 2 volumes (Baton Rouge: Louisiana State University Press, 1966);

"Ernest J. Gaines," in *Contemporary Novelists,* edited by James Vinson (New York: St. James Press, 1972), pp. 236-237;

Miller Williams, ed., *Contemporary Poetry in America,* includes poems by Aubert (New York: Random House, 1973);

Arnold Adoff, ed., *Celebrations: An Anthology of Black Poetry,* includes poems by Aubert (Chicago: Follett, 1979);

Edward Field, ed., *A Geography of Poets: An Anthology of the New Poetry,* includes poems by Aubert (New York: Bantam, 1979);

"Balls and Chain" and "There Were Fierce Animals in Africa," in *Contemporary Southern Poetry,* edited by Guy Owen and Mary C. Williams (Baton Rouge & London: Louisiana State University Press, 1979), pp. 17-18;

"James Weldon Johnson," in *Writers of the English Language,* edited by James Vinson (New York: St. James Press, 1979).

PERIODICAL PUBLICATIONS: "Black American Poetry: Its Language and the Folk Tradition," *Black Academy Review,* 2 (Spring/Summer 1971): 7-8;

"Ernest J. Gaines' Truly Tragic Mulatto," *Callaloo,* 3 (1978).

Alvin Aubert's work as a poet, editor, and publisher places him at the center of creative activity among Afro-Americans during the last three decades. He stands as a chronicler of the black literary experience. Since 1975, as publisher and editor of *Obsidian: Black Literature in Review,* Aubert has provided an outlet for many Afro-American scholars and creative writers. His own poetry is often elliptical and curiously dispassionate, as if he wants only to capture objectively the occasion that provided the emotional impetus for writing the poem and to leave the evaluation of that moment's meaning to the reader. His poetry is distinguished by its uniqueness within the historical period in which it was written: while many of the black poets who published during the late 1960s and early 1970s wrote angry, didactic poems, he wrote somewhat allusive poems that always suggest more than they directly convey.

Alvin Bernard Aubert was born to a working-class family in Lutcher, Louisiana, in 1930. He was the last of Albert and Lucille Roussel Aubert's seven children. From all indications Aubert was greatly influenced by his father and, by his own admission, found favor in his status as the unexpected youngest child. His childhood experiences, rich in Louisiana folk culture, would later find their way into his poetry through regional diction and themes which revolve primarily around his relationship with his father and the presentation and exploration of characters from his childhood. Poems drawn from Aubert's childhood include "Economics," "Photo Album," and "Three for the Old Man," all of which appear in *Against the Blues* (1972). The actual language of Aubert's childhood is clearest in the dialects of Southern characters, for example, in "Whispers in A Country Church" and "Testament," which appear in the same volume.

In 1944, at the age of fourteen, Aubert dropped out of high school and worked in a general store in Lutcher for three years. In 1947 he joined the army, where he remained until 1954. In 1948 he married his first wife with whom he had a daughter, Stephenie. He completed a GED high school level test in 1947, and in 1955 he entered Southern University in Baton Rouge, Louisiana, from which he graduated in 1959 with a bachelor's degree in English and a minor in French. In 1960 he earned a

Alvin Aubert was born in Louisiana and taught English literature at Southern University in Baton Rouge. Now he teaches Afro-American literature at State University College in Fredonia, New York.

The first poem he wrote was "Nat Turner in the Clearing," in 1963, before William Styron's novel made Turner's slave revolt common knowledge. Writing the poem triggered Aubert's poetic efforts, which culminated in the book **Against the Blues.**

About black poetry Aubert says, "All of Afro-American literature is grounded in Afro-American folk culture.

"The people in this country of African descent had to begin all over again and create their own culture, which was inevitably a folk culture. They have created a literature that is more closely identified with the masses of black people." He says the role of the black poet is to help black people to see themselves in a new perspective, "to get them to affirm everything productive of their presence here, and also to put things of a negative nature in perspective."

AGAINST THE BLUES, by Alvin Aubert—$1.50

BROADSIDE PRESS

12651 Old Mill Place **Detroit, Michigan 48238**

Against the Blues

Poems by Alvin Aubert

BROADSIDE PRESS $1.50

Covers for the 1972 book of poems about which one critic wrote, "Aubert . . . reaches back in time to create his vision of a tough, dangerous, but never worthless world."

master's degree from the University of Michigan and returned to Southern that year and remained as an instructor there for ten years. Aubert remarried in 1960; his wife, Bernadine Tenant, is from Collinston, Louisiana. They have two daughters, Miriam and Deborah.

While teaching, he also did graduate work in sixteenth- and seventeenth-century English literature at the University of Illinois from 1963 until 1964 and again from 1966 until 1967. At the same time he wrote poetry. Aubert's interest in writing poetry began and was largely nurtured during the days at Southern. His poems appeared in the major Afro-American publications, most notably *Black World, Black Scholar, Black American Literature Forum,* and the *Journal of Black Poetry,* as well as in publications that were not directed at black audiences, such as *Discourse, Prairie Schooner,* and the *Iowa Review.*

In 1972 Aubert's first volume of poetry was published by Broadside Press (an important force in black poetry in the 1960s). The poetry in *Against the Blues* largely derives its themes from Aubert's personalized landscape of rural Louisiana. The following lines from "Whispers in a Country Church"—"Who's that dark woman/Sittin next to the preacher/Eyeing his feet?"—take us directly into any one of countless black churches in the South. This poem, like several others in the volume, achieves universality through its personalized portrayal of a relatively local incident of random gossip. In "Economy," Aubert recalls a white youth "clutching the pull of a red wagon," selling "gutted coons/and possums kept from flies/And delicate eyes/By old newspapers." The industrious youth sells his products to black people for "Money down on a new red bike." As the poem proceeds, Aubert's observations become an entrance to a generally accessible childhood experience of economic exploitation and calculated industriousness.

The first poem of the volume, "Bessie," differs from most of the poetry in the collection in that it serves as a cultural apology: "Bessie Smith,/Enable me./But first forgive./Forgive my late arrival." Aubert ultimately meshes the personal apologetic plea with a wider one: "Forgive Mississippi, Bessie./Forgive Mound Bayou, U.S.A./Forgive." Having made Bessie Smith a cultural heroine in this poem, Aubert proceeds to a more characteristic mode of presentation in the volume's next poem, "Bessie Smith's Funeral," in which description of physical objects—"Smoke-white walls,/An artless trim of brown,/Windows unadorned"—is mixed with nonmaterial reality—"spirits are abroad in the splintery pews,/Restless in the drafty aisles." The merging of material and spiritual worlds, as well as an economy of words which omits transitions between these worlds, is what gives this poem the elliptical quality characteristic of most of Aubert's poetry.

Against the Blues received mixed reviews that stressed Aubert's craft. Tom Dent, a fellow poet and Louisianian, observed that "Reading this book is like being exposed to a series of dazzling word images that lead us finally to . . . well, a let down. Most of Aubert's poems seem impersonal, life observed from a safe reflective distance rather than lived through the emotions." Nonetheless, other reviews were laudatory. According to an unsigned review that appeared in *Kliatt,* Aubert demonstrated William Carlos Williams's observation that "a poem is a small (or large) machine made out of words." Aubert's concern with manufacturing led James Schokoff to describe the world of Aubert's poetry as "tough, dangerous, but never worthless."

In 1972, the kind of poetry that Aubert wrote was not especially in vogue with many younger black poets who still adhered to the black aesthetic that emerged from the black arts movement of the 1960s. Aubert's most political poem in *Against the Blues,* "Nat Turner in The Clearing," is without the didacticism that characterized much of the poetry written during this period. He ends his poem: "I let fall upon these pale remains/Your breath-moist word, preempt the winds, and give/Them now their one last glow, that some dark child/In time to come might pass this way and, in/This clearing, read and know." This patient waiting for social change contrasts sharply with Don L. Lee's (Haki Madhubuti) "poem to complement other poems" in which he admonishes Afro-Americans to "change," to "read a change. live a change. read a blackpoem./change. be the realpeople." Lee's style and message were the norm. Aubert continued to write more inferential and ambiguous poems while he made plans for the literary journal he had always dreamed of publishing and editing.

He moved to the State University of New York at Fredonia in 1970, and it was from there that *Obsidian* was launched in 1975. Aubert succeeded in assembling an impressive editorial board which included Kofi Awooner, Ernest Gaines, Blyden Jackson, Saunders Redding, and Darwin Turner. The first issue, which included contributions by novelist Leon Forrest, poet Lorenzo Thomas, and literary critic Houston Baker, was well-received.

Nineteen seventy-five also saw another milestone for Aubert; his second volume of poetry, *Feeling Through,* was published by Greenfield Press.

Some of the poems in this volume—such as "Inquest" and "Spring 1937"—continue in the vein of the bulk of the poems in *Against the Blues*. They are personal reflections of specific events. But Aubert broadens the personal dimension to include more cultural heroes and heroines as themes for poems. In "Notes for a Future Memory," he reflects on the death of Malcolm X, and in "Dayton Dateline," he reflects on the life of Paul Laurence Dunbar. Despite the differences in theme, the style of these poems is similar to his earlier poems, particularly in terms of the way they conclude. The end of "Note for A Future Memory," which reads "we watched them re-play/the undeciphered death/of Malcolm," is more reflective and less proscriptive than most of the poems written by Afro-Americans on the occasion of Malcolm X's assassination. For example, Carolyn Rodgers's "Poems for Malcolm" provides a representative contrast to Aubert's Malcolm poem. She writes: "I'm asking for real poems for Malcolm/Black poems for Malcolm." She concludes, "I want us to be a Black Nationhood poem/for/El Hajj Malik El Shabazz." In "Dayton Dateline," Aubert continues the plea for forgiveness we see in "Bessie." He says to Dunbar: "this is my offering,/paul. simple, barely edited. and may/your painstaking soul forgive me." In each instance, the conclusions trail off into an ambiguous realm which turns back on itself.

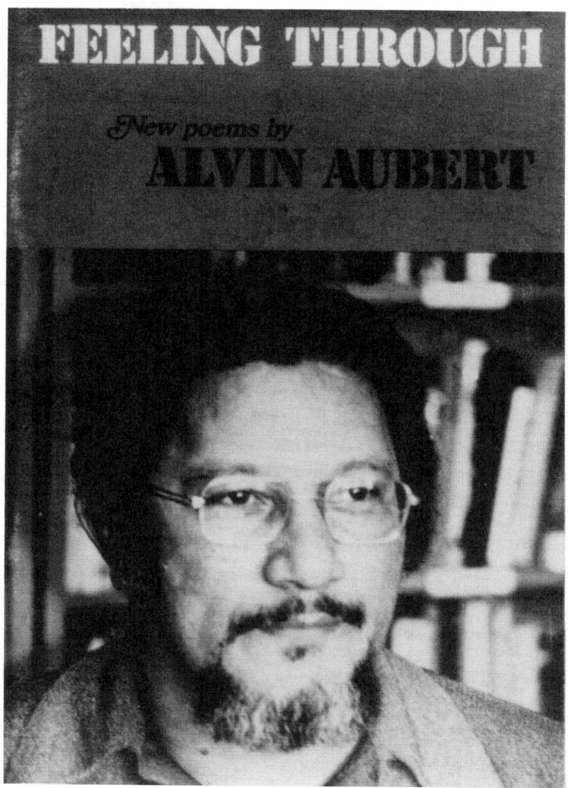

Reviews of Aubert's second collection of poetry praised the musicality of his work.

Generally though, this volume is distinguished from the previous volume in its attempt to deal with the aesthetic and political issues of the time. "Black Aesthetic," "Dialogue in 3 Acts/Speak Critic and Poet," "For Mark James Essex," and "There Were Fierce Animals in Africa," for example, though contextualized by contemporary history, are filtered through Aubert's elliptical style. "Black Aesthetic" reads like an allusion: "way i see it/and i'd do it/if i could paint—/remember the show/that french dude did? nude/coming down steps?—/something like that./only/it'd be up/not down. and out./black man coming out/of himself. up./and like i said, out." Aubert departs from his usual style in this poem in his decision to write in lowercase letters and in the decisions he makes concerning punctuation; the periods in the middle of lines have the effect of creating the staccato rhythm that was current in black speech and writing during the late 1960s and early 1970s. However, even as he responded to the black arts movement (the title comes directly from the center of the black arts movement's theoretical assumptions), Aubert's aesthetic, as revealed in this poem, was not as direct as that of most black poets writing in the period. Amiri Baraka (LeRoi Jones), for example, expounded a far more direct aesthetic in his poem "Black Art": "We want a black poem. And a Black World./Let the World be a Black poem/And let all Black people speak this Poem/Silently/or LOUD."

Critical reaction to *Feeling Through* was similar to that to *Against the Blues* in its emphasis on Aubert's craft, particularly the ways in which he skillfully captured music and feeling. Herbert Woodward Martin's review in the *Three Rivers Poetry Journal* notes that Aubert's "use of language is music on the order suggested by Wallace Stevens in 'Peter Quince at the Clavier.'" The reviewer concludes this observation by asserting that "Music is feeling . . . not sound" and that, as the book's title indicates, Aubert's poetry is a sensitive and honest pursuit of feeling. The turns and discoveries of this pursuit, even as it confronts average events, are musical. Jerry Ward, in his review of the book, makes similar observations. "The poems in *Feeling Through* are informed by clarity, wit, and the easy rhythmic flow of human speech."

Aubert has been quite successful in obtaining grants to do creative work and to publish *Obsidian*, which has consistently been well-received. In 1959 he was Woodrow Wilson Fellow at the University of Michigan, and in the summer of 1978 he was Bread Loaf Scholar in poetry at the Bread Loaf Writers Conference. In the summer of 1973 and again in 1982 Aubert received a grant from the National Endowment for the Arts to devote time to writing. The most recent grant is meant to allow Aubert to complete a new volume of poetry tentatively titled "New and Selected Poems." In 1979 Aubert received the Editors Fellowship from the Coordinating Council of Literary Magazines to publish *Obsidian.*

Aubert's poetry is distinguished by his attention to craft and the extent to which the focus of his work ran counter to currents of Afro-American poetry of the late 1960s and the early 1970s.

References:

Tom Dent, "Against the Blues," *Black Collegian,* 4, no. 2 (1973);

Kliatt (November 1972): 103;

James Schokoff, "Aubert's Poems Have Depth," *Buffalo Courier Express,* 8 June 1973, p. 22.

Gerald William Barrax

(21 June 1933-)

Lucy K. Hayden
Winston-Salem State University

BOOKS: *Another Kind of Rain: Poems* (Pittsburgh: University of Pittsburgh Press, 1970);

An Audience of One: Poems (Athens: University of Georgia Press, 1980);

The Deaths of Animals and Lesser Gods (Lexington, Kentucky: Callaloo, 1984).

OTHER: Robert Hayden, ed., *Kaleidoscope: Poems by American Negro Poets,* includes poems by Barrax (New York: Harcourt Brace Jovanovich, 1967);

Denise Levertov, ed., *Out of the War Shadow,* includes poems by Barrax (New York: War Register's League, 1967);

Paul Carroll, ed., *The Young American Poets,* includes poems by Barrax (Chicago: Follett, 1968);

Abraham Chapman, ed., *New Black Voices,* includes poems by Barrax (New York: New American Library, 1971);

Robert Hayden, David Burrows, and Frederick Lapides, eds., *Afro-American Literature,* includes poems by Barrax (New York: Harcourt Brace Jovanovich, 1971);

Arnold Adoff, ed., *The Poetry of Black America,* includes poems by Barrax (New York: Harper & Row, 1973);

Stephen Henderson, ed., *Understanding the New Black Poetry,* includes poems by Barrax (New York: Morrow, 1973);

Guy Owen and Mary C. Williams, eds., *New Southern Poets: Selected Poems from Southern Poetry Review,* includes poems by Barrax (Chapel Hill: University of North Carolina Press, 1974);

Owen and Williams, eds., *Contemporary Poetry of North Carolina,* includes poems by Barrax (Winston-Salem, N.C.: John F. Blair, 1977).

Gerald W. Barrax was one of many young black poets who raised their articulate voices during the 1960s. In 1970, his poems from that period appeared in a slim volume entitled *Another Kind of Rain.* A decade later, he published a second volume of verse, *An Audience of One* (1980). His artistic growth during that decade is worthy of note. Although both collections have similar themes and images, in the second volume Barrax speaks with a stronger imaginative voice, which is not nearly as derivative of other poets as that in his first volume. His poetic techniques, especially in *Another Kind of Rain,* are similar to those used by many of the other young black poets of the 1960s: free verse, irony, humor, typographical stylistics, metaphysical poetry, and diction teeming with "street talk" or "soul talk," often aimed at shocking the bourgeoisie, both black and white. Many of the poems in both books express his perceptions of the special characteristics of the black experience. He does not seem wholly to concur with Haki Madhubuti's statement that the

Gerald Barrax (photograph by Linda B. Walters)

black poets of the 1960s "look upon themselves as black men or black women first, then as poets." Rather, Barrax's blackness and his poetic imagination are integral parts of each other, together shaping much of his poetry.

Gerald Barrax was born in Attalla, Alabama, on 21 June 1933, to Aaron Barrax and Dorthera Hedrick Barrax. He has one brother, Harold, who is younger. In 1944 his family moved to Pittsburgh, where he lived until he moved to North Carolina in 1969. From 1953 to 1957, he was a radio mechanic in the U.S. Air Force, serving as airman first class. From 1958 to 1967, he was a clerk and carrier at the U.S. Post Office in Pittsburgh. Over the next few years Barrax worked in a variety of occupations, as a steel mill laborer, cabdriver, and awning hanger. In addition to working, Barrax also attended Duquesne University from 1959 to 1963 and received a B.A. degree in English, although he had first majored in journalism. He worked for a while as a substitute teacher in the Pittsburgh public schools. In 1967 he enrolled at the University of Pittsburgh for graduate work in English and received an M.A. in 1969. That same year he moved to North Carolina, where he has been working toward a doctorate in English at the University of North Carolina, Chapel Hill.

From 1969 to 1970 Barrax was an English instructor at North Carolina Central University (Durham). Then in 1970 he joined the faculty at North Carolina State University (Raleigh), where he is currently a professor of English. His honors and awards include the 1972 Broadside Press Award, the Bishop Carroll Scholarship for Creative Writing, a gold medal award from the Catholic Poetry Society of America, and the 1983 Callaloo Creative Writing Award for Nonfiction Prose.

To provide material for his poems in *Another Kind of Rain* as well as in subsequent work, Barrax mines his wide experiences, particularly the experience of being black. In commenting on blackness and death, the two major themes in his work, Barrax states, "They are implicit in all my responses to people and the world I live in and in everything I write." His view of blackness is not limited to one perspective; in *Another Kind of Rain*, Barrax employs many different personae in describing life for blacks in America. In "For a Black Poet," he uninhibitedly celebrates blackness:

Beautiful as
a Black poempoetperson should be who
  knows what beauty lurks in the lives of men who
  know what Shadow falls between promise and
  praise.

Like his contemporaries who embrace the black aesthetic, Barrax believes that blackness is all-important. Unlike some of his militant contemporaries, he tried diligently to avoid excessive rhetoric, exhortation, speechmaking, ranting and raving; and this excessiveness he parodies in the opening lines of this poem—

BLAM! BLAM! BLAM! POW! BLAM! POW!
RATTTTTTTAT! BLACK IS BEAUTIFUL, WHI
TY! RAATTTTTTTAT! POW! THERE GO A HON
KIE! GIT'M, POEM! POW! BLAM! BANG!

Barrax explains his position in this way: "I AGREED with all that my brother and sister poets were saying; but I wanted not to have to SAY it, but to make the reader FEEL it through his senses, his emotions. There was need for the rhetoric and exhortation; the TIME needed it, the PEOPLE needed it. But the poetry didn't. Too much potentially good poetry was betrayed by speechmaking. You'll notice that I can't always resist it myself, but I do it (I hope) aware of the risk I'm taking. And I always consider it a weakness in *my* poetry. There are better poets than I, of course, who can write with rhetorical sophistication, who are exhortatory, and still turn it into poetry. But there are not many, and I'm not one of them." Clearly "Filibuster, 1964" qualifies as one of the poems in which Barrax could not resist "speechmaking." In it he inveighs against legislators, both Democrats ("jackasses") and Republicans ("rebel pachyderm") for filibustering against legislation for civil rights—"While you talk/ we discover better ways of dying/than you ever invented for murdering boys." With a final bitter thrust, he refers to the Klansmen among their constituencies:

When you have done
and your last shard of eloquence falls
from
the
air
the applause you'll hear will be one hand clapping
of your hooded constituent
horribly grinning in the gallery.

The black experience, however, is not all *Sturm und Drang;* it has its lighter side. For example, in "The Dozens," Barrax assumes a voice that accentuates the levity of the oral initiation experience he portrays in the following scene:

Big Boy (Sophisticated, worldly-wise with the knowledge learned from listening to the hip talk of other big boys):

Yo momma yo momma yo momma
yo mom ahhh yo maaa yo mommmmmmmmmm
UHma
momma yo yo mommamommamomm
ahhhhhh yo momma yoooOOOOOHHHHH
MAN
yo MOMMA!

Little Boy (The Innocent who hasn't heard the hip talk of the Big Boys. He doesn't understand why there are tears in his eyes, but he knows, vaguely, that he must reply):

An' . . . an' . . . and you is ANOTHER one!

Blackness continues to be a major theme in *An Audience of One,* in which vastly different aspects of the black experience are addressed. "Narrative of a Surprising Conversion," illustrative of Barrax's

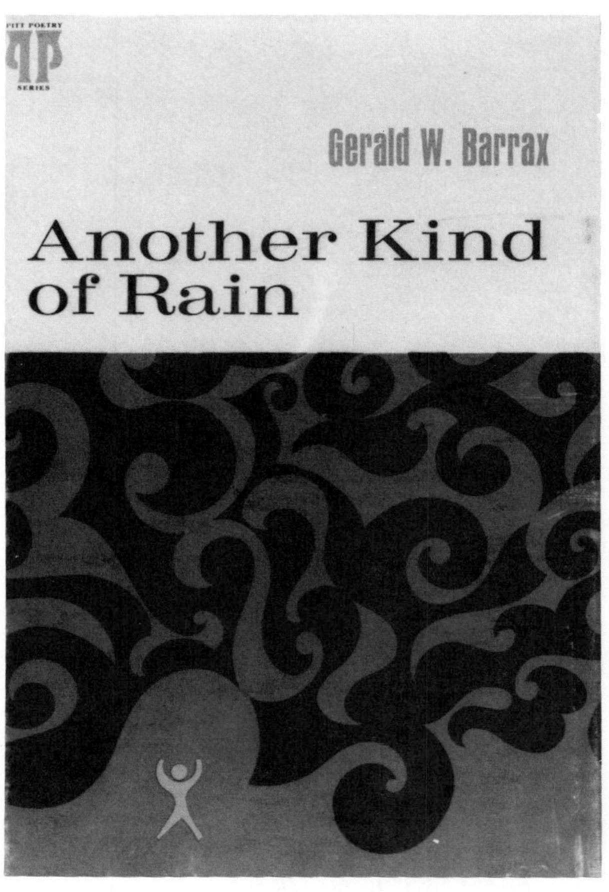

Front cover for Barrax's first book. According to the poet, "Blackness and death are implicit in all my responses to people and the world I live in and in everything I write."

controlled and economical way of presenting a meaningful narrative, tells of a young man, attending an integrated Northern high school, who, although aspiring to be a professional, was told by his guidance counselors that his aptitude tests revealed he should do something with his hands, like carpentry. Satirizing and dramatizing the counselors' evaluation, Barrax has the boy turn to dealing, stealing, and ultimately killing to illustrate how adept he is with his hands. "Body Food," a more abstract poem, discusses the black man's racial heritage in America in historical and philosophical terms, highlighted with fitting metaphors:

If then it is in the blood of some of us
to lust after the ears the tails the snouts
the feet the maws & even the
chitlins of the filthy beast
forgive us: with these
& the greens cornbread & molasses
than transubstantiated into the bones

brain & flesh of the black household gods
who brought us through the evil
rooted in this land,
    we honor them
in the heritage of their strength.

The last five lines could easily be an evocation of Aeneas, carrying his small household gods with him as he flees flaming Troy; the universality of this allusion adds heroic dimensions to the American blacks' ability to survive. Although Barrax's concern with racial heritage seldom causes him to look to his African ancestors, in "Another Fellow," however, he addresses the belief of some Africans in ancestor-worship and reincarnation. In reflecting on a snake's discarded skin, he recalls that his African ancestors would have welcomed the snake to their huts, believing it to be a reincarnation of a deceased relative: "My ancestors, considering its immortality,/Would've welcomed it with food and drink/When it came as spirit of the living-dead from the forest/To visit their huts. . . ."

Barrax confesses that sometimes he speaks as a "vulnerable mortal and sometimes as a vulnerable black American." His poems on blackness are just as poignant as those dealing with his second major theme: death. Clearly "Obits" with its three subdivisions—"Deaths Yesterday," "Previous Deaths," and "Deaths Elsewhere"—exemplifies this theme. Combining sobriety with wit, the poem reveals the regularity with which Barrax read the obituary column in the newspaper, as in this quotation containing his third reference to that activity: "I awoke one morning late missing the world/got the paper and started reading thru:/all deadlines made   promises kept   I found it/in sect. 3, p. 4, col. 2."

"The Passage to Shiva" in *An Audience of One* addresses not only Barrax's awareness of death but the poet's reverence for all life, including that of a dog. Although he takes seriously the fact that he accidentally killed a dog when his car struck it at night on a North Carolina road, he adds a mock heroic quality to the narrative by alluding in the title to Shiva, the Hindu god of destruction and reproduction, and by querying, "What apocalypse did I bring?" He laments that the dog has been sent to "eternal good hunting/where the scent was 'forever warm/and still to be enjoyed.' " The words from Keats's "Ode on a Grecian Urn" dignify the poem and intensify its mock heroic quality. Moreover, this poem evinces the poet's flexibility in handling the theme of death, which, although on the surface is treated lightly, was not so regarded by him; for on the return trip he drove during the day, in an attempt to avoid killing another animal.

Addison Gayle, Jr., has stressed the importance of serious and eclectic scholarship for proponents of the black aesthetic. Herein lies the key to Barrax's development. Clearly he is an avid reader, for his poetry is replete with allusions to and images from world literature—Hebrew, Greek, English, French—the sciences, music history, and other areas.

In *Another Kind of Rain* Barrax is decidedly eclectic; many poems in this volume are generously endowed with quotations by Shakespeare, Tennyson, Yeats, Eliot, and Cummings. Conversely, in *An Audience of One* Barrax is far less derivative, thus indicating greater assertiveness and self-assurance as he honed his poetic skill. Yet still apparent in this volume is Barrax's ability to invoke universal themes by drawing upon the great traditions of literature as well as the mundane occurrences of modern life, as for example, in "The Only Way My Dumb Flesh Knows." The controlling image is the camera, an image that recurs in five poems in *An Audience of One.* With his camera, the poet snaps several "centerfold" type pictures and because he has perfected his techniques, at least his photographic ones—

getting myself time and distanced in place with you
to picture that lovely beast with two backs
or reversed, the androgynous anthropophagi
creature from another country
where lovers grow loving heads between their legs
  clilic

Barrax clearly alludes here to the taunts made by Iago to Brabantio, when he informed the father that his daughter, Desdemona, had married Othello:

BRABANTIO
What profane wretch art thou?

IAGO
I am one, sir, that comes to tell you your daughter and the Moor are now making the beast with two backs.

The classic image of tragic love becomes the image of the hermaphroditic cannibal, which in turn is superimposed upon the familiar image of the tangled bodies of two lovers.

Sterling Brown had identified "franker and deeper self-revelation" as one of the chief interests of Harlem Renaissance poetry; Stephen Henderson cites it as being equally important to contemporary black poetry. Autobiographical allusions and self-revealing imagery actually predominate in Barrax's poems, yet, he maintains a sufficient distance so that his poems do not degenerate into emotional confessionals. For example, in "Efficiency Apartment," in *Another Kind of Rain*, a poem with an ironic and paradoxical title, the poet, divorced from his first wife, Geneva Lucy, whom he had married in 1954, and missing their three sons, remembers happier days, when he teased Dennis Scott (b. 1955), Gerald William, Jr. (b. 1961), and Joshua Cameron (b. 1963) when they returned home from school—

I'd keep
them waiting outside the
back door asking who
they were *Is that*
you Sam Harry Joe?
and they'd fall all
over each other shrieking

no daddy
it's *us!*

Sad and alienated, the father sometimes telephones them and talks with each son, but not with their mother—

Hello, Hello. hello.
what were you doing
how is school
are there grapes on the vine yet
I'll see you soon I dont know
goodnite goodnite goodnite
no tell her goodnite for me

The tension in the last line is touching.

"The Postal Clerk Mourns His Lost Love" also builds upon Barrax's informal autobiography. Recalling his own experience as a postal clerk in Pittsburgh, Barrax creates the persona of an unrequited lover who is so disconcerted that he sends "a letter for Ohio A-L God knows where." The poem appropriately opens with lyrics of the song "I love my baby, but my baby don't love me."

An Audience of One, also sometimes autobiographical, chronicles changes in his marital status. "I Travel with Her" tells of his traveling between marriages to Paris and London with a lady from St. Vincent Island (West Indies), Joan Dellimore, whom he later married in 1971. "The Fourth Son" provides a speaking picture of his parenting the three sons by his first wife—"fathers sometimes need excuses to hold/the warmth they love, I never did"—and also of the pathos of the miscarriage by his second wife of a fetus which a microscopic examination revealed as being a fourth son. Later Barrax and his wife became the parents of two daughters (Shani Averyl, born on 31 December 1974, and Dara Hillary, born on 5 September 1978). His poem "Shani" is named in honor of the first daughter—"Shani: the wonder, the surprise, the start-/ling event." The poem recalls not only the sorrow of losing "the fourth son" but, fortunately for him and his wife, also the joy of expecting a new baby and later of informing his parents in Pennsylvania of her arrival: "your paternal kin remained exiled/in winter and cities,/still the alien places/ long after the Great Migration/from the black soil of our origins." He concludes the poem by saying that the three sons from his first marriage come for thirty days each year "to make us whole again." This poem receives its tensile strength from the antipodal pull of its contrarieties: the miscarried son and the full-term daughter, the Caribbean maternal grandparents and the American paternal grandparents, the North (to which his parents had migrated many years before but where they still feel alien) and the South (to which he has returned and where Shani was born), his first marriage and his second marriage. "Confession," like "Shani," is also addressed to his beloved daughter. This poem recounts, in a poignant narrative, the fear that she was seriously ill until medical tests verified that she was not. Fortunately her family's grief was unwarranted in fact, but the drama of the poem is intensified as a result of the tension between life and death.

In each volume of verse appears a poem about a black historical figure. Contemporary poets who embrace the black aesthetic frequently use historical themes as a means of raising the consciousness of blacks, as well as celebrating their heroes. "For Malcolm: After Mecca" appears in the first volume; "King: April 4, 1968," in the second. In the latter poem, Barrax combines black history with autobiography. His subtle development of the theme of black heroes and his impassioned rhetoric should be noted. His only reference to Dr. King's assassination is the oblique comment: "but when I learned that non/violence kills you anyway." Instead of emphasizing King's assassination, the poet recounts how he has developed an anathema for killing. He recalls how repulsive for him was the killing of hogs in Alabama and how he was traumatized by shooting a robin when he was fourteen. But he was so vehement about Dr. King's assassination that he wishes he could retaliate—

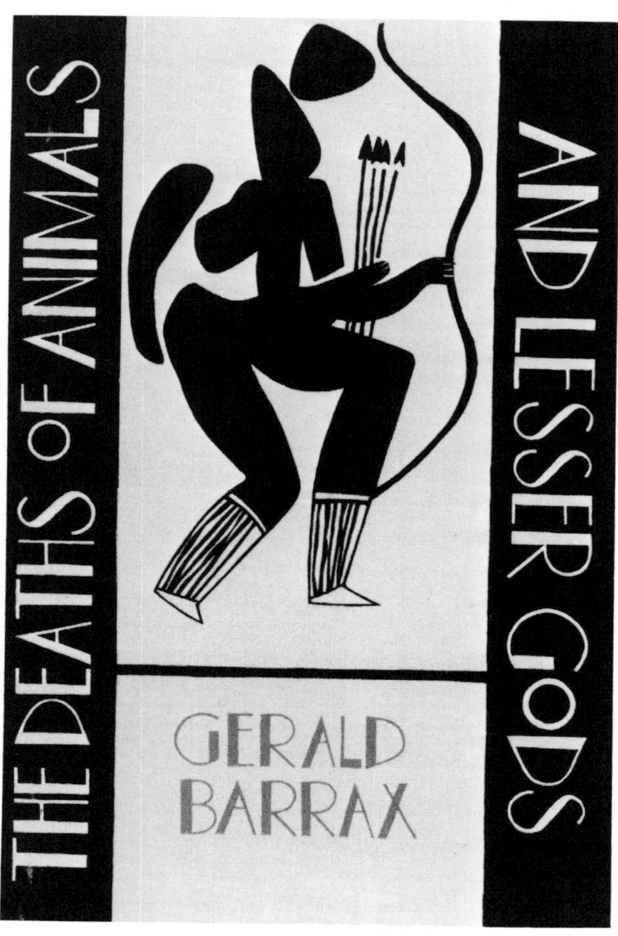

Front cover for Barrax's 1984 collection of poems, many of which draw from mythology and mysticism

But I am
me. What ever made me made
you, and I anesthetize the soft thing
to stop squirming when
you do it brothers I shout
righton, righton, rightON
my heart is with you
though my stomach is still in Alabama pig
pens.

This stanza builds up to a crescendo of "rightON" and then diminishes with an earthy comment about his Alabama childhood.

Barrax's work is also in concert with much black poetry of the 1960s in its handling of the theme of existentialism. Blyden Jackson observes that many black poets of the 1960s accepted wholeheartedly this philosophy: "They scorn, that is, the doctrines of determinism which have dominated the counsels of the intellectually respectable in our scientific twentieth century. Like the existentialists, the militants refuse to concede that man is what he is because heredity, or environment, or the two in combination, if not some other set of external forces, make him so. With the existentialists the militants assert that men choose themselves, and thus their worlds, a circumstance which means also that any man may change his choice and, accordingly, his world." Barrax begins "Another Way of Dying" with an epigraph from Camus's *The Myth of Sisyphus,* and the poem is primarily a working through of that quotation, whose thesis is "The body's judgment is as good as the mind's."

Recently, Barrax has been concentrating on teaching and writing poetry. *The Deaths of Animals and Lesser Gods,* his third volume of poetry, was published in 1984. This accelerated productivity augurs well for his future as a poet; for, having evinced earlier his improved poetic skill and a more confident voice, Barrax undoubtedly will acquire an ever-increasing reading public, who will continue to enjoy his poems and will motivate him to be even more prolific.

Joanne M. Braxton

(25 May 1950-   )

Edward T. Washington
Boston University

BOOK: *Sometimes I Think of Maryland,* as Jodi Braxton (New York: Sunbury Press, 1977).

OTHER: Lucille Iverson and Kathryn Ruby, eds., *We Become New,* includes poem by Braxton (New York: Bantam, 1975);
Arnold Adoff, ed., *Celebrations,* includes poem by Braxton (Chicago: Follett, 1977).

Joanne M. Braxton is a young and talented scholar-poet who has accomplished a good deal in a short time. Although similar in certain respects to the new black poets of the 1960s and early 1970s, Braxton nonetheless strikes out in new directions in style and theme that may suggest new directions for Afro-American poetry more generally.

Joanne Margaret Braxton was born in the old Freedman's Hospital in Washington, D.C. She grew up in Lakeland, a small town fifteen miles outside Washington. She is the only daughter of Harry McHenry Braxton, Sr., a retired machinist, and Mary Weems Braxton, a clerical worker and later a homemaker. The Braxtons also had three sons: Harry Braxton, Jr., Douglas Weems Braxton, and James Alfred ("Billy") Weems (deceased). Also living during Braxton's earliest years were her two grandmothers, Emma Margaret Harrison, and Mary Elizabeth ("Miss Maime") Weems. Family ties are significant thematically in Braxton's poetry; in fact, they are the central element of her creative process. As Braxton commented: "My grandmothers taught me family history and genealogy, and told me stories they had heard about slavery; tales of horror and strength. This oral tradition constitutes the source of my artistic consciousness and my personal strength."

Braxton received her B.A. degree in Literature and Writing from Sarah Lawrence College in New York in 1972, and her Ph.D. in American Studies at Yale University in 1984. Her thesis, "Autobiography by Black American Women: A Tradition Within a Tradition," complements not only her special relationship with her family but also her artistic interests in reconstructing and preserving folk traditions from the black past, particularly the Hoodoo folk magic form.

A scholarship student at Sarah Lawrence College in Bronxville, New York, from 1968 to 1972, Braxton was selected as a Danforth Fellow in Afro-American Literature in 1971. In 1975, she was educational consultant to the Connecticut Commission on the Arts, Poets and Writers in the schools program. Additionally, she has participated in a Connecticut Library Tour sponsored by the Academy of American Poets. She has taught American literature and modern fiction at Yale, and creative writing at the University of Michigan. From 1976 to 1979, she was a Junior Fellow in American Studies and Poetry with the Michigan Society of Fellows. In 1980, she assumed duties as an assistant professor of English at the College of William and Mary in Williamsburg, Virginia.

Braxton's volume, *Sometimes I Think of Maryland,* was published in 1977 under the pseudonym Jodi Braxton, a name she no longer uses. The most notable stylistic quality of these poems is their lyricism. Unlike the public and exhortative voices of her immediate predecessors, the new black poets, Braxton's tone is almost invariably private and reflective. One might expect that lyricism in her several love poems, but the personal element is prominent, too, in "place" poems such as the title poem and in poems ostensibly about other people, such as "Miss Maime" and "Black Sheba." Even in the complex trio of mythological poems entitled "Conversion," Braxton's lyricism reflects her introspective sensibility. In an interview, she tells how, at age twelve, she wrote her first poem in her "secret place" in a local wood; and even now she does her best writing in the more private hours of late evening and early morning.

Another point of style which differentiates Braxton from the plain-speaking and pragmatic 1960s poets—Ishmael Reed, Michael Harper, Henry Dumas, and Larry Neal, notwithstanding—is her extensive use of symbolism. In many of the poems in *Sometimes I Think of Maryland,* Braxton provides the reader with a stream of abstract images whose relationships to one another are not always immediately clear. Take, for example, the opening stanza of "The Palace at Four A.M.":

i live in a house
where birds fly in and out
there are no chairs
the lights are always on
our picture window walls reflect
rotting oranges
a pus swollen stream
where two legged carnivores collect
to stop my passage
into the world of the living

Only in the last three lines of this stanza do we begin to see that this poem is a social critique of a bleak and hostile modern world.

The most difficult poems of all, however, are the Hoodoo "Conversion" trio, some of Braxton's own favorites. From "Conversion I" we have:

reach blues ancestor
astral bird
startling grace of white
flapping strangely slow
like spirits ride
into streaked morning
cirrus and sunrise arching
night's baptismal blackness

These lines are not easily penetrated, but here, as is most often the case, Braxton uses associated symbolic images to create a mood that supports her mythological reconstruction of the familial and ancestral past.

A third stylistic feature of Braxton's verse (one more akin to the 1960s black poetry) is its sensuousness. Almost every poem exudes an earthy seductiveness that describes the sight, smell, sound, and touch of people, or of the natural world. From "Conversion II," for instance, we have:

pulp of nausea
woman of lips that tremble
hair full of mud
bed slept clothes and wash night purple love
come glide to the swamp

i the woman nude with serpents
and a saucy rhythm to guide love

And part of "Miss Maime," a poem to her grandmother, reads:

No straight lines but drooping shoulders
And old hands chewed a red-brick brown
Hands that healed my bee stings
With three different kinds of leaves and love
Offset by two skinny yellow bowed legs
Knotted with brown spots

Then there is the poised and poignant love poem "In Case You Forget":

A spectacle of evening color
Binds me to you

Tender I touch the teasing tan
Slick glimmer of perspiration

I like you when you sweat

A sensuous style enables Braxton to address in graphic and feeling terms her central interests: her Maryland home, her close-knit family, her intimate relationships. Additionally, when she explores ancestry or tradition in mythological terms, sensuous diction helps her to create a mystical mood that calls forth a vivid image of the past. This is the case with "Call Her Back," an incantatory plea for the return of the brave spirit of black womanhood:

call her back
paddled blistered burned
to miscarry master's whim

and the children that came
black strong bawling
and of your flesh anyway
you suckled by day and suffocated by night
to save them from slavery
touched by the spirit

Beyond the stylistic features, two strengths of Braxton's poetic technique are her verbal dexterity and her use of rhythm. Although her expression is not consistently powerful, much more often than not she presents us with a striking image or metaphor, made possible by deft word selection and pithy economy. For example, she refers to a fertile and wishfully expectant female as "a woman who bleeds with the moon"; or she describes the drama of a sunrise as a time when "the morning bursts/a belly of swollen light"; or her vision of a pair of sensual thighs that "ripple like some porto novo/ seaside walking rite." Similarly, when Braxton creates poems with song in mind, she encourages cadence and rhythm to join with word choice to communicate a message that is both vivid and resonant. She works in lyric jazz and blues rhythms, but in

"Poem for Blackboys in Floppy Tie-Die Hats Who Try to Relate to Sisters on Off-Nights" (where she sounds most like a 1960s poet), she takes advantage of the natural musicality of Afro-American speech patterns to put forth her tirade against black cool dudes who exercise different standards toward white and black women:

As I walk by

You, who in imitation of life
Was sidling up to white thighs
Five seconds before
Yeah, I saw you
Asking to buy that gray broad
A soda at Blimpies

Now you scream "Sister"
For some sure come-on
Like for a nickel
We can go around the corner
Into the shadows
For a bump and grind

In contrast with the freshness of the diction and rhythm in Braxton's work, structurally the poetry is not overly innovative, especially when set beside the plethora of radical forms brought forth by her immediate predecessors. Braxton writes in free verse and uses little or no punctuation, yet her stanzas are neat, balanced, regular, and formal, particularly in the shorter poems. In those poems in which she departs from a conventional pattern, the resulting form is not especially surprising. Exceptions here would include her blues lyrics, and "Rising," a poem whose increasingly severe economy signals, inversely, a rather momentous aesthetic climax.

Braxton's critics frequently call attention to her abilities as a cultural myth-builder (especially in the Hoodoo tradition), and to the womanly strength of her poetry. Curiously though, no one has acknowledged the lyrical sense of loss that occurs in many of her best poems. This motif is significant in Braxton's work, because it reveals the close relationship that exists between her life and art.

Braxton endured painful losses during the writing of the poems in *Sometimes I Think of Maryland;* she lost one of her all-important grand-

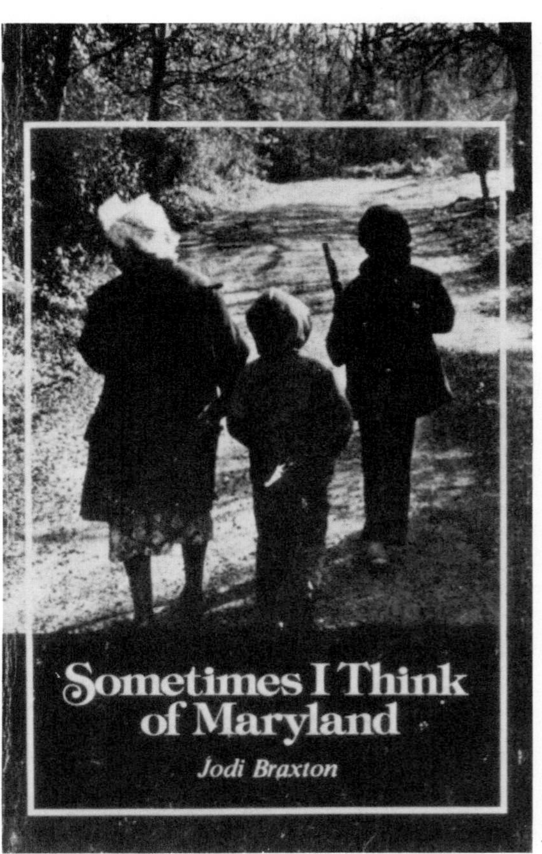

Covers for Braxton's only published poetry collection to date

mothers, Mrs. Weems, and she watched the health of her father (the person who first encouraged her to "do something important") deteriorate with Parkinson's disease. Away from home she saw shifting economic and demographic patterns lead to the sale of the old house in the woods where she had grown up. Then too, in the 1970s, Braxton, like many other people, watched the black activism that helped to shape her values fade into apathy.

Given these events, it is not surprising that a sense of loss works its way into Braxton's poetry. Of the earlier poems, written during her time at Sarah Lawrence, "Miss Maime" is a thoughtful reminiscence about a cherished family member back home in Maryland. Another early poem, "Let the Day Come," involves the poet's need to transcend the anguish and loneliness of this world; then, mindful of a lost grandmother's chilling stories of the past, "Call Her Back" pleads for the return of the lost wisdom and fortitude of America's slave mothers. Similarly, "Do You Know Jesus, His Only Son, Our Lord" laments the New World despair that has cut black women adrift from the wholeness and beauty of the ancestral past.

Of the poems written after college, "Sometimes I Think of Maryland" is a meditation upon the passing of "big old houses" (one house in particular), of childhood, and of a bounteous country life. Here Braxton uses personal observations on her changing hometown to symbolize a loss of security, tradition, and well-being that any reader may identify with:

i place my head next to earth
and listen deep for voices
recognition/memory
song
close my hand over empty soil
where once grew corn collards
and tomatoes 2 lbs. big

Another poem of this later period is "Suicide Poem #3," a chilling sensual loss poem:

the purple breast of morning
wails at my feet
wails at my feet

*****

there is darkness upon my womb
and blood is the fruit of my lungs

Similarly, political poems like "On Turning Around" and "Whatever Happened to Black America Or: The Setzuan Invisibility Black and Blues" bemoan the loss of the spirit, progressivism, and leadership of the 1960s; and two love poems, "Contact Contract" and "October 29, 1972 1:45 And On," deal, respectively, with an unfulfilling relationship and a relationship in which the poet's lover has gone, leaving her alone but still wanting his child:

the sex the sound
the baby please
please please

when will you
come again?

One poem in particular that illustrates how Braxton's real life losses can influence, even determine, the direction, meaning, and style of her poetry is "Black Sheba." Inspired by Braxton's genealogical research, "Black Sheba" is a mythological poem of praise to the poet's great-great-grandmother who had been a mystical Hoodoo conjurer replete with snakes. Poetically, as well as historically, Sheba extends the matrilineal bloodline, bringing the poet one step closer to her ancestral origins. As the poem moves toward its end, it rises and expands in intensity, and the poet gains strength, pride, and courage from the acknowledgment of the blood bond between Sheba and herself:

you's a black queen Sheba
great black great grandmom
i love the you
that works in my flesh
African woman, i love you
yeah, and i know you be giving me strength
you pushed a baby carriage
full of African gods

However, an unexpected twist occurs in the final couplet:

give 'em to me
'cause i need 'em

Rather than allow the poem to blossom out and soar, the poet redirects the expansiveness downward and inward, shifting the focus from the mythical, almost magical Sheba to the comparatively mundane real world problems of the poet. In fact, this highly lyrical shift to the historical present focuses so much attention upon the unspoken needs of the suddenly (and ironically) vulnerable poet, that Sheba, the grand subject of the poem for twenty-six lines, is in danger of being lost herself, here at the climactic close of the poem. This is quite a sacrifice for a myth-giving artist to make in this situation, and one can only surmise that the poet's sense of loss is sufficiently weighty to compel the inclusion of the anguished lyric couplet.

Since the publication of *Sometimes I Think of Maryland,* Braxton's losses have not abated: death claimed her second grandmother, Emma Margaret Harrison, her brother, Billy Weems, her adviser and friend at Yale, Charles T. Davis. Not surprisingly, the poems that Braxton has published since her book all involve the idea of loss or separation: "Progression" is a eulogy to her brother Billy, and "Chief Crazy Horse" is an ode on her absent cousin Kwesi Ballagon. "[W]ater rushing over the ford" is a poem about how one copes with a long distance love relationship. To note only the pervasiveness of loss in Braxton's poetry, however, does not do justice to the full scope of her work: for while her poetry does admit loss, it does not ever lose hope. Often in a different poem, or even in the very poem that acknowledges a need, Braxton seeks to repair, replace, or transcend personal, familial, and historical rents.

At times, this mending process is carried out in a scholarly fashion; for instance, Braxton incorporates a childhood lullaby into "Sometimes I Think of Maryland" because it echoes a traditional slave song she came upon in her research. Or, as is the case with the "Conversion" poems, she consciously resurrects the language and tone of the Hoodoo tradition to both preserve and reinvigorate this past spiritual legacy. She writes in black musical idioms to maintain and extend their already strong traditions.

Then too, there are family poems written in honor of grandmothers, aunts, brothers, and cousins that also center on some loss. Yet these poems function as concrete verbal restorations that the poet (and everyone, from a mythological standpoint) will always have to soothe the pain of the original loss. That these poems do in fact work this way is best seen in the poem "Miss Maime" (subtitled "An old Colored woman whose picture I take out at three o'clock in the morning between calculus and Brecht"). Here Braxton sets down some carefully chosen remembrances of her grandmother that culminate in the epiphanic line "Gingerbread woman topped by a crown of snow." To be sure, this word picture of Maime begins with the pain of separation; yet from that loss has arisen a tangible, renewed Maime in the form of a poem. The words will provide as much comfort in the future as the photograph has provided in the past.

In like fashion, on the most intimate level, Braxton writes about both the pains of love and its joys, not only in poems expressing sexual fulfillment but also in tender imagistic tribute poems such as "In Case You Forget" or "Your Innocence Tells on You in Early Morning." Even in the later poem "[W]ater rushing over the ford," Braxton makes her peace with an absent lover by focusing her emotional attention upon the happy moments the lovers spend together.

Finally, in "Rising," a poem that epitomizes Gwendolyn Brooks' description of Braxton's poetry as having "economy, elastic vigor, and young excitement," Braxton reveals that beyond expressing loss, her poems exist to repair and even transcend all forms of privation; that is, for Braxton, the very process of writing a good poem, even one fraught with pain or apprehension, helps to effect a cure:

i am a fire
i am a bird/afire
out of control
rising to the sun

birthing poems
in soul writhings of
fresh peace

call the name
and light the incense
i am going to burn

Braxton's losses are voids filled in some measure by her ability to "birth poems." In this book of poetry, which is arranged thematically to suggest movement from vulnerability to strength, from loss to fulfillment, the final lines of the last poem, "Conversion III," are definitive:

this is why i came
into the marsh/to forget
men women houses pain

to burn my clothes
and make me a cover
of snakeskin and prayer

an altar in the wood

More broadly then, Braxton's poetry should be seen as curative poetry—she herself refers to her creative expression, at least in part, as therapeutic or self-healing. Related to this same concern is Braxton's interest in holistic medicine and natural forms of healing. The connection that brings the essence of Braxton's poetry to the fore, however, is the fact that this interest actually began in childhood when she watched her grandmother prepare herbal teas and remedies, folk forms of today's holistic medicine. Braxton calls upon similar forms as healing, restorative elements in her poetry. Small wonder then that Braxton says that her grandmothers' heritage, tradition, and culture are the foundation for, not just her personal strength, but her poetic inspiration as well.

Public reaction to Braxton's poetry has been favorable. She is frequently asked to read publicly (although increasingly she is sought to lecture on her academic work), and she has shared the stage with such luminaries as Alexis Deveaux, Sonia Sanchez, Pauli Murray, and Alice Walker. Likewise, her reviewers, while acknowledging the flaws perhaps endemic to a beginning poet, speak encouragingly about the prospects of her future endeavors. As critic Jerry Ward says of her work as an Afro-American poet: "It is clear that Braxton is testing out things here, searching for those areas of experience that are right for her voice. I suspect that she will do for the insufficiently explored body of Afro-American hoo-doo materials what Ai did with cruelty, what Jayne Cortez does with surrealism, what Sherley A. Williams does with the blues."

Since *Sometimes I Think of Maryland,* Braxton has channeled her energies toward the completion of her academic program at Yale. The many poems she has published subsequently are not radically different in theme, style, or tone from the earlier poems. One exception though with respect to style is "[W]ater rushing over the ford," which, unlike her previous poems, is saturated with near rhyme. More might be said about this poem, but the point is that, since one of Braxton's goals is to work more "art" into her poetry, "[W]ater rushing over the ford" may signal a start in that new direction.

Even with this modest development in her style, her innovative work with folk traditions, and the positive critical reception, it is difficult to predict what we might receive from Braxton in the future. Although she insists that she will "always write poetry," and that she will concern herself much more with the creative arts as time becomes available to her, her commitment to academic research and scholarship will continue to vie with her interest in poetry for her full attention. At this point, what we have from Joanne Braxton are a goodly number of fine poems—and the hopeful likelihood of more and even better poetry in the future.

Reference:

Jerry W. Ward, "At the Edges of the Eighties," *Obsidian,* 5 (Spring/Summer 1979): 135-137.

Margaret T. G. Burroughs

(1 November 1917-   )

Mary Jane Dickerson
University of Vermont

SELECTED BOOKS: *Jasper, The Drummin' Boy* (New York: Viking, 1947; revised edition, Chicago: Follett, 1970);

Did You Feed My Cow? Rhymes and Games from City Streets and Country Lanes, collected by Burroughs (New York: Crowell, 1955; revised edition, Chicago: Follett, 1969);

Whip Me Whop Me Pudding and Other Stories of Riley Rabbit and His Fabulous Friends (Chicago: Praga Press, 1966);

What Shall I Tell My Children Who Are Black? (Chicago: M.A.A.H. Press, 1968);

Africa, My Africa (Chicago: DuSable Museum, 1970);

What Shall I Tell My Children: An Addendum with a Letter from Ruwa Chiri (Chicago: DuSable Museum, 1973).

OTHER: *For Malcolm: Poems on the Life and Death of Malcolm X,* edited by Burroughs and Dudley Randall (Detroit: Broadside Press, 1967);

Woodie King, Jr., ed., *The Forerunners: Black Poets in America,* includes poems by Burroughs (Washington, D.C.: Howard University Press, 1981);

Erlene Stetson, ed., *Black Sister: Poetry by Black American Women, 1746-1980,* includes poems by

Burroughs (Bloomington: Indiana University Press, 1981).

Artist, teacher, museum director, and poet, Margaret Taylor Goss Burroughs has spent much of her life actively encouraging an appreciation for the African heritage of Afro-Americans. In the early phase of her career, from the late 1940s through the 1960s, she worked in Chicago primarily as an artist and art teacher. Her prints and watercolors earned her several prizes and a reputation as a promising painter. For example, she won an honorable mention in 1947 for a print exhibited at Atlanta University, which also awarded her first prize in its Watercolor Purchase competition in 1955. During the same period, her concern with the education of youth combined with her interest in the visual arts in the production of two illustrated books for children, *Jasper, The Drummin' Boy* (1947) and *Did You Feed My Cow?* (1955). However, beginning in 1961 with her founding of the Ebony Museum of African-American History in honor of Jean Baptiste DuSable (the first permanent settler in Chicago), Burroughs became active in the Chicago black arts movement in literature, and she became more visible as a writer. Her poetry began to appear along with that of younger poets—Haki Madhubuti (Don L. Lee), Carolyn Rodgers, Eugene Perkins, Sterling Plumpp and others involved in the Organization of Black American Culture. Although she has not received the attention given either to them or to her contemporary Gwendolyn Brooks, who has been a critically acclaimed poet since the 1940s, Margaret T. G. Burroughs has carved out a place for herself as a poet whose work reflects a keen awareness of the multiple dimensions of Afro-American life and history. Her poems, focusing frequently on Africa and its legacies among blacks in America, have developed out of her lifelong commitment to preserving and enriching black culture.

Born 1 November 1917 in St. Rose, Louisiana, a small community outside of New Orleans, she is the daughter of Alexander and Octavia Pierre Taylor, who, participating in the post-World War I migration to Northern urban areas, moved to Chicago in search of greater economic opportunities. The experience of her emigré parents is the subject of a poem in her first volume of poetry, *What Shall I Tell My Children Who Are Black?* (1968):

> My father was a man of the soil.
> He was born among the red dirt furrows of Louisiana.
> His face was the earthy color of dirt.
> His brow grew lined like the furrows that he tilled
> And which his father had tilled before him.
> His hands bore the dirt stains to his death.

Although Alexander Taylor found work in a railroad roundhouse after his arrival in Chicago, he remained connected to the rural South and to his heritage as a farmer. Octavia Taylor exchanged work as a domestic in Louisiana for the same in Chicago:

> My mother worked all of her natural life.
> Worked in the big house in Ama, Louisiana
> Worked for two pale old ladies in Hyde Park, Chicago
> Divided her time for twenty years, taking care
> Of them and watching out for us the best she could.

In simple, eloquent language, Burroughs conveys the quality of the lives of her parents, to whom she also dedicates the volume, and by extension she suggests the experience of other rural Southerners who made their way to Chicago, but found little improvement in their condition there.

However, for Margaret Taylor as for other children of Southern emigrés, the city did provide opportunities unavailable in the South. After graduating from Englewood High School in 1933, she attended Chicago Normal College and in 1937 received a teaching certificate for elementary grades. Two years later, she received an Upper Grade Art Certificate from the college, by then renamed Chicago Teachers' College (now Chicago State University). That same year, 1939, she married Bernard Goss and began to concentrate on her own art work, while teaching elementary school (1940 to 1946). After the birth of her daughter Gayle, she continued with her education in art, completing a bachelor's degree in art education in 1946 and a master's in art education in 1948, both from the Art Institute of Chicago. By the time she finished her training, she was divorced (1947), had already embarked on a teaching career at DuSable High School that would last for twenty-three years (1946-1969), and had published her first book, *Jasper, The Drummin' Boy* (1947), which she illustrated. Throughout the 1950s, Burroughs pursued her dual career as an artist and an educator. She spent one year (1953) studying at the Institute of Painting and Sculpture in Mexico City; in addition, she took graduate courses during the summers at Teachers College of Columbia University (1958-1959). Her abiding concern, in availing herself of the opportunities that her parents did not have, was in developing herself and her students as fully as possible. As she herself put it in her "Open Letter to Black Youth of Alabama and Other Places": "self awareness must be buttressed with knowledge of black heritage if it is to have meaning. . . . One must study and dig for it."

Burroughs's vision of preserving the heritage of blacks extended beyond teaching and painting. She saw, as well, the need for "some kind of institution dedicated to preserving, interpreting and displaying our heritage," she said in recalling the founding of the Ebony Museum of African-American History in 1961. Together with Charles Gordon Burroughs, whom she had married in 1949, Burroughs began the museum in her home, because she recognized that if such an institution would come into existence, "we would have to create it ourselves." During the first year of operation, the new museum attracted more than five hundred people. Encouraged by the response to her effort and made determined by her experience as a public schoolteacher who saw the exclusion of her people from traditional texts, Burroughs invested much of her energy in raising funds for the museum, which she believed would enrich the lives of blacks, particularly youths, whose self-esteem was being undermined. In school texts, she observed that "there was nothing about our glorious past in Africa and very little about our immense contributions to the growth of this country. . . . Africans were portrayed in the crudest of manners. . . . 'How could we expect to develop healthy concepts about ourselves if we kept getting force-fed that inaccurate, racist material?' I asked myself." She answered her own question with the establishment of the DuSable Museum, for which she was executive director for twenty-four years. In that capacity Burroughs worked to develop a collection that today includes not only African and Afro-American art but also primary references, manuscripts, and personal papers, along with over 10,000 books related to the history and culture of Africans and Afro-Americans. Since 1973, the museum has had a permanent home in a building secured from the Chicago Park District; it contains 20,000 square feet of space and will soon obtain an additional 40,000 square feet. According to Burroughs, the museum serves over 100,000 people annually by offering tours, films, lectures, writers' seminars, poetry festivals, and research programs.

Her attitude toward the DuSable Museum and her own mission is succinctly expressed in a poem to her grandson Eric Toller:

> I have become highly conscious of our folk heritage
> and lore
> For I realize that it is my duty to pass it on to you.
> So lately, I have been going over songs and rhymes and
> games
> Of our people, and the stories of our great heroes and
> heroines,
> Like Tubman and Truth, Douglass, Gannet and
> Wheatley and more.
> For it is up to me to acquaint you with these noble
> ancestors.

The poem from *What Shall I Tell My Children Who Are Black?* suggests as well a reason for Burroughs's turning to the writing of poetry in the 1960s. During that period of activism among nationalists and pan-Africanists in Chicago and across the country, poetry that drew upon the familiar folk traditions of blacks and that espoused the necessity of a positive black identity became a primary means of reaching black audiences, young and old alike. Burroughs, while not abandoning her work in sculp-

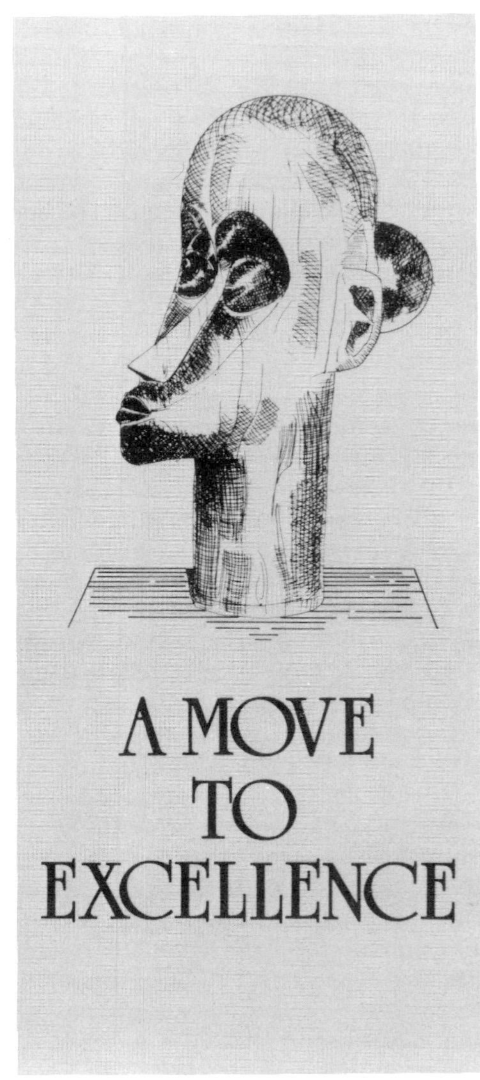

Leaflet for the museum which promotes African-American community arts and culture as well as African history. Burroughs founded the museum in her home.

ture, oils, acrylics, and batik, recognized the power of poetry in achieving her goal of transmitting a vital African-American culture. In poetry and prose poems, she felt able to convey her messages, which she called "statements which the time I live in compelled me to make."

During the 1960s, Burroughs wrote poems and read her work at the DuSable Museum, but the first major appearance in print of her poetry was in 1967, when "Brother Freedom" was published in *For Malcolm: Poems on the Life and Death of Malcolm X,* an anthology edited by Burroughs and Dudley Randall that celebrated and eulogized Malcolm X (El-Hajj Malik El-Shabazz). Her poem expressed the themes that were to become the dominant ones in her poetry: the heroic nature of Afro-American experience; the achievement of African and Afro-American culture; and the continuity in the heritage of blacks, especially as exemplified by the lives of African and Afro-American freedom fighters. The imagery in "Brother Freedom" transforms Malcolm X into a Christ-figure whose promise is "snuffed out" by "Judas guns": "Lay him down gently, lay him down slow./Swathe him in linen, wrap him just so." However, it also emphasizes his relationship to the Muslim faith and the traditions of Islam: "Turn his young face toward Mecca's soft glow./Our fallen warrior, our Brother Freedom."

In spirit and in hope, Malcolm "swirls around us/In the vital air, inspiring all/Who seek, salute Freedom":

> Immortal now, he sits in fine company
> With L'Overture and Joseph Cinque
> With Vesey, Turner and Prosser
> Lumumba and Evers and others. Brother Freedom.

The expression is characteristic of Burroughs's poetry, which is direct, accessible, and evocative, because her primary concern lies with reaching black people of all ages, and most especially the young.

For Malcolm was an important anthology, in that it brought together what Burroughs and Randall called an "honor roll" of black poets: those well-known, such as Gwendolyn Brooks, Amiri Baraka (LeRoi Jones), Margaret Walker, and Robert Hayden; those becoming recognized, such as Clarence Major, David Henderson, Larry Neal, Sonia Sanchez, and Mari Evans; and those yet unknown, such as David Llorens, Joyce Whitsitt, Nanina Alba, and Burroughs herself. In all, forty-three poets were included. Moreover, the volume was the first of its kind; all of the poems were dedicated to and focused on a single black hero, who, as Randall and Burroughs concluded in their introduction, took "full manhood rights by the Black-man."

The collaboration was inspirational for Burroughs, for the following year she published her first volume of poetry, *What Shall I Tell My Children Who Are Black?* (1968). In his introduction Chicago poet Haki Madhubuti (Don L. Lee) captured the spirit infusing all of the works in the book: "The prose and poetry of this book, beautiful black words and images, is contagious and if read seriously, will infect the reader with a black disease: black pride. In keeping with the times and with herself, Mrs. Margaret Burroughs paints beautiful black pictures with the same alphabet that is so often used against black people." The poems aim to develop a sense of pride in the accomplishments of blacks, but they also evoke the reality of the oppression suffered by blacks. The poetic voice is a personal one speaking in a proselike idiom directly to the reader. For example, in the extended monologue "Everybody But Me," the subject is the freedom, rights, and privileges assured citizens in a democracy, yet denied blacks: " 'You say that you believe in Democracy for everybody,/ . . . for dogs and cats and others and everybody,/Everybody, but me.' " Historical names and references in the first half of the poem form a catalogue of moments in the development of a democratic society; Washington and Lincoln, the Declaration of Independence, the Constitution, and the Bill of Rights all emphasize the aspects of American life from which blacks have been excluded. The second half of the poem presents the contributions made and the piety displayed by blacks who have not changed their conditions:

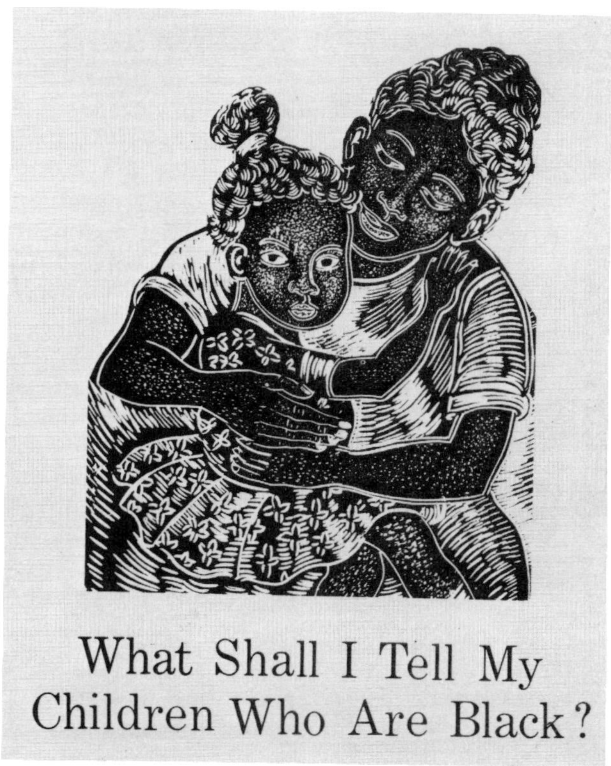
What Shall I Tell My
Children Who Are Black?

Lithograph by Burroughs from her volume of poems for children

> My father told me that in World War I they sent out a call for everyone including me and we had to go over to fight the Kaiser to keep the world free and safe for Democracy for everybody.
> When I got home I was hurt to find that they really did mean everybody, Everybody, but me.

The last stanza is a call to action: "from here on I'm/going to get together/with you and my sisters and brothers black and white all/over the country and over the world and we're going to/put up a terrific fight until we win . . . and when/we say peace and freedom for everybody it will mean/Everybody, everywhere." The poem concludes with a dream of victory and inclusion, "It will mean me."

More properly prose than poetry, "Everybody

But Me" is indicative of both the strength of Burroughs's messages and the weakness of her expression. While her prose poems stir empathetic responses, they are not memorable. They suggest that Burroughs's sentiments in *What Shall I Tell My Children Who Are Black?* were shaped not only by the author's commitment to improving the conditions of Afro-Americans but also by her determination to fight oppression among all groups of people. Burroughs had visited Europe and the Soviet Union in 1965 and led a delegation of Afro-American artists on tour of Russia in 1966. Deeply affected by her travel, she stated that her credo was "the betterment of life for all mankind and especially my people." She perceived that "betterment" meant what V. I. Lenin had called "the finest cause in the world, the fight for the liberation of mankind," and she quoted his statement in her 1967 biographical note for the anthology *For Malcolm.* In her poems that appeared a year later in *What Shall I Tell My Children,* she is guided by that credo and its underlying ideology.

Burroughs views the poet as a secular prophet who is especially conscious of the working classes of whatever color. She sees an inextricable connection between politics and art, as she acknowledged in a statement in *The Forerunners: Black Poets in America* (1981): "I am honored to be included as a 'literary godparent of today's black poets' or a 'forerunner'. . . . This properly acknowledges the continuity of our people in the struggle against oppression. . . . Black poets, from Phillis Wheatley to Margaret Walker and beyond, have played their significant roles by using their pens as their weapons. . . . The poets are in the vanguard. If you would stay, thwart progressive change, silence the poets, for if left to their own devices they will prepare the ground for and help to usher in the new order."

Burroughs's poetry after *What Shall I Tell My Children* reveals significant development in form and technique that may be due in part to her finding a voice and material more uniquely her own. A series of educational experiences contributed to her development as a poet. During 1968, she taught African and African-American art history at the Chicago Institute of Art; at the same time, supported by a fellowship from the National Endowment for the Humanities, she held an internship in museum practices at the Field Museum in Chicago (1967-1968). During the summer of 1968, she received a travel grant to Africa from the American Forum for International Study. Her stay was in Ghana, but she also visited other West African countries. The following year, she participated in an American Forum for International Study program at the University of Ghana. Her tenure in Ghana further stimulated her interest in black culture, but, importantly, it provided her with concrete experiences upon which she could draw for her creative work. One tangible result of her experiences on the African continent was her second volume of poetry, *Africa, My Africa* (1970). Inspired mainly by her stay in Ghana, these poems were written primarily during the summer of 1968, and they represent the most effective poetry Burroughs has published thus far.

Africa, My Africa is a skillfully structured sequence of eighteen poems that begins with an Afro-American's joyful arrival on the "home" continent in "African Welcome," and that portrays that arrival as a fulfillment of identity in "On My Return Home": "At last I've linked the circle round." However, in "Home Again," the theme of the Afro-American as a stranger in African society introduces the complexity that reverberates throughout the volume—the African-American is home, but not *at* home:

> I have come home . . . I am yet a stranger
> I wandered over the land in search of my own
> In and out of the slums and Zongas of the cities, I go
> Through the stalls of the crowded Makalo, I go
> Along the emerald hedged roadways, I go
> From one red walled village to the other, I go
> Until I reached one that seemed to be mine
> Expecting to be welcomed I poured libation
> To the spirits of my ancestors
> But they gave no sign of greeting. . . .

The poems chronicle the returned individual's experiences of Africa as an Afro-American, and they conclude in "Farewell Africa," "The Odum Tree," and "You Came From Over the Ocean" with a necessary departure "to your faraway home," "Over the ocean to your adopted home." What Margaret Burroughs attempts in these poems is reminiscent of what Countee Cullen attempted earlier and what Robert Hayden achieves later in *American Journal:* the merging of personal history with the larger framework of the African-American experience which is both an extension of and a separation from an African experience of memory and desire. In *Africa, My Africa,* Burroughs exercises great control over her language to produce poetry of subtlety and meaning. Her poems go as far as any contemporary poems about Africa to evoke the ambiguities of Africa in the consciousness of black Americans. They invite comparison with the Afri-

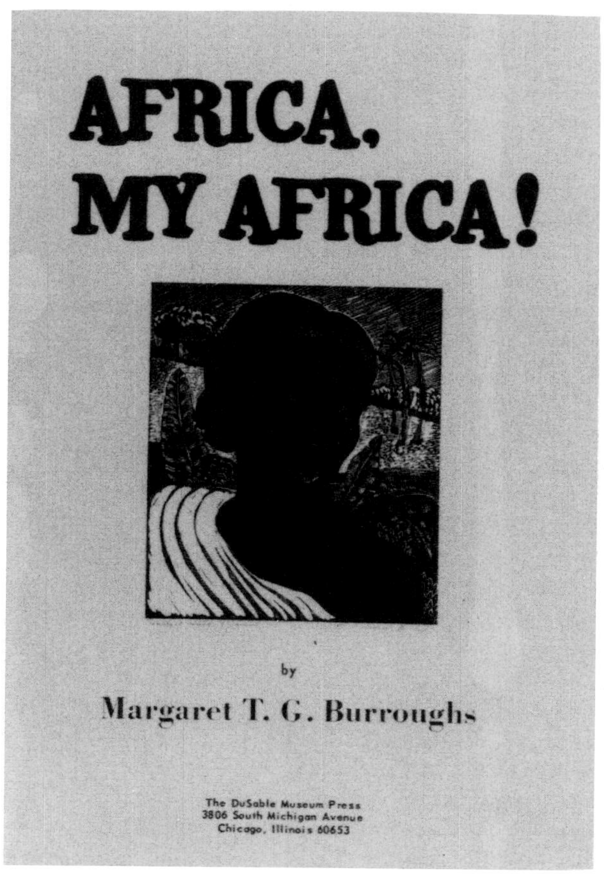

Title page for Burroughs's 1970 book which reflects, according to her husband, the "love and humanity for the people from whom we have sprung."

can poems of another Chicago poet, Margaret Danner, who not only is Burroughs's contemporary but also shares her feeling about the complex meaning of Africa for the Afro-American. In the foreword, the poet's husband, Charles Gordon Burroughs, says, "The poem tells us about Africa with love and concern for people and humanity without claiming to grasp and understand the blackness of our ancestral home." In their honesty about preconceptions versus reality and their sensitivity to people and place, the poems instruct by means of a confluence of emotions and images, a confluence that liberates Burroughs from the ideological constraints of her earlier poetry.

The best poems in the volume are those that render the Afro-American of the late 1960s black revolution in the United States confronting both an historical Africa and a contemporary African society in transition. "In Joe and Juliana's Living Room—Accra, Ghana" describes how "With a flip of the dial . . . /The age old message of the drums of home/And the rhythms of the high life of now" can fill a living room in an African home simultaneously with sounds from the "Hi-fi" of "Chicago three thousand miles across the ocean," and "With rhythms of my soul folks from home": Lady Day (Billie Holiday), Nat King Cole, Duke Ellington, and Louis "Satchmo" Armstrong or Abbey Lincoln and Max Roach. The reality is that Accra, "Johannesburg, Harlem,/Newark, Watts, Detroit and Chicago" are all mixed and fused in music and rhythms that echo backward to ancestors and forward to future generations on both continents. "The Fetish Priestess" and "Of Mercedes Benzes and The Big Coke" play upon the materialism invading the developing African world. "Madam Honoré the fetish priestess of Larte," depending upon ancient rites, "Effects cures, divines fortunes and solves problems"; however, "the only Mercedes Benze in town/Sits outside her door, and in her/Carpeted living room after her seances are over/She herself is transformed by the TV magic." Mercedes Benzes and Coca-Colas are Burroughs's symbols for the modernization of Ghana: "Drink, Drink drink the big, big coke. The African/Who is somebody or the African who aspires to be somebody/Always drinks the big, big Coke. And uses Ponds, and chews/Wrigleys." Yet she uses these symbols to reveal not only an African being corrupted by the rush toward a westernized future but also an Africa stratified by enormous differences in economic conditions:

And swank ranch style houses with television aerials
And sleek office buildings complete with air conditioning
And garbage strewn streets with slop swirling in the gutters
And curried chicken and filet mignon at the Ambassador
And ground nut soup with little meat, much yams and long gravy
And wretched clapboard villages in the bush. . . .

The contradictions in "progress" that cause Burroughs to juxtapose "ancient lorry wagons packed with poor folk" and "chauffeur driven Mercedes Benzes" in "Of Mercedes Benzes and The Big Coke" also cause her to reflect on the slave castles still standing along Cape Coast and on their meanings for Afro-Americans, as in "Elmina" and "Capecoast Castle Thoughts." In the two poems, the persona contemplates slave castles erected for the purpose of holding Africans captured for the slave trade until they could be loaded into ships bound

A recent photograph of Margaret Burroughs

for the Americas. "But for you where might I be?" the descendant of those who survived the middle passage asks in the reflective "Elmina." However, in "Capecoast Castle Thoughts" there is both anger and pain as the persona asks, "a castle for whom?" and labels the place a "bloody fortress/Permitting only two escapes, slavery or death." One of the strongest poems in Burroughs's canon, "Capecoast Castle Thoughts" follows the persona as she becomes one with those once imprisoned, re-enters the past, "shriek[s] in anguish and despair," and feels shackles and chains, lashes and whips, until "driven the hundred steps/out from the dungeon and down to the sea/And thence to the waiting ships," she breaks the nightmarish reverie and concludes the powerful poem.

In the years since 1968 when she first visited Ghana, Margaret Burroughs has returned many times to Africa, traveling in Egypt, Ethiopia, Kenya, Tanzania, Dahomey, Togo, Nigeria, Morocco. And her itinerary has taken her to countries where enslaved Africans arrived after crossing the Atlantic—Haiti, Jamaica, Trinidad. These travels have reinforced her dedication to an African identity and heritage which are visible not merely in her poetry but in her inspirational life's work, in her teaching the young, creating art, directing the DuSable Museum, and sustaining other artists and writers. In these facets of her life, as much as in her poetry, Burroughs has made her greatest contribution. She has already received numerous awards, including an honorary doctorate of Honoris Causia (1972) from Lewis College, Lockport, Illinois, for her work. Recently named Emeritus Director of the DuSable Museum, Burroughs currently provides cousultation and other support services to the arts community through her newly formed agency, The Burroughs Group. Always active and stimulated to perform the tasks necessary for a vital future, she plans to compile a volume of poems dedicated to Paul Robeson, and a collection of games from Africa, both intended to link past with present and, thereby, enlarge the possibilities for understanding Afro-American experience.

Reference:

Salim Muwakkil, "A Solid Monument," *In These Times* (27 February-12 March 1985): 24-23 [*sic*].

Lucille Clifton

(27 June 1936-   )

Wallace R. Peppers
University of North Carolina at Chapel Hill

See also the Clifton entry in DLB 5: *American Poets Since World War II.*

BOOKS: *Good Times: Poems* (New York: Random House, 1969);

Some of the Days of Everett Anderson (New York: Holt, Rinehart & Winston, 1969);

The Black BC's (New York: Dutton, 1970);

Everett Anderson's Christmas Coming (New York: Holt, Rinehart & Winston, 1971);

Good News About the Earth: New Poems (New York: Random House, 1972);

All Us Come Cross the Water (New York: Holt, Rinehart & Winston, 1973);

Don't You Remember? (New York: Dutton, 1973);

Good, Says Jerome (New York: Dutton, 1973);

The Boy Who Didn't Believe in Spring (New York: Dutton, 1973);

An Ordinary Woman (New York: Random House, 1974);

Everett Anderson's Year (New York: Holt, Rinehart & Winston, 1974);

The Times They Used to Be (New York: Holt, Rinehart & Winston, 1974);

My Brother Fine with Me (New York: Holt, Rinehart & Winston, 1975);

Three Wishes (New York: Viking, 1976);

Everett Anderson's Friend (New York: Holt, Rinehart & Winston, 1976);

Generations (New York: Random House, 1976);

Amifika (New York: Dutton, 1977);

Everett Anderson's 1-2-3 (New York: Holt, Rinehart & Winston, 1977);

Everett Anderson's Nine Month Long (New York: Holt, Rinehart & Winston, 1978);

The Lucky Stone (New York: Delacorte, 1979);

My Friend Jacob, by Clifton and Thomas DiGrazia (New York: Dutton, 1980);

Two-Headed Woman (Amherst: University of Massachusetts Press, 1980);

Sonora Beautiful (New York: Dutton, 1981);

Everett Anderson's Goodbye, by Clifton and others (New York: Holt, Rinehart & Winston, 1983).

Lucille Clifton (photograph © 1982 by Layle Silbert)

PERIODICAL PUBLICATIONS:

FICTION

"It's All in the Game," *Negro Digest,* 15 (August 1966): 18-19;

"The Magic Mama," *Redbook,* 134 (November 1969): 88-89;

"Christmas is Something Else," *House and Garden,* 136 (December 1969): 70-71;

"The End of Love is Death, the End of Death is Love," *Atlantic,* 227 (March 1971): 65-67.

NONFICTION

"We Know This Place," *Essence,* 7 (July 1976);

"If I Don't Know My Last Name, What is the Meaning of My First?: Roots, The Saga of An American Family," *Ms.,* 5 (February 1977): 45.

Thelma Lucille Sayles Clifton was born in Depew, New York, on 27 June 1936 and was educated at Fredonia State Teachers College, Fredonia, New York, and at Howard University, Washington, D.C. She began composing poems and writing stories at an early age and has been much encouraged by an ever-growing reading audience and a fine critical reputation. In many ways her themes are traditional: she writes of her family because she is greatly interested in making sense of their lives and relationships; she writes of adversity and success in the ghetto community; and she writes of her role as a poet.

Clifton's first book of poems is a varied collection of character sketches written with third person narrative voices. The ironically titled *Good Times* (1969) presents a variety of realistically drawn family and inner city community portraits. Throughout the volume Clifton seems to make conscious efforts to combat the negative images associated with inner city life by reminding us that whatever the strictly socioeconomic characteristics of the community, home is what it is called by those who live there: "we hang on to our no place/happy to be alive/and in the inner city/or/like we call it/home." One poem in particular, "Good Times," sets the mood of the volume:

> My Daddy's paid the rent
> and the insurance man is gone
>
> ....
>
> My Mama has made bread
> and Grampa has come
> and everybody is drunk
>
> ....
>
> oh children think about the
> good times

A determined optimism and an infectious gaiety in the face of the adversities of ghetto life permeate the collection. This is not to say, however, that Clifton fails to point out tragic figures in the community. Lane, in "Lane is the Pretty One," is said to be the best-looking colored girl in town. Like the aging central figure of "Miss Rosie," she is a sad figure having suffered much abuse because of her beauty and never having been allowed to develop her human potential. "Robert" presents a different type of tragic personality, the familiar fawning Uncle Tom-like figure. There are other portraits of tragic males, such as the young men who have lost their way and spend much of their time at the local poolroom: "don't it make you want to cry?" The carefully drawn portraits seem valid and authentic in their depiction of heroism and tragedy.

Good News About the Earth (1972) is Lucille Clifton's second volume of poems. The good news seems to be that "we as people have never hated one another." The news is certainly refreshing, although the evidence presented for this point of view can be distressingly disappointing. There is, too, the good news, as in *Good Times,* that the community has always had heroes, people who manage to lead lives worthy of emulation despite the most trying conditions. Two such poems are appreciations of Eldridge Cleaver and Richard Penniman, "Little Richard." Unfortunately, these poems and others in the same vein are period pieces from the 1960s and, in general, have not aged well.

An Ordinary Woman (1974) is Clifton's third and most popular collection of poems. Written in the same ironic, yet cautiously optimistic spirit as her earlier published work, this collection of forty-five poems is lively, full of vigor, passion, and an all-consuming honesty. Viewed as a single body of writing, the poems take as their theme a historical, social, and spiritual assessment of the current gen-

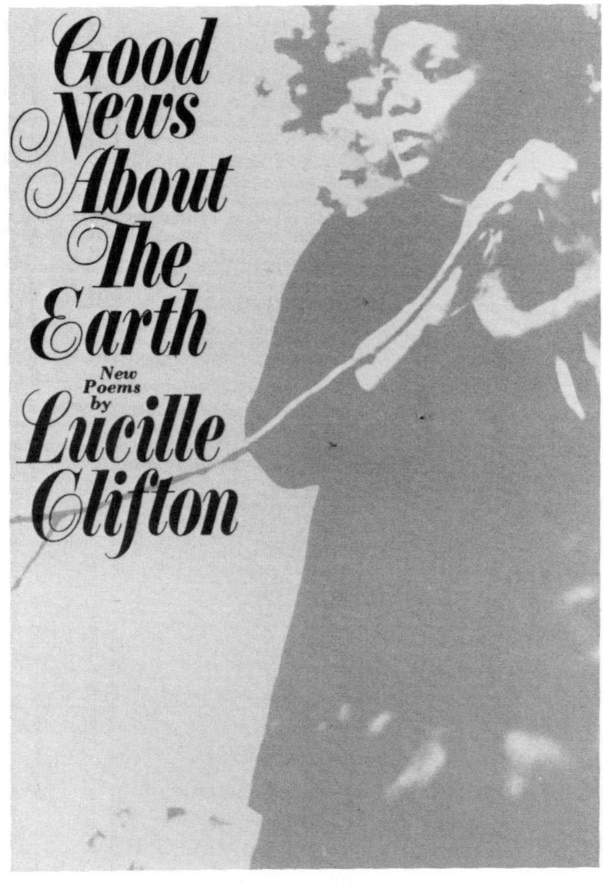

Dust jacket for Clifton's 1972 poetry collection, dedicated to "the dead of Jackson and Orangeburg and so on and so on and on"

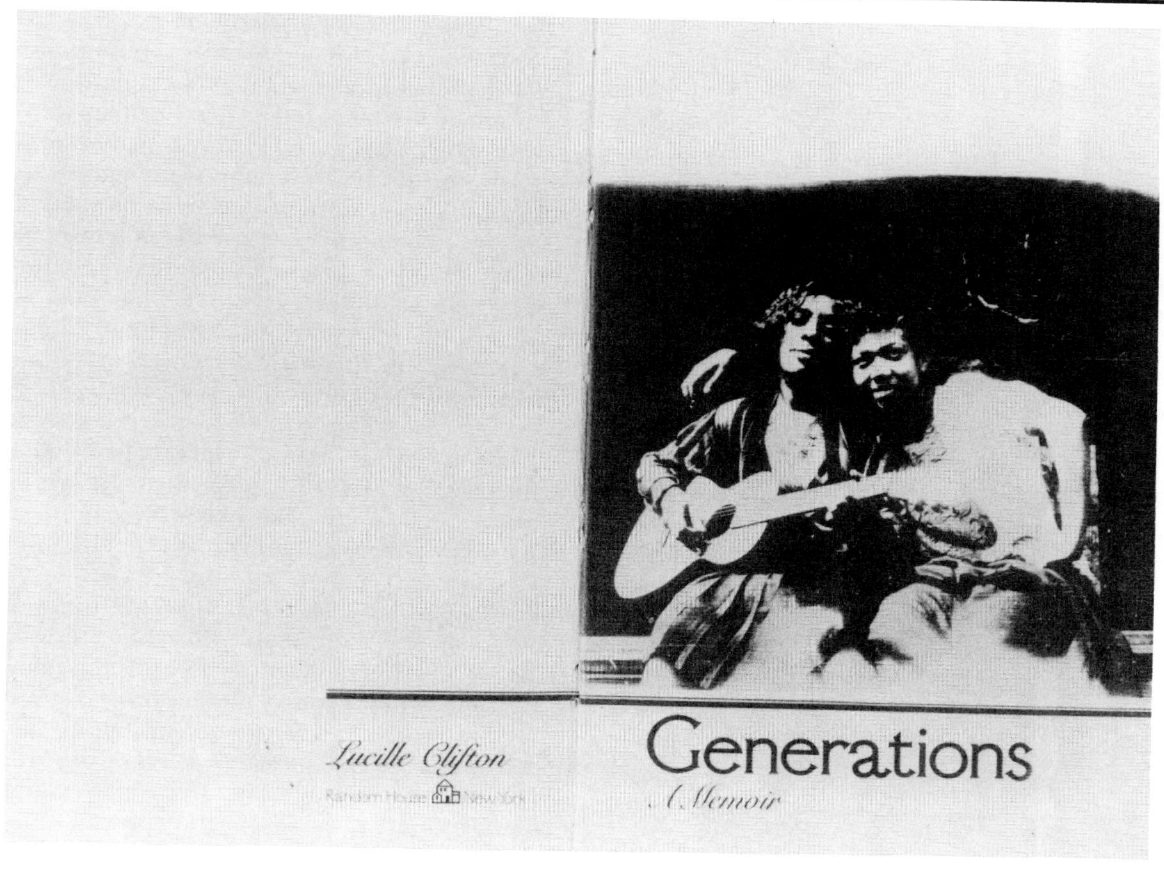

Title-page spread for Clifton's 1976 memoir

eration in the genealogical line of Caroline Donald, born in Africa in 1822, and Sam Louis Sale, born in America in 1777. It is an assessment, the significance of which derives, in large measure, from Clifton's quite subtle, unique, and personal definition of "ordinary." The title is intentionally provocative; its primary purpose is to alert even the most experienced Clifton reader to expect the extraordinary in the mundane.

The source and inspiration for the volume, and perhaps for the full corpus of Clifton's work, is the poet's great great-grandmother, Caroline Donald. Clifton shares the full story of "Caroline" and her descendants in her 1976 memoir, *Generations*. Caroline was a remarkable woman who, along with her mother, sister, and brother, had been kidnapped from her home in Dahomey, West Africa. Anything but ordinary, the Dahomean woman endured. Caroline not only survived this difficult and harsh introduction to America, but she managed to instill in members of her family, and the local black community at large, important and lasting principles of faith, dignity, intelligence, and integrity.

Her child Lucille carries the distinction of having been the first black woman legally hanged in Virginia. Lucille, called Lucy, waited patiently near the bend in a secluded country road and calmly shot the white father of her only son, Genie. Clifton offers no motivation for her violent act. Lucy remained on the spot until the inevitable mob appeared. Seeing the only daughter of the much-respected Caroline, they restrained their initial impulses, took Lucy to jail, and then tried, and hanged her. Even in those dark days, Caroline Donald is recorded as having been strong and courageous.

Lucy's son, Genie, was the father of Samuel, who married Thelma Moore: they are the parents of Thelma Lucille Sayles Clifton, the poet. It is here with Lucille and her husband Fred and their six children—Sidney, Fredrica, Gillian, Alexia, Channing, and Graham—that Clifton begins her poetic examination of the generations descended from Caroline Donald. Clifton moves backward in time from the present. Using an especially successful technique, *An Ordinary Woman* is direct and honest, almost brutal. Without the slightest evasion, Clifton

Clifton's great-grandmother, hanged for murdering her white lover. The story is told in Generations.

looks upon her own life and the lives of her family and community.

In the signature poem from the collection Clifton announces that this year, the year of her assessment, her thirty-eighth year, finds her reflective and somber. "Plain as cake," she says, "an ordinary woman":

i had expected to be
smaller than this,
more beautiful,
wiser in Afrikan ways,
more confident,
i had expected
more than this.

The sentiment is familiar. The strong sense of general disappointment coupled with the sinking suspicion that one's life has missed the mark strikes responsive chords in many readers. And worse still, from the speaker's point of view, is the growing realization that this enormously unsatisfying condition is probably permanent. This realization is reinforced by what might be called ordinary folk wisdom. Such wisdom has it, as a matter of settled principle, that at about forty (thirty-eight is uncomfortably close) most people have become all that they ever will become. Remembering ordinary wisdom may be the key to a clearer understanding of what Clifton is up to.

In this instance Clifton has used ordinariness as an effective rhetorical device. By taking a rather ordinary experience, one that is often personal and very private, and talking about the problem as it has arisen in her life, or, more precisely, in the life of the persona, Clifton has elevated the experience into a public confession. This confession may be shared by and with almost anyone experiencing the developing certainty that life is not ideal. It is this shared sense of situation, an easy identification between speaker and reader, that heightens the notion of ordinariness and gives both the poem and the collection an added dimension.

Repeated references to the family unit also reinforce Clifton's special concept of the ordinary. Across many cultures the family is an established unit of social organization. In the poem its use as a recurrent symbol has a redemptive function. Clifton's mother, after all, died at forty, a sad woman who, by the evidence of her own testimony, lived a substantially unfulfilled life. However, Clifton's immediate family, with all of its warts, has remained strong and vibrant. That at least one of Clifton's mother's children has reared such a family seems to vindicate and to redeem the life of the mother. An added benefit of the redemptive quality associated with the poet's family is the attendant hope that is engendered—the hope that no matter how desperate the family beginnings were, the possibility of survival is more than real. For Clifton, who is engaged in a quest for understanding, there is the additional hope that the peace of an examined life awaits her at the end of this period of questioning.

"In the Evening" and "Forgiving my Father" are two poems from *An Ordinary Woman* which are devoted to Clifton's preoccupation with making sense of the relationship between her mother and her father. The task is extremely important to Clifton because the answers provide clues to meaningful questions. Clifton's memory of her mother is that of a devoted and caring homemaker, a parent who was always careful to add a special loving touch to everything under her control at home. The irony is that this care and concern seem never to have been enough, certainly not enough to keep her alive, but more disturbingly, not enough to keep her husband fully satisfied at home. A union which ought to have been a wonderful marriage quite obviously went terribly wrong. Toward the end of her life what is most apparent is that she was such an "unfinished" person. Nonetheless, the mother was able to transmit to her children the importance of the proper care of family. The lessons made a lasting impression on the poet. "I can see you now," the narrator of "In the Evening" recalls, "our personal nurse":

placing the iron
wrapped in rags
near our cold toes,
you are thawed places and
safe walls to me as i walk
the same sentry.

If the experience of *An Ordinary Woman* is ordinary, it is not because it is in any way trivial or unimportant, but because it validates many traditional experiences. For example, despite her personal disappointment with her father, and despite a contemporary feeling among black women poets of malice toward men, Clifton treats the black man with appreciation and as an important component of the family.

Clifton's view of herself is both ordinary and extraordinary. She sees herself as a poet compelled to create, and she expresses this notion in many of the poems in *An Ordinary Woman.* In "The Poet," for example, she describes her special impulse as an imaginative person in almost classical terms: "i beg my bones to be good but/they keep clicking music." In much the same vein in her "Love Poem," she insists that she did not choose to be a poet, rather the demons chose her. "Demon, Demon, you have dumped me/in the middle of my imagination/. . . i will have you/have you have you." It is interesting to note that it is a transcendental calling which she credits for her poetic inspiration. This is a circumstance which helps explain her emphasis on spiritual things in this poem and in others.

In the *Two-Headed Woman* (1980), Clifton's most recent published poetry, a significant number of poems explore philosophical or religious themes. These poems show some of Clifton's finest writing and certainly contain some of her most memorable lines. "To the Unborn and Waiting Children" is one such poem which asks a familiar question: why am I in the world? "i went into my mother as/some souls go to church, for the rest only," Clifton says, in a very effective line that captures her sense of powerlessness associated with being in the world. Just as there is no rest, physical or spiritual, for some regular churchgoers, there is no rest for those beginning life; for one day the newborn will be cast into an often unfriendly world of someone else's design. It is a state of affairs to which there is no real alternative. Clifton continues with a line that captures the inevitability of the life struggle: "there is no such thing/as a bed without affliction." Though the proposition is no doubt true, a soul's search for some relief from the world's affliction is what motivates the poet's thinking and writing along these lines. The effort is certainly a determined one as she devotes some of her strongest writing to the problem.

In addition to the heavy emphasis on religious themes in *Two-Headed-Woman,* there are a variety of other themes covered in the volume. Clifton again treats the relationships of family: there is another tribute to the memory of her mother; there is a rather complicated poem in which she explores her feelings toward her father, "Forgiving Father." There are two very interesting poems which address the problem of the special strength that must be summoned when an individual decides to find his or her own way, "Friends Come" and "To Joan." The latter is a tribute to the fourteenth-century French saint who, with all the attendant risks, at long last had to listen to her private voices. Joan had to cling to the certainty that her calling was a heavenly one when there were other possibilities which her neighbors were swift to point out. It was her sustaining faith which brought her through her tribulations, and it seems to be Clifton's point that it is precisely this degree of strength and faith that is required to sustain an "examined life."

There is a line in the poem "Admonition," from *Good News About the Earth,* which would serve well as an introduction to Clifton's substantial work in literature for young readers: "children/when they ask you/why is your mama so funny/say/she is a poet/she don't have no sense." One may not take the line literally since she certainly puts a lot of effort into making sense of the world for a young audience. At present Clifton has published more than sixteen books for young readers. One of her most durable characters is little Everett Anderson, a young black boy whose realistic life experiences give the character vitality. In order to survive, for example, Everett must understand and accept the death of his father (*Everett Anderson's Goodbye,* 1983) and the remarriage of his mother (*Everett Anderson's 1-2-3,* published in 1977). *Sonora Beautiful* (1981) is slightly different. In this story the young protagonist is white. We know this because the book is beautifully illustrated and these illustrations clearly identify the persona. The story is about a remarkable family of mother, father, and little girl who come to appreciate the value of a loving home.

Lucille Clifton has a volume of poetry and several pieces of short fiction in progress. She promises to be as prolific in the future as she has been in the past and to continue exploring her favorite themes—family, faith, and hope. In *Generations,* a very young Genie asks his grandmother how they can hope to survive a particularly difficult time. The ever-confident Mammy Ca'line simply smiles and replies, "Don't you worry, mister, don't you worry." The optimism is appropriate not only for the descendants of Caroline Donald but for the wider audience of Clifton enthusiasts as well.

Charles E. Cobb, Jr.

(23 June 1943-)

Clara R. Williams
Mercer University

BOOKS: *In the Furrows of the World* (Tougaloo, Mississippi: Flute Publications, 1967);
Everywhere Is Yours (Chicago: Third World Press, 1971);
African Notebook: Views on Returning 'Home' (Chicago: Institute of Positive Education, 1971).

OTHER: "Whose Society Is This?," in *Thoughts of The Young Radicals* (Washington, D.C.: New Republic, 1966);
"Ain't That a Groove," in *Black Fire: An Anthology of Afro-American Writing,* edited by LeRoi Jones and Larry Neal (New York: Morrow, 1968);
Todd Gitlin, ed., *Campfires of the Resistance: Poetry From the Movement,* includes poems by Cobb (Indianapolis: Bobbs-Merrill, 1971);
"Nation," in *The Poetry of Black America,* edited by Arnold Adoff (New York: Harper & Row, 1973).

PERIODICAL PUBLICATIONS:
NONFICTION
"Making An African Bantutstan," *African World Newspaper,* March 1972;
"Zambia In the Sun," *Black Books Bulletin,* 1, no. 4 (1973): 4-7;
"Atlanta to Zimbabwe," *Southern Exposure,* 9 (Spring 1981): 85-88;
"After Rhodesia, A Nation Named Zimbabwe," *National Geographic,* 160 (November 1981): 616-651;
"The Remarkable Mr. Mugabe," *Black Enterprise,* 12 (January 1982): 43-44;
"Marking Time in Grenada," *National Geographic,* 166 (November 1984): 688-710.
POETRY
"Nation #3," *Journal of Black Poetry,* Pan African issue, 1, nos. 14-19 (1970-1971): 13-14.

Charles E. Cobb, Jr., poet and free-lance writer, is a dynamic personality in the literary world. As a writer, he has given audiences *In the Furrows of the World* (1967) and *Everywhere Is Yours* (1971), books of poetry that reflect his resolute views regarding the racial barriers confronting oppressed peoples everywhere. His involvement with the civil rights and the antiwar movements of the 1960s served as a springboard for his poetic and narrative creativity. His themes arise out of the injustices and inequities suffered by people throughout the world. Cobb is also well-known for his professional contributions to *National Geographic* and *Black Enterprise* magazines, for which he has composed numerous excellent articles on Third World nations. From 1976 to 1979 he also served as foreign affairs news reporter for National Public Radio.

Born in Washington, D.C., to the Reverend Charles E. Cobb, Sr., and Martha Kendrick Cobb, he was the oldest of four children. His father's Methodist ministry took the family to Kentucky, North Carolina, Massachusetts, and various other states. One effect all of this traveling had on young Cobb was to make him sensitive to his surroundings; he became aware of the injustices suffered by his people. His works reflect this awareness. In 1961, he started studying in the Afro-American program at Howard University. Shortly thereafter, in the spring of 1962, he left Howard and migrated south to begin his affiliation with the Student Nonviolent Coordinating Committee (SNCC) in Mississippi. In the spring of 1973 he returned to Howard's University Without Walls and studied there through 1976.

There were many human rights issues ballooning at the time Cobb made this transition, and he could not ignore his own personal, political interest. For Cobb to establish an association with SNCC meant that he would become physically involved in the civil rights movement; this was of the utmost importance to him. He discusses his reasons for joining SNCC in his 1965 article "Whose Society Is This?" "Somehow, I have to shake free enough to determine and do a work that is mine. For determining and doing a work that is mine, implies living a life that is mine, a living that only I can make if it is to be mine. The living that I must do, cannot be given to me in any sense, unless I am willing to accept the terms of the giver. I have found space to do that in the Student Non-violent Coordinating Committee, and in that sense, participate in what SNCC is to be, since it is people doing work." In an interview with Howell Raines, Cobb disclosed many of the abuses he and other workers suffered while engaged in voters' registration rallies and organizational group efforts for blacks in the 1960s. He had truly become physically involved.

In the Furrows of the World, his first book of poetry, is a commentary upon his experiences with SNCC from 1962 until 1967. Cobb's poems in this volume were written while he was living in several Southern cities, including Atlanta, Tougaloo, Birmingham, and Mobile.

Gren Whitman, an organizer for the Inter-Faith Peace Mission in Baltimore, Maryland, and an active member of SNCC during the 1960s, says in his review of *In the Furrows of the World* that the book was not complete. Cobb agrees that this work "begins in struggle and ends in struggle, with interludes of peace woven through the fabric of words and photographs. When Black America's struggle is finished, when Black children will look in a mirror and see a symbol of resistance, a symbol of beauty, blessed by the color of their skin and the strength of their heritage, then this book will be finished." This powerful excerpt from "Furrows" reiterates that view:

And i suppose
it will come
someday,
this thing
this black i am
that has to battle now

to
be

We, will not have to say
someday
nor fight
for
what we are

We will be
simply
be

We

Cobb focuses in this volume on the many signs of racial unrest in the United States during a time when black America was engaged in more visible means of securing equal rights. "L. A.-The Order of Things," one of the most compassionate poems in *In the Furrows of the World,* confronts the reader whose values are inverted and whose vision is limited: "It is you/who feels the pain/for a burning

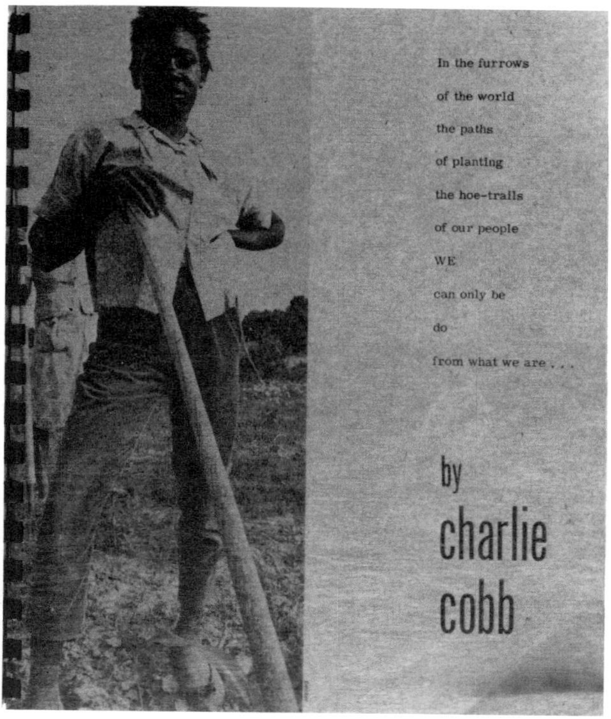

Title page for Cobb's first poetry collection, written between 1962 and 1967 while he lived in the South and worked for SNCC (photograph by Bob Fletcher)

supermarket/and cannot/hear the cries/of a hungry child."

From 1968 to 1969, Cobb was associated with the Center for Black Education in Washington, D.C. In 1969 he became involved in the founding of Drum and Spear Press, a black publishing venture in that same city. Cobb served on the Board of Directors during the five years of the press's existence. His involvement with Drum and Spear took him to Tanzania, East Africa, where he was able to promote the firm's publishing endeavors, along with other organizations "attempting to establish a presence in Africa." Such undertakings "are important because they begin to illustrate in Africa that Black American institutions can work for and from Africa," Cobb said.

Cobb began to formulate his ideas for his nonfiction work, *African Notebook: Views on Returning 'Home'* (1971), while in Tanzania. One of his most self-revealing works, it asserts his attitudes and philosophies about the black American/African relationship. Deeply concerned with the communicative process between black Americans and Africans, Cobb fears that "one of the most destructive elements of our condition is the separation and fragmentation that exists between us." He admits that "There is a tendency among Blacks in the United States, largely due to existing conditions, to harbor a fairly romantic view of the African continent. This prevents us from really seeing what is there, and what the implications of what is there mean, in terms of the kind of work we can do." This volume raises the questions that have important social and political consequences for black Americans and Africans. He points out that American blacks in Africa "have no really fixed collective relationship to Africa except in the vague, highly romanticized sense of being 'lost brothers.' Africa has not yet been confronted with how it should function in terms of African people outside Africa." From 1971 to 1972 Cobb continued to voice his commitment to the examination of African/American ties through a series of short articles about Africa which were published by the Third World Press. In 1971, Cobb's poetry collection *Everywhere Is Yours* was published. "To Vietnam," a literary observation of his spring 1967 visit to Vietnam, is a social poem. Cobb alludes to the strong Vietnamese nationalism prevalent in Hanoi during his visit. His admiration for this country besieged by political turmoil, but unified in spirit, resounds from beginning to end. We hear Cobb's implied comparison between the Vietnamese experience and his own:

carpets cover many floors
where i come from
but none kiss the sky.

i have never known before
fields that filled the hungry.

i have never stood free,
to sun, to son.

wind has never sung song
of nation
in my Black face

In the same book of poetry, "Nation No. 3" describes a search for ancestral lineage. Cobb declares in his poem that Africa is "home" to many, certainly for him. "As today I stand, son to mother Africa." There is a constant reminder that this homeland exists for mankind to rediscover. Cobb believes that a greater exposure to new ideas can benefit a racially torn United States. He feels that Africa embodies important values and can offer an abundance of new ideas to the black community. He expresses these convictions in the poem: "In searching, stumble to you Africa,/as a child torn from the womb,/slung to die, as without milk./ /Minds eye wanders to where I have never been in looking/for where we can be. . . ."

"Koyekwisa Ya Libala (a song of celebration to Anne and Marvin)" is a beautiful wedding chant included in *Everywhere Is Yours.* It demonstrates Cobb's joyous side, and it celebrates blackness and unity with nature, as well as union between people:

He seemed so old; as all the ages of his people.
Older than when his people began.

Was young when the sun first reached down with its
yellow arms
to embrace the earth.

In lines across his face was written all the tales
that time can tell.

He was black. Black as the blackest depths of the
universe. Black,
as the deepest depths of soil. And in the same harmony
as sun to soil. In the harmony of all living things,
all things that are,
and all things that are to be,
Shaded by a cotton tree he sat
softly singing to the silences.

As a political writer, Cobb's commitment and

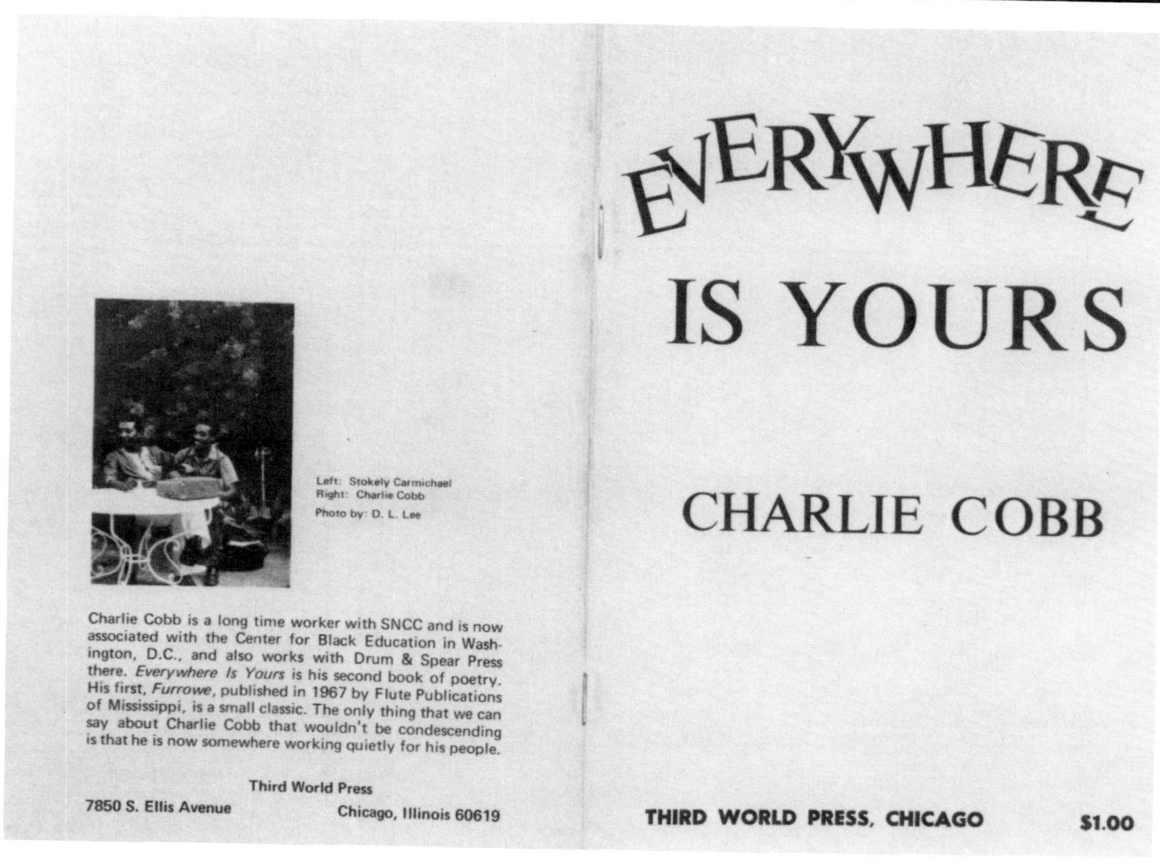

Left: Stokely Carmichael
Right: Charlie Cobb
Photo by: D. L. Lee
Charlie Cobb is a long time worker with SNCC and is now associated with the Center for Black Education in Washington, D.C., and also works with Drum & Spear Press there. Everywhere Is Yours is his second book of poetry. His first, Furrowe, published in 1967 by Flute Publications of Mississippi, is a small classic. The only thing that we can say about Charlie Cobb that wouldn't be condescending is that he is now somewhere working quietly for his people.
Third World Press
7850 S. Ellis Avenue
Chicago, Illinois 60619
EVERYWHERE
IS YOURS
CHARLIE COBB
THIRD WORLD PRESS, CHICAGO
$1.00

Covers for Cobb's 1971 collection of poems, depicting the black American "as a child torn from the womb" of Africa

devotion to oppressed peoples are evident in his work. He is a sensitive writer with compassion for others and allegiance. His writings exemplify determination and fortitude, coupled with abrasive tendencies and literary freedom.

Many of Cobb's political and social themes and his literary style are similar to those expressed in the works of other writers of color of the 1960s, including Nikki Giovanni, Haki Madhubuti (Don L. Lee) and Amiri Baraka (LeRoi Jones). They were writers of their time, and their work exemplifies the struggle to secure human rights within the political framework through artistic expression. Cobb's style of using minimal capital letters, staccato phrasing, and little or no punctuation is also seen in other black writers' compositions. Typographical, grammatical, and syntactical experimentation gave these writers a way to play artistically with the established terms of language, much as their political experimentation was geared toward changing the terms of established society. Gren Whitman notes in his review that Cobb seldom makes use of capital letters because he does not want to be reminded of "anyone else you have to call 'cap'nmisterbossmansir." He has no affinity with periods as they are indicative of an ending.

From 1976 to 1979, Cobb served as Foreign Affairs News Reporter for National Public Radio.

Over the years, Cobb's publications have shown growth and maturity. His writings have mellowed, a far cry from the fiery nature of his earlier originals. Cobb has also broadened his literary base as a free-lance writer for *National Geographic* and *Black Enterprise* magazines, as he accepts assignments on location in such places as Zimbabwe and Jamaica. His work continues to exemplify his love and respect for his people; there is no doubt that he is dedicated to writing the truths of the political, economic, and social problems confronting black Americans as well as citizens of the Third World.

References:

James Forman, *The Making of Black Revolutionaries:*

A Personal Account (New York: Macmillan, 1972), pp. 297-299, 387;

Angela Jackson, "Everywhere Is Yours," *Black World,* 21 (February 1972): 91;

Howell Raines, *My Soul is Rested* (New York: Putnam, 1977), pp. 244-248;

Mary Mace Spradling, ed., *In Black and White: A Guide to Magazine Articles, Newspaper Articles and Books* (Michigan: Gale Research, 1980), p. 195;

Gren Whitman, "Book Without A Label," *Nation,* 206 (22 April 1968): 547-548.

Sam Cornish

(22 December 1935-)

Jon Woodson
University of Rhode Island

SELECTED BOOKS: *In This Corner: Sam Cornish and Verses* (Baltimore: Fleming-McCallister Press, 1961);

People Beneath the Window (Baltimore: Sacco, 1964);

Generations, and Other Poems (Baltimore: Beanbag Press, 1964); enlarged, published as *Generations* (Boston: Beacon Press, 1971);

Angles (Baltimore: Beanbag Press, 1965);

Winters (Cambridge, Mass.: Sans Souci Press, 1968);

Your Hand in Mine (New York: Harcourt, Brace & World, 1970);

Sometimes (Cambridge, Mass.: Pym-Randall Press, 1973);

Grandmother's Pictures (Lenox, Mass.: Bookstore Press, 1974);

My Daddy's People (Newton, Mass.: Educational Development Center, 1976);

Sam's World (Washington, D.C.: Decatur House Press, 1978).

Sam Cornish (photograph by Phyliss Ewen)

OTHER: LeRoi Jones and Larry Neal, eds., *Black Fire: An Anthology of Afro-American Writing,* includes poems by Cornish (New York: Morrow, 1968);

Chicory: Young Voices from the Black Ghetto, edited by Cornish and Lucian W. Dixon (New York: Association Press, 1969);

Clarence Major, ed., *New Black Poetry,* includes poems by Cornish (New York: International, 1969);

Harry Smith, ed., *Smith Poets,* includes poems by Cornish (New York: Horizon Press, 1969);

The Living Underground: An Anthology of Contemporary American Poetry, edited by Cornish and Hugh Fox (East Lansing, Mich.: Ghost Dance Press, 1969);

George Plimpton and Peter Ardery, eds., *American Literary Anthology 3,* includes poems by Cornish (New York: Viking, 1970);

Ted Wilentz and Tom Weatherly, eds., *Natural Process,* includes poems by Cornish (New York: Hill & Wang, 1972);

Arnold Adoff, ed., *One Hundred Years of Black Poetry,* includes poems by Cornish (New York: Harper & Row, 1972);

A Penguin Anthology of Indian, African, and Afro-American Poetry (London: Penguin, 1973);

David Alan Evans, ed., *New Voices in American Poetry,* includes poems by Cornish (Cambridge, Mass.: Winthrop, 1973);

Adoff, *Celebrations: A New Anthology of Black American Poetry,* includes poems by Cornish (Chicago: Follett, 1977).

Sam Cornish emerged as one of the numerous Afro-American poets who gained an audience during the revolution in the arts that took place in the late 1960s. Because his work was anthologized by LeRoi Jones and Clarence Major, Cornish came to be associated with poets who embraced a black aesthetic. During the late 1960s and early 1970s, he presented a body of technically proficient poems that were appreciated for their simplicity, directness, and honesty. Cornish made it all too clear what it was to be a black American. Not as public a figure as several of the writers in the black arts movement, Cornish produced some of the most profound work to come out of that group. Though his work reflects the dictates of the black aesthetic, with its emphasis on popular speech, social protest, and the celebration of black culture, it is never at the expense of craft, insight, and individuality. Because of the intelligence and clarity of his poems, Cornish has won the interest of a wide reading audience and the admiration of poets of differing schools.

Samuel James Cornish was born to Herman and Sarah Cornish. He and his brother, Herman, Jr., grew up in Baltimore, Maryland. He left Douglass High School after his first semester, taking his education into his own hands. In "Winters," a long prose-poem in *Generations* (1971), he wrote of his early life with his mother and grandmother:

> All that keeps with me is the silences of my childhood winters when the absence of my father kept me close to the first two women in my life. Being alone with them, my brother and I were close for two boys, and they grew the same way. It was like the four of us in the world, living through meal time and seasons. . . . It was the most natural thing being without a father. You just never saw him in the house. Suddenly you were moving around doing things. This is how it begins. It's like you were always there, and he never was. . . . Being raised by two women who thought they were going to be left behind when the men in the family grew up, growing among two aging women who regretted their marriages was the background that made and separated my brother and me. When I want to remember him, it is always a matter of starting with the words or images of the women, who after our father's death, raised us. These women raised us on two things: chicken and God.

Cornish spent time in the Medical Corps in the United States Army from 1958 to 1960, and he attended Goddard College in Vermont. From 1966 to 1970 he was a writing specialist with the Neighborhood Centers in Baltimore. He also worked for an insurance company and in several bookstores in the Boston area. He was a consultant on children's writing for the Educational Development Center in Newton, Massachusetts, in their Open Education Follow Through Project. With Lucian W. Dixon, he edited *Chicory: Young Voices from the Black Ghetto* (1969), which developed into a series published by the Enoch Pratt Free Library (Community Action Program) in Baltimore.

Throughout the books of poems that Cornish has written, his concerns have remained the same. His view of the world takes in the cosmos of everyday experience, the human complexities of love, fear, and hope. *Generations,* the title of his first collection, proclaims his abiding concern with the lives of people. The poems range in subject from the pain of a boy growing up without a father to the love of a class of children for their teacher. A teacher of children himself, Cornish has also published books for children, and his interest in young lives is an antidote to the anger that comes through in many of his poems. Most of his poems confront individual suffering: the death of Malcolm X, the death of Martin Luther King, Jr., the murder of Black Panther Bobby Hutton, the struggles of Harriet Tubman, Frederick Douglass, John Brown, and Rosa Parks. Cornish shows that America has always been a land of crisis and social chaos. His work is an individual's record of tragic events.

In later poems, Cornish treats the lives of men and women who were prominent in the long struggle for civil rights: Marcus Garvey, Sojourner Truth, George Jackson, A. Philip Randolph, and Mary McLeod Bethune. He accords equal attention

Covers for Cornish's 1964 collection of poems, People Beneath the Window

to the anonymous suffering of working women, slaves, and people that pass in the street. A major theme throughout the poems is the portrayal of the people that Cornish knows best: his absent father, his mother, his brother, and his grandmother. He has also written about his mother-in-law, his wife, and himself. His treatment of himself is largely concerned with his own childhood memories, although he does pay some attention to his own failings as a parent and as a husband.

Nineteen sixty-eight was a year of great activity for Cornish. He was engaged in readying an expanded collection of his poetry, *Generations,* which had been published originally in 1964 as a sixteen-page pamphlet. He was awarded a poetry prize by the Humanities Institute of Coppin State College for his influence on "the Coppin poets." He was also awarded a grant by the National Endowment for the Arts. His influence was felt by more established poets, such as Hugh Fox, who dedicated *The Living Underground: An Anthology of Contemporary American Poetry* (1969) to Cornish "who originated the whole idea of this anthology one afternoon sitting around drinking beer at John's Pond, Cape Cod, in the summer of 1968." Ruth Whitman, a Boston poet, acknowledged Cornish's abilities in her preface to *Generations:* "Through succeeding years of writing, learning, editing, teaching, he has never lost this original honest and direct access to his subject matter. But his subject has not only been that of a black boy growing up in Baltimore who sees everything with the intense childlike eye of a poet, or of a young man entering adulthood, marrying, extending his personal and interracial relationships, as all men do. Of far more importance, his subject is also the tragic history of his race, the human race, the black race." *Generations* was well received, drawing favorable comments from Michael Hefferman in *Midwest Quarterly:* "Sam Cornish has managed, by pure artistry, to create a book of human perceptions." The poet Maxine Kumin also praised the volume: "Behind the clean lyric lines there stands a man who is harsh and honest in his blackness, gentle and perceptive in his humanity."

Generations takes up public and private themes from an individual point of view. Never in these poems are there the workings of abstract forces; men and women cause all things that happen. History is always shown as the experience of single persons. In "Slave Burial" the whole of the institution of slavery in America is reduced to simple facts: "when/you wear/dead man's/clothing/you die/in a part/of them." The civil rights movement is concretized as the individual heroism of Rosa Parks: "i walk for my children/my feet two hundred years old." Cornish is able to enter into the lives of public figures and to restore their uniqueness, but he is at his best when he employs contemporary experiences as his subject matter, for in the historical pieces he is limited to known facts, and often the material is too well-known to allow for a forceful impact. The accuracy of Cornish's perceptions is most powerful in poems like "Low Income Housing" in which poverty is treated in terms of what happens to poor people: "there is a cop on the corner/he breaks your teeth when he comes into the house/he says the jew is counting money." Likewise, events of national consequence are dealt with meaningfully as personal experience, as in "Crossing Over into Delaware During the Newark Riots," which records that violent event as it interpenetrates the poet's reality: "in the air/the wind is spreading." The best poems in *Generations* are the most personal. Cornish's poems about his family are filled with compelling details that provide the shock of recognition; for example, in "Your Mother," he writes

> she checks the dirt
> under the butcher's
> fingernail her feet
> slip in water
> and fish scales
> hamburger looks
> dead behind dirty
> counter glass
> flies
> even in the winter
> live here.

Winters, a limited edition chapbook that was also published in 1968, captures Cornish's movements back and forth between Baltimore and Boston. In his foreword, Ron Schrieber, a critic and editor, states that "The poet draws his images from what he knows best—the people and streets and houses of Baltimore, the New England landscape, his own home." Importantly, Schrieber also points out that "The poems in *Winters* show Sam Cornish

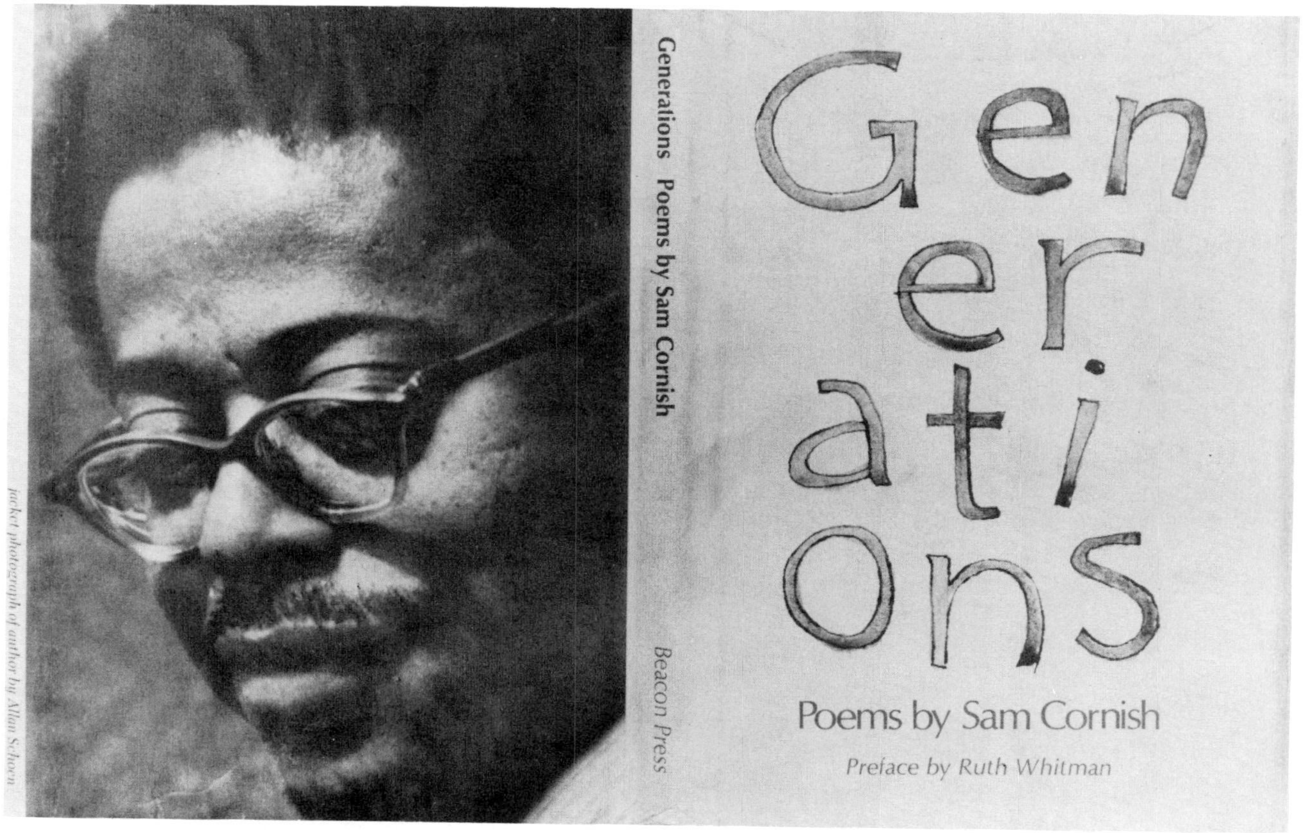

Dust jacket for the 1971, expanded version of Generations. *According to Clarence Major, the poems "are clear and sharp, with no excess fat."*

at his gentlest." It is as though by leaving Baltimore behind and traveling to New England Cornish was for a time able to inhabit a more serene frame of mind. There are some poems in *Winters* that maintain the harsh tones of the poems in *Generations*, but in Massachusetts it is nature that threatens: "she wants/to sleep/with her door/open/but i have/ seen the woods." *Winters* gives glimpses of the poet relaxing with his family in "Summer Home." In one untitled poem, the lines grow uncharacteristically long and the poem does little more than present a picturesque scene: "rows of ships sailboats and tourist shops."

In 1973 Cornish moved from Cambridge to Baltimore again. While in Baltimore he was associated with writing programs at Edmondson High School and Coppin State College. His influence can be seen in *Express Yourself* (1973), an anthology of student writings from Edmondson and in *I Speak* (1973), poems by students at Coppin. During 1973, Cornish's third volume of poems, *Sometimes*, was published by a small press in Cambridge, Massachusetts. The poems in *Sometimes* reflect life in New England in specific locations: "South End Boston," "Cape Cod," and "Vermont Where White Students, Poets and Radicals Live and Expect to Meet Blacks Skiing Cross-Country." *Sometimes* is as angry a book as was *Generations*, showing the poor people of Boston as *Generations* showed the poor of Baltimore. Even Cape Cod no longer affords the poet an escape: "Cocktail hour/and talk is not the same/as a walk through the city/as yards of wooden chairs/ and unfed children/who wonder what the second/ language/is."

Although the subjects of the poems in *Sometimes* vary from World War II, the Vietnam War, marriage, death, and working for a living, there is a consistent concern with poverty and spiritual emptiness. Wherever the poet turns he must confront the fact that the world is not perfect, that life is difficult for most people. The most successful poems in *Sometimes* face these facts directly. In "For" there is a catalogue of shocking incidents written "for" the perpetrators: "whoever called me coon from the safety of/his dark baltimore room." "For" concludes in amazement that in the face of these abuses and injustices "only three cops were killed in Ohio."

Cornish's fourth collection of poems, *Sam's World*, was published in 1978. This work is his largest collection of poems, and they continue the concerns voiced in his first collection, *Generations*. Thematically, the poems take in his family, Afro-American historical figures, slavery, and Africa. New themes that are explored in *Sam's World* are the lives of musicians (Scott Joplin, John Hurt, and Bessie Smith) and the army. Many of the poems in this collection are concerned with the lives of women, either because they are famous, or because they are anonymous. The two most provocative poems concern women who are essentially "invisible": the poems serve to make them visible. These poems, "In a Red Dress" and "Her Face in the Street," are reminiscent of the poems of William Carlos Williams in their closeness of observation and establishment of the importance of the lives of insignificant people. In "Her Face in the Street" a dead woman "looks like a woman i have always known/there is a policeman in the street/trying to look like a man/afraid of his car." Never humorous, and seldom satiric, these poems make use of a bitter irony that is something new in Cornish's work. Throughout *Sam's World* the poems force the reader to feel that something must be done about the situations that poor people find themselves unable to escape.

As in *Generations*, the poems in *Sam's World* that are based on historical themes are remote and lacking in conviction. The achievements of these poems are that they keep the past alive and they show that history is always rooted in the living experiences and struggles of individuals like Frederick Douglass and Harriet Tubman. Cornish is at his best when he is speaking in his own voice. However, one exception to this is "In a Red Dress" where he visualizes a slave woman who washes a floor "a hundred years ago." He recreates her in telling detail, concluding with the revenge that fills her mind:

> she pretends
> to be quiet
> her mind is grinding
> glass
> pissing in the evening meal.

Sam's World contains some of Cornish's best writing to date. The high quality of this work has been noted by E. Ethelbert Miller, the Washington, D.C., poet, critic, and editor of *Hoodoo* who reviewed the collection in *Callaloo*. Cornish has received consistent praise for his poems; his work may be found in several anthologies and appears regularly in such journals and reviews as *Berkshire Anthology, Blacksmith Anthology, Natural Process Anthology, Massachusetts Review, Poetry Review, Liberator, Journal of Black Poetry*.

Cornish has said that he writes to communicate with audiences, and his books have been favorably received by both readers and poets because of the accessibility of his writing and his stylistic clarity. He is presently living in the Boston area, where he continues to write, give readings, and to operate the Fiction and Literature Bookstore in Brookline, Massachusetts. Cornish has currently completed manuscripts for a study of Booker T. Washington and an anthology of contemporary and historic black writers.

Reference:

Eugene B. Redmond, *Drumvoices: The Mission of Afro-American Poetry, A Critical History* (Garden City: Anchor/Doubleday, 1976).

Jayne Cortez

(10 May 1936-   )

Jon Woodson
University of Rhode Island

BOOKS: *Pissstained Stairs and The Monkey Man's Wares* (New York: Phrase Text, 1969);
Festivals and Funerals (New York: Bola Press, 1971);
Scarifications (New York: Bola Press, 1973);
Mouth on Paper (New York: Bola Press, 1977);
Firespitter (New York: Bola Press, 1982);
Merveilleux Coup de Foudre Poetry of Jayne Cortez & Ted Joans (France: Handshake Editions, 1982);
Coagulations: New and Selected Poems (New York: Thunder's Mouth Press, 1984).

RECORDINGS: *Celebrations and Solitudes: The Poetry of Jayne Cortez* (Strata East, 1975);
Unsubmissive Blues (Bola Press, 1980);
There It Is (Bola Press, 1983).

OTHER: Orde Coombs, ed., *We Speak as Liberators: Young Black Poets,* includes poems by Cortez (New York: Dodd & Mead, 1970);
Arnold Adoff, ed., *The Poetry of Black America: An Anthology of the 20th Century,* includes poems by Cortez (New York: Harper & Row, 1972);
Abraham Chapman, ed., *New Black Voices,* includes poems by Cortez (New York: New American Library, 1972);
Lindsay Patterson, ed., *A Rock Against the Wind: Black Love Poems,* includes poems by Cortez (New York: Dodd & Mead, 1973);
Quincy Troupe and Rainer Schulte, eds., *Giant Talk,* includes poems by Cortez (New York: Random House, 1975);
Homage a Leon Gontran Damas, includes contribution by Cortez (Paris: Présence Africaine, 1979);

Jayne Cortez (photograph © 1984 by Layle Silbert)

Erlene Stetson, ed., *Black Sister: Poetry by Black American Women, 1746-1980,* includes "Orisha," "Phraseology," "Orange Chiffon," "Under the Edge of February," "So Many Feathers," "In the Morning," "Grinding Vibrato" by Cortez (Bloomington: Indiana University Press, 1981);

"In the Morning," in *Powers of Desire: The Politics of Sexuality,* edited by Ann Snitow, Christine Stansell, and Sharon Thompson (New York: Monthly Review Press, 1983);

Amina Baraka and Amiri Baraka, eds., *Confirmation: An Anthology of African American Women* (New York: Morrow, 1983).

Although she has published many volumes of poems and her work has appeared in several anthologies and in numerous periodicals, Jayne Cortez is best known as a performer of her own poetry. Her association with the Watts Repertory Theatre Company in Los Angeles is, perhaps, responsible for her concentration on the oral delivery of her poems. This focus is complemented and amplified by her feelings for the performance styles of a number of black musicians and singers, such as Billie Holiday and Charlie Parker. Cortez's ability to chant her poetry using evocative, jazz-influenced vocalizations has marked her as a creative artist uniquely able to reach audiences for whom books of poetry have little appeal. Her reputation has grown by means of her contact with audiences at poetry festivals, universities, and writers' conferences, and her record albums have been favorably reviewed in popular magazines.

Jayne Cortez was born in Arizona and reared in Watts, California. Cortez participated in writing groups during the 1960s and was the artistic director of the Watts Repertory Theatre Company from 1964 to 1970. Since 1967 she has lived in New York. From 1977 to 1983 she was writer in residence at Livingston College of Rutgers University in New Brunswick, New Jersey. Cortez has traveled and read her poetry throughout North America, Latin America, Africa, and Europe. She has a son, Denardo, by jazz musician Ornette Coleman.

Cortez began publishing during the 1960s when the civil rights and antiwar movements dominated American life; she has continued to produce poems which testify to her active participation, as an artist, in the struggle for human freedom. Cortez has combined the oral styles of black speech with a range of musical traditions, from African praises and Afro-American folk blues to experimental jazz: she has developed a style of poetry that is emotionally dynamic and technically versatile. She has written with increasing force and mastery of the many indignities that alienated and divided people must bear: poverty, dehumanizing labor, imprisonment, violence, and sicknesses of the spirit. Cortez's poetry is a protest against lost chances for love, against the horrors of life in crowded cities, and against the weakness of those who submit to colonialism, imperialism, and political repression. The bitterness and rage that she expresses are balanced with praise for the artists, laborers, visionaries, and leaders who work toward a revolution in which "everything/in this world changes."

Pissstained Stairs and The Monkey Man's Wares (1969), Cortez's first collection of poems, has musicians as the subjects of many of the poems. "The Road" alludes to the death of the blues singer Bessie Smith, and other poems give glimpses of Leadbelly, Charlie Parker, Ornette Coleman, Clifford Brown, Sun Ra, Billie Holiday, John Coltrane, and Fats Navarro. She emphasizes the deaths that some of these musicians met through drugs and she confronts the bleakness of many of their lives. Cortez writes of blues and jazz artists because for her they constitute a pantheon of revolutionary heroes and heroines who have prepared the way for the new order that they sing about. Love and sexuality are also major themes in *Pissstained Stairs.* Love is generally unrequited and sex is portrayed more as an irresistible physical need than as an act of mutual pleasure; there is nothing of the puritanic or conventionally romantic treatment of sex in these poems.

The style of the poems in *Pissstained Stairs* is unique, but varied. The poems differ in length; within the poems line lengths vary, and there is little shown in the way of formal control. Most of the poems consist of fragmentary snatches of blueslike cadences that attempt to create the spontaneous speech of ghetto dwellers. The poems present the details of lives lived too closely crowded together: odors, noises, and excretions. The most successful poems are "Race," which bitterly condemns black male homosexuality in unflinching detail, and "Suppression," which uses long, parallel lines to catalogue the nightmarish sensations of unfulfilled sexual desire. *Pissstained Stairs* placed Cortez among the poets of the black arts movement, and Haki R. Madhubuti (Don. L. Lee) calls her one of the poets whose work "continued to deafen us."

Festivals and Funerals (1971), Cortez's second collection of poetry, was praised by Eugene B. Redmond in *Drumvoices: The Mission of Afro-American Poetry, A Critical History* (1976) for being "Musical, daring, ambivalent, complex and technically dexterous." The volume extends Cortez's concerns with love and celebrations of sexuality, but the poems exhibit a move to more theoretical concerns: colonialism, African nationhood, revolution, mythology, and the role of the artist in revolutionary politics. The poems are more personal, and the mediating influences of larger-than-life figures are not as important. Life is directly confronted in such poems as "Screams," "Pearl Sheba," and "I Would Like To Be Serene." Other poems are occasional and address the themes of assassination and the culture of colonialism. *Festivals and Funerals* presents poems with relatively regular lines, and the language is raw, vital, and in touch with people who see themselves as poised between the extremes of creation and destruction. The most accomplished poems in the book are monologues, such as "I'm A Worker," in which the voice of a worn-out garment worker is convincingly rendered: she asks "do you think a revolution is what i need?"

Jayne Cortez's third book, *Scarifications* (1973), treats new subjects: the Vietnam War, a visit to Africa, police killings, the Attica revolt, New York City life, and the assassination of Kwame Nkrumah. Many of the poems are short, ironic commentaries, and the longer poems use irony to play down the escalation of violence, as when napalm is called "A New Cologne." The subject of genocide is treated ironically when Wounded Knee is compared to ankles damaged by platform shoes. The poems in *Scarifications* are tighter in form than earlier ones, even when presenting images motivated by madness and desperation. The subject of Africa gives Cortez a chance to write of life in more romantic terms; in "Ife Night" the beauties of nature are directly presented. In "Orisha" and "Back Home in Benin City" images of exotic settings are fused into tense and impassioned songs of praise.

Mouth on Paper (1977) shows that Cortez has continued to develop as a poet. This volume takes up many of the same themes of the former collections, and there are poems about jazz: "Rose Solitude," written for Duke Ellington, and "Chocolate," written for a trumpet player. *Mouth on Paper* includes poems on Africa, "Ogun's Friend" and "For the Brave Young Students in Soweto," and there are poems about slain heroes and heroines: Henry Dumas, Christopher Okigbo, and Alberta King. Revolution is invoked in "For the Brave Young Students in Soweto" and in "Brooding."

The poems in *Mouth on Paper* are consistently longer than those in previous collections, and the intention seems to have been to provide sustained texts suitable for being read aloud. The length of the poems in the volume gives the reader time to build the themes, line by line, into structures that nearly approach jazz solo improvisations in their achievement of complexity and variation of sound.

In "Mercenaries & Minstrels," the generalized tormentors of earlier poems, such as "To A Friend" *(Scarifications)*, which tells of "the mutilation of things," have been made concrete and given a name: "A mercenary like Rolf Steiner/will split open your head with a bottle of I. W. Harper." Likewise, those who reject a revolutionary solution to social problems have been identified: "so don't tell me/to get down on my knees/and roll around singing mammy like ben vereen." Cortez's fragmented imagery has been integrated into the realistic details of the lines and invested with an exactitude that works to make horror horrible where before the effect was merely strangeness: "he'll cut off your legs/fire-up your thighs/and twist your balls/into an american eagle and swastika emblem for his bi-centennial."

In Cortez's poems, oppression is oppression whether it is found in Africa or in the United States.

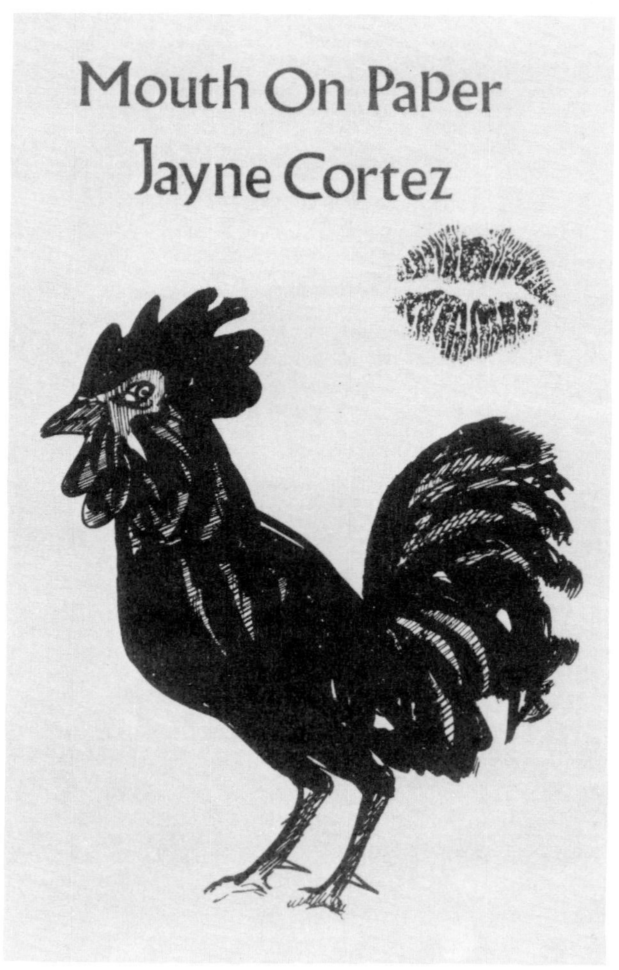

Front cover for Cortez's 1977 poetry collection

This view was symbolized in *Festivals and Funerals,* for example, in the lines "who killed Lumumba/ what killed Malcolm"; in *Mouth on Paper,* it is made concrete. In "For the Brave Young Students in Soweto," Cortez details the similar fates of blacks in New York and in South Africa: "When I look at this ugliness/and see once again how we're divided and/ forced into fighting each other/over a funky job in the sewers of Johannesburg/divided into labor camps/fighting over damaged meat and stale bread in Harlem. . . ." There is clearly only a single people in her view.

Mouth on Paper also includes poems that attempt to make music; in "Chocolate" there are such lines as "aye ya ya ya ay yo Chocolate" that seek to imitate the trumpet sounds that she also describes with words. Although these lines work on the page because they are not overdone, they are actually oral fragments that allow Cortez's voice to simulate a trumpet solo when she reads the text aloud. Another oral technique that works is the simulation of choral responses. Nearly every line in "For the Poets" ends with an added sound, which works like a response: "I need a canefield of superstitious women a/fumes and feathers from Port Lobito a." The range of sounds has been carefully restricted (a, ah, oh, huh, uh-huh), and they do not move the attention away from the words of the poem. These extra sounds lend a semblance of mystery to the poem, as though some ritual were taking place.

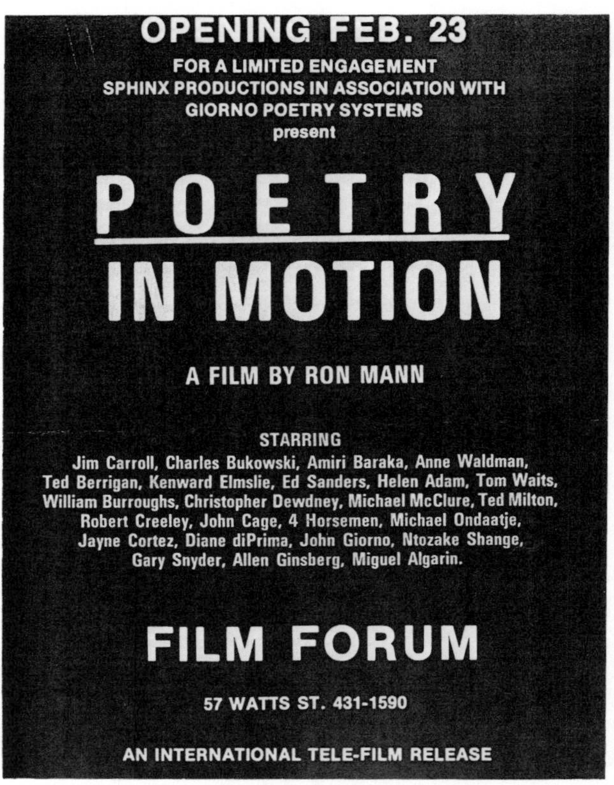

Advertisement for a 1982 film in which Cortez reads her poetry

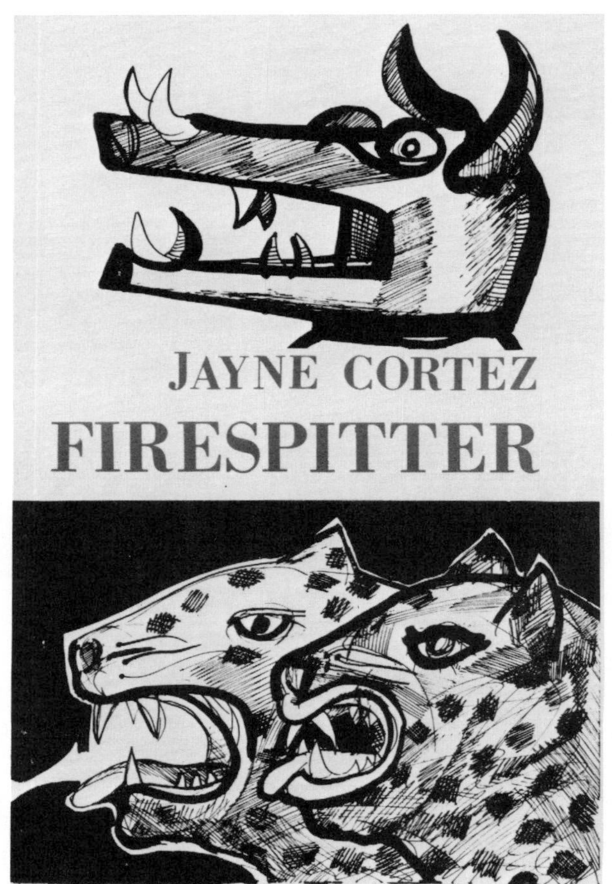

Front cover for Cortez's 1982 collection of poems, many of which were inspired by the Nigerian people Cortez met at the second World Black and African Festival of Arts and Culture (FESTAC).

The poems in *Mouth on Paper* are the culmination and clarification of the themes and subjects that Cortez had been concerned with throughout all of her earlier writing: familiar objects (sander, drill, grinder, drill press, hacksaw, brick ax); flesh (bald spot, toes, chin, penis, mouth, breasts, knees, shoulders); emblems of violence (bullets, razors, cyclone, explosion, smoke); and fluids (blood, cataracts, lizard juice, mucous, spit, goober oil, mud, cognac, champagne, sweat). These materials are blended into new combinations in each line ("peach brandy spit") so that they build up surprising images that give an improvisational effect. These recombinations of things into images also cause the poems in *Mouth on Paper* to simulate the poetry of African praises.

"Ogun's Friend" in particular stands out as an acknowledgement of the influence of the African praise form. This poem includes exclamations like "Yo " and "Hey" at the beginning of several of the stanzas, and the stanzas themselves are catalogues of repeated sensory experiences: "i saw," "i heard," "i smell," "i feel." The poem is perhaps as African in content and execution as is possible when the medium is American language. In this poem, Cortez is at her best in the use of shocking combinations to create images ("I smell some ratheads in here") and in her approximation of the African appreciation of force and physical vitality ("Whose that one so brown and fine/Ogun's friend . . ."). Even though the poem uses the name of an African deity throughout the lines, the language is Afro-American, the use of the exotic is never false, and the poem details an understanding of human limits in an ultimately mysterious universe with authority and good humor.

In 1982, Cortez's collection *Firespitter* was published. The poems combine a mature expression of earlier themes and forms with a sociopolitical awareness. The poetry of Cortez has moved from the somewhat chaotic style of free verse, with an emphasis on black speech that was common to many of the Afro-American poets of the 1960s, to the controlled evocation of otherness employed by the American surrealist poets. Cortez has been published in the surrealist journal *Arsenal* and has also been included in the City Lights publication *Surrealism and Its Popular Accomplices*. It is noteworthy that the American surrealists are aware of the affinities between blues and surrealist art both in their affirmation of the power of sex and in their protest against social repression. Blues, jazz, African art, and the writing of the Negritude poets have all been declared surrealist in form and content by American surrealists. By being linked to this school, Cor-

$6.95 ISBN : 0-938410-20-2 (pbk.)

Poetry/Black Studies

Thunder's Mouth Press, Box 780, New York City 10025

Cortez has been and continues to be an explorer, probing the valleys and chasms of human existence. No ravine is too perilous, no abyss too threatening for Jayne Cortez. A thrilling collection.
Maya Angelou

Since this collection was drawn from a fine career, it is inevitable that the result is simply a fine piece of work. It demonstrates Ms. Cortez's versatility and mastery of language. These poems pulsate with a certain rawness that is sometimes bitterly angry but always eloquent, and the results are relentlessly powerful.
Gloria Naylor (winner 1983 American Book Award)

Jayne Cortez is an energy, a nourishment, a Black Nation song.
Gwendolyn Brooks

Covers for Cortez's 1984 collection which includes new poems that were intended to be chanted aloud

tez has not given up anything or moved away from her past creations. She has been discovered for what she is—an artist committed to the same revolutionary program as the surrealists and one who has employed many of the same materials and methods as André Breton, Ted Joans, and other poets of the surrealist school.

The range of Cortez's development can be appreciated in *Coagulations: New and Selected Poems* (1984). Although many of the new poems in the collection share the raw, sometimes violent language and vision of the poems reprinted from other volumes, they also display a density, or compactness, of form and expression. Cortez has explored the limits of written poetry. She has moved consistently toward texts that ask to be chanted aloud, in contrast to much recent poetry that is actually prose written in short lines. It is for this reason that Cortez has continued to make records of her work. As far back as 1976, Eugene B. Redmond was able to see that her writing in *Pissstained Stairs* and *Festivals and Funerals* "is especially rich in its interweavings of music." He spoke of her "earth-woman musicality." Redmond also recognized the intellectual content of her writing and placed her work in the category of "Deeper, searching, and more profound poetry" noting that she "wades into the intense intellectual and psychological realm of blackness."

References:

Don L. Lee, "Toward a Definition: Black Poetry of the Sixties," in *The Black Aesthetic,* edited by Addison Gayle, Jr. (Garden City: Anchor Books, 1972);

Eugene B. Redmond, *Drumvoices: The Mission of Afro-American Poetry, A Critical History* (Garden City: Anchor/Doubleday, 1976).

Victor Hernández Cruz

(6 February 1949-)

Pamela Masingale Lewis
Ohio State University

BOOKS: *Papo Got His Gun! and Other Poems* (New York: Calle Once Publications, 1966);

Doing Poetry (Berkeley: Other Ways, 1968);

Snaps (New York: Random House, 1969);

Mainland (New York: Random House, 1973);

Tropicalization (New York: Reed, Cannon & Johnson, 1976);

The Low Writings (San Francisco?: Lee/Lucas Press, 1980?);

By Lingual Wholes (San Francisco: Momo's Press, 1982).

OTHER: LeRoi Jones and Larry Neal, eds., *Black Fire: An Anthology of Afro-American Writing,* includes poems by Cruz (New York: William Morrow, 1968), pp. 436-437;

Arnold Adoff, ed., *City in All Directions,* includes poems by Cruz (New York: Macmillan, 1969), pp. 60-61;

Walter Lowenfels, ed., *In a Time of Revolution: Poems from Our Third World,* includes poems by Cruz (New York: Random House, 1969), p. 26;

Clarence Major, ed., *The New Black Poetry,* includes poems by Cruz (New York: International Publishers, 1969), pp. 45-46;

Adoff, ed., *Black Out Loud,* includes poems by Cruz (New York: Macmillan, 1970), pp. 64-69;

Alan Lomax and Raoul Abdul, eds., *3000 Years of Black Poetry,* includes poems by Cruz (New York: Dodd, Mead & Co., 1970), pp. 260-261;

Adam David Miller, ed., *Dices or Black Bones,* includes poems by Cruz (Boston: Houghton Mifflin, 1970), pp. 36-44;

Ishmael Reed, ed., *19 Necromancers from Now,* includes contribution by Cruz (Garden City: Doubleday, 1970), pp. 57-74;

Stuff: A Collection of Poems, Visions & Imaginative Happenings from Young Writers in Schools—Opened & Closed, edited by Cruz and Herbert Kohl, afterword by Cruz (New York: World Publishing, 1970);

Abraham Chapman, ed., *New Black Voices: An Anthology of Contemporary-Afro-American Literature,* includes poems by Cruz (New York: New American Library, 1972), pp. 238-240;

Alfredo Matilla and Iván Silén, eds., *The Puerto*

Rican Poets: Los Poetas Puertorriqueños, includes poems by Cruz (New York: Bantam Books, 1972), pp. 208-216;

Adoff, ed., *The Poetry of Black America,* includes poems by Cruz (New York: Harper & Row, 1973), pp. 506-511;

Paul Breman, ed., *You Better Believe It: Black Verse in English from Africa, the West Indies and the United States,* includes poems by Cruz (Baltimore: Penguin Books, 1973), pp. 516-518;

Maria T. Babin and Stan Steiner, eds., *Borinquen: An Anthology of Puerto Rican Literature,* includes poems by Cruz (New York: Knopf, 1974), pp. 440-446;

Janice Mirikitani and Luis Syquia, et al., eds., *Time to Greeze,* includes poems by Cruz (San Francisco: Glide Publications, 1975), pp. 165-167;

Quincy Troupe and Rainer Schulte, eds., *Giant Talk: An Anthology of Third World Writings,* includes poems by Cruz (New York: Random House, 1975), pp. 193-194, 487;

Steve Cannon, ed., *Jambalaya: Four Poets,* introduction by Cruz (New York: Reed, Cannon & Johnson, 1976).

PERIODICAL PUBLICATIONS:

POETRY

"Papo Got His Gun," *Evergreen Review,* 11 (August 1967): 73-80;

"Three Poems by Victor Hernández Cruz," *Ramparts,* 7 (24 August 1968): 51-52;

"The Champagne of Cocaine" and others, *Yardbird Reader,* 1 (1972): 99-102;

"You Gotta Have Your Tips on Fire," *Village Voice,* 19, 31 October 1974, p. 56;

"The Latest Latin Dance Craze" and others, *Revista Chicano Riquena,* 3 (Summer 1975): 12-14;

"Caffeine Gardeens" and others, *Greenfield Review,* 4, no. 3/4 (Autumn 1975): 70-71.

FICTION

"The Plumbers," *Black Scholar,* 12 (September-October 1981): 18-19.

According to Donald E. Herdeck, editor of a critical encyclopedia on Caribbean writers, writers like Piri Thomas and Victor Hernández Cruz have been at the forefront of a movement of "neo-rican" writers. The Neorican (or Nurican or Nuyorican) writers are Puerto Ricans, says Faythe E. Turner, "who have been born or have spent their formative years on the United States mainland, who write in an idiomatic English influenced by Spanish and Black English, and who derive mainly from the working class. Their literature," she continues, "is a Puerto Rican examination of their status on the mainland, the reality of life here, and the traditions they consider to be part of their familial past. . . ." While Thomas has gained eminence through his novels *Down These Mean Streets* (1967) and *Savior, Savior Hold My Hand* (1972), Cruz's forté is poetry, written primarily in English rather than in Spanish.

Now in his mid-thirties, Cruz has reached a diverse and large audience. His poems have been translated into five languages and have been included in no fewer than fifteen anthologies—mostly Afro-American. They have also appeared in avant-garde magazines like *Ramparts* and *Yardbird Reader,* in periodicals published in Spain and Latin America, in an operetta written by a world-famous composer, and on New York City buses. Cruz has written four volumes of poetry and has published three. He has lectured at colleges and universities across the country. He has appeared in street productions with a theater group which he cofounded, has read his poetry in Europe, and has edited at least two reviews and one collection of juvenile poetry.

Cruz's works are a radical attempt to clarify the reality of *el barrio,* Spanish Harlem, from which he comes. His words become tools with which he carves portraits of the mainland most Americans have never seen. At the same time, using nature, rhythm, lyric, sensual imagery, and sometimes Spanish diction, he seeks to help the reader better understand himself in order to "reshape the world."

Victor Hernández Cruz was born in Aguas Buenas, Puerto Rico, on 6 February 1949, to Severo and Rosa Cruz. Like thousands of other islanders, his family migrated to the mainland for economic reasons brought about by colonialism and the industrialization of the island. When Cruz was six his family moved to the Lower East Side of Manhattan, one of New York City's minority enclaves designated *el barrio.* Shortly after the move, his parents divorced, the aftermath of which brought hardship and heartache to Cruz, his mother, and sister, Gladys. Cruz says of that time, "Life was harsh and hard . . . because of things to overcome . . . and insults to take." Cruz's mother continued to support and hold the family together, an effort he prizes because it gave him a "sense of pride and strength," and brought "glory to [his] work."

Around the age of fourteen, Cruz began to write. He describes it as a "disease spreading throughout" his young mind. His fascination with books increased his interest in writing and the "power of words began to seep into [him]."

At seventeen Cruz had written his first book of verse, *Papo Got His Gun* (1966), while still a student at Benjamin Franklin High School. *Papo Got His Gun,* which means Papo has his awareness, showed the beginnings of creative energy for Cruz, or more aptly, nervous energy. Cruz and a few friends carried a mimeograph machine up six flights of stairs to print *Papo Got His Gun* under the name Calle Once (Eleventh Street) Publications. Copies of the collection were distributed to stores to be sold for seventy-five cents each. Surprisingly, while only five hundred copies were printed, one copy fell into the hands of Fred Jordon of *Evergreen Review,* an avant-garde New York magazine. *Evergreen* subsequently ran a seven-page spread using a few poems from *Papo* and photographs from *el barrio.*

In Papo one hears the voice of a teenager grappling with identity, life, and death. He writes of his experiences in the streets and beyond, of his dreams and visions. The death of friends is a common occurrence for the young poet, as in "Louie Is Dead": "I remember you Louie/you was still in school/and we used to sit on stoops and jive/ . . . but no more/ . . . Louie is dead." He writes also of his role as poet in "A LETTER TO JOSE":

Joe i been fighting
not the way we used to fight with the Sportsmens
but with words that must be as sharp as blades

Other themes include the rape of America, nature, street and school educations, bitterness, anger, "fast" girls, and the *barrio* hero, as in "The Life of Juan Gonzales." The persona views Juan as "something savage," "yet beautiful and clean," a view incomprehensible to the Fifth Avenue dweller. Cruz's themes are effectively rendered by his use of simile, contrast, repetition, narration, rhythmic and lyrical lines, vivid, colorful language, and humor. His use of poetry as his weapon is one of his most vehement statements. In "A LETTER TO JOSE," he says:

there are people who say my story is dying
but i'm going to stick with it
cause i know they are wrong . . .
cause i know you're still in the ghetto
and mama is there
and Tito has been killed by it

In *Papo Got His Gun* Cruz is not afraid to expose the ugly side of life, or the beauty and vitality he sees within it. One senses that Cruz's vocation as poet was firmly established by the time he was seventeen.

Six months before he was to have graduated in 1967, Cruz left Ben Franklin High School. The following year he cofounded the East Harlem Gut Theatre, located on 104th Street in New York. Gut Theatre was a Puerto Rican collective composed of actors, musicians, and writers. Cruz's "plays" were performed in the streets. Gut Theatre closed after one year of operation.

Cruz joined *Umbra* magazine in 1967 as an editor. *Umbra* had been founded by David Henderson, Calvin Hernton, and Tom Dent on the Lower East Side in 1962. The magazine was published by an artists' collective, the Society of Umbra, part of the black literary movement of the 1960s and 1970s. When Cruz became associated with *Umbra* it was largely under the editorship of David Henderson who had moved the magazine to California. Among the magazine's contributors were Ishmael Reed (who was to become Cruz's close friend), Larry Neal (another friend), Nikki Giovanni, Amiri Baraka, Toni Cade Bambara, Quincy Troupe, Hernton, and Cruz. Many of these writers went on to publish works in varied literary genres as well as to edit Afro-American anthologies at the height of the black power movement. Cruz's works were frequently anthologized during this period. After years of struggle over editorial policy, *Umbra* folded in 1969. A special Latin/Soul issue was *Umbra's* last publication. Cruz coedited and translated works for this issue.

In 1968 three of Cruz's poems appeared in the prestigious *Ramparts* magazine. Two of his poems appeared in an Afro-American anthology, *Black Fire,* edited by Baraka (LeRoi Jones) and Larry Neal, at the request of Neal who knew Cruz from *Umbra.*

Cruz left New York for the West Coast, moving from one focal point of the American counterculture scene, the Lower East Side, to another, Berkeley, in 1968. He left because of the "pressure of street life and family." Since then, "a back and forth relationship with the East and West has been going on . . . with the balance tipping toward the West" in recent years. Cruz went to Berkeley to "hang out," but found himself in the middle of a cultural revolution where he was "able to pursue books and ideas." California was a writer's haven; Cruz interacted with other artists and read many of the authors whose subjects and styles were to influence his works. Among these were Baraka, Richard Wright, Ralph Ellison, Franz Fanon, Cesar Vellejo, Pablo Neruda, as well as Ernesto Cardinal and Octavio Paz, whom Cruz considers "two very perceptive poets of this continent." The influence of musicians Tito Puento and Eddie Palmieri y Cortijo can be seen in Cruz's highly rhythmic and lyric verse.

A teaching job subsequently developed in a Berkeley experimental public school, directed by Herbert Kohl, author of *36 Children* (1967). For about six months Cruz taught a group of junior high school boys how to survive as men, which he felt would help them write well, too. Out of this experience Cruz wrote "Doing Poetry," one single poem published as a four-page pamphlet. In one section of "Doing Poetry" Cruz expresses his views of his role as poet. He portrays life "thru ugly ugly cuts/or beautiful dreams." He is undogmatic in his writing:

> god would not make anything bad or dirty. some peo-
> ple
> make dirty things happen tho.
> i see what's in the world & sing it
> like god.

Sections of "Doing Poetry" appear in Adam David Miller's anthology of Afro-American literature *Dices or Black Bones*, published in 1970. A section of the poem, also, is included in German composer Hans Werner Henze's operetta *Voices: a Collection of Songs for Two Vocalists and Instrumental Groups* (1973). Another of his poems, "The Electric Cop," is put to music in this operetta, which was first performed in 1974 by the London Symphony at the Queen Elizabeth Hall in London. In 1978 the Contemporary Music Players performed the operetta at the San Francisco Opera House.

Another publication issuing from the Other Ways experience was *Stuff: A Collection of Poems, Visions & Imaginative Happenings from Young Writers in Schools–Opened & Closed* (1970), which Cruz coedited with Kohl. *Stuff* uses poetry, prose, and illustrations by children, teens, and adults, but focuses mostly on the work of teens. Some of Cruz's own verse and prose appear in *Stuff*, including a section from "Doing Poetry" which is used as the afterword.

Cruz began work on his first major publication, *Snaps*, in 1968 while living in a 72nd Street East Harlem Building owned by jazz musician Miles Davis. Part of his time was spent writing and part was spent tutoring youths in basic education skills in a program through Columbia University. Of all his poetry, *Snaps*, published in 1969, has received the

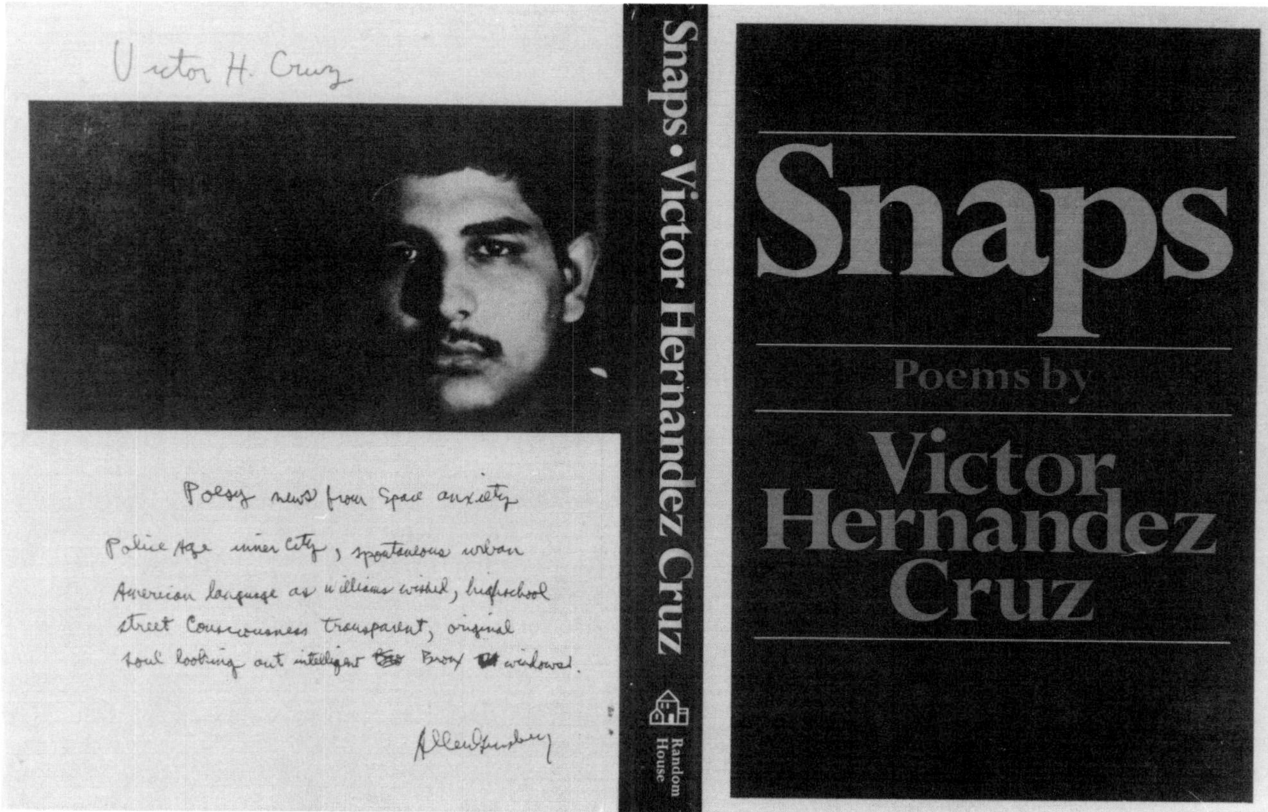

Dust jacket for Cruz's first major collection of poetry

widest critical reception, perhaps because it was his first work published by a major company, Random House, or perhaps because it sold 6,000 copies.

In *Snaps* Cruz still works out of a nervous energy, and he is looking for direction. Yet, there is a tighter form of control in his language. He says he "was trusting my voice and my mind." Among his themes are the rejection of white American values, death, poetic potency, "hanging out," the spirit world (*espiritismo*), and New York City street life. Cruz uses plain, simple language as he indicts the American dream in "IS A DEAD MAN": "hopeless/useless/is a dead/dead world/they selling/here." One notes techniques of rhythm (*ritmo*) and lyric (*música*), as well as a sense of ongoing movement in "latin & soul": "thru universes/leaning-moving/we are traveling/where are we going/if we only knew." Cruz's "Free Spirit" imitates freedom of movement and rhythm in dance (*mambo*), especially by repetition.

you are already there
nothing stopping you
you are magic
magic
magic
espiritu libre
espiritu libre

In one part of a thirty-two-stanza poem, "The Eye Uptown & Downtown," Cruz's persona literally becomes an eye seeing the daily happenings of the city. Stanza thirty is glaringly realistic:

death everywhere
coat cut
throat slit
smash against a wall
blood
wallet three feet away
empty.

In contrast Cruz is able to have hope through poetry as a means of social reform. Cruz's poem "today is a day of great joy " is one of the strongest statements the poet makes regarding the power of the word:

when poems start to/knock down walls to/
choke politicians/when poems scream &/
begin to break the air

that is the time of/true poets   that is/
the time of greatness

Critics were positive in their reception of the use, in *Snaps*, of abrupt, spontaneous, and compact snapshot imagery and its gnawing realism. *Snaps* was lauded, also, for its control of space. Some saw Cruz's language as forceful, immediate, and refreshingly uninhibited. Others viewed his themes as repeats of 1960s Beat poetry, but lacking fresh angles. These critics deemed his verse most successful as poetry when there was no social commentary. Critics of his snapshots saw them as limiting his poetic craft because of the abstractions. Some pointed out an unwillingness to omit detail and a tendency toward repetition, both leading to monotony. Others viewed Cruz's language as too predictable and too fearful of risk-taking, suggesting ambivalence within his cultural and poetical identity. One critic even suggested that *Snaps* was not poetry at all. Though ambivalent in their appraisal of his work, most critics seem to agree that *Snaps* was a necessary work for the American public and literary establishment because of its unadulterated portrayals of city life and Cruz's unconventional poetic technique.

One has to question criticism regarding Cruz's social commentary and the validity of his snapshot imagery, repetition, and unusual diction, because Cruz dispels the poetic traditions which critics seek to force upon him. Editors Miguel Algarin and Miguel Piñero (*Nuyorican Poetry: An Anthology of Puerto Rican Words and Feeling*, 1975) suggest that the Nuyorican poet must "extend poetic traditions" because of his role in the community. He "fights with words," and so must redefine and recreate language in such a way as to capture experience—no matter how extreme—realistically. Cruz himself denounces critics who seek to force a poet into a particular style: "They try to make you into something they can understand, then they can go home feeling OK. But with me, they went home without understanding me."

Cruz's comments appeared in a joint interview with close friend and critic Clarence Major, author of *The Dark and the Feeling* (1973). Both were attending the Summer Institute on Black Excellence at Cazenovia College in Cazenovia, New York, in 1969 as token Puerto Ricans among black writers and a predominantly black audience. The message he delivered at the conference was that Puerto Rican culture is a rich blend of three cultures: Indian, Spanish, and African. The mixture of the three, with their foods, music, religion, rhythm, and mythologies bring beauty and flavor to his work.

Dance and rhythm of African culture within Puerto Rico are treated in Cruz's poem "african things," published in *Negro Digest* in 1969, and later

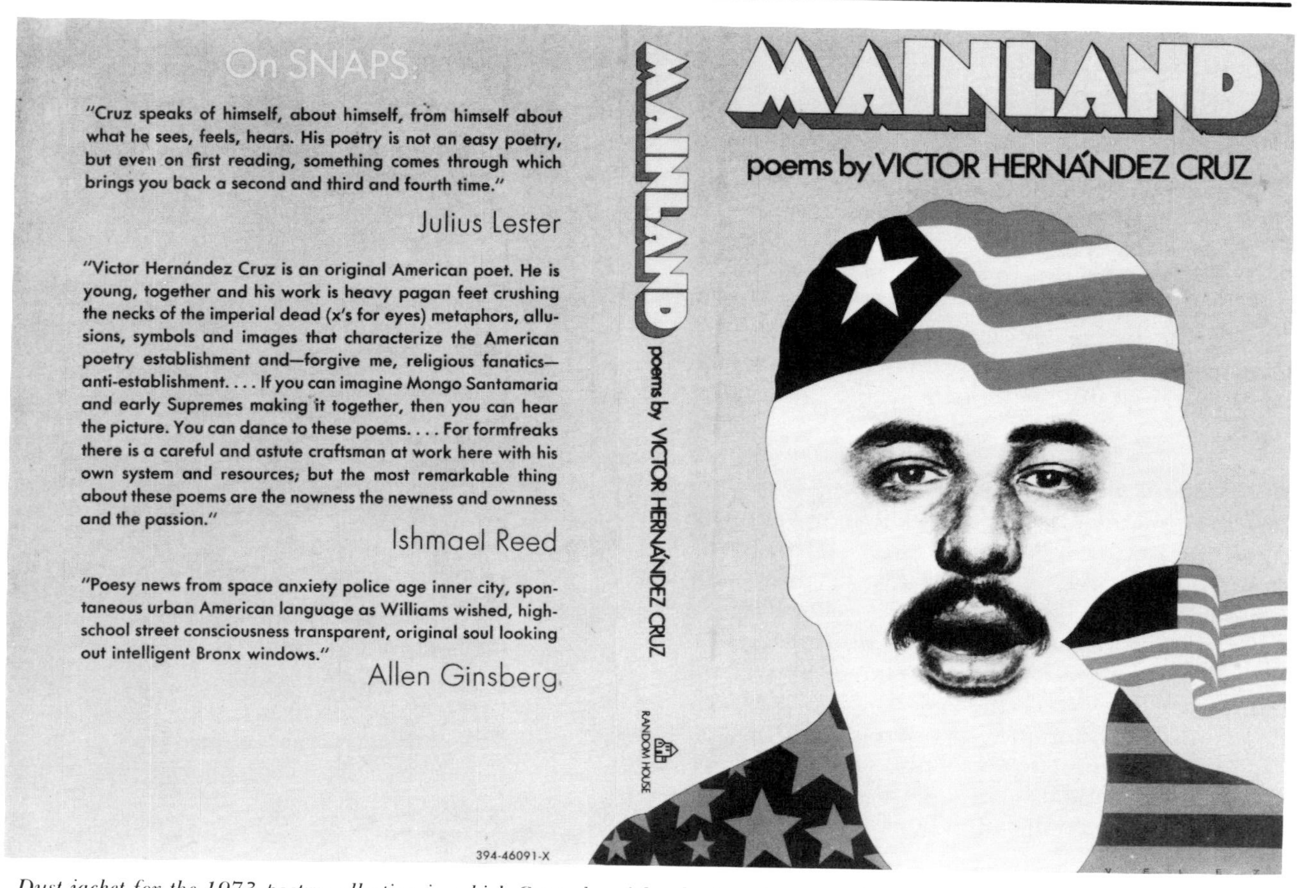

On SNAPS:
"Cruz speaks of himself, about himself, from himself about what he sees, feels, hears. His poetry is not an easy poetry, but even on first reading, something comes through which brings you back a second and third and fourth time."
Julius Lester
"Victor Hernández Cruz is an original American poet. He is young, together and his work is heavy pagan feet crushing the necks of the imperial dead (x's for eyes) metaphors, allusions, symbols and images that characterize the American poetry establishment and—forgive me, religious fanatics—anti-establishment. . . . If you can imagine Mongo Santamaria and early Supremes making it together, then you can hear the picture. You can dance to these poems. . . . For formfreaks there is a careful and astute craftsman at work here with his own system and resources; but the most remarkable thing about these poems are the nowness the newness and ownness and the passion."
Ishmael Reed
"Poesy news from space anxiety police age inner city, spontaneous urban American language as Williams wished, high-school street consciousness transparent, original soul looking out intelligent Bronx windows."
Allen Ginsberg
394-46091-X
MAINLAND
poems by VICTOR HERNÁNDEZ CRUZ
RANDOM HOUSE
MAINLAND
poems by VICTOR HERNÁNDEZ CRUZ

Dust jacket for the 1973 poetry collection in which Cruz chronicles the American experience from the Puerto Rican point of view

in his second book of poetry, *Mainland* (1973). That year, also, Cruz's poetry appeared in *The New Black Poetry*, edited by Major, as well as in two other Afro-American anthologies, *City in All Directions* and *In a Time of Revolution*. Sections of an incomplete novel, *Rhythm Section / Part One*, appeared in Reed's anthology *19 Necromancers from Now* in 1970. Cruz's verse also appeared in at least three other anthologies that same year.

Many other publications featured Cruz's poetry in the early 1970s, including two journals dedicated to Third World artists, *Confrontations* (1971) and *Mundus Atrium* (1973). *Confrontations* was edited by Quincy Troupe, who also used Cruz's works in his anthology, *Giant Talk* (1975). The journal *Yardbird Reader*, edited by Reed, featured two of Cruz's poems in 1972. His poems also appeared in the anthologies *New Black Voices* and *The Puerto Rican Poets*, both in 1972, and in *The Poetry of Black America* and *You Better Believe It* in 1973.

Cruz taught a poetry workshop as guest lecturer at the University of California at Berkeley in 1972. His classes involved discussion of his own work and works of his favorite poets. He also served as an instructor in ethnic studies at San Francisco State College. His classes emphasized Hispanic poetry and literature from Mexico and Puerto Rico.

Cruz's most notable publication of the early 1970s was his second book of verse, *Mainland*. In this collection Cruz is less concerned with the glimpses of life in *el barrio*, and more readily develops longer images of his experiences elsewhere. Cruz's persona travels East to West through the U.S. mainland, as Cruz himself had traveled. Here, imagery is far more focused and much more sensual than in *Snaps*. Again, one sees the intermingled African, Indian, and Spanish cultures throughout his verse, as well as a mixture of Spanish and English diction. Always, one senses movement through the familiar *música*, *ritmo*, and *mambo*. In *Mainland* Cruz invokes his reader to combine the senses and to mix the natural and supernatural in order to recapture the experience of the Bronx, Chicago, Detroit, Las Vegas, San Francisco, and other cities.

Mainland's first poem, "You Gotta Have Your

Tips on Fire," also published in the *Village Voice* (October 1974), appropriately encourages the reader to be ready to utilize vitality at all times while one can:

> You gotta have your tips on fire
> You never will be in the wrong place
> For the universe will feel your heat
> And arrange its dance on your head

Within the universe, one can tap into a vibrant force to experience life at its fullest. He seems to imply, moreover, that this poetry helps one get one's "tips on fire."

"En La Casa De Verta" (In Verta's House) was published in a cookbook entitled *Vibration Cooking* by Verta Mae Grosvenor (1970). The poem mixes different cultures, "hot sauce/street beans/caribbean rice on the fire/with african juice warmin. . . ." The end result, of course, is Puerto Rico, an island culture formed by the "centuries and centuries/of sea exploration and mixing. . . ." Cruz's glimpses of the cities on the mainland are accurately descriptive and humorous. In "Berkeley/Over," he says Berkeley is "A town of philosophical habits/Cold turkey would kill it. . . ." Cruz laments civilization's assault on nature in "The Ways of San Francisco": "Wire lines all over the town/distract the sky. . . ." On the other hand, Nature is enhanced by the trolly car's dance: "The train cha chas on two/straight lines. . . ." In "Chicago/3 Hours" one hears music in

> Traffic chaos—
> That melody of a fast moving
> civilization

Chicago humorously comes alive in Cruz's descriptions: "For the famous breeze/Bacardi light//a spirit walks the bridge with/cement still tied to his legs." "Las Vegas" is the "City of coins/George Washington and Lincoln/Slide into your slot machines . . ." and "The poor middle aged men/Lose their hair/At the tables. . . ." "African things" highlights the spirit world: "african spirits/dance & sing in my mother's house. in my cousin's house, . . . " while Cruz's persona is like a spirit in "from the Secrets II":

> This morning I move like the river
> moves
> In and out of rooms like the warm
> wind passing through.

Here, the river is part of the universal movement flowing through everything. In "Séis Amarrao" the poet returns to his native Puerto Rico, to his grandmother's home, to experience her world.

> This town holds my grandmother
> In her ancient dreams
> Sewing dresses and cooking food
> Somewhere in a quiet street
> within

The serenity of the town contrasts sharply with the towns on the mainland.

> Quiet in the night of memories
> Quiet in the valley over the mountain
> Quiet like the lines of Caquax.

Reviewers of *Mainland* were pleased to see themes which departed from the New York experience. They marveled at the presence of multiple cultures in Cruz's poetry. One critic noted that the *Mainland* voice is "more developed" and less self-conscious than that of *Snaps,* but felt the abstractions were inappropriate for the sensuous imagery. On the whole, *Mainland* was lauded by critics for its diverse themes and the ease with which Cruz exposes the underside of mainland U.S.A.

Cruz received a Creative Artists Program Service (CAPS) grant in 1974 in order to write his third volume of poetry. The purpose of the grant was to enable New York State artists to create new work or to finish work in progress. One of the poems used in this volume, "El Tropical Club," was included in an anthology prepared by the CAPS program.

Also in 1974 selections from *Rhythm Section/Part One* were published in an anthology of Puerto Rican literature, *Borinquen* (1974), the aboriginal name for the island of Puerto Rico, meaning "The Land of Proud Men." His poems also appeared in an anthology of minority literature, *Time To Greeze* (1975), and in two journals, the *Greenfield Review* and *Revista Chicano Riquena.*

Cruz married in 1975. His wife, Elisa Ivette, bore him a son, Vitin Ajani, the same year. Cruz became a contributing editor of *Revista Chicano Riquena* in 1976. A book for which he wrote the introduction, *Jambalaya: Four Poets,* was published that year, as well. *Jambalaya* was edited by Steve Cannon, a former editor of *Umbra.*

Two of Cruz's poems, "The Where Is What Is" and "Side 19," appeared on New York City buses in 1976 through the Poetry in Public Places Contest. The contest was sponsored by the American International Sculptors Symposium. The poems were placed on 1,000 city buses. Cruz was fortunate in that his were among the twelve poems selected from 6,000 entries. "Side 19" also appeared in Cruz's third volume of poetry.

Cruz returned to San Francisco in 1976. At that time he became associated with the San Francisco Neighborhood Arts Program, and worked with schools, senior citizens centers, prisons, and city festivals. The job provided support while Cruz completed his third volume, *Tropicalization* (1976). *Tropicalization* "took wings" and released Cruz's creative energies with a greater ease in style. While *Mainland* reveals a picturesque journey through the United States, using heightened sensual imagery to glamorize the otherwise mundane countryside, *Tropicalization* reveals Cruz's efforts to inject a Latin American joie de vivre into North America, an act of tropicalizing. One sees brisk, witty, and proverbial poems depicting New York City life. Unlike the poems in *Snaps*, these portraits are not as rigid, for Cruz injects humor through the varied means of survival he recreates. These experiences are triumphs because of the will to survive. One finds, moreover, some of the same themes—New York street life, the spirit world—as those seen in *Snaps*, yet these are given a new vitality by Cruz's extended imagery.

Cold weather is one subject Cruz uses to reveal the humor and pathos of survival. "Side 6" quips about New York weather that was so cold "one day/in January" that Doctor Willie who "was broke like a mango/tree in Alaska" would not bend down to pick up a dollar bill. In "Side 3" the imagery is strong and vivid, and the tone sardonic:

> Out of the avenue comes a heavy overcoat
> That needs a cigarette
> Go smoke Con Edison Bro

"Song 3," from "Three Songs From the 50s," contrasts mainland cold with island warmth:

> There was still no central heating
> in the tenements
> . . . .
> We used to think about my uncle Listo
> Who never left his hometown

On *Mainland:*

He has returned to the mother, the source, the tropical cradle, and he has found God. Hernandez Cruz's creation is soul poetry, and as such, it is a direct avenue to the Ultimate Creator. God is the fountainhead of poetry and music. the common rhythm that runs through Hernandez Cruz's poem is "la salsa de Dios". By pursuing the secrets of his Puerto Rican-African heritage he has ultimately achieved a universality and a brotherhood with all men."

—*Nicolas Kanellos*

". . . Hernandez Cruz is the most alive new poet I've come across in several years. . . The poet doesn't go anywhere; he just stands there. Really it is probably better not to say "the poet"—maybe "the singer" or "the man"—because the voice in the poetry detaches itself from a writer named Victor and becomes sheer creative force."

—*John Brushwood*
Kansas City Morning Star

"MAINLAND is a beautiful, moving work; fun to read and an absolute joy to re-read. Victor Hernandez Cruz is the real thing: an original poet with a vision and music all his own expressed in an idiom that is electrifyingly American. The present collection should firmly establish him as one of the most gifted young voices on the contemporary poetry scene."

—*Al Young*

Reed, Cannon & Johnson : $4.95

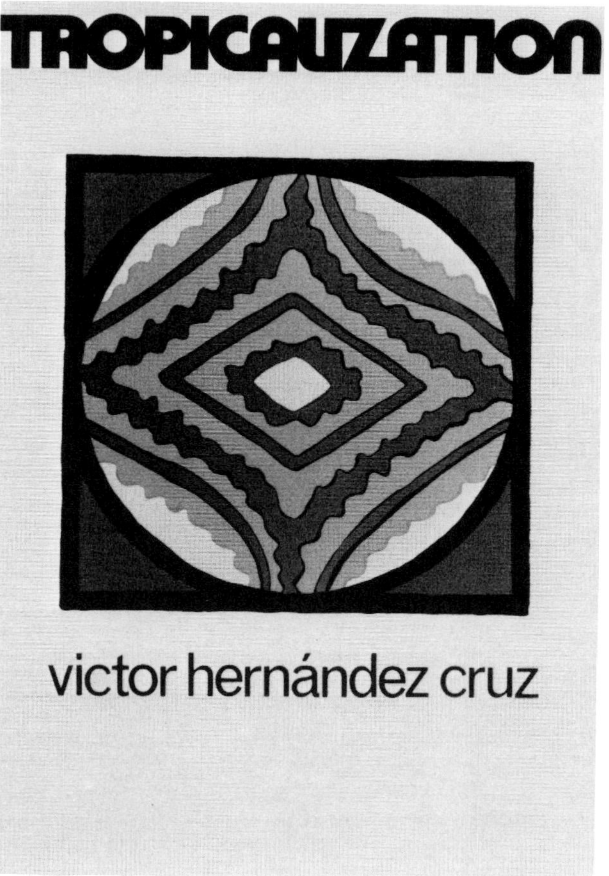

Covers for Cruz's 1976 volume of poetry and prose narratives that examines survival techniques in el barrio

We'd picture him sitting around
cooling himself with a fan
In that imaginary place
called Puerto Rico.

Here, one senses Cruz's attempts to tropicalize the tenements; the persona seeks to bring Puerto Rican warmth, emotional as well as climactic, to New York City's *el barrio*. One notes also the barrier, indicated by "imaginary place," between the present and the past which mainland Puerto Ricans face.

Cruz's glimpses at everyday life take one's mind off the harsh realities of survival. "Side 31" notes a Coney Island sign "That reads: Come inside and see the Invisible Man." "Side 18" shows one of the "crazies," a man waiting for a building to come by so he can "jump in." "Side 20" rejects Oscar Lewis's controversial *La Vida*, a lurid and somewhat pathetic sociological study of Puerto Ricans in New York and San Juan, published in 1965. Cruz writes

I found Oscar Lewis'
Tape recorder
Behind a pizza shop in the Bronx
And they wouldn't give me
Ten dollars for it
At the pawn shop

He speaks of dance in "Side 12," revealing two cultural traditions:

Manhattan dance Latin
In Spanish to African rhythms
A language lesson
Without opening your mouth.

Movement and *ritmo* seem to dominate his imagery.

Critics praised *Tropicalization* for its bilingual diction, its style, and its energy. Cruz's imagination ran more freely, yielded more greatly developed images, and revealed a stronger grasp of his craft, as well as a liberation of himself as poet. Critics saw *Tropicalization* as more innovative and fresher in its approach to themes than were *Snaps* and *Mainland*.

Cruz won another CAPS grant in 1978 to write fiction. That year some of his short fiction work was published in two other avant-garde reviews, *New World Journal* and *Invisible City*. A short novel, "Novenas," was also written through the grant. "Novenas" has never been published.

In 1979 Cruz took part in the One World Poetry Festival in Amsterdam, Holland, and gave poetry readings in Germany and France the same year. He was invited back to the Festival the following year, along with poet Allen Ginsberg.

Cruz's second child, Rosa, was born in 1980. That same year, "The low writings," a short story, appeared in *Mango*, a journal of Chicano literature. "The low writings" was subsequently published in pamphlet form and in an issue of *Numbers* magazine (1981?), which devoted an entire issue to Cruz's works. The *Black Scholar* published fiction by Cruz in 1981, as well.

In 1982 Cruz was working full-time on a collection of poetry and prose, *By Lingual Wholes*. Many of the poems in this collection have political undertones. "Bacalao and Society" addresses the colonialism of the Portuguese through the metaphor of the dried cod, *bacalao*, eaten on board the exploring vessels, and still used today in Hispanic cuisine. "Borinkins in Hawaii" comments on the exploitation of Puerto Rican migrant workers by the Hawaiian plantation system. One short narrative, "Don Arturo: A Story of Migration," briefly uses the Cuban revolution as a backdrop to the persona's story, while "*Merenque* in History" speaks of Puerto Rican colonization. Cruz often injects humor into these serious subjects.

The book is written in English, Spanish, and a hybrid language, "Spanglish" (Spanish syntax and English diction). It explores the experiences of a mind shaped by two languages, for example poems

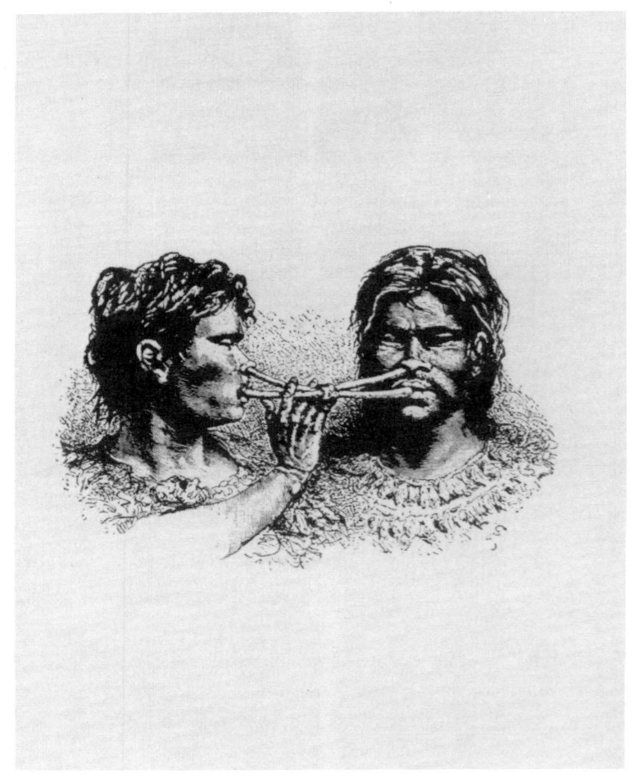

Engraving from By Lingual Wholes, *Cruz's 1982 collection*

like "Ver-sion/cion" are written in both English and Spanish; "Hearing Inside Out" is written with English diction and Spanish syntax; and there are narratives written primarily in English but using some Spanish diction. Cruz describes the dual nature of *By Lingual Wholes* as a tightening process which uses precision in its delivery. "Bi-Lingual Education" captures the essence of this experience for Cruz. Picturing the persona before a mirror, Cruz warns him not to look at himself:

> lest you see yourself
> your tongue hanging out
> like a carpet
> where two ladies
> are sprawled   entwined
> They come to eat you
> in doubles
> They chew you
> till you are
> a strong and perfect 1.

Cruz seeks the readers' wholeness as well as his own, so that we might revisualize our world as he does his world. One couplet in "A Gang of Shorties" expresses this view: "Sophisticated street where style erupts: some say slums/Those who cannot see will not hear the drums."

By mid-1982 Cruz had completed his first novel, in which he seeks to recreate his parents' world in a Puerto Rican village. He uses information from his parents and other relatives, including actual names of people his mother knew. He also incorporates imaginary objects—fruits and trees—to help reconstruct the village life.

Cruz's hybrid culture of Spanish, African, and Indian influence seems to have left him open to new visions and vehicles of art. He feels the true artist can create from anything in the universe, and need not be limited by culture or literary genre. He is now creating more fiction—short stories and novels—than poetry. One expects, moreover, that Spanish will appear more frequently in his works as a means of redefining and controlling the English language.

Cruz has become a leader among Neorican writers, setting a trend for other Neorican and non-Puerto Rican poets with his "Span-glish," *ritmo, mùsica, espiritismo, mambo,* and nature imagery. In fact, his dependence upon nature as a theme causes some critics to regard him as a naturalist; others view him as a surrealist á la Garcia Lorca. His imagination and spontaneity are deemed crucial to his genius.

Poets Allen Ginsberg and Ishmael Reed praise

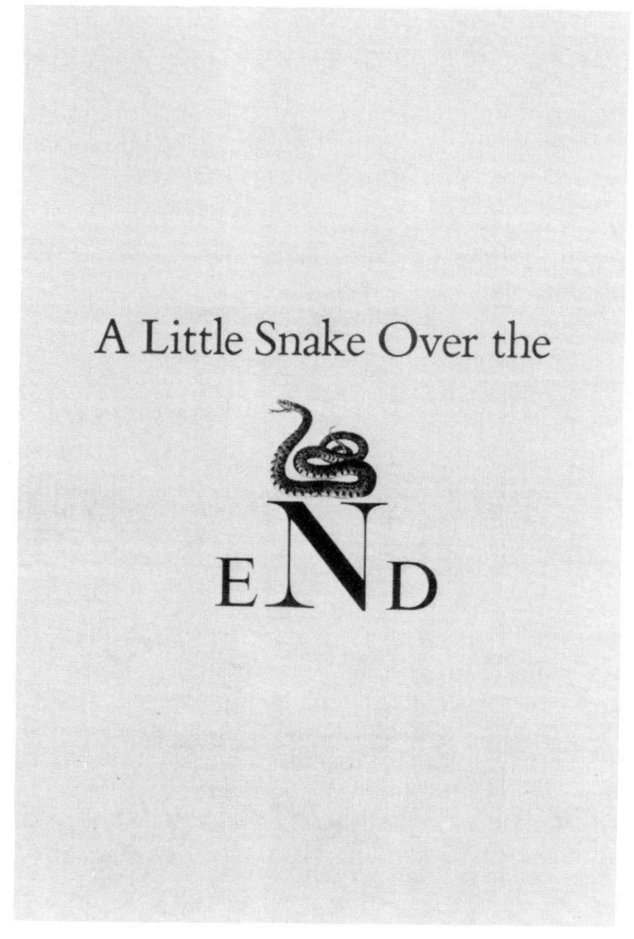

Closing illustration from By Lingual Wholes *that demonstrates Cruz's playful handling of language*

Cruz's originality, Reed being especially complimentary of the astuteness of his poetic craftsmanship and the passion with which he writes. Critic Eugene Redmond has described him as an "important American poet," along with such diverse writers as Gwendolyn Brooks, Jóse Montoya, Michael Harper, Sylvia Plath, and Robert Lowell. That his work has appeared in some of America's most prestigious, avant-garde, and scholarly periodicals gives credence to this view. Certainly Cruz's poetry and prose are important to the American literary scene, for they explore and expose American society, and they use human imagination to break down cultural barriers, to create new perceptions of reality, and to "formulate new visions for the future."

Interviews:

Walt Sheppard, "An Interview with Clarence Major and Victor Hernández Cruz," in *New Black*

Voices, edited by Abraham Chapman (New York: New American Library, 1972), pp. 545-552;

Victor Rosa, "Interview with Victor Hernández Cruz," *Bilingual Review,* 2 (September-December 1975): 281-287.

References:

Faythe E. Turner, "Puerto Rican Writers on the Mainland: The Neoricans: A Thematic Study," Ph.D. dissertation, University of Massachusetts, 1978, pp. 120-134;

Barry Wallenstein, "The Poet in New York: Victor Hernández Cruz," *Bilingual Review,* 1 (September-December 1974): 312-319.

Margaret Esse Danner

(12 January 1915-)

June M. Aldridge
Spelman College

BOOKS: *Impressions of African Art Forms* (Detroit, Mich.: Broadside Press, 1960);

To Flower (Nashville, Tenn.: Hemphill Press, 1963);

Poem Counterpoem, by Danner and Dudley Randall (Detroit, Mich.: Broadside Press, 1966);

Iron Lace (Millbrook, N.Y.: Kriya Press, 1968);

The Down of a Thistle: Selected Poems, Prose Poems, and Songs (Waukesha, Wis.: Country Beautiful, 1976).

OTHER: Rosey E. Pool, ed., *Beyond the Blues: New Poems by American Negroes,* includes poems by Danner (Lympne, Kent: Hand and Flower Press, 1962);

Arna Bontemps, ed., *American Negro Poetry,* includes poems by Danner (New York: Hill and Wang, 1963);

Dudley Randall and Margaret Burroughs, eds., *For Malcolm: Poems on the Life and the Death of Malcolm X,* includes poems by Danner (Detroit, Mich.: Broadside, 1967);

Brass Horses, edited by Danner (Richmond, Va.: Virginia Union University, 1968);

Regroup, edited by Danner (Richmond, Va.: Virginia Union University, 1969);

Patricia L. Brown Johnson, et al., eds., *To Gwen With Love,* includes poems by Danner (Chicago: Johnson Publishing Company, 1971);

Dudley Randall, ed., *The Black Poets,* includes poems by Danner (New York: Bantam, 1971);

Robert Hayden, et al., eds., *Afro-American Literature: An Introduction,* includes poems by Danner (New York: Harcourt Brace Jovanovich, 1971);

Richard Barksdale and Keneth Kinnamon, eds., *Black Writers of America: A Comprehensive Anthology,* includes poems by Danner (New York: Macmillan, 1972);

Arnold Adoff, ed., *The Poetry of Black America: Anthology of the 20th Century,* includes poems by Danner (New York: Harper & Row, 1973);

Stephen Henderson, ed., *Understanding the New Black Poetry,* includes poems by Danner (New York: Morrow, 1973);

Erlene Stetson, ed., *Black Sister: Poetry by Black American Women, 1746-1980,* includes poems by Danner (Bloomington: Indiana University Press, 1981).

RECORDING: Danner and Langston Hughes, *Writers of the Revolution.* Black Forum (BB 453).

A poet who has not yet received the critical acclaim of some of her contemporaries, Margaret Danner has nonetheless made substantial contributions to the development of Afro-American literature. Author of five volumes, editor of two, and represented in numerous anthologies, Danner, like Gwendolyn Brooks and Mari Evans, bridges the gap between the poets who came to adulthood in the 1940s and 1950s and those who, like Nikki Giovanni and Sonia Sanchez, ushered in the black arts movement of the 1960s. The few critics who have written about Danner's work praise her highly for her exotic and exact images, her subtle protest poems, and her message that black Americans should preserve, appreciate, and celebrate their

African heritage. Sometimes compared to Langston Hughes for her frequent thematic focus on Africa, and to Brooks for her subtlety, irony, and images, Danner is a meticulous poet who has continued writing over several decades.

Margaret Esse Danner was born 12 January 1915 to Caleb and Naomi Esse of Pryorsburg, Kentucky. The young Danner began writing poetry in junior high school, where she won first prize for "The Violin" in a poetry contest when she was in the eighth grade. In later poems, she would make references to the Stradivarius and Guarnerius violins that are the central images of that early poem. Although she was not to become a published poet until much later in her life, Danner nevertheless continued to write.

She attended Englewood High School in Chicago, where the family had relocated. Her college career was spent at Loyola and Northwestern Universities, and her creativity was nurtured under the guidance of Karl Shapiro and Paul Engle. The formative years in Chicago and her association with writers there inspired Danner to return to that city after several years in Detroit in the 1960s. However, Danner's first significant recognition as a poet came in 1945, when she won second prize in the Poetry Workshop of the Midwestern Writers Conference held at Northwestern University.

While in Chicago, she became affiliated with *Poetry: The Magazine of Verse,* in 1951. Danner initially worked as an editorial assistant for this avant-garde journal, which continued its long tradition of introducing new poets to the American public. The journal published a series of four of her poems, entitled "Far From Africa," which has become the most popularly anthologized of her poems. The publication resulted in Danner being awarded a John Hay Whitney fellowship in 1951, which was intended to support a trip to Africa scheduled for that year; she delayed the trip, however, until 1966.

After serving as editorial assistant to *Poetry* from 1951 until 1955, Danner was promoted to assistant editor, the first black person to hold that position. She is certain that it was Karl Shapiro who influenced the magazine to promote her, and she recalls the association with *Poetry* as one of the most rewarding experiences of her life. She served as assistant editor from 1956 until 1957.

Although some details about Danner's life are certain, others are sketchy. Initially married to Cordell Strickland, she was subsequently married to Otto Cunningham. She and Strickland have one child, Naomi, who resides near her in Chicago. Naomi's son, Sterling Washington, Jr., has become the inspiration for many of Danner's poems. She calls them the "Muffin poems." Although readers share the joy and pride the doting grandmother feels, they are also allowed a glimpse into more substantive matters; the Muffin poems range over a variety of subjects, as evidenced by titles such as "Black Power Language" and "Muffin, His Baba and the Boneman."

It was perhaps her success with *Poetry* that took Danner away from Chicago. In 1961, she went to Wayne State University in Detroit to begin one of the many positions she has held as poet-in-residence at various universities. Her trek to Detroit led to the direct involvement in community artistic organizations that would characterize her for many years to come. She found an empty parish house near Detroit's King Solomon Church and persuaded the minister, Dr. Boone, to allow her to establish a community arts center there. Boone House, opened in 1962, has been described as a "lively center for the arts," especially for the children for whom it was specially conceived. Poets who helped Danner in various ways at Boone House were Dudley Randall, Robert Hayden, Hoyt Fuller, Owen Dodson, and Naomi Long Madgett.

During this period, Danner also became active in the Baha'i faith. From 1964 until 1966, she was the touring poet with the Baha'i Teaching Committee. Although she has an impressive number of poems about or that make references to the Baha'i faith, Danner cannot be called a religious poet; rather, the Baha'i faith is either an important idea or image in a poem, rather than the theme of it. For example, "Here and In That Same Light" is a fifteen-line poem in which she sees the "highest light within/the Baha'i sky." In another poem, "the eclectic patterns of the Baha'i Temple" in Wilmette prove to her that "lace has the strength of immortality." From a perusal of references to the Baha'i faith, which she shared with Robert Hayden, it is clear that she sought more to extol the beauty of faith than to describe it as a personal experience, for beauty becomes its own kind of religion.

Danner's association with Randall led to their collaborating on a volume, *Poem Counterpoem,* in 1966. The volume consists of twenty poems, ten by Danner and ten by Randall, on alternating pages, in which they essentially conduct a dialogue with each other. Two of the paired poems, both entitled "Belle Isle," are on the same subject—an area in Detroit. The other paired poems treat similar subjects, ranging from the civil rights movement, to old age, to black heritage. "Ballad of Birmingham," in which Randall uses the frame of a familiar folk game, "Mother, May I," to depict the disastrous consequences of four little black girls' request to go to church, is paired with Danner's "Passive Resistance," in which she questions the value of turning the other cheek when she really desires to fight back: "I want no more of this humility." She "bows low," but maintains that such posturing must have been "much easier for God's son." A similar note is sounded in "This is an African Worm," in which the worm, representative of blacks in America, can only "crawl, and wait," rather than striking out against its oppressors; both poems illustrate the quiet, reflective strain of protest characteristic of Danner's poetry.

Poem Counterpoem is one of the highlights of the collaborative efforts of the Detroit poets. Randall, founder and publisher of Broadside Press, joined with Danner, Hayden, Dodson, and others in making Detroit "alive and alert to literature," as Danner described the environment. Editors, publishers, and creative artists, they all formed an important part of the black arts movement of the 1960s, but Danner was cited as being special. Paul Breman, writing in "Poetry into the Sixties," referred to her as "the doyenne of Detroit's black letters."

In 1966, Danner was able to make the long delayed trip to Africa. She went to read some of her poems at the World Exposition of Negro Arts in Dakar, Senegal, and stopped off in Paris to see the exhibition of African art; the trip became one of the highlights of her life. It is evident from her poetry that Africa was very much a part of Danner's consciousness and poetry long before she visited there; her visit sharpened her aesthetic sensibility. Several critics have praised Danner's African poems because they, more than any other category of her poems, form her strongest aesthetic and philosophical statements. Broadus N. Butler, writing at the beginning of *Impressions of African Art Forms* (1960), Danner's first volume of poetry, suggests that her poems "probe into the social body and perform a kind of midwifery to assist the present rebirth and transformation of appreciations and valuations of Negro and African art." In a paper entitled "Margaret Danner and the African Connection," delivered at the 1980 meeting of the National Council of Teachers of English, eminent scholar Richard Barksdale posed and explored the question of the distance from "Beale Street to Benin City" in Danner's poetry. The blues connection suggested by Barksdale's phrasing reiterates the ties between Africans and Afro-Americans.

Danner's trip to Africa represented a culmination of the awards she had received to that point and that she would continue to receive during the decade of the 1960s. In 1950, she had received grants from the Women's Auxiliary of Afro-American Interests and from the African Studies Association. In 1960, she received a grant from the American Society of African Culture; in 1961, an award from the African Studies Association; and in 1965, the Harriet Tubman Award. After her trip to Africa, she received an award from Poets in Concert in 1968.

The end of the 1960s found Danner in a different environment. From 1968 to 1969, she was poet-in-residence at Virginia Union University in Richmond, Virginia. One of the historic black colleges, Virginia Union gave Danner another firsthand opportunity to put her politics into practice. While at Virginia Union, she edited two anthologies. *Brass Horses,* the first of the two, appeared in 1968, and *Regroup* appeared in 1969.

Danner's third single volume of poetry, *Iron Lace,* was published in 1968, another achievement for that energetic decade. Throughout this period, Danner appeared at various writers conferences and poetry festivals. Perhaps the most publicized of these was the Phillis Wheatley Poetry Festival, organized by poet/novelist Margaret Walker and held at Jackson State College (now University) in November of 1973. Danner was among eighteen prominent black women poets invited to read from their works and participate in discussions on the current state of poetry. The event received national attention, with *Black World* publishing an article on it in February of 1974 and *Ebony* magazine following suit with a photographic essay in March of 1974.

The 1970s also saw the publication of another volume of poetry by Danner; selected and new poems, *The Down of a Thistle,* dedicated to Robert Hayden and introduced by Samuel Allen, appeared in 1976. The heavily illustrated volume contains several memorable poems that make use of African images and symbols. The title poem is typical; in African culture, Danner notes, "thistles are accorded reverence" and they wear their "shaded down as fluffy tiaras." The thistles imported to "dress and bless . . . offices and homes" are prized much more than the symbolic thistle-like slaves, who:

having had no royal passage
were seized and thrown into 'holds'
slumping over humps of humiliation, degradation,
making spines of their many lumps
in order to protect their crowns.

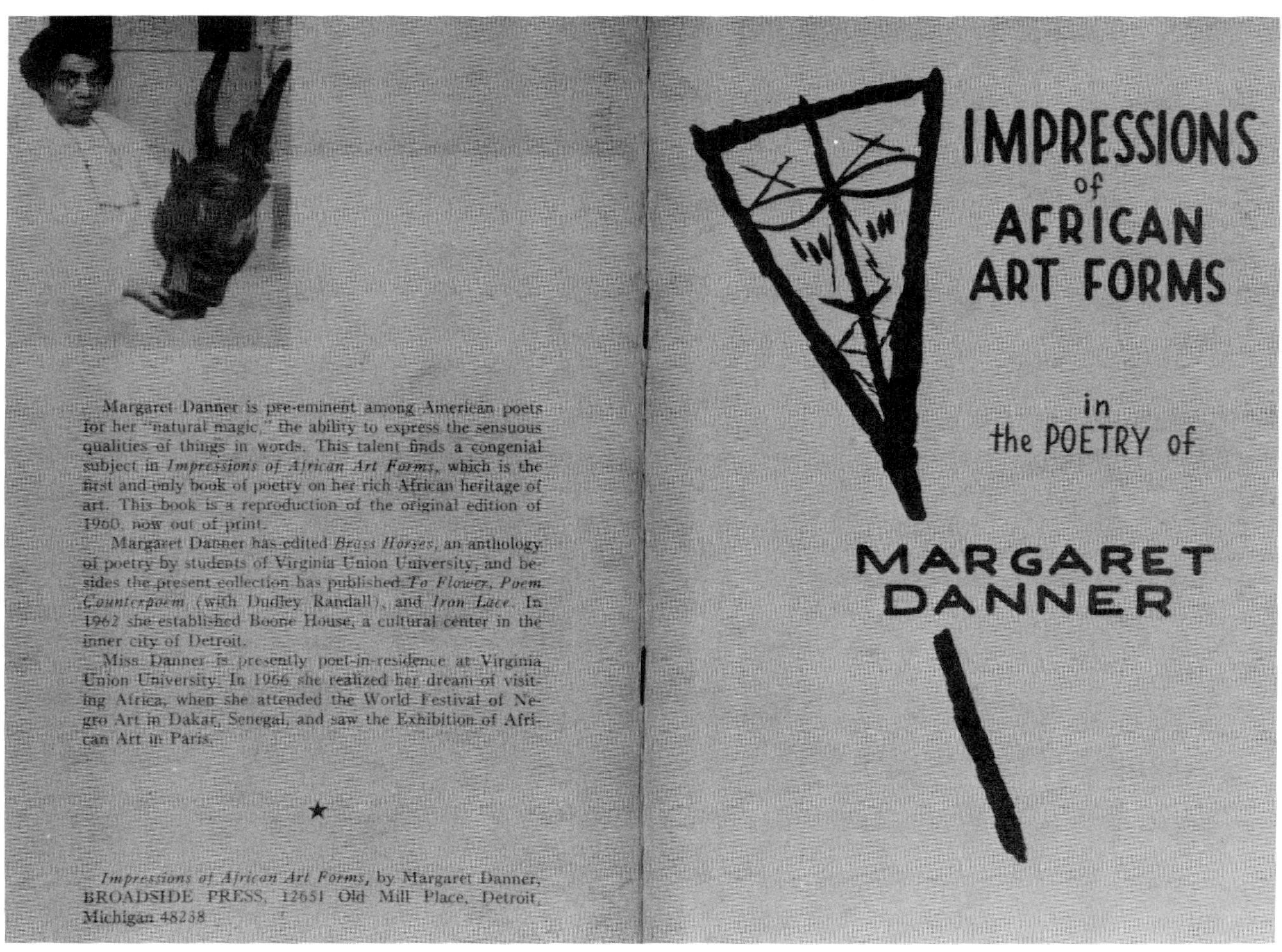

Margaret Danner is pre-eminent among American poets for her "natural magic," the ability to express the sensuous qualities of things in words. This talent finds a congenial subject in *Impressions of African Art Forms*, which is the first and only book of poetry on her rich African heritage of art. This book is a reproduction of the original edition of 1960, now out of print.
Margaret Danner has edited *Brass Horses*, an anthology of poetry by students of Virginia Union University, and besides the present collection has published *To Flower, Poem Counterpoem* (with Dudley Randall), and *Iron Lace*. In 1962 she established Boone House, a cultural center in the inner city of Detroit.
Miss Danner is presently poet-in-residence at Virginia Union University. In 1966 she realized her dream of visiting Africa, when she attended the World Festival of Negro Art in Dakar, Senegal, and saw the Exhibition of African Art in Paris.
★
Impressions of African Art Forms, by Margaret Danner, BROADSIDE PRESS, 12651 Old Mill Place, Detroit, Michigan 48238
IMPRESSIONS
of
AFRICAN
ART FORMS
in
the POETRY of
MARGARET
DANNER

Covers for the Broadside Press "reproduction" of Danner's first book, a twenty-page collection of poems in which "African culture and its representatives are uncaged from the safe captivity of the Exhibition area," according to Emilie Newcomb, the introducer of the volume

Instead of being prized and having their true virtue recognized, modern thistles (black people) are avoided and devalued. To achieve her multiple associations, Danner skillfully intertwines images, rhythm, and the legacy of Africa and the middle passage.

A poem that illustrates her subtle use of color imagery is "And Through the Caribbean Sea," in *Poem Counterpoem*, where hues of black and red predominate. Danner comments on the legacy of black people who, "like shades that were first conjured up/by an African witch-doctor's ire," live "in a huge kaleidoscope world" where they must constantly seek the color of their true identity. "Indigo for the drum and the smoke of night,/tangerine for the dancing smudged fire," signs of African heritage, have been shifted: the indigo is now reflective of the blue sky of the Goths, tangerine "became the orange of the tango" and "the red of the Susy Q." We traded one pattern for another, Danner asserts:

> Until, who questions whether we'd be prone to yearn
> for a Louis Quinze frame, a voodoo fire,
> Rococo, Baroque, an African mask or a Gothic spire
> or any style of any age or any place or name.

Haki Madhubuti (Don L. Lee) accurately comments in *Dynamite Voices* (1971) that the "references or allusions which are not African are meant to indicate a loss of identity."

The African poems constitute the most significant group of Danner's poetry. They touch on a wide range of topics, and some overlap with other categories of her poetry, especially her protest poems. "This is an African Worm," for example, vividly illustrates the use of an African symbol which, transformed by the "iron lace" of Danner's poetic sensibility, becomes a strong symbol of protest. Danner deftly paints an image of a worm that "will not stride, run, stand up/before the butterflies, who/have passed their worm-like state," and that ultimately can only "crawl and wait." While crawling and waiting are reminiscent of Milton's "They also serve who only stand and wait," the line at the end of Danner's poem portends hopelessness and immobility, the peculiar plight of black people in America who refuse to or who cannot stand up for their rights.

Perhaps the most anthologized of Danner's protest poems is "The Elevator Man Adheres to Form," in which a black male Ph.D. operates an elevator. The poem is chosen for anthologies not because it represents the body of Danner's poetry, but because of the tremendous impact created by a very effective blending of tone, theme, and rhythm. Yet the protest is aimed toward the black man as much as toward white American society. While Danner implies that the society is probably responsible for such a well-educated black man being underemployed, she is also critical of the black man who seems overly acquiescent in the unbecoming role he has had to adopt. "I see these others boggling in their misery/ and wish this elevator artisan would fill his flourishing/ form with warmth for them and turn his lettered zeal/ toward lifting them above their crippling storm."

One of Danner's most successful protest poems is "The Endangered Species," which is also the title of a section in *The Down of a Thistle.* The poem is a carefully wrought structure of ideas and images in which the endangered species, a pearl, is less valued by "most modern pigs" because it is "such a sooty stone." Those who know the value of "lovely black pearls" cannot "polish and mold their bizarre beauty to beads" alone. Other images in the poem refer to the "hooves" of the modern pigs, connoting an image of the devil when later the "Caster" makes a "protégé of the pearl/to help it shine full blown." Thus the modern pigs scorn the pearl while the caster, presumably with allusions to the Fisher of men as well as to the Maker of man, accepts the black man, the endangered species of the title.

Danner's poetry, as a whole, is more a celebra-

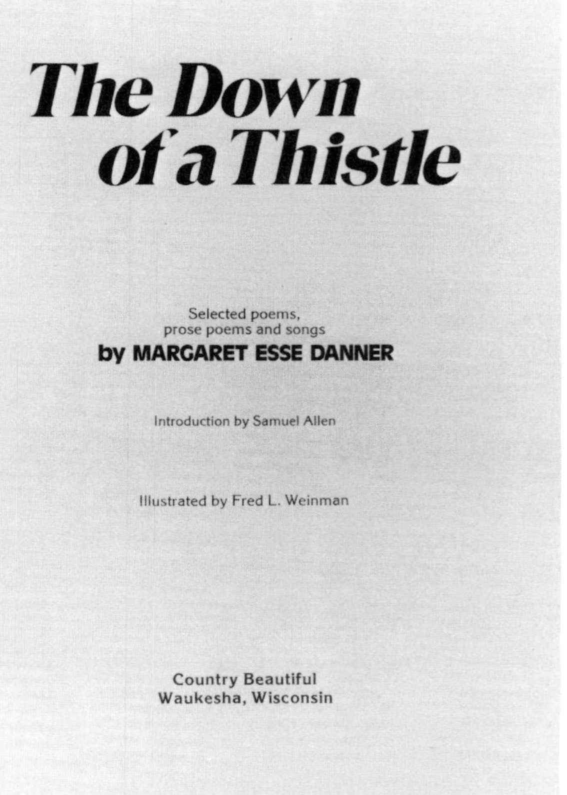
The Down of a Thistle

Selected poems, prose poems and songs

by MARGARET ESSE DANNER

Introduction by Samuel Allen

Illustrated by Fred L. Weinman

Country Beautiful
Waukesha, Wisconsin

Frontispiece and title page for Danner's 1976 volume of poetry, which is dedicated to Robert Hayden tion of black people than a sustained protest of their plight. Whether she celebrates them as poets, sculptors, or other artists, she glories in the beauty of blackness. "In a Bone White Frame" underscores her philosophy; she must make two paintings, not spend time acquainting herself with "ming blue, peach, pastel, white," which obviously symbolize alien cultures and concerns. She must focus on "this huge mahogony oil" that "occupies [her] through every cell," because she "loves it" and what it represents in the history of suffering black people. Though the cost of that preoccupation might be dear, the commitment must not waver. She states in "Inheritance for Muffin" that she cannot leave her grandson gold beyond that contained in a watch or ring, but she can leave him an "exquisitely carved Benin Bronze" or a "Senufo Firespitter Mask" that might suggest Rome or "other classic places," "but that were in reality conceived from steak bones on Beale Street/in Memphis, Tenn." The African continuity, that "immense, shining cultural highway leading from Beale Street down through the stressful centuries back to Benin," as Barksdale describes it, must hold against other influences. That cultural highway makes Danner's poetry unique.

As a group, the African poems are superior to Danner's other poems, and they will undoubtedly form the basis for her future reputation. Samuel Allen has observed that Danner's poetry "rejoices" and that she "eloquently affirms, . . . more seasoned wisdom, a resurrected Black and African identity." Though Danner now finds it difficult to write poetry because of encroaching blindness, her perseverance is just as strong as her links to Africa. As a contributor to Afro-American literature and especially to the black arts movement, and as a poet who clearly understood the ties to African heritage, Danner will be remembered not only as a writer but as a guardian of culture.

References:

Leonard Pack Bailey, ed., *Broadside Authors and Artists: An Illustrated Biographical Directory* (Detroit, Mich.: Broadside, 1974);

Richard Barksdale, "Margaret Danner and the African Connection," paper delivered at the annual meeting of the National Council of Teachers of English, Cincinnati, Ohio, 22 November 1980;

Haki Madhubuti (Don L. Lee), *Dynamite Voices I: Black Poets of the 1960s* (Detroit: Broadside, 1971);

Eugene Redmond, *Drumvoices: The Mission of Afro-American Poetry, A Critical History* (Garden City: Anchor/Doubleday, 1976).

Henry Dumas

(20 July 1934-23 May 1968)

Carolyn A. Mitchell
University of Santa Clara

BOOKS: *Ark of Bones and Other Stories,* edited by Hale Chatfield and Eugene Redmond (Carbondale & Edwardsville: Southern Illinois University Press, 1970; London & Amsterdam: Feffer & Simons, 1970);

Poetry for My People, edited by Chatfield and Redmond (Carbondale & Edwardsville: Southern Illinois University Press, 1970; London & Amsterdam: Feffer & Simons, 1970); republished as *Play Ebony: Play Ivory,* edited by Redmond (New York: Random House, 1974);

Jonoah and the Green Stone, edited by Redmond (New York: Random House, 1976);

Rope of Wind and Other Stories, edited by Redmond (New York: Random House, 1979).

OTHER: "Mosaic Harlem," "Knock on Wood," "Cuttin Down to Size," in *Black Fire: An Anthology of Afro-American Writing,* edited by LeRoi Jones and Larry Neal (New York: Morrow, 1968);

Arnold Adoff, ed., *Black Out Loud: An Anthology of Modern Poems by Black Americans,* includes poems by Dumas (New York: Macmillan, 1970);

Adoff, ed., *The Poetry of Black America: Anthology of*

the 20th Century, includes poems by Dumas (New York: Harper & Row, 1973);

Adoff, ed., *Celebrations: A New Anthology of Black American Poetry,* includes poems by Dumas (Chicago: Follett, 1977);

Eugene B. Redmond, *Griefs of Joy: Anthology of Afro-American Poetry for Students,* includes poems by Dumas (East St. Louis: Black River Writers, 1977).

Henry Dumas's personal and creative life flashed brilliantly across the social and political sky of the 1960s, leaving behind an extraordinary, but incomplete legacy of fiction and poetry which has been meticulously organized and edited by Eugene Redmond, well-known poet and critic who worked with Dumas at Southern Illinois University. Under Redmond's guidance, Dumas's poetry and fiction have been posthumously published by Southern Illinois University Press and by Random House. Redmond and others have also adapted Dumas's poetry and prose to the stage.

Henry Dumas was born in Sweet Home, Arkansas, on 20 July 1934. He migrated to New York City's Harlem at the age of ten, attended public schools and graduated from Commerce High School in 1953. Dumas started at City College (now part of the City University of New York), but interrupted his studies in 1953 to enter the Air Force. He was stationed at Lackland Air Force Base in San Antonio, Texas. Little is known about his early life in Arkansas, but vignettes of the South which are vividly told in his unfinished novel, *Jonoah and the Green Stone* (1976), and in his short fiction suggest what his childhood experiences may have been. Beyond rendering his observations of Southern life, Dumas captures the psychological tenor of the black experience there.

Henry Dumas married Loretta Ponton on 24 September 1955, when he still had two years of his military service remaining. He was discharged from the Air Force in 1957; his first son, David, was born on 20 June 1958. Dumas enrolled at Rutgers University in New Brunswick, New Jersey, pursuing a full-time program for approximately two years, and exploring courses in etymology and in sociology before finding his natural place in English. Perhaps the responsibilities of a growing family and the increasing social and political chaos of the civil rights movement added to Dumas's decision to curtail his studies and to continue at Rutgers as a part-time student until 1965, when he left the University without completing his degree.

The early 1960s were a crucial time in Dumas's life. His second son, Michael, was born on 24 August 1962. Loretta Dumas speaks of her husband's growing involvement with the civil rights movement, which she feels deflected his interest from the intense study of religion which he started in the 1950s. Dumas then combined part-time study with his job as an operator of printing machines at IBM, a position he held from 1963 to 1964. While continuing to study, work, and write, Dumas found the time to take clothing and supplies to the occupants of tent cities in Mississippi and in Tennessee. The political commentary in these actions are manifestations of Dumas's understanding of and commitment to black people. These actions provide the basis for much of his writing in this period which captures the particular ethos of the South. It is an ethos that is grounded in poverty, deprivations, and oppressions—all realities that made the civil rights movement necessary.

Henry Dumas (photo by Clem Fiori)

Dumas's short story "Rain God," published in *Negro Digest* in January 1968, begins with three young boys hurrying home ahead of a coming rainstorm. The premise of the story is an old folktale which posits that when sunshine and rain occur simultaneously, the devil is beating his wife. Blue, the young narrator, believes the tale and is afraid of the devil, so he lags behind his friends, Cud and Ned. He thinks, "Cud is ahead because he ain't afraid of the Devil, but I am, and we are running along the fence and Cud is leaping over. . . . Ned is standing near the stump waving at us like he found the greatest secret in the world, and I am standing higher on the post . . . so that I can see if I can *see* the Devil beating his wife. If I can see from here, I am staying here." The three boys, having found a rotten tree stump with a hole in the center, see "two figures, like little carved dolls, on top of that old stump. . . . dancing in the light around the center hole. . . ." Blue sees the devil "dressed in red, swinging a whip, snorting smoke when a raindrop strikes, striking the other on the back." He sees the devil's wife, dressed in white, fall into the hole. "But she catches the edges of the stump and the Devil pulls her up . . . and I am watching him straddle her, and then I hear a scream and the wind is slashing me with rain." Cud and Ned run ahead of Blue who knows the devil is chasing him. They meet Blue's father, hurrying to complete his chores before lightning starts. Blue's father, hearing Ned mention that it is "rainin' and sunshinin' at the same time," says, "Rain under the sun, you stick a pin in the ground, and put your ear to it and you can hear the Devil beating his wife." Blue is anxious to have his father know that he has not just *heard* the devil, he has *seen* him beating his wife.

Blue's father senses that something unusual has happened to the boys, and Blue feels that he is patient with them because he, too, perhaps sees the devil coming down the road. The father's answer to their question "How come he beating her?" reminds the reader that the essential purpose of folklore is to provide answers to the unanswerable. Blue says of his father's response, "he tells us the truth, and truth is because it is raining and sunshining at the same time."

"Rain God," narrated in the first person singular, reveals Blue's point of view through a stream of consciousness technique. Blue is one with nature, for he does not just see and reflect on nature, he *is* nature. He says, "I am a waterfall flying off that post and I must be a river because the fence is shaking and trembling and shaking like the dead trees did in the stream when we were fishing." When he sees the two figures dancing on the stump, he says, "I feel the rain spirits soaking into me."

The theme of union with the natural world occurs often in Dumas's work, for example, in his poem "Root Song," from *Play Ebony: Play Ivory* (1974), in which the poet says, "Once when I was a tree/flesh came and worshiped at my roots./My ancestors slept in my outstretched/limbs. . . ." In the poem, as in the short story, there is harmony between the human being and landscape that provides the foundation from which the mystical experience unfolds. In the story Blue's oneness with the earth's mysteries makes his belief in the fantastic possible. In the poem the oneness with the tree is the metaphor which allows the poet to return to his ancestral roots.

"The Crossing" in the collection *Ark of Bones and Other Stories* (1970) moves to the sense of danger and attendant fear that often dominates the lives of black people in the South. In this story, three young children, Jimmy, Bubba, and Essie, walking home from Sunday school, externalize and displace their deeply rooted fear of imminent danger. They tease one another, which seems typical enough until Bubba mentions Emmett Till, the Northern teenager who was actually lynched in 1953. Dumas effectively combines the fictional preoccupation of Jimmy, who wants to scare Bubba's sister, Essie, by throwing her into the creek, with the historical reality of Till's story. Bubba says to Jimmy, "Naw. You must think she looks like Emmett Till. . . . White folks throwed him in for good!" Bubba then shares his child's version of the atrocity with Jimmy, who had never heard the story. The recounting of Till's story is the verbalization of past danger which makes it possible for the children to confront their fear of present danger, since danger is woven ominously into the landscape, the atmosphere, the very fabric of black/white relationships in the South.

Dumas describes the crossing and the surrounding landscape in language so ominous that the utter vulnerability of the children is frighteningly apparent. Theirs is not the usual childhood fear of witches and goblins or wicked stepmothers created by nursery rhymes and fairy tales. It is the specific fear experienced by children who know that their lives can be senselessly snuffed out at any minute by people who despise them for their very blackness. Therefore, their "fairy tale" is the story of Emmett Till. Jimmy, Bubba, and Essie must face social reality at an early age.

The sense that Dumas must have literally or figuratively had some of these same experiences is one way to account for the power and accuracy of this story and others like it, such as "Rope of Wind," "Thrust Counter Thrust," and "Double Nigger," in which the unfolding of black life and events is al-

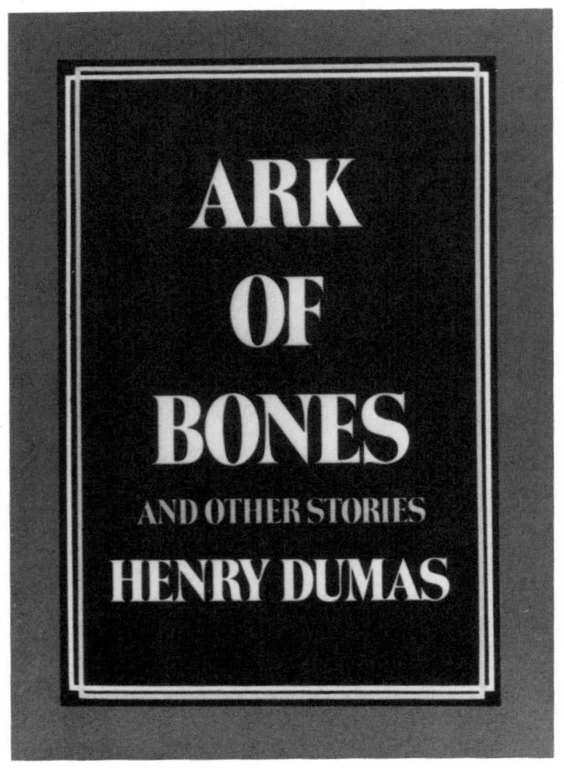

Dust jacket for the 1974 trade publication of Dumas's first book, originally published in a limited edition by the Southern Illinois University Press in 1970, two years after Dumas was shot to death in Harlem by a policeman

ways set against the common fear of blacks that white people are out to do violence against them.

"A Boll of Roses," though incomplete according to Eugene Redmond, is an exquisitely balanced story about Northern civil rights workers who come South to organize the voter drive and to open schools. The story graphically reveals the plight of poor Southern blacks, their utter determination to improve their circumstances, and the potential danger they face from Southern white people who see the Northerners as "outside agitators."

Layton Fields, the central character, is a high school student who must take time off to pick cotton; and his personal story is presented against the backdrop of the civil rights work. Layton becomes infatuated with Rosemarie Stiles, a young, black civil rights worker, and his attraction for her underscores his poverty, his ignorance, and his lack of social grace. He prepares to meet Rosemarie, despairing over and rejecting his shoddy clothes. He resolves, nonetheless, to approach her and plucks a rose to present to her. When Layton finally meets her, he accosts her with the words, "What you think you doing coming down here to mess with niggers? I bet this the first time you ever see a cotton field." These are hardly the appropriate words for a young man in love. Layton, an awkward boy, just beginning to interact with girls, is put soundly in his place with her response, "Well, I certainly didn't come out here to talk with no dirty mouthed mannerless thing like you."

Rosemarie's remark is a painful reminder of the class problems that isolate blacks from one another; it is a commentary on the complexities of American society, which were made more apparent by the civil rights movement. The issues of race, caste, and class have serious implications for the development of black/white and black/black relationships. Ironically, Rosemarie's snub does more to motivate Layton to change his life than the crusading of the organizers. He sees the need to change as a very personal, social move—not an intellectual or political one. Layton leaves Rosemarie: "The sun was heavy on him. He liked the way it felt. He knew he was going to pick some cotton today. He was going to get that money, o yeah, he was going to get it, and he was going to go to school. He might even buy him some clothes. That's right." Layton now remembers his mother and her prayer that he finish school; he "thought of his mother's pinched face, the other night. A pain had knotted there so long that it was part of her look. He wanted to change that face. He wanted his mother to smile. He knew what he would do." The "boll" of roses is as useless to Layton in his courting of Rosemarie as a boll of cotton is to the sharecropper who reaps no reward from his picking. Thus, Layton, knowing that his mother would appreciate a rose, resolves to give the flower to her, the more influential woman in his life.

That Rosemarie Stiles sees Layton as a "dirty mouthed mannerless thing" indicates how far her world is from his. She does not understand that Layton is a product of the soil, a man-child whose life is captured in Dumas's poem from *Play Ebony: Play Ivory,* "Son of Msippi," part of which reads:

> Up
> from Msippi I grew.
> Up
> from the river of pain.
> . . . .
> out of the loins of the leveed hands
> muscling its American vein:
> the great Father of Waters,
> I grew
> up,
> beside the prickly boll of white,

beside the bone-filled Mississippi
rolling on and on,
breaking over,
cutting off,
ignoring my bleeding finger.

The Rosemaries of the world may never understand, but the poem reveals the integrity, strength, courage, and sense of worth of the sharecropping man. Though the Mississippi River rolls "on and on,/ignoring the colored coat I spun/of cotton fibers," still the son "grew,/wailing a song with every strain." He is clear about the value of the coat he spins because he has done his job well and in it is America's prosperity. He is clear about the song he sings for it is evidence of his spirit and his resilience.

Jonoah and the Green Stone, Dumas's unfinished novel (which was to have been part of a trilogy entitled "Visible Man"), begins with the story of six-year-old Jonoah battling to stay alive during the worst flooding of the Mississippi River in Southern memory. The story follows Jonoah's growth into adulthood and his participation in the civil rights movement. The boy's journey is long and complex, taking him into the "wilds" of Harlem and into activities that are hinted at as being less than savory; yet, his character is drawn with such insight and compassion that his potential is still apparent, even in the fragment. The sum total of his experiences—good and bad—forge his character and become his strength. The novel is brilliantly structured around the biblical stories of Noah and Jonah, for Jonoah is both Noah, the builder of the Ark and the survivor of the flood, and Jonah, the reluctant prophet who winds up in the belly of the whale.

Jonoah has a love-hate relationship with the Mississippi, for the flood kills his mother, his father, and his would-be rescuer, Old Man Hearth. Jonoah, wracked by a fever, also comes close to drowning, and he describes the memory of the experience: "For the rest of my life, that first flood was alive in my mind, forming me, and driving me. Of all the times that I played and fished on the mud banks of the river, none beat upon my soul and my body as did the times when I had to go down into the water to save my life." The river destroys and restores, and Jonoah must acknowledge this paradox, making peace with it. His "ark" is a flat-bottomed johnnyboat and when he awakens from the fever, the boat is running swiftly in the flood, unattended because Mr. Hearth has been swept away. Jonoah is rescued by the six-year-old Jubal, who is mature beyond his years. Jubal, his sister, Ruby, Papa Lem, and Mamada come aboard the

Front cover for the 1974 trade paperback publication of Dumas's posthumously published poems, first collected in a limited edition by Southern Illinois University Press in 1970

"ark"; they become Jonoah's family. Jonoah, like Noah, survives the flood and matures under the inspired nurturing of Mamada and Papa Lem, his newfound parents.

Jonoah loses his moral direction in the wilderness of the North. He is caught up in the wantonness of city life, yet is aware of the political and social turmoil swirling around him. The development of the story is especially sketchy at this point, but Jonoah's symbolic relationship to Jonah is apparent, for he finds himself "trapped inside the belly of some demon creature whose sides and dimensions were elusive: a nightmare." Jonoah succumbs to the lure of Harlem and the evil of his friend, Hoodoo. But Jonoah retains a vestige of his early spirit; he begins to focus on the racial war going on in Mississippi and he "hears" the voice of his Mamada singing in Arkansas. He leaves Harlem, the belly of the whale, to join his family in battle. Jonoah's revelation is that you "cant kill a man unless he wants to die. When you kill a body then you aint killing a man. . . . You cant see a man unless he wants to be seen. . . . You cant kill a man if he's a man. Whether he's a black or brown or red or yellow or white or *anything man,* you cant kill him. . . ." Jonoah's message seems to be that the spirit of men lives in the actions they perform; but, given the incomplete nature of the novel, it is not clear how Dumas intended to resolve his version of the conflict between good and evil. And, the meaning and significance of the "green stone" are not fully apparent. Nevertheless, the vision which informs *Jonoah and the Green Stone* is powerful. As a commentary on the history of black people that makes the civil rights movement absolutely essential in their bid for freedom, the novel is a potential masterpiece.

During his time at Lackland Air Force Base, Dumas taught Sunday school classes, and it is perhaps during this period that his interest in Christianity crystallized. He began an intense and searching scrutiny of the Protestant denominations and probably began to combine this study with the mature assessment that Afro-American belief systems and folkways are sometimes different from mainstream traditions. For example, one difference is the way in which biblical stories are personalized and woven into folktales and myth. Dumas writes sophisticated versions of these "weavings" when he combines the Noah/Jonah story in *Jonoah and the Green Stone* and the Noah/Ezekiel story in "Ark of Bones." Music is also a foundation of black American tradition, and Dumas's study would have enabled him to discover or to rediscover the place of gospel music in Afro-American religion. According to Loretta Dumas, he had an extensive collection of gospel music which included such geniuses of the art as the Five Blind Boys from Mississippi, the Swan Silvertones, and the Dixie Hummingbirds. Dumas immersed himself not only in gospel but also in the spirituals, the blues, and jazz, in which gospel is rooted. Thus, music and religion are intertwined as theme and motif in Dumas's fiction and poetry.

This combination of interests is especially evident in "A Boll of Roses," where music is Layton's mother's mainstay in her personal and communal struggle. Her deep and basic faith is revealed as she listens to the "deep rhythmic pulse of gospel music" coming from the Five Blind Boys; and, it is the background harmony for the civil rights theme.

The thematic purpose of the story "The Voice," from the collection entitled *Rope of Wind* (1979), is to address the question of the existence of God. But music, once again, is the motif, for the story is about a group of young men in Harlem who sing gospel and blues. They are unable to sing now because their lead singer, the "voice" of the title, became ill and died of spinal meningitis. The ritual of mourning brings them to question God's color, purpose, and even his existence in their effort to understand what entity could allow Spencer to die.

The theological answers to the question of God's existence and purpose offered by a Jewish scholar and a Catholic priest do not match Spencer's grandmother's simple avowal that "the Lord blesses good singing." The boys catch the spirit of Arnold, a member of the group who picks the guitar, and they began to sing: "We sang from our souls, and before long everybody was standing round listening. Spencer's mother was trying not to cry. And then all of a sudden Blake caught a note, and we all heard it and we came to his aid. We got to feeling good, and the people backed us up with some hand-clapping. Spence should have been there then, because we were all singing and making one voice." Spencer's death unites the boys and his voice becomes their voice. In the "one voice" is an affirmation of the continuity of life, and their affirmation of God's existence.

In the poem "KEF 25," from *Play Ebony: Play Ivory,* Dumas uses music not only to honor the unity of the sacred and the secular in the Afro-American community but also to locate the roots of that music in the majestic African past. Dumas writes:

> the swan silvertone singers
> pulled chords of blue and purple
> like the velvet robe of king Nkoko
> sounding in their sounding
> of gut and Benin strut
> paying no mind to the bean
> and unseen mama walkers and owl
> talkers laying it up close
> to the night pose perching
> peeking seeing
> all the silvermoon lies of throat
> and tongue splitting
> in the unknown

Here, Dumas uses color metaphors to describe the harmony ("pulled chords of blue and purple") of the gospel sounds made by the "swan silvertone singers." The harmonic colors are like the colors in the royal robes of "king Nkoko"; the chords are like the bold instrumentalism and the dancing of the ancient African kingdom of Benin. The poem suggests the unknown power of the spiritual music is in

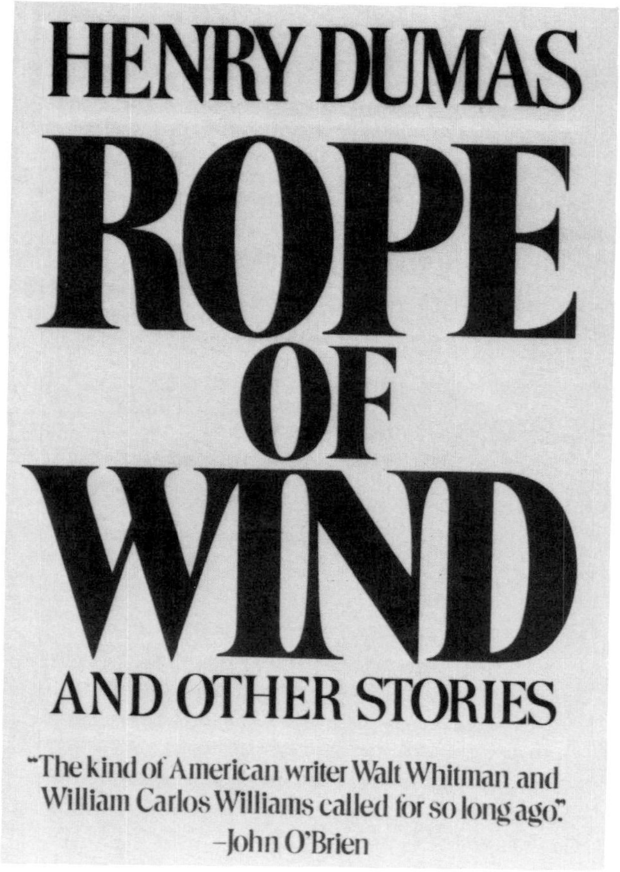

HENRY DUMAS
ROPE OF WIND
AND OTHER STORIES
"The kind of American writer Walt Whitman and William Carlos Williams called for so long ago."
–John O'Brien

Dust jacket for the second collection of Dumas's stories, these written between 1957 and 1965. Ark of Bones *and* Rope of Wind *comprise twenty-one of the thirty-six stories found among Dumas's papers after his death.*

its ability to validate itself while acknowledging the presence of its worldly, secular counterpart.

Dumas was so fascinated with black music as a historical and evolutionary force that he studied for a time with the visionary black jazz musician, Sun Ra, who believes that music is a cosmic force of unmeasured power. Dumas's story from *Ark of Bones* "Will the Circle Be Unbroken " reflects his understanding of this belief. In this powerful tale Ron, Tasha, and Jan, three white people, attempt to enter the Sound Barrier Club. Jan is a tenor saxophonist who has jammed before with Probe, the black master of the new music. Though he knows that white people are not allowed into the club, Jan decides that he will "talk to Probe personally. He had known many Negro musicians and theirs was no different from any other artist's struggles to be himself, including his own." Jan thinks about his friends, who "were two of the hippest ofays in town, and if anybody could break the circle of the Sound Club, it would be friends and old friends of friends."

Jan reveals his latent racism when the doorman, holding a sign that reads "We cannot allow non-Brothers because of the danger with extensions," bars his entrance to the Club. Jan is arrogant and skeptical about the idea "that all the spades believed this thing about the lethal vibrations from the new sound." He and his friends are finally admitted with the help of a white policeman.

The musicians begin to create a circle of music which approximates the magic circle of the universe. Probe plays his saxophone, tightening and balancing the circle, preparing the "womb for the afro-horn" whose "vibrations were beyond his mental frequencies unless he got into deeper motives." Probe gets into "deeper motives," and Dumas attempts to capture the cosmic forces tapped by the music: "*Inside the center of the gyrations is an atom stripped of time, black. The gathering of the hunters, deeper. Coming, laced in the energy of the sun. He is blowing. Magwa's* [the drummer's] *hands. Reverence of skin. Under the single voices* [sic] *is the child of a woman, black. They are building back the wall, crumbling under the disturbance.*" The music is an affirmation of African life as it is celebrated in ritual; the wall is perhaps symbolic of the circle that used to protect African people and culture, here (as elsewhere) threatened by the disturbance created by Jan, Ron, and Tasha. Dumas borrows from the belief that all life, hence all life properties—from science, to math, to music—began in Africa. At any rate, when Probe summons his "first statement from the afro-horn," the rare cosmic instrument of which there are only three, Jan, Ron, and Tasha are killed instantly, and one is reminded of the occult belief of the ancient, secret, religious societies founded on the principle of the magic circle that all outsiders break at their own peril. "Will the Circle Be Unbroken" is an effective and powerful tribute to the cosmic teachings of Sun Ra.

No commentary on Dumas's religious/spiritual vision would be complete without mention of "Ark of Bones," from the collection of the same name and "The University of Man," from *Rope of Wind.*

"Ark of Bones" borrows from the biblical stories of Noah and Ezekiel and in Dumas's hands becomes the archetypal picture of Afro-American suffering. Headeye, who is the chosen man whose name suggests the wisdom of the third and seeing, knowing eye, leads the young narrator, Fish, down to the river's edge where a rowboat ferries them out to an ark. In the spirit of the fantastic which characterizes the myth, no explanation is offered for the presence of the ark. And Fish, accepting the presence of the vessel without question, describes the scene: "All along the side of the ark them great black men were hauling bones from that river. It was the craziest thing I ever saw. I knowed then it wasn't no animal bones. I took a look at them and they was all laid out in different ways, all making some kind of body and there was big bones and little bones. . . . I shut my mouth then. I knowed I was on to somethin, I had fished out somethin.

I comest to think about a sermon I heard about Ezekiel in the valley of dry bones."

"Ark of Bones" is a parable in which Fish watches the workers on the ark "fish out" the bones of Africans stolen from the homeland and destroyed in the "service" of America. The Mississippi River is the depository for all the bones of all lynched black people, and the story at this point parallels Dumas's poem "Son of Msippi," especially the lines "Up/from Msippi I grew./Up/from the river of pain/Cane-sweat river-boat/nigger-bone floating." Fish discovers as he climbs the steps into the ark that each bone bears a date; the first he notices is 1608, then 1944 (the year he was born), and 1977. Headeye instructs Fish in the protocol, reminding him (Fish is reluctant because he knows he is a sinner) that he has been "called."

As Fish descends the stairs into the hold of the ark, he sees: "Bones. I saw bones. They were stacked all they way to the top of the ship. I looked around. The underside of the whole ark was nothin but a great bonehouse. I looked and saw crews of black men handlin in them bones." The irony is that this is not Noah's ark of survivors, but a floating version of Ezekiel's valley of dry bones.

Headeye has come to be initiated into the sacred ranks of those who talley and record each skeleton fished from the Mississippi River, a task which insures that the dead will not be forgotten; therefore, their dying will not have been in vain. Fish-Hound is to witness the initiation and then return to the people as a prophet. The priest says to Headeye, "Son, you are in the house of generations. Every African who lives in America has a part of his soul in this ark. God has called you, and I shall annoint [*sic*] you." The truth of the priest's words is apparent, because Headeye and Fish discover upon their return that "the white folks had lynched a nigger and threw him in the river."

Headeye now returns to the ark for good and Fish says, "People been askin me where'd he go. But I only tell em a little somethin I learned in church. And I tell em about Ezekiel in the valley of dry bones. . . . I never told em about the Ark and them bones. It would make no sense. . . ." In this story, all the metaphors that Dumas uses throughout his poetry and fiction merge. The dual meanings of bones, river, rain, and flood tell a complex story, for Dumas combines an understanding of Afro-American suffering with a special vision of Afro-American spirituality, thus making "Ark of Bones" one of the most powerful stories he has written.

Dumas's interest in religion included non-Christian beliefs, and "The University of Man" is a fine example of this interest. The story is like an ancient Zen koan, in which Tyros the American, who has worked for twenty years as a watch repairer, sets out on a journey saying, "It is the quest for knowledge that is holy, and not the knowledge itself." After much traveling, Tyros comes upon a man digging a trench toward a river. The gist of the story is revealed in a marvelous dialogue between Tyros and the digger that is reminiscent of the Artist of Kouroo, who appears (defying time while seeking perfection) in the conclusion to Thoreau's *Walden*. The conversation between the two men concludes with the words of the worker: "With the knowledge gained at the university with no name, one does one's work and there is no end to it. Knowledge flows as time flows. This is my work . . . this canal and this river."

As he talks to the man about the nature of education and knowledge and the place of the "university," the true meaning of his quest becomes apparent to Tyros who resolves to "go to the university and get the tools of his mind and soul sharpened, and then . . . come back to the place on the river and . . . help the man. And if the man were gone or dead, then he would gather all the tools of his soul and he would do the man's work." The story depicts movement away from the goal and success orientation that often plagues modern Christian belief and turns upon the sense of paradox that develops intuitive understanding, which is central to Zen belief. The act of digging seems like a mindless, senseless, selfish, wasteful act calculated to benefit only the digger, because only he seems to understand his own action. But the discipline implicit in the act connects the digger with the eternal which is the selfless source of true knowledge. The importance of the story is that the person who would discover this answer to the act of digging, must also dig.

Mrs. Dumas reveals her husband to have been a man of magnetic energy and electrifying intensity, who seemed to be awake even when asleep. He was a person of great depth who, in her words, was so alive and interesting that if a group of people were stranded on a desert island with nothing to do, they would be fully occupied because of the range of his intellectual interests and his perpetual mental and physical motion. He was always "on" and nothing was too mundane or arcane for his critical eye. Even when he turned to television for relaxation, whether watching the evening news or cartoons, he critiqued the programs for their underlying intent and moral impact on viewers. He constantly sought the actual and hidden meanings of the information disseminated by television, because of its ability to influence all people—black and white, young and old.

Since Dumas neither relaxed nor socialized, the intensity that characterized his personal and creative life probably accounts for the remarkable number of manuscripts left by him; every moment when he was free of other obligations was spent writing. In a sense, he was obsessed, feeling compelled to write. Loretta Dumas reports that her husband felt that he did not choose to write, but that writing chose him. The literary manifestations of this personal and intellectual intensity are apparent in many stories, but in none so graphically as in "Rope of Wind."

In "Rope of Wind," Johnny B discovers that Reverend Westland is to be kidnapped and lynched. Johnny is unable to forewarn Westland, and the criminals succeed in abducting him. Johnny chases the kidnappers' car, running on foot behind it, mustering superhuman strength and summoning intuition to help when strength fails. Thus, he is able to keep up with the car, but is unable to save Reverend Westland's life. He does, however, save the body from the barbaric mutilations that are part of the lynching ritual. Johnny then retraces his route, racing the ten return miles to tell friends and family where to find the body. Only indomitable will keeps him going, and when he completes his mission, his heart bursts from the unnatural exertion, and he dies—having sacrificed his life to spare the others, because "he wanted to be with Westland, for when he told Lance and Jubal what had happened, then they would all want to die just like him." Johnny B gives his life so that Lance and Jubal will not feel that they have to die with Reverend Westland. Like "Ark of Bones," "Rope of Wind" reveals Dumas's unusual vision in a way which shakes the foundation of traditional storytelling. Thus, Johnny B makes it possible for those who remain alive to avenge the dead man, for he tells exactly where the criminals are. And, he preserves

The Garvey-Dumas One Love Celebration

P R O G R A M

5:00 p.m.-7:30 p.m.........LIBATION CEREMONY

Dr. Elkin Sithole, Ethnomusicologist
Professor,
Inner City Studies

WELCOME AND INTRODUCTIONS

Dr. Gloria J. Latimore, President
BAD Enterprises

Kiarri T.-H. Cheatwood
Celebrated African Poet

Gypsi-Fari
Leading American-based Root Rock Reggae Band

7:30 p.m.-8:30 p.m.........INTERMISSION

8:30 p.m.-11:00 p.m.

GUEST ARTISTS

Prof. Sterling Plumpp,
Assistant Professor, Black Studies
University of Illinois - Chicago

Hon. Charles L. James, President
UNIA and ACL

Sister Poet Jayne Cortez, Poet and Recording Artist

Eugene Redmond, Poet and Essayist

Gypsi-Fari

BENEDICTION

Rev. Al Sampson, Pastor
Fernwood United Methodist Church

ONE LOVE! ONE HEART! ONE DESTINY!

The Hon. Marcus Garvey

Saturday, November 12, 1983

THIRD BAPTIST CHURCH
1551 W. 95th St.
Chicago, IL

5:00 - 11:00 PM

Program for the 1983 celebration of Marcus Garvey and Henry Dumas at the Third Baptist Church in Chicago

the sanctity of the human body in death by denying the murderers the opportunity to mutilate it. But what sets the story apart is the telling image of Johnny pushing himself to the point where he is still running, but is rid of the restricting body, for the people "saw him coming at dawn. They saw human spirit coming out of the past. They saw their own souls age before their eyes. Johnny B came like a ghost, wavering in the road, stumbling and falling."

If his blues poem "Machines Can Do It Too (IBM Blues)" is any indication, Dumas was deeply attuned to the usurpation of human life by machines. The poem catalogues machines that "walk and talk/even sing a song to you," and machines that "fly and cry,/even wave bye bye to you/They gott'em to make you happy/gott'em to make you blue." The most telling line is "I got to leave this old country/when they machines doing everything." Dumas's poem approaches the true raunchiness of the blues with the last stanza:

Let me tell you people, tell you what I have to
Let me tell it like it is people,
tell you what I have to do
If I find a machine in bed with me,
that's the time I'm through

The poem combines the old-fashioned blues musical cadence and verbal innuendo with deep perception about the danger implicit in runaway automation where machines might take over all human activities, even the most intimate.

The poem was surely inspired by Dumas's job as a machine operator at IBM. After his year at IBM, Dumas followed more humanitarian occupations as a social worker for the state of New York from 1965 to 1966, as an assistant director of Upward Bound at Hiram College in Hiram, Ohio, in 1967, and as a teacher-counselor and director of language workshops which were a part of the experiment in higher education at Southern Illinois University in 1967 to 1968. Clearly, a humanitarian instinct is reflected, too, in his ongoing involvement with the civil rights movement. Perhaps these appointments, like the time in the military and at Rutgers University, were avocations, and therefore, secondary to Dumas's call to write. From 1953 to 1968, he was active on the "little magazine" circuit, both as a contributor and as an editor, publisher, and distributor. He was affiliated with magazines such as the *Anthologist, Untitled, American Weave,* and the *Hiram Poetry Review.*

Poetry for My People was published in 1970 by Southern Illinois University Press under the joint editorship of Hale Chatfield, who had been at Rutgers University with Dumas, and Eugene Redmond, who had been Dumas's colleague at Southern Illinois University. The preface in this volume is by Amiri Baraka (LeRoi Jones) and the introduction is by Jay Wright, whose friendship with Dumas also dates back to Rutgers University. In 1974, Random House reissued the volume under the more meaningful and poetic title *Play Ebony: Play Ivory,* the title poem in the collection. Eugene Redmond is the sole editor of this edition, and the volume retains only the introduction by Jay Wright from the original collection.

Dumas's poetry falls into roughly four categories: revolutionary poems that clearly reflect the black political idiom of the 1960s; nature poetry in which the poetic voice is transfigured into natural elements; poetry in which the poet captures the bittersweet humor and the risqué paradox that characterize the blues; and poems that are akin to parables and aphorisms through which lessons are taught.

The power of Dumas's vision is more readily apparent in the last three categories; most of the revolutionary poetry borders on the stridency and rhetoric that so quickly dates the works. But there is a lyricism in the remainder of the work that identifies him as a major poet.

Henry Dumas's poetry and fiction effectively capture the reality of Afro-Americans in both the rural and the urban environment. His work is infused with integrity, new vision, and spirituality that place him in a league with Jean Toomer on the earlier end of the historical scale and with Ernest Gaines and Alice Walker on the contemporary end of the scale. His integrity is apparent in the fact that he did not cater to current literary fads, although he wrote about contemporary issues. He did not "sell out" by rushing into print, as evidenced by his unpublished manuscripts, although he was interested in being known and read. The stereotypes and clichés that often appear in literature are conspicuously absent from his writing, for Dumas constantly sought new ways to tell the story of his people's lives.

Henry Dumas died on 23 May 1968, at the age of thirty-four, the victim of a policeman's bullet. Mystery shrouds the event which occurred on the Harlem platform of the New York Central Railroad. According to some accounts, the policeman, employed by the Transit Authority, alleged that Dumas was acting erratically and suspiciously. Dumas was said to be singing aloud and when approached by the policeman, placed his hands in his pockets—a gesture which led the officer to think he had a gun. In later biographical commentaries, Dumas's death is characterized as one of "mistaken identity." He was killed just as he began to mature as a writer, and before he was able to organize and edit his work. He left behind a vast body of work that is yet to be published.

In 1970 Arnold Adoff included a poem of Dumas's in his anthology *Black Out Loud.* Adoff says in the preface to this volume: "There are many revolutions taking place in our country today. Some carry with them noise and smoke and blood. They explode in headlines and newscasts. Poets make revolutions with their words and craft. An exciting poem can have the power of a fist. It can help bring about changes that are strong and meaningful." This quotation captures the value of Henry Dumas as a writer and as a person. His gift is twofold: it is a gift of words, and it is the ultimate gift of blood.

References:

Stephen Henderson, *Understanding the New Black Poetry: Black Speech and Black Music as Poetic References* (New York: Morrow, 1973);

Clyde Taylor, "Henry Dumas: Legacy of a Long-breath Singer," *Black World,* 24 (September 1975): 4-16.

Ebon
(Leo Thomas Hale/Ebon Dooley)

(25 January 1942-   )

Rhonda V. Wilcox
DeKalb Community College

BOOK: *Revolution: A Poem* (Chicago: Third World Press, 1968).

TELEVISION: "Wrightsville, Georgia," in "The Poetry of *The Black Nation,*" Cable Atlanta, February 1982.

PERIODICAL PUBLICATIONS: "A Poem to My Brothers Killed in Combat or something about a conversation with my father after Rev. King was killed," *Negro Digest,* 18 (February 1969): 90-91;

"The Mighty John Hancock or: The Bigger They Are—the Harder They Fall," *Negro Digest,* 18 (September 1969): 20;

"The Return to Order: The Peace Terms," *NOMMO,* 1 (Fall 1969): 37;

"The Bust," *Potlikker,* 1 (1976): 23-24.

Quintessentially an activist poet, Ebon is probably still thought of by many as a 1960s poet, with everything identification with that decade implies. One of the Chicago poets who flourished in connection with the OBAC Writers Workshop in the late 1960s and early 1970s, he is best known for his efforts of that period.

Ebon was born Leo Thomas Hale, the oldest child of Leo and Beatrice Hale of the small farming community of Milan, Tennessee. Son of a schoolteacher and the grandchild of middle-class farmers, he went to Nashville's Fisk University on an early entrant scholarship. In college he was nicknamed after the character in a popular song: "Hang down your head, Tom Dooley." The name Tom Dooley stuck until around 1963, when he chose the name Ebon (pronounced Ē-bŏn) after a pioneering black South American aviator. Ebon's activism might be said to have begun with his work as managing editor of the Fisk literary magazine and newspaper (which included Nikki Giovanni as a freshman reporter). He went on to further activism when, as a regional honors scholar, he entered Columbia Law School in 1963. In New York he saw two very different sides of the larger world, as a law school management trainee at Manufacturers' Hanover Trust and as a member of the Law Students' Civil Rights Research Council and volunteer for the Harlem community action project of Har-you-act. At the first Black Power conference in Newark, he was impressed by the Chicago delegation; unable to get a large enough scholarship to go on to graduate school in business after his 1967 graduation from Columbia, he went to Chicago as a VISTA legal volunteer.

Ebon's reputation rests mainly on one small

Ebon (photograph by Anne P. Tinker)

but solid book of poetry. *Revolution* (1968) was written over a period of two years in the Chicago of the late 1960s. While Ebon found Chicago "a very depressing experience in many ways," he also found it an even more vibrant intellectual, political, and artistic community than he had found in New York. He witnessed the Chicago Democratic Convention of 1968, worked with youth gang leaders of the "main 21," and counseled local citizens in their struggles for civil rights. The heart of Ebon's Chicago experience was the OBAC (Oh-bah-see) Writers Workshop (Organization for Black American Culture), founded in 1967. It included future luminaries such as Johari Amini (Jewel Latimore), Haki Madhubuti (Don L. Lee), and Carolyn Rodgers. The young writers were entertained regularly by Gwendolyn Brooks, whom Ebon acknowledges as one of his greatest influences. The Writers Workshop developed an aesthetic manifesto that was based on both artistic and social awareness. It particularly focused on the need to free black literature from the aesthetic criteria established for traditional Western works.

Revolution expresses both the aesthetic freedom and the social anger of that background. It is a collection of separate poems written at intervals over two years; but they represent "a continuous sort of experience": "the poems are a poem," as the introduction says. Ebon groups the poetry in a pattern: "4 poems loving US. a warning. 4 poems watching THEM. a request. 4 poems describing their death. a question." The very titles of the poems formally express the struggle to break through boundaries and, at the same time, to see the world from a plurality of perspectives: "Viet Nam Cotillion or Debutante Ball in the Pentagon or The Statue of Liberty Has Her Back to Harlem"; "The Easter Bunny Blues or All I Want for Xmas is the Loop"; ". . . . . Or Love Song to a Whore or America the Beautiful or An Historical Account of the Movement 1619 Tomorrow or . . . ." As Ebon said recently, "the titles are poems themselves."

While the poems written in celebration of blackness do not rise above the ordinary (with the exception of "To Our First Born or The Prophet Arrives: 'minnie lou had a boychild this morning!' "), the poems of anger in *Revolution* are memorable. These are the poems which prompted Carolyn Rodgers to call Ebon "a master of the gory"; more than that, he is both visually and intellectually provocative. Consider first the picture suggested, and then the different interpretations played upon, by the use of enjambment in "The Prophet's Warning or Shoot to Kill":

for I have seen
the faces of the enemy.
and they are red,
and white,
and blue.
patriotically evil faces . . .

Detroit he calls "that/pale/cold/white/unfeeling/pus/ of america's cancer," isolating words to force the reader to see the fullness of their implications; and he evokes nightmare images to describe the Whore of America: "when she smiled/it was a time of death/and giggling angels;/of love songs and/trembling virgins,/baptized and diseased/like carnivorous cadavers/playing shuffleboard in sunday school." "I saw them bayonet/her spine/and pin her 16th birthday/to a cross." Like Stephen Crane, who described the Civil War without having been there, Ebon graphically visualizes Vietnam. And

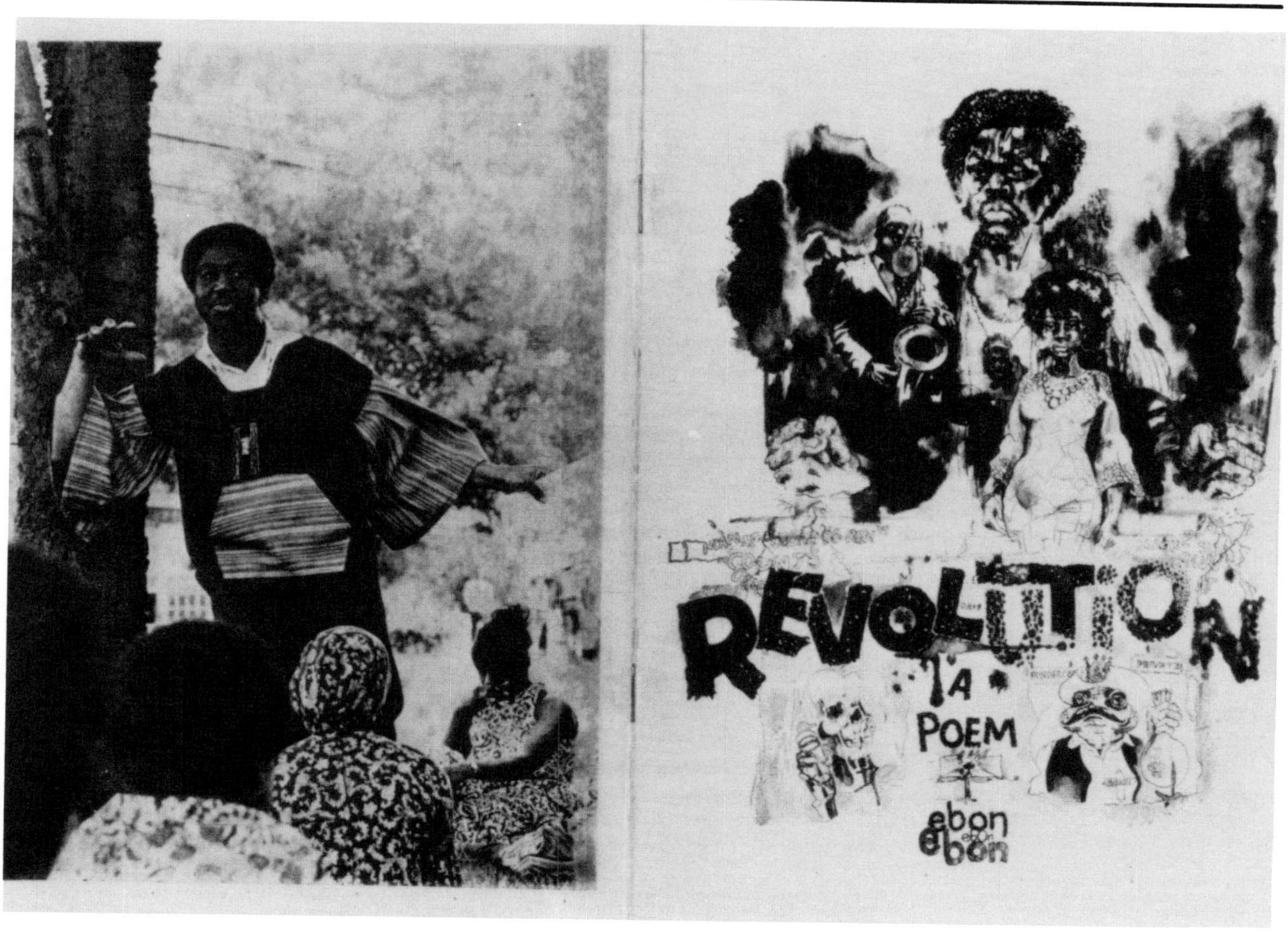

Covers for Ebon's 1968 volume of poetry which he calls "a version of history. a scream which describes what I see."

while he indicts Lyndon Johnson (in "Portrait of King Toad or Home on the Range") as he honors Malcolm X ("Chicago/Summer/68. Part I: For Malcolm"), his work is never simple propaganda. It is real poetry—sharp vision and skillful use of language and mechanics metamorphose into something richer when applied to the culturally resonant subjects Ebon chooses.

Other poems of this period evince similar skill. "The Mighty John Hancock or: The Bigger They Are—the Harder They Fall" is a violent and yet wonderfully cathartic vision of the imagined collapse of the newly erected John Hancock Building. "The Return to Order: The Peace Terms" is a clear-cut example of one of Ebon's favorite devices, the reversal of traditional Western imagery of black and white, with white the sign of evil (a device effectively employed in *Revolution*). "A Poem to My Brothers Killed in Combat or something about a conversation with my father after Rev. King was killed" is a moving expression of a surfeit of frustrated indignation: "I cannot cry this time/he said./ and I nodded to agree."

After Chicago, though the quality of his work did not decline, Ebon's production slowed, as the activist poet gradually came to give more time to activism than poetry. In September of 1969 he went to Atlanta to take over the management of the Timbuktu Bookstore, which had been opened by Abdul Al Kalimat (Gerald McWorter). After its failure (the Chicago branch survives), he managed Uhuru, another bookstore specializing in Afro-American works until 1974. He was involved in the establishment of the Atlanta Center for Black Arts and was on the board of directors of the Southern Education Program, formed to recruit black teachers from the North for local colleges. As a CETA worker, he began teaching at Atlanta's Neighborhood Arts Center in 1975 and later was its acting director for nine months.

One production of the Neighborhood Arts Center was *Potlikker* (1976), a collection of writings

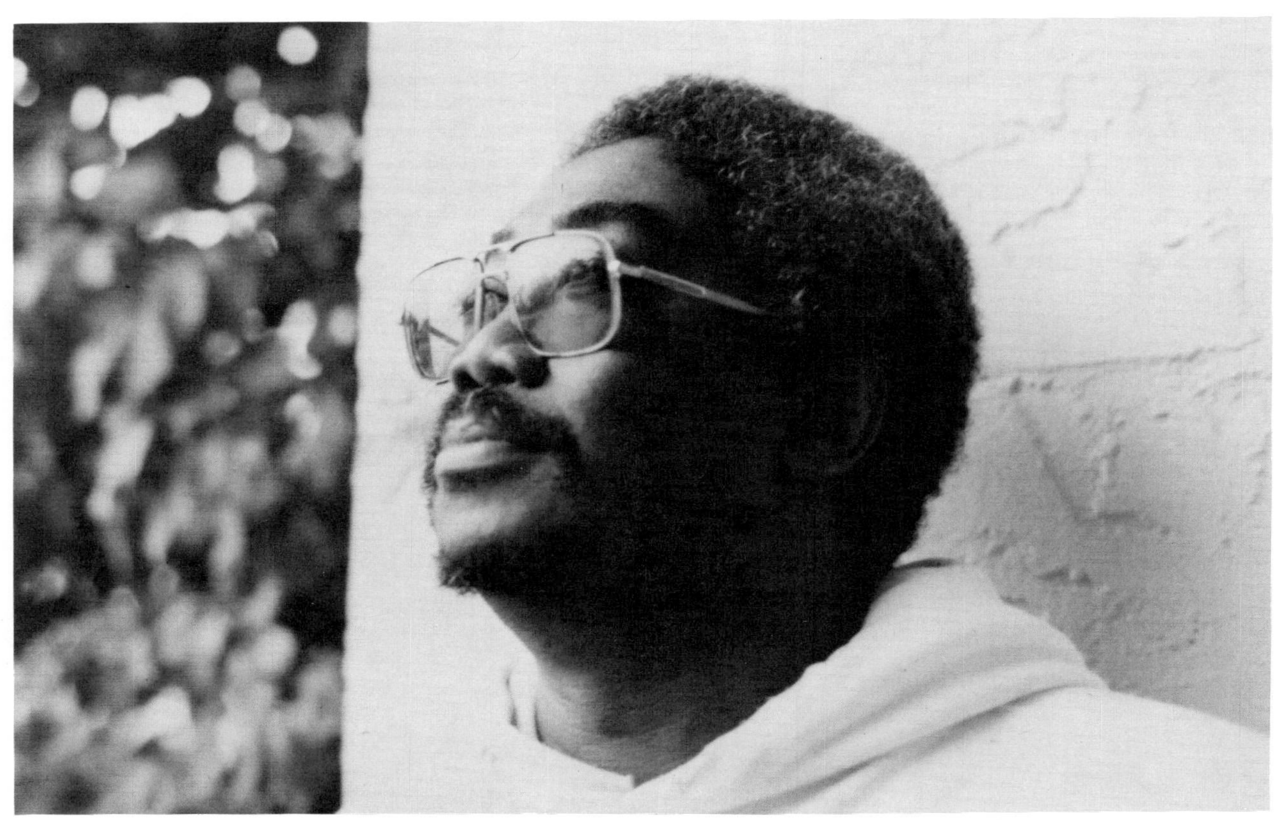

Ebon, August 1984 (photograph by Anne P. Tinker)

and artwork which included "The Bust" by Ebon. This piece, described purposefully in the table of contents as a "short story" (in line with the OBAC tenet of breaking the bounds of traditional forms), is a poem with as strong a social orientation as any of Ebon's work, but derived from no single historical incident; it is instead an attempt to render imaginatively a typical situation. As in the case of all of Ebon's work, it is sensorially vivid: "Poems come to me as visual images in the first instance," he says, and with him we see a vicious little cop as he "carrie[s] his weapon/like a snarling dog/on a straining leash," and feel "the concrete wall growing moist beneath [the] palms" of the wrongly arrested "school boy and june bug." The poem/story's ending, in which the policeman's partner is killed, is similar in its violent wish-fulfillment to "John Hancock"—although, being more realistic, it is an uglier resolution of anger. But the anger never overcomes the poetry; instead, they serve one another.

A more recent example of Ebon's work, "A Poem to Wrightsville" (retitled "Wrightsville, Georgia"), illuminates another aspect of his poetry. In *Dynamite Voices: Black Poets of the 1960's* (1971), Don L. Lee describes Ebon's "deep voice bouncing out like a Black barker at a secret blood rite." Ebon is consistently aware of the poem as performance. As a New York law student, he frequented the haunts of musicians; as a Chicago poet, he performed with musicians, reciting his words as they improvised. He traveled around the country giving planned and impromptu readings with other OBAC poets. In this later piece, he consciously incorporates audience response into the poem. First read at a 1980 benefit for the people of Wrightsville, it uses a refrain which had been the rallying cry of the townspeople as they fought depredations against their civil rights: "Ain't taking no more!" The Wrightsville citizens cheered and rose to their feet as their own words were delivered by the poet. It was true performance poetry and communal performance at that.

This combination of art and social purpose distinguishes Ebon's life. He still writes; he has a book-length collection of poems ("Chicago Black") as yet unpublished, and has begun to work on a novel. But his most creative work today is in the management of groups that encourage artistic and social expression. Three times past president of Atlanta's WBIG community radio station and vice-president of the Little Five Points (Atlanta) Community Association, he became in 1984 the director of the newly formed Southeast Community Cultural Center of Atlanta. This man whom Nikki Giovanni called one of her "heroes" has become primarily a teacher and inspirer of others. Ebon's small body of published work will continue to be valued on its own merits; the numerous reprintings of his poems in various anthologies bear witness to that fact. But he will also be remembered as an influence on the artists who follow him. He was one of the originators of an artistic movement whose intensity may have weakened, but which nevertheless has broadened, as it spread from a few cultural centers to communities all across the United States.

References:

Leaonead P. Bailey, *Broadside Authors and Artists* (Detroit: Broadside Press, 1974), p. 45;

"Chicago's OBAC: Portrait of Young Writers in a Workshop," *Negro Digest,* 17 (August 1968): 44-48, 79;

Nikki Giovanni, "Revolution," *Negro Digest,* 18 (August 1969): 95;

Don L. Lee, *Dynamite Voices: Black Poets of the 1960's* (Detroit: Broadside Press, 1971), pp. 41-43;

Carolyn M. Rodgers, "Black Poetry—Where it's at," *Negro Digest,* 18 (September 1969): 7-16.

James Andrew Emanuel

(15 January 1921-   )

Douglas Watson
Oklahoma Baptist University

BOOKS: *Langston Hughes* (New York: Twayne, 1967);

Dark Symphony: Negro Literature in America, co-authored and edited by Emanuel with Theodore L. Gross (New York: Free Press, 1968);

The Treehouse and Other Poems (Detroit: Broadside Press, 1968);

Panther Man (Detroit: Broadside Press, 1970);

How I Write/2 (New York: Harcourt Brace Jovanovich, 1972);

Black Man Abroad: The Toulouse Poems (Detroit: Lotus Press, 1978);

A Chisel in the Dark (Poems: Selected and New) (Detroit: Lotus Press, 1980);

A Poet's Mind, edited by Jean McConochie (New York: Regents Press, 1983);

The Broken Bowl (New and Uncollected Poems) (Detroit: Lotus Press, 1983).

RECORDINGS: *The Treehouse and Other Poems,* Broadside Voices, 1968;

Panther Man, Broadside Voices, 1970.

OTHER: "The Future of Negro Poetry: A Challenge for Critics," in *Black Expression: Essays by and about Black Americans in the Creative Arts,* edited by Addison Gayle, Jr. (New York: Weybright & Talley, 1969);

"Fever and Feeling: Notes on the Imagery in *Native Son,*" in *Richard Wright's "Native Son": A Critical Handbook,* edited by Richard Abcarian (Belmont, Cal.: Wadsworth, 1970);

"Blackness Can: A Quest for Aesthetics," in *The Black Aesthetic,* edited by Gayle (Garden City: Doubleday, 1971);

"The Short Fiction of Langston Hughes" and "The Literary Experiments of Langston Hughes," in *Langston Hughes: Black Genius,* edited by Therman B. O'Daniel (New York: Morrow, 1971);

"Christ in Alabama: Religion in the Poetry of Langston Hughes," in *Modern Black Poets: A Collection of Critical Essays,* edited by Donald Gibson (Englewood Cliffs, N.J.: Prentice-Hall, 1973);

"The Challenge of Black Literature: Notes on Interpretation," in *The Black Writer in Africa and the Americas,* edited by Lloyd W. Brown (Los Angeles: Hannessey & Ingalls, 1973);

"Racial Fire in the Poetry of Paul Laurence Dunbar," in *A Singer in the Dawn: Reinterpretations of Paul Laurence Dunbar,* edited by Jay Martin (New York: Dodd, Mead, 1975);

"Black Poetry for a New Century," in *Interculture: A Collection of Essays and Creative Writing,* edited by Sy M. Kahn and Martha Raetz (Vienna: Braumüller, 1975).

PERIODICAL PUBLICATIONS: "Emersonian Virtue: A Definition," *American Speech,* 36 (May 1961): 117-122;

"Langston Hughes' First Short Story: 'Mary Winosky,' " *Phylon,* 22 (Fall 1961): 267-272;

"The Invisible Men of American Literature," *Books Abroad,* 37 (Autumn 1963): 391-394;

"America Before 1950: Black Writers' Views," *Negro Digest,* 18 (August 1969): 26-34, 67-69;

"Renaissance Sonneteers," *Black World,* 24 (September 1975): 32-45, 92-97.

James A. Emanuel is a poet who vividly captures black experience and sensibilities. With academic and racial integrity, he has sought in both prose and poetry to preserve and expand the heritage of black American writers. His personal and poetic development, especially during the 1960s and 1970s, reveals a growing consciousness of the roles of the black American poet and a maturing vision of the racial fire that informs his work. To date, Emanuel's poetry has been afforded insufficient critical attention, and for many scholars his reputation continues to depend upon early and very competent critical works. However, his keen, sensitive perceptions of youth and love and heart-rending images of pain and racial oppression have made his poems favorites of those who have read them, and the thematic variety and technical skill that characterize the body of his poetry promise his eventual recognition as an indispensable figure in black American poetry. For few other poets has the relation between personal experience and the poem—the process of the poem's creation—captured so great an interest; yet, the poems are not merely personal, for Emanuel is fully aware of his audience's diversity and of the traditions to which his poems owe thanks and allegiance. The result is that Emanuel's work stands and will stand as testimony to his often painful heritage—racial, American, and universally human—and to his struggle to achieve, through poetic skill, images of identity true to that heritage. The body of his work is a lode which younger poets would do well to mine.

James Andrew Emanuel was born in 1921 in Alliance, Nebraska. The fifth of seven children who gathered around their mother as she read in the evenings, James was early stirred by the language of the Bible and the dramatic appeal of stories from magazines like the *Saturday Evening Post.* Also, the poetic rhythms of Paul Laurence Dunbar's work and the prose movements of Booker T. Washington's *Up from Slavery* were planted during these family sessions. Such stirrings, reinforced by his reading "practically all of the western and adventure and sports novels" in the Alliance library, caused him to entertain ambitions of becoming a writer. As a boy he memorized much popular poetry, and he also wrote poems and short stories. The stories, mostly of the detective and mystery variety, were soon destroyed as inadequate; as for the poetry, when Emanuel's junior high school principal made him read his Thanksgiving poem on the auditorium stage, he vowed to himself to write no more. Fortunately, the vow was not kept.

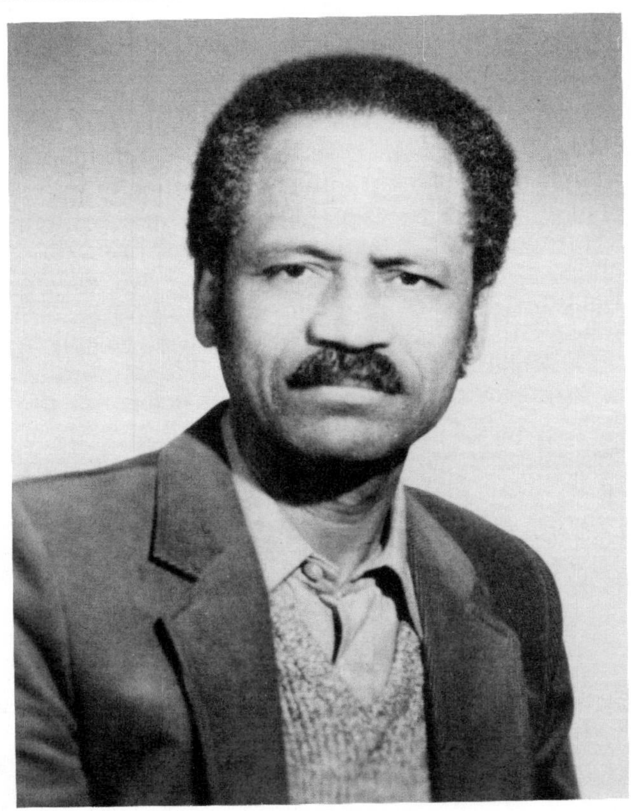

James Emanuel

That his boyhood and adolescence in Alliance were little scarred by racism is a fact which Emanuel says owes less to the town's egalitarianism than to the more ideological drift of his family conversations and to his general popularity and success in school. A straight-A student and valedictorian of his class, he graduated in 1939 with confidence that he could manage a successful life. This confidence is reflected in various bold steps he took to obtain work and money for schooling. Before and after graduation, he worked on several farms and ranches in Nebraska. The distasteful memories of one such job—slopping hogs on the William Batt farm—would later contribute to the poem "Three Chores: One Country Day," a poem "sifted . . . [from] among the tumbleweeds, snakes, and endless prairie lands of . . . adolescent summers." While still a teenager he also worked as an elevator operator in Denver, Colorado, and in Des Moines, Iowa, and as baling machine operator and weighmaster in Rock Island, Illinois. In 1942, at the age of twenty, he was in Washington, D.C., as confidential secretary to General Benjamin O. Davis, who was then in the War Department as the Assistant Inspector General of the U.S. Army. After two years in that position, Emanuel decided to go into the Army to earn enough money for college, and he did wartime duty as a staff sergeant with the 93rd Infantry Division in the Pacific.

At the end of World War II, Emanuel entered Howard University in Washington, D.C. Again, academic excellence characterized his work; his bachelor's degree in 1950 was awarded summa cum laude. While at Howard, he found encouragement for his writing ambitions. He published several poems in college anthologies and campus newspapers, and the beginning chapters of a novel written during his freshman and sophomore years were praised by campus visitor Pearl S. Buck.

In 1950 Emanuel moved from Washington to Chicago, where, in the same year, he married Mattie Etha Johnson. He began work on the master's degree at Northwestern University while working as civilian chief in the preinduction section of the Army and Air Force Induction Station. He held the job until near the end of his academic work, but resigned it when he became convinced that he had been passed over for promotion because of his race. At Northwestern, he again found encouragement for his writing. One teacher, Joel Hunt, praised him for the portrait of the mother in his novel, and two of his poems were published in a campus journal. Professor Zera S. Fink read his first serious poem, "Sonnet for a Writer," to a Wordsworth seminar in which he was enrolled and followed the reading with the pronouncement that "Mr. Emanuel is a poet." Indeed, that poem eventually won a citation for merit from *Flame* magazine after its 1958 publication in *Phylon*. The novel, after two rejections, was set aside. In 1952, Emanuel was awarded a John Hay Whitney Fellowship which supported his final year of work at Northwestern, where he received the M.A. degree in 1953, and his first year of work toward the Ph.D. degree at Columbia.

The move to New York and Columbia might be seen, had later events occurred differently, as a prelude to a stable and largely satisfying academic career in New York City. From 1954 to 1956, Emanuel taught at the Harlem YWCA Business School while taking course work at Columbia. In 1957, before beginning the study of Langston Hughes's work which would be his dissertation, he accepted a job as instructor of English at City College of New York. Afterward, he began to write poetry as regularly as time allowed. This work was encouraged by occasional publication in *Phylon* and the *New York Times*. The development of a personal friendship with Hughes in 1959 offered Emanuel not only keen insights into the man whose work he both studied and admired but it offered him a respected and highly competent reader for drafts of his own early poems, a reader whose suggestions were usually taken to heart. The years at Columbia taught Emanuel an academic preference for close reading as opposed to historical criticism; this is reflected in early published essays like "Emersonian Virtue: A Definition" (1961). In 1962, when he received the Ph.D. degree from Columbia and was promoted to assistant professor at City College, James Emanuel knew academic success and recognition; he held promise as an analytical critic and occasional poet; he found personal support in the love of his wife and his seven-year-old son, James, Jr. He was a black man who, apparently without major interruption, had managed the obstacles to personal and vocational success.

Several events of the early and middle 1960s began to alter the course of Emanuel's career and to point him toward a primary commitment to a poetry grounded in consciousness of his own racial identity. He had known black writing from his childhood, but the literary models for his earliest work had been traditional English masters—Keats, Shakespeare, Wordsworth. His first conscious influence had been the hard, vivid poetry of Hopkins, whose "purpose of squeezing 'all the water' out of his words" he admired, but he sought not to imitate anyone. The subjects of the earliest poems had little if anything to do with race. But in his study of Langston Hughes, Emanuel began to realize the lack of attention paid to black writers in general; he learned to admire Hughes's purpose of " 'illumination' of the condition of Black Americans" and resolved to carry it on in his own work. He began to read more and more widely from the work of black authors. From this reading came the 1963 essay "Invisible Men of American Literature" and other later works intended to uncover important but unacknowledged black writers and to set them in their broader literary contexts. Emanuel's personal crusade for recognition of a generally disesteemed black American literature led also to his initiating, in 1966, the first course in black poetry to be taught at CCNY. The intense reading and research which went into the course's preparation paid dividends in several essays, in his book-length study of Hughes published by Twayne in 1967, and in *Dark Symphony* (1968), a major anthology of black American writing (the first such book in thirty years) presented in historical perspective, coauthored and edited with colleague Theodore L. Gross. Each of these tasks testified to Emanuel's desire to help black writers "possess their own heritage"; but, aside from the service done to other writers, there can be little doubt of the works' value to his own poetic development—the focusing on his racial identity, the assumption of a mantle of race consciousness, and a growing awareness of an attention to his literary forebears and contemporaries.

Another event of the mid-1960s was to shake Emanuel from any relative comfort of his personal perspective on race. Amidst a school integration struggle in 1966 he filed for a post on the Mount Vernon, New York, school board and was inducted into the world of racial politics. When he attempted to manage an all-black campaign with a platform that argued for the teaching of black literature in New York schools, and when he employed tactics such as a black boycott of local merchants, he came under both public attack and private scrutiny. The story of the former underlies the poem "To the Negro Children of Mount Vernon," an appeal to "understand what I have done" as an act of consciousness raising; the story of the latter is the key to "For 'Mr. Dudley,' a Black Spy." The severe paranoia resulting from fear of invasion by such treacherous figures as Mr. Dudley is indirectly blamed by Emanuel for the eventual breakdown of his marriage to Mattie. The entire campaign episode kindled a hatred for injustice and treachery which has since burned both within and beyond the issue of racism and which has continued to appear in the poems of more recent years.

After *Langston Hughes* and *Dark Symphony,* and in the midst of publication of essays in *Phylon, Black World* and elsewhere, Emanuel's first volume of poetry was published. *The Treehouse and Other Poems*

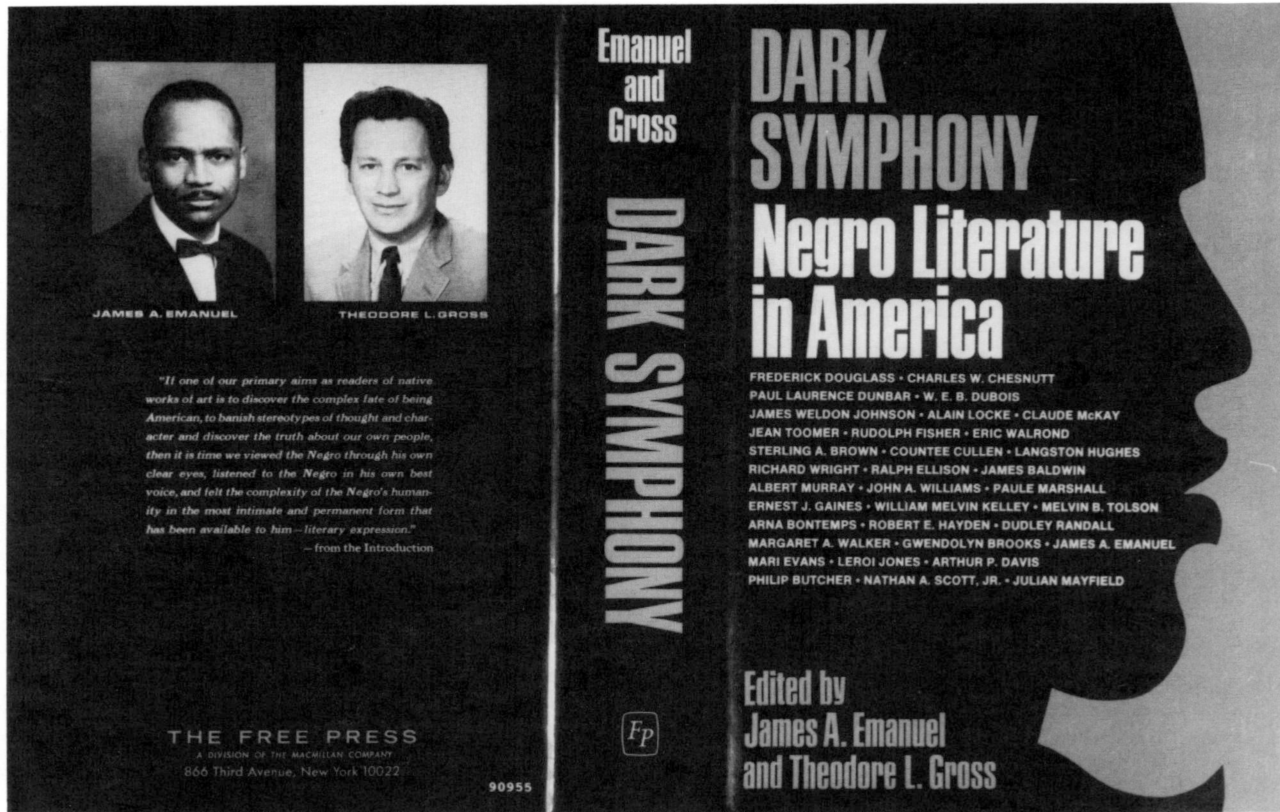

Dust jacket for the 1968 anthology which presents black American literature in historical perspective

(1968), published by Dudley Randall's Broadside Press, included several poems that had appeared earlier in periodicals and anthologies. The volume is a synthesis of Emanuel's broad thematic concerns for the innocence, energy, and pain of youth, for miscellaneous events of the black experience and the context of racism that affects them, for the powerful and creative force of the imagination, and for the complex activity of the black writer as a metaphor for an active human intelligence. The poems of *Treehouse* are sometimes serious, sometimes ironic, sometimes lyrical, but never light. Almost uniformly they employ traditional patterns of rhythm and rhyme, but occasionally reflect blues and jazz forms learned first, perhaps, from the poetry of Langston Hughes.

In the poems of youth, Emanuel celebrates the "powers which children grow and shine/And give away like flowers," but he is always aware of a hovering darkness that restrains such shining. In "The Voyage of Jimmy Poo," he projects a "bathtub sea" of childhood imagination, a sea where "Young Neptune dashed the waters/Against enamel shore,/And kept the air a-tumbling/With bubble clouds galore." Still, such child's play is restricted, and "soon the voyage ended./The ship was swept away/By a hand that seemed to whisper,/'No more games today.' " Similarly, in "Fishermen," a poem that recalls the poet's fishing trips with his son, the progression is from the three-year-old with innocent imagination, "curled sleeping" beside his father or "squirm[ing] to my armpit in the poncho," to the thirteen-year-old who is "uncurled," "thinned . . . hard," a "manchild . . . fishing far from me." Childhood is wonderful but fleeting; it is never simple. As the poet says in "The Young Ones, Flip Side," "Put off, or put on/Youth hurts. And then/It's gone."

Not all the poems of *Treehouse* are obvious in their racial concern, but, as Emanuel's friend Marvin Holdt has pointed out, most poems in the first section of the book do reflect aspects of the black experience in America, treated with bitterness and revolt. "Nightmare," the opening poem, recalls a surreal image like that in the grandfather episode of Ralph Ellison's *Invisible Man*. The sleeper tells of seeing a face come "Back from the dead"; it "Leaned forward" and "laughed./ . . . just laughed/ At my tears." This haunting vision, merciless and comic, does not have to be understood as the poet's painful racial heritage, but as such, it depicts a consistent tension that figures into the more obviously racial poems which follow it.

Among the names and faces that float through the racial memory of these poems is that of Emmett Till, a fourteen-year-old black boy from Chicago murdered by a group of white men and thrown into the Tallahatchie River in 1955 after he allegedly whistled at a white woman in Mississippi, where he was visiting. In the poem, written in 1963 "in twenty-seven minutes and never changed," Emanuel links the historical event to "That bedtime story/Of the fairy/River Boy/Who swims forever,/ Deep in treasures,/Necklaced in /A coral toy." Both Emmett's and the fairy boy's stories possess auras of unreality, yet Emmett Till's is factual and documented by newspaper and magazine clippings and photographs; its horror "Won't be still." The fate of Emmett Till is extended to other unnamed black victims in the poem "Where Will Their Names Go Down?" It asks the fate of "Our bloodied boys/ Sunk link by link/ . . . In the Tallahatchie, the Mississippi, and the Pearl." But resolution is found not in a submergence of history into fairy tale, but in a conscious commitment of the living to redeem the memory of the dead—"we rise to fiercely shake a chain of days/That blurry hang across that dying scrawl." It is a commitment that recalls Emanuel's own academic purpose—to help black writers and readers to recover and possess their heritage.

Other race-related poems in the volume are worthy of attention. "Negritude" is a catalog of associations with blackness, among which are "the brotherhood of pain," "the diary of the mind," and "a burden bravely chanted." In a brief, jazzy poem, "The Negro," Emanuel protests the word "Negro" and the stereotype of black men as "Eyes a-saucer,/ Yessir bossir,/Dice a-clicking,/Razor flicking." The poem's key line turns on the grammatical distinction between the definite and indefinite articles: "The-ness froze him/In a dance./A-ness never/ Had a chance." "For Malcolm, U.S.A.," in which the poet claims that "Malcolm was/My native land," affirms a racial identity by figuratively recalling the black hero. Most tribute pieces, generally not the best of his work, will probably fall from the poet's canon, but "For Malcolm, U.S.A." will stay, as it does in *A Chisel in the Dark* (1980). "Stop Light in Harlem" looks toward a later tendency to avoid patterned forms and to depend almost exclusively on free verse lines. "Get Up, Blues" and "A View from the White Helmet" are also interesting for their musical experimentation.

The poems of *Treehouse* which most directly explore the poet's mind are "A Negro Author" and "The Treehouse." In the first, Emanuel speaks from inside the head of a black poet concerned with the task of satisfying two very different audiences and aware of the self-denial involved in either playing one's response off against the other's or in allying completely with one and denying the other. The poet is trying to assert a personal poetic purpose, but faces the contradiction that a commitment to aesthetic integrity rather than to racial ideology may leave him no audience at all.

> I wrote something black today.
> I wonder what Negroes will say
> about it.
> Tomorrow I'll do something white
> If I can hold my pen just right
> throughout it.
>
> I'd rather be devoutly me,
> Do my writing in a tree,
> Watch it seep up into leaves—
> Whose beauty no one misconceives.
>
> Yet, what will Negroes say (and whites)
> About a man who only writes
> Leaves—of a color hard to name?
> I'm treed, in this peculiar game.

The poet's concern for balance is reflected in the internal division of the initial stanza and in the carefully matched rhymes throughout. Though the pattern of the poem disguises it, the concern is that of the jazz soloist, defining his musical identity by a middle passage between melodic regularity and atonality. This middle ground is the treehouse of the man/poet, a region not necessarily chosen, but in which creation is possible, if not necessary.

The figure of the treehouse is a central one for Emanuel; he came to it in 1959 as "a theoretical refuge to which every hard-pressed man should be allowed to retreat." As his original conception of the figure suggests, it is more general and perhaps optimistic in its external reference than the poet's tree in "A Negro Author"; however, it is safe to say that for Emanuel, the poet is the archetypal hard-pressed man. And if the poet is not intentionally the central figure of the poem, nevertheless, all of its dynamics seem to work well for him. "The Treehouse" is almost entirely concrete in its imagery, yet the central figure is clearly an abstraction, a place in the mind. It is a space in which perspective may be gained on the past and the future, where the poet may mediate the immediate and the eternal, but it is not a space, a refuge, to be gained without compensating loss. Thus, the movement from "house below" to "house above" is made on "perilous stairs" from which the man/poet may fall into an abyss of unreality; the treehouse refuge comes not naturally, but as a "green splice in the humping years"; and the "twilight flash/Of luminous recall" is achieved only after a loss of actual sexual power in the presence of which "every moving thing/was girl-shaped." To understand youth's innocence and energy, one must, it seems, also know their loss. In the end, the poet's, the thinking man's drama of life is acted out on the "perilous stairs" amid connections of power and loss, here and wherever, now and forever, self and universal.

Among the final poems of *Treehouse* are several lines which affirm the necessity of gracefully accepting a perilous stairs existence. In one, acceptance of time as "the gift we learn to take" disdains protest for a recognition of natural limits. "After the Record Is Broken," a poem about heroes which draws on Emanuel's adolescent years in Nebraska, urges the reader not to forget the "lesser men" of the past in the midst of the "higher, faster, farther" achievements of the present. "Genesis" likewise acknowledges the complexities of human history in its affirmation not only of final achievements but of preliminaries: "I like the hand that strokes the babe/Before it whips the boy," and "I like the pause that guards a friend/Before the tongue that tells." "I Touched the Hand of a Soldier Dead," a poem grown from Emanuel's World War II experience, is reminiscent of Hardy's "The Man He Killed," but possesses less of irony and more of human compassion. Touching the hand of the dead soldier, the poet notes that "It looked not like an enemy,/Nor like a friend." His response is simple: "I dug a shallow grave/ . . . I said a prayer . . . And pulled some sampaquita flowers/To mark the place." He resolves the experience and the volume with another recognition of limited achievement, of inevitable conflict: "I never knew the victory./But I knew the war."

Critical response to *The Treehouse and Other Poems* was slight. In one of the few published reviews of the book, Darwin Turner noted that "These are quiet poems," and that "the quiet is especially noticeable when it is contrasted with the shrieks and shouts of other Broadside authors, such as Don Lee and Dudley Randall." Indeed, the poems of *Treehouse* do reveal a quieter, cooler voice than is heard in Emanuel's next book, *Panther Man* (1970). They are generally premiddle 1960s compositions and thus reflect a distance from racist oppression never again possible after the 1966 school board campaign.

Even as *Treehouse* was released, Emanuel was headed for the University of Grenoble, France, where he was to hold, during 1968 and 1969, his first Senior Fulbright Professorship and spend his first year of sabbatical leave from CCNY. Hoping to "brush into oblivion the harshly debilitating memories of the [previous] two and a half years," the poet, with his wife and son, moved into a seven-room chalet in Seyssins in the Belledonne range of the Alps. For at least three months during the winter of that year, Emanuel worked productively on such diverse poems as "Fourteen," "For 'Mr. Dudley,' a Black Spy," "Item: Black Men Thinking," and "Flirtation," but in general the year in Seyssins was a period of deteriorating family relationships and painful reminders of scars inflicted by American racism. In "Snowflakes and Steel," Emanuel's unpublished autobiography, he speaks of his wife as a victim of racial recriminations, driven to intermittent insanity and "irregularly tensing whole days and nights with incredible and often dangerous whimsies." He feared for his son's personal safety and for his own, and even took the precaution of sleeping in the chalet's attic office, furniture piled against the door to block any surprise entry. Although near the end of the year the three traveled together by car from Grenoble south into Spain and Italy, north into Sweden and Denmark, the trip was marred by accident and embarrassment and offered neither recovery nor reunion. At the end of the first Fulbright year, Emanuel could count among his accomplishments several finished poems and an increased knowledge of black American culture and history gained in preparing lectures for his university classes. He returned to New York not having brushed aside the memories of racial injustice, but stirred even more deeply, more personally, by the violence and debilitation of such injustice. The next years back in New York were unhappy ones, marked by further deterioration of his marriage and only a little redeemed by the insights gained from his City College students, to whom his second volume of poems, *Panther Man*, was dedicated in 1970.

Emanuel was aware that *Panther Man* contained a different kind of poetry than he had previously written. In the preface, he calls the volume "a reflection of personal, racially meaningful predicaments" compelled by "my feelings about the most abysmal evil in the modern world: American racism." Indeed, its poems, all except the tribute to Langston Hughes written between June 1968 and August 1970, burn with a harsher fire than any in *Treehouse*. Technically, they are poems which depart from traditional patterns. The poet was aware of a need "to harmonize my current poetic style with the disharmony of my experiences. I needed a no-jive, no-bullshit style: no pretty rimes, no fake capitals, no rounded corners when the edges had actually been jagged; nothing but felt truth on my own terms, come what may." What is perhaps most remarkable about *Panther Man* is that its often ironic, often bitter reflections are still touched by a human delight in youth's exuberance and man's will to endure.

The title poem decries the 1969 killing by Chicago police of Black Panthers Mark Clark and Fred Hampton. In lines which mirror his commitment to a new style, Emanuel muses on the fate of his "Panther Man" protagonist:

Wouldnt think
t look at m
he was so damn bad
they had t sneak up on m,
shoot m in his head
in his bed
sleepin
Afroed up 3 inches
smilin gunpowder.

In the end, the poet calls on the murdered Panther to "Get up/and fight that cracker-back/back m gainst the wall/of YOUR room/where YOU sleep/ with YOUR dreams/ . . . if THATS the way he is /even yr GHOST/can take m." Read against earlier poems like "Emmett Till" and "Where Will Their Names Go Down?," "Panther Man" demonstrates a thematic progression regarding racism, but it would be a mistake to overlook the equally dramatic progression of Emanuel's poetic line. This same willingness to dare new ways echoes through the protagonist's response to his restrainers' warnings in "Old Black Men Say": "Im gonna rile them folks/ like I been riled,/gonna be a fool/maybe,/whatever they raised—/them old Black men."

As in *Treehouse*, there is deep respect in *Panther Man* for the power of the poetic process to shore up one's world and to assert one's identity. "For the 4th Grade, Prospect School: How I Became a Poet" is a response to a question posed by a young listener who had heard Emanuel read during one of his many visits to elementary school classrooms. The images of the poem are associated with children's losses—a kite broken loose, a top fallen into a gutter, a dog run away. Against these material losses, Emanuel asserts the power of poetry to bind up and hold one's valued possessions in memory—"I tie together things I know/and wind up with a poem to show." The regular rhythms and rhymes of the poem reflect both its relatively early composition

(June 1968) and its subject of binding together. But poetry's ability to preserve by holding together is only one of its powers asserted in *Panther Man.* Poetry may also be a weapon for unleashing inner rage, as in "Black Poet on the Firing Range." There Emanuel projects a poet "shootin from the hip/ gettin off bullets cant be heard/till they hit Whitey's mind," and he challenges the black poet to "Go head, Black on—/guess trigger time for real/dont make/no noise." Marvin Holdt has appropriately used these lines to ally Emanuel with Thoreau, Gandhi, and Martin Luther King in a "family of activists in nonviolence," but it is the power of poetry and not simply of nonviolence that they most solidly affirm.

The harshest words of *Panther Man* are found in the ironic tribute poem, "For 'Mr. Dudley,' a Black Spy." "Mr. Dudley" is a name given by Emanuel to a black man he is convinced carried out CIA-like espionage activities against him and his family during and after the 1966 school board campaign. He is addressed as "Harlem dud," capable of playing "whatever role/Master Whitey Big/kicked on you," and he evolves into a symbolic Judas able "to bug the private hearts" of those who are "Black but not your kind." Finally, the poet offers his bitter tribute: "For you, 'Dudley,'/and your beardless, baubled clan,/these loathings/to suck on." The paranoia induced by the Dudleys of Emanuel's past contributes also to "Item: Black Men Thinking," a poem which describes the poet's shock at reading the statement "the CIA poisoned Richard Wright. . . ." The poem traces the shock of awareness, of possibility of horror even greater than the mind can comprehend, and the slow adjusting of the mind to the horror—"the scar becoming slowly man,/nerved to clash with monsters." The suddenness with which knowledge comes is also central to "Black Humor in France: For Etha," a poem that recalls a day in Grenoble when the poet's wife, her face masked in the white of soap lather, leapt from behind him to shout "BOO!" into his ear. Her "White folks scareya, hunh?" taunts his surprise, and he must regain his balance before he is able to make a rational response—"dont come up behind me;/makes me nervous since the war." But in the final lines, the poet redefines the situation in his own mind, this time in deeper, more complex racial terms: "but didn't say when war began/nor dare count all those faces/clean and white/that came up from behind." Such conditioned caution is seen as part of the uniquely black experience in "Whitey, Baby," where the poet taunts "Whitey" with "What CHU know/bout stayin in the dark/cause ya cant blieve nothin/nobody says. . . ?"

The poems of *Panther Man* that celebrate vitality and understanding include "Fourteen" and "Sixteen, Yeah," both inspired by Emanuel's son's restless energy, and "Crossover: for RFK," a poem in which Emanuel uses the perspective of Juan Romero, a young Mexican-American present at the assassination of Robert Kennedy, to pay tribute to the senator's rare vision of a possible human community that "crossed-over" any distinctions of race or wealth. Similarly, in "Christ, One Morning," the man of vision "teaching love" is perceived as "spied on, kissed, spit on,/pushed atop the world,/speared still with hate/but eyes forgiving, wondering."

At least two poems from *Panther Man* recall the perilous stairs, the middle passage existence of "The Treehouse." In "Cat on a Tree," the title of which at least accidentally recalls the image of "Christ, One Morning," a brief bus ride vision of an apparently terrified white cat clinging to the trunk of a tree reminds the persona of "a blk cat I know." The "cat" is at ease in the tree, "nuzzlin the bark/ goin round the trunk playful/ . . . he coolcatnumber 1/up in snow aint been found yet/ . . . changin trees and gettin closer to the ground/the higher he climbs." The black cat's ease on the tree trunk is related to the survival instincts of the protagonist in "Black Man, 13th Floor" who, with "12 floors below me, 12 above," is "bettin on my life squeezin out/crawlin through some other stinkin/ middle passage."

Like *Treehouse, Panther Man* attracted little critical notice. Emanuel turned to other tasks in keeping with his commitment to preserve the heritage of black poetry. By 1970 he had suggested to Dudley Randall the Broadside Critics project, a series of monographs on the contributions of black poets to American literature. When Randall agreed that the project should be pursued, Emanuel was named general editor, and in that capacity, from 1970 to 1975, he saw through the press five volumes, including studies of Countee Cullen, Claude McKay, and Phillis Wheatley. Another project begun in 1970 to 1971 was his analysis of the process of poetic composition which was to become part of the book *How I Write/2* in 1972. In it he explored, by way of analysis and interviews, several poems by himself, Haki R. Madhubuti (Don L. Lee), Sonia Sanchez, Gwendolyn Brooks, and Nikki Giovanni. Emanuel's interest in recording and analyzing the processes of composition did not stop with *How I Write/2*; it is present in the surprisingly

4 June 1972, Toulouse 5:45 p.m. - 6:40
1st version
[Toulouse Poems]
For Alix, Who Is Three

Foreign country of your eyes
picture-book blue
as the lake you fingered as you read
and taught me simple words
like clé (like key),
chocolate milk breath
curled up in smiles
for such a stranger in the room
who animal by animal
and thing by thing
even with their names on the page
had to be told again
like clé (like key),
your voice half gone to bed
comes back transformed in faces that I knew
or all one changing face and changing years
one or a few or many
as pages turn and doors swing wide
row behind row until...

And there again is Alix,
who is three
who
in foreign country of her eyes and chocolate smile
gave me the key
the clé
I will throw away
if I ever want
to lock those doors again.

First draft for the poem that Emanuel says was "inspired by a three-year-old French girl," and which "freed my creativity dammed up for over two years by racism in the U.S.A. and led to a stream of poetry written in Europe" (courtesy the author) precise time notations on draft copies of his poems, and it is the moving force behind the composition of "Snowflakes and Steel: My Life as a Poet, 1971-1980."

As 1966 had begun a period of awakened terror for Emanuel, so 1971 began a series of departures. As he left New York in August 1971 for Toulouse, France, and an appointment at the university there, he was alone, headed for a "foreign environment where every uncertainty would be matched by the promise of growth, the possibility of rebirth." He sought to clear out his life and make it "fit for poetry." Not until 1978 did such fitness show itself in a published volume of poems, but that book, *Black Man Abroad: The Toulouse Poems,* tells the story of his dramatic struggle out of personal pain and poetic stagnation, through "revival and reorientation," and toward revolutionary activity. In Toulouse from 1971 to 1973, he taught classes and directed theses, some dealing with black American literature; professional support and friendship came from university colleagues Marvin Holdt, Anthony Suter, and Lee Audhuy, but the pivotal figure in his Toulouse world and throughout the decade of the 1970s was Marie-France Bertrand, whom he met in the spring of 1972. A travel guide and librarian, she became his redemptive companion in travel and love, and "Le Barry," the home of her lawyer mother, became a refuge to which he could retreat from various madnesses outside. It is to Marie-France that *Black Man Abroad* is dedicated, and it is she who stands behind its poems of love.

In the fall of 1973, Emanuel was back at CCNY. It was a nightmare period in which threats of physical injury and confiscated property eventuated in divorce from Mattie and in complete loss of contact with his son. Among the bitter consequences of his divorce suit was the theft of literary papers, among which were Langston Hughes's letters and manuscripts and the drafts of his own early poems. Temporary escapes to London and Le Barry relieved the 1973-1974 school term, and when he returned to New York in the fall of 1974 from a summer of travel through Europe with Marie-France, she accompanied him. He received a Fulbright appointment at the University of Warsaw, Poland, for 1975 to 1976, and she joined him there. Oppressive teaching and living conditions in Warsaw led eventually to Emanuel's revolutionary protest against university officials and to his broad sympathy for the common people of Poland. The assertion of his human rights in the face of oppression was nothing new for the poet; it belied a consistent concern for upholding the dignity of the individual.

After the Warsaw year and a summer in France, Emanuel returned to New York. He taught at City College during the next two years, but escaped to Toulouse each Christmas and for the summer in between. A personal highlight of the period was his participation in the World Black and African Festival of Arts and Culture in Lagos, Nigeria, during January 1977. He had read his poems often in Europe and America, but the thirty-minute reading at FESTAC, because of its connection to worldwide black cultural awareness, was special. After a productive period of writing in the summer of 1977, Emanuel was ready to offer a new gathering of poems. Through friend Lance Jeffers, he contacted Naomi Long Madgett of Lotus Press, and she, believing Emanuel to have been one of the best of the then-defunct Broadside Press authors, readily agreed to publish the new book, *Black Man Abroad,* in 1978.

The poems of *Black Man Abroad* are typically longer, more personal, and more difficult than the poems of the earlier books. The difficulty lies partly in the personal references of the poet (who takes the risk knowingly, believing that the poems should come "feelingly . . . out of his own life"), but it also lies in the attempt to carry off a more complex vision of life's inconsistencies and incongruities than is found in earlier poems. In the best of the poems, the attempt is remarkably successful.

The book is arranged in four sections: "The Toulouse Poems, Parts I & II," "The Warsaw Experiment," and "Occasionals." The first section, subtitled "It Was Me Did These Things," traces a psychological journey toward acceptance of diverse expressions and sensibilities of love. After an initial poem about the casual risks of living and the inevitable pain of betrayed love and failed idealism come two celebrations of innocence inspired by Alix Cordesse, three-year-old daughter of a Toulouse friend. In the first, Emanuel recalls Alix as she who "gave me the key / the *clé* / I will throw away / if ever I want to lock my doors again"; in the second he wishes her happiness—"what will sweeten to the touch / seeming little, being much." He says that the vision of Alix permitted a reopening of his life to love after the painful losses of past years, but in "Didn't Fall in Love" it is clear that a residuum of caution and pain still prevents easy commitment to a new love object. Commitment does come in the poems most directly addressed to Marie-France, of which "For Mees" is the most memorable. Amid reflections on their travels together, Emanuel speaks of her "gentle hand . . . / rebuilding me luminous and possible," of her as "the pit and shaft and

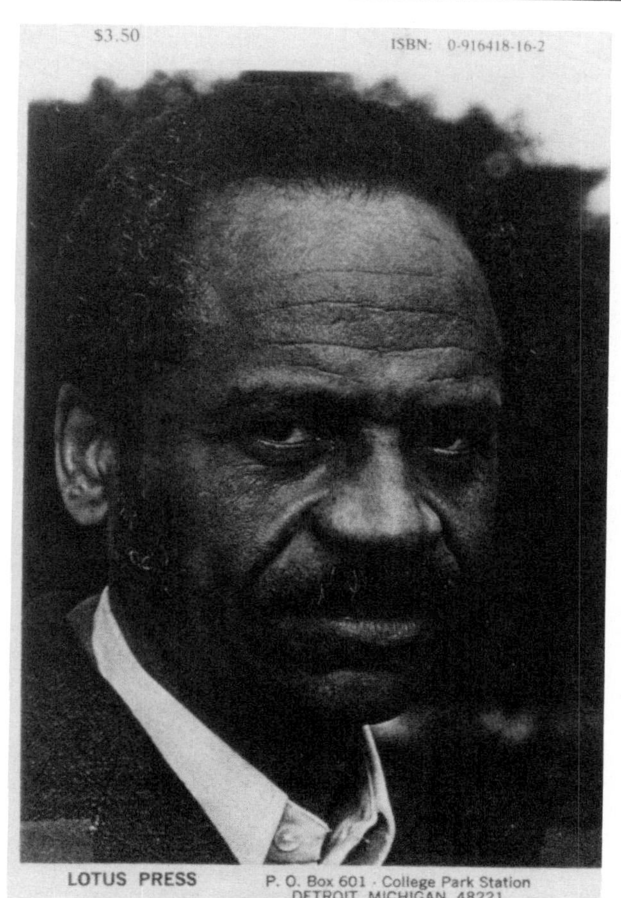

Covers for Emanuel's introspective 1978 poetry collection

gleam of sun/in some dark mine of me." "La Dame, at the Throw-Away Fire" tells of helping an old woman sift through piles of "junk" accumulated over many years. The woman repeatedly checks the poet's and his young companion's intentions to burn "her breathing treasures we would junk entire." When the job is completed, they form "a silent ring/around the laggard fire" in which burn the "trifles" the old woman has permitted it. It is not clear whether the would-be destroyers of the souvenir hoard she loves fully understand "what *Madame* had lived to learn:/We throw away the best we get/but bury what we save,/while flames in us give jewel-life/to all we know of grave." "La Dame, at the Throw-Away Fire" is a strong poem which, like the earlier "Old Black Men Say" and the later "For Young Blacks, the Lost Generation," springs from a tension between one's heritage and the desire for freedom from it. As always, Emanuel affirms the value of heritage without condemning the restlessness of those who would deny it.

From love expressed and observed, the poems turn to a definition of self in several poems which explore relationships of flesh to spirit and action to idea. In "Clothesline, rue Marie" the body is called "crank and tendon of my will to be"; though the poet wishes to "ungirth all the bounds of me," he recognizes that only the "clothes-line" man of wind, or spirit, can achieve such an escape. Inversely, in "My Animal: Accident at Pas de la Case," the animal nature of man is lauded for carrying the poet beyond his rational limits of pain and fear. Self is defined in terms of time and experience in "Chanteuse de Restaurant, Toulouse," which recalls an evening with friends when a young, expressive singer-guitarist performs her song, "dimly wondering/ if our older bones/had ever lain in her grass/ . . . that greened for her in single sun/and greyed so quickly into song." The situation and the complex of relationships that emerge between idea, song, singer, and audience recall those in Wallace Stevens's "The Idea of Order at Key West," but

Emanuel's primary concern is the distance between love acted and understood. The singer knows the exuberance of love, but doubts that her old listeners ever have; the poet understands not only the exuberance but the mature commitment.

"Flowers for a Real-Gone Girl" and "Goodbye No. 1" address the fragility of love, the first in a wish for "flowers that don't live long," the second in darker considerations of the loss of love's beauty through concern over love's posturings. The latter is Prufrockian in its uncertainty but not in its experience; Emanuel's lovers may fumble awkwardly, but they have known love, though theirs is now only a "beauty that has been." In love's "crazy scrapbook" there is room, too, for toughness and humor. "Topless, Bottomless Bar, Manhattan" presents a naked, gleaming dancer, a figure of exploited loveliness, as she "bottomed slow on hips downsettling like a spinning coin/and squatted squarely in the face of one/who gawked at what she closely opened to his eyes," and in the whimsical "Ass on the Beach, in Spain," the physical beauty of bikinied bodies so dazzles the poet that "my narrow bed tonight turns to remember."

Part II of "The Toulouse Poems," "The Ones Who Did It," contains poems of a black sensibility. Their language is harsher, more jagged than that of other poems in the volume. The title poem of the section is an interrogation—"ARE YOU THE ONES WHO DID IT?"—of any readers who have contributed to the heritage of enslavement and racism, but the crime turns out to be transformable into something not wholly destructive: "Your hate received's a load to build on,/pile with lumber of my life." "Kickass" tells of various encounters with a prince of violence who has "magic powers/of travel and disguise," but comes to "nightmare . . . though twice upon a time/he was a King." It is the tale of violence repaid by violence until earth is "nearly done to death." Perhaps Emanuel's most complex poem about the self-conscious identity of the black poet is found in "After the Poetry Reading, Black." It arises from a white listener's expression of disappointment, at the end of a reading, because the poet is "not Black enough" in his images, not strident enough in his racial effusions. Much of the poem is a surreal monologue spoken by the poet's "Trans-a-lator," his ironic piercer of the veil of white talk. It is clear that the disappointed listener had sought not poems of human experience, but reinforcement of his racial stereotypes, and the Trans-a-lator's explanation carries the poet back through many false identities foisted upon him by audiences, black as well as white, but the poem ends in an affirmation of self-identity which transcends the misintentions and misperceptions: "I knew/what I meant."

The "Warsaw Experiment" section consists of four poems that recall the poet's year in Poland; they are poems of empathy for his colleagues and for the common folk of Poland as well, but the personal experiences on which they lean seem less clearly transmuted into a broader vision than those behind other poems in the volume. Among the "Occasionals" which close the book, the most memorable is an airport poem that recalls the nature of the poetic world which Emanuel inhabits, a world in which "so much begins in pain" but in which there is "a stair,/climbable to passage through/to loosenings, to air," a world in which "reachings, heftings of the doubt" are "the waiting truth,/ . . . believable as air."

During January of 1978, Emanuel continued to write while preparing in Toulouse for a Paul Laurence Dunbar conference in Baltimore in February. At the conference, where he presented some of his poems, he renewed many old acquaintances and spoke of parallels between Dunbar's poetic career and his own. At the end of the spring semester, he left New York for France and London. Even continuing legal troubles over his stolen literary papers could not completely suppress his pleasure at the sabbatical leave he was beginning. From July to December 1978, he worked in London; after Christmas at Le Barry, he settled in Paris. There he wrote poems that would comprise much of the 1980 volume, *A Chisel in the Dark*. Between travels, he also continued to read publicly. In America, recognition of his work began to come in the form of critical attention and award. During 1979, *Black American Literature Forum* published Marvin Holdt's article on his work, and the American Biographical Institute named him among their "Notable Americans." In 1980 to 1981, as Visiting Professor at the University of Toulouse, he taught courses on his poetry and directed theses on black literary figures.

With the Broadside editions of *Treehouse* and *Panther Man* generally unavailable, *A Chisel in the Dark,* published in July 1980, does the service of reprinting twenty-two of the early poems. More significantly, the format facilitates a handy measure of Emanuel's growth into a mature poet in full possession of his powers. Gwendolyn Brooks's acknowledgment of "great gallops forward" evidenced in *Chisel's* poems is appropriate. The book title, from a line in "Sonnet for a Writer," which in 1958 had brought the poet his first literary recognition, is itself a rich and appropriate image of Emanuel's poetic purpose; the poems are expressions of his role as shaper in the diverse materials of darkness—blackness, pain, oppression, and the unknowns of life and love. It is the role of the speaker who says in "Officer Liz and the Poem," "Flickerings are all the light I get/to finish what I do" in "my place where anguish lives/in fumblings for the word." In "Stiff Roses Bring Their Simple Wish," he affirms the reality of beauty despite his awareness of its artificial, manipulated expressions. In "El Toro," he affirms the necessity of power. In a line that recalls the "Black on" of "Black Poet on the Firing Range," he commands the great black bull to "stay terrible." Like the distance between beauty and terror, the distance between regularity and randomness defines a space in which the poet works. In "Worksheets, Flat No. 9" the poet writes of practicing "dual rhythms"—"one set for the street alone," "the other . . . offhand, random/ . . . with a motion of its own," so as to face "the surfaces/night had pulled down."

Two very different black experience poems are in *Chisel.* "White-Belly Justice: a New York Souvenir" is a vitriolic attack on the lawyer who caused Emanuel such anguish during and after his divorce proceedings; it is a careful, understandable, perhaps inevitable response to the court-related events that occurred between 1974 and 1978, but its inclusion in the book is unfortunate. It surpasses "For 'Mr. Dudley,' " in venom, but lacks the earlier poem's keenness and consistent purpose. One can only weep for the experience that makes such poems seem necessary. In contrast, "For Young Blacks, the Lost Generation," contains some of the finest sketches of black young people and their forebears in any poetry. Reminiscent of the earlier portraits of his restless, energetic son, these relate the helplessness of urban youth crying out for recognition and power, but the power of the poem comes from the thrusting of these images of lost ones against a rich background of their enslaved forefathers. The poet's achievement, consistent

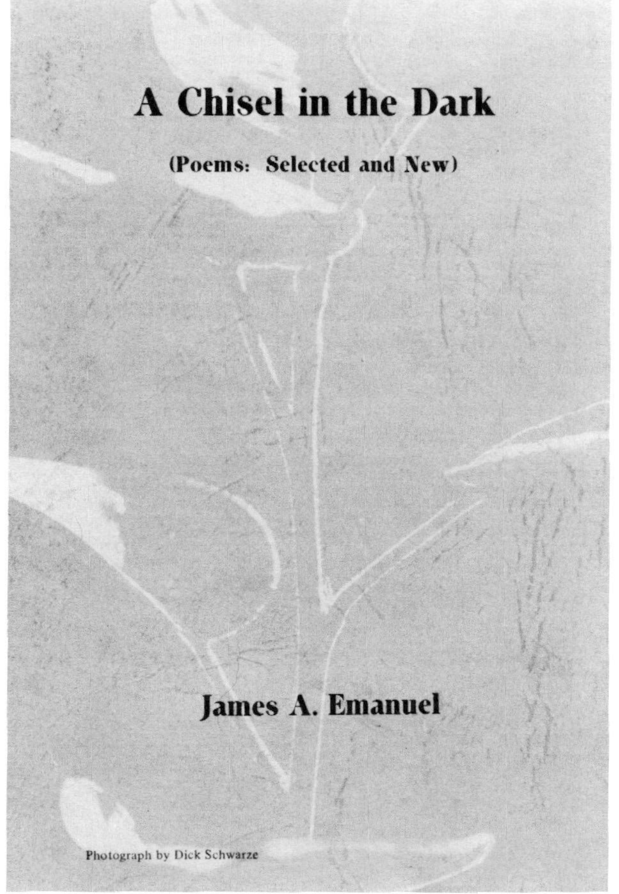

Covers for Emanuel's fourth collection of poems which takes its title from his first published serious poem, "Sonnet for a Writer": "To stray across my own mind's half-hewn stone/And chisel in the dark, in hopes to cast/A fragment of our common self, my own. . . ."

with his career's central purpose, is to remind those who would claim "Them old slaves ain't none of me" that they must possess the heritage of their fathers "and theirs before them/back to the one/ who held the vomit tight/against his teeth," because the survival and identity they seek depend upon it as understanding depends upon pain.

The closing poems of *Chisel* express a mature acceptance of life's trials and incongruities. They are poems which only a poet come painfully to terms could write. In "Three Chores, One Country Day," a long story of apprenticeship to "dank Necessity," he ends thus:

It takes me all my life and all my strength
to do three chores:
to slop these hogs despite the boar,
find beauty down in barnyard lore,
and claim for love some patches on the grass.

In the final poem of the book, "He Shall Be Nameless," there is still another acceptance of man's role:

the business of a man
is voyaging far from childhood sweets,
flowering new transactions shore by shore,
becoming captain, crew, and weathered sail. . . .

Such a faith seems a fitting product of the poet's life.

After completion of *A Chisel in the Dark*, Emanuel remained in Europe, living in Paris, but traveling elsewhere to read his work and to visit new countries. From 1981 to 1982, he completed *A Poet's Mind* (1983), edited by Jean McConochie, an anthology of some of his poems with text and exercises, for use by foreign students of English. In 1982, he returned to New York and CCNY to teach out the years required for his retirement. While there, his next collection, *The Broken Bowl* (*New and Uncollected Poems*) (1983), was published by Lotus Press. The composition dates of the poems range from 1946 to 1982 (the majority are new). Among the poems are examples of familiar motifs: tributes, travel scenes, celebrations of children and innocence, everyday events lucidly depicted, terrors remembered and traditions revered. The title poem of the book illustrates a poetic progression typical of Emanuel's style: a simple event in the present triggers a memory, and the memory expands until, interrupted by another simple event in the present, it yields a present made richer, more deeply emotional, by the remembered dimensions of the past. A grandmother of eighty recalls from

Emanuel, Christmas 1984 on the grounds of "Le Barry," "the country home of friends in . . . southwestern France, where I have written much poetry since 1972"

her dishwashing sink the pain and loss of her childhood. The broken bowl that triggers her memory becomes the emblem of her life, but she is recalled from the dark knowledge of the past by the innocent remarks of her granddaughter. The grandmother turns to the innocent claim on her attention and wipes away "the thought/of some old splendid thing,/now finished,/unbroken/in its time."

While he taught at City College and awaited the publication of *The Broken Bowl*, the poet was himself recalled to a part of his past that had slipped away. His son Jimmy, to whom he had written early poems of joy and celebration of youth, but from whom he had been estranged since his divorce, had experienced as an adult a period of drug dependency. The poet, returning from a vacation in January 1983, learned that his son, anguished by his severe brutalization by San Diego police, had committed suicide. With the company and support of Marie-France, Emanuel taught classes and began to assemble his literary papers for a permanent library collection. He retired from CCNY at the end of 1983.

Now living in France, "earth-citizen" Emanuel is able to exercise his first loyalty to poetry, "the ultimate expression of an individual's appreciation of human life."

Interviews:

Houston A. Baker, Jr., *Road Apple Review,* 3 (Winter 1971-1972): 24-30;

Tape recorded interviews for archival collections: Fisk University (Nashville); Hatch-Billops Collection (New York).

References:

Houston A. Baker, Jr., *Contemporary Poets* (New York: St. Martin's, 1980);

Marvin Holdt, "James A. Emanuel: Black Man Abroad," *Black American Literature Forum,* 13 (Fall 1979): 79-85;

Ann Semel and Kathleen Mullen, *Black American Poetry: A Critical Commentary* (New York: Monarch Press, 1977).

Papers:

The collection at the Jay B. Hubbell Center for American Literary Historiography, Duke University, Durham, North Carolina, among other items, includes a 458-page manuscript autobiography, with photos, entitled "Snowflakes and Steel: My Life as a Poet, 1971-1980."

Mari Evans

(16 July 1923-   )

Wallace R. Peppers

University of North Carolina at Chapel Hill

BOOKS: *Where Is All The Music?* (London: Paul Breman, 1968);

I Am A Black Woman (New York: Morrow, 1970);

JD (Garden City: Doubleday, 1973);

I Look at Me! (Chicago: Third World Press, 1973);

Rap Stories (Chicago: Third World Press, 1973);

Singing Black (Indianapolis: Reed Publishing Company, 1976);

Jim Flying High (Garden City: Doubleday, 1979);

Whisper (Berkeley: University of California Center for African American Studies, 1979);

Nightstar: 1973-1978 (Los Angeles: Center for Afro-American Studies, UCLA, 1981).

PLAY PRODUCTIONS: *River of My Song,* Indianapolis, Lilly Theatre, Childrens' Museum, 1977; Chicago, Northeastern Illinois University, Center for Inner City Studies, 1977;

Eyes (Adapted from Zora Neale Hurston's *Their Eyes Were Watching God*), New York, Richard Allen Cultural Center, 1979; Cleveland, Karamu Theatre of the Performing Arts, March-April 1982.

OTHER: James A. Emanuel and Theodore L. Gross, eds., *Dark Symphony: Negro Literature in America,* includes poems by Evans (New York: Free Press, 1968);

Abraham Chapman, ed., *Black Voices: An Anthology of Afro-American Literature,* includes poems by Evans (New York: New American Library, 1968);

Anita Dore, ed., *The Premier Book of Major Poets: An Anthology,* includes poems by Evans (Greenwich, Conn.: Fawcett Publications, 1970);

Edna Johnson, ed., *Anthology of Children's Literature,* 4th edition, includes poems by Evans (Boston: Houghton Mifflin, 1970);

Alan Lomax and Raoul Abdul, eds., *3000 Years of Black Poetry: An Anthology,* includes poems by Evans (New York: Dodd, Mead, 1970);

Richard A. Long and Eugenia Collier, eds., *Afro-American Writing: An Anthology of Prose and Poetry,* includes poems by Evans (New York: New York University Press, 1972);

Chapman, ed., *New Black Voices: An Anthology of Contemporary Afro-American Literature,* includes poems by Evans (New York: New American Library, 1972);

Raoul Abdul, ed., *The Magic of Black Poetry,* includes

poems by Evans (New York: Dodd, Mead, 1972);

Stephen Henderson, *Understanding the New Black Poetry: Black Speech and Music as Poetic References,* includes poems by Evans (New York: Morrow, 1973);

Arnold Adoff, ed., *Black Out Loud: An Anthology of Modern Poems by Black Americans,* includes poems by Evans (New York: Dell Publishing Company, 1975);

Black Women Writers (1950-1980): A Critical Evaluation, edited by Evans (Garden City: Anchor/ Doubleday, 1984).

PERIODICAL PUBLICATIONS:

FICTION

"Third Stop in Caraway Park," *Black World,* 26 (March 1975): 54-62.

NONFICTION

"In the Time of the Whirlwind: I'm With You," *Negro Digest,* 17 (May 1968): 31-36, 77-80;

"Blackness: A Definition," *Negro Digest,* 19 (November 1969): 19-21;

"Contemporary Black Literature," *Black World,* 19 (June 1970): 4, 93-94;

"Behind the Green Door," as E. Reed, *Black Enterprise,* 7 (February 1977): 27-32;

"The Nature and Methodology of Colonization and Its Relationship to Creativity: A Systems Approach," *Black Books Bulletin,* 6 (August 1979): 10-17;

"Decolonization as Goal; Political Writing as Device," *First World,* 2 (November 1979): 34-39.

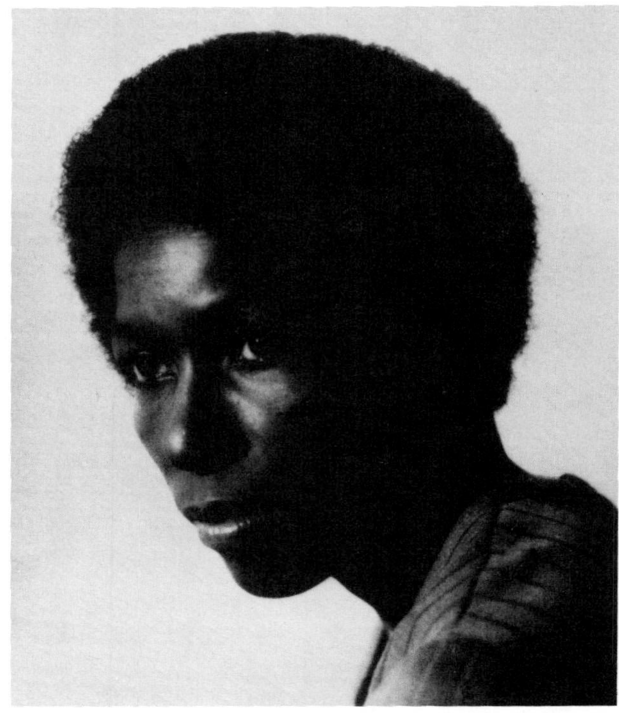

Mari Evans (courtesy Schomburg Center for Research in Black Culture, The New York Public Library, Astor, Lenox, and Tilden Foundations)

Mari Evans has become as much of a household name in the 1980s as Nikki Giovanni was in the 1960s. Her volumes of poetry, her books for adolescents, her work for television and other media, and her recently published volume on black women writers between 1950 and 1980 ensure her a lasting place among those who have made significant contributions to Afro-American life and culture. Teachers and scholars initially focused their attention on Evans in 1970 when *I Am A Black Woman* was published. The volume heralded the arrival of a poet who took her subject matter from the black community, and who celebrated its triumphs, especially the focus on the beauty of blackness that characterized the black arts and civil rights movements, and who would mourn its losses, especially the deaths of Martin Luther King, Jr. and Malcolm X. Identified through subject matter and stylistic experimentation with the poets of the 1960s, Evans has continued, through television, recordings, radio, play productions, and lectures, to illustrate her commitment to black arts and black people.

Evans was born in Toledo, Ohio, on 16 July 1923. She says that "no single entity really influenced" her life as did her father, who saved her "first printed story, a fourth-grade effort accepted by the school paper, and carefully noted on it the date, our home address, and his own proud comment." That tribute to her father appears in the essay "My Father's Passage," which is included in *Black Women Writers (1950-1980): A Critical Evaluation* (1984); Evans notes that her father had died two years before the writing of the essay.

After attending public school in Toledo, Evans enrolled at the University of Toledo where she studied fashion design, a profession that did not hold her interest for long. Although she had intentions of writing, she did not consciously decide to be a poet. "I drifted into poetry thought by thought," she writes; "it was never intentional."

Evans has combined her interest in poetry with an extended career in academia and other areas of community and professional life. She has taught at various universities, beginning in 1969 when she spent a year as instructor in African-

American literature and writer-in-residence at Indiana University/Purdue. From 1970 through 1978, Evans was assistant professor and writer-in-residence at Indiana University, Bloomington; from 1972 until 1973, she combined her Indiana job with an appointment as visiting assistant professor at Northwestern University. Her academic career continued with visiting assistant professor appointments at Purdue University (1978 to 1980); at Washington University in St. Louis (1980); and at Cornell University's Africana Studies and Research Center (1981 to 1984); she was also designated distinguished writer while at Cornell. Evans is currently associate professor and writer-in-residence at the State University of New York at Albany.

Her diverse, nonacademic career includes a five-year stint as producer, writer, and director of the highly acclaimed television program *The Black Experience*, at WTTV, Channel 4, Indianapolis (1968-1973); consultancies with the National Endowment for the Arts (1969-1970) and the Bobbs-Merrill Publishing Company (1978-1983); director of the Literary Advisory Panel for the Indiana Arts Commission (1976-1977); and membership on the board of directors of the First World Foundation.

Though Evans is reticent about providing information about her life, she does indicate that she is divorced and the mother of two sons, both of whom are now adults. She has been active in community affairs, serving as a choir director, as a long-term member of the board of management of the Fall Creek Parkway YMCA, and as a board member of the Indiana Corrections Code Commission. These activities are a testament to her firm belief that artists must be involved in the community.

Evans writes across four genres: poetry, dramatic literature, the essay, and short fiction; but she has found her finest voice in the writing of poetry. In addition to her four volumes of published poetry, she has produced six juvenile texts, five plays (the choreographed version of two of her plays, *A Hand Is on the Gate* and *Walk Together Children*, have had successful off-Broadway runs), numerous critical essays, and a short story. She has a novel in progress. Her work has appeared in over thirty textbooks and a variety of languages, including German, Swedish, French, and Dutch, as well as in the standard British and American editions.

Evans's development as a technically skilled artist with a strong social commitment and a marked clarity of poetic vision can be observed in three of her volumes of poetry: *Where Is All The Music?* (1968), *I Am A Black Woman* (1970), and *Nightstar: 1973-1978* (1981). Her first book of poems, *Where Is All The Music?*, barely suggests Evans's eventual concern for social relevancy; of the twenty-four poems in *Where Is All The Music?*, only three—"The Alarm Clock," "Black jam for dr negro," and "Who can be born black"—treat themes that are incontrovertibly "activist." However, even in these three poems, our primary interest is not thematic; rather, these pieces are significant because of the well-crafted first person personae, effective linguistic devices, apt diction, and strong characterizations.

"The Alarm Clock," for example, presents a persona who tells of being awakened quite suddenly by the alarm clock. The jolt from the clock reminds him of another jolt, a sadder and crueler awakening when a waiter denied him service at a public restaurant. Both jolts are sources of considerable distress, and this distress is certainly the thematic focus of the poem. However, it is the poem's simple and accurate diction that sustains and heightens it. "Alarm Clock/sure sound/loud/this mornin'," the speaker says:

remind me of the time
I sat down
in a drug store
with my mind
a way far off

The language, particularly the clear syntax, makes the poem eminently readable. The colloquial use of the verbs "remind" and "sound" and the expression "a way far off" have the effect of enhancing the sense of realism of the speaker and the poem. However, Evans does not overload the poem with excessive dialect. The speaker does not say, for example, "sho" for "sure" or "sto" for "store."

Evans presents a more fully delineated character in another early poem of social relevancy, "Black jam for dr negro." The poem's thematic focus is the speaker's rebellion against adopting what he views as middle-class social affectations. He prefers "his natural self." The speaker realizes that his style of speech and the casual character of his general demeanor embarrass his companion, a person greatly concerned with social appearances, and this realization sets up the dramatic verbal confrontation in which the speaker demonstrates his superior mind and firmer grasp of social reality. The companion never responds, but the reader is assured of his humiliation.

"Black jam for dr negro," is a poem with a clearly discernable social message, but the chief poetic accomplishment is technical. Through adept

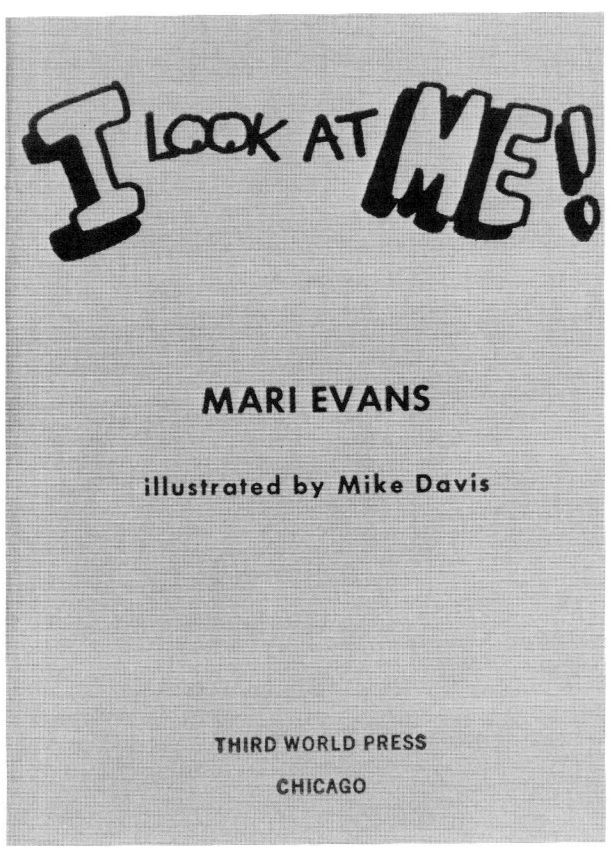

Cover for Evans's 1974 reader for two-year-olds

choice of language and the technique of creating line breaks in counterpoint to natural syntax, Evans effectively suggests the rhythmic speaking style of the persona and creates a tension between form and content. These nine lines contain five "rest" positions, in which punctuation would usually appear, for example, after the words "afro," "down," "thang," "first," and "up."

> Pullin me in off the corner to wash my face an
> cut my afro turn
> my collar
> down
> when that aint my
> thang I
> walk heels first
> nose round an tilted
> up

Evans uses this technique throughout the thirty-six line poem. It is an interesting method of poetic construction and one to which Evans returns in *I Am A Black Woman* and *Nightstar*. The remaining poems of *Where Is All The Music?* do not prefigure the predominant thematic interests of the later Evans.

Her early, ambitious focus is primarily twofold: to record the emotional vicissitudes of the individual soul; and to document the difficult, but necessary, struggle to form meaningful human relationships. These lines of grief and personal loss are from "I can no longer sing": "the fluid beauty/which once fled my soul/to hang quicksilvered/in the mote-filled/air/has gone." The individual in conflict is recorded in "Conflict": "I know with pain/the Me that/is, and I/inbreathe/this anguish deep/upon my heart." The individual in control is recorded in "The Silver Cell": "I have/never been contained/except I made/the prison, nor/known a chain/except those forged/by me." In "Here . . . hold my hand," Evans addresses one's need for human closeness, even in silence: "here/hold my hand./since/there is nothing/we can/say." The theme is repeated in "Marrow of my bone": "Fondle me/caress/cradle/me/teach me there/is someone." Occasionally, Evans uses comedy to advance this very serious theme:

> Where have you gone
> with your confident
> walk your
> crooked smile the
> rent money
> in one pocket and
> my heart
> in another . . .

The concern with problems of the individual is a pervasive theme in *Where Is All The Music?*, but with *I Am A Black Woman*, the reader becomes aware of Evans's social awakening. "I am a black woman," she says in the poem from which the volume takes its title: "Look/on me and be/renewed." The rhythm and phrasing are reminiscent of a line from Shelley's "Ozymandias": "Look on my works, ye Mighty and despair!" This romantic inverted echo reminds the reader of Evans's earlier poems, but in this instance, the individual struggle has a broader significance. The poet chooses a public persona to work through her understanding of what it means to be black in the Western world, and she hopes to inspire others through their witnessing her quest. The evidence for this broadened perspective can be found in the poem itself:

> I lost Nat's swinging body in a rain of tears
> and heard my son scream all the way from Anzio

It is evident that the pronominal references are meant to be symbolic—neither the poet nor the persona has seen Nat's body or had a son in Anzio—of a more universal black experience.

In her effort to move from the treatment of strictly individual concerns in her poetry to a treatment of themes of wider community interest, in *I Am A Black Woman,* Evans includes a number of poems the personae and the settings of which are well-known. Often referred to as domestic poems, these poems are about the women of the community, black women. "When in Rome," "7:25 Trolley," and "BeAtrice Does the Dinner" use strong visual imagery and suggestive language to create recognizable characters engaged in believable activities. This realism is achieved not so much through a reliance on the power of the imagination, but rather through the poet's sure knowledge of the subjects and the setting. One of the most enduring domestic images in all of *I Am A Black Woman* is of little Theodore, who, tiring of the suffocating isolation of his aunt's home, executes a daring "Escape," the poem's title. Theodore opened the screen door . . .

> and ran ran ran ran ran ran ran
> ran ran ran ran ran
> ran ran ran ran ran
> it
> took seven
> Other Kids
> to catch him:
> gently—for
> they greatly admired
> his defiance

The poem's appeal is directly related to the simplicity of language and the familiarity of the character.

The poems of *I Am A Black Woman* raise serious issues. "The Great Civil Rights Law A.D. 1964" addresses the question of the effectiveness of legislation designed to improve the quality of life in the community. "The Emancipation Of George Hector (a Colored Turtle)" speaks of the problem of political and social diversity in the community. In addition, there are the poems of exhortation, "Speak the Truth to the People," for instance, and moving political monologues in the spirit of "The Rebel" and "The Insurgent."

Nightstar, Evans's most recent volume of poetry, shows a fully matured dedication to the community. In the earlier poems, she had searched for an effective and appropriate role for artists and, in this volume, she presents her findings. In "once again the poets," Evans suggests that poets committed to social realism have four responsibilities: to listen, watch, warn, and tell. She believes the very best of the committed poets attempt all four, but Evans says that the poet who takes on even one of these responsibilities makes an important contribution to the survival and development of the community.

Front cover for a lecture brochure

According to Evans, authentic voices of the community are what committed poets listen for; voices that tell the stories of lives; voices that are sometimes brutal or angry, confused or loving, yet real. Though the poet is a careful, attentive listener ever attuned to meaningful shifts in nuances, Evans understands, too, that listening is not enough. Poets must also keep an analytical eye on the events of the community. This constant vigil provides the empirical base from which an artist makes generalizations about the nature, structure, function, and meaning of community life, as well as the direction of important social and cultural changes. But most importantly, a poet's watch provides the high ground from which he or she may shout warnings. Evans understands the poet's duty to warn the people of impending danger as a critical responsibility of the artist who is politically responsible.

Having the responsibility to warn the people leads quite naturally to the fourth and final poetic duty of the committed artist: a poet must tell. This special telling is distinguished from the more prosaic, factually detailed recording of the historian. For the poet, language is the tool for freezing the insight, arresting the message, highlighting the lesson. The use of language in this way is a use for which historians have little patience or time. Evans has said more specifically: "I insist that Black poetry, Black literature if you will, be evaluated stylistically for its imagery, its metaphor, description, onomatopoeia, its polyrhythms, its rhetoric. . . . My primary goal is to command the reader's attention. I understand I have to make the most of the first few seconds his or her eye touches my material. Therefore, for me, the poem is structure and style as well as theme and content; I require something of my poems visually as well as rhetorically. I work as hard at how the poem 'looks' as at crafting; indeed, for me the two are synonymous."

The artist is preeminently a teacher who perfects his or her technical skills to find the most effective vehicle for the message. It is this special poetic telling to the people, and especially to the young people of the community, that is an important requirement of the committed, dedicated, serious artist.

In *Where Is All The Music?*, Evans began developing the technical apparatus she would need as a poet. In *I Am A Black Woman,* she discovered the effectiveness of the domestic scene. Now, in *Nightstar,* she has formulated a creed. This volume shows her confidence as well, and she continues to fashion memorable lines: "I was not really/left behind/my face my eyes/part of my smile remained," Evans says in "I was not really left behind." In *Nightstar,* the domestic scenes are more closely related to the folk-life of the community; for example, in the poems reminiscent of the Frankie and Johnny ballads, "One More Black Belt Gone" and "The Street

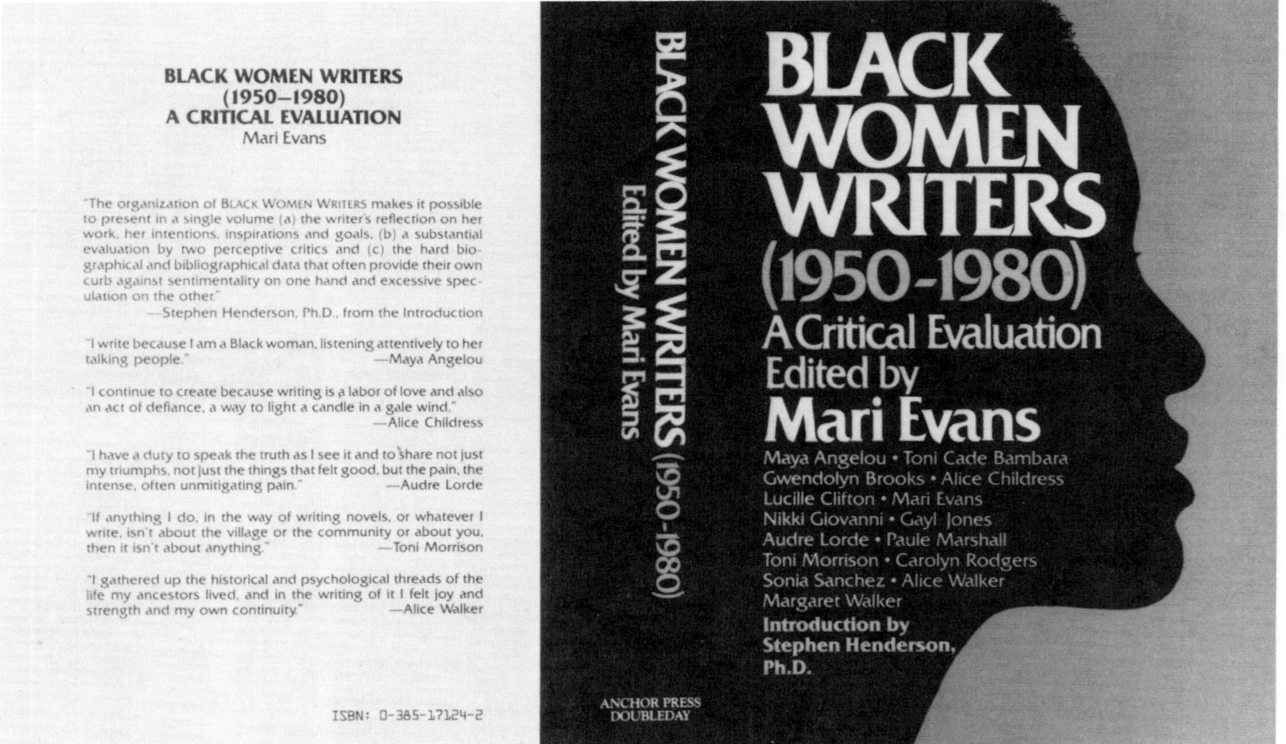

Dust jacket for Evans's 1984 critical history of fifteen contemporary authors

Lady," as well as in numerous celebrations of the blues and blues musicians, "Blues in B♭," "Black Queen Blues," and "Cellblock Blues." But the principal focus of *Nightstar* is the celebration of community heroes as in the Nicodemus poems, the Africa-centered Daufuskie poems, and the poems dedicated to lesser-known community personalities, "Oriki: For James Mark Essex and the Others," for example.

During her career, Mari Evans has received more honors and awards than can be numerated here. She received a John Hay Whitney Fellowship in 1965, a Woodrow Wilson Grant in 1968, and an award in 1970 for the Most Distinguished Book of Poetry by an Indiana Writer. She was awarded an honorary degree from Marion College in 1975, an Outstanding Woman of the Year Award (Bloomington, Indiana, 1976), and a National Endowment of the Arts Creative Writing Award (1981 to 1982). She has also been a fellow at the MacDowell Colony in Peterborough, New Hampshire (1975).

Mari Evans is a member of the community of black writers for whom writing has come to be an expression of a personal as well as a social responsibility. In discharging her personal responsibility, Evans creates work that is original and that enriches the cultural life of the community. She understands her responsibility as a solemn duty to create works that analyze, if not suggest solutions to the economic, political, and cultural issues facing the community. For Evans, it is a question of being faithful to a commitment to bear witness in difficult times. It is not a burdensome responsibility. After all, in her own words,

> Who
> can be born
> black
> and not exult!

Julia Fields

(January 1938-)

Mary Williams Burger
Tennessee State University

BOOKS: *Poems* (Millbrook, N.Y.: Kriya Press, 1968);

East of Moonlight (Charlotte, N.C.: Red Clay Books, 1973);

A Summoning, A Shining (Scotland Neck, N.C., 1976);

Slow Coins (Washington, D.C.: Three Continents Press, 1981).

PLAY PRODUCTION: *All Day Tomorrow*, Knoxville, Tenn., Knoxville College Drama Workshop, 1966.

OTHER: R. Baird Shuman, ed., *Nine Black Poets*, includes poems by Fields (Durham, N.C.: Moore Publishing Company, 1968), pp. 66-79.

PERIODICAL PUBLICATIONS:

POETRY

"For Poets," *Negro Digest*, 14 (September 1965): 60;

"Georgia Douglas Johnson," *Negro Digest*, 15 (October 1966): 48;

"Boxer," *Negro Digest*, 16 (February 1967): 48;

"Poem," *Negro Digest*, 17 (September/October 1968): 62-64;

"Three Poems—Seizing, Big Momma, The Policeman," *Black World*, 21 (September 1972): 46-48;

"Spring," *Black World*, 23 (September 1974): 76-77;

"Jonah's Wail," *Black World*, 23 (May 1974): 53;

"Alabama Suite—The Letter X, Sin, Mary, Art, I Loves a Wig," *Black World*, 24 (February 1975): 41-47;

"Thoughts Is What You Asked For," *Callaloo*, 4 (October 1978): 52;

"Mr. Tut's House: A Recollection," *First World*, 2 (1979): 38-39.

FICTION

"Ten to Seven," *Negro Digest*, 15 (July 1966): 79-81;

"Not Your Singing Dancing Spade," *Negro Digest*, 16 (February 1967): 54-59;

"The Hypochondriac," *Negro Digest*, 17 (July 1968): 61-65;

"No Great Honor," *Black World*, 19 (June 1970): 66-70;

"The Plot To Bring Back Dunking," *Black World*, 22 (August 1973): 64-71;

"August Heat," *Callaloo*, 4 (October 1978): 37-45.

NONFICTION

"The Green of Langston's Ivy," *Negro Digest*, 16 (September 1967): 58-59.

Julia Fields

Julia Fields emerged as a poet and creative writer in the 1960s, but her works are seldom identified with the themes of social turmoil, the bold language of racial confrontation, the defiant stance of black cultural separatism, and the daring iconoclastic artistic forms that marked the black arts movement and dominated the writings of other young black poets of the era. Fields, nevertheless, is an important representative of the cultural and artistic renaissance that gave birth to her writings, not only because her poems and short stories probe the political, social, and moral status of black people, but because they are saturated with their authentic language, sensibilities, values, rituals, and myths. Against a background of surging and resurging black consciousness and aesthetics, her works capture and reflect the folk spirit in black life, shatter the illusions of history, and demystify sacred areas of Southern life and black experience; she liberates, therefore, the feelings, mind, and spirit of her readers and audiences no less than her more stridently militant peers. In a poem from *Slow Coins* (1981) entitled "East of Moonlight," Fields has written,

> in the space between wars
> i wish to tell some stories to the young
> and i wish to make vivid again the memory
> of the old, to speak with farmers who are
> holy men, no quack farmers but those poets
> who kneel in the dust and shell it through
> their fingers. . . .

She is indeed an artist who tells stories, recording in poetic form what she has observed and known of her people's time and place in history.

Julia Fields grew up in Perry County, Alabama, in the large family of Maggie and Winston Fields, variously described as a preacher, farmer, and storekeeper. Fields spent her childhood years, it has been noted, in streams and wildflowers. She was a shepherdess; she picked cotton, read books, wrote poems, and painted in watercolors, nurturing, no doubt, the searching, visual quality which permeates her writing. There is also music in her background. Although she was not allowed to listen to rhythm and blues on the radio, she heard the music of the church every Sunday and Wednesday, and its strong, vibrant movement is discernible in her poetry and prose.

School for Fields intermingled with jobs such as washing dishes, peddling vegetables, waiting tables, and working in a factory. After graduating from Robert C. Hatch High School in Uniontown, Alabama, she went away to the "staid Presbyterian walls" of Knoxville College in Tennessee, where she graduated with a B.S. degree in 1961. While she was a student, majoring in English and acting in campus plays, Dr. Rosey E. Pool visited her campus and, in 1962, published two of Fields's poems in an anthology of black literature entitled *Beyond the Blues*. These poems, "I Heard a Young Man Saying" and "Madness One Monday Evening," were the first of Fields's works to appear in a nationally distributed publication. "I Heard a Young Man Saying" received favorable responses, and it was republished in several journals and as a broadside in 1967 by Broadside Press in Detroit.

For several years after her graduation from Knoxville College, Julia Fields taught at Westfield High School in Birmingham; but, she commented in *Beyond the Blues,* "I have one ambition: to be a poet." Growing and developing in her craft, she spent a brief period in New York and a summer in residence at the Bread Loaf Writers' Conference at Middlebury College, Vermont (she received the M.A. in English from the Bread Loaf School in 1972). She also traveled to England and Scotland to attend the University of Edinburgh in the summer of 1963.

With Dr. Pool's encouragement, Fields sent some of her poems to Langston Hughes. His positive response and encouragement laid the foundation for a continuing influence on her and her writing. In "The Green of Langston's Ivy," she describes Hughes as a "beautiful, brilliant and loving man who continued to help the younger poets even through the political discrediting and over the so-called gulf of generations." In the same essay, written in tribute to Hughes following his death in 1967, she recalls her first encounter with the poet several years earlier at a party to celebrate his acceptance of the Spingarn Award. When he asked her what she was drinking, she recalls, "having come recently from the Black Belt [to New York] and being in complete awe of SIN, I said 'coca cola.' He looked at me in his smiling manner and replied, 'A writer can't make it on coca cola.' " Fields recognized and clearly never forgot the impact of seriousness imbedded in the humor of his remark. Like Langston Hughes, she learned to convey seriousness in humor and to create the "shocks of defiance" that she also had admired in his poetry since her days at Knoxville College when she read his poems to a room full of her friends far into the night.

In 1964, the two poems which had been published in *Beyond the Blues* appeared in Hughes's anthology, *New Negro Poets, USA,* firmly establishing Julia Fields's place as a young black poet to be acknowledged, even if she was not applauded. Indeed, Julia Fields did not receive high critical acclaim or enjoy widespread popularity at this early point in her career, but her works did begin to appear regularly in the journals of black literature and culture, and in most of the anthologies that were published after Pool's and Hughes's pioneering collections of the works of young black poets. By the time she had published her first thin volume of poems in 1968, the year in which she also received a grant from the National Endowment for the Arts, two poems under the heading, "Poems: Birmingham 1962-1964" had been published in *Massachusetts Review* and *Negro Digest* (1965); and the first of her short stories to be published, "Ten to Seven," had also appeared in *Negro Digest* (1966). It was followed in 1967 by "Boxer," a poem on and in Muhammad Ali's proud and defiant style; and a short story entitled, "Not Your Singing Dancing Spade," which concerns the identity crisis of a black performer who has been very successful in the American mainstream. The personas and narrators of these works introduce the questioning mood in Fields's poems and stories, and reveal the author's attempt to "travel behind the eyes" of her heroes into their consciousness to explain the changing land and people in the South, the effects of the civil rights and cultural movements on black folks and, no doubt due partly to her brief sojourn in New York, the effects of urbanization on black people.

During the last half of the 1960s, two poets whom Fields admired—Georgia Douglas Johnson and Langston Hughes—died, as well as several black political leaders including Malcolm X and Martin Luther King, Jr. Her poems written in tribute to them are poignant expressions of sadness and of the spirit and quality she admired in each. In the "Georgia Douglas Johnson" poem, the qualities seem to be vibrant color and detail. In "Poet," written on Hughes's death and included in the September, 1967 edition of *Negro Digest* dedicated to the poet, it is integrity, or the certainty that "the heart of the poet is not for sale." In another tribute, "Langston Hughes," published in R. Baird Shuman's *Nine Black Poets,* the spirit admired is the "pure poet with the loving heart." Her poems eulogizing Malcolm X and Martin Luther King, Jr. are also tributes to the ideals they dared to represent. In the King poem, which is actually for poets, she remembers Malcolm, Mack (Parker), Medgar (Evers), and then Martin as "One dangerous dreamer gone"; and calls for an end to poets writing eulogies, questioning their effectiveness: "Is this what we—/The "Intellectuals"—/Offer as our share to the ages?" and "The Poets bend/Over sheets of paper/ . . . Their little eulogies/Eloquent, impotent/Polished, meaningless/One by one . . ./The dead are burying the dead."

According to the available evidence, Julia Fields has not written another eulogy. However, the last three years of the 1960s represent an important and productive period for Fields. She was one of nine "aspiring black poets" selected by R. Baird Shuman for inclusion in his anthology, *Nine Black Poets* (1968). Rating her as a well-disciplined writer, Shuman included twelve of Fields's poems in the collection, among them her tribute to Langston

Hughes, and "Aardvark," a poem about Malcolm X's method of self-education. Most of the poems that she contributed, however, are tender and sensitive impressions of her surroundings, prompting Shuman to compare her works to those of Anne Spencer and Emily Dickinson.

Even more significant in 1968 was the publication of her first book, *Poems,* which received generally positive responses from critics, most notably Don L. Lee (Haki Madhubuti). In *Dynamite Voices* (1971), he points out the "superbly satiric" poems in the book, such as "Lily Black Blonde From Wig Haven Among the Urinals," and Fields's very good use of ironic contrast in "Harry Rosenbloom I Give You Back Your Chauffeur and Your Grey Limousine," "Possessed of these cool skyscraper rows of," and "Testimonials." "Testimonials," which, along with "High on the Hog," continues to be among her best-crafted and highest-rated poems, is a dramatic narrative which effectively creates and communicates the distance between the views of Aunt Sally, who loves cleanliness so much that even the voodoo doll found among her belongings after her death is clean and new, and her young, modern niece who tells the story from an ironic yet warm and emphatic point of view, indicating that the young lady respects the tradition represented in her great aunt's ideals, and will carry it on—to an extent. "Testimonials" vividly reveals the morally strict traditions and rituals of rural Southern black folks, mocking them with reverence and humor in much the same way that Langston Hughes's Jesse B. Semple stories both celebrate and satirize black experience in the urban North.

The two qualities Fields admired in Langston Hughes's writing, seriousness in humor and shocks of defiance, are at the core of "High on the Hog" as well as "Testimonials." "High on the Hog" was first published in *Negro Digest* in 1969, and is generally acknowledged by critics to be a masterpiece of irony in its daring to defy the defiance of the 1960s movement. It points out that some aspects of ethnic culture (soul food, for instance) and political stances (revolution) are being over-romanticized by the upsurge of black consciousness, and the narrator, having experienced the real thing, has earned the right to do and eat whatever she likes.

Described in 1970 by R. Baird Shuman as a gifted poet who lives far-removed from the literary centers to which writers often flock, Julia Fields had, by this point in her life, returned to live in the South. She also had left high school teaching to serve as poet-in-residence at Miles College in Birmingham before moving to North Carolina, where she retained a residence until going to Washington, D.C. in the late 1970s. Throughout her career as a writer, and in addition to the diverse occupations she has assumed along the way, Fields has always been a teacher, spending brief periods as poet-in-residence, lecturer, or instructor at Miles College; Hampton Institute in Virginia; St. Augustine College in Raleigh, North Carolina; East Carolina University in Greenville, North Carolina; Howard University in Washington, D.C.; and the University of the District of Columbia. Her poems about teachers, however, are among the bitterest of her satires. With irony seldom relieved by humor, as it is in most other instances, and with the animal imagery one finds in her poems on fascism, racism, and violence against humans and the land, she has written poems about "make-believe humanists" who grave-monger and scramble visions into nightmares; about "soul-begging pseudo-scholars, prim intellectuals," who conspire to sell the hearts of Zora Neale Hurston and other black poets to make good appearances in public places; and about "the wretched old thing in a grey dress" and "the perverse old thing in a miniskirt" who confer upon others the meaning of John Donne's work.

Poems on the subject of parasitic scholars, however, are neither her major nor her most compelling works. Julia Fields is a highly complex woman who maintains a strong sense of individualism in her creative efforts. There is no evidence, for example, that she was ever a member of any of the poetry movements, workshop groups, or arts centers that flourished in the 1960s and 1970s, except the group that gathered around Georgia Douglas Johnson for her home-based workshops. Julia Fields read at black arts conferences and writers workshops and was, in 1979, a member of the First World Speakers/Lecturers Bureau as well as, according to its announcements, a founder of and consultant to the Learning School of the American Language, but she remains something of a loner. In a statement appearing in *Broadside Authors and Artists* (1974), Fields is quoted as saying, "I wish to work with other black artists so as to be able to use the themes (on the American 200th year celebration) either in my poems for musical compositions, paintings, dances, mime and songs . . . but since it is impossible to work with others in my isolation, I hope that I can at least share my work and dream with some college. But since colleges are dead to creativity . . . I hope that I can at least publish it for commercial reasons."

Julia Fields's works, like those of most black poets, have not received significant commercial reward, but she is unquestionably a versatile artist. She has written a full length play, *All Day Tomorrow,* which was produced and performed in the Knoxville College Drama Workshop in 1966 to benefit the school's alumni fund, and she has written fiction and poetry on many different subjects. Among them are poems and stories on the South, the environment, unemployment, war; the meaning of peace, the arms race, and women who will not let their sons grow up. Her subjects range from women who never felt someone's fingers being broken against their skulls, and women who lament the terror of the day, but always have a good word for the Lord, to women who want to die in a state of enviable cleanliness. She writes about gluttony; how black black really is; the deliverance through death of black heroes; poets who are not for sale; the encroachment of urbanization on the South; the necessary ritual in black folk life, particularly the religious life; and about nature, history, white folks, racism, violence, sin, love, death. As Mercedese Broussard notes in one of the few reviews of Fields's poetry, "Ms. Fields is not Julia one-note; she has many themes."

For the consistently superior quality and consciousness of her work, Julia Fields was awarded the Seventh Conrad Kent Rivers Memorial Fund Award in 1972 by the editors of *Negro Digest.* They cited in particular her poem, "High on the Hog," which she had read recently on a nationally televised program, "Soul," and "Not Your Singing Dancing Spade," a short story that has been included in three different publications, including *Black Fire: An Anthology of Afro-American Writing* (1968), considered by some to be the landmark text of the 1960s black arts movement. In reviewing the anthology, one critic rated Fields's story as less moving than another story in the collection, but as a provocative narrative which questions the general melting pot myth of America as a grey world with

Covers for Fields's 1973 book which ends with her definition of poetry as "a form of will. It is a determination to be in the world while giving to it and loving it. It's also a wishing after some kinds of beauty to be born."

room in it for all people to attain the American dream. It also searches very briefly through several specific myths, including the idea of black women as Caldonias and Sapphires; the feeling that black is an ugly color; and the distaste among some Negroes for the authentic songs, dances, and physical features, such as lips, hair, and noses of black people. The awakening of the hero to genuine pride in his ethnic heritage is provoked by his maid's declaration that "the first best beauty in the world is Black."

"Not Your Singing Dancing Spade" is the only one of Fields's short stories which, along with "How Black" and several other poems, directly probes the identity problem, a prevalent theme of the black arts movement. In Fields's poetry, the idea of self-love and pride in the color of one's skin is seldom treated in the specific, formulaic manner of "Not Your Singing Dancing Spade." More often, black consciousness and pride are underlying parts of the character's being, as they are for August Future in "The Plot to Bring Back Dunking" (1973), and for the people Fields portrays in poems such as "Priestess Aretha" and "Mrs. Rosa." When there is some confusion in the character's perspective, Fields often clothes the question of black pride in superb irony, mocking the old-fashioned values of the rural, usually older, black folk with reverence and humor, while probing into and exposing the illusory qualities in the socially progressive values of the younger, often urbanized blacks. "August Heat" (1978) and "The Common Is Versus the Common Ain't" (1981) are strong examples of this perspective, with Mrs. Carrie Vale and Mrs. Mellie Morris contrasted to the son and daughter of each, Mr. Ghit Vale from "Windy City" and Miss Annie Mae Morris from college. Mrs. Vale and Mrs. Morris, as well as their neighbors, Mr. Nelson and Brother Leroy, seem to know nothing about the contemporary political issues facing black people, but their attitudes and values are models of black tradition and they have no problems of identity and self-love. The point Fields makes in these stories is that the folk values of older people like Mrs. Vale provide strength, security, and continuity; and the younger ones who know this always come back to the source of these values, if only for a summer vacation.

Julia Fields's second volume of poetry, *East of Moonlight,* was published in 1973 by Red Clay Books in Charlotte, North Carolina. It includes many poems in the tradition of her earlier book, *Poems.* "By the Day Ladies," for instance, reflects the poet's great respect for the genuine folk spirit, for the ladies whose souls are deep in original human credence, who do not have time to "raise a yell," but have hearts primed for sacrificial fire. As in many of her works, the point is that in the fervor and romanticism of the movement, the true character and spirit of the people may be overlooked. *In Drumvoices* (1976), Eugene Redmond acknowledged the publication of *East of Moonlight* and other works by Julia Fields, and placed her among the few good black poets who voluntarily live in the South, noting her searching spirit and praising the "subtle dart, but direct power" that he finds in her poetry, especially earlier poems such as "High on the Hog." The "subtle dart" is a major technique in her poetry, for while Fields never sought to be revolutionary, she does seek to tell the truth, to get to the heart, in her own way, of black experience. As she had noted in response to a question on the black aesthetic posed to her and other black writers in 1968 by the editors of *Negro Digest,* "In the future, the only relevant literature will be that which has gone directly to the heart of Blackness."

Julia Fields received recognition and encouragement from several other poets during this period, particularly Robert Hayden, who had included her work in his 1967 anthology, *Kaleidoscope,* and Clarence Major, who cited her in *The Dark and Feeling* (1974) as one of several "particularly good" poets in his own age group, and as one of the best black women poets on the scene. Major further describes Fields as one of the most intellectually crisp poets of her generation, noting that her images are always sharp and strong.

A Summoning, A Shining, published in 1976 by Fields, in Scotland Neck, North Carolina, and dedicated to Hayden, Redmond and Majors, further established the poet's mastery of the "subtle dart" and sharp imagery, and illustrates the thematic power she often achieves by infusing an historical perspective into poems which are ostensibly impressions of her surroundings. The poetry in this volume is uneven, as reviewer Mercedese Broussard suggests in her references to the "minuses of mechanics," but it contains thoughtful and subtly complex works. In one of several "Small Songs to Moral Beauty" that Fields has written, an old building being torn down by "the boys on the yellow beasts" makes the poet wonder whether it is possible to save old buildings, or even an old woman or an old man—that is, to preserve history—unless one is a mythmaker. In another poem, "Great Buildings in Their Slumber," she notices that great old edifices do not sway and bend with the historical moments of the present such as bombings, suicides, wars, and assassinations, and are not bothered by bats, gulls, and tourists. However, a breeze sands

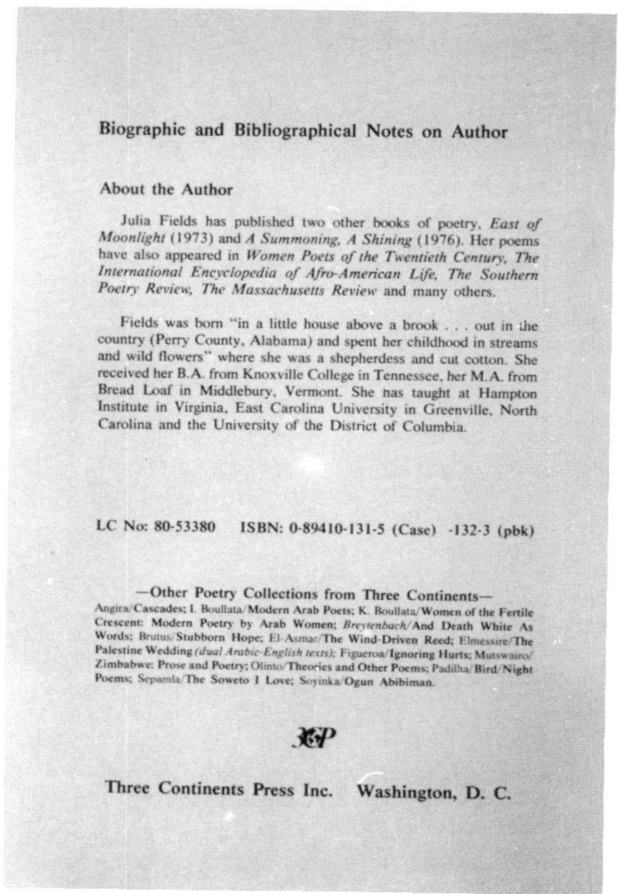

Biographic and Bibliographical Notes on Author

About the Author

Julia Fields has published two other books of poetry, *East of Moonlight* (1973) and *A Summoning, A Shining* (1976). Her poems have also appeared in *Women Poets of the Twentieth Century, The International Encyclopedia of Afro-American Life, The Southern Poetry Review, The Massachusetts Review* and many others.

Fields was born "in a little house above a brook . . . out in the country (Perry County, Alabama) and spent her childhood in streams and wild flowers" where she was a shepherdess and cut cotton. She received her B.A. from Knoxville College in Tennessee, her M.A. from Bread Loaf in Middlebury, Vermont. She has taught at Hampton Institute in Virginia, East Carolina University in Greenville, North Carolina and the University of the District of Columbia.

LC No: 80-53380 ISBN: 0-89410-131-5 (Case) -132-3 (pbk)

—Other Poetry Collections from Three Continents—
Angira/Cascades; I. Boullata/Modern Arab Poets; K. Boullata/Women of the Fertile Crescent: Modern Poetry by Arab Women; *Breytenbach*/And Death White As Words; Brutus/Stubborn Hope; El-Asmar/The Wind-Driven Reed; Elmessire/The Palestine Wedding *(dual Arabic-English texts)*; Figueroa/Ignoring Hurts; Mutswairo/Zimbabwe: Prose and Poetry; Olinto/Theories and Other Poems; Padilha/Bird/Night Poems; Sepamla/The Soweto I Love; Soyinka/Ogun Abibiman.

3CP

Three Continents Press Inc. Washington, D. C.

Covers for Fields's 1981 poetry collection which takes its title from her poem "Great Buildings in Their Slumber": "They sleep through the picturesque / cameos / of old women selling fish and gritty fruit / in quick streets / To whoever has slow coins."

the confident corners of a great building, and ruffles the fine essence of a grain of its stone. There is telling symbolism and irony in the small imperceptible act of nature which changes and disturbs the great old building while momentous events mean nothing.

"Mr. Tut's House: A Recollection," published in *First World* in 1979, is probably the best example of Fields's interest in the illusory nature and the mythical power of history, and of her ability to infuse a significant historical perspective into a contemporary event—in this case, the touring exhibition of the ancient Egyptian King Tutankhamen and her memory of a neighbor named Mr. Tut. "Mr. Tut's House: A Recollection" takes its readers not only back into the narrator's life when she was nine years old, but back into the deep reaches of her cultural history. It is a long, narrative, slightly mystical poem written in two parts. The first part offers vivid, visual details of the sights along the route to Uniontown, Alabama, in 1947, particularly Mr. Tut's house. Mr. Tut cut gravestones by hand. His house is remembered more clearly by the now-grown-up narrator than she remembers Mr. Tut, of whom no one talks anymore, and the stones, which also are no longer mentioned. Yet, despite the years and changes in industry and people, "Mr. Tut's house was there." Shifting to the 1977 exhibition of King Tut in Washington, D.C., the poet sees the golden death mask of the ancient king and recognizes his kinship to Mr. Tut of Uniontown, whose stare, she now remembers, was electric and yellow like the eyes of the mask, the symbol of the king's permanence, just as the house has given Mr. Tut continued life. The continuity between them and the poet's feeling of kinship to them ("My brother—you are older than I who am older than you") suggests the importance of history and the continuum of time that Broussard identified in Fields's earlier poetry in *A Summoning, A Shining.*

Julia Fields's finest volume of poetry and "prose poems," *Slow Coins*, was published in 1981 by Three Continents Press. It reprints several poems that have been cited frequently for their excellence, and others that are bound to be also; and it adds newer examples of the themes and techniques introduced and explored in her three earlier books. Divided into nine sections—Very Personal, People, The South, The North, The State and Science, Indians, Nature, Prose Poems and Other Poetry, and The Many Worlds We Wander Through—*Slow Coins* begins slowly and tenderly, touching with light dignity, sadness, or disdain, subjects close to the heart, and progressing to some of her most thoughtful works such as "East of Moonlight," "Eden ½ Mile," "New South," and several poems on inanimate symbols of Southern heroes and values—"Bronzes," "Bronze Horses in the Park," and "Lee." Also included in *Slow Coins* are several of Fields's poems on urbanized blacks, most of whom are women, except in "Black Super Bad From Down North," a poem in which North is really "Up South," and super bad people have rented cars and rented minds. Among the women whose conditions and values Fields sensitively explores are a woman of questionable sanity who eats rain; young and gifted prostitutes who stand in "two's and three's and four's like soft, lost birds" in "Vigil"; the affluent woman whose "orange hair and almost-pucci dress" are contrasted to the narrator's natural hair and skin; the "jolly, fat widows"; Anita who has a "swinging weekend father"; and Muriel who has endured so much—her factory job, the lonely violent streets, and the sneers and leers of her neighbor and her neighbor's husband—but who stands high, "because some things can't hardly make Miss Muriel cry." Fields's mastery of irony reaches an unquestionable peak of excellence in *Slow Coins*.

Retaining her tendency to clothe critical comment in irony, Julia Fields also uses detailed dramatic characterizations of people, places, and events in *Slow Coins* to explore the meaning and impact of history, and to reveal the folk heritage bequeathed to black people by the Southern environment and its older citizens—more, it is implied, than was given to them by the political fervor and the cultural renaissance of the 1960s and 1970s. Pursuant to the purpose stated in "East of Moonlight," Fields has said, "I travel to places behind their eyes to see the meaning of tomorrow." Suggesting a spiritual and moral purpose rather than a political one, she reveals the contradictions in sacred areas of our thoughts and rituals such as love in "Man, My Mate"; the South in "Mississippi Green or Something is Unfinished Here, Emmett Till"; and nature in "Green," "Birmingham," "Georgia Suite," and other poems in which the colors and forms of nature reflect the things that have happened in the South, and harsh images are used to "vomit back remembrances of the life on the land."

Fields at the time she wrote Slow Coins

Slow Coins, which must presently be considered Julia Fields's major work, contains another important element, although critics generally have not associated it with her. The black arts movement of the 1960s and 1970s gave us many, many poems and stories written in black dialect, but it would be difficult to find very many which surpass in authenticity and natural flow the Southern folk language in Fields's writing. From "Big Momma" (1972) to "Thoughts Is What You Asked For" (1978), and most of the testimonial and narrative poems in *Slow Coins*, the texture, rhythm, and idiom of oral black language are created, often without the dialect and without grotesque spellings and other typographical maneuvers which either caricature or completely miss the force and beauty of the language. In *Slow Coins*, "Shooting the Big Hookey" and "How Black" exemplify the poet's ability to capture the force and beauty of the language almost solely through the texture and movement created in the works. "How Black" is a poem which rhythmically recites some of the standard signifying tales passed among black people to make a very serious and, some might have said a decade earlier, revolutionary point. It defiantly (and humorously) exposes the myths and tales surrounding black skin color. At the same time, it reverses the meaning not only of the myths but of the (then) overexoticized quality of blackness. In fact, the narrator, who is black in theory and fact, is so black that her black is light—insight. Her confrontation with the myths and the new popularity of her color purges its negative image. In addition to its theme, the proud, sassy tone and the use of familiar folk materials give "How Black" its power and authenticity. "Shooting the Big Hookey" details the struggles of 76-year-old Mr. Taylow, who feels himself to be "in the way of fate," to carry out the business of old age with dignity, an important motif in Fields's testimonies of the old. "Shooting the Big Hookey" is a moving study in the psychology of old age fading to a stop, or shooting the biggest hookey of all—death. As in "How Black," this "prose poem," as she calls it, is written in vivid, unadorned detail and authentic language which retains, as history and art must, the dynamic cadences and idioms of the people and the times.

Julia Fields has said "the black experience seems the most intense experience in the modern world. It is better that black people write it ourselves. . . ." Quite simply, that is what she does, and will likely continue to do, but always from the perspective of history—present, past, and future—with shocks of defiance, darts of irony and superb satire. Her difference from many other contemporary poets, and therefore a major part of her significance to the times in which she writes, is that she sees a major and lasting dimension of the "intense black experience" in the memory of the old and in the farmers who kneel in the dust (i.e., people who are close to the earth); and she believes it is too early to celebrate.

References:

Leaonead P. Bailey, ed. *Broadside Authors and Artists* (Detroit: Broadside Press, 1974), p. 51;

"Black Writers' Views on Literary Lions and Values," *Negro Digest,* 17 (January 1968): 25;

Mercedese Broussard, "Blake's Bard," review of *A Summoning, A Shining, Callaloo,* 1 (December 1976): 60-62;

Don L. Lee, *Dynamite Voices: Black Poets of the 1960s* (Detroit: Broadside Press, 1971): 63-65;

Clarence Major, *The Dark and Feeling: Black American Writers and Their Work* (New York: The Third Press, 1974): 41-42;

Eugene Redmond, *Drumvoices: The Mission of Afro-American Poetry, A Critical History* (Garden City: Anchor/Doubleday, 1976).

Calvin Forbes

(6 May 1945-)

Robert A. Coles
Fordham University

BOOKS: *Blue Monday* (Middletown, Conn.: Wesleyan University Press, 1974);

From the Book of Shine (Providence, R.I.: Burning Deck Press, 1979; Copenhagen: Razorback Press, 1980).

OTHER: "Lullaby for Anne-Lucian," "Reading Walt Whitman," in *The Poetry of Black America: Anthology of the Twentieth Century,* edited by Arnold Adoff (New York: Harper & Row, 1972);

Abraham Chapman, ed., *New Black Voices,* includes poems by Forbes (New York: New American Library, 1972);

X. J. Kennedy, ed., *Messages: A Thematic Anthology of Poetry,* includes poem by Forbes (Boston: Little, Brown, 1973);

"Gabriel's Blues," in *The Poetry Anthology, 1912-1977,* edited by Daryl Hine and Joseph Parisi (New York: Houghton Mifflin, 1978);

Frank Stewart and John Unterecker, eds., *Poetry Hawaii: A Contemporary Anthology,* includes poems by Forbes (Hawaii: University Press of Hawaii, 1979);

Keith and Rosemarie Waldrop, eds., *A Century in Two Decades: A Burning Deck Anthology, 1961-1981,* includes poems by Forbes (Copenhagen: Burning Deck Press, 1982).

Since the publication of his collections of poems, *Blue Monday* (1974) and *From the Book of Shine* (1979), Calvin Forbes has emerged as one of the prominent black voices to have developed out of the 1970s. Commanding ever more critical attention, his is a new and original voice. Winner of a 1973 Bread Loaf Writers' Conference Fellowship, 1974 Fulbright Grant, 1982-1983 National Endowment for the Arts Fellowship, 1984 D.C. Commission on the Arts Fellowship, as well as other awards, Forbes creates a distinctive poetry that is both experimental and complex. He communicates a philosophy, indeed a highly moral philosophy, as well as the thoughts and emotions of a writer whose artistic ability and vision are still expanding.

Much has gone into the process that shaped Forbes's life and art. He was born on 6 May 1945 and raised in Newark, New Jersey, the seventh of eight children of Jacob and Mary Short Forbes. He attended public schools in Newark, matriculated for a short time at Rutgers University, and pursued creative writing at the New School for Social Research in New York City. At the New School, Forbes began to learn his craft and to grow intellectually by studying with poet Jose Garcia Villa and by reading the books he stacked while working at the New School and New York public libraries.

Forbes decided to broaden his education and knowledge by traveling. Heading west to see America, he hitchhiked throughout most of the states of the Union and lived briefly in Hawaii and Mexico. Despite having left his former school, family, and friends, Forbes found these years instrumental in his development as a serious writer. He now lived his art through a sense of commitment to the discipline, craft, and an honest vision of his experiences. During his travels, Forbes also wrote and published his first poems in *Poetry* (1968) and the *American Scholar* (1968). Later, a number of his poems appeared in an anthology of Hawaiian poetry.

Beginning in 1970, Forbes taught creative writing and Afro-American literature at Emerson College in Boston for three years. After he published *Blue Monday,* he left Emerson in order to accept an assistant professorship in English at Tufts University, Medford, Massachusetts. In 1974, he took a leave of absence from Tufts and, under the auspices of the Fulbright organization, lectured in Denmark, France, and England. Upon returning to America in 1975, he resumed his duties at Tufts until 1977, when, again, he departed to complete an MFA degree at Brown University, Providence, Rhode Island. In 1982-1983 Forbes was appointed guest lecturer in Afro-American literature at the University of the West Indies, Kingston, Jamaica. Currently he is teaching creative writing and poetry at Howard University, Washington, D.C.

Forbes's subjects are often universal and familiar. The poet Michael Harper notes that many of Forbes's poems are about "heroism, tradition, improvisation." But Forbes's treatment of such themes is often unconventional. For example, Forbes indeed treats the subject of heroism in such poems as "Blind Date with a Voice," in which "Shine met a girl named Glow who stole/The night from the moon." Such courage deserves to be noticed. And Forbes does write of tradition, specifically the traditions of the folk experience of black Americans. He writes of the so-called blues people, unashamed of expressing themselves; he writes of "fantasy people," whose "Shattered lives spread across centuries/Like crumbs thrown to pigeons." And he treats the theme of improvisation from the point of view of the poet who must improvise constantly when he reads to an unappreciative audience: "For a sentimental moment, the way Bo Jangles/Used to dance, I lift my big feet/And I do the poet's shuffle."

But he writes about other subjects as well, for example, Maoists and political hypocrites: "they See Mao/and wear pajamas, they land in Jersey/City and their blond comrades feed them." He sings, too, of the creative process which he celebrates in "Hope against Hope," a piece that expresses the hope of artistic creation surviving and transcending a hopeless universe. And Forbes articulates his private experiences: "there's no place to hide; the faster I pray/the slower I go"; his mother, "Pale as the familiar cream and tea, you/Float past history and into a cup"; his father, "you lost yourself/In the night gambling/With nothing to show"; his friends, lovers, and the home in which he was raised: "Come away from the streets where you/Claw your childhood out of the/sidewalk."

Probably the most striking quality of the poems in *Blue Monday* and, to a lesser extent, *From the Book of Shine,* is their metaphoric and synecdochical complexity, reminiscent of the work of John Donne and Gwendolyn Brooks. Forbes is skillful in the way he suggests double, and sometimes, triple layered meanings through tight control over

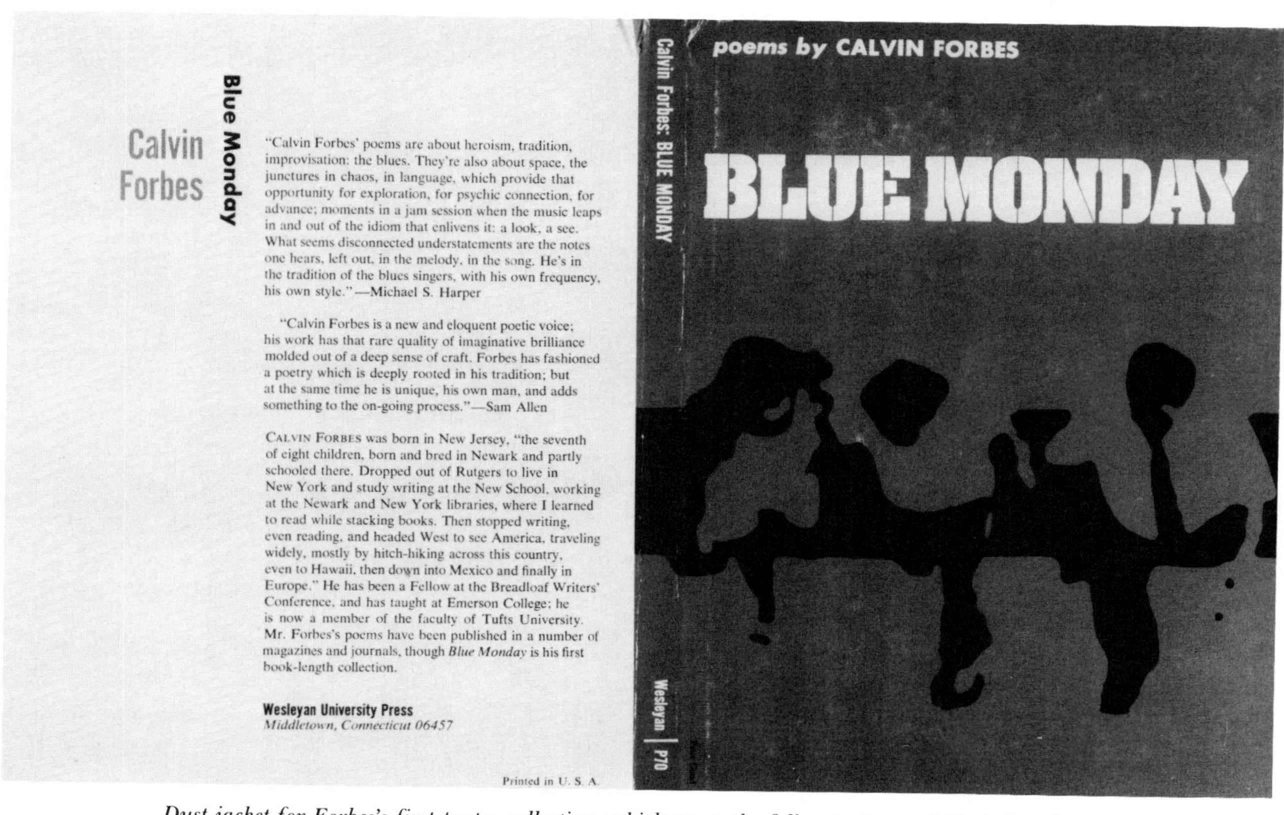

Dust jacket for Forbes's first poetry collection, which treats the folk experience of black Americans

simile and metaphor, both of which spark clear, powerful phrases and images. Forbes is a master of the figurative device of the conceit. He can take a single metaphor or simile and extend it by forming a multiple series of image clusters similar in meaning, yet different in the manner of their construction. And taking these clusters as a whole, within a single poem, Forbes works them into a unified pattern. In short, any single part becomes a synecdoche which implies the whole of the poem. The whole, in turn, can suggest the parts, as well as primary and secondary meanings which suffuse the entire work. Content, as a result, becomes integral and inseparable from form.

This highly experimental yet controlled structural approach is demonstrated in the poem "Outside the City," one of the least complex poems in which this figurative approach is used. The poem opens with the metaphor:

> The fields are darker than dimples
> Streaking in a curving line . . .
>
> On my side of the map mud softens
> Like a forgotten face; acres
>
> Of wheat bow like heads
>
> Of slaves . . .

"Fields," "mud softens," "acres of wheat" provide a visual setting of a countryside, which is compared with images of race and the memory of oppression: "darker than dimples," "a forgotten face," "heads of slaves." Forbes creates a pattern of metaphors, all of which extend the images of the observed countryside and the collective black experience.

Forbes continues this pattern through six stanzas. For instance, the countryside also includes a yard: "the yard's drying/Crust cracks like a spine"; "the fence/Rots like the hull we sailed/In"; and the mountains "look like/Scraped knuckles." The overall effect of these image clusters is to evoke a racial memory of the history which has placed the Afro-American into Euro-American mainstream. Ironically, Forbes strikes a contrast between a supposedly humane environment, "country," with a supposedly pernicious environment, "city." Here the traditional, associative roles of city and country are reversed.

In the poem "Europe," from *Blue Monday,* the central conceit is a chessboard upon which Europe manipulates and controls contemporary society: "The traditional pawn breaks/Castles, achieves early equality/And wins but his heart is empty." In the fablelike "Killer Blues," in the same volume, the central images are of animals: "Blackbird, blackbird, where's/ Your nest now that Mister Rat ate/ Your family. . . ." The blackbird suggests black America which is being feasted upon by Mister Rat, white America.

Forbes admits he has been influenced by John Donne, Gwendolyn Brooks, and Philip Larkin, all of whom he vigorously studied and whom he feels have aided in "my quest for form, control, and complexity." By no means does Forbes subscribe to imaginative excess and spontaneous bursts of emotion. Langston Hughes has also been an important influence on his work, particularly in the use of the blues tradition and the folkloric heritage of Afro-Americans.

Yet, one should not take the Hughes influence too far for there are some fundamental differences between the two poets. First, though they both spring from the blues tradition, Hughes often imposes a classical 4/4 measure, twelve-bar pattern, with an overall rhyme scheme of AAB on his blues poetry, as if the poem itself could almost represent a blues lyric in musical form. For example, in "Bound No'th Blues," Hughes writes:

> Goin' down the road, Lawd,
> Goin' down the road.
> Down the road, Lawd
> Way, way down the road.
> Got to find somebody
> To help me carry this load.

Here, Hughes expresses four beats to a line, where two lines represent a bar, three bars per stanza, and there are four stanzas in the entire poem. Notice, too, the rhyme scheme AA ("road," "road"), B ("load"). Again, this pattern is repeated in each of the remaining three stanzas.

Forbes, on the other hand, represents the mood and tone of blues rather than the structure of the blues lyric itself. In Forbes's blues pieces, and he has many of them, he reveals the bitter and tragic blues quality through such lines as:

> How many times have you put vaseline on
> Your face, the winter making you grey
>
> As a confederate uniform; and the wind
> Drawn tears on your face leaves a thin grey
> Line marching to your mouth. And you
> Wonder where the black went. . . .

Here, significantly, one notes a second important difference between Hughes and Forbes. That is to say, Forbes's vision, his mood and tone, is bleaker than Hughes's. Whether Hughes uses blues structure or representative voice, as in his Jesse B. Semple series in which Semple's comments and views about life and race represent similar views of "common" and "ordinary" blacks, Hughes always exudes humor along with the pain and hurt. Not so for Calvin Forbes. Even where Forbes's similarity to Hughes is strongest, in Forbes's Shine ("a black Everyman") and Hughes's Jesse B. Semple, Forbes displays no apparent sense of humor; hence, his vision is a more despairing one. Nevertheless, Hughes and Forbes are similar, despite Forbes's grim world, in that they both represent Afro-American reality from the juncture of race awareness and everyday experiences of black folks.

Forbes's poetry has appeared in journals such as: *The Yale Review, The American Scholar, Poetry Magazine, Black World, The Iowa Review, Prairie Schooner,* and others. He continues to write poetry, but is currently completing a novel he started in 1982 under an NEA fellowship.

Nikki Giovanni

(7 June 1943-   )

Mozella G. Mitchell
University of South Florida

See also the Giovanni entry in *DLB 5, American Poets Since World War II.*

BOOKS: *Black Feeling, Black Talk* (New York: Black Dialogue Press, 1967);
Black Judgement (Detroit: Broadside Press, 1968);
Black Feeling, Black Talk/Black Judgement (New York: Morrow, 1970);
Re: Creation (Detroit: Broadside Press, 1970);
Gemini: An Extended Autobiographical Statement on My First Twenty-Five Years of Being a Black Poet (Indianapolis: Bobbs-Merrill, 1971);
Spin a Soft Black Song Poems for Children (New York: Hill & Wang, 1971);
My House: Poems (New York: Morrow, 1972);
A Dialogue: James Baldwin and Nikki Giovanni (Philadelphia: Lippincott, 1973; London: Joseph, 1975);
Ego-Tripping and Other Poems for Young People (New York: Lawrence Hill, 1973);
A Poetic Equation: Conversations Between Nikki Giovanni and Margaret Walker (Washington, D.C.: Howard University Press, 1974);
The Women and the Men (New York: Morrow, 1975);
Cotton Candy on a Rainy Day (New York: Morrow, 1978);
Vacation Time: Poems for Children (New York: Morrow, 1980);
Those Who Ride the Night Winds (New York: Morrow, 1983).

RECORDINGS: *Truth Is On Its Way,* Right-On Records, 1971;
Like a Ripple On a Pond, NikTom, 1973;
The Way I Feel, Atlantic Records, 1974;
Legacies, Folkways Records, 1976;
The Reason I Like Chocolate, Folkways Records, 1976;
Cotton Candy on a Rainy Day, Folkways, 1978.

OTHER: *Night Comes Softly: An Anthology of Black Female Voices,* edited by Giovanni (Newark, N.J.: Medic Press, 1970).

PERIODICAL PUBLICATIONS: "Black Poems, Poseurs, and Power," *Negro Digest,* 18 (June 1969): 30-34;
"The Planet of Junior Brown," *Black World,* 21 (March 1972): 70-71.

Photograph by Yvette LeRoy (courtesy Schomburg Center for Research in Black Culture, the New York Public Library, Astor, Lenox and Tilden Foundations)

Nikki Giovanni is an important and extremely popular literary figure who came into prominence on the American scene as one of the most noted poets of the new black renaissance which began in the 1960s. Since that time she has grown tremendously from the open, aggressive, and explosive revolutionary tendencies that characterized her early verses to expressions of universal sensitivity, artistic beauty, tenderness, warmth, and depth. Accompanying this steady growth in artistic quality as a poet has been her attainment of wide popularity and acclaim as a lecturer in the black community and on college campuses around the country. Especially revered for her easy blending of curse-words into her most elegant speeches, she has become somewhat of a folk hero, and has been called the "Princess of Black Poetry." On her frequent speaking tours she attracts overflowing crowds. Addressing such a crowd at Wilberforce University in 1972, where she received an honorary Doctor of Humanities degree, she laughingly pointed out that her shocking language had helped bring her to that moment; the graduating seniors gave her a standing ovation. She herself has served as professor of English at Livingston College of Rutgers University in New Jersey and at Queens College of City University of New York as professor of Black Studies. She has traveled broadly, in Africa, Europe, and the Caribbean, and has received numerous honors and awards. Her record album *Truth Is On Its Way* (1971), in which she recites some of her poetry to the background of gospel music, was among the top best-selling albums of that year. Her poetry also demands and has received much critical attention.

Giovanni was born Yolande Cornelia Giovanni, Jr., in Knoxville, Tennessee, the younger of the two daughters of Gus and Yolande Giovanni. Even as early as four years of age, she was brave, assertive, and forceful, and idolized her older sister, Gary, whom she was determined to "protect." When she was very young, her family moved to Wyoming, Ohio, a suburb of Cincinnati. Her mother and father, who was from Cincinnati, had met while students at Knoxville College. In Cincinnati, Giovanni's mother served as a supervisor for the Welfare Department and her father served as a social worker. Louvenia Terrell Watson, Giovanni's maternal grandmother, seems to have exerted a tremendous influence upon Nikki. She was assertive, militant, and terribly intolerant of white people. She and Giovanni's grandfather, John Brown ("Book") Watson, a schoolteacher in Albany, Georgia, were urged to leave that city for fear of Louvenia's being lynched for her outspokenness. They left hurriedly one night in a buggy, lying concealed under a blanket, and settled in Knoxville, where Giovanni's mother, Yolande, and two other daughters were born. Giovanni revered her grandmother, with whom she lived during her sophomore and junior years at high school. Louvenia Watson had taught her responsibility to her own people.

Seriously disaffected with what she considered the trivial and insincere regard for humanness that seemed to exist in marital relations, Giovanni decided early that marriage was not for her, at least not at that time. She then concentrated her energies on developing her career as a writer. She was deeply concerned about her own identity as a person—who she was and what her purpose in life should be. She was very proud of her sister Gary, who was especially gifted in music, but she had a difficult time establishing herself as a poet. She was imaginative, given to fantasizing and intellectual speculation. She says that her fantasy life went on with a "different personality emerging all the time." This side of her was balanced by absorption in hearty reading—about fifty books a year, including Ezra Pound, T. S. Eliot, Richard Wright, Greek and Roman mythology. She attended an Episcopal school, where she was not too fond of the white teaching nuns, who on one occasion called Richard Wright's *Black Boy,* which she had read as a seventh grader, a trashy book. Her decision to become a writer was based on the recognition of and desire to develop her intellectual and imaginative gifts rather than to stifle them in a typically middle-class domestic situation. Therefore, having a strong affinity for family life but not desiring to be inhibited by a possibly inhospitable marriage, Giovanni made the conscious choice to have a child out of wedlock. Her son, Tommy, was born to her while she was visiting her parents for Labor Day in 1969. He became the center of her life, and in 1971, she dedicated to him her first book of poems for children, *Spin a Soft Black Song.*

The 1960s were a tumultuous decade for all of America. Producing many emotional highs and lows, they abounded in mass movements and rebellious demonstrations, as well as in shocking occurrences. In the area of civil rights there were sit-in demonstrations, freedom rides, and the Voting Rights Act, which was accompanied by numerous voter registration projects. The National Association for the Advancement of Colored People (NAACP), the Southern Christian Leadership Conference (SCLC), the Student Non-Violent Coordinating Committee (SNCC), the Congress of Racial Equality (CORE), and many other black-oriented groups were in full action, fighting for the liberation and equality of black people and competing for recognition in the black community and the nation. It was also an era of marches on Washington and in other places under leaders such as Martin Luther King, Jr., Stokely Carmichael, Floyd McKissick, and James Forman.

It was a time of transformation from this mild-

Dust jacket for Giovanni's 1971 children's book. In the Introduction she says, "That's Charles and me—when we were little. We don't look as happy now. . . . We tried to remember what we were like and what we did."

er form of liberation struggle to black power and liberation and black revolutionary efforts. Elijah Muhammad, Malcolm X, and the Nation of Islam stirred black people to move toward radical self-assertion and revolutionary change. Malcolm X, Medgar Evers, John F. Kennedy, Martin Luther King, Jr., and Robert Kennedy were all felled by assassins' bullets. Riots and rebellion sprang up in Watts (Los Angeles), California; Newark, New Jersey; New York City; Nashville, Tennessee; Chicago, Illinois; Detroit, Michigan; Washington, D.C.; and in other cities across the nation. Antiwar demonstrations and rebellion erupted on the college campuses around the country. To say the least, it was an exciting time to be a student on a college campus.

At the beginning of this period of upheaval, Nikki Giovanni, a small, quick, harsh, gentle girl of seventeen entered Fisk University in September 1960. Coming from a middle-class family residing in a suburb of Cincinnati, Ohio, she was then a Goldwater supporter who had read much of, among other books, Ayn Rand, cheap novels, and fairy tales. Yet, she was in a state of growth. She did not like Fisk, whose social life did not appeal to her. (During the early 1960s, it might be noted, Fisk was widely known for its intelligent, relatively well-off young women who would more than likely marry one of the graduates of Meharry Medical College in the same Nashville area. Less privileged young women and men attended Tennessee State University of the same city.) Giovanni did not approve of the dean of women whom she referred to as "bitchy," and the following Thanksgiving she rushed home to her grandmother's in Knoxville without getting the dean's permission. Upon her return to school, Giovanni was placed on probation. But her attitude did not change, for in February, she was released from the school for having an "attitude" which did not "fit those of a Fisk woman." Her grandfather died in April, and after the funeral, Giovanni returned to Cincinnati with her mother, strongly regretting, however, having to leave her grandmother alone.

In 1964, Giovanni, true to her contradictory nature, returned to Fisk University and became respected as an ideal student. These were some of her most active years. She developed her literary talents, and edited *Elan,* a campus literary magazine. She also became politically active; in 1964, she was sufficiently politically aware to found a chapter of SNCC on the Fisk campus. This activity is the first evidence of her interest in black power, for this act followed Stokely Carmichael's declaration of "Black Power" on a freedom march down a Mississippi highway in 1963. What marked the radical shift from the conservative Goldwater stance to that of black power is not quite clear. It might be conjectured, however, that her encounters in the Southern environment and her close observations of the progressive developments in the nation of the civil rights demonstrations, especially in the South, along with the great popularity of Malcolm X and the Nation of Islam around the country, among other things, captured the imagination and enthusiasm of this sensitive young woman.

While at the university, Giovanni also took part in the Fisk Writers Workshop under the direction of the celebrated author John O. Killens, who no doubt inspired her literary talents as well as contributed to her awakening as a black liberationist. On 4 February 1967, she graduated magna cum laude, with honors in history. Unfortunately, her grandmother's death followed closely upon this happy occasion—on 8 March of the same year. Spiritually, artistically, and politically awakened, Giovanni was profoundly affected by this incident. It stirred in her a sense of guilt and shame both for the way in which society had dealt with this strong, sensitive woman, to whom she had been so close and who had deeply influenced her life, as well as for the way she herself had left her alone to die. It may be assumed that it was this great attachment to Louvenia Terrell Watson that makes Giovanni cherish so much the friendship of women over fifty years old, and causes her to be quite sensitive to the needs and aspirations of the women who fill much of her poetry.

After graduation Giovanni had gone home to Cincinnati. The news of her grandmother's death came as a shock, for she had been planning to drive down and bring her back to Cincinnati for a visit only two days later. And she felt she should have been there with her when she died. When her father called and gave her the news Giovanni became ill and remained so throughout the funeral. Weighing heavily on her conscience was also the fact that she believed strongly that it was "progress" which had killed Louvenia Watson. Earlier, the street on which Louvenia Watson had lived, Mulvaney Street in Knoxville, had been located in a development area of a Model Cities project. Louvenia Watson had been forced to move to make way for a new shopping mall, convention center, and expressway. Though it had a bigger backyard and no steps to climb, the new house on Linden Avenue was never home to her. Giovanni felt her grandmother died because "she didn't know where she was and didn't like it. And there was no one there to give a touch or smell." No doubt, her sensitivity to the reality of this situation aroused in Giovanni an awareness of the helplessness of other humans under similar social conditions and served as a significant cause of the anger evident in her early verse.

In June of the same year, 1967, Giovanni planned and spearheaded the first Cincinnati Black Arts Festival, thus initiating an awareness of arts and culture in the black community, and becoming a prime mover in the struggle for the awakening that was characteristic of the period. This effort evolved into The New Theatre, a black indigenous theater movement. Deeply engrossed in community organization and the concepts of black nation-building, and not advancing herself occupationally or professionally, Giovanni was told by her mother, who was a supervisor for the Welfare Department, that she would either have to get a job or go to graduate school. Feeling that either of these alternatives would interfere with her black liberation activities, Giovanni tried every means to evade the issue. She consulted with her father, from whom she hoped to receive sympathy, but discovered the avenue of escape lay elsewhere; she resolved to attend graduate school.

With a Ford Foundation Grant, she attended the University of Pennsylvania School of Social Work and later entered the School of Fine Arts at Columbia University. In 1968, she received a National Foundation for the Arts Grant and served as assistant professor of English in the SEEK Program of Queen's College. In the same year, she lived for a time in Wilmington, Delaware, where she started a black history workshop in the black community, thereby continuing her activist involvement.

Out of these involvements grew her first two books, which were published successively, *Black Feeling, Black Talk* (1967), and *Black Judgement* (1968), later combined into one volume. The first book, *Black Feeling, Black Talk,* contains mostly black consciousness-raising, chatty lyrics, monologues, and ritual recitations, some relating to her personal experiences as a black liberation advocate and many of these dedicated to black persons and groups whom she felt contributed to her own development. These poems seem to represent a kind of ritualistic exorcism of former nonblack ways of thinking and an immersion in blackness. Not only are they directed at other black people whom she wanted to awaken to the beauty of blackness, but also at herself as a means of saturating her own consciousness. For instance "Poem (No Name No. 2)" is a six-line poem which reads like an incantation:

Bitter Black Bitterness

Black Bitter Bitterness
Bitterness Black Brothers
Blacker Yet Bitter
Get Black Bitterness
NOW

This type of exorcistical chant is expanded in "The True Import of Present Dialogue, Black vs. Negro," which aims also for a psychological reversal of the state of one's mind:

Nigger
Can you kill
Can a nigger kill
Can a nigger kill a honkie
Can a nigger kill the Man
Can you kill nigger
Huh? Nigger can you
kill

The poem continues with daring questions, interspersed with ironic allusions to violent actions blacks have committed for the nation against their own color across the world and ends with the command: "Can you learn to kill WHITE for BLACK/ Learn to kill niggers/Learn to be Black men."

Another poem is of a confessional nature, "A Short Essay of Affirmation Explaining Why (With Apologies to the Federal Bureau of Investigation)." As the title suggests, it affirms blackness and ends on a humorous note: "I'm into my Black thing/And it's filling all/My empty spots/Sorry 'bout that,/ Miss Hoover." One poem in this collection, "Word Poem (Perhaps Worth Considering)," goes beyond Giovanni's vision of violent change to a vision of rebuilding:

As things be/come
let's destroy
then we can destroy
what we be/come
let's build
what we become
when we dream

And a few other poems in the volume are surprisingly full of pleasant remembrances of warm human contacts and feelings of personal intimacies, joys, and sorrows: "You Came, Too," "Poem (For TW)," "Poem (For BNC No. 1)," "Poem (No Name No. 1)." The volume opens with a reminiscence of a black arts conference in Detroit. "Detroit Conference of Unity and Art (For HRB)" is dedicated to H. Rap Brown, prominent revolutionary figure on the American scene during the time who was charged with inciting riots. The poem recalls the cherished topics of the conference (the possibility of black-

Covers for Giovanni's pivotal 1968 collection which marks the growth of her revolutionary consciousness

ness, inevitability of revolution, black leaders, black love, black men and women) and climaxes with the revealing quatrain: "But the most/valid of them/ All was that/Rap chose me."

Giovanni's genuine poetic talent is clearly exhibited in this first volume in her clever and skillful play with words to create humor, chagrin, irony; convey feelings of hatred, love, tenderness, and moods of loneliness, sadness, joy. However, in this early stage of her commitment of her talent to the service of the black revolution, her creativity is bound by a great deal of narrowness and partiality from which her later work is freed. The capacity for growth, incidentally, is a singular quality exhibited in her works as a whole. A steady progression toward excellence in craftsmanship is one of the key elements in her development.

Her second work, published in 1968, *Black Judgement,* is pivotal, and contains the germ of later ideas. Already in it, for instance, is the tension between the private artistic self, which she masks by excessive revolutionary rhetoric, and the public, communal, political self. Later works show the partisanism fading into a universal outlook and identity along with the growth in individualistic artistic skill and perception. But first, the revolutionary fire had to run its course. And *Black Judgement* is an extremely important book in this regard, because it reflects what seems to be a kind of death and rebirth in the artist's life in which she is baptized in the revolutionary spirit and rhetoric and finally awakens later to a healthier self and world consciousness. This experience is marked by two great events of the 1960s: the assassinations of Martin Luther King, Jr., and Robert F. Kennedy. The poems are dated and some make direct reference to the events.

The tragic death of King on 4 April 1968 enraged and embittered her and stirred in her a deep desire for revenge, as the heavy-handed prose piece, "Reflections on April 4, 1968," exhibits. It was written the very next day and records her initial reaction in such incendiary statements as: "What can I, a poor Black woman, do to destroy America?" "The Assassination of Martin Luther King is an act of war." "May his blood choke the life from ten million whites." These aggressive sentences are balanced by broader reflections scattered about on the deeper ironies of the situation, such as: "Let us pray for the whole state of Christ's church"; "Let America's baptism be the fire this time" (an allusion to Baldwin's *The Fire Next Time* and to the black spiritual about the biblical flood); and "This is a thirsty fire they [America] have created. It will not be squelched until it destroys them." Referring ironically to America's notion of itself as the promised land and its people as the chosen, she closes the piece with a call to black people for some form of saving action, reinforced by allusion to King's favorite hymn, "Precious Lord—Take Our Hands—Lead Us On." Giovanni obviously separated the man from his methods. Showing disrespect for his tactics in the earlier "Poem for Black Boys," written two days before his assassination, in "Reflections . . ." two days later she is plunged into deepest melancholy at the news of his murder. A number of the other poems reflect stages of religious melancholy Giovanni undergoes as a result of the tragic occurrence. Five days later in "The Funeral of Martin Luther King, Jr.," after attending the funeral in Atlanta, she expresses chagrin at the words on King's headstone: "Free At Last, Free at Last/But death is a slave's freedom." And contrary to the claim of critics that her early poetry was lacking in a sense of hope for the future, she concludes the poem with, "We seek the freedom of free men/And the construction of a world/Where Martin Luther King could have lived and preached non-violence." Three days after the funeral we find her moving deeper into spiritual despondency.

"A Litany for Peppe," written on 12 April 1968, is a perverted parody of the genuine religious ritual, reminiscent of Christ's Sermon on the Mount, especially the Beatitudes. Its disconnected recitations mingled with a refrain is suggestive of mental distraction combined with a studied call for avenging actions. For instance, it begins with: "They had a rebellion in Washington this year/ because white people killed Martin Luther King/ Even the cherry blossoms wouldn't appear." This is followed by the refrain: "Black Power and Sweet Black Peace." Another section about riots is followed by "And sweet peace to you my child," juxtaposed ironically with "Blessed be machine guns in Black hands." The poem closes with the perverted beatific refrain, "Blessed is he who kills/For he shall control this earth."

This macabre vision is balanced by a rather pleasing and wholesome prose-poem about the author's life while growing up. "Nikki-Rosa," which has long been Giovanni's most cherished creation, was written on the same day as "Litany." It focuses on the joys and pleasantries of growing up in a black home in spite of poverty and some unhappy occurrences. She recalls gratefully such things as: "how happy you were to have your mother/all to yourself and/how good the water felt when you got your bath"; "how much you/understood their feelings/ as the whole family attended meetings"; "and though you're poor it isn't poverty that/concerns you"; "it isn't your father's drinking that makes any difference/but only that everybody is together and you/and your sister have happy birthdays and very good Christmasses/and I really hope no white person ever has cause to write about me/because they never understand Black love is Black wealth and they'll probably talk about my hard childhood and never understand that/all the while I was quite happy."

A few weeks after King's funeral, still brooding in the same state of melancholy, Giovanni wrote "The Great Pax Whitie," a perversion of a black sermon and a parody of the Pax Romana. It opens with a parody of Genesis: "In the beginning was the word/And the word was/Death./And the word was nigger/and the word was death to all niggers/And the word was death to all life." Punctuated with the refrains of "peace be still" and "ain't they got no shame," the poem catalogues America's sins of violence as well as those of the Western world in general, making allusions to the holocaust. It closes with a sense of horror at the same violence which took the life of John Kennedy, Malcolm X, and Martin Luther King.

So the great white prince
Was shot like a nigger in Texas
And our Black shining prince was murdered
like that thug in his cathedral
While our nigger in Memphis
was shot like their prince in Dallas
and my lord
ain't we never gonna see the light.

A few days later Giovanni becomes the little girl again back home in Knoxville with "daddy," "grandmother," "going to church and listening to gospel music," as she writes "Knoxville, Tennessee" (17 May 1968): "I always like summer/best/you can eat fresh corn/from daddy's garden/and okra/and greens/and cabbage/and lots of/barbecue/and buttermilk/and homemade ice-cream./ . . ." Like "Nikki-Rosa," it is a return to the source, to the beginning, to the mother's womb, so to speak, from which a glorious rebirth is to be expected.

But before that could take place another national tragedy occurred which only intensified Giovanni's despondency, the assassination of Robert F. Kennedy on 6 June 1968, a few weeks after "Knoxville" was written. The poem "Records" was written in response to this occurrence:

how i feel about a
family
being wiped out
trying to explain
that they have nothing
against bobby
he's white
millionaire
several times over
so it must be me
they are killing

The subtlety of this assumption leads her to advocacy of retaliation as a means of self-protection:

this country must be
destroyed
if we are to live
must be destroyed if we are to live
must be destroyed if we are to live.

"Adulthood," written on the same day, is a monologue detailing certain phases of the author's life up to the present time. It is concentrated as well as comprehensive and may be looked upon as describing the evolution of a revolutionary. It begins with the girlhood stage of wonder ("i was meaningless/and i wondered if life/would give me a chance to mean") and records the changes in the teenage stage of dating, the young adult stage of college, and commitment and black awareness. Then she cites her involvement in artistic pursuits and black cultural activities as a means of aiding black liberation:

for a while progress was being
made along with a certain
degree
of happiness cause i wrote a book and found
a love
and organized a theatre and even
gave some lectures on
Black history
and began to believe all good
people could get
together and win without bloodshed

Then the author begins to ritualistically catalogue a series of tragic deaths and regretful happenings that shattered her faith and transformed her into an indignant revolutionary; "a for real Black person who must now feel/and inflict/pain." The events include the deaths of Dag Hammarskjöld, Patrice Lumumba, President Diem, Kennedy, and a number of other killings prior to and including King and the second Kennedy brother, the arrests of

LeRoi Jones (Amiri Baraka), and H. Rap Brown, and the flight of Stokely Carmichael.

Giovanni's emergence from this "night-journey" is seen in later works, but hopeful signs of it appear in a few of the poems in this collection, especially those dealing with pleasant remembrances of her childhood days and wholesome family relations. The harshness of the revolutionary verses of some of these poems overshadows certain other more lyrical images such as in "Beautiful Black Men" and the personal, perceptive, and revealing monologue "Woman Poem." Both of these poems were written on 10 September 1968. A few lines from each should illustrate the point. "Black Men" sounds like a jazz song:

i wanta say just gotta say someting
bout those beautiful beautiful beautiful
outasight
black men
with the afros
walking down the street
is the same ol danger
but a brand new pleasure—.

"Woman Poem" is written in the chatty dialogue of an average woman:

you see, my whole life
is tied up
to unhappiness
its father cooking breakfast
and me getting as fat as a hog
or having no food
at all and father proving
his incompetence
again
i wish i knew how it would feel
to be free.

Her first two books brought Giovanni to critical attention as one of the three leading figures of the new black poetry between 1968 and 1971 (the other two were Don L. Lee and Sonia Sanchez). Their works, and the works of others, were variously described as hate poetry by Arthur Davis in 1973; humanistic protest by Richard K. Barksdale in 1973; nation-building poetry by R. Roderick Palmer in 1971; positive in celebrating blackness and the need for dynamic change by A. Russell Brooks in 1971; rooted in the love of black people and an affirmation of life, posing a tension between hatred and love, life and death, thus constituting a real vitality (Bernard W. Bell, 1971); and, as Don L. Lee himself said in 1971, as reflecting awareness of the values of black culture and commitment to the revolution.

Having been awarded the Harlem Cultural Council on the Arts grant and cited in the *Amsterdam News* as one of the ten most admired American women, Giovanni in 1969 began to emerge from her state of grief and shock. Before she became an associate professor at Rutgers University, Livingston College, while she was living in Manhattan, she had made a crucial decision. Since family life had always been of the utmost significance in her life, and having consciously determined not to get married soon, the twenty-five-year old author deliberately chose to have a child. Her son, Thomas Watson Giovanni, was born on 31 August 1969 of the year she was at Rutgers. The birth of her son constituted the turning point in her life; as she returned from her mother's house in Cincinnati where her son had been born, she began to center her whole self around her relationship with Tommy.

In 1970 Giovanni founded the publishing cooperative, NikTom, Limited, and collected, edited, and published a volume of poetry by black female poets, a number of whom were prominent—Gwendolyn Brooks, Mari Evans, Jewel C. Latimore (Johari Amini), Carolyn Rodgers, and Margaret Walker.

Her third volume of poetry, *Re: Creation,* published in 1970, was not significantly different in tone, content, and style from the first two: it contained black revolutionary verse. In 1970, also, her first two books were reissued in a combined volume by William Morrow Publishers. In the meantime, between 1969 and 1971, Giovanni had traveled to the Caribbean to such places as Haiti and Barbados, and wrote the autobiographical work *Gemini: an Extended Autobiographical Statement on My First Twenty-Five Years of Being a Black Poet* (1971), and her fourth book of poetry, *Spin a Soft Black Song Poems for Children* (1971), dedicated to her son. With the publication of these two works a significant change takes place in her as a person and as an artist.

In these two works we see evidence of a more developed individualism and greater introspection, and a sharpening of her creative and moral powers, as well as of her social and political focus and understanding. This is true especially in *Gemini,* where it is obvious she now takes herself more seriously as a poet and a woman, as well as a revolutionary. Giovanni here attempts to clarify, in a number of poetic, polemical, descriptive, critical essays her stance on many issues. As her poetry is not traditional, neither is this book a conventional autobiography. She calls it "An Extended Autobio-

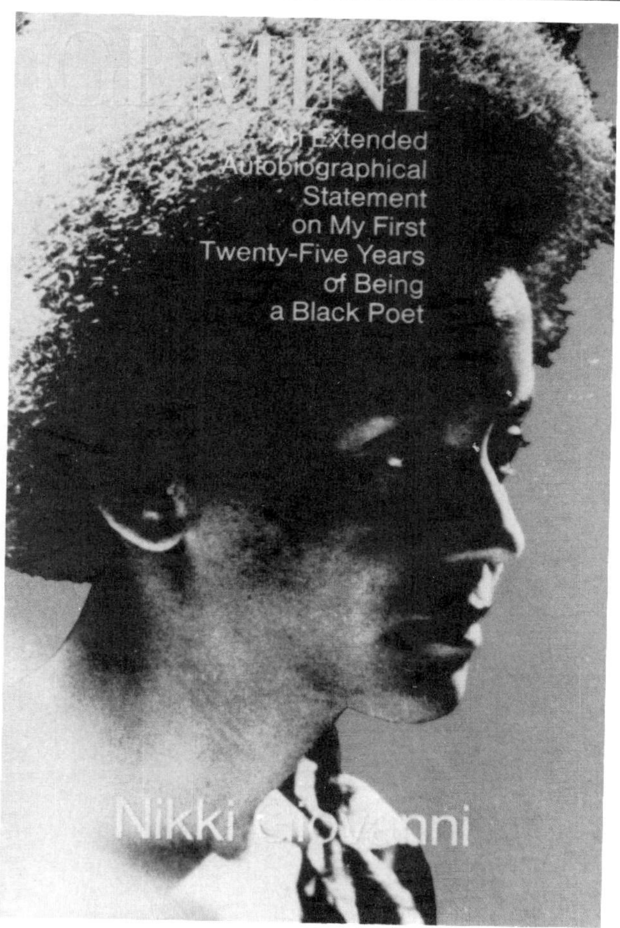

Dust jacket for Giovanni's 1971 volume of essays in which, as Lonne Elder III has said, "she dares to confront personal and emotional danger"

graphical Statement on My First Twenty-Five Years of Being a Black Poet." One understands that being a poet is what she is about; it has been a part of her very nature from infancy onward. Also important is the fact that she is a *black poet.* Rather than a completely chronological report and clarification of her development, *Gemini* gives us a piecemeal characterization of the author from the presentation of bits and pieces of her various experiences of growing up, going to college, working, getting involved with black liberation, having a baby, traveling, and so on. The book also characterizes the members of her family, including her grandmother and grandfather, as well as her mother, father, sister, and nephew. In addition, we get essays and prose pieces, some previously published in magazines, which explain and defend her views on various subjects and persons, including black literature, music, Angela Davis, and Lena Horne.

Of particular interest are the two articles "A Revolutionary Tale" and "Don't Have a Baby till You Read This," both of which are perceptive, half-humorous, sometimes rambling stories of incidents occurring in critical phases of her life—becoming a revolutionary, deciding to go to graduate school, and having a baby. The former was written and published in June 1968 in *Negro Digest,* and the latter appears for the first time in this volume. Both reveal warm, sensitive, charming sides of the artist's nature and the wholesome, loving, sharing family environment in which she was raised. The artist's ability to weave tales of her own life as though they were those of a fictional character and entertain and captivate her audience with humor and insight is remarkably displayed.

In the first story we learn that it was her roommate Bertha who was influential in the author's transformation from the Ayn Rand-Barry Goldwater mentality to black activist-revolutionary; that subsequently she converted her mother and father by getting them to read Frantz Fanon, Stokely Carmichael, H. Rap Brown, John O. Killens, Amiri Baraka, Larry Neal, and others. In the second story, she confesses that she did not discover that she was pregnant until she was in the fourth month, while visiting in Barbados; that her heart had stopped temporarily during the birth of her son by cesarean section; and that her newly born son was gladly welcomed into a supportive, loving, caring family.

Finally, in the chapter entitled "It's a Case of . . . ," she reflects on her travels to California, Haiti, Barbados, on Angela Davis, among others, groups, and social and political issues, and here Giovanni shows signs of considerably modifying her personal, social, and political views, as well as the direction of her intellectual and emotional growth. For instance being black did not help her in Haiti, for even in this black nation she was open to being preyed upon as a foreigner. She enjoyed Barbados much more, but still realized she was not simply in a black country, but also in a foreign land. As a result of pondering on subjects related to these journeys, she modified her views of West Indians in the United States as being exploiting immigrants. "I bobbed up and down in the water and thought about how beautiful a people is at home. I would have hated West Indians had I not visited Barbados. I fully understood and agreed with Harold Cruse about that."

She began to formulate a humanist world view and to see individuals, including herself, of course, in terms of their places in the scheme of things. "The state of the world we live in is so depressing.

And this is not because of the reality of the men who run it but it just doesn't have to be that way. The possibilities of life are so great and beautiful that to see less wears the spirit down." Facing this reality, she begins to sort out meaningful responses to the situation: "It's like the more you move toward the possible, the more bitter you become toward the stumbling blocks. I can really understand why people don't try to do anything. It's not really easy, but if you have to deal with energy it's a much more realistic task to decide not to feel than to feel. It takes the same amount of time but not to feel is ultimately more rewarding because things always come back to that anyway. . . . You were a fool." Whether one agrees with her or not one sees that she is figuring things out for herself, that she is preparing herself for tremendous personal growth. "The truth is that there is this shell around you, and the more you say, 'All right, you can come in' to someone, the more he questions the right of the shell to exist. And if you fall for that and take it away, he looks at your nakedness and calls you a whore. It's an awful thing when all you wanted was to laugh and run and touch and make love and really not give a damn." *Gemini* received mixed reviews.

Spin a Soft Black Song, published the same year and dedicated to her new son, contains some thirty-odd poems recounting the feelings of black children about their neighborhoods, American society, and themselves. These poems well represent the tenor of the black experience and convey interesting insights into it and life in general. However, in spite of the author's attempt to emulate the language of childhood and convey the thoughts from a childlike point of view, the ideological bent of the works is anything but childish. One can see Giovanni's increase in skill and movement toward a wider and more humane ideal in her writing.

Also, in 1971, Giovanni soared to national popularity and fame by the recording of her album *Truth Is On Its Way,* in which she reads some of her poetic creations against the background of gospel music provided by the New York Community Choir. Ellis Haizlip, producer and director of the WNET/TV show "Soul," was instrumental in getting Giovanni to become involved in the venture. The earlier popularity of shows he had done with women writers reading their own poems induced him to experiment further and to suggest to Giovanni the possibility of combining gospel music with her work. In July she introduced the recording before a crowd of 1,500 during a free concert at Canaan Baptist Church in Harlem. Its reception was sensational and, surprisingly, converted listeners who otherwise had rejected the new black poetry as being offensive and antagonizing. In a May 1972 article in *Jet* she explained, "I wanted people to take not just my poetry, but something I thought was a valid comment on my poetry which was gospel music." Her desire to relate her poetry not to street music but to church music, she explained, was expressive of a new aim in her life, to get inside institutions and effect changes in and through them. For the same reason, she joined the National Council of Negro Women, founded by Mary McCleod Bethune, and is very active in it today.

Giovanni's album became a top-selling record and was a hot number on radio stations around the country. The author was in great demand for making personal appearances nationally. Ever since that time, she has had a busy schedule, making the rounds especially on college campuses. *Mademoiselle* magazine presented her with an award for outstanding achievements; Omega Psi Phi fraternity presented her an award for her outstanding contribution to arts and letters. In November, 1971 she became ill from too much travel.

In 1972 she was featured on the covers and within the pages of numerous magazines, including *Ebony, Jet, Harper's Bazaar,* and *Publishers Weekly.* She was presented the keys to Gary, Indiana, and Lincoln Heights, where the mayor proclaimed 14 April Giovanni Day. It was "marked with a motorcade led by Mayor James E. Lowry and other elected city officials, a dinner at St. Simon's Church and a ceremony before an overflow crowd at Lincoln Heights High School, where Mayor Lowry read the proclamation from the city fathers and citizens." The National Association of Radio and Television announcers presented her an award for the Best Spoken Word Album; Prince Matchabelli presented her its Sun Shower Award (for women who achieved new heights in their careers in 1971); the National Council of Negro Women granted her a life membership and scroll; and she became a part of the National Black Heroines for PUSH.

In April of the same year, she was presented with an honorary Doctorate of Humanities degree by Wilberforce University. In an article in *Jet,* she says she was startled by the Reverend Leon G. Sullivan's description of her as "this fine, young woman who walks in truth and who brought a measure of wisdom to all who've seen what she's written." As she walked to the podium she thought to herself, "Now, all these graduating brothers and sisters are going to feel that I'm telling them that they could be honored just by saying mother———."

In 1972, also, her new book of poetry *My House,* appeared, evidencing a remarkable change in her writing. She briefly commented on this change: "I'm into a very personal thing, now, and I have a two and a half-year-old-son, and I'm more settled." As for this change in her focus, she declared, "Only a fool doesn't change. Only the mass of the earth remains the same. It has not changed in weight since it was formed, but yet, it is a constantly changing thing."

Having visited Africa and Europe in July 1971 with Ida Lewis (who wrote the foreword to *My House*), Giovanni had further modified her views of the world and herself. The individualism in her earlier works that was either separate from or in tension with her political ideology now comes to the fore and blends with a modified political stance, and in most cases, it supplants the narrow revolutionary conception; and Giovanni's creative genius abounds. Rhythmic, lyrical qualities, vivid imagery, shifting moods, tones, and atmospheres, and the liquid flow of words and phrases combine to reveal the author's enormous skill.

In *My House,* Giovanni turns more from the outside issues to thoughts of home and family and extended family, love, and humanness. The poems are personal and autobiographical, all dated, written mostly in 1971 and 1972, and are grouped under two headings "The Rooms Inside" (twenty-three poems) and "The Rooms Outside" (thirteen poems). In the first section the poems concentrate on the warmth, pleasures, and comforts of home and family, intimate relations, personal thoughts, and love. The second section is about people (mostly black) beyond the home environment, and the struggles and issues they have to face. The predominant form is the monologue, revealing the mood and innermost thoughts of the personas in descriptive, rhythmical language.

The author's changing attitude is expressed in

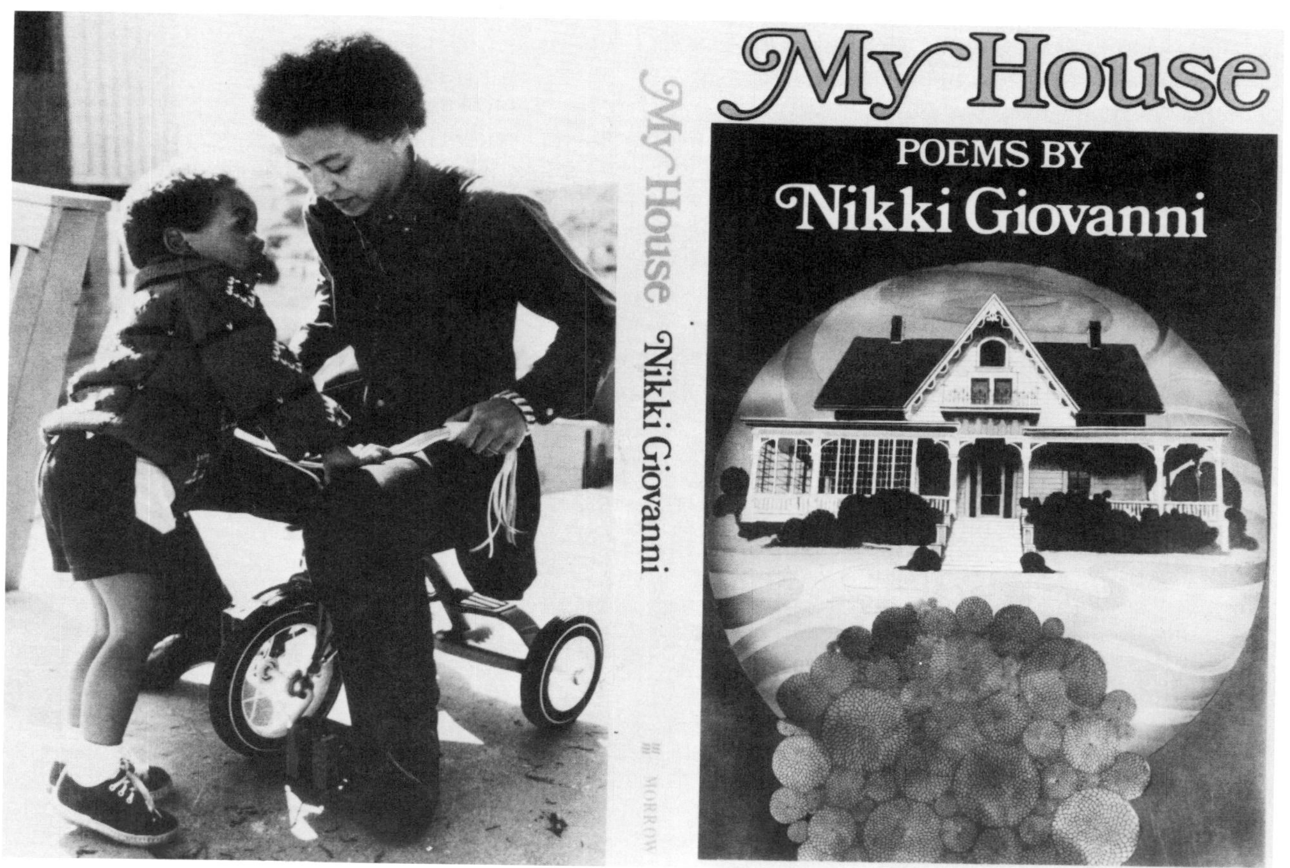

Dust jacket for Giovanni's 1972 book of love poems. When critic Thomas Lask noted the "sharp modulation in tone" of these poems from the stridency of her earlier work, Giovanni laughingly called herself "a muted militant."

"Categories." Thinking back on occasions of seeing an "old white woman" and wanting to relate to her as a person, but finding it impossible to because of the great psychological distance, the poet concludes:

if she weren't such an aggressive
 bitch she would see
that if you weren't such a Black one
there would be a relationship but
 anyway—it doesn't matter
much—except you started out to
 kill her and now find
you just don't give a damn cause
 it's all somewhat of a bore
so you speak of your mother or sister
 or very good friend
and really you speak of your feelings
 which are too personal
 for anyone else
 to take a chance on feeling.

The "too personal" feelings, in fact, are often exposed in the poems of *My House,* for example, in the direct physical imagery of "When I Nap": "i lay at the foot/of my bed and smell/the sweat of your feet/in my covers/while I dream." In "Africa I" the reader is invited to share the creative exuberance of the persona: "on the bite of a kola nut/i was so high the clouds blanketing africa/in the mid morning flight were pushed/away in an angry flicker/of the sun's tongue." In contrast, the closing words display the delicacy of the speaker's interaction, with her mother, "and something in me said shout/and something else said quietly/your mother may be glad to see you/but she may also remember why/you went away."

One of Giovanni's closest friends, Ida Lewis, comments in the foreword to *My House* on the author's focus on family and individualism: "one key to understanding Nikki is to realize the pattern of her conviction. The central core is always associated with her family: the family that produced her and the family she is producing. She has reached a simple philosophy more or less to the effect that a good family spirit is what produces healthy communities, which is what should produce a strong (Black) nation."

In 1973 Giovanni collected and edited a volume of her poems especially for young people, *Ego-Tripping and Other Poems for Young People.* It consists chiefly of poems appearing in previous volumes. The title poem characterizes the general tone of the rest in the volume. Proud, boasting, filled with hyperbolic imagery, the poem fairly struts up and down the page. The speaker is an omniscient female god: "I was born in the congo/I walked to the fertile crescent and built/the sphinx"; she continues "I sat on the throne/drinking nectar with allah," "My daughter is nefertiti," "My son noah built new/ark and/I stood proudly at the helm." The poem ends in a sudden shift to the words of a popular blues song: "I am so perfect so divine so ethereal so surreal/I cannot be comprehended/except by my permission/I mean . . . I . . . can fly/like a bird in the sky. . . ."

Giovanni's popularity was still growing. She was cited in the *Ladies Home Journal* as Outstanding Woman of the Year for Youth Leadership, and she received a National Book Award Nomination for *Gemini.* Her collaborative volume with James Baldwin, *A Dialogue,* was published. Two years earlier on 4 November 1971, in London, England, the two authors had taped a conversation for the television program "Soul." The videotape was shown in two installments on 15 and 22 December 1971. The two authors revised and edited the transcribed tape which appeared in this published volume. What is significant is that Giovanni and Baldwin represented two generations of black writers who were deeply affected by and involved in the black movement for liberation, but who were of different ideologies and philosophies. It was a dynamic meeting of minds on such subjects as religion, black men and women and love, America and black people, junkies, the American society and hope, the black movement, literature, criticism and the art of writing. All in all the dialogue is quite interesting and closes on a genuine note of hope.

One year after the successful dialogue with Baldwin, in October 1972, Giovanni appeared on the Paul Laurence Dunbar Centennial program at the University of Dayton, in Ohio, along with Margaret Walker and other writers reading from Dunbar's work. Giovanni and Walker had an almost electrifying effect on their audiences. During the occasion Giovanni accepted a challenge from a participant to do a "Conversation Book" with Margaret Walker. She had for a number of years had a great admiration for Margaret Walker, especially in appreciation for her poem, "For My People." Therefore, in Walker's home in Jackson, Mississippi, in November 1972, and in Washington, D.C., in January 1973, between them, the two poets discussed a range of subjects, and the conversations were published in the volume, *A Poetic Equation: Conversations Between Nikki Giovanni and Margaret Walker* (1974). This encounter was much more potentially explosive than the one with Baldwin, for

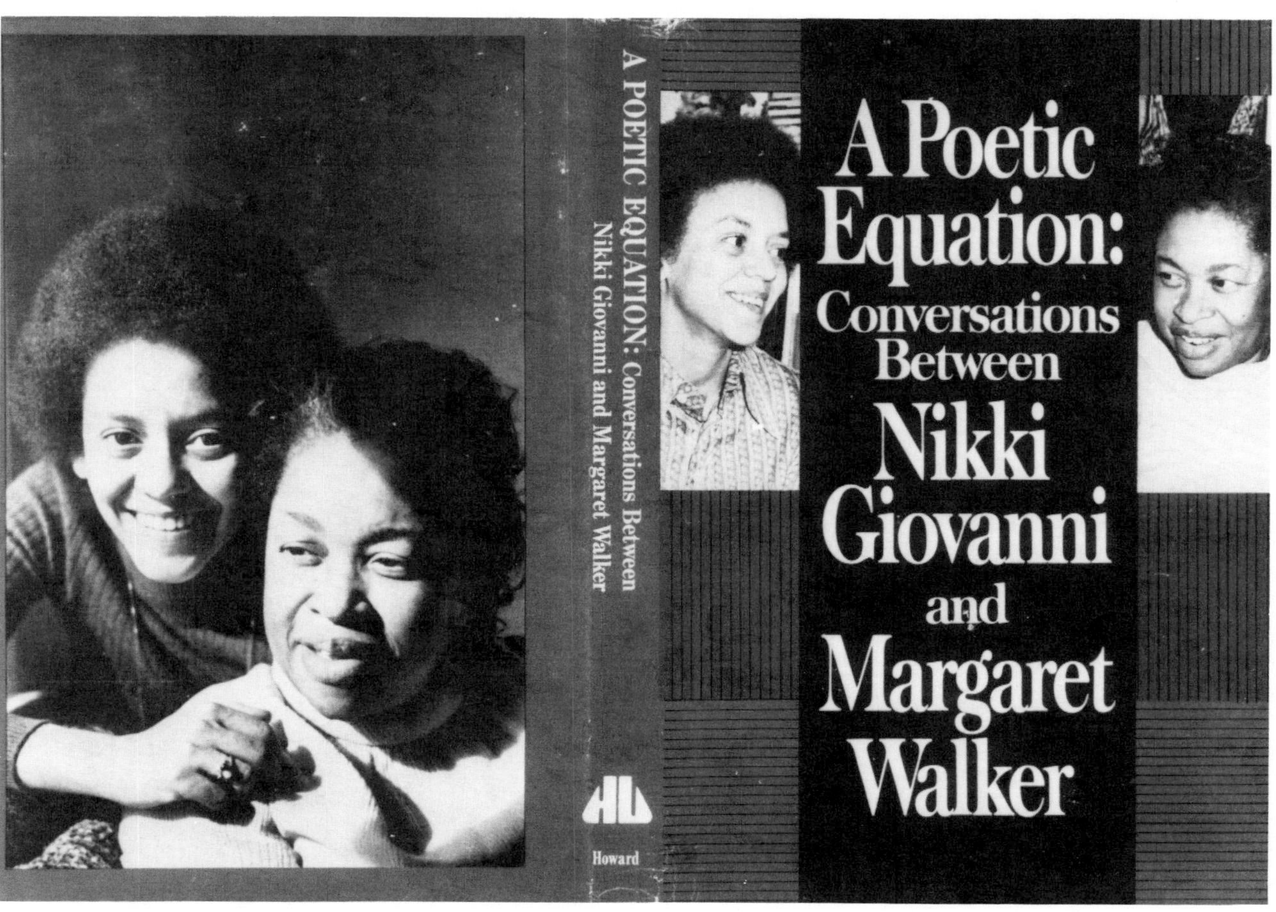

Dust jacket for the 1974 transcription of two tape-recorded sessions in which Giovanni, "a product of the 1960s and 1970s," and poet Margaret Walker, shaped by the 1930s and 1940s, discuss, in the editor's words, everything "from Superfly *to the possibilities of genocide"*

although the two poets admired each other immensely, they came from sharply different settings and orientations.

The Preface to the book defines the contrast between the two minds. Of Walker, we are told: "Margaret Walker had decided to sow her seeds in the South (her home is Jackson, Mississippi) after finding the northern soil of Chicago and New York interesting, but not the kind of stuff from which her roots are grown. She is a woman who reflects the values of a generation of blacks steeped in scholarship (and proud of it), who experienced the Depression, World War II, the rise of the American Communist Party and McCarthyism, and a racial perspective which had its own particular kind of radical and conservative aspects." Of Giovanni, on the other hand, we are told: "And Nikki Giovanni, a virtual embodiment of the sixties and seventies: controversial, in constant physical and mental movement; not only unafraid to explore the dichotomies of the times and of herself, but determined to lay them bare. Her sensibility thrives in an urban world, and she has shored up her life forces to not only survive but direct it."

The resultant book consists of six chapters of exciting intellectual encounter between two women of high intelligence. The subjects discussed include the methods of the black liberation movement, thoughts on writing and criticism, war, the black woman, and black people and their future in America. Clearly the differences come through in Walker's humanism and theological stance and Giovanni's more radical stance concerning violence and self-defense as opposed to degradation, the views the two have of each other's writing. On a number of issues the poets reached an agreement. Both especially endorsed the changes in society regarding sex roles and the role of the family. Giovanni expresses the belief that "sex-derived roles" do not work in the community. She recommends "getting rid of them!" The discussion ends on a hopeful note that stresses the need for black people to take responsibility in getting things straight in America.

The publication of *The Women and the Men* in 1975 marks another milestone in the life and career of Nikki Giovanni. In this collection of poems, we find that she has permitted to flower fully portions of herself and her perception which had been evident only in subdued form or in incompletely worked-through fragments. Ideas concerning women and men, universal human relatedness, and the art of poetry are seen here as being in the process of fuller realization in the psyche of the author. Furthermore, the delicate, charming, poetic expression they are given in these verses show superior skill and mature creative development. The artist has evidently relaxed the revolutionary restraints on her artistic talents and is now allowing her full creative powers to blossom.

The poems are included under three divisions: "The Women," "The Men," and "And Some Places." The first and second divisions are devoted to full poetic expression of the interests and insights she briefly dealt with in the pivotal work *Black Judgement* ("Beautiful Black Men" and "Woman Poem"), that were issues in her dialogues with Baldwin and Walker, and that ran through (as a minor theme) most of her previous works. In the first division, "Revolutionary Dreams" (a dramatic monologue), describes surrender to natural powers and sums up her shift in focus from "militant," "radical," dreams of political takeover to an emphasis on self-realization: "If I dreamed natural/ dreams of being a natural/woman doing what a woman/does when she's natural/i would have a revolution."

In a review in *Best Sell* in January 1976, Robert McGeehin responded quite positively to this volume, especially to the poems in the first division. He referred to them as a "startling group of

POETRY $2.95

The Women and the Men

This is the third book of poems by one of America's most popular poets. The poems in this volume cover a large period in Nikki Giovanni's life and display in full measure the gifts that have made her so appealing to her large following: her warmth, her conciseness, her passion, and her wit. Above all, they display Nikki Giovanni's caring for the people, things, and places she has observed and touched and captured.

Praise for Nikki Giovanni's Earlier Books of Poetry:

MY HOUSE
"Nikki Giovanni has . . . become one of the most potent voices of our time. Her message is universal and the rhythm and language of her poetry can be compared favorably with that of the finest poets of the past. She is a beautiful and complete human being with a genius for describing the human condition."
—*Minneapolis Tribune*

BLACK FEELING, BLACK TALK/BLACK JUDGEMENT
"Nikki Giovanni is sometimes gentle, sometimes angry, and always moving."—JULIUS LESTER in *The Guardian*

Cover illustration by James Barkley
Cover typography by George Romero

MORROW QUILL PAPERBACKS
105 Madison Avenue, New York, N.Y. 10016

0-688-07947-4

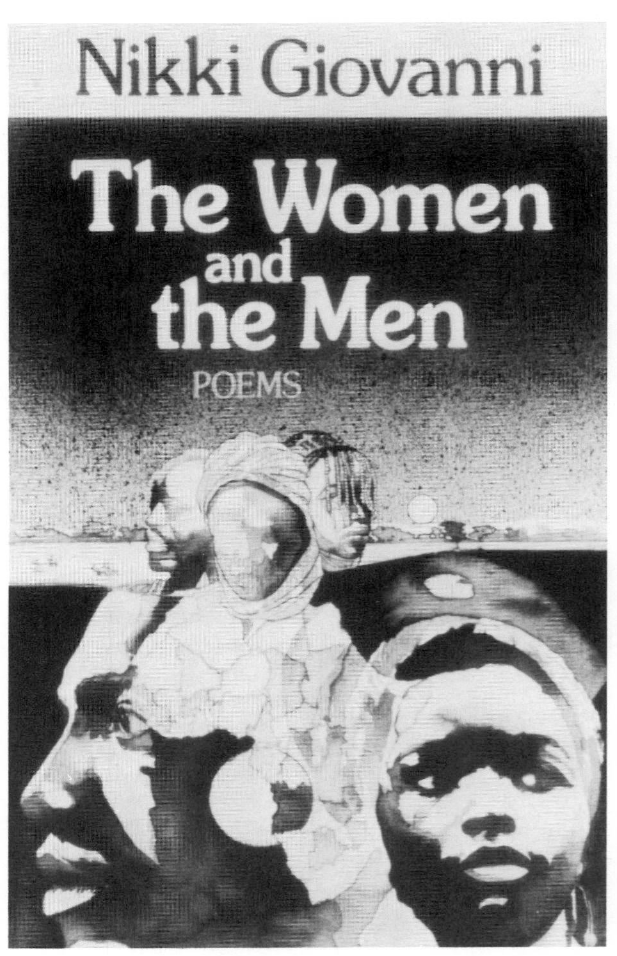

Covers for Giovanni's 1975 poetry collection, in which she considers the qualities that link all people

poems," primarily portraits, "clear and honest expressions and statements of Black womanhood and repetition that would make for easy musical scoring." McGeehin is right. For instance, "The Women Gather" is a dirge reflecting on the contradictions of life. "Each Sunday" tries to capture the serious philosophical thinking of a woman waist-deep in domestic affairs. "The Genie in the Jar (for Nina Simone)" is a beautiful song celebrating creativity. Also included is "A Poem for Aretha" and "Ego-Tripping."

In the second division, "The Men," the author's haunting desire to understand black men, strongly presented in her dialogue with James Baldwin, has seemingly dissolved in a submission to simply loving them in joy and appreciation. The imagery of this section is unique and skillfully chosen and combined, often with musical word arrangements reflective of jazz and blues songs. "The Way I Feel" concludes, "in my mind's eye you're a clock/and I'm the second hand sweeping/around you sixty times an hour/twenty-four hours a day." "Kidnap Poem" declares, "if i were a poet/i'd kidnap you/put you in my phrases and meter/you to jones beach." "Poem" ends with the phrase "with the relief of recognition/i bend to your eyes/casually/raping me." "Autumn Poem" closes after a reflection on an earlier love-making scene, with "i am a leaf/falling from your tree upon which i was/impaled."

The last division, "And Some Places," reveals a mellowed revolutionary revisiting some places and her former self and detailing new insights and new perceptions. "Africa" depicts a land describing itself as a "teller of tales/a dreamer of dreams" of freedom and hope and joy, the resolving of tensions between "blacks and Africans" who will walk "side by side in a new world/described by love and bounded by difference/for nothing is the same except oppression and shame." "A Very Simple Wish" expresses surprise at the simple fact "that it's easier to stick/a gun in someone's face/or a knife in someone's back/than to touch skin to skin/anyone whom we like." After summarizing the need for blending all the world's people and differences into one harmonious whole, the poem concludes "i want to make a quilt/of all the patches and find/one long strong pole/to lift it up/i've a mind to build/a new world/want to play." Finally, the author's simple, artistic view of her craft is summarized in "Poetry": "poetry is motion graceful/as a fawn/gentle as a teardrop/strong like the eye/finding peace in a crowded room." A poem, she continues, "is pure energy/horizontally contained/between the mind/of the poet and the ear of the reader/if it does not sing discard the ear/for poetry is song."

By 1976 and 1977, America showed signs of turning inward, away from the raucous times of the 1960s and early 1970s. The me-generation limped to the foreground. Many black revolutionaries were simply overwhelmed by the sudden turn of events of a new era; old tactics of marches, demonstrations, riots, rhetoric, and burnings had lost their appeal. Some revolutionaries were able to change their tactics to suit the times of economic and energy crises and political repression. Some became more introspective and began to sort out a new, relevant approach to life. Nikki Giovanni survived this lull in the black liberation struggle, because she had already begun to cultivate the inner resources she possessed and always remained open to spiritual, intellectual, artistic, ethical, as well as political growth. These years found her still traveling, writing, and developing and sharpening her skills and perceptions.

In 1978, she published *Cotton Candy on a Rainy Day,* perhaps her most sobering book of verse yet. It contains thoughtful and insightful lyrics on the emotions, fears, insecurities, realities, and responsibilities of living. The extended metaphor of the title poem, "Cotton Candy on a Rainy Day," is rather apt. The insubstantial, fleeting quality of life is cleverly depicted in relation to her personal growth and social involvement, and the necessity for change occasioned by the 1970s. "Don't look now/I'm fading away/into the gray of my mornings/or the blues of every night," it begins. Characterizing the 1970s as "loneliness," she calls it "The sweetest soft essence/of possibility/never quite maturing." Somehow, the incompleteness of the liberation movement of which she was so intricately a part arouses a sense of loneliness, boredom, futility, in which she sees herself as fragile and incomplete: "I am cotton candy on a rainy day/the unrealized dream of an unborn idea."

The fragile aspects of the human condition are reflected in other poems such as "The New Yorkers," which describes scenes of men and women in various troublesome stances of life. "Crutches" and "Boxes" reflect life's desperation: "emotional falls always are/the worst/and there are no crutches/to swing back on." "I am a box/on a tight string/subject to pop/without notice." "Age," "Because," "Their Fathers," and "Life Cycles" are examples of her philosophical reflections on life that are so prevalent in this volume. The author's new sober attitude toward life is aptly described in "Fascinations": "finding myself still fascinated/by

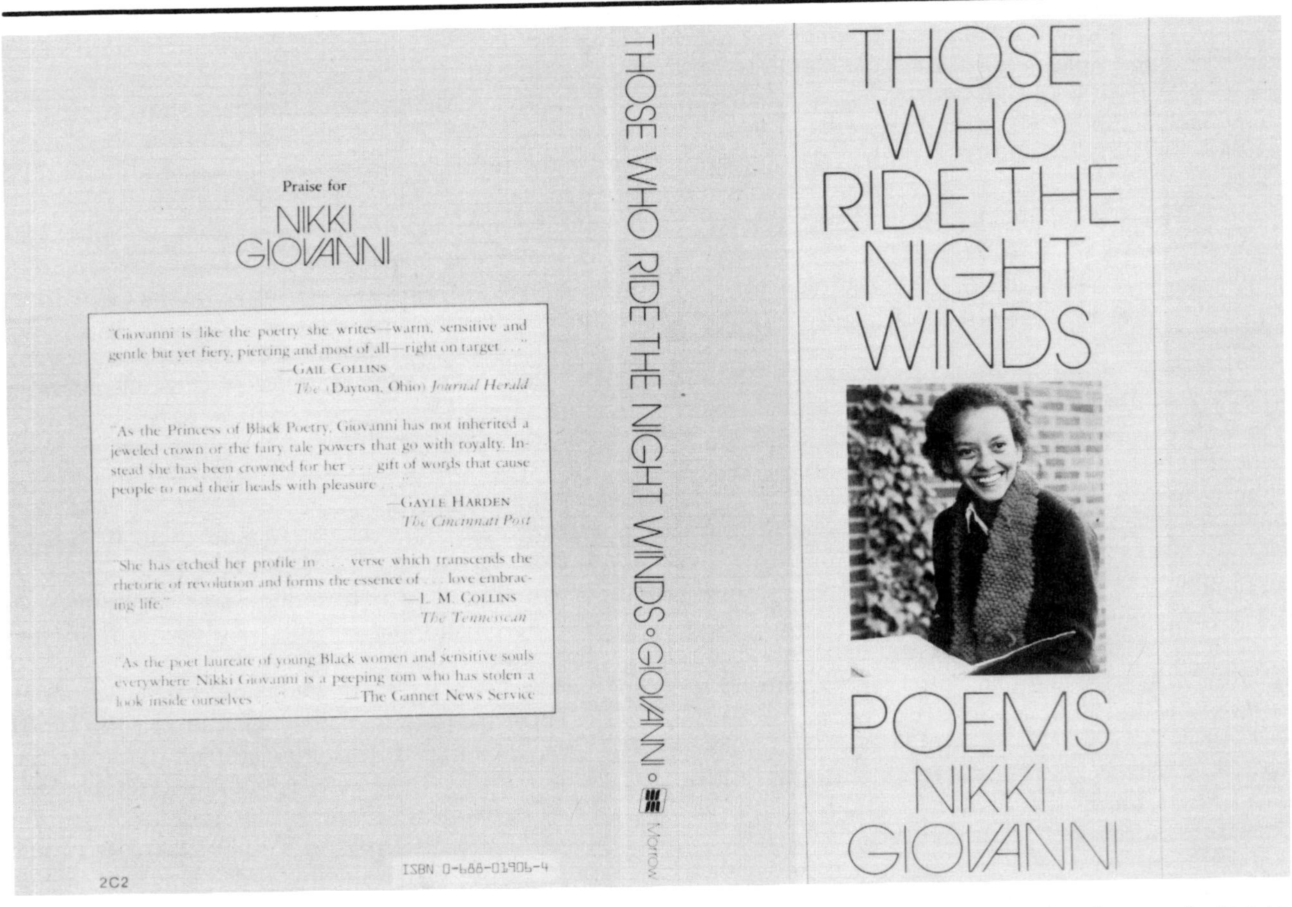

Praise for
NIKKI GIOVANNI
"Giovanni is like the poetry she writes—warm, sensitive and gentle but yet fiery, piercing and most of all—right on target . . ."
—GAIL COLLINS
The (Dayton, Ohio) Journal Herald
"As the Princess of Black Poetry, Giovanni has not inherited a jeweled crown or the fairy tale powers that go with royalty. Instead she has been crowned for her . . . gift of words that cause people to nod their heads with pleasure . . ."
—GAYLE HARDEN
The Cincinnati Post
"She has etched her profile in . . . verse which transcends the rhetoric of revolution and forms the essence of . . . love embracing life."
—L. M. COLLINS
The Tennessean
"As the poet laureate of young Black women and sensitive souls everywhere Nikki Giovanni is a peeping tom who has stolen a look inside ourselves . . ."
—The Gannet News Service
ISBN 0-688-01906-4
2C2
THOSE WHO RIDE THE NIGHT WINDS • GIOVANNI
Morrow
THOSE WHO RIDE THE NIGHT WINDS
POEMS
NIKKI GIOVANNI

Dust jacket for Giovanni's 1983 volume of poems dedicated to "those who ride the night winds—who are the day trippers and midnight cowboys—who in sonic solitude or the hazy hell of habit . . . are determined to push us into the next century, galaxy—possibility. . . ."

the falls and rapids/i nonetheless prefer the streams/contained within the bountiful brown shoreline/i prefer the inland waters/to the salty seas/knowing that journeys end/as they begin."

Paula Giddings, who wrote the introduction to *Cotton Candy,* titled "A Woman of the Seventies," sees the volume as completing Giovanni's cycle of dealing with society, others, and finally herself. This pensive, introspective, plaintive work "speaks of loneliness, personal emptiness, and love which is not unrequited but, even worse, misunderstood and misbegotten."

In 1978, the same year of this publication, Giovanni's father, Gus, suffered a serious stroke. Realizing the dilemma this put her family in, Giovanni and her son, Tommy, moved from their New York apartment back to Cincinnati to be with her parents, still, however, maintaining a small apartment in New York. Her father was moved to California to stay with her sister, Gary, for a convalescence. Giovanni proved her genius for home and family life by fixing up the basement of her family home to include a living area, work space, bedroom, and bathroom; she cooks, shops, washes her car, and plays football with her son.

In 1980, Giovanni published *Vacation Time: Poems for Children,* a delightful collection, totally free of ideology, full of bubbles, joy, animals, flowers, birds, sunshine, rainbows, stars, and the light fantastic. One may be dazzled by the smooth way she drops all political and personal concerns and completely enters the world of the child and brings to it all the fanciful beauty, wonder, and lollipopping. In 1983 *Those Who Ride the Night Winds* was published by William Morrow.

In this book Giovanni has adopted a new and innovative form; and the poetry reflects her heightened self-knowledge and imagination. Written in short paragraphs punctuated with ellipses reminiscent of telegraphic communication, most of the poems appear to be hot off the mind of the author. Yet, the style also suggests the halting flow of perceptive thought. "If you want to share . . . a vision . . . or tell the truth . . . you pick up . . . your pen . . . and take your chances. . . ," she writes in "Lorraine Hansberry: An Emotional View." This is what she herself has done. Her vision concerns specifically those who have the courage to seek change, to take a risk, about those "who ride the night winds" and "learn to love the stars . . . even while crying in the darkness. . . .": Lorraine Hansberry, John Lennon, Billy Jean King, Martin Luther King, Jr., Robert Kennedy, Phillis Wheatley. In most cases the poems are meditation pieces that begin with some special quality in the life of the subject, and with thoughtful, clever, eloquent, and delightful words amplify and reconstruct salient features of her or his character.

Such is the case with "The Drum," which invokes the Pied Piper, Kunta Kinte, and Henry David Thoreau in a rhythmic reflection upon Martin Luther King, Jr.'s "Drum Major for Peace" speech. In "This Is Not For John Lennon," she contemplates the artist as "an astronaut of inner peace" who "celebrated happiness, gave word to the deaf . . . vision to the insensitive . . . sang a long low note when he reached the edge of this universe and saw the blackness . . . poetry. . . ." Not all of the poems are written in the telegraphic style; a few free verse pieces are more traditional. All the poems are not about famous persons. Some of the pieces are built upon everyday people and events: mothers, children, skydiving, love, anniversaries. In fact, the most impressive and delightful poem in the book is titled "I Wrote a Good Omelet":

I wrote a good omelet . . . and ate a
hot poem
after loving you
Buttoned my car . . . and drove
my coat home . . . in the rain . . .
after loving you
I goed on red . . . and stopped on
green . . .
floating somewhere
in between . . .
being here and being there . . .
after loving you.

Having had a rapidly and steadily changing writing career over the past decade and a half, Nikki Giovanni has exhibited tremendous creative, intellectual, ethical, and political growth. Much is to be expected of her in the future, as each publication in the past has proven to be a progressive manifestation of her true genius.

References:

Peter Bailey, "Nikki Giovanni: I Am Black, Female, Polite," *Ebony* (February 1972): 48-50;

Richard K. Barksdale, "Humanistic Protest in Black Poetry," in *Modern Black Poets: A Collection of Critical Essays*, edited by Donald B. Gibson (Englewood Cliffs: Prentice-Hall, 1973), pp. 157-164;

Bernard W. Bell, "New Black Poetry: A Double-Edged Sword," *CLA Journal*, 15 (September 1971): 37-43;

A. Russell Brooks, "The Motif of Dynamic Change in Black Revolutionary Poetry," *CLA Journal*, 15 (September 1971): 7-17;

Arthur P. Davis, "The New Poetry of Black Hate," in *Modern Black Poets: A Collection of Critical Essays*, edited by Donald B. Gibson (Englewood Cliffs: Prentice-Hall, 1973), pp. 147-156;

Don L. Lee, *Dynamite Voices: Black Poets of the 1960s* (Detroit: Broadside Press, 1971), pp. 68-74;

Gwen Mazer, "Nikki Giovanni," *Harper's Bazaar* (July 1972): 50;

Jeanne Noble, *Beautiful, Also, Are the Souls of My Black Sisters; A History of the Black Woman in America* (Englewood Cliffs: Prentice-Hall, 1978), pp. 197-198;

R. Roderick Palmer, "The Poetry of Three Revolutionists: Don L. Lee, Sonia Sanchez, and Nikki Giovanni," *CLA Journal*, 15 (September 1971): 25-35;

Stephanie J. Stokes, " 'My House': Nikki Giovanni," *Essence*, 12 (August 1981): 84-88;

Cordell M. Thompson, "Nikki Giovanni: Black Rebel with Power in Poetry," *Jet* (25 May 1972): 18-24.

Papers:

A selection of Giovanni's public papers are at Mugar Memorial Library at Boston University.

Michael S. Harper

(18 March 1938-)

Norris B. Clark
Colgate University

BOOKS: *Dear John, Dear Coltrane* (Pittsburgh: University of Pittsburgh Press, 1970);

History Is Your Own Heartbeat: Poems (Urbana: University of Illinois Press, 1971);

Photographs: Negatives: History as Apple Tree (San Francisco: Scarab Press, 1972);

Song: I Want a Witness (Pittsburgh: University of Pittsburgh Press, 1972);

Debridement (Garden City: Doubleday, 1973);

Nightmare Begins Responsibility (Urbana: University of Illinois Press, 1975);

Images of Kin: New and Selected Poems (Urbana: University of Illinois Press, 1977);

Rhode Island: Eight Poems (Roslindale, Mass.: Pym-Randall Press, 1981);

Healing Song for the Inner Ear: Poems (Urbana: University of Illinois Press, 1984).

OTHER: *Chant of Saints: A Gathering of Afro-American Literature, Art, and Scholarship,* edited by Harper and Robert B. Stepto (Urbana: University of Illinois Press, 1979);

The Carleton Miscellany: A Ralph Ellison Festival, edited by Harper and John Wright, 28, no. 3 (Winter 1980);

"My Poetic Technique and The Humanization of the American Audience," in *Black American Literature and Humanism,* edited by R. Baxter Miller (Lexington: University Press of Kentucky, 1981), pp. 27-32.

Photograph ©1984 by Layle Silbert

Michael S. Harper

The publication of *Images of Kin* (1977), Michael S. Harper's seventh book of poetry in eight years, established him as one of America's most prolific writers. His major significance as a poet is widely recognized among black Americans as well as among white Americans, from Pulitzer Prize winning poet Gwendolyn Brooks *(Annie Allen,* 1949), to the young Armenian poet Peter Balakian, to the conservative critic Edwin Fussell: "This is very likely the finest poetry now being written in a woe-begotten and woe-begone country—perhaps the best since John Berryman. . . ." In his mid-forties, Harper has achieved distinction as a poet because, as Brooks has stated, his "poetry is vigorous as well as brilliant. It has unafraid strength. Although technically dextrous, it differs magnificently from the customary methodical product of today. . . ." Yet, what distinguishes Harper as a unique poet is a distinctive voice that captures the colors, mood, and realities of the personal, the racial, and the historical past, and a philosophy that bridges the traditional schism between black America and white America. As Roger B. Henkle wrote, in nominating Harper for the Israel J. Kapstein endowed chair at Brown University, "Michael Harper is one of the most influential voices among Black artists, and intellectuals in America. . . . But as deeply grounded as Michael Harper is in the Black experience, his poetry speaks to all readers . . . it is a highly sensitive voice, indeed a passionate one; it is expression that resonates with the idioms of American culture." Harper's distinctive voice and philosophy, evidenced by the critical acclaim received by *Dear John, Dear Coltrane* (1970), *History Is Your Own Heartbeat* (1971), *Nightmare Begins Responsibility* (1975), and *Images of Kin,* provide American literature with a modern poetry that combines the fact that one is both a black American and an American—W. E. B. Du Bois's dual consciousness. As Harper suggests, the Afro-American tradition and the American tradition are not mutually exclusive; indeed, they are interlinked, and "being a Black poet and an American poet are two aspects of the same story, two ways of telling the same story. I'm both/and, not either/or." Harper's poetry, especially since he is primarily a narrative poet, illustrates a responsibility to the heroic traditions which are not only connected with one's personal idioms and one's racial province but also are interlinked with all American idioms and ethnic provinces. As a unique contemporary poet who rejects the dualisms of a Judeo-Christian tradition, he integrates and combines black idioms, black traditions, and black literary motifs with the larger picture of American lexicon, American landscapes, and American institutions. Language is, thus, the magical device, and his poetic voice is clearly an attempt to follow the contemporary muse as well as to speak about the personal and historical truth to all people, no matter what. Harper's poetic vision primarily manifests itself in the Afro-American literary tradition, the oral-musical traditions of the blues, jazz, and spirituals. Thus, as John Callahan writes, he "is a poet of simplicity in the midst of complexities, affirmation in the midst of tragedy. . . ." Unlike many of the black poets who emerged during the 1960s and 1970s, Harper is not a poet of obscenities, racial slogans, polemics, or "revolutionary poetic devices"; he is a poet of racial and cultural dualism who has turned his "double-consciousness in the veil" into a source of truth and beauty unlike most contemporary black poets.

Michael S. Harper was born at his parents' home in Brooklyn, New York, in 1938. That event was of great significance because his grandfather Roland R. Johnson delivered him and because he was the first male child on either side of his family. Harper's father, Walter Warren Harper, was employed as a postal worker and supervisor; his mother, Katherine Johnson Harper, worked as a medical stenographer. Although they were not wealthy, they did have a good record collection which first interested Harper in music, a source for his poetic creations. At the age of thirteen, Harper's family, which included Jonathan Paul, his younger brother, and his sister, Katherine Winifred, moved to a predominantly white neighborhood in West Los Angeles, an area in which the homes of some black families had been bombed during the early 1950s.

Upon entering Susan Miller Dorsey High School, Harper was placed in an industrial arts program rather than an academic program; his father "had to come to the school to straighten out a counselor" about his son's ability. Because of an extreme case of asthma, inherited from his mother, Harper not only spent the summer of 1951 sitting up in a chair but also later failed gym because he would not "strip down." As a consequence of the unsatisfactory grade in gym, he was kept off the honor roll; thus, he stopped worrying about becoming a scholar, became a newspaper boy, learned the streets and the neighborhoods, and tried to figure out how not to become a doctor.

Throughout his early career, Harper had been encouraged to study medicine and had two role models in his family, the grandfather who had delivered him and his great-grandfather Dr. John Albert Johnson, a bishop in the African Methodist Episcopal Church and a missionary to the dioceses of South Africa from 1907 to 1916. Although Harper, as his poetry illustrates, had a serious interest in medicine, literature, and history, he was only a marginal student but an extremely good standardized test taker. Although he wrote a few poems, mostly doggerel, as he claims, in the back of his English class, his intense interest in poetry and history remained primarily dormant in high school. He destroyed those early efforts and switched to prose and short dramatic forms until he was almost through college. Following his graduation from high school in 1955, he attended Los Angeles State College from 1956 to 1961. While in college, Harper worked full time as a postal worker at a facing table, "the middle-class equivalent to the pool hall." That work experience, "the real beginning of my life," exposed him to many blacks who had been as well educated as his father was, but were unable to advance according to merit or ability in white American society. Similarly, while in college pursuing a formal premedical course, he was ill-advised by a zoology professor to give up medicine under the assumption that blacks could not make it to medical school. Those experiences of racism and rejection in his own life and in the lives of his family members and black acquaintances helped to form his conception of a schizophrenic American society.

Harper claims that while he was in college, John Keats's (1795-1821) *Letters* and Ralph Ellison's *Invisible Man* (1952) prepared him for the Iowa Writers Workshop in the winter of 1961. Although those works were leading Harper to poetry, he also was particularly influenced by a course entitled The Epic of Search in which the classics, from *The Odyssey* to *Invisible Man,* provided a historical view of man's quest for self-assertion. While in Iowa City, known as the Padre by black students because he wore two hats in the library to keep warm, possibly symbolic of his increasing concerns about the concept of dualism, Harper encountered writer Ralph Albert Dicky and painter Oliver Lee Jackson. At Iowa, Harper became more acutely aware of racial differences, because blacks were restricted to living in segregated sections. That experience, combined with the exclusion of blacks from the curricula of his earlier high school and undergraduate academic preparation, increased his awareness of the fragmentation of society. As the only "blood" enrolled in both the poetry and fiction classes at Iowa, Harper first began to write poetry seriously. After spending a year at Iowa, Harper returned to Los Angeles to student teach at Pasadena City College in 1962. Although previously enrolled in the Creative Writers Program at Iowa, Harper had to return to take his comprehensives in English in 1963 and to receive the masters in English from Iowa.

Harper first taught at Contra Costa College, San Pablo, California, from 1964 to 1968; was a visiting professor at Reed College and Lewis and Clark College from 1968 to 1969; and was an associate professor of English at California State College (now University), Hayward, from 1969 to 1970. In 1970, he submitted his first book of poetry, *Dear John, Dear Coltrane,* to the "U.S. Poetry Prize" sponsored by the University of Pittsburgh. Even though his work—evaluated by Gwendolyn Brooks, Robert Penn Warren, and Denise Levertov—did not win the prize, the University of Pittsburgh Press published *Dear John, Dear Coltrane,* which received a National Book Award Nomination in 1971. Although he had published poems in various journals—*Carolina Quarterly, Quarterly Review of Literature, Poetry Northwest, Southern Review, Negro Digest, Poetry,* and *Midwestern University Quarterly*—with the publication of *Dear John, Dear Coltrane* Harper's formal career in poetry was launched.

Harper received a tenured appointment as an associate professor at Brown University in 1970 but took a leave of absence to pursue a postdoctoral fellowship at the Center for Advanced Studies at the University of Illinois from 1970 to 1971. Since 1970, Harper has been employed by Brown University as a professor of English; he was promoted to full professor in 1974, and served as director of the Graduate Creative Writing Program until January 1983, when he received the Israel J. Kapstein Professorship of English at Brown. Harper also has been a visiting part-time professor at Harvard (1974 to 1977), a visiting professor at Yale (Fall 1976), a Benedict Distinguished Professor of English, Carleton College in Northfield, Minnesota (Spring 1979), an Elliston Poet, Distinguished Professor at the University of Cincinnati (Fall 1979).

Harper has received a National Institute of Arts and Letters Creative Writing Award (1972); a Guggenheim Fellowship in 1976; a National Endowment for the Arts grant (1977); and a Massachusetts Council Creative Writing Award in 1977. He participated in the bicentenary exchange with England, 1976; read at the Library of Congress in 1975 and 1976; and traveled to Ghana, South Africa, Zaire, Senegal, Gambia, Botswana, Zambia, and Tanzania on an American specialist grant in 1977. Harper has also traveled to Germany, Egypt, Scandinavia, and Mexico. In addition to travel and awards, he has been a creative writing judge for the New York State Council on the Arts (1977) and the National Book Award (1978).

Harper's primary emphasis is exploring the dual-consciousness of being a black American poet and an American poet by unifying the racial past into a meaningful whole with the present. "I don't believe in either/or. I believe in both/and," Harper has said, "I'm not a Cartesian poet." To transcend the "Cartesian" polarity of either/or, Harper focuses on race as a metaphor and as a challenge of assertion in the honoring of kinship relationships—personal, familial, communal, national, and international—as a way of linking the past with the present moment, the living with the dead, black America with white America, and Afro-Americans with black Africans. His poetry, which encompasses multiple topics, links art with experience, "to speak about time and place and my own people as a kind of metaphor [which] can be extended and applied to everybody . . . if one can only find the key; and there are keys." Many of the keys to extending the black American experience as a central motif, which Harper relies upon, evolve structurally from the oral, musical traditions of black America, especially blues, spiritual, and jazz forms.

Harper has always had an interest in music

and in music as an enactment of ritual: "my mother was Episcopal my father Catholic; I was a Baptist because of the great singing." Harper's interest in music began when, as a child, he was not permitted to play the collection of 78s his family owned. That prohibition insured his interest. He grew up being familiar with the music of Bessie Smith, Louis Armstrong, Duke Ellington, Billie Holiday, as well as jazz greats such as Thelonious Monk, Sonny Rollins, Miles Davis, and Bud Powell, and most especially, Charlie Parker. Those influences provide him with an architectonic impulse to create. In fact, in *Dear John, Dear Coltrane* Harper pays tribute to numerous musicians; for example, "Alone," dedicated to Miles Davis, is the only poem Harper had written in his worksheet at Iowa and the only one he had kept from his earlier writings.

Both blues and jazz rhythms, Harper says, require a mastery of form and instrument in order to improvise upon thematic texts and make them new in terms of human experience. It is necessary to establish a delicate balance between a personal identity and a group identity, to be an individual as well as a member of the collective. Harper's poetry does precisely that: It "counterpunches to the values of things and of human beings. . . ." With icons of heroism and resistance to oppression by black Americans implicit in all of his work, he testifies to all human efforts and achievements, specifically to black American values inherent in the making of American society.

The basis of Harper's poetic technique is modality, a term difficult to understand abstractly, but one which can be felt subjectively through Harper's works which are poems of performance; that is, they are meant to be sung or read aloud. His poetry, as he claims about *Dear John, Dear Coltrane,* is rhythmic rather than metric.

In an interview with Abraham Chapman, Harper said that in his poetry, modes "are forces. . . . Modality is always about relationships; modality is also about energy, energy irreducible and true only unto itself. What that means is that the Cartesian analogical way of looking at the world will not do for modality. A mode is true only unto itself and can only be understood inside the modal-

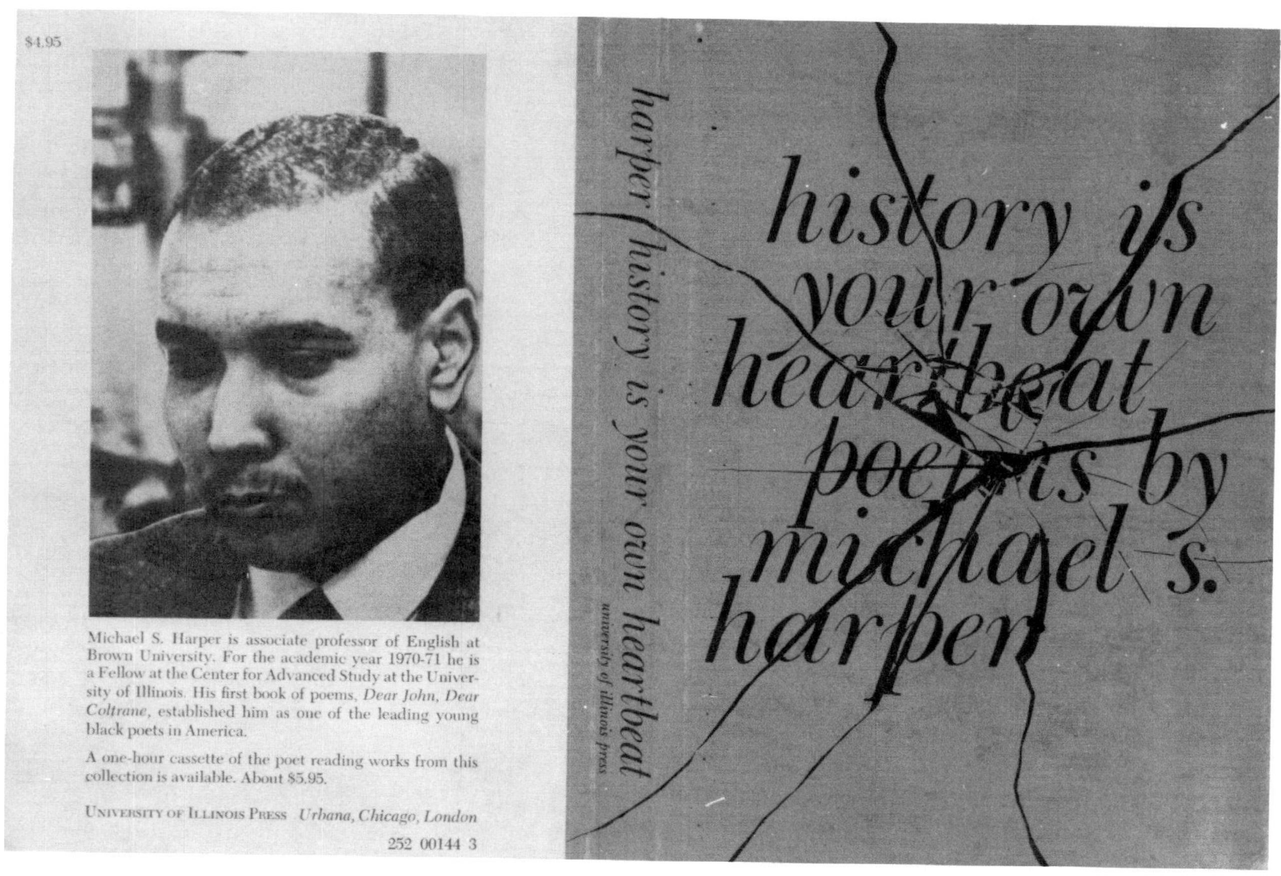

Dust jacket for Harper's 1971 poetry volume which uses history in the sense that T. S. Eliot suggested in A Sacred Wood: *"no poet, no artist or any art has his complete meaning alone"*

ity . . . the Western orientation of division between denotative/connotative, body/mind, life/spirit, soul/body, mind/heart, that is a way of misunderstanding what modality is: 'modality is always about unity.' " Harper poetically provides a key to modes in "Corrected Review":

> Our mode is our jam session
> of tradition,
> past in this present moment
> articulated, blown through
> with endurance,
> an unreaching extended
> improvised love of past masters
> instruments technically down

Modes, as Harper explained, are difficult to fully comprehend outside of themselves; for example, it is difficult to talk about war in the mode of peace. *Muntu: The New African Culture* (1961) by Janheinz Jahn was influential in Harper's concept of modes.

Another informing principle in Harper's poetry is his reliance upon historical myth as an open-ended structure. To Harper, when myths are true and vital, they remain applicable to continuing human experience, not limited to or isolated from historical experiences. Implicit in this view is Harper's belief in man as basically spiritual and in the universe, although diverse, as holistic, not fragmented. It also suggests that man is a reflection of his environment and the environment is a reflection of man. Harper's interest in open-ended myth is a result of his keen awareness of racism and American injustices: "the fantasy of white supremist America with its closed myths has always been a fantasy of a white country. Out of that kind of fantasy came genocide, Indian massacres, fugitive slave laws, manifest destiny, open-door policies, Vietnam, Detroit, East St. Louis, Watts, the Mexican War, Chicago and the Democratic Convention of 1968."

Modality and open-ended myth structures are theoretical concepts that run counter to the theoretical poetic stance of the mainstream (mostly white) whose ideas have dominated American literary criticism in this century. The New Critics believe the poem should be judged as an object in and of itself, and that a poem needs nothing outside itself—like a knowledge of history—to be understood. For Harper, the New Critical approach limits the necessary healthy tension between the internal and external factors of the poem, between the present and the past. Modality and myth also correspond to music which is internal and external to the poem, has a historical past as well as a present moment. They are not pragmatic or abstract like jazz and the blues. The poetic musical and mythic modes can revive the past through the readers' inner feelings, by creating a new sense of time and by arranging a historical awareness. In Harper's vision, playing a musical number or reading a poem fuses the past with the present moment, uniting disparate but complementary moments into a unified whole. Harper has been characterized as being a poet of the paradoxical—but not a poet of paradox—for the external world of objective reality and the internal states of subjective consciousness fuse. His approach to the dramatic or narrative moment is influenced by Keats and Ellison. For Harper, then, poetry recaptures in written or recorded forms the present moment of personal experience which is a microcosm reflecting and extending itself to the universal experiences of his people and their past traditions.

Such a complicated and abstract poetic philosophy as Harper has espoused has led to criticism of him as a writer who wants to create a world vision rather than to pay attention to the techniques of art. The first is true, but certainly Harper's concern with technique, especially the concrete image, is evident throughout his poetry. Harper primarily writes in free verse forms and relies upon musical rhythms to enhance his images as extended metaphors, especially in his earlier poetry. Unlike many other poets, Harper has always maintained that his poetic influence has been primarily musical, although he acknowledges he has studied white American poets—William Carlos Williams, Walt Whitman, T. S. Eliot, Robert Lowell, Theodore Roethke—as well as black American poets—Paul Laurence Dunbar, Langston Hughes, Countee Cullen, Robert Hayden, Gwendolyn Brooks, Sterling Brown. Ironically, it was F. Scott Fitzgerald who taught him that "jazz, essentially a black form could be a comment on character and plot." In reaction against traditional forms, Harper employs such techniques as sprung syntax (an approximation of natural speech patterns), enjambment (the placement of closely related words in different lines), modulated line lengths (closely regulated and measured), blues refrains, idioms, and cadence, "sour" or off-notes, irregular repetition, imbalance and variation of words, phrases, clauses, and lines. Joseph Raffa points out, in a comment that applies to all musicians and poets who improvise on the traditional, "Harper's utilization of traditional verse forms is ironical. The movement away from convention and traditional form reflects his predisposition to run things back a different way thereby creating an original voice in contemporary poetry."

Michael Harper's first book of poetry, *Dear John, Dear Coltrane* (1970), was originally to be entitled "Black Spring" after a poem in the collection. Since Henry Miller's book by that name was already published, Harper reluctantly changed the title. *Dear John, Dear Coltrane* is a compilation of ten years of work and represents Harper's "struggles with maintaining a kind of hold on one's stylistic controls with voice, with idiom, with line, with imagery, with consistency of diction." Although the title suggests the collection of poems is about John Coltrane, the reason for Harper's hesitancy in using that title, it is not; rather, Coltrane is a fundamental source of inspiration for the text, as well as an underlying influence in many of his later poems. Harper first encountered John Coltrane when he was quite young and maintained a friendship with him until Coltrane's death in 1967. The title is not merely a gratuitous reference to a musician; it is a statement of love for one whose vision and wholeness provided an inner power to sustain the struggle: "a love supreme." Typical of Harper's use of the personal symbol which becomes communal and universal, "Brother John," the volume's first poem, is dedicated to John O. Stewart, a fiction writer friend of Harper. The voice of the poem is Coltrane's. The voice not only sets the tone for the text, but more important, it resonates with another chord, the voice of literary character Father John from Jean Toomer's *Cane* (1923). Father John's lament—"O th sin th white folks 'mitted when they made the Bible lie"—articulates Harper's vision of the hypocrisy of the white church in America and clarifies his attempts to destroy the cultural barriers that lead to social schizophrenia.

The thematic aim of this collection of seventy-two poems is one of redemption, which Harper expresses in terms of the unique black American experience, the painful and private existence symbolized by the black musician who frequently is at his best when he is down and out. "Been down so long, down don't bother me." Reminiscent of the blues, refusing to accept discord, the poetry also suggests the redemptive nature of man's creativity—like singing or acting to alleviate pain, agony, and sorrow. Harper's view here is quite close to W. E. B. Du Bois's in "Sorrow Song" in *The Souls of Black Folks* (1903), and to the precepts of black religious tradition. Throughout this collection is an underlying theme of the need for individual self-assertion, the human imperative which enables people to transcend their travails in the face of personal and historical suffering. The assault upon one's humanity is answered through restatement and artistic process:

> Black man:
> I'm a black man;
> I'm black; I am—
> A black man; black
> I'm a black man:
> I'm a black man;
> I'm a man, black—
> I am—

In the assertive, musically represented moment, the modality is personal, communal (black traditional), and universal. The call to assert oneself is a dominant motif from "Brother John" to the last poem in the collection, "Biafra Blues."

In general terms, the *Dear John, Dear Coltrane* collection of poems can be divided into three basic categories. The first group contains poems about kinship relationships or extended family relationships, which include friends and musicians such as Charlie Parker, Miles Davis, Billie Holiday, and James Brown. The most moving and best poems are those which have an intensely personal meaning to Harper, and thus to all humankind. For example, "Reuben, Reuben," the poem about his own loss of a son, testifies to Harper's need to transcend his own pain, as musicians have done, by providing himself with a creative response to the horror:

> I reach from pain
> to music great enough
> to bring me back, . . .
> a brown berry gone
> to rot just two days on the branch
> we've lost a son,
> the music, *"jazz,"* comes in.

Geographical poems evolving out of Harper's travels to Mexico in the summer of 1967 with his wife and son and his attempt to locate himself in a time and place as an extension of man's history make a second grouping of poems. Historical or political poems are in the last category. These pieces use central incident, such as the Lewis and Clark expedition in "Clark's Way West: Another Version," or a more modern incident, as in "American History":

> Those four black girls blown up
> in that Alabama Church
> remind me of five hundred
> middle passage blacks. . . .

As Harper has stated, "I did not see many voices of my own ancestors ably represented in our literature and I wanted to do my part to testify to their effects and achievements. . . ."

In essence, *Dear John, Dear Coltrane* represents Harper's attempt to connect personal and family experience, and the history of his people, with universal questions of self-assertion and transcendence—but never failure or despair. Although some critics have suggested *Dear John, Dear Coltrane* is a confusion of voices, there is a clear resonant voice in the text that unifies the disparities: "I want to testify to a love supreme, a love which personally and communally provides unity amid diversity, especially in America where the American Dream is death. *Dear John, Dear Coltrane* is—a love supreme, a love supreme which transcends death"; "we ached for song you'd concealed/with your own blood. . . ."

History Is Your Own Heartbeat (1971), Harper's second book of poetry, received the Poetry Award of the Black Academy of Arts and Letters in 1971. The volume is both similar to and an extension of *Dear John, Dear Coltrane;* history and myth become interlaced with Harper's personal history as a central theme. This text more clearly illustrates Harper's belief that one must retrieve and reclaim one's past; one must find or establish a connection with others. *History Is Your Own Heartbeat* is a much more personal and narrow text than the expansive *Dear John, Dear Coltrane;* yet, it also is a testament to and unadorned statement about the nature of American society. Harper uses history more explicitly in this text, especially in section two, where he delineates his indebtedness to individuals he has known in order to establish a link between himself, his past—and theirs—and the present moment.

The book of poems is divided into three parts. The first, entitled "Ruth's Blues," is a twenty-poem section which uses his mother-in-law's, Ruth Buffington's, medical history with gallstones as an extended metaphor for the collective amnesia—denial of kinship relationships—from which Americans suffer. The illnesses of Ruth become symbolic of the illnesses of individuals, especially whites, who frequently internalize and deny multiple cultural influences, thus allowing their behavior to be marked by delusion and by intellectual and emotional deterioration. The section provides an orchestrated historical picture or anatomy, expressed in contemporary idiomatic modes of speech and in medical jargon, of Ruth's quest for physical and psychological health. A symbol of Harper's faith in humankind and some Americans, and in a tribute to her personal strength, Harper's Ruth rises above her anemic condition and cultural sterility to make contact with those in her extended family. They in turn make contact with her. The hospital and the clinical descriptions in this section, adroitly used "to draw attention, to shock my reader with detailed, medical closeness and approximation," emphasize the literal *process* of seeking health and spiritual wholeness. The quest then metaphorically leads to a discovery or rediscovery of the bonds of friendship and kinship. Using a hospital to represent American potential to build something new, he says: "We reconstruct lives in the intensive/care unit. . . ." The intensive care unit is necessary to heal the sick, to provide a way station for the wounded so they can make contact with the living even though dying.

The second section, "History as Personality," consists of twenty-eight poems which focus on the eternality of music, color, race, and culture. It reconciles black traditions in the family with natural history. Harper suggests the need to create a viable continuum for children, the future. His epigraph from "Choice of Colors" is by the musical group The Impressions, and it is seminal to this section as he provides a panorama of personalities who have been instrumental in opening his awareness of the dynamic, personal, and aesthetic processes of growth. The array "is devoted primarily to people I've known whom I owe in various ways." This section opens with "Martin's Blues," which reemphasizes the needs and strengths of the individual and the group: "We shall overcome/some day—/Yes we did!/Yes we did!" Thematically it takes one back to the Ruth section. "History as Personality" also begins to illustrate Harper's concern for double-consciousness as "Madimba: Gwendolyn Brooks," a double-conscious sister in the veil, is praised for her ability to destroy one's cage, "the first act of liberation." Following W. E. B. Du Bois, Harper uses the veil as a metaphor for racism, and he raises the question pertinent to black Americans in a diseased and intolerant society: "If you had a choice of colors, which one would you choose? To be an American (white) or to be a Negro?" In Harper's aesthetics, to choose either/or produces a schism between one's history, one's culture, and ultimately in one's personality. This section, which ends with "Don't Explain: 'Culture as Science as Language as Cannibal,' " moves further away from the question of a double-conscious sensibility to one of cultural disunity and stereotype perpetuated by the written word. Implicit in this section is Harper's idea that language—words—can be used to build or to destroy. Myth as lie is, indeed, perpetuated by language. Personalities, culture, and language are intertwined as individuals are linked to others via extended family relationships. To bridge the separation between individuals, races, and culture, Harper suggests people must deal with their histories and see the relationship between the single beating heart and all hearts, between the single historical story and all stories. Reassessing history can help one to overcome disillusion, frustration, and ignorance just as music can enable one to transcend pain through jubilation.

Section III, "High Modes," dedicated to Oliver Lee Jackson, a black painter with whom Harper spent some time at Iowa, is the most complicated of the three sections in *History Is Your Own Heartbeat.* The aim of this section is to transform classical images and myths into modal myths and images much as a painter would visualize or revitalize a vision. Significantly, the first poem, " 'Bird Lives': Charles Parker in St. Louis," recounts Parker's personal history and his continuing titanic influence on others, although he is, literally, dead. Quite important to Harper's vision, Parker, similar to the heroes in the preceding section, remains alive and vital in the consciousness of the poet. " 'Bird Lives' . . ." addresses the question of racism, myth as stereotype, and Harper attempts to work out a cosmic vision by juxtaposing war and oppression with its antithesis, music. Nevertheless, music, painting, and poetry—the creative product (artifact)—are repositories of statements, statements without explanation, but replete with historical connotation. Also important in this section is Harper's nonacceptance of the traditional dichotomies of culture as represented in "Zeus Muse: History as Culture." As Harper points out, the poet-doctor (perhaps in subconscious analogy to his text) William Carlos Williams suggests in *The American Grain* (1925) that history for Americans began with enslavement, murder, and blood, rather than with great ideals or classic literature. This entire section moves from remembering the dead past to reclaiming it by literally and figuratively returning to one's roots: "Black Man Go Back to the Old Country." With that line, repeated fourteen times in italics within forty lines, Harper emphasizes the need for cultural and racial continuity; that continuity is not merely derived from white America and black America; it is also derived from Africa—or the continuum of one's history—as well.

History Is Your Own Heartbeat means one must claim one's history, one's past; and the poet, in keeping with T. S. Eliot's guidelines in "Tradition

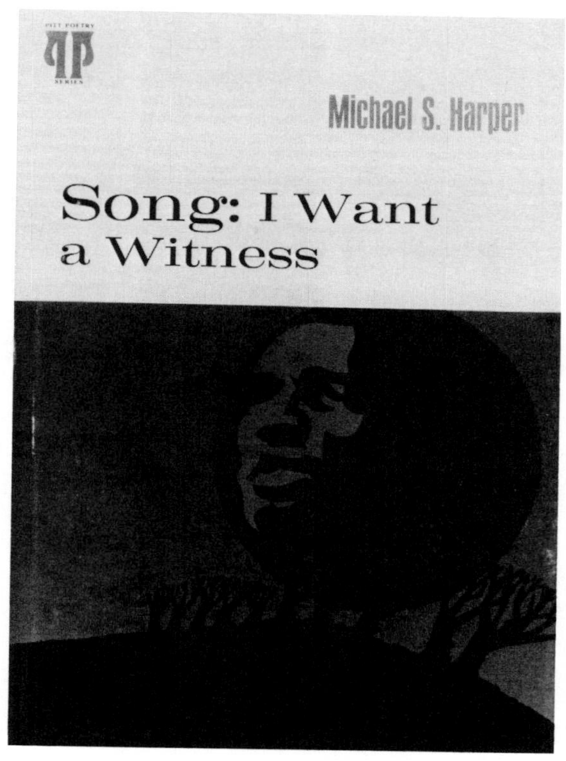

Dust jacket for Harper's fourth collection. He expresses his view of the connection between poetry and history in lines of the opening poem, "When there is no history/there is no metaphor. . . ."

and the Individual Talent" (1920), must obtain one's past by great labor. Harper was significantly influenced by Eliot's *The Sacred Wood* (1920) which he read in graduate school. After all, "no poet, no artist or any art, has his complete meaning alone." As *History Is Your Own Heartbeat* suggests, there is a relationship between the heartbeat of an individual and all heartbeats, between the artist and his ancestors, black and white, between their traditions and his. Thus, man or the poet can transcend his own physical and spacial limitations by returning to and accepting his heritage:

And we go back to the well: Africa,
the first mode, and man, modally,
touched the land of the continent,
modality: we are one; a man is another
man's face, modality, in continuum,
from man, to man, "contact-high," to man,
"contact-high," to man, high modes, oneness

Achieving oneness, diversity amid unity, will reduce the schizophrenia that divides man against himself and others. That in itself is a healing process.

Song: I Want a Witness (1972) continues the trend Harper establishes in the previous collections. As the foreword to the first section states, "When there is no history/there is no metaphor." In brief, Harper uses black religious tradition as a source and a substratal metaphor to testify to the historical black experience. The minister (or poet) calls upon his congregation to take another look at the way they live through descriptions of Old Testament fire and brimstone in hopes of having them achieve salvation, and New Testament love and peace and unity. Harper's "scene is about power,/terror, producing/love and pain and pathology;/in an army of white dust,/blacks here to 'testify'/. . . and redeem, and redeem. . . ."

This text is divided into five sections. The first section and the last, the foreword and the afterword, are the same except for the treble repetition of the lines in the last section. The repetitive exhortation of the last section suggests a need, an urgency, to bear witness to the assault upon nature, native Americans, blacks, the land, and the nation. Throughout Harper's poetry is a sense of man being assaulted (insulted) by forces from without. Witnesses who testify become involved, in a spiritual sense, and can thus transcend or overcome travail beyond their control.

Section II, "Homage to the New World," opens with an epigraph, "Nightmare begins responsibility," the title of Harper's sixth book of poetry, and consists of fifteen poems with a focus on kneading (needing) and baking bread (birth) in the hearth as an extended metaphor of man's interdependence and interconnections with others. Included in this section are clear references to Harper's personal history, although the poetry is less socially oriented than his earlier works. Juxtaposed among images of love and warmth, symbolized by Harper's loving wife, to whom the text is dedicated, and the hearth or kitchen, are images of the exterior: the cold, icy winter landscape, the slowly thawing spring. Tranquility and serenity, devoid of social or political pressures or assaults, is the tone of this section. Yet, the last poem, "Homage to the New World," dramatically shifts the mood from quiet and calm, even though images of death continuously recur, to one of tension as the outside world invades the private consciousness of the poet. The narrator, as does his friend, who comes to deliver a message, becomes fully aware of America's history—a gun, cocked by "our next-door animal-vet neighbor." As Harper explained, "Homage" was written after he had spent a year at the Center for Advanced Study at the University of Illinois. "It had been a painful year for me but also a very meaningful one—one that I grew about." Implicit in this section is an awareness of external reality imposing itself upon internal consciousness, producing pain and terror in the nucleus of love. In many ways, man is disinherited from society.

Section III of *Song: I Want a Witness* is a critique and commentary on William Faulkner's short story "The Bear." "Love Letters: The Caribou Hills, The Moose Range" is about an actual hunting episode in Alaska; but more important, it is a commentary on Faulkner's mythologizing of the hunt, man's violent quest as heroic. Images of violence fill this section which treats man's being disinherited from the land and nature; the sport of hunting not only kills needlessly the hunted, but it can also kill or bruise the hunter. The poet narrates the hunt as he comments on the self-destructive nature and alienation of man. "I hold moral/convictions/top priority/in people." This section, although difficult to comprehend, is important because it also suggests that language and traditions can obfuscate meaning and reality; literature needs to take an ethical position. In a moral position reminiscent of the native American view, Harper believes, "One does not sell the earth upon which the people walk."

Section IV of the text, "Photographs: Negatives" had been published in a limited edition of five hundred texts under the title, *Photographs: Negatives: History as Apple Tree* (1972). The only differences between this section and the separate publication are the reversed order of two poems; in *Song: I Want a Witness,* "At the Cemetery" appears before "Utility Room" and the dedication. The separate text was published and dedicated to Harper's wife, Shirl, to commemorate the birth of their daughter, Rachel. In *Song: I Want a Witness* the section opens with the epigraph, "Nightmare begins responsibility," and establishes the theme of the native American as the root of America: "The Indian is the root of an apple tree;/history, symbol, presence: these voices/are not lost on us, or them." Harper steps inside the native American sensibility to build and extend a kinship relationship to the past. The native American provides meaning for Harper personally and communally. His great-great grandmother was the daughter of a Chippewa chief of Dalhousie, Canada; he lived on a native American burial ground for six months without knowing it; and, in the context of white American culture, the native American is as alienated as is the black American. The section, divided into nine poems, also links the personal history of the narrator with the history of

PHOTO GRAPHS: NEGA TIVES: HIS TORY AS APPLE TREE *a poem by* Michael S. Harper

Dust jacket for the limited edition of Harper's 1972 collection of poems

white America: Roger Williams and John Winthrop. Stalwarts of early, authoritarian, American culture are linked to the land, to the past, and memories in the present. As is characteristic of Harper, the central image is an organic metaphor that grows and transcends time by bridging present and past, and diverse peoples: native Americans, Puritan American historical figures, blacks, and Harper himself. In "History as Appletree," he says:

As black man I steal away
in the night to the apple tree,
place my arm in the rich grave,
black sachem on a family plot,
take up a chunk of apple root,
let it become my skeleton,
become my own myth:
my arm the historical branch,
my name the bruised fruit,
black human photograph: apple tree.

Nicely combined in this passage is the recurring notion of development in three modes: photography, history, and family evolution.

In *Song: I Want a Witness* the American symbol of the stalwart oak is replaced by the apple tree, one that not only bears witness (fruit), but extends to link the nation. The poems in this section are mostly written in the language of photography, and the progress of the section is analogous to the process of photography from developing "The Negatives," to the picture of "History As Appletree." Images appear and seem to develop slowly like a still photograph. Harper visualizes, brings out of darkness, the false, narrow mythology of New England and suggests a multiple heritage for America. Black, white, and red (earth, flower, and fruit) are all conjoined in the historical continuum of America. "The Appletree" was the original title Harper wanted to use for the text.

Debridement (1973) is Harper's fifth book of poetry, and it has been considered his most unevenly written and least well-crafted book. The title is taken from an army medic's term for the cutting away of dead, gangrenous, or contaminated flesh to avoid infection of the healthy tissue. Significantly and appropriately in Harper's vision, this text is dedicated to his three living children and to his two sons who died in early childhood, Reuben Masai and Michael Steven. The text is divided into three parts. Part I, "History as Cap'n Brown," consists of twenty poems in which Harper brings to life the idea that John Brown was not, as myth depicts him, a fanatic who would risk the lives of his men in a foolish cause. The text opens with John Brown because of the heroic stance and the notions about manhood, especially about black manhood, he embodied. Harper always writes about heroism manifesting itself in various actions. In a way, John Brown functioned as a poet because he was able to envision others outside of his experience, outside of his cultural circumstances and yet, to give them, by assumption, the same meaning he ascribes to himself. Harper narratively provides a new insight into John Brown, not as insane, but as being passionately and morally committed to a humane cause. This section on Brown further illustrates Harper's concern with myth as lie and the past being realized in the present consciousness of the artist. Nicely intermixed in this section on Brown are black heroes unknown to most who read or study American history. As Harper has stated, very few blacks or their accomplishments were presented to him during his education. There are alternative subjective and objective voices which emphasize the breach in the cultural identities and the legacies of the past between black America and white America. Also juxtaposed to the intense and fiery passion history has attributed to Brown is the tone of quiet, steady resolve and determination. Interspersed throughout is the veiled language of black American slaves with strong biblical overtones, historically accurate in the black American oral tradition. What is equally important in Harper's eulogizing of John Brown's heroism is the strong sense of indebtedness Harper illustrates we all have to the numerous blacks whose fight for freedom and liberty parallel Brown's own: Harper names them in "Manual For the Patriotic Volunteer":

> "Odd Fellows": DeGrass, McCune Smith,
> Purvis, Vashon, Woodson, the Langstons,
> Gen'l Tubman, Henson, Douglass,
> Loguen, Payne, Ogden, Ward,
> Garnet, Redmond, Bibb: black Heroes all.
> . . . .
> We wrote our names on the hideout walls
> hung by the heavens in blood

Unlike most of Harper's books of poetry, *Debridement* has a more significant impact when read as an extended narrative rather than as individual poems, and the second section, in particular, reads best as a single unit. "Heartblow" consists of ten poems which focus on the "uneven wattage" of Richard Wright's prose. Similar to the Brown section, this one explores how, and possibly why, Wright dealt his own death—heartblow. Although numerous critics acclaim Wright as the best black American writer, Harper raises reservations or objections to Wright's adherence, consciously or unconsciously, to the romantic-schizophrenic stereotypes of racial sexuality and aggression. Despite those reservations, including Wright's misrepresentation of black history, Harper pays tribute to the best naturalist novel in America, *Native Son* (1940); thus, Wright is a literary hero even though Bigger Thomas is too much hysteria and stereotype and not enough controlled anger. He does not have the vision of the double-conscious brother in the veil. Harper juxtaposes this section, which incorporates Wright's Marxist perspective, to the section on Brown, a moral and political activist. Wright responds to racial assault with the pen, Brown with the sword.

The title section of the book, "Debridement," moves into present time by presenting a fictional American hero: John Henry Louis. This narrative sequence recounts how an intelligent black American, the winner of a Medal of Honor, ultimately debases himself, regains his self-respect, and becomes the victim of racism. He is shot while attempting to collect the symbolic debt black Americans are owed by American capitalism and exploitation, money owed to him by a white businessman. The ending is tragic, but not ironic since John Henry's life is the black American experience—one which coerces the victim into becoming a victimizer through exploitation. In this section, Harper alternates short prose passages with units of verse. The language, appropriately, is suggestive of military field surgery and the operating room. Without explicit comment on the mythical John Henry, the steel driving man who kills himself and is killed psychologically, Harper allows this John Henry to survive psychologically, although he is killed nonetheless. The psychological perspective is an important one in these poems; short poem fragments, reflective of a disjointed psyche, are interspersed throughout the narrative, and psychological reports on John Henry's mental stability are substituted for headlines in newspapers (the headlines to which heroes or villains are entitled). This section completes the circle of myth as lie. Together the three heroes, all outsiders to the political and moral system established in America, must contend with their dreams and responsibilities to self and to community. In essence each has asserted his manhood—moral, literary, or patriotic—only to be awakened from his dream through his death. Thus, past and present heroes are victims of myth and racism.

Nightmare Begins Responsibility (1975), the logical sequel to *Song: I Want a Witness* and *Debridement*, has been considered Harper's richest book in range and in variety of selections. The volume is predicated upon Harper's realization that one must act when he awakens from his dream. In fact, since people continually live nightmares, it may be that they can only awaken from nightmares through action—political, literary, or personal, as in *Debridement*. Throughout Harper's earlier poetry runs the idea that the American dream or manifest destiny are inoperable concepts for minorities in white America because of inherent racism, cultural indifference, and man's failure to assume a collective responsibility for the land, environment, and other people. *Nightmare Begins Responsibility* takes this vision one step further into landscapes of ruin, sickness, and alienation which, as in his first two books of poems, man can only transcend by having the courage to assert himself in the face of victimization and travail. In essence, *Nightmare Begins Responsibility* is a commentary on mankind "not being responsible to very complicated and complex bloodlines that have gone into the making of America."

Again, Harper organizes the collection by

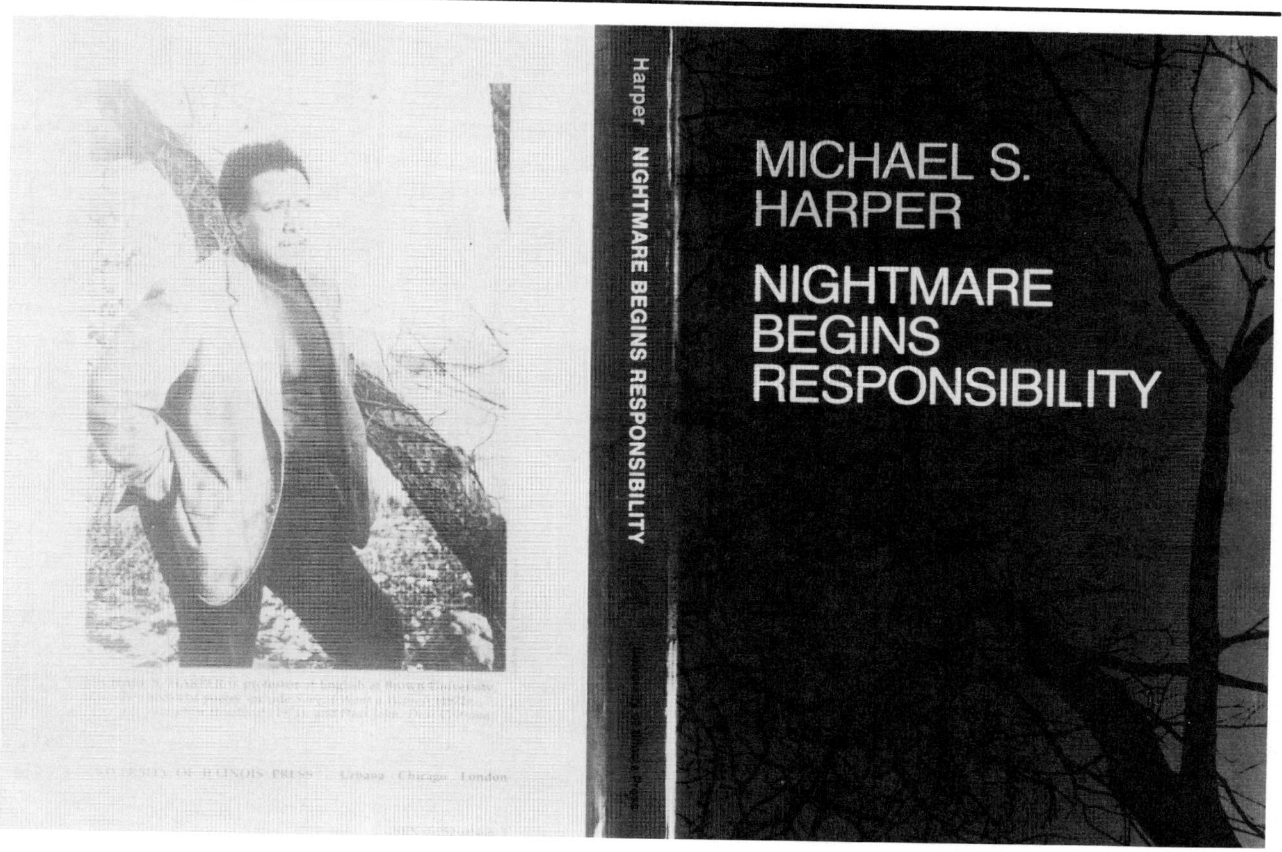

Dust jacket for the 1975 poetry volume which takes its dedication from the title poem: "say it for two sons gone,/say nightmare, say it loud/panebreaking heartmadness:/nightmare begins responsibility"

groupings. The first of five is "Kin" which establishes the kinship or modal units of the individual, family, community, and nation. Those relationships continue to provide a means to heal the disparity and disunity of America's nightmare. Harper opens the section with the blues-jazz idiom of "Kin," and he ends with "Kin 2—one more time—(unblue version)." The eight aphorisms which begin this section establish the theme that survival is the duty and responsibility of man, as in *Debridement.* In his struggle man faces his pain and agony and frees himself from despair and heals himself by never accepting it.

Section II, "Approximations," for Ralph Albert Dicky (1946-1972), a poet and MFA student at Iowa and a friend of Harper, treats death as the violator of kinship relationships. The acts of communication and poetic recreation become the bridges which link the living with the dead. The very process of writing is a way of assuming responsibility and a way of establishing a spiritual connection: "We must conjure you/with poems," Harper says in "Memorial." "Cryptograms," the next section, begins with coded messages from Jean Toomer's "Essentials" *(Cane).* The "need to find a method for developing essence and perfecting being" is Harper's concern here. This grouping of poems is witty, epigrammatic, and deceptively simple.

"Nightmare Begins Responsibility" is the fourth section. In each of the six poems in this section, a responsibility, a decisive action is taken, for example, in the form of his grandfather (Charles Joseph Harper) facing down a white mob inspired by the movie *The Birth of a Nation,* or Jackie Robinson's heroism in baseball. Harper suggests that wisdom is to be shared by all and that the poet's duty is to share his personal vision for the collective good: "say it for two sons gone,/say nightmare, say it loud/panebreaking heartmadness:/nightmare begins responsibility."

The fifth section, "Sterling Letters," is dedicated to Professor Emeritus Sterling A. Brown of Howard University, a friend, mentor, and hero of Harper. Harper first encountered Sterling Brown's recordings in a library in San Francisco and was influenced by Brown's poetry in *Southern Road*

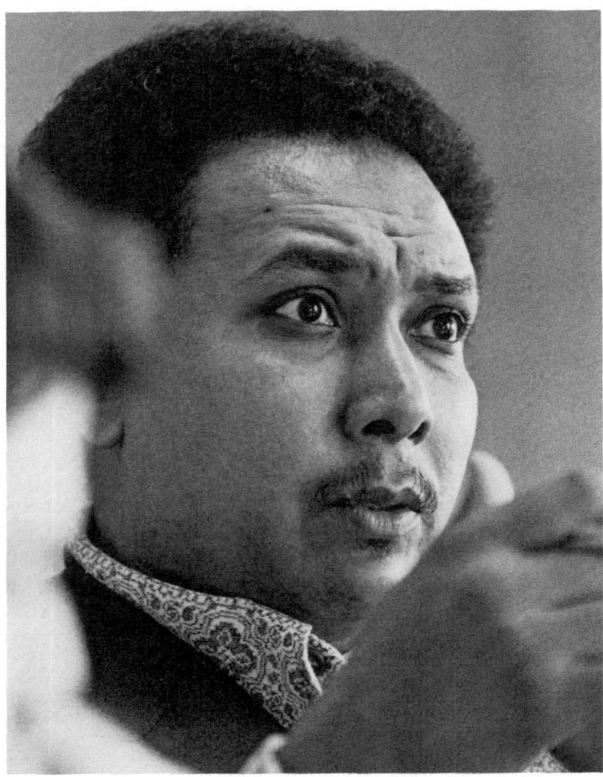

Harper in 1977 (courtesy of University of Illinois Press)

(1932). Brown is Harper's valued visionary, as are the eleven other heroes in this section—athletes, gospel singer, writers, and wife. Brown is symbolic of all of them because he has kept the Afro-American folk tradition alive, as Harper is doing in establishing a continuum of the black American artistic tradition. Indeed, Brown becomes a living poem as do historical figures like Crispus Attucks because their lives and circumstances are emblematic of others' lives and others' efforts. In "Br'er Sterling and the Rocker" Harper says:

> Any fool knows a Br'er in a rocker
> is a boomerang incarnate; look at the blade
> of the rocker, that wonderous crescent
> rockin' in harness as poem.

This section also establishes Harper's tie with other writers—living and dead: Paul Laurence Dunbar, Zora Neale Hurston, Ernest Gaines, Robert Hayden, and Leon Forrest. The connection is the renewing process of creating art. Overall, this group of poems focuses on the artist who has gone beyond nightmare to triumph and to share the power, beauty, and grace of an art form.

Because the range of *Nightmare Begins Responsibility* is vast, it is less coherent as a piece than Harper's other texts. Some critics, unjustifiably, have assessed it as filling space with unintelligible poems (cryptograms). But in the face of his earlier texts, what is significant and comprehensible in this volume is Harper's continued effort to unite different aspects of the black American community into a unified whole. Stylistically, *Nightmare Begins Responsibility* is Harper's richest and most artful poetry—from terse aphorism to rich allusion, from folk diction to the diction of the ivory tower.

Images of Kin, Harper's 1977 book of poetry, received the Melville-Cane Award and was nominated in 1978 for the National Book Award. It is primarily a collection of Harper's best and most representative poems from his earlier texts. Except for the first two sections, "Healing Songs" and "Uplift from a Dark Tower," the selections are in reverse chronological order, carrying the reader back to the distant past. "Healing Songs," as the title suggests, continues Harper's passionate testimonial to the history of his people and restates the necessity of reenvisioning myth. And he continues to evaluate his place and the place of others in the tradition of literary art. "Tongue-Tied in Black and White," for example, is an attack upon inconsistencies or inaccuracies of writers, specifically the poet Theodore Roethke, who use the black idiom. As Harper has stated, he reads white authors to see how they make use of form, as well as to evaluate black character and motivation. Yet, Harper, in comments similar to those he made about Richard Wright in *Debridement,* establishes an affectionate bond, despite differences, between himself and others. Harper can accept the social complexities which exist, and he is comfortable in not denying a dual tradition as many white American writers and black American writers have done. In this text Harper continues to be a poet of harmony—accepting unity and diversity—rather than discord. What is necessary, from Harper's point of view, is to free oneself from the dark tower and to make connections. *Healing Song for the Inner Ear* (1984) is Michael Harper's eighth book of poetry. It is his first book published since 1977 when *Images of Kin* appeared. This text is divided into five sections, and it continues to delineate personal history as a central theme. As with his other books of poetry, Harper respectfully pays tribute to folk heroes, musicians, poets, family, and friends. Clearly there is a sense of commitment to the sanctity of life, a keen awareness of the injustices inflicted upon all humankind. The

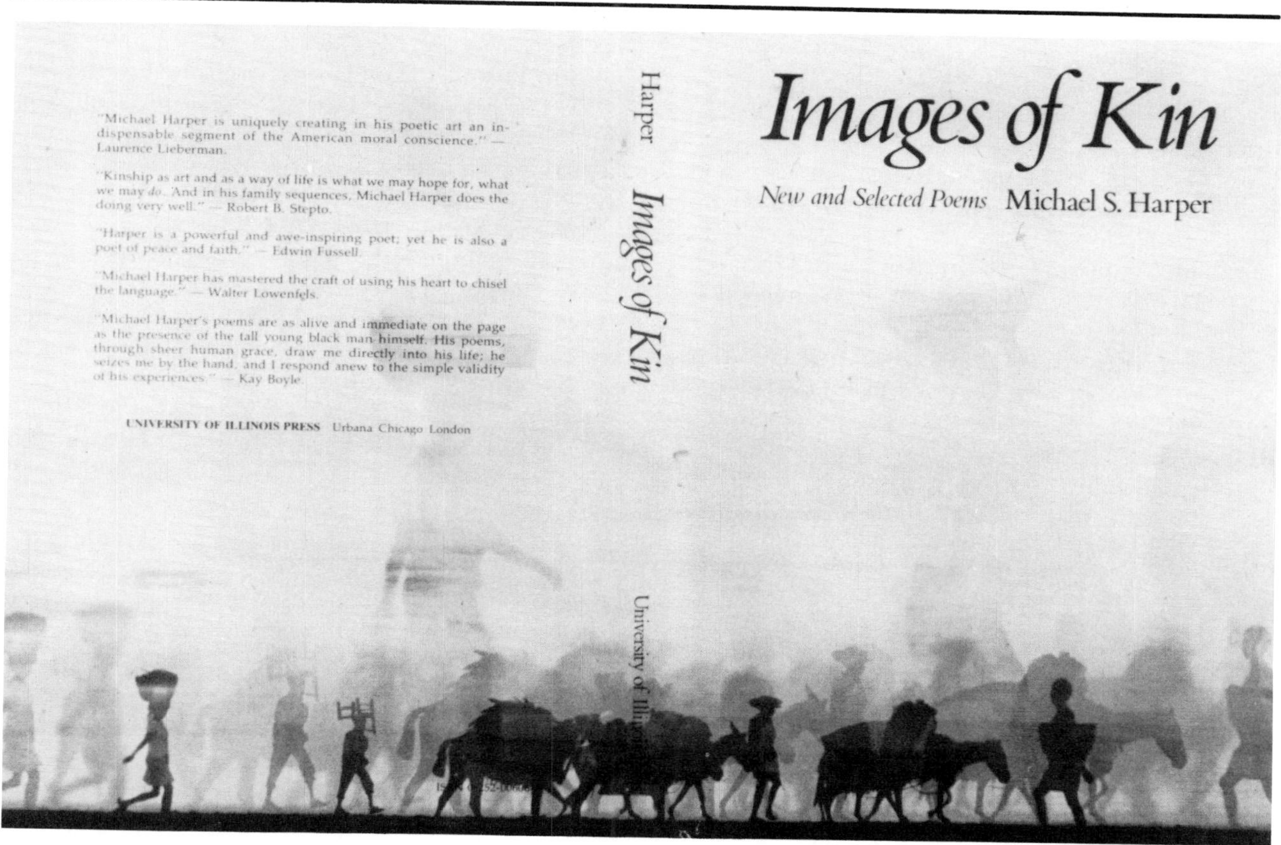

Dust jacket for Harper's 1977 book. Edwin Fussell calls his work "very likely the finest poetry now being written in a woe-begotten and woe-begone country."

poetry in this collection is more international in scope as it reflects experiences in places as far removed as Stockholm, Soweto, Saratoga Springs, and Mount Saint Helens, as "Monuments to history and pain. . . ." Again, Harper conveys a liberating vision in his desire to link together all that he loves, to celebrate the full range of the black American experience, to question the myths and lies of historians, politicians, sociologists, and writers, and to seek his own liberation and personal freedom through artistic expression. This collection of poems is immediately personal, and although it relates the individual experiences to the universal, it has a tendency to be slightly obscure and academic. Yet, it is moving and humanitarian, especially the poems on racial inequities in South Africa. The history and consciousness of music, its evocation of triumph through pain tie together the poems of this volume: "I pursued the songless sound" to sing "Salaams of becoming:/A LOVE SUPREME."

Although most of his accolades have been from the traditional establishment and most of his damnation has been from advocates of a black aesthetic (Amiri Baraka once referred to him as the "rhythmless Michael Harper"), Harper's poetry maintains a balance between the racially and culturally destructive forces on the one hand and artistic sensibilities on the other. In many ways, Harper is neither a black poet nor a white poet; as he freely acknowledges, he uses both traditions and heritages rightfully his and America's to create images of power and beauty. As Harper continues to create, to establish links, he probably will continue to bear witness to the distortions of history, misconceived ideas, reductive myths, and arbitrary separation of humans into stereotyped categories. Without question, Harper will continue to delve into the past and to balance it with his present consciousness. He will continue to use the whole range of his experiences and bring to bear on them the full weight of his intellect and the intensity of his emotions. As T. S. Eliot says, "The historical sense compels a man to write not merely with his own generation in his bones, but with a feeling that the whole of literature

. . . has a simultaneous existence and composes a simultaneous order. . . ."

Interviews:

John O'Brien, "Michael Harper," *Interviews with Black Writers* (New York: Liveright, 1973), pp. 95-107;

Abraham Chapman, "An Interview with Michael S. Harper," *Arts in Society,* 2 (Fall/Winter 1974): 463-471;

James Randall, "An Interview with Michael S. Harper," *Ploughshares,* 7, no. 1 (1981): 11-27.

References:

John F. Callahan, "The Testifying Voice in Michael Harper's *Images of Kin," Black American Literature Forum,* 13 (Fall 1979): 89-92;

Edwin Fussell, "Double-Conscious Poet in the Veil (for Michael S. Harper)," *Parnassus* (Fall/Winter 1975): 5-28;

Laurence Lieberman, "Derek Walcott and Michael S. Harper: The Muse of History," *Yale Review,* 62 (October 1973): 284-296;

Arnold Rampersad, "The Poetics of Michael S. Harper," *Poetry Miscellany,* 6 (1976): 43-50;

Robert B. Stepto, "Michael S. Harper, Poet as Kinsman: The Family Sequences," *Massachusetts Review,* 17 (Autumn 1976): 477-502;

Stepto, "Michael Harper's Extended Tree: John Coltrane and Sterling Brown," *Hollins Critic,* 13 (June 1976): 2-16.

David Henderson

(1942-)

Terry Joseph Cole
Fiorello H. LaGuardia Community College

BOOKS: *Felix of the Silent Forest* (New York: Poet's Press, 1967);

De Mayor of Harlem (New York: Dutton, 1970);

Jimi Hendrix: Voodoo Child of the Aquarian Age (New York: Doubleday, 1978); condensed and revised as *'Scuse Me While I Kiss the Sky: The Life of Jimi Hendrix* (New York: Bantam, 1981);

The Low East (Richmond, Cal.: North Atlantic Books, 1980).

PLAY PRODUCTION: *Ghetto Follies,* San Francisco, Buriel Clay II Memorial Theatre, 1978.

OTHER: Langston Hughes, ed., *New Negro Poets: USA,* includes poems by Henderson (Bloomington: Indiana University Press, 1964);

Hettie Jones, ed., *Poems Now,* includes poems by Henderson (New York: Kulchur Press, 1965);

Walter Lowenfels, ed., *Where is Vietnam? American Poets Respond,* includes poems by Henderson (Garden City: Anchor/Doubleday, 1967);

LeRoi Jones and Larry Neal, eds., *Black Fire: An Anthology of Afro-American Writing,* includes poems by Henderson (New York: Morrow, 1968);

Umbra Anthology 1967-1968, edited by Henderson (New York: Society of Umbra, 1968);

Anne Waldmen, ed., *The World Anthology: Poems from the Saint Marks Poetry Project,* includes poems by Henderson (New York: Bobbs-Merrill, 1969);

Hughes and Arna Bontemps, eds., *Poetry of the Negro 1746-1970,* includes poems by Henderson (New York: Doubleday, 1970);

Ted Wilentz and Tom Weatherly, eds., *Natural Process: An Anthology of New Black Poetry,* includes poems by Henderson (New York: Hill & Wang, 1970);

Nick Harvey, ed., *Markin Time: Portraits in Poetry/San Francisco,* includes poems by Henderson (San Francisco: Glide, 1971);

Woodie King, Jr., ed., *Blackspirits: A Festival of New Black Poets in America,* includes poems by Henderson (New York: Vintage, 1972);

Jerome Rothenberg and George Quasha, eds., *America A Prophecy: A New Reading of American Poetry From Pre-Columbian Times to the Present,* includes poems by Henderson (New York: Random House, 1973);

Ronald Gross, Quasha, et al., eds., *Open Poetry: Four*

David Henderson (photograph ©1983 by Anthony Barboza)

Anthologies of Expanded Poems, includes poems by Henderson (New York: Simon & Schuster, 1973);

Janice Mirikitani, et al., eds., *Time to Greez: Incantations from the Third World,* includes poems by Henderson (San Francisco: Glide/Third World Communications, 1975);

Umbra/Latin Soul 1974-1975, edited by Henderson (Berkeley: Society of Umbra, 1975).

PERIODICAL PUBLICATIONS: M. Horovitz, ed., "Azania for Thee: We," in *New Departures: Second International Poetry Olympics,* no. 14 (England 1982);

"Avenue C Blues," *Race Today: Britain's Leading Black Journal,* 14 (April/May 1983);

"Prose," "Tuffgong," "Third World," "Portraits of the Road," *Hambone,* no. 4 (Fall 1984).

If any author may be nominated as the literary heir of Langston Hughes, David Henderson deserves the honor. His poetry makes use of personal experience, popular culture, and European and American mythologies to create a new mythology for the people of Harlem and the castaways on Manhattan Island. Like all mythmakers, Henderson is at once a fabulist, sociologist, and historian. In a 1972 interview he describes himself as a "griot," assuming the mantle of the traditional African storyteller and chronicler.

Henderson was born in Harlem in 1942 and was raised there and in the Bronx. He later lived in the East Village on the edge of the Bowery, a section of New York populated by artists and derelicts alike. While in New York he attended The New School for Social Research, Bronx Community and Hunter Colleges of the City University. From 1964 to 1965 he also attended the East-West Institute in Cambridge, Massachusetts. He published his first poem in a citywide newsweekly, the *Black American,* in 1960. He was a founder of the *East Village Other* (an alternative newspaper) out of which grew the Underground Press Service, which during the 1960s networked articles of common interest among radical, literary, and political publications.

In 1962, with Thomas Dent, Albert Hayes, Calvin C. Hernton, and others, Henderson founded the Society of Umbra which in 1963 began publishing *Umbra* "out of racial and social awareness," a magazine described in its first editorial as an outlet "for unpublished and infrequently published ethnic writers" as opposed to "best sellers" and "literary spokesmen of the race situation . . . popular in commercial press and slick in-group journals." The first issue of *Umbra* was anything but slick, printed in offset on carefully chosen, heavily-textured paper. It sported a cover by budding artist Tom Feelings and included poems by Julian Bond, Oliver Pitcher, Lerone Bennett, Raymond Patterson, Julia Fields, and Alice Walker. Over the years it has served as an initial showcase for such talents as Nikki Giovanni, Ishmael Reed, and Quincy Troupe. To the first issue, editor Henderson contributed three poems: "Time & Atavism," "The Ofay & the Nigger," and "Black is the Home."

Henderson's early poetry is awkwardly self-conscious with neither the personal intensity nor the dense imagery of the poems in his first book, *Felix of the Silent Forest* (1967). "Time & Atavism" is the most personal, describing the relationship between Henderson and a younger brother. The language is often archaic as opposed to figurative, "My young brother lies long abed." The other two poems show first sparks of Henderson's mythmaking ability. In "The Ofay & the Nigger" archetypal characters converse at a party in the spirit of "Northern Hiptitude":

> they must obey
> PARLANCE
> -the god of interracial
> love/understanding
> & Northern Mongrelization

"Black is the Home" uses the European myth of

Mount Olympus as an implied metaphor for an America bent on genocide through disdainful disassociation from a people. Conversely the negative energy of America's evasion is channeled by black men and women into the creation of some things positive: strong black gods, such as an anthropomorphized History, along with determined martyrs for the American dream who daily join the black pantheon.

In 1967 the Poet's Press published two thousand copies of *Felix of the Silent Forest.* In the book's introduction Amiri Baraka (LeRoi Jones) describes Henderson's poetry as a "world echo" full of "strength and beauty" particular to the black experience. He contrasts the poetry of the collection with the lyrics of the Beatles, observing they "can sing 'Yellow Submarine' because that is where they, and all their people (would like to) live. We (black folk) are in the streets . . . somewhere in the world." Jones concludes that Henderson's writings are "local epics with the breadth that the emotional consciousness of a culture can make."

The poetry of *Felix of the Silent Forest* is powerful in its use of taut, often ironic, images built on careful use of description. These poems herald the jazz poetry of *De Mayor of Harlem* (1970) but contain a concreteness which makes their collection superior to the second book. In the title poem, popular culture, folklore, and myth merge to create and animate a worn Felix the (black "cool") cat, dethroned as the cartoons' black god of mirth, no longer immune to the superstitions and stereotyping with which his kind (black cats/black people) are associated. He becomes a metaphor, not only for disinherited black Americans, but for anyone once loved and discarded. Felix "walks the City hungry in every sense," haunting greasy spoons and:

wondering if
anyone he loves
wonders where he is.

"Boston Road Blues," early in the same volume, gives a good example of Henderson's ability to set a scene using ironic contrast: "Ride a speeding Bonneville/along this main street/and you will see the Negroes waiting on either side/on stoops on dinette and aluminum chairs/like the retired/bop cap and sneakered Jews/of the Grand Concourse." The most telling words are "waiting" and "retired" since one implies looking for opportunity and the other the ostensible reward of a fulfilling professional life. The piece moves from lyric to narrative in its second section, telling the

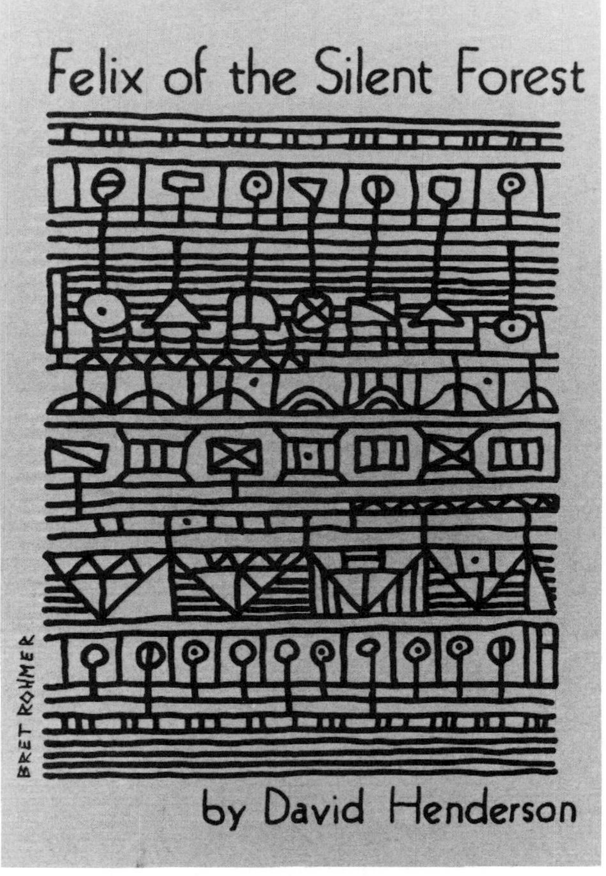

Front cover for Henderson's 1967 collection of poems. In the Introduction Amiri Baraka (LeRoi Jones) calls Henderson's poetry "the world echo."

autobiographical "legend" of Henderson's sojourn as a member of a singing group à la Motown's Temptations and their many clones:

our quartet calling ourselves Starsteppers
(perhaps to insure a goal
other than a ghetto)

Myth and autobiography fuse for effective description in the moody piece entitled "poem" which recreates a holiday visit home and speaks of "the worn crotch of the alabaster moment" in which the poet sadly becomes aware of the effects of distance, time, and experience on familial relationships. He notes, "I am too big/I move from room to room like a giant."

"They Are Killing All the Young Men," dedicated "to the memory and eternal spirit of Malcolm X," is an angry complaint about the lack of coverage, indicative of a lack of respect, given by the popular media to the assassination of Malcolm X. The death of Malcolm X is described by Henderson as "the end of a personal era" in the introduction to *De Mayor of Harlem;* it is a grisly event which will recur many times in his poetry as he attempts to make sense of it; as such it becomes an allegorical reminder of the negative energy expended in the irreverent treatment of black life by American institutions, energy which forces the creation of positive contemporary black myths and mythic figures.

In 1967 Henderson served as a consultant for the National Endowment for the Arts, and during that summer worked with the Free Southern Theatre in New Orleans. In 1968 he traveled to Berkeley, California, where he served on the Board of Directors of the University Without Walls and served as an artistic consultant to the Berkeley Public School System. Returning to the Northeast, he worked with the Teachers and Writers Collaborative housed at Columbia University in New York City and through 1970 taught at the City College of New York first in the SEEK program, then in the English department, and finally, as poet-in-residence. At the University of California, Berkeley (1970-1972), Henderson taught English and Afro-American literature, and at the University of California at San Diego (1979), he lectured for the Literature department.

Henderson's introduction to *De Mayor of Harlem* describes it as a collection of "poems, documentaries, tales, and lies" written between 1962 ("Elvin Jones Gretsch Freak," "Bopping," "So We Went to Harlem" also appear in *Felix of the Silent Forest*) and 1970. The first cluster of poems, 1962-1966, are the most powerful because of Henderson's ability to manipulate the reader using detailed sensory descriptions; however, the later poetry draws a strength of its own when recognized as "jazz poetry," riffs of relevant but staccato images, bare, stark, reaching for myths existing in the collective unconsciousness of black people. Henderson describes jazz poetry as "the language of the man of the moment; it's improvised; it's street language . . . African 'talking drums'—the basis of jazz—were one of the world's first mass communications systems. People related to those rhythms in a unified way."

"De Mayor of Harlem" appeared before the

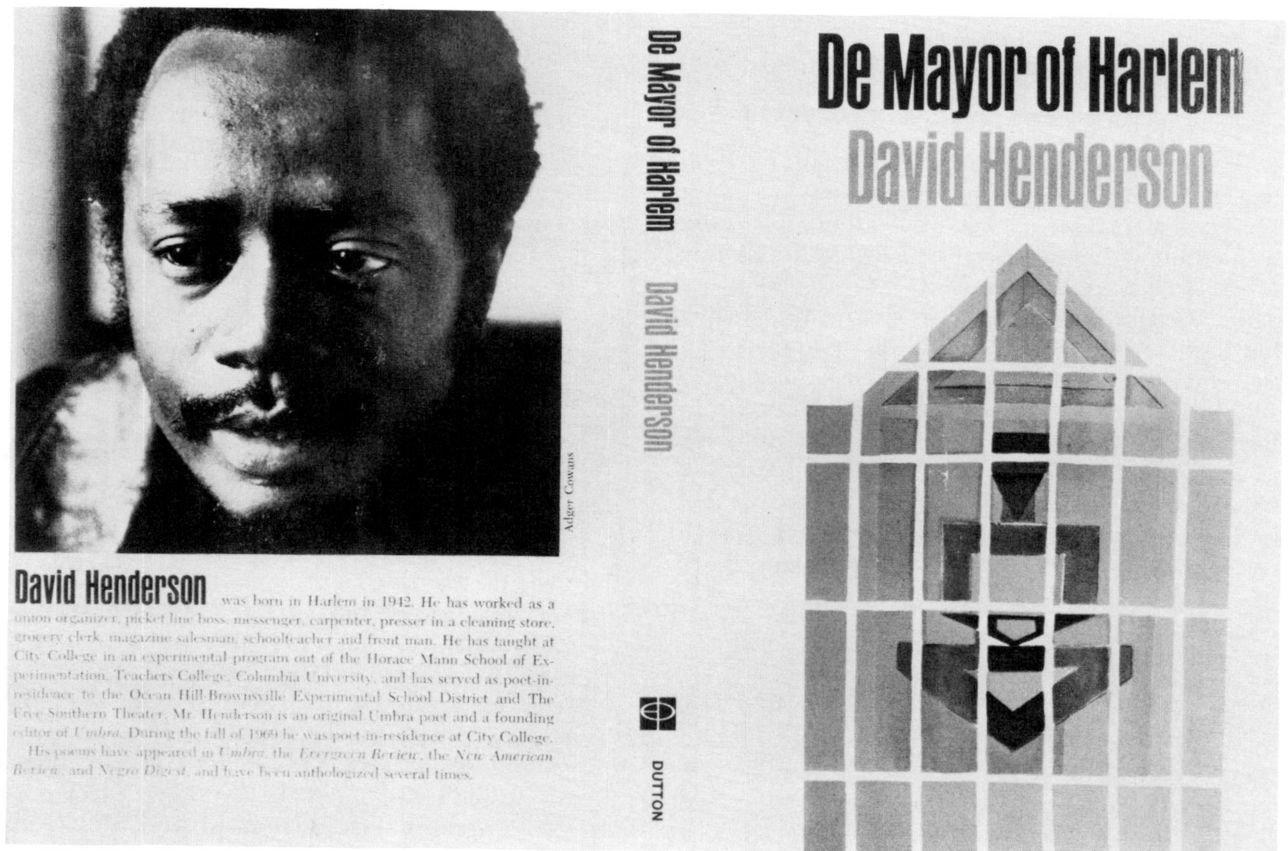

Dust jacket for the 1970 book that Henderson says "covers seven years of poems, documentaries, tales, and lies"

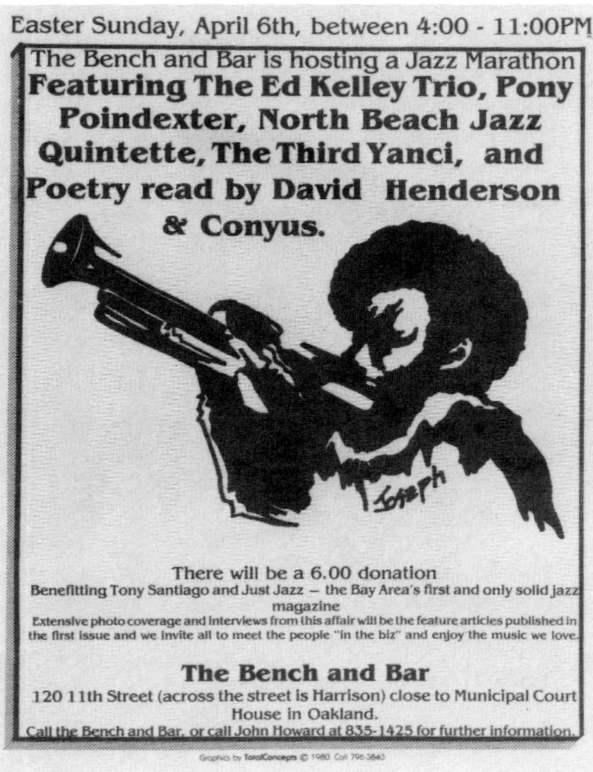

Flyer advertising a 1980 reading by Henderson

book was published, in *Umbra Anthology 1967-1968* in a slightly different form and entitled "Walk with the Mayor of Harlem." Especially noticeable is the ironic shift in the poem's tone caused by the change in the article spelling from "the" to "de," showing again the need to discard old myths and mythic heroes for new. Historically, the elected position of the Mayor of Harlem (held by such luminaries as Bill "Bojangles" Robinson and Willie Bryant) has been politically powerless, existing, to Henderson, as another false idol created to sop the attention of black Harlemites, a placebo who serves as a symbol of institutional America's benign neglect. In the poem, *de* Mayor of Harlem is simply a silent figure of a past era, wandering amid the life-filled, myth-creating Harlem streets:

walk with de mayor of harlem
find no   find no
                              find not
many of the millions
        of the downtown boston blackies
fancy of james bond
in psychedelic robert hall clothing
. . . .

        tell me like it is
the memory of sky watch
sun dance drum chant body ruba
taut are the signals thru the skin
thru bones
hard as the forgotten legions
of/the
giant bushmen

The book's first section reveals the scope of Henderson's role as griot. Some poems are commemorative, recalling such events as the Pope's visit to Harlem and a Marcus Garvey Day parade. Others, titled "documentaries," review events such as the 1964 Harlem riots and their aftermath, from a black perspective:

I see police eight to one
        in its entirety Harlem's 2nd Law of Thermodynamics
        Helmet
        nightsticks bullets to barehead
        black reinforced shoes to sneaker
Am I in Korea?

"A Documentary on Airplane Glue" directs attention to a social ill instead of a single event: "Sometimes I wonder how the effects of the glue was discovered/could it have been an eleven-year old . . . piecing & glueing & piecing/gasping with slight exasperation/& then suddenly wonderfully/soaring/ultimately away."

Some pieces include the word "saga" in their titles and elaborate on the significance of a communal event. The "Saga of the Audubon Murder" mythically links and contrasts the birth of George Washington with the assassination of Malcolm X. "The Last Set Saga of Blue Bobby Bland" is a found poem which reports a showdown on the stage of the Apollo Theatre between blues singer Bobby "Blue" Bland and his audience when a drunken woman with an afro climbs onstage and begins to insult Bland's process hairstyle.

Rhythm and blues images give way to jazz in the second and third sections of the book. Some of the poems are portraits of jazz musicians, such as Theolonious Monk and John Coltrane, which attempt to place them in the new cosmology Henderson is creating. Jazz rhythms syncopate the poems and images suffer, becoming more jumbled, relying more on the reader's ability to make connections: "chant chant sheet glass windows/glaciers of upper kingdom/stark screams shatter glass/runs the tracks under trees of lightning/hung out over red trailers."

There are sentences and passages in the late poems which quickly come to life and wrestle with the imagination, even as Henderson chooses to remain dynamic by wrestling with new forms. His "Harlem Anthropology," the final poem in *De Mayor of Harlem,* opens with comic pride that would make Langston Hughes laugh: "harlem you got some big legs!"

Henderson's latest collection, *The Low East* (1980), is a celebration of his return to New York's Lower East Side (nicknamed "Alphabet City" because the avenues have letter names). In this collection, written over several years, he attempts to define this section of the city, even as he had Harlem in *De Mayor of Harlem.*

In this volume the matured poet questions his life roles and experiments with his craft. There are more portraits than narratives here: characters such as Mad "Mambo" and Vera Goode come alive through the precision of slice-of-life description. There are a few prose poems, notably "Charlie at the Vanguard" which reflects Henderson's love of jazz. While there is a caution in the poems, a meditativeness not present in the earlier works, Henderson has not lost faith in his griot's role as "cheerleader," unveiling the pride of the people in the community. Henderson comments in the poem "Blue Horizon": "we will win/because our cause/is just/because we cherish/human beings/as the closest expression/to the wonders/of all of Gods/creations."

David Henderson was a recipient of the Great Lakes College Association of New Writers Award in 1971. His poetry has found a place in many anthologies, and in 1978 the Library of Congress began tape-recording Henderson reading his work. He presently commutes between Berkeley and New York City, spending his time teaching and editing. He has completed an unpublished collection of poems largely about his California experience, "Berkeley Trees," written between 1969 and 1984. He is also writing a nonfiction prose book about reggae music.

Interviews:

Diane Middlebrook, "David Henderson's Holy Mission," *Saturday Review* (September 1982);

Kofi Natambu, Interview with David Henderson, in *Solid Ground: A New World Journal,* no. 7 (Winter 1984).

Everett H. Hoagland III

(18 December 1942-)

Linda E. Scott

BOOKS: *Ten Poems: A Collection* (Lincoln University, Pa.: American Studies Institute, 1968);

Black Velvet (Detroit: Broadside Press, 1970);

Scrimshaw (New Bedford, Mass.: Patmos Press, 1976).

OTHER: "Night Interpreted," in *The New Black Poetry,* edited by Clarence Major (New York: International, 1969);

H. N. Rosenberg, ed., *Patterns,* includes poems by Hoagland (Idlewild, 1970);

"Love Child—A Black Aesthetic," "My Spring Thing," "The Anti-Semanticist," "It's a Terrible Thing," in *The Black Poets,* edited by Dudley Randall (New York: Bantam, 1971);

"Prologue," "Georgia—It's the Gospel Truth," in *A Broadside Treasury,* edited by Gwendolyn Brooks (Detroit: Broadside Press, 1971);

"The Anti-Semanticist," in *New Black Voices: An Anthology of Contemporary American Literature,* edited by Abraham Chapman (New York: Mentor, 1972);

Ron Welburn, ed., *Dues: An Anthology of New Earth Writings,* includes poems by Hoagland (Emerson-Hall, 1973);

Quincy Troupe and Rainer Schulte, eds., *Giant Talk: An Anthology of Third World Writings,* includes poems by Hoagland (New York: Vintage Books, 1975).

PERIODICAL PUBLICATIONS:

POETRY

"Fertility Doll," *Negro Digest,* 18 (September 1969): 37;

"Music," *Black World,* 24 (September 1975): 67;
"America: An Allegory," *Black World,* 24 (October 1975): 55-57;
"Goree," *American Poetry Review,* 12 (July/August 1983).

FICTION

"Table Talk," *Black World,* 23 (June 1974): 76-80;
"Manchupa Suite," *Black World,* 23 (August 1974): 53-58.

Everett Hoagland's poetry is a celebration of Afro-American history and culture based on the thematic and aesthetic assumptions of the black arts movement. The differences between his collections of poetry suggest his artistic maturation and the concretization of the values of the black aesthetic.

The son of Everett Hoagland, Jr. and Estelle Johnson Hoagland, he was born on 18 December 1942 in Philadelphia, Pennsylvania, where he spent his youth. Hoagland received a bachelor's degree from Lincoln University in Pennsylvania in 1964, having been a recipient there of the Silvera Award for Creative Writing. He taught English at Harding Junior High School in Philadelphia from 1964 to 1967. His other early teaching experiences included the Operation Headstart program in Philadelphia during the summer of 1965 and English classes in Philadelphia's Adult Evening School from 1965 to 1966.

In 1967 Hoagland returned to Lincoln University where he served as assistant director of admissions until 1969. In 1968, the American Studies Institute at Lincoln published his first volume of poetry, *Ten Poems: A Collection,* and for the 1968 to 1969 year, he was named one of the Outstanding Young Men of America.

In 1969 Hoagland moved to California, where he lived for two years. He served as assistant to the director of the Black Studies Center of Claremont College. He was also an instructor in African-American poetry, and he was poet-in-residence for the Black Studies Center. While in California, he also worked as coordinator and teacher of Afro Culture and Society in the Chino Institute for Men, instructor of American and black literature at Mount San Antonio College, and English instructor for Claremont College's summer Upward Bound program.

In 1970, Hoagland's best-known collection, *Black Velvet,* was published by Broadside Press. He entered the Creative Writing Program at Brown University as a University Fellow in 1971 and received his M.A. in 1973.

Hoagland was an instructor of humanities in the preenrollment program at Swarthmore College in 1972. He has been a professor of English at Southeastern Massachusetts University since 1973. In 1975, he was the recipient of a Creative Artists Fellowship from the Massachusetts Arts and Humanities Foundation. From 1979 to 1982, Hoagland was a weekly columnist for the *New Bedford Standard-Times.* He is currently a contributing editor for the American Poetry Review.

Everett Hoagland (photograph by John Scheckler)

Hoagland is divorced and the father of four children, Kamal, Nia, Ayan, and Reza. He is a member of the Baha'i faith, "and/but a Black American," he adds, "which says it all."

Although there has not been much critical response to Hoagland's poetry, the frequent appearance of his work in anthologies indicates a reader appreciation for his work. Unfortunately, his first collection is not readily accessible, so it is difficult for readers to assess his earliest writing style. Thus, an analysis of his writing career must begin with his first widely circulated work, *Black Velvet.*

Published in 1970, the collection bears the unquestionable influence of the black arts movement. Hoagland was enmeshed in an artistic environment that encouraged and embraced expressions of reality. His poetry emphasizes the unity of black people and the shared aesthetic heritage which is implicit in all aspects of black life. Hoagland's poetry does not exhibit the specific political preoccupations of writers such as Amiri Baraka (LeRoi Jones) and Haki R. Madhubuti (Don L. Lee), but it does share the sense of racial pride that

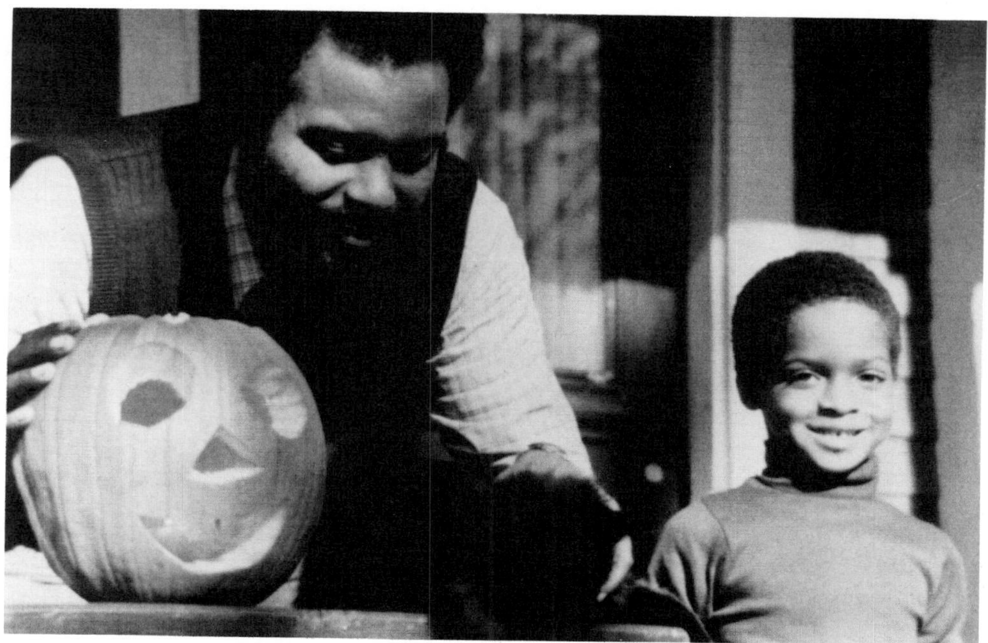

Hoagland and son, five-year-old Kamal, Halloween 1978

permeates the works of William J. Harris, Quincy Troupe, and fellow Philadelphian, Larry Neal. These poets use language that is both ironic and infused with a joyful appreciation of the sounds and senses of black life and culture. Hoagland says his work was strongly influenced by the work of Sterling Brown and Robert Hayden, whom he feels are the best and most eloquent epic poets, and by Jayne Cortez and Ntozake Shange for their inventiveness with language. For Hoagland, black art is black life—a concept made explicit in *Black Velvet*'s opening poem:

our art is beyond reproach but never beyond reach
its in the streets not the colleges what we can't
learn we don't teach and what we don't learn ain't
worth it we got what it takes.

Black women are central to the volume. The collection is dedicated "to sisters everywhere" and its themes are frequently advanced by women. Hoagland admires their beauty and the heritage they embody. In the frequently anthologized poem "Fertility Doll," he addresses the world's ambivalent perception of black women:

from the hottentot
i remember a harvest somewhere
and follow her
walk with wondering
why europe put her
simultaneously
in a kitchen and a
museum.

Women are both subject and metaphor for Hoagland. In "Sunrise Brown/Amanecer Moreno," images of the desert are used to describe a woman. In "Tropical Landscape," the African continent is described through images of women. In both poems, the metaphor and subject merge and become indistinguishable.

Hoagland consistently employs images and metaphors that evoke the senses. "Love Child: A Black Aesthetic" typifies Hoagland's use of sensuality in its description of the sexual act and the birth of a child. Furthering the metaphor, the birth of a child becomes analogous to artistic creation,

POP! a black pearl from god brand new small brown
sugar lump velvet little wild rabbit burnished gold
nugget rock a bye rock a bye sweet blackberry pie
and honey love syrup soul soft fur brown round little
cup of rum nectarous distillation of the words "i
love you" . . . godly milky mystical nascency succulent
miracle.

In "The Anti-Semanticist," Hoagland denies the ability of language to communicate anything meaningful. He claims he is not concerned with adjectives, nouns, or metaphors. Reality is the only thing deserving attention. Specifically, he is interested in whether a woman is spiritually beautiful—not whether she is physically beautiful. In addition, he values her pride and her ability to love—attitudes that cannot be expressed in language,

there is little definition i need
indeed
it matters only that there is
black power
in your loving.

The uniqueness of Hoagland's early poetry is rooted in his use of Afro-American music. The language of the blues and the rhythms of jazz propel his words. Madhubuti has described Hoagland's poems as "Otis Redding rhythms that won't stop dancing." His repetitious alliteration and rhymes are simultaneously frenetic and smooth. Outlined by ironic contradictions, their effect is that of lyrical dynamite, "opulent oracle—it's a terrible thing!/ my, my/pink and purple butterfly/fine as you want to be!/sly sleepin' creamy creepin' soul stabbin' dippin'/dabbin'. . . ."

Hoagland does not limit his musical references to the traditions of black Americans. He presents a bemused response to classical music: "Fucgue [sic] in B(lack) Minor" is a verbal and rhythmic mockery of Johann Sebastian Bach's repetitive tempos and tunes. Hoagland even amends the adoration of God found in Bach's work,

god is black is christ
was black and good is black
and evil's not and lack of black is blank
and give us back
and black give back
to black
and black is back
and black is black is black is black is black
oh yea-a-a-h!!

In 1974 and 1975, Hoagland published four original works in *Black World.* In 1974 the magazine had bestowed upon him the Gwendolyn Brooks Award for Fiction. Hoagland's work in this monthly periodical is interesting when considered in retrospect because it reveals a poet in transition. The subjects of the poems are actual people: Nate Shaw and Joan Little; the writing style is more narrative and prosaic than it was earlier, but the forms are more experimental; for example, his fiction incorporates poetry. The concerns expressed in this material are more political and historical than those of his earlier work. The stories and poems published in *Black World* were never anthologized and remain obscure, but as harbingers of Hoagland's later work, they offer significant insights.

With the publication of his next collection, *Scrimshaw* (1976), Hoagland earned a permanent position in the canon of Afro-American poetry. *Scrimshaw* revives thematic and stylistic trends established in *Black Velvet* and unveils a more introspective view of people and events.

Completed after his graduation from Brown University's Creative Writing program, this collection bears the influence of the program's director, poet Michael Harper. Harper's influence is most evident in Hoagland's emerging sense of history. Subtitled "A Celebration of the American Bicentennial," much of *Scrimshaw* is a revision of the events surrounding the American Revolution and America's founding fathers. Hoagland echoes Harper's notion that an understanding of history is fundamental to individual identity and destiny in "Georgia On His Mind,"

At the bar
the black man
picks up his glass
the way he picked cotton.
Gin oils Eli Whitney's machine.
His tongue is cotton,
his mind is a cotton gin,
his life a mill wheel on
the river, oils the machine
His soul is a boll weevil.

In 1976, this person has no identity other than that bestowed upon his ancestors two centuries ago. Black Americans cannot escape the historical fact of slavery, and its legacy will remain at the core of the soul.

The concept of a soul—a spiritual home—is central to *Scrimshaw.* In "The Path of Bones," Hoagland explains how the title of his collection conveys this theme. The concept of a scrimshaw, originally an article carved from a piece of whalebone ivory, is expanded by Hoagland to include all expressions of individuality. It is a thoughtful creation, having profound implications for the creator,

Scrimshaw as braille for the ear
to hear the sea-rocked Path of Bones, a keyboard,
  lining the Middle Passage
home.

Music continues to be implicit in Hoagland's

poetry, although the music in *Scrimshaw* is more of a long blues cry than the staccato repetition of *Black Velvet.* This difference is most apparent in "Solo: Blowing," which translates the story told in a horn player's solo,

african avenues in the mine my mind the street was
an african termite mounds of sounds too much diz-
zying color too much riotous ritual-I'm In Another
World
I'm Riding On The Moon And Dancing On The Stars At
Nighttime.

In the poem's conclusion, Hoagland presents a new definition of the black aesthetic,

sunk into the navy blues IS the music is black A PRISM
the blind are bright buoys on an ebb-tide of eye BLOW-
ING
is the ability to concentrate while wandering within
the elastic frameword of A DREAM when you mine your
mind it's scrimshaw TO THE BONE TO THE
BONE. . . .

Through these lines Hoagland suggests that black music and art are prisms which reflect and reverse light, thus defining and creating rather than being defined and created by others. Black art is deliberate and thoughtful, even when it appears to be erratic and spontaneous. It is limitless, coming from and aiming toward the very essence of black culture.

This is a different aesthetic than that presented in *Black Velvet.* Interestingly, *Scrimshaw* includes the opening stanza of "Love Child: A Black Aesthetic" and entitles it "Bopping: Brown Sugar." The inclusion of this variation might suggest that the sensual and sensuous aspects of black life are only a part of the culture and do not completely define it.

The poems in *Scrimshaw* are more conventional than those in *Black Velvet.* They include standard punctuation and capitalization. They are longer and more narrative, and they rely less on sensual images and word plays. The greatest contrast between the two collections lies in the immense sobriety of *Scrimshaw.* Hoagland embraces his heritage and the people of his race, but like the protagonist in "The Weight . . . Faith and Charity," he appears to have lost the hope which lightened his early poems.

The perspective expressed in *Scrimshaw* is one which views art as a direct correlation of history. A black poet in America in the 1970s shares experience with minority Americans such as Paul Cuffe,

Hoagland with daughters Nia (front) and Ayan

Quamany, Prince Goodwin, Plato Turner, and Cato Howe, who fought for America's freedom in the 1770s without obtaining their own. Hoagland's piercing vision of America emerges in the repetition of two refrains throughout *Scrimshaw,*

I tremble for my country when I remember God is just.
. . . .
Manumissions: Death, the Great Emancipator.

Finally, Hoagland issues a statement of strength and solidarity that should serve as a warning to all people who attempt to dehumanize others,

We are dust.
Rock is the placenta of time.
But rock can be shattered.
You cannot break dust,
it defies the hammer.
Chisels cannot carve up
-on it. Its stuff will not
make good statues of your heroes.
Heroes are made of it.
Blown up? Explosives never destroy it.
It cannot be slung or thrown.
Primitive
but it can kill you.

In his most recent poetry, Hoagland extends his concerns to incorporate black Americans' African heritage. An unpublished collection dedicated to his children, ". . . Here . . . ," is marked by a sense of kinship with family members and all Africans.

Subtitled "Celebration," the poems are inspired by a family trip to Senegal. Images of African land and history dominate the collection. In "Goree," these images are heightened by contrasts with images of contemporary black Americans.

You crawl out into the light
of the setting sun, face the western horizon
and, stripping as you go, hanging your watch,
and jeans, western shirt and shoes on your white
shadow, you wade into
the east shore of the Middle Passage—

that hyphen between African
and American—and
the surf hisses and steams off you
like water around white hot iron.

Everett Hoagland's concern for humanity has grown through the years. Accompanying it is an outrage at all that has thwarted the development of human beauty. The result is a poetry which seeks to teach as well as to entertain. As it is informed by Afro-American history and culture, his poetic style has become an eclectic fusion of agit-prop, historical narrative, and bebop.

While Hoagland has not published enough to be judged conclusively, his very survival as a poet has been a significant contribution to Afro-American culture. His career verifies the fact that the black arts movement was not a momentary trend that could be easily abandoned. The rich ferment of the period had a permanent impact, having introduced and nurtured young artists such as Hoagland who would continue to grow and create from its substantive base.

Reference:

Don L. Lee, *Dynamite Voices: Black Poets of the 1960s* (Detroit: Broadside Press, 1971).

Angela Jackson

(25 July 1951-)

D. L. Smith
Williams College

BOOKS: *Voo Doo/Love Magic* (Chicago: Third World Press, 1974);

The Greenville Club, in *Four Black Poets* (Kansas City, Mo.: Bk Mk Press, 1977);

Solo in the Boxcar Third Floor E (Chicago: OBAhouse, 1985).

PLAY PRODUCTIONS: *Witness!* Chicago, Showcase Theatre, March 1978;

Shango Diaspora: An African-American Myth of Womanhood and Love, Chicago, Parkway Community House Theatre, October 1980;

When the Wind Blows, Chicago, October 1984.

OTHER: Carolyn Rodgers, *How I Got Ovah:New and Selected Poems,* foreword by Jackson (Garden City: Doubleday, 1975);

"Basementmusic," "For Our Rising," "From a Speech . . .," in *15 Chicago Poets* (Chicago: Yellow Press, 1976), pp. 57-62.

PERIODICAL PUBLICATIONS:

POETRY

"george, after all, means farmer," "Doubting Thomas," "Monroe, Louisiana," *Callaloo,* no. 5 (February 1979): 84-86;

"One Kitchen," "Divination," "Wave for the Man Wherever the Song Is," "Invocation," "Who Would Trade It," "The Bloom Amid Alabaster Still," *Obsidian,* 5 (Winter 1979): 87-92;

"Solo in the BoxCar, Third Floor E," "Solo for an Alto," *Black Collegian,* 1 (April/May 1980): 121;

"The Spider's Mantra," "The House of the Spider," "Spider Divine," "The Itsy Bitsy Spider Climbs and Analyzes," "In Her Solitude: The Inca Divining Spider," "The Spider Speaks on the Need for Solidarity," "Why I Must Make Language," *Open Places,* no. 37 (Spring/Summer 1984): 3-11.

Photograph by Jim Curley

FICTION

"Dreamer," *First World*, 1 (January 1977): 54-57;

"Witchdoctor," *Chicago Review*, 28 (Winter 1977): 76-82;

"From *Treemont Stone*," *TriQuarterly*, no. 60 (Spring 1984): 154-170.

Angela Jackson is generally recognized as the most versatile and richly talented of the writers to emerge from Chicago's Organization of Black American Culture (OBAC) Writers Workshop during the 1970s. She is the author of three volumes of poems, several short stories, a popular romance (coauthored pseudonymously), and a novel in progress. Despite her versatility, however, she is known primarily as a poet and especially admired for her technically deft, densely metaphorical, and constantly inventive language. She is also celebrated as a brilliant reader of her own poetry and fiction. Apart from her purely literary accomplishments, Jackson is known for her role as the coordinator and sustaining presence in the OBAC Workshop after Hoyt Fuller's departure in 1976.

Jackson, the fifth of nine children, was born in Greenville, Mississippi, to George and Angeline Jackson. Her parents moved to Chicago while she was a small child. Consequently, she grew up in Chicago and developed a sense of language which was fundamentally Southern yet tempered by urban and Midwestern influences. While she was an undergraduate at Northwestern University, Jackson began to receive literary recognition. In 1973 she received the Conrad Kent Rivers Memorial Award, a literary prize bestowed annually by *Black World*. In 1974 Northwestern awarded her both the Edwin Schulman Fiction Prize and an Academy of American Poets Prize.

Despite her education at Northwestern, her most important literary influence was her involvement with the OBAC Workshop, which she joined in 1970. OBAC, a community-based organization, was founded to encourage "the conscious development and articulation of a Black Aesthetic." In keeping with this general goal, the Workshop pursued three explicit objectives: "(1) the encouragement of the highest quality of literary expression reflecting the Black Experience; (2) the establishment and definition of the standards by which that creative writing which reflects the Black Experience is to be judged and evaluated; and (3) the encouragement of the growth and development of Black critics who are fully qualified to judge and to evaluate Black literature on its own terms, while at the same time, cognizant of the 'traditional' values and standards of Western literature and fully competent to articulate the essential differences between the two literatures." Led by Hoyt Fuller, the editor of *Black World*, the workshop's founding members had included such distinguished poets as Haki Madhubuti (Don L. Lee), Carolyn Rodgers, and Johari Amini (Jewel Latimore). While the OBAC writers were strong individuals, they shared a set of concerns and a general sense of style which marked them as a distinctive "school" or movement. Angela Jackson's own style developed out of this context.

This influence is readily apparent in her first

book, *Voo Doo/Love Magic* (1974). She herself notes: "i am more than grateful for the grooming and growth allowed me in the workshop; for the dedications i have gained as a Blackperson and the commitment to Black/craftsmanship and Black/communication." She dedicates the book to her family, to members of OBAC, and to Hoyt Fuller. *Voo Doo/Love Magic* is a collection of fifteen poems, mostly concerned with a longing for love, family experiences, and the exploration of cultural resources. Yet even more fundamentally, it is an experiment in style. These poems are ebullient in spirit, and deeply rooted in Afro-American vernacular speech. The main technical challenge which they pose is the dilemma of how to capture the authentic rhythms and inflections of vernacular speech, yet at the same time to produce a language which is creative, not merely imitative.

These poems succeed remarkably well at capturing the mannerisms of vernacular speech, but the spacing and virgules which Jackson uses to indicate inflections may mystify the uninitiated reader. Sometimes, indeed, they seem gratuitous, as in these lines from "Woman Walk/Down a Mississippi Road":

> i wuz the young april after noon
> breathed into this mississippi
> breeze /n fold/ed myself
> into the fresh/ ness of his arms.

Here, one needs the poet's own remarkably subtle ear to reproduce the rhythmic pattern; and even then, these lines rely too much on the inflections for them to stimulate other interest. Even a reader who can distinguish between the inflections of "afternoon" and "after noon" or "fold/ed" and "fresh/ness" may conclude that this passage offers more sound than substance. The best poems, however, skillfully combine authenticity and creative resourcefulness.

An example of a well-balanced poem is "Second Meeting," which suggests African antecedents to an encounter between a young man and woman in a Chicago subway car. It begins:

> memba the time . . .
> we met at home
> that slow age ago. one day.
> me.
> with a water jar balanced
> on my head/
> to fetch from the river
> and u
> an u wuz
> hone/n a spear for the
> hunt that nite

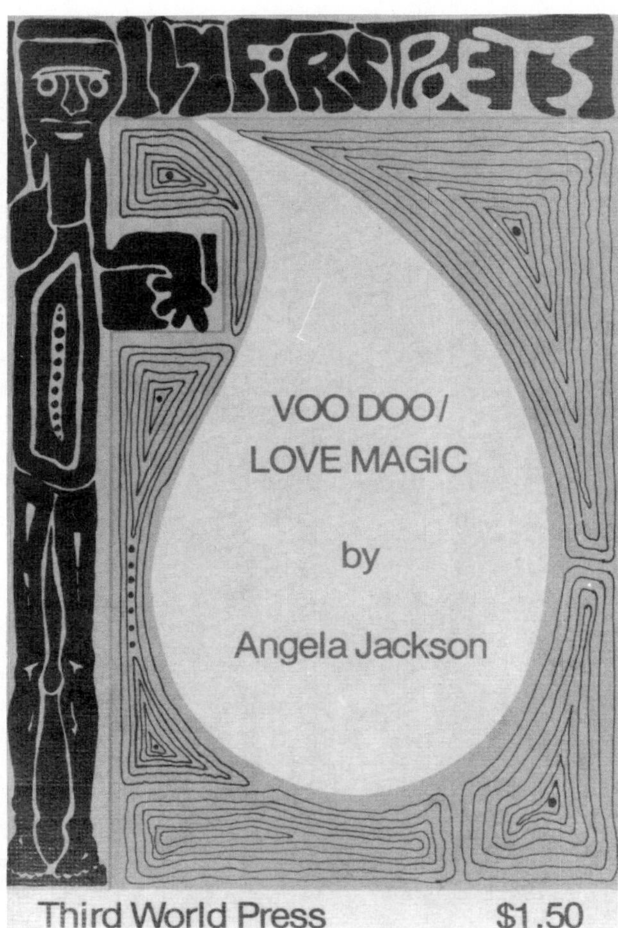

Cover for Jackson's 1974 collection of poems, in which she experiments with style

In the middle section of the poem, the female speaker recollects their previous life in Africa and reminds the young man of it with her smile. He responds, haltingly:

> (don't i know u
> from
> sum/
> where??
> u said. and
> i nod/ed softly: yes.
> afraid i'd tip/ ova
> the water jar
> i always think
> is
> balanced
> on my head . . .

This poem works because the inflections and pauses, the general sense of style, are not just mannerisms. They are part of the subject of the poem, which is concerned with how personal style is mediated through deeper cultural memory. The subtle and precise language used here typifies Jackson at her best. Another of her special talents, one which appears only occasionally in these poems, is her ability to create what Stephen Henderson has called "mascon" images: that is, images which evoke a dense cross-section of Afro-American experience. For example, the speaker of "lovin u rite" promises to

> make home as home as buttermilk an
> cornbread outta mayonnaise jar.

The "home" here is "downhome"—the Deep South—where people do, indeed, relish the delicacy which she describes. Her love, by implication, will strike a resonance equally deep.

In her concern with Afro-American vernacular speech, Afro-American music ("Make/n My Music"), the continuity of African culture, and the endeavor to make serious art accessible to a popular black audience, Angela Jackson's work reflects directly the influence of OBAC and Hoyt Fuller. Yet her poems are never polemical, as Madhubuti's often are, and like Carolyn Rodgers, she often grounds her politics in a call for strong community ties and a general love for black people (for example, "because we failed"). Also, like Rodgers, she sharply criticizes the hypocrisy of people whose militancy is merely talk ("Revolution"). Nevertheless, even in this first book, she exhibits a distinctive, highly personal voice. No one has developed a more complex and subtly modulated vernacular-based poetic diction than she. In *Voo Doo/Love Magic* her command of rhythmical language is most apparent. In her next book, *The Greenville Club* (1977), her gift for creating complex metaphors blossoms.

During the mid-1970s she became active with the Poets-in-the-Schools Program in Illinois and she began to be frequently demanded as a reader. As her inclusion in *15 Chicago Poets* (1976) demonstrates, her reputation had grown beyond the context of OBAC. *The Greenville Club* was published in *Four Black Poets,* a collection of chapbooks bound into a single volume. Most of these poems express reminiscences of growing up in an urban, black community, and they cover a broader range of perspectives than the previous collection. They exhibit a more restrained style and, generally, a greater maturity.

The opening poem, "The Cost of Living," exemplifies this volume's strengths. It begins:

> The cost of living
>   is far
>   too high
> life will split you along your back
> like the fisherman's wife who tears
> the blackspine from the
>   shrimp
>   for her gumbo

This poem, addressed to a black man, is about the need for love and the consequence of not having it. Love, in the poem, spares one from the cost of living alone: to risk being split open like a shrimp. Given an alternative, the poem concludes, "the heart cannot afford/such expensive feasts." Even more striking than the poem's message, however, is the poet's creation of metaphor. In comparing the black man to a shrimp, the poet stresses the destructive power of the world around us, which not only humbles but emasculates black men. The brilliant coinage "blackspine" is both physical strength (backbone) and blackness (cultural heritage and identity). Finally, gumbo requires lots of shrimp, and black men, this image implies, are as vulnerable and expendable as shrimp. (Gumbo, incidentally, is both a Bantu word for okra and a classic dish in soul food cuisine. "Gumbo," therefore, links African and Afro-American cultures.) In sum, the poet evokes castration without mentioning the knife and expresses a political consciousness without a word about politics. Such richness and subtlety of meaning are typical of Jackson's mature work.

In contrast to *Voo Doo/Love Magic*'s celebratory exuberance, several poems in *The Greenville Club* evince a preoccupation with the elusiveness and destructive power of love. "Brokenhearted, Alabama" presents an especially memorable portrait of a woman driven mad by love. Its densely evocative opening lines describe her:

> bananapeelings her bruisedskin
> brushing against her hair a bitten sun
> running its noon
> she shades her face
> worrybunched and blotched
> and waits
> it's too much. they heard her say.

This acute awareness of pain also extends into Jackson's treatment of political topics. One of her most memorable poems is "from a speech delivered in freedom hall on afrikan liberation day: words from

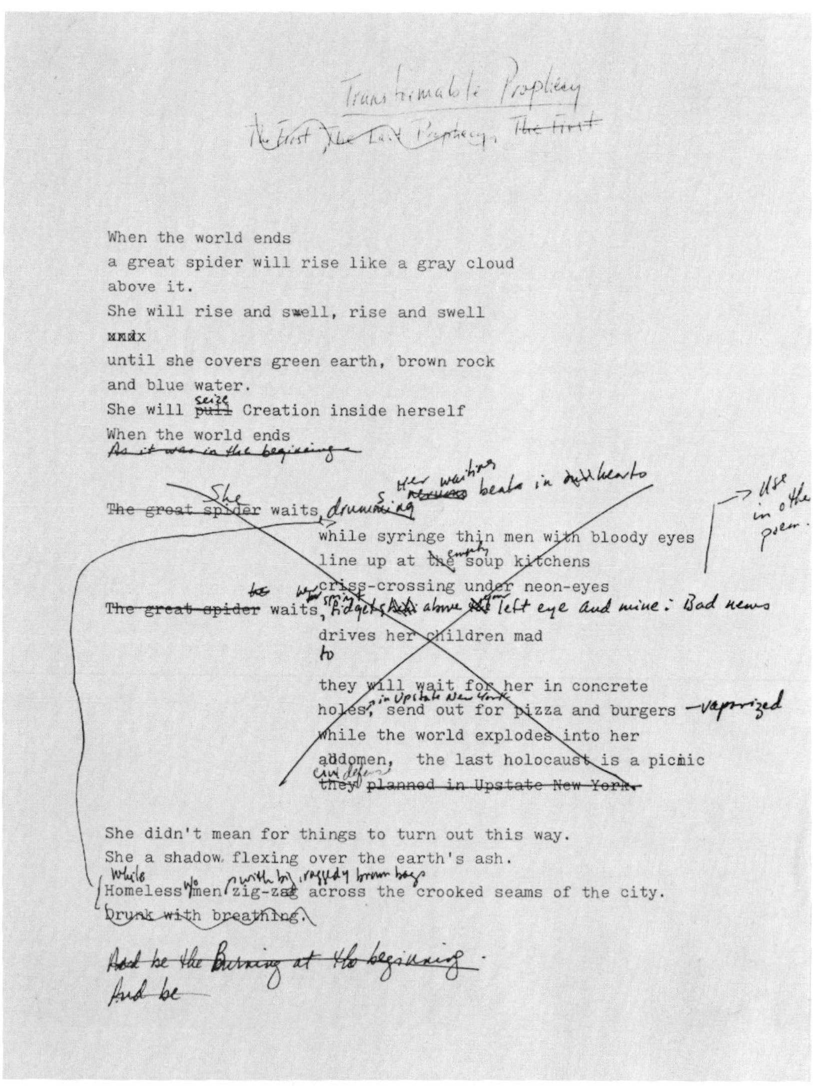

Transformable Prophecy

When the world ends
a great spider will rise like a gray cloud
above it.
She will rise and swell, rise and swell
until she covers green earth, brown rock
and blue water.
She will pull seize Creation inside herself
When the world ends
As it was in the beginning

The great spider She waits, drumming her waiting beats in our hearts
while syringe thin men with bloody eyes
line up at the empty soup kitchens
criss-crossing under neon-eyes
The great spider waits, fidgets above my left eye and mine: Bad news
drives her children mad
they will wait for her in concrete
holes, in Upstate New York send out for pizza and burgers —vaporized
while the world explodes into her
abdomen, the last holocaust is a picnic
they planned in Upstate New York.

She didn't mean for things to turn out this way.
She a shadow flexing over the earth's ash.
While Homeless men who zig-zag with ragged brown bags across the crooked seams of the city.
Drunk with breathing.

And be the Burning at the beginning.
And be

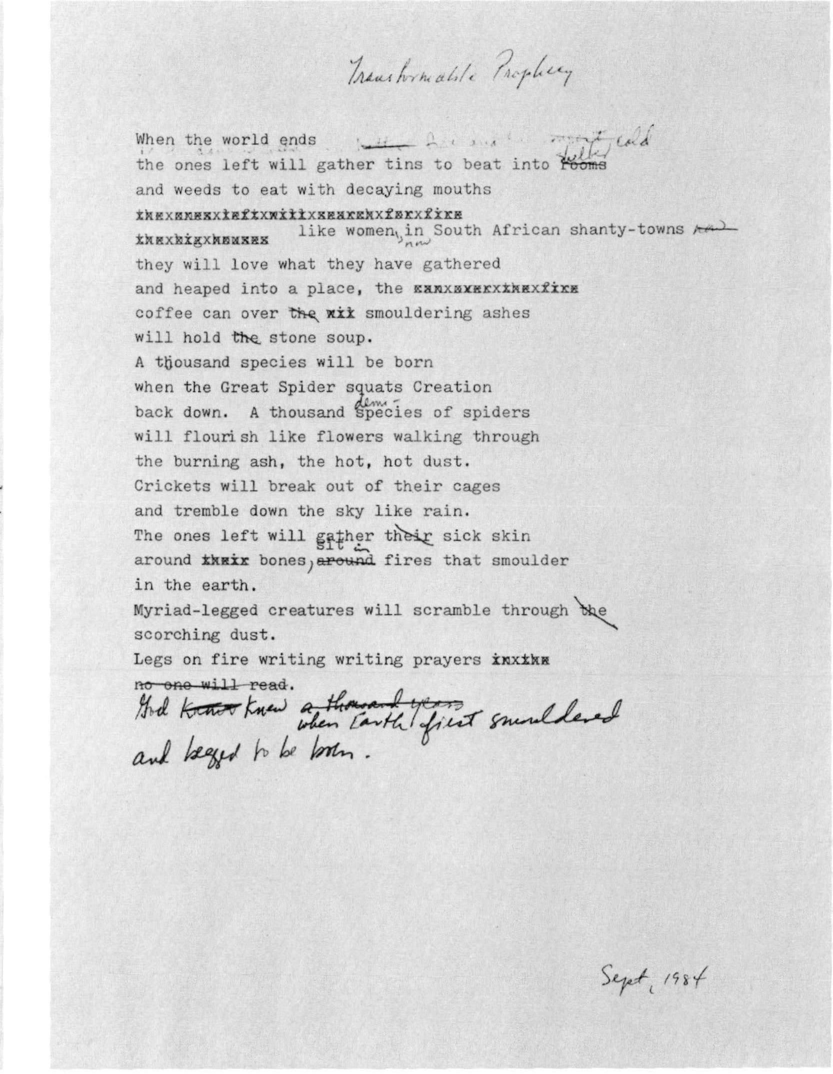

Transformable Prophecy

When the world ends
the ones left will gather tins to beat into rooms shelters
and weeds to eat with decaying mouths
like women now in South African shanty-towns
they will love what they have gathered
and heaped into a place, the
coffee can over the smouldering ashes
will hold the stone soup.
A thousand species will be born
when the Great Spider squats Creation
back down. A thousand demi-species of spiders
will flourish like flowers walking through
the burning ash, the hot, hot dust.
Crickets will break out of their cages
and tremble down the sky like rain.
The ones left will gather sit in their sick skin
around bones, around fires that smoulder
in the earth.
Myriad-legged creatures will scramble through the
scorching dust.
Legs on fire writing writing prayers
no one will read.
God knew when Earth first smouldered
and begged to be born.

Sept, 1984

First draft for a recent poem by Jackson (courtesy of the author)

Transformable Prophecy

When the world ends
a great spider will rise like a gray cloud
above it.
She will rise and swell, rise and swell
until she covers green earth, brown rock,
and blue water.
She will seize Creation imside herself
when the world ends
in the last days between the fire and the cold
the ones left will gather tins to beat into shelter
and weeds to eat with decaying mouths
like women in south african shanty-towns.
They will love what they have gathered among ghosts
and heaped into a place.
The coffee can over smouldering ashes
will hold stone soup.
A thousand species of decay will be born
when the Great Spider squats Creation
back down. A thousand demi-species of spiders
will flourish like flowers walking through
the burning ash, the hot, hot dust.
Crickets will break out of their cages
and tremble down the sky like rain,
twitching on the ground, while the sky turns cold.
The ones left will gather sick skin around bones,
sit in fires that smoulder in the earth.
Myriad-legged creatures will scramble through
scorching dust,
legs on fire writing writing prayers God knew
when earth first smouldered, squalled
and begged to be born.

*

*Change to "squatters-towns."
More accurate, shanty too
Irish derivative.

21.

Revised final draft for "Transformable Prophecy." Jackson says, "The final copy . . . has a rather new note, indicating a change I felt needed to be made on a supposedly complete poem" (courtesy of the author).

a welfare mother." A masterpiece of understated outrage, this poem expresses the response of poor women to those who impugn their integrity:

> the
> president
> is a welfare-chiseler
>
> he
> chip away my sons life
> scale
> his years
> like flakes from fish
>
> cluttering the kitchen floor
> with tears

These shocking images make the president a symbol for the most exploitative aspects of an oppressive system, which wreaks "nonchalant" destruction in the lives of poor people. Protesting forced abortions, the speaker quips:

> he flush my daughters
> futures
> down the clinic toilet

Finally, adding another sardonic twist to the "chiseler" image, the poem reaches its crescendo of contempt with the factual observation: "he pay no income tax." Jackson concludes this blistering poem by simply repeating the opening lines. This incisive and mordant poem, like most of *The Greenville Club,* reveals a sensitive, clear-headed, and fiery poet at the height of her powers.

In her most recent book, *Solo in the Boxcar Third Floor E* (1985), Jackson continues her earlier thematic concerns. These new poems are spoken in the voices of various tenants in an apartment building, not in the poet's own voice. In this respect, *Solo* seems very closely related to the fiction writing which has been Jackson's dominant concern during the 1980s.

Jackson's fiction, like her poetry, is especially notable for its sharp images and metaphorically rich language. Indeed, her novel in progress, "Treemont Stone," grew out of an unpublished series of narrative poems called "A House of Extended Families." (*The Greenville Club* is actually a part of this larger collection.) Some of her ideas, originally conceived as poems, apparently demanded fictional treatment. In her fiction, Jackson's primary concern has been to capture the quality of her characters' lives through a precise and evocative rendering of their own use of language. Though she writes beautiful, descriptive prose, her most memorable trait as a fiction writer is her ability to create voice and to let the characters speak for themselves. Her most notable early stories include "Dreamer," which appeared in the premier issue of *First World* (1977) and "Witchdoctor," which appeared in *Chicago Review* and won an Illinois State Arts Council Award in 1978.

The following passage from "Witchdoctor" illustrates the most memorable qualities of Jackson's prose. It describes the protagonist's thoughts after a final tryst with her adulterous, but deeply cherished, lover:

> I rose, laughed, left and rinsed by body. Foamed between my legs with a face towel. Water fell from my faucet. I sang that man from under the last cover. I bathing. He sleeping bones and lost semen. I hummed across the water cupping under my breasts. I scattered scents and singing. His name was steam. I tempted him to wash my back; to touch mahogany into ashy fire. I beckoned him from bed through the closed bathroom door. He did not come. I slapped at his silence with a dry towel: frisked my free body. Calling to him.
>
> I stood in the doorway searching for him. The stripped bed was an empty white page. The rest of his poems were written in this silence I am constantly reading inside my head.

Like her poems of this period, her stories evince a poignant awareness of the pain associated with unrequited love. The power of these stories derives not from the movement of plot, but from the vividly present consciousness of her characters and their sense of themselves, of each other, and of the world.

The performances of Jackson's dramatic work have been enthusiastically received. *Witness!,* an "anthology" of her poetry and prose, was performed in Chicago and Milwaukee by the Ebony Talent Readers Theatre in 1978 and 1979. Her full-length poetic drama, *Shango Diaspora: An African-American Myth of Womanhood and Love* (produced in 1980) has been produced in several cities, including Chicago (1980, 1981, 1984), Cleveland (1982), and New York (1982). The New York production was directed by Woodie King, Jr., at the New Federal Theatre. King described the play's one-week run as "stupendous." Based on a long sequence of poems, *Shango Diaspora* chronicles a young woman's initiation into the mysteries of sexuality and love. It utilizes a freely interpreted version of African mythology as well as the blues and various other elements of Afro-American culture. While *Shango Diaspora* might be compared to Ntozake Shange's *for colored girls who have considered suicide/when the rainbow isn't enuf,* its general style more closely resembles such plays of Federico García Lorca as *Blood Wedding* and *Don Perlimplín.*

Angela Jackson received international recognition when she was selected to represent the United States at the Second World Festival of Black and African Arts and Culture (FESTAC) in Lagos, Nigeria (1977). Her work has been included in Dial-a-Poem and Poetry-on-the-Buses, and in 1979 she received one of two premier Illinois State Arts Council Creative Writing Fellowships. The following year she received a creative writing fellowship from the National Endowment for the Arts. She was listed in *Outstanding Young Women of America* in 1979, and *Ebony* magazine, in its August 1982 issue, included her among "Women to Watch in the 1980s." In 1983 she received the second Hoyt W. Fuller Award for Literary Excellence. Beginning in September 1983, she became Writer-in-Residence at Stephens College in Columbia, Missouri. She was elected Chairperson of the Board of Directors for the Coordinating Council of Literary Magazines (CCLM) during 1984. *Solo in the Boxcar Third Floor E* received an American Book Award from the Turtle Island Foundation in 1985.

Among her recent publications, an excerpt from "Treemont Stone" has appeared in *Tri-Quarterly* (Spring 1984), and a selection of poems from her forthcoming book, "The House of Spider," appeared in *Open Places* (Spring 1984). A new play, *When the Wind Blows,* was produced in Chicago in October 1984. A full-length volume of poems, "The Midnight Market of Memory and Dream," has been accepted for publication by Third World Press, but at the time of this writing, no publication date has been set. At present, Jackson is completing another book of poems, "Dark Legs and Silk Kisses." She is also doing final revisions on "Treemont Stone." Her long-range projects include editing an anthology to commemorate the twentieth anniversary of OBAC in 1987.

References:

Edith Herman, "Verse Things Could Happen When a Poet Visits the School," *Chicago Tribune,* 30 May 1977, II: 5,7;

"Women to Watch," *Ebony,* 37 (August 1982): 56.

Lance Jeffers

(28 November 1919-19 July 1985)

David F. Dorsey, Jr.
Atlanta University

BOOKS: *My Blackness Is the Beauty of This Land* (Detroit: Broadside, 1970);

When I Know the Power of My Black Hand (Detroit: Broadside, 1974);

O Africa, Where I Baked My Bread (Detroit: Lotus, 1977);

Grandsire (Detroit: Lotus, 1979);

Witherspoon (Atlanta: Flippin Press, 1983).

OTHER: "The Dawn Swings In," in *The Best American Short Stories–1948,* edited by Martha Foley (New York: Houghton Mifflin, 1948), pp. 157-171;

Percy Johnston, ed., *Burning Spear,* includes poems by Jeffers (Washington: Jupiter Hammon, 1963), pp. 25-37;

R. Baird Shuman, ed., *Nine Black Poets,* includes poems by Jeffers (Durham: Moore, 1968), pp. 116-144;

"The Death of the Defensive Posture: Toward Grandeur in Afroamerican Literature," in *The Black Seventies,* edited by Floyd Barbour (Boston: Porter-Sargent, 1970), pp. 253-263;

R. Baird Shuman, ed., *A Galaxy of Black Writing,* includes fiction by Jeffers (Durham: Moore, 1970);

"Afroamerican Literature: The Conscience of Man," in *New Black Voices,* edited by Abraham

Chapman (New York: New American Library, 1971), pp. 506-513;

Al Young and Ishmael Reed, eds., *Quilt 1*, includes poems by Jeffers (Berkeley, Cal.: N.p., 1981), pp. 49-51.

PERIODICAL PUBLICATIONS:

FICTION

"Keep your Tears Inside," *Quarto* (Winter 1951);

"Tomorrow," *Dasein* (March 1961): 50-72.

NONFICTION

"Bullins, Baraka, and Elder: The Dawn of Grandeur in Black Drama," *College Language Association Journal*, 16 (September 1972): 32-48.

The corpus of black American literature is characterized by extraordinarily varied rhetorical forms, all devoted to articulating the real, human condition of a people who bear a unique and harassed relation to their own nation. In this corpus the poetry of Lance Jeffers is particularly significant for its individuality so squarely rooted in the traditions of black expression. In themes, images and vision, but in linguistic freedoms as well, Jeffers's poetry is securely faithful to an aesthetic whose boundaries and potentials it constantly extends and defends.

Lance Jeffers was born the only child of Henry Nelson and Dorothy May Flippin, on 28 November 1919, in Fremont, Nebraska. His mother's father, George Albert Flippin, took Jeffers from his parents when he was one year old, and reared him in Stromsburg, Nebraska. Jeffers lived with his grandfather and his wife (who was white) until the grandfather's death in May 1929. There can be no doubt that Jeffers was permanently influenced by the personality of this strong-willed and defiant black medical doctor, living in an almost exclusively white environment, with both unwilling and grateful white patients. It seems significant too, in retrospect, that during this period Jeffers did not experience membership in a black community with sizeable numbers of peers and adults.

During the rest of his formative years, simple physical distance also complicated Jeffers's relationship to a black community. In the summer of 1929 he moved to the home of his mother and stepfather, Forrest Jeffers. Forrest Jeffers was also a defiantly strong, black man, but without the social standing, income, or more subtle resources of a respected professional. He was a maintenance man in a white, San Franciscan apartment building; he, his wife, and then his stepson dwelled in the basement apartment. The inevitable constrictions, indignities, and resentments Jeffers experienced contrasted sharply with his midwestern beginnings, and were for many years, even into adulthood, interpreted by the boy as a meanness of spirit in shocking contrast to the expansive, dominating authority of the grandfather. However, in later years, even before this error was acknowledged, Jeffers's poetry evinced a profound consciousness of heroic grandeur crimped by meanness of circumstance. This theme, of course, is an abiding motif in black American literature, but Jeffers voices it in a uniquely impassioned and clarion way. It is, for example, the single unifying theme of his first volume, *My Blackness Is the Beauty of This Land* (1970), in which "Black Soul of the Land" describes an old black man and includes the lines: "and in the humble frame bent with humiliation and age,/ there stood a secret manhood tough and tall/that circumstance and crackers could not kill. . . ." Similarly "The Song" begins

> When I was a janitor's stepson among the
> wealthy whites,
> my color hung from my skin like a razor gash,
> my shame was a needle left inside my heart by
> an enemy surgeon,
> my love an amputated limb I carried about
> under my arm.

The poem ends, speaking of Saunders King, the blues singer, "he sings the mastery of a folk who bent slavemasters to their/need and planted their love unhidden in the soil."

Except, then, for one gratifying year at Tuskegee Institute High School, circumstances beyond anyone's control denied Jeffers an unencumbered immersion in black community life, but assured him, after the age of ten, full experience of the anomalies of being black in white America. His stepfather actually instructed him to forego his neighborhood white, inevitably prejudiced friends, and seek out blacks, however distant. The warm and lasting acceptance from black working-class children and adults which he found in San Francisco and even in the nearby town of Healdsburg is indicated in poems and a book's dedication forty years later.

Another anomaly in Jeffers's life was music. In Nebraska, from the age of five, Jeffers had studied piano. In the one-room basement apartment was a grand piano; his mother continued to teach him classical piano music. But at fifteen, Jeffers's steady, required practice was supplanted by an incessant new interest. With the phonograph pulled

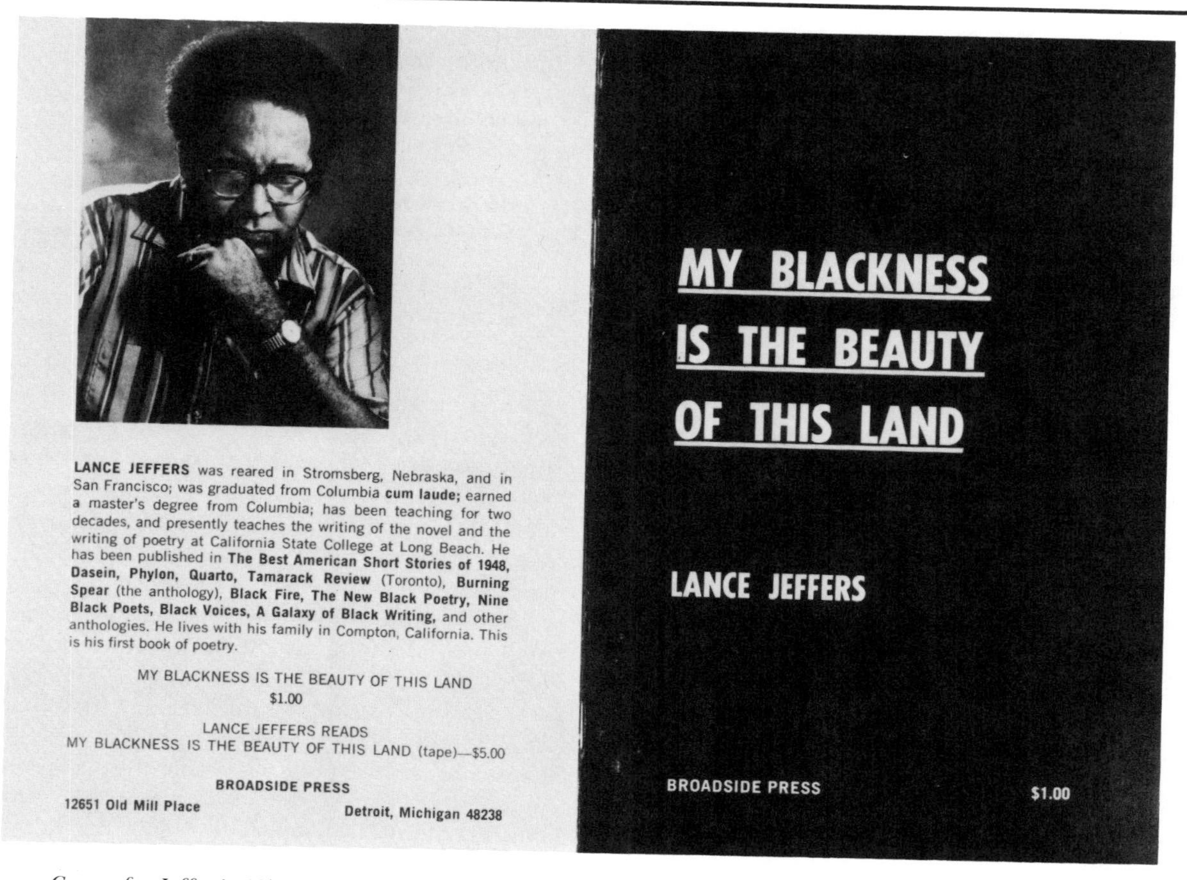

LANCE JEFFERS was reared in Stromsberg, Nebraska, and in San Francisco; was graduated from Columbia cum laude; earned a master's degree from Columbia; has been teaching for two decades, and presently teaches the writing of the novel and the writing of poetry at California State College at Long Beach. He has been published in The Best American Short Stories of 1948, Dasein, Phylon, Quarto, Tamarack Review (Toronto), Burning Spear (the anthology), Black Fire, The New Black Poetry, Nine Black Poets, Black Voices, A Galaxy of Black Writing, and other anthologies. He lives with his family in Compton, California. This is his first book of poetry.
MY BLACKNESS IS THE BEAUTY OF THIS LAND
$1.00
LANCE JEFFERS READS
MY BLACKNESS IS THE BEAUTY OF THIS LAND (tape)—$5.00
BROADSIDE PRESS
12651 Old Mill Place
Detroit, Michigan 48238
MY BLACKNESS
IS THE BEAUTY
OF THIS LAND
LANCE JEFFERS
BROADSIDE PRESS
$1.00

Covers for Jeffers's 1970 poetry volume, the theme of which is the heroism and endurance of black Americans

up beside the piano, Jeffers labored to imitate the jazz of Teddy Wilson. Playing jazz became a practice and a fulfillment in being black; and his pleasure and competence in playing jazz have remained throughout his life.

In the course of his adolescent evolution, Jeffers transferred among three high schools before graduating in 1938. Adjusting to college life posed similar difficulties, and he attended three colleges in the San Francisco area (including the University of California at Berkeley) before joining the army in January 1942.

Jeffers's adulthood begins, therefore, in an army at war. After eleven months he was commissioned a lieutenant in the Medical Administrative Corps. He served in Europe from 1944 to 1945, and he was discharged in January 1946. In May of that year he married Camille Jones, whom he met in England where she was a social worker who directed a Red Cross center for soldiers. (They have a son born in 1956.) Then began a period of concerted effort toward an academic and literary career. By 1951 he had earned from Columbia University both a B.A. (cum laude) in English and an M.A. in English Education, and his short story "The Dawn Swings In" had been published in *The Best American Short Stories–1948*.

Jeffers began teaching in 1951. Except for one-year stays at the University of Denver and the University of Toronto as a graduate student, he taught only briefly at many colleges, some predominantly black and others not. His assertive principled independence seems to have dictated this peripatetic existence, although everywhere his dedication and capacity as a teacher and writer have been recognized. Since 1974, however, he has remained at North Carolina State University, where he is currently full professor of English. These years have also been his most artistically productive to date.

Although it is always suspect to link the distinctive qualities of poetic genius to biographic data, in Jeffers's case the life provides a possible explanation for both the intense love for the black communal spirit and his iconoclastic individuality of expression. When tracing the influence of events on another aspect of Jeffers's poetic voice, we are on sturdy ground. In 1959 Jeffers divorced Camille Jones and married Trellie James. Almost the entire corpus of his poetry has been produced since this date. The inspiration of Trellie Jeffers is evident not only in the dedications of all the books and in the twenty-four published poems about her, and the others about their three daughters, but more subtly in the thematic and stylistic links between those poems and many others. It is no exaggeration to compare the figure of Trellie to Dante's Beatrice as paragon, arbiter, consolation, and guide. The overwhelming differences lie in the immediacy, the physicality, and the unflinching reality of the womanhood and the poetry. In the often anthologized paean "Trellie," for example, Jeffers's persona says:

From the old slave shack I chose my lady,
. . . .
in song as causeful as the fiery center of the earth,
in love as muscular as the thighs of
darkskinned god who cradled Africa to his chest,
in love as nippled as the milk that flows from Nile to
sea. . . .

Lance Jeffers's poems began appearing in anthologies in 1962. The first copious collection was twenty-four poems in the seminal anthology of Howard University Poets, *Burning Spear* (1963), edited by Percy Johnston. But it was a black press devoted to poetry which published his first volume, in 1970. This volume is named after an already much anthologized poem, "My Blackness Is the Beauty of This Land." The poem and its companions display many of the characteristics which mark the entire corpus of this poet. They were written over a span of a decade. (Half had already appeared with twenty-four others in *Nine Black Poets* (1968) edited by R. Baird Shuman. Since many of the poems in Shuman's volume do not appear in any other volume, they are useful for tracing the evolution of Jeffers's own tastes.) The theme of *My Blackness Is the Beauty of This Land* is the awesome courage and endurance of blacks in the face of occasionally spectacular, but constantly vicious abuse from whites. The concept of beauty, while sculpted into detailed physical descriptions, is always presented as the external manifestation of inner character. The speaker's own defiance, like that of all other personae, is never bare of tenderness, determination, and full awareness of vulnerability. The ethical soul always assailed is the subject of Jeffers's art. Though it is not at all stylistically typical, "The Afroamerican Face" encapsules the thematic unity.

The black face has greater weight;
a horny boot of scorn its freight

The black face bears sweeter fruit;
grief lies at its deepest root

The black face has finer grain
to see through wounds that are stilled by pain

The black face is sod for rage,
and seamless sweetness in another age.

Such a theme requires that individual poems, no matter how strident, capture the poignancy of struggle, hurt, and need. None of the poems is a genuine narrative, but because they focus on character at specific moments, they allude to personal narratives, implicit biographies. This allusive scope is part of the means by which each persona becomes paradigmatic of the race itself. Occasional citations of known and unidentified names (Vietnam, Mrs. Williams, Birmingham, Chaney) have the same effect.

Jeffers also applies nature imagery to particulars in a way that makes them generic as well. The language of these poems is within the black contemporary tradition, particularly in evincing sincerity, an important criterion of the black aesthetic. Jeffers, himself, has said that sincerity is his first criterion for great poetry. But in art, sincerity can only be conveyed through artifice, that is, through the use of forms which, by convention, suggest sincerity. Jeffers, like many black poets, achieves the impression of sincerity through specific rhetorical devices. For example, he relies heavily on litanies with parallel clauses or parallel sentences, each introduced by anaphora and sustained by alliteration. Furthermore, he uses the first person pronoun in almost every poem; the poet declares himself, his feelings and ruminations, regardless of the topic. By contrast, the contemporary black aesthetic considers rhyme and meter to be artificial, contained, and hence, inherently insincere. Thus despite one sonnet in twenty-six poems of *My Blackness*, rhyme and obtrusive meter have limited frequency and functions. A typically black use of rhyme occurs in the poem "Prison." There a passionate but involuted metaphor of Southern oppression as a prison has uneven, unrhymed stanzas. The metaphor is followed by five sharp curses, each a rhyming couplet. Both rhyming vilification and rhyming conclusions to unrhymed poems are salient conventions of sincerity according to black aesthetic traditions.

Close analysis of his poetry reveals that Jeffers uses much internal or subtle end rhyme and metrical regularity. For example, in "Let My Last Breath Be Immortal Sandals: For My Children" the lines end with the words: ears/tears/love/ears; feet/flesh/fruition/feet, but there is no impression of rhyme whatever. Or the covert rhyme may be between the last *accented* syllable of one line and the very last syllable of the next, or between the end of one line and the caesura of the next.

Similarly, Jeffers employs meter with subtlety. Meter conveys a sense of balance and graceful force, but the modern black aesthetic tends to regard metrical regularity as a mark of insincere, academic poetasting. Jeffers achieves the grace of meter while maintaining the air of sincerity by placing a few carefully variant syllables in otherwise metrical verse. In the first three lines of "She Takes the Lion's Head," for example, only one syllable interrupts the iambic pattern, and only two do so in the last, emphatic line. The uneven length of the lines, and the points emphasized by accented syllables together obscure the poem's reliance on meter for its grace and force:

> What skin this black maiden has upon her breast,
> What simple tales of kindness her body tells!
> By the riverside she takes the lion's head upon her lap,
> and extracts the fangs one by many one!

In such ways as these Jeffers has remained squarely but atypically within the black tradition.

Abraham Chapman's *New Black Voices* (1971) includes four poems by Jeffers which he later rewrote or revised. Their transmutation gives clear evidence of a quantum leap in Jeffers's aesthetic development. With *When I Know the Power of My Black Hand* (1974) emerges a major and startling poetic voice which both challenges and confirms the black aesthetic.

The title poem is shorn of its earlier self-pity and fortified by shorter lines, more subtle parallelism, and more grandeur. The first strophe employs anatomical imagery which, in the second, is woven with nationalist allusions to make a stunning tapestry of determined hope. "Trellie" is revised in many smaller ways to produce a tighter, finer poem. Together these poems are fair representatives of the mature Jeffers style.

The prevailing theme of *When I Know the Power of My Black Hand* is again endurance in the face of oppression, with the emphasis remaining, of course, on American oppression of blacks. But the scope becomes global and historical: Indian massacres, Vietnam, Buchenwald, Peru. The exploration of human experience and feeling is immensely more inclusive and more acute. The immediate abuse and response are typically not the focus of the poem, but its setting, the context which enriches whatever is the poem's true subject. For example, a poem on the commitment required of a school teacher is rescued from eviscerating universality by the one well-placed word, "blackness." "Breath in my nostrils" captures the exuberance of a "breasty spring day." Only in the last line do we learn that the person "lifting his head to a wildhorse tilt" is a slave. In the fifty-one poems there are innumerable portraits of human character and choice. Therefore, although the sensibility is monochromatic, the scope is panoramic.

The vocabulary of images similarly expands, drawn primarily from human anatomy and cosmic nature. The variety, the oxymoronic aptness, and the daring lexical ingenuity of this imagery become the most salient feature of Jeffers's language. Stars "dip their hands into a night sky." A "broken black man" has "an ocean in his viscera which he never sailed"; a bold one "flung up a cathedral on heaven's floor." Serenity swims "acres of lake" in a "majestic" shoeshiner's brain; blackness is a Niagara falling "down the thoroughfare of my brain." Love "searches [a teacher's] throat for signs of poison"; "fear is vulture's eggs caught in my throat." There is compelling grandeur in the metaphors themselves (Niagaras, elephants, pyramids, "the polar seats of planets") and grandeur in the verses of heroic length and rhetoric:

> no redwood tree is a shadow to the stature of
> their sweetness,
> [but] a wounded deer may weep their longing
> and their love.

Another hallmark of Jeffers's style is idiosyncratic and often paradoxical images. Readers may simply understand their plain meaning ("blackwheat voice"), their allusion to tradition ("stride heaven's streets by hearing my own heart quake," or "a woman rebuked and scorned"), or their context ("promises of violence/assault my skin" meaning "my determination to commit violence tingles my flesh"). Jeffers makes liberal use of new forms that are mostly compounds, and function shifts which preserve meter and density: corpse-head, bluecool, hutted (dwelling in a mere hut), many cloudedness, knife-y, rivery. Actually it is their integration into the wrenching imagery and surprising thought which makes them seem so numerous and original: "Thus the eye of murder winked from my sea last night:/by my victories whipped to graceful upswim suddenly,/maddened by the feel of being starved by peace and beauty:/so slipped murder quickly to the surface of my sea."

When I Know, therefore, presents a distinctly individual voice that is yet within the parameters of contemporary black style. In its heavy reliance on alliteration, anaphora, litanies, grammatical parallelism supporting whole stanzas and whole poems, the poetry is conventionally black. In lexical liberties and in the preponderance of imagery from nature and the generative parts of the body and in the penchant for oxymoron, the poetry is *sui generis.* In the prevailing theme of America's moral morass, the poetry is typical, but unique in its focus on different characters, classes, and crises. Finally, the speaker of these poems is always the poet; it is with the poet that the reader identifies, witnesses, and empathizes. It is the poet's sensibilities we are asked to share. While this limitation is in no way typical of black poets, the sense of immediacy, reality, thus conveyed is a criterion earnestly required in the aesthetic.

O Africa, Where I Baked My Bread appeared in 1977 while Jeffers was in his fourth year at North Carolina State. It is his largest collection. Like its first poem, this book is itself "the lyric of all the disinherited of the land," but there are many more autobiographical poems. They fit into Jeffers's change in emphasis from themes of survival amidst oppression to the intricacies of love—sexual, familial, and social.

Poems with a sexual motif are fringed with political commentary to a degree reminiscent of the early poetry of Dennis Brutus. In November 1976, Jeffers toured Cuba in a group formed by *Black Scholar* magazine and led by its editor, Robert Chrisman. A group of ten poems, "The Flesh of the Young Men Is Burning" recounts the visit in fairly propagandistic prose. Most other poems are character sketches, also woven with political themes.

The black aesthetic (at least as articulated by scholars) rejects the concept of aesthetic distance, supplanting it with the canon of commitment, Jeffers's "sincerity." Yet *O Africa,* even with its confessional poems, is more crafted and less a cry of the heart than earlier works. The motif of oppression is less pervasive. No longer is the poet's feeling always the true subject; frequently now the speaker-poet disappears from the poem. For the first time several poems speak from within their characters. Indeed the poet himself sometimes becomes a character to be viewed, like others, from the outside. There are more anecdotal and occasional poems, and more experiment with architectonics. "Tuskegee, Tuskegee," for example, though autobiographical, has all these developments.

Jeffers's language in *O Africa* is much less idiosyncratic than in *When I Know.* Parallel constructions are both more common and more direct. For emphasis whole lines may be immediately repeated. The grammar is straightforward. Most metaphors are clear; there is a strong resurgence of rhyme, which in many poems occurs only at the poem's final cadence to mark the concluding antithesis, didactic message or emotive intensity.

Jeffers evidences a growing concern with the poem as artifact in *O Africa;* but, because grammar and imagery are clearer, the reader finds more incontestable places where meaning falls into a quicksand metaphor. There are also infelicities of rhythm which suggest the creator's sacrifice of form to meaning. Yet, when the poetry is read aloud in the tradition of black recitation, all such rhythmic "problems" can be resolved by musical lengthening, rests, or grace notes. That is, as with the poetry of Maya Angelou and many other modern black poets, proper comprehension and appreciation require a familiarity with black oral tradition.

The poems in *O Africa* make frequent reference to sexual anatomy. This emphasis must be taken (along with violence) as the major metaphoric representation of Jeffers's poetic vision. Through it is filtered much of his perception of persons, ethics, and social forces, in short, the human condition. It is arguable that black tradition does not find in this the prurience or obscenity that it would necessarily bear in contemporary white American literature. In black verbal arts such imagery is both allowed and understood, not required nor even expected. However, it is also true that it offends the sensibilities of much of the black reading public. Nonetheless this figurative and literal emphasis on genitalia and sexuality must be taken as Jeffers's use of a resource that would be expressed differently in other cultures.

With his residence in Durham, North Carolina, then, Jeffers has experienced the most settled period of his life, and with it his poetry has flourished in variety and complexity. In this evolution *O Africa* shows a retreat from the idiosyncratic imagery and language of *When I Know,* but more creative experiment in other aspects of poetic form. In 1979, *Grandsire* carried the evolution further. It contains the long title poem and nineteen others. About the same time it appeared the poet was revising his novel, *Witherspoon* (which Jeffers reports that he first composed from 1963 to 1970). This may not be merely coincidental, for the most notable feature

Covers for Jeffers's 1979 collection of narrative poems

of *Grandsire* is its new narrative and dramatic skill.

In earlier books, only the briefest stories are sketched from start to end. Usually the reader is shown only disconnected elements of a scene or plot. Personae are presented like caricatures, that is, some parts are copied meticulously, while other parts are reduced. But in several short poems of *Grandsire* Jeffers for the first time displays a thorough mastery of poetic narrative. Typically there is a short scenario with characters described, motives reported, and a climactic denouement interwoven with moral comment. In "Woman Giving Out Leaflets," for example, twelve lines suffice to report every relevant element of a street encounter, including the didactic import. Such devices as anaphora, alliteration, and litanies are more subtle and less plentiful but are common enough to remain Jeffers's most obvious allegiance to black rhetorical tradition.

However, the poem "Grandsire" is the crowning achievement. It invites comparison with Pindar's odes for its lyric force wedded to the narrative sweep of epic. The subject is Jeffers's own grandfather, an Achilles more proud, self-willed, and hot-tempered than the mortals around him. He is also a medical doctor. With flashbacks and epic delays, the account of his life covers the period from 1876 to 1928. His relations with wives and lovers, his consequent bouts with white neighbors, laws and lynchers, his indiscriminating will to heal, and his autonomous sense of duty are all described as for a "giant . . . who walked the plains of Nebraska like a fearless god!" Most other characters have brief, crystalline appearances, bristling with precise delineation, but acting as foils of Grandsire's power. Two wives, however, one white and one black, are compassed at the tragic meeting point of choice, challenge, character, and chance.

Grandsire as a whole maintains the heroic mold of "Grandsire." The language, characterization, poetic stance are all larger than life. The subject matter returns to the parochial confines of blacks in the United States. The poetic structures continue the eclectic and successful experiments of *O Africa.*

Witherspoon portrays a conventional preacher who, in the stress of responding to a town's racial crisis, grows to a revolutionary sense of social and Christian duty."The Blues and Rachmaninoff" is a volume of poetry which is not yet published. The title poem concerns a black female psychiatrist confronting her own past and the constrictions of racial prejudice on the lives of her patients.

Lance Jeffers's poetry is an important and striking expression of black contemporary poetics. Yet, because it is so unique, it offers interesting evidence for the flexibility and potentials of a communal aesthetic. It is even more important, however, as a unique and passionate reflection of black life in the United States.

Interview:

Doris Laryea, "A Black Poet's Vision: An Interview with Lance Jeffers," *College Language Association Journal,* 26 (June 1983): 422-433.

Ted Joans

(4 July 1928-)

Jon Woodson
University of Rhode Island

See also the Joans entry in *DLB 16, The Beats: Literary Bohemians in Postwar America.*

BOOKS: *Jazz Poems* (New York: Rhino Review, 1959);

All of Ted Joans and No More (New York: Excelsior, 1961);

The Hipsters (New York: Corinth, 1961);

Black Pow-Wow: Jazz Poems (New York: Hill & Wang, 1969; London: Calder & Boyars, 1973);

Afrodisia: New Poems (New York: Hill & Wang, 1970; London: Calder & Boyars, 1976);

A Black Manifesto in Jazz Poetry and Prose (London: Calder & Boyars, 1971);

The Aardvark-Watcher: Der Erdferkelforscher [bilingual edition] (Berlin: Literarisches Colloquium Berlin, 1980);

Merveilleux Coup de Foudre Poetry of Jayne Cortez & Ted Joans (France: Handshake Editions, 1982).

OTHER: Elias Wilentz, ed., *The Beat Scene,* includes poems and statement by Joans (New York: Corinth, 1960);

Arna Bontemps, ed., *America Negro Poetry,* includes poems by Joans (New York: Hill & Wang, 1963);

Paul Breman, ed., *You Better Believe It: Black Verse in English,* includes poem by Joans (Baltimore: Penguin, 1973).

PERIODICAL PUBLICATIONS: "First Papers on Ancestral Creation," *Black World,* 19 (August 1970): 66-72;

"Natural Africa," *Black World,* 20 (May 1971): 4-7;

"The Langston Hughes I Knew," *Black World,* 21 (September 1972): 14-18.

Public poet, jazz musician, surrealist painter, expatriate wanderer, and cultural revolutionary, Ted Joans was one of the chief creators of the Beat Generation in the 1950s. Joans has been a popular poet since 1958 when, living in New York's Greenwich Village, he first began reading at the Seven Arts Coffee Gallery and in private homes as one of the Rent-A-Beatnik poets. He was originally associated with other well-known Beats: Jack Kerouac, Gregory Corso, Allen Ginsberg, Amiri Baraka (then LeRoi Jones), and Bob Kaufman. Joans organized the New York City Beats in order to raise money for most of their little magazines, but always the "man alone" he was never published in any of them. Because of his refusal to send his work to magazines and publishing houses, he has not been widely published. Despite the passage of the Beats from popular attention, Joans has, like Ginsberg and Baraka, maintained a following by continuing

Ted Joans (photograph by Chris Felver)

to set the tone for a lifestyle that rejects middle-class conventionality in a quest for a "moral revolution."

Ted Joans was born 4 July 1928 in Cairo, Illinois, the son of a riverboat entertainer. Joans was educated at Indiana University, from which he received a bachelor's degree in Fine Arts-Painting in 1950. From Indiana, he went to New York City. In the "Last Words" to *All of Ted Joans and No More* (1961), Joans described his life in New York's Greenwich Village:

> Like man, I came to the Village scene after doing the school bit in Indiana, Kentucky, Illinois, came here to paint and I did, and still do, I have exhibitions almost annually on Ten St. with the avant-garde, used to throw big surrealist costume balls and gigantic birthday parties, got married and saw the birth of four masterpieces that ex-wife and I created, Daline, Teddy, Terry and Jeannemarie, after four years, divorce, blues, beat bread, then split for Europe, Middle East and Africa, fell in love in Tangiers and the European people and the African People, plan to take my love to Morocco with me and live there. . . .

Despite his absence from the little magazines, during the time that he lived in Greenwich Village, Joans was written about in *Life, Time, Sepia,* and *Ebony* magazines. He received additional publicity from articles about him in the *New Yorker, Holiday, Whisper, Pic,* and from appearances on television programs, and in two movies.

In her introduction to *All of Ted Joans and No More* (1961), Mrs. I. D. Klar points out that "He is not only a spokesman for the new Negro but also a spokesman for the Beat Generation." She further describes him as "a poet of love and dadaism." His poetry is a partial product of the bebop era in jazz music; Joans derived his public image from the hip mannerisms of the bebop musicians, and this influence penetrates his poetry: "He has always stated that he is not a poet and that he is just a mere Jazzaction spokesman." His poetry shows the influence of Walt Whitman, Langston Hughes, and the poets of the Beat school, Bob Kaufman in particular. Throughout Joans's irreverent writings there are celebrations of sexuality, jazz music, African culture, and social revolution. His poetry is equally a vehicle for social protest; his favorite targets are racism, sexual repression, and injustice.

All of Ted Joans and No More was published as a farewell to America and to the Beat scene which Joans felt had become too commercialized. The volume contains the texts that Joans had been reading aloud in Greenwich Village coffeehouses during the 1950s and 1960s. His performances were "successful financially if not esthetically" according to Klar. Though Joans was a vibrant figure on the Village scene, life in America constantly grated against his sensibilities. Having already traveled widely in Europe and Africa, Joans resolved to leave the United States at about the time his first book of poems appeared:

> I am very much in love and plan to split before snow falls on New York's Greenwich Village uncurbed dog sidewalks, I hate cold weather and they will not let me live democratically in the warm states of the United States, so I'm splitting and letting America perish in its own vicious puke or letting America find and live that Moral Revolution that I hoped would happen.

All of Ted Joans is a collection of forty jazz poems that reflects the often casual publishing style of the Beat writers. The book was printed on pink paper and bears collage material in the margins surrounding the poems. Just as many of the poems show the influence of André Breton, the French surrealist theoretician and poet, the marginal illustrations show the influence of Max Ernst, the originator of surrealist collage technique. Like Ernst, Joans employed engravings cut out of medical books and such Victorian travelogues as *Heroes of the Dark Continent* (1890). As with Ernst's collages, the effect of the graphics is the presentation of mysterious dramas laden with subliminal sexuality.

The poems in *All of Ted Joans* are varied in style, ranging from freewheeling catalogues of associated material to prose monologues. Joans is at his best in poems that use parallel lines in which every line begins with the same phrase; in "Je Suis Un Homme" every line begins with "I am a man," and in his most widely anthologized poem, "The .38," each line begins with "I hear." Another technique that he used to structure his long oral poems is the short repetend. In "Travelin" he repeats the title after each stanza:

In Washington D.C. I hurried off
the greyhound bus and practically ran
the mile and half to the Lincoln
memorial, where I hastily rushed up
the steps, and with all my strength
spat long distance into the statue's face.
TRAVELIN

Most of the poems in *All of Ted Joans* are designed for an oral delivery in a coffeehouse setting; meant to be entertaining, they are comical, shocking, and based on subjects derived from popular culture. In the best poems of this type, for example, "Let's Play Something," the poet uses a child's pretend game to portray the world that the Beats turned their backs on:

let's play something
let's play that we are all safe!
let's play that we all work from 9 to 5/and we are
caught up in the ratrace, like trying to pay for
that splitlevel/with the inevitable wall to wall
carpet, and trying to keep up with the new car
payments/on the flashy car, color t.v., hi-fi,
wash-n-dry, deep freeze, airconditioned cool
breeze, more bills and bills, psychiatrists
bills and other keeping up with the Jones's
ills!

All of Ted Joans is a self-consciously Beat book that concludes with a short lexicon of Beat terminology (spade, baby goose, A-trainer) to aid the

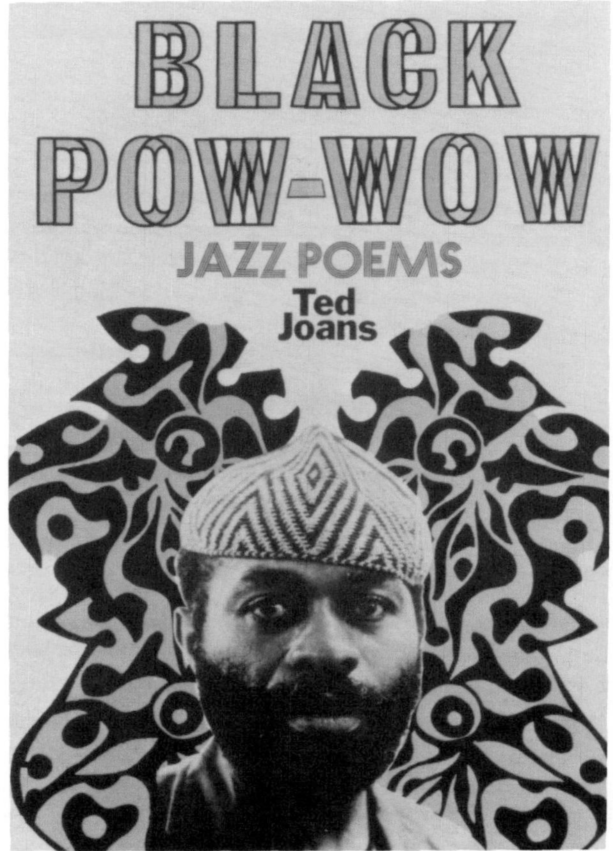

Dust jacket for Joans's 1969 collection. André Breton said Joans was "the only Afro-American surrealist."

uninitiated reader. Although Klar has said that the influence of surrealism is apparent in Joans's work, that influence seems only superficial. Joans says, "I am a man I kissed André Breton on Rue Bonaparte in Paris . . ." in order to establish his connection to that movement. And in poems such as "Open Wide Your Legs" there is some use of free association in the imagery:

Open wide your legs
because the rhinoceros herd has begun the parade
of savage splendor
and seven umbrellas lie pressed against the breast
of an earth worm

These poems lack the originality of Bob Kaufman's more inspired "wacky" images, and Joans's surrealistic efforts are not as successful as his colloquial poems in the style of Whitman.

Leaving New York in 1961, Joans traveled to Tangiers, Morocco, and took up residence with his new wife. He continued to explore Africa, taking

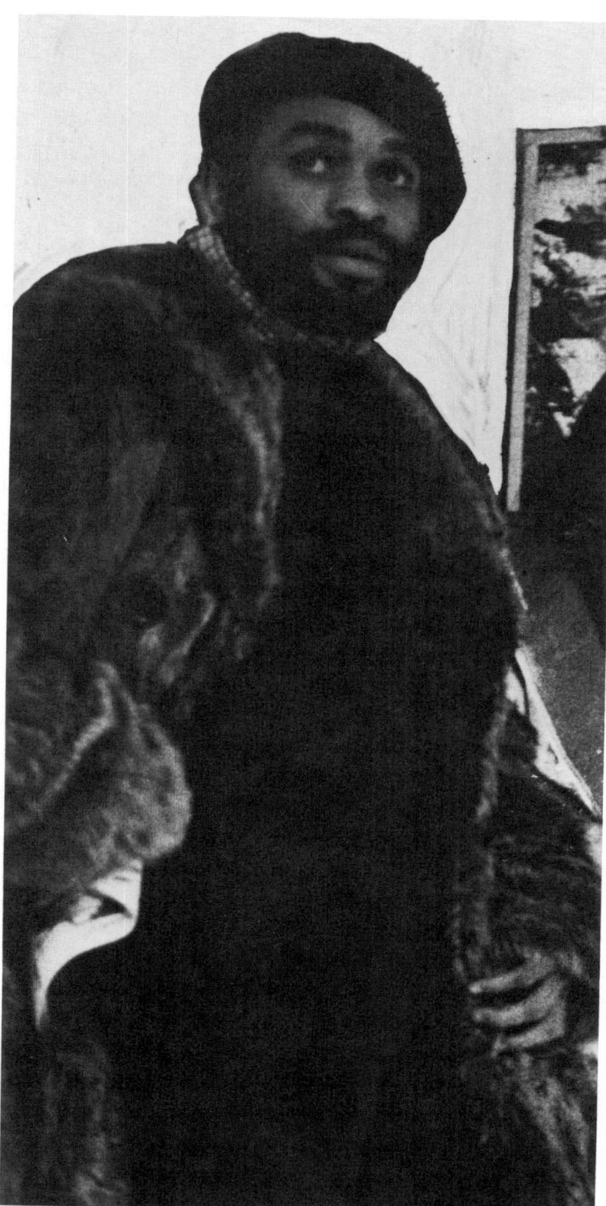

Ted Joans (courtesy Schomburg Center for Research in Black Culture, The New York Public Library, Astor, Lenox and Tilden Foundations)

ships to various ports and going inland by train. He often traveled on foot; in 1962 he wrote a long poem, "Afrique Occidental," while in Timbuktu, Mali. The poem describes his wanderings:

> As I lay here in a tent and write as I think
> Greenwich Village is long way off, with its
> coldwater flat and sink
> I have traveled a long way on the Beat bread
> I made
> Now I'm deep in the interior of Africay,
> the only Afroamerican spade

During the next several years, Joans established a pattern of moving to European cities such as Paris, Copenhagen, and Amsterdam in the summer months and moving back to Africa in the winter months. In Europe he moved among a wide circle of friends which included the painter Bob Thompson and writer Melvin Van Peebles. Joans also associated with visiting Afro-Americans, such as Langston Hughes. Cecil Brown, in his novel *The Life and Loves of Mr. Jiveass Nigger* (1970), describes the way Joans lived in Europe. Brown has thinly disguised Joans by calling him Ned Green:

> When he saw Ned's face, the full, round beard, the hairline that receded back into the baldness of his head, he knew this was the Ned Green on the front of the thin book of beat poetry he had read some long time ago back in New York. He told the poet he had read his book, and the poet was very pleased, more pleased than one would think a poet should be about a thin volume of verse that's interesting but not that great.

Joans established Amsterdam as his European headquarters by renting a small room from the Dutch surrealist artist Toni. While continuing to write poems, Joans also painted, but he supported himself largely by selling African masks and sculptures which he collected on his travels through Africa. He also took on commercial writing assignments and produced some of Arthur Frommer's *Europe on Five Dollars A Day*.

Black Pow-Wow: Jazz Poems (1969) reflects a shift in Joans's poetry; he had become interested in the black arts movement that was reshaping Afro-American literature, and new issues entered his work. Joans's long-standing interest in Africa made him a pioneer contributor to the new style of poetry being written in the United States during the 1960s and 1970s. However, his influence is difficult to measure directly because he did not appear in any of the landmark anthologies of that period (*Black Fire, Black Voices,* and so on). He was, however, connected with the writers seeking to originate a black aesthetic, and his work is included in *For Malcolm,* edited by Dudley Randall and Margaret Burroughs and published by Broadside Press in 1969.

The dedication of *Black Pow-Wow* reads: "For you/I offer/THIS Poem/For You/Are In/DEED/IN/NEED OF A/black poem." The book includes some of the best poems from *All of Ted Joans and No*

More. Black Pow-Wow also contains a number of poems exhibiting revolutionary rhetoric, showing that Joans abandoned the Beat posture of passive contemplation: "occultism, rejection of the Establishment, and an existential view of life. . . ." *Black Pow-Wow* is a call for collective violence, containing poems such as "Lets Get Violent," "Revenge," "Not Yet Uhuru," "Promised Land," and "Black February Bloodletting." Though these poems were not new to Joans's canon, his earlier ones had presented individual actions and his notion of a possible revolution had been vague and more a matter of surrealist doctrine. The language of *Black Pow-Wow* was not Beat; it used an idiom closer to Afro-American dialect, and employed up-to-date terminology and the rhetoric of black power. Joans's second volume of poems was a marked attempt to reach across the Atlantic in order to urge on black Americans in their quest for the moral revolution that he had advocated since the 1950s.

The influence of surrealism on the poems in *Black Pow-Wow* was slight; there is only one poem, "Nadja Rendezvous," that shows a slight influence. That poem was dedicated to André Breton and described Joans's relationship with the father of surrealism. The poem itself is simply a listing of meetings between the two poets and contains only a few surreal images: "The revolver the white haired revolver is still loaded." Joans's efforts in *Black Pow-Wow* were wholly directed toward producing poems accessible to black American readers.

By the end of the 1960s, the culture of America had so altered that Joans felt that he could return to his native land; the climate of revolutionary change attracted him. In one poem in *Black Pow-Wow*, "Believe You Me," he was able to write:

I am going back
I am black but I'm going back
A young Russian poet I once read,
"a poet should be where the action is"
I am going back
I am going to return
to the land of Burn, Baby, Burn!

The poem concludes:

But I'm not afraid and I'm too damn tired to run
I am going back

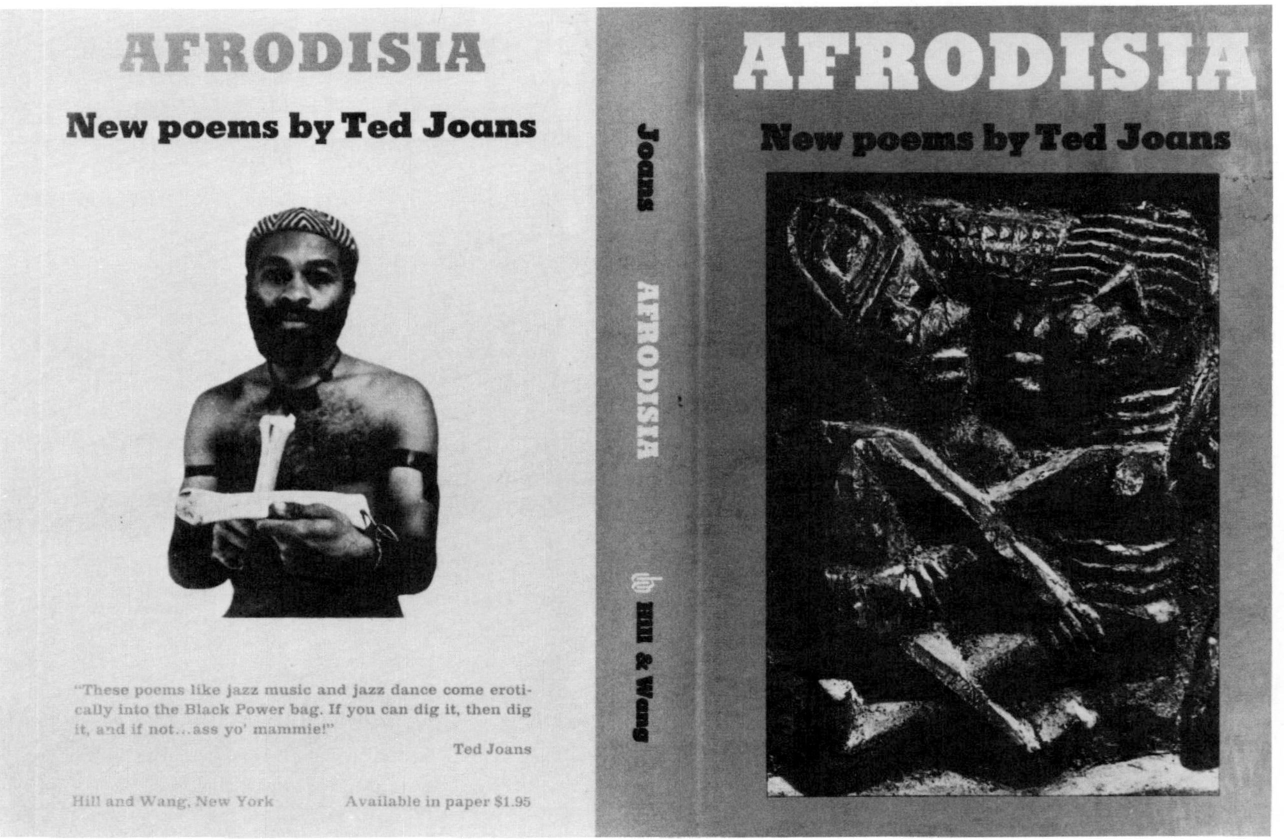

Dust jacket for Joans's 1970 book of poems, of which half are about Africa and half are dedicated to Eros

with a mission up my sleeve
Let's call it jazz poetry
JAZZ IS NON-VIOLENT
yeah thats what I want white America to believe
I'm going back!

Afrodisia (1970) contains poems dating as far back as 1962 and written in Europe and Africa. The poems are largely about African themes as the book was designed for the audiences that Joans read to during an extensive tour of America that he conducted during the early 1970s. He traveled widely, reading to the large audience for black poetry that had been created by such innovators as Haki Madhubuti (Don L. Lee) and Amiri Baraka (LeRoi Jones). Joans was invited to read for and to be recorded by the Institute for the Arts and Humanities in Washington, D.C. His participation in the vital cultural movement of this period motivated him to write in "Home":

back with
my black
tribe again
yes it is good
to be back
with my tribe again

Afrodisia is divided into two sections, "Africa" and "Erotica." The "Africa" section contains poems that range in subject from descriptions of the African landscape ("Souk," "Palm Tree," "Tide of March") to poems that advocate revolution ("Okay, You Are Afraid of Africa," "To Every Free African," "No More Space For Toms"). Most of these poems are merely programmatic gestures, such as "The African Ocean," which proclaims:

I know your real name
this name I'm proud to reveal
I free you from that slave name Atlantic
AFRICAN OCEAN! AFRICAN OCEAN!

The most successful poems in the "Africa" section of *Afrodisia* are personal, describing Joans's own experiences in Africa. There are a number of long pieces that describe travels throughout Africa: "Afrique Accidentale," "Shave & Haircut & A Circumcision," "Still Traveling," "As Don Took Off At Dawn," "Sand," and "My Trip." "My Trip" is the closest thing to an autobiography that Joans has published. The poem begins with "I have been to the desert" and concludes:

Front cover for Joans's 1980 bilingual poetry volume

Turning up here and showing up around there
after having been several months up Europe
yonder confuses the white abuses of the blacks
Smiles and deceit can always cheat their fears and
conceit Africa big Africa wide Africa is my
other side The true side that I do not want to
hide That is my trip

The poems in *Afrodisia* that take Europe as their subject are protest poems expressing rage at things which happened long ago. "Dutch Treatment" uses a pun (Dutch treat) as an ironic emphasis to underscore a threat against the country that in 1619 began the slave trade to North America:

Holland you must hear
the price you pay is not
too dear Pay it now
before it is too late Pay
the price or join South
Africa's future fate!

These poems are more thoughtful and original than his militant poems, but they are technically limp and politically simplistic.

The poems in the "Erotica" section of *Afrodisia*

are introduced by a statement of intent; Joans writes erotic poems in order to emancipate Americans from "anti-erotic" attitudes. The poems date from the Beat 1950s in Greenwich Village when sexual repression was symbolic of all of modern ills. The poems are written in the loose style of Beat poetry and are either too personal or too occasional to stand on their own. One poem, however, a play on the word "continent," does achieve Joans's erotic intent; this poem is a tour de force of erotic detail that describes the intimate exploration of a woman's body: "I want, I shall, I must cross your body continent/I trust that my trip is mutually hip/My tongue shall be my means of travel." The poem is liberating, truly erotic, and shows great poetic inventiveness and imagistic power.

Because Ted Joans is a black poet who began his career as a Beat and became an expatriate, he has been able to provide American readers of poetry with a unique perspective of their culture; Joans writes as a trebly alienated insider. His poetry has kept pace with his personal development, but there has not been a major shift in his style of writing throughout his career.

Joans has learned to appreciate group activity. Despite the seemingly personal nature of his poetry, he has not really shown himself: "I have gained entrance into secret societies in Africa: sorcerers/marabouts/and magicians turned me on They who decorated me with gris gris I still call myself Ted only because you wouldn't understand who I really am now." Joans has not been widely acknowledged critically, but his influence on Afro-American writers has been great. His style of colloquial, jazz poetry is the common ground of black poetry as it has been written and defined since the mid-1960s. Joans remains a popular poet and many look forward to his long-promised autobiography "Spadework." Like his mentor Langston Hughes, Ted Joans is a poet of the people who has used the jazz idiom to create a style of poetry that has gained wide popular acceptance because of its fluidity, honesty, and vitality.

Bob Kaufman

(18 April 1925-   )

Jon Woodson
University of Rhode Island

See also the Kaufman entry in *DLB 16, The Beats: Literary Bohemians in Postwar America.*

BOOKS: *Abomunist Manifesto* (San Francisco: City Lights, 1959);

Does the Secret Mind Whisper? (San Francisco: City Lights, 1959);

Second April (San Francisco: City Lights, 1959);

Solitudes Crowded with Loneliness (New York: New Directions, 1965);

Golden Sardine (San Francisco: City Lights, 1967);

Watch My Tracks (New York: Knopf, 1971);

The Ancient Rain: Poems 1956-1978 (New York: New Directions, 1981).

TELEVISION: "Coming from Bob Kaufman," *Soul* (NET, 1972).

OTHER: Arnold Adoff, ed., *City in All Directions,* includes poems by Kaufman (New York: Macmillan, 1969);

Clarence Major, ed., *The New Black Poetry,* includes poems by Kaufman (New York: International, 1969);

Langston Hughes and Arna Bontemps, eds., *The Poetry of the Negro 1746-1970,* includes poems by Kaufman (Garden City: Doubleday, 1970);

Alan Lomax and Raoul Abdul, eds., *3000 Years of Black Poetry,* includes poems by Kaufman (New York: Dodd & Mead, 1970);

Adoff, ed., *The Poetry of Black America,* includes poems by Kaufman (New York: Harper & Row, 1972).

Many readers view Bob Kaufman as the unsung patriarch of the Beat poetry movement of the 1950s and 1960s. Although somewhat neglected critically in America, his work is not unknown and

Bob Kaufman (photograph by Richard Morris)

appears in more than thirty anthologies. Major white poets such as Lawrence Ferlinghetti, Kenneth Rexroth, Allen Ginsberg, and Gregory Corso, as well as Beat-turned-black-nationalist-poet Amiri Baraka (LeRoi Jones) enthusiastically took their cues from Kaufman's innovations. However, they have not been as quick in recognizing his influence. Kaufman's poems were instrumental in spreading the values and existentialist bohemian life-style of the Beat generation throughout Europe, where his work has been well received, and, eventually, throughout the United States.

Bob Kaufman was born in New Orleans to an Orthodox Jewish German father and a devout Catholic mother, descendant of a woman who was brought to America on an African slave ship. He was the eleventh of thirteen brothers and sisters. Raised in New Orleans in the traditions of the church and the synagogue as well as in the voodoo beliefs of his grandmother, he eventually identified strongly with the philosophy of Buddhism. He attended elementary school in New Orleans and left home at the age of thirteen to work at sea. During his eventful twenty years in the U.S. Merchant Marine, he cultivated an intense taste for literature. Settling in California in the late 1950s, he became one of the founders of the burgeoning literary scene of the West Coast. Shortly after moving to San Francisco Kaufman was married. It was only at the insistence of his new wife, Eileen, that Kaufman began to keep a written record of his poetic creations. So absolute was Kaufman's dedication to the automatic sources of poetry and to oral improvisation that he often neglected to document his work. Many of his published poems are transcriptions of tape recordings made in coffeehouses and in other Beat gathering places.

The development of Bob Kaufman's poetry, and of Beat literature in general, cannot be viewed properly without understanding its relationship to modern jazz music. Kaufman's broadsides, such as *Abomunist Manifesto* (1959), and first book of poems, *Solitudes Crowded with Loneliness* (1965), became overnight classics of the Beat generation. Kaufman's poems popularized a style that emulated the mannerisms and existential image associated with bebop, an avant-garde approach to jazz improvisation and a bohemian way of life that resisted the commercialization of jazz by record companies and imitation by white musicians. Adapting the harmonic complexities and spontaneous inventions of bebop to poetic euphony and meter, Kaufman became the quintessential jazz poet. Many of Kaufman's poems employ the jargon of bebop, improvisational structure, as well as allusions to and the influence of such musicians as Charlie Parker, Dizzy Gillespie, and Miles Davis.

Ishmael Reed once described Parker as a "musical innovator and bad boy genius"; Kaufman was attracted to Charlie Parker for those qualities. Using jazzlike word improvisations based on the phrases of jazz solos, Kaufman's poems also show the influence of Lord Buckley and King Pleasure. Both Buckley and Pleasure experimented with words, but their works appeared only as records. Kaufman's poems also show a marked influence of the modernist literary schools that emphasized the irrational, surrealism, and Dadaism. Borrowing from surrealism, which advocated revolutionary politics, Kaufman instilled an attitude of social protest into Beat poetry. Despite the use of protest themes, however, Kaufman's poems show an alienated, apolitical rejection of conventional society. The poetry expresses the range of the Beats' values: madness, voluntary poverty, a search for holiness, primitivism, and spontaneity.

Bob Kaufman first began to publish poetry in the late 1950s, shortly after he left the Merchant Marine. Kaufman's life in San Francisco's North Beach centered on the Bagel Shop, where he held court. The Beats of the North Beach area were committed to an unconventional life-style. Kaufman horrified his neighbors with his unruly antics, for example carrying his son Parker in his clarinet case; and he soon became the target of beatings and harassment by the city police.

Kaufman's earliest publications, all appearing in 1959, were the poems *Abomunist Manifesto, Second April*, and *Does the Secret Mind Whisper?*. Having originally appeared in *Beatitude* magazine, they were later published separately as broadsides by City Lights, the primary publisher of Beat writing. All three of these long poems convey a posture of disaffiliation and alienation through a tone of understated irony. The poems are marked by unusual juxtapositions of historical events and personalities. Kaufman also uses catalogues of surreal images, and verbal and prosodic experiments with jazz rhythms in line forms derived from the style of Walt Whitman:

> I want to be buried in an anonymous crater inside the moon.
> I want to build miniature golf courses on all the stars.
> I want to prove that Atlantis was a summer resort for cave men.
> I want to prove that Los Angeles is a practical joke played on us by superior beings on a humorous planet.

Abomunist Manifesto is a sequence of imaginary "documents," "notes," and "excerpts" from what purports to be a recently discovered religious movement. References within the poem suggest that Kaufman got the idea for his "manifesto" from the flurry of interest that arose over the discovery of the Dead Sea Scrolls. The poem is an indictment of a contemporary society that can learn nothing from history. In Kaufman's view the Beats, like the ancient Essenes, are persecuted by the authorities. Kaufman also uses his poem to show that the intolerance of modern society toward nonconformists is justified by their misinterpretation of religion. Since the Beats were dedicated to a program of disaffiliation, they never produced a serious document that was a collective Beat manifesto; a Beat manifesto would have been entirely contradictory. In one sense, Kaufman's poem is the closest thing to a manifesto that a member of the Beat generation could produce. In actuality the *Abomunist Manifesto* is an antimanifesto that ridicules the entire enterprise of formulating a system of beliefs; "Abomunism's" chief tenet is "Abomunists join nothing but their hands or legs, or other same." In Abomunism, "Abomunists vote against everyone by not voting for anyone." Beneath the poem's ironic humor and word play, Kaufman shows that the poem is a protest against the cold war, the stockpiling of atomic missiles, sexual repression, and the systematic hypocrisy of a society that pretends to care about spiritual values while preparing for nuclear war.

The other two broadsides published by City Lights in 1959, *Second April* and *Does the Secret Mind Whisper?*, are more determinedly surrealistic and lyrical than the *Abomunist Manifesto*. In both *Second April* and *Does the Secret Mind Whisper?* one surprising image follows upon another, in a technique reminiscent of the one developed by André Breton and the French Surrealists. Kaufman's poems use the catalogues in the hope that the cascading images are able to transform and renew the mind by jarring it into a more perceptive grasp of reality.

Abomunist Manifesto and *Second April* were included in Kaufman's first volume of poems, *Solitudes Crowded with Loneliness*. One of the poems in this collection, "Bagel Shop Jazz," won Kaufman a nomination for the Guinness Poetry Award and appeared in the fourth volume of the *Guiness Book of Poetry* in 1961. "Bagel Shop Jazz" is a relatively realistic description of Kaufman's San Francisco bohemian milieu. The poem lists the cast of characters inhabiting the typical Beat scene. There are the "mulberry-eyed girls," "turtle-neck angel guys" engaging in their favorite pastimes, "mixing jazz with print talk . . . lost in a dream world/where time is told with a beat." The poem expresses the fervent rejection of conventionality practiced by the Beats. Like many of the poems in *Solitudes*, "Bagel Shop Jazz" celebrates the Beats' attempt to find a new source of truth in jazz music. The poem, however, contrasts the upbeat mood of a search for ecstasy and vision with the dejected mood that comes from the attention of the surrounding society: "The guilty police arrive."

An important theme developed by the poems in *Solitudes Crowded with Loneliness* is the struggle between the truth and the lies of governments and other of society's institutions. Many of the poems in *Solitudes* celebrate the heroes who struggled against conventionality. Kaufman's heroes include Hart Crane, Albert Camus, Guillaume Apollinaire, and Allen Ginsberg, with whom he founded *Beatitude* magazine in 1959. In Kaufman's view, truth is doomed to fail in its struggle with the world shaped

CITY LIGHTS BOOKS

THE ABOMUNIST MANIFESTO was first published serially in John Kelly's glad magazine, BEATITUDE, and is the first and last word from the abominable snowmen of modern poetry.

BOB KAUFMAN is the author of SECOND APRIL, a black illumination soon to be published by CITY LIGHTS BOOKS.

35¢

© 1959 by BOB KAUFMAN

CITY LIGHTS BOOKS are published at 261 Columbus Avenue, San Francisco 11, California, and distributed nationally to bookstores by PAPER EDITIONS CORPORATION. Overseas distributors: W. S. HALL & CO.

Printed at the TROUBADOR PRESS, San Francisco

ABOMUNIST MANIFESTO

BOB KAUFMAN

Covers for Kaufman's 1959 poem, which ridicules the process of creating systems of belief

by middle-class values. A poem that Kaufman wrote while in prison speaks of "The Battle of Monumental Failures raging/Both hoping for a good clean loss." The Beats hoped to find in jazz a therapy that would cure the sickness of the human spirit, and Kaufman's poems helped to spread this idea. The primitivism evident in Kaufman's poems is typical of the jazz poets of the 1920s and may have been derived from Langston Hughes's poetry. The poem "Battle Reports" ends with lines that show jazz's victory over the repressive society of the modern city: "Attack: the sound of jazz./The city falls."

Kaufman's *Solitudes Crowded with Loneliness* became an overnight classic of the Beat generation and was important in spreading the movement throughout the United States and across the Atlantic to England and France. The collection was published as a pocket-sized volume in France and immediately achieved a reputation in Europe rare among books of poetry by foreign poets. Leading French magazines reviewed the book, so that Kaufman was considered to be among the greatest black American poets. His poetry was also well received in England. His American reception, however, was not favorable, and Kaufman's poetry was ignored by academic critics and editors of anthologies. Despite this exclusion from scholarly circles, Kaufman's poetry was some of the most popular work of that period. *Solitudes Crowded with Loneliness* was widely read by those sympathetic to the life-style of the Beats. It is currently in its sixth printing.

Kaufman left San Francisco for New York in the spring of 1960. He had been invited to read at Harvard University. He had also begun work on his first book, but his years in New York were filled with poverty, addiction, and imprisonment. "Blood Fell on the Mountains," composed upon his return to San Francisco in 1963, portrays his sorrow and disillusionment. "Small Memoriam for Myself," written the following week, became a final supplication; three days later, Kaufman took a ten-year Buddhist vow of silence prompted by the assassination of President Kennedy.

The phrase "Golden Sardine," scrawled on a scrap of brown wrapping paper in a bundle of Bob Kaufman's manuscripts, was used as the title of his second book of poems; *Golden Sardine* (1967) was edited out of Kaufman's scattered fragments of manuscripts. By the time the volume was published, Kaufman was well into a decade of silence during

$1.25

"GOLDEN SARDINE" scrawled on a scrap of brown wrapping paper found in a bundle of Bob Kaufman's manuscripts in a Moroccan-leather portfolio from which this second book of his poems is chosen—"Golden Sardine" floated loose in a stream of tattered papers & visions—"Golden Sardine" the image of the poet himself, brown paper skin torn & tossed South of Market, San Francisco, where he sleeps in a beat-up hotel named for Yankee Civil War general . . . Bob Kaufman was first published in Beatitude Magazine in San Francisco in the late 1950s. His broadsides, "The Abomunist Manifesto," "Second April," and "Does the Secret Mind Whisper" were separately published by City Lights and then included in his first book, SOLITUDES CROWDED WITH LONELINESS, published by New Directions in 1965. This book was translated and published in France in a big pocketbook edition and immediately achieved a notoriety rare among books of poetry by foreign poets, with features in leading French revues such as l'Express, La Quinzaine, Jeune Afrique, and Jazz Magazine. Today in France Kaufman is considered among the greatest Negro-American poets alive in spite of his continuing exclusion from American anthologies, both Hip & Academic.

THE POCKET POETS SERIES
GOLDEN SARDINE
BOB KAUFMAN
NUMBER TWENTY ONE

Covers for the 1967 poetry collection, which was published well after Kaufman had begun his decade of silence

which he neither spoke nor wrote. *Golden Sardine,* which was edited by Mary Beach, is a collection of poems that range from the energetically surreal filmscript of "a horror movie to be shot with the eyes" to an eloquent, restrained Buddhist prayer, "Saraswati." The poems deal with some of the Beats' favorite themes: the struggle to express artistic truth, the need for protest, and the pain and sadness of life. Of the poems in *Golden Sardine,* the most successful combine elliptical construction and wacky imagery with a tone of relaxed resignation. One poem, "Crootey Song," abandons language altogether in an attempt to reproduce a bebop scat improvisation. Many of the poems in *Golden Sardine* are of a fragmentary, unfinished nature that results from their spur-of-the-moment, jazz-inspired creation.

Having maintained his silence for over ten years, Kaufman stunned a local gathering by breaking into dramatic speech on the day the Vietnam War was ended. In this way, Kaufman once again demonstrated his concern with historical events, a consistent theme in his poetry. During the next five years, Kaufman composed some of his most provocative and challenging poems. The work written during this period was collected, along with some earlier writing, in Kaufman's third volume, *The Ancient Rain: Poems 1956-1978* (1981). In 1978, Kaufman abruptly renounced writing and withdrew once again into silence. Just prior to resuming his vow of silence, Kaufman told Raymond Foye, the editor of *The Ancient Rain,* "I want to be anonymous . . . my ambition is to be completely forgotten." Kaufman's tendency toward self-effacement is a theme expressed in a number of the poems in *The Ancient Rain.*

Bob Kaufman's impulse to withdraw from society is partly attributable to his disgust with the decadent state of the contemporary world. Kaufman, like the other Beat writers, was heavily influenced by the philosophy of Buddhism, which advocates a rejection of the material world as the only solution to the world's problems. In such poems as "The Poet" and "I am a Camera," Kaufman shows that while "creation is perfect" it is man who is responsible for destroying the earth: "The American/sun called the atomic bomb is/being dropped on all enemy/cities by the American sun."

The poems in *The Ancient Rain* that were written between 1973 and 1978 are much more expressive of religious mysticism than Kaufman's earlier poems. Whereas the early poems were concerned with jazz, Kaufman's later poems are more concerned with literary themes. Kaufman speaks of the Spanish poet Federico Garcia Lorca, who had been mentioned in several of Kaufman's earlier poems, but who now takes on a central role in the 1973 to 1978 group of poems. Kaufman speaks of his identification with Lorca in his long poem "The Ancient Rain": "I thought because Lorca said he would let his hair grow long someday crackling blueness would cause my hair to grow long." In "The Night that Lorca Comes," the Spanish poet is endowed with the attributes of a savior. Other poems from this period do not directly refer to Lorca, but are clear imitations of Lorca's style. Kaufman's mysterious "Oregon" echoes Lorca's "Somnanbule Ballad" and also mentions the Spanish poet by name: "I am talking to Lorca. We/Decide the Hart Crane trip, home to Oregon. . . ."

Kaufman's appreciation of Lorca matured over the years. In "Lorca," a poem from the 1956 to 1963 group, Lorca is described in Harlem and in the Spanish Civil War. In the 1973 to 1978 poems, Lorca is clearly a transcendant figure who symbolizes rebellion and sacrificial death. In addition to Lorca, Rimbaud and Hart Crane are also important to the later poems in both style and content. Both of these visionary poets, like Lorca, died young, and Kaufman's inclusion of these personalities in his poems shows his fascination with this powerfully romantic theme. The notion of a sacrificial death recurs throughout much of Kaufman's poems, for example in "The Poet," "I am a Camera," and "Oregon." In Raymond Foye's opinion, the poems written between 1973 and 1978 are "simple, lofty, and resplendent." Kaufman's later poems show him to have changed his attitude radically during the silent years. There is none of the ironic understatement and verbal play so characteristic throughout the poems in *Solitudes Crowded with Loneliness* and *Golden Sardine.*

Even when Kaufman had been working actively as a poet he had done very little to promote himself beyond a local following in North Beach. Despite his low profile, however, he was drawn into notoriety by the efforts of the more public relations-oriented of the Beats. Lawrence Ferlinghetti was especially helpful in gaining Kaufman a national reputation because of the wide distribution of his City Lights publications. Because Bob Kaufman is so closely associated with the major writers of the Beat generation, his poetry has been widely anthologized, and his reputation and influence have continued to grow. Kaufman's books have maintained good sales, and his influence on Afro-American poets of the 1960s and 1970s is apparent in many of the poems in LeRoi Jones's and Larry Neal's watershed anthology, *Black Fire.*

Kaufman's influence on Ishmael Reed's poetry is easily seen. Reed, an influential writer and anthologist, has none of Kaufman's attitude of disaffiliation; however, poems like "I was a Cowboy in the Boat of Ra" show Kaufman's influence in Reed's use of the Beat style, the use of Egyptian subject matter, and in the playful approach he has toward language. Reed's literary magazine at times prints poems by Kaufman, and his name comes up in poems by other *Yardbird* poets. Other poets who show Kaufman's influence in their work are Jayne Cortez, Gil Scott-Heron, and David Henderson.

Bob Kaufman, like other Beat writers, has attained the status of a living legend. To some, Kaufman has been a Beat angel, King of North Beach; to others a Buddhist prophet and poet. Pierre DeLattre sees Kaufman as a man with a "Rimbaud complex": he wanted to speed things up and to die young. DeLattre said of Kaufman, he was "The greatest poet on North Beach and he wasn't all that great, but he was a great poet, was Bob Kaufman." He characterizes Kaufman's lapse into silence as the result of Kaufman's addiction to methedrine: "For ten years he was completely out of it . . . only now is [he] just beginning to recover to an extent to be able to articulate again." Kaufman has continued to maintain his public presence in San Francisco by giving poetry readings with Gregory Corso, Lawrence Ferlinghetti, and other Beat writers. Kaufman, to whom the coinage of the word Beatnik has been attributed, is remembered by readers as an original Beat poet and an important influence on contemporary American poetry.

References:

Steve Dossey and Donna Wood, "An Interview with Pierre DeLattre," in *Beat Angels*, edited by Arthur Knight and Kit Knight (California, Pa.: the unspeakable visions of the individual, 1982);

James A. Emanuel and Theodore L. Gross, eds., *Dark Symphony: Negro Literature in America* (New York: Free Press, 1968);

Raymond Foye, "Editor's Note," in Bob Kaufman's *The Ancient Rain: Poems 1956-1978* (New York: New Directions, 1981);

June Jordan, ed., *Soulscript: Afro-American Poetry*

(New York: Doubleday, 1970);
Eileen Kaufman, "Laughter Sounds Orange at Night," in *Beat Angels*, edited by Arthur Knight and Kit Knight (California, Pa.: the unspeakable visions of the individual, 1982);
Eugene Redmond, *Drumvoices: The Mission of Afro-American Poetry, A Critical History* (Garden City: Anchor/Doubleday, 1976).

Etheridge Knight

(19 April 1931-)

Shirley Lumpkin
Marshall University

BOOKS: *Poems from Prison* (Detroit: Broadside Press, 1968);
Black Voices from Prison, by Knight and others (New York: Pathfinder Press, 1970); originally published as *Voci Negre Dal Carcere* (Bari, Italy: Giuseppe Laterza & Figli, 1968);
Belly Song and Other Poems (Detroit: Broadside Press, 1973);
Born of a Woman. New and Selected Poems (Boston: Houghton Mifflin, 1980).

When his first poetry collection, *Poems from Prison,* was published in 1968 by Dudley Randall's Broadside Press, Etheridge Knight was an inmate in Indiana State Prison; his work was hailed by black writers and critics as another excellent example of the powerful truth of blackness in art that the black arts movement, then reaching its height of influence, was promoting. Gwendolyn Brooks wrote of the strong presence of blackness and maleness in Knight's poetry, and in her preface to his *Poems from Prison* she prophetically identified the enduring characteristic of Knight's poetry: "Vital. Vital./This poetry is a major announcement." When he was paroled, Etheridge Knight continued to write the poetry he had begun to write in prison in 1963. "Poeting," as he would call it, became a center for his life, and his work became important in Afro-American poetry and poetics and in the strain of Anglo-American poetry descended from Walt Whitman. Thus, a black poet whose work reflected the prison, the male experience, and the aesthetic of the 1960s continued to write into the 1980s, absorbing more and more of the Afro-American, Anglo-American, European, and African literary traditions into a body of poetry capable of forming a passionate, loving connection with black and white readers. A believer in the trinity of poet-poem-people, Knight seeks and often achieves a responsible and specific language true to his human experience. Using oral premises to govern his style, he consciously strives to create communion and communication with audiences through the words of his poetry as written and as spoken in his numerous readings of his work. Speaking of what is often ignored or left out of poetry, Knight succeeds in reaching his audiences and making them feel and see anew the meaning of experience.

Born in Corinth, Mississippi, on 19 April 1931, to Etheridge "Bushie" and Belzora Cozart Knight, Etheridge Knight grew up in Paducah, Kentucky, with four sisters and two brothers. The bleakness and harshness of his life outside his family circle are reflected in his descriptions of his teenage years spent learning various toasts and other oral repartee from the men with whom he frequented the streets, bars, and poolrooms, quitting school after the eighth grade, and running away. The emotional anguish he experienced resulted in his addiction to narcotics and his enlistment in the army at seventeen in an attempt to escape the pain. Of these years he says: "I didn't finish the white man's high school—ran away from home instead; later, when I was seventeen years old, I joined the army disillusioned and got hooked. . . ."

During his army stint from 1947 to 1951, Knight served as a medical technician and saw active service in Korea where he received a "psyche/wound." While the remainder of his service in Guam and Hawaii was not wartime duty, the pain and disillusionment which he had experienced before his enlistment were aggravated by his wound.

Hence his narcotics addiction continued after his discharge, for reasons Knight again best describes: "I died in Korea from a shrapnel wound, and narcotics resurrected me." This resurrection, however, eventually led to what Knight called another death, a ten to twenty-five year indeterminate sentence in 1960 for a robbery committed in Indianapolis, Indiana, to support his habit. Until November 1968, when he was granted a parole, Knight served his sentence primarily in the Indiana State Prison in Michigan City, Indiana. Here "disillusioned and hooked," Knight found the resurrection which was to keep him attuned to life and love: poetry. He became a poet in prison: "I died in 1960 from a prison sentence & poetry brought me back to life."

When he went to prison Knight was an accomplished toast-reciter, and he refined his expertise in the traditional oral Afro-American art while there. Toasts are long narrative poems, usually in rhyming couplets, memorized and told by black men primarily to each other in certain male gatherings. Sexual exploits, drug activities, and violent aggressive conflicts involving a cast of familiar folk figures like Shine, the black stoker on the Titanic, or the signifying monkey, or junkies, whores, and pimps are related by the teller. Using street slang, drug and other specialized argot, and often obscenities in a creative call and response mode with a participating audience who comment and insert or make stanzas of their own, the toast-teller must be a master improviser in the genre to hold his audience's attention and must have an excellent sense of what makes characters and situations dramatically appealing.

In prison Knight not only told toasts masterfully, but also began to apply his understanding of the subjects, characters, and language of toasts, his ability to make them, and his knowledge of their aesthetic to written poetry. According to Knight, it was the telling of toasts out of prison and in that gave him a sense of himself and his community and a knowledge of what poetry is and can do. Since toast-telling brought him into genuine communion with others, he felt that poetry could simultaneously show him who he was and connect him with other people. Even in prison, Knight found community: "You know, we had a community and it was because of poetry—that's what brought me into communion with other people."

Consequently, by 1963, Knight had begun writing and submitting poetry for publication. By 1965, he had developed a specific ambition about writing. In the notebook he kept while in prison he wrote: "I will write well. I will be a famous writer. I will work hard and my work will be good. I will be a famous writer. My voice will be heard and I will help my people."

Knight's people, his black audience, were part of his conception of writing from the beginning; but in order to reach and help them he had to battle the formidable creativity-killing environment of prison and to utilize the time he had forced upon him to read prodigiously and to learn about words. While imprisonment worked against the creative process because he was painfully sensitive to his brutal environment, Knight persevered and developed connections with black poets, writers, and publishers, particularly Gwendolyn Brooks who visited Indiana State Prison for a reading, read Knight's work, and corresponded with him to offer advice; Sonia Sanchez, whom Knight corresponded with and married upon his release from prison in 1968; and Dudley Randall, whose Detroit-based small black press, Broadside, brought out Knight's first book of poems.

Thus, Knight's first two books, *Poems from Prison* (1968) and *Black Voices from Prison* (1970), were written and put together in the same contexts: prison life and the emergence of the black power ethic in the social, political, behavioral, and aesthetic worlds. *Poems from Prison* consists entirely of Knight's poems, while *Black Voices from Prison* is composed of Knight's work in poetry, nonfictional and fictional prose and the work of other inmates of the prison who are listed as coauthors.

The poems in the 1968 *Poems from Prison* are best described by Gwendolyn Brooks's incisive preface as "certainly male—with formidable austerities, dry grins, and a dignity that is scrupulous even when lenient." She wrote of the work's "centers of controlled softness" and a "warmth" that is "abruptly robust," the "blackness, inclusive, possessed and given; freed and terrible and beautiful." The poems recreate the conditions that black males experience, especially in prison, where they are sexually, physically, and mentally oppressed, brutalized, and separated from all those they love. The poems also give pictures of the heroes who emerge from this literal metaphor for the oppression that all blacks suffer; black men like Malcolm X and Hard Rock are heroes because they bring freedom and hope to others living in harsh conditions even if they themselves are destroyed. But heroes like Dinah Washington and Langston Hughes are present in the poems too, and Knight's warm and softer side is represented by lovers and family members and nature in his haiku poems. Always, however, the speaker is separated from warmth by stoney prison walls and guards or more subtle forms of oppression, usually racial.

As Gwendolyn Brooks also noted, the "effortless" music of the poems is actually "exquisitely carved." The poetic texts show Knight's concern with form, his attempts to control his wordiness by taking Brooks's suggestion that he write some haiku, his development of vocabulary, and his study of the techniques, styles, and works of poets like Langston Hughes, Gwendolyn Brooks, Dudley Randall, Amiri Baraka (LeRoi Jones), Emily Dickinson, Walt Whitman, and Robert Bly.

As a result, Knight's first slim volume contains poems which have been continually reprinted in poetry anthologies and which remain some of the best poems he has written. His Malcolm X poems, "For Malcolm A Year After" and "It Was a Funky Deal," and "Hard Rock Returns to Prison From the Hospital for the Criminal Insane," "He Sees Through Stone," "As You Leave Me," "The Violent Space," and "The Idea of Ancestry" render archetypal experiences and people in Afro-American history through powerful, critically acclaimed language.

As his Malcolm X poems memorialized and immortalized the historical Malcolm X by bringing the meaning of the death of the man to life, the "Hard Rock" poem brings the fictional Hardrock to life with what Robert Bly has called Chaucerian power. Reprinted in Knight's *Born of a Woman. New and Selected Poems,* "Hard Rock" presents the modern, prison version of the "bad" or "mean" "nigger," meaning a man who fights racism and oppression; Hardrock is a tragic figure since the modern technology of brain surgery has destroyed the character that beatings and prison could not.

What renders the picture of Hardrock even more powerful is the first person plural persona's voice which uses black, prison, and standard vocabulary to explain what Hardrock's destruction means to the "we" speaking in the poem. The prisoners "all waited and watched, like a herd of sheep," to see if Hardrock had become a docile "good nigger"; the speaker says they "wrapped" themselves "in the cloak/Of his exploits" since Hardrock was their "Destroyer, the doer of things,/We dreamed of doing but could not bring ourselves to do"; for the "fears of years, like a biting whip,/Had cut deep bloody grooves/Across our backs." The doubly tragic destruction of Hardrock the individual and of the hope he represented for others is memorably communicated through the vitality of the characters, although some readers, like Bly, are disturbed by the iambic meter of the poem that does not seem to do the characters or the experience justice.

In "He Sees Through Stone," reprinted from *Poems from Prison* in *Born of a Woman,* Knight creates another archetypal prisoner, the "old one," the aged and ageless black survivor who helps the frightened young blacks by his innate power. The language and lines are lean and suggestive, the images powerful, and the speaker, an "I" in the prison population who is neither the old man nor the "black cats" who circle him, is subtle, unobtrusive and effective.

Lean and powerful images also characterize the love poems in the volume, particularly "As You Leave Me" and "The Violent Space (or when your sister sleeps around for money)." In each of these poems the first person persona describes a beloved woman oppressed into prostitution. In "As You Leave Me" the woman is a lover and in "The Violent Space" the woman is a sister. Through concentrated, yet simply descriptive words which come from the details of daily life—like beer foam on the lips, and Johnny Mathis records, wasp stings, and a repeated refrain "Run sister run—the Bugga man comes!"—the speaker in each poem chronicles his inability to stop the oppression of his beloved. As the woman goes out to sleep with men, many white, for money, the speaker sings his song and takes his pain to a reefer or the twisted spoon of the heroin addict.

Of the good poems in *Poems from Prison,* the one which has been most lauded and most frequently anthologized is "The Idea of Ancestry," sometimes called one of the best poems that has been written about the Afro-American conception of family history and human interconnection. In this poem, Knight used what came to be his trademark in punctuation, the slash mark, along with commas, colons, occasional unusual spellings, and spacing of words to indicate how the voice should sound saying the lines. He also found a particularly effective combination of the vocabulary of the drug culture, of black slang, and of concrete images to make the idea of ancestry come alive. The reader can see the speaker staring at the forty-seven pictures of his family members pasted on his prison wall and trace the details of the speaker's remembered connections with them. Equally, the reader is, like the speaker, brought up short during the warm, flowing intermingling of lives by the "gray stone wall," one of those stark, concrete, and vigorous images which Knight creates, that, like the speaker's drug addiction, separates the speaker from those he loves and to whom he is connected. A powerfully complex experience of the essential

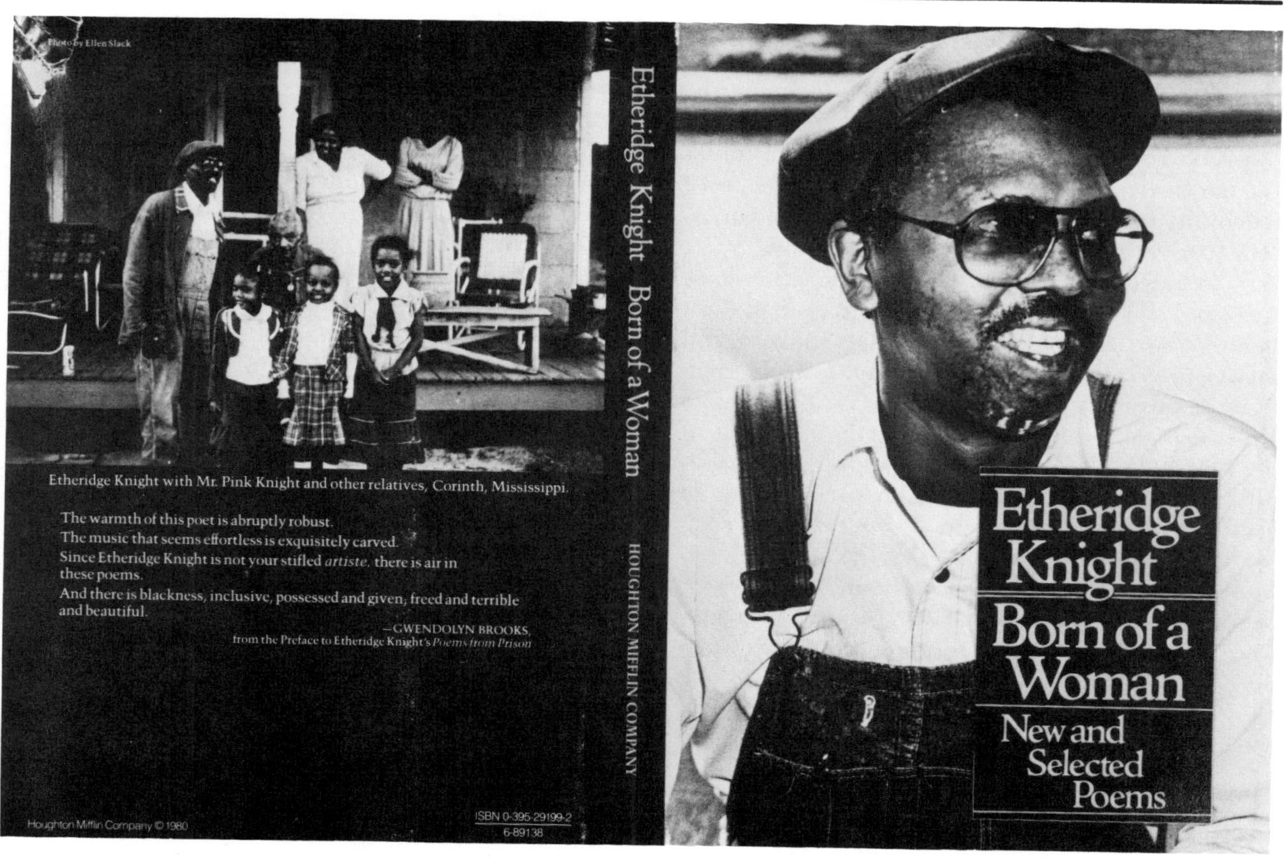

Dust jacket for Knight's 1980 book of poems, which takes its title from the Book of Job: "Man that is born of a woman is of few days and full of trouble."

loneliness and relatedness of a man who is at once "all of them," but different from them, and having "no children to float in the space between" is created through the structure and language of the poem.

Black Voices from Prison, released in English in 1970, although first published in Italian in 1968, was, like *Poems from Prison,* written with a major theme of the necessity for freedom, especially in an oppressive society that consigns black men to prison and many black women to prostitution and separates them from loving themselves and each other. With one notable exception, "A WASP Woman Visits A Black Junkie in Prison," the Knight poems in this volume are the same as those in *Poems from Prison.* What is added is Knight's prose, essays on the history of prison and the injustice done to some inmates, notebook excerpts and letter exchanges with fellow prisoners, and a short story, "No Time to Mourn," in which Knight graphically depicts how the oppression of prison has destroyed the emotional life and soul of a black "lifer," Jake, who must live by the code "no sweat, no trouble" even when facing the death of his last living relative. The work of other prisoners that is included reveals the same oppression, the violence and rape in prison, the injustice of how black men are treated, and the emergence of the new black consciousness brought into the prison by the "young black cats" who refuse to submit or be Uncle Toms, as they called it, in the face of white oppression. This black consciousness, the prison equivalent of the outside black power movement, was presented by Knight and the prisoners in the volume as the force which could offset and stop the soul-destroying effects of racism and prison.

These two books were composed by Knight with a specifically black audience in mind, for as Knight said in a 1968 *Negro Digest* symposium, the black artist should be accountable only to black people and should sing to them of their own deeds and misdeeds and make his heart beat with the same rhythm as the hearts of his people. These two volumes certainly beat with the heart of black male prisoners and make freedom a prerequisite for black life. However, something else was happening in this work as well. Knight was learning about the relationship of freedom to what all artists in an oppressive society must do. As he was to say after his release from prison, all artists must have a theme of freedom; and "the main things that freedom operates from are mobility and communication."

While the specifics of black prison experience were and still are important to Knight, even in *Black Voices from Prison* he saw possibilities for love and poetry to create a certain temporary kind of freedom, a possibility reflected in "A WASP Woman Visits A Black Junkie in Prison." In this narrative of the meeting of two people who had no "denominator," "common or uncommon," between them, an exchange across seemingly insuperable barriers occurs. Managing to "summon up the fact that both were human," a conversation took place which brought "no resurrection and truly/No shackles were shaken" but did bring some temporary softness to the black junkie in his prison.

In the late 1960s and the early 1970s Knight's work was primarily praised in print by black critics and poets Gwendolyn Brooks, Dudley Randall, and Haki Madhubuti (then Don L. Lee) who directed attention to the greatness of Knight's work in a tradition of literature stemming in part from Jean Toomer; Knight's incorporation of typically black themes like the memory of ancestors and the destruction of the black man or the "mean nigger" by the system; and Knight's effective use of formal versification and original use of punctuation, rhythm, and precise images to create a musical, oral effect in his work. Some of the black critics, like Madhubuti, had reservations about Knight's use of "dictionary words" and references to Greek classics, but Knight's poetry was generally enthusiastically embraced by blacks and reprinted in the numerous anthologies of black literature and black poetry which began appearing in the late 1960s and the 1970s.

Meanwhile, by 1969 Etheridge Knight had been paroled from prison, had married Sonia Sanchez and enlarged his family to include her children and all the people he was meeting in freedom. Living outside prison as a black poet from 1969 to 1972, Knight held various university jobs. He was writer-in-residence at the University of Pittsburgh, then at the University of Hartford, and then at Lincoln University. In addition to being a poet and instructor, Knight also became more actively involved in editing, serving as poetry editor for *Motive* magazine. His work brought him recognition, and he started to receive awards, honors, and grants, such as a National Endowment for the Arts grant in 1972 and a Guggenheim Fellowship in 1974. The Guggenheim was particularly significant, since it signaled the direction Knight was moving in during the 1970s. He was granted the Guggenheim on the basis of a proposal he had made to study the oral traditions, the speech and music he had grown up with, which form the legitimate basis of black poetry, as evidenced in the work of poets like Langston Hughes, Sterling Brown, and so many others.

Knight found freedom invigorating and used his new mobility to communicate with a wider community and to develop even further the range of possibilities for black oral poetic techniques, this time with a greater emphasis on rhythm and sound. He broadened his audiences, partially as a result of the many new contacts he had and the many readings he gave. In the 1970s he felt that his poetry was "also important to white people because it evokes feelings. It has importance in a country like this where we share so many common experiences." What had been a vague possibility in the 1968 work had become a reality in the 1970s work. Knight never repudiated his concerns and statements of the late 1960s, because his later emphasis on context as important to understanding poetry—his poetry—came out of the common history and images that blacks share. He saw his later poetry as less narrow than his 1960s work, and he was comfortable with the idea that since the new black poets rooted their poetry in life and had no absolute doctrines, his aesthetic would change and evolve just as life did without becoming less black. His poetry was to be a "belly song," the poetry of feeling, since Knight believes the seat of human feeling is the belly where one first feels fear, love, joy, and pain.

Pain was certainly a part of Knight's life and work in freedom, for freedom could not end his personal difficulties. His marriage to Sonia Sanchez dissolved, his problems with women, loneliness, drugs, drinking, violent and oppressive racism, and living continued. But now, the bad times rocked in some kind of rhythm with the good, for during this same period, he began a marriage with Mary Ann McAnally with whom he had two children. In 1973 he brought out a new book of poetry with Broadside Press, *Belly Song and Other Poems,* which incorporated his new experiences and interests into the continuing structure of the aesthetic for writing poetry he had developed in prison.

Prominent in this collection is Knight's written version of the Shine toast he had learned. "Dark

Prophecy: I Sing of Shine" is Knight's poetic version of the traditional toast about how the black stoker on the Titanic saved himself, when the ship sank, by resisting all the blandishments of the racist world which, until this moment, had hated him. Knight does not transcribe, but writes a version which emphasizes what dark brothers should learn from Shine. It is religion, in the form of the preacher Shine had to kill in Knight's poem, that is the greatest barrier between a black man and his freedom, although the temptations of money and sex are still significant.

This collection also has an ancestor poem about Knight's relationship to his past. In "The Bones of My Father" a concrete image of bones, with multiple significance in Afro-American preaching, spirituals, and reading of the Bible, is wedded to the voice of the speaker who recounts modern black and white inability to experience connection with the bones of the fathers. The young black men are nodding in a drug-induced stupor on the stoops of tenements, and the young white "long-hairs" are searching for, but alienated from, the promise of resurrection in the bones. Thus, the persona's father's bones remain grinning and unrisen on the bottom of the Tallahatchie.

Knight's rhythmical experimentation and growth are evident in the poem "Ilu, the Talking Drum." Considered by Robert Bly to be one of the best poems of the last fifty years because of its original and intense use of rhythmical sounds, the poem came out of Knight's summer spent with Nigerian poet and playwright Wole Soyinka, who taught him how the African drum uses pulse beats and the tone of the human voice to communicate. In the poem the subjects—"15 Nigerians and 1 Mississippi nigger,"—are dying in the dead, threatening darkness of Mississippi. Their menace was actually that of stoney whiteness or racism, and they are resurrected through the rhythmical sounds of the drum which Knight reproduces in a stanza of "Kah-doom" lines that are particularly powerful when read.

Knight's use of his own autobiography is also quite evident in *Belly Song* poems. Some of those feelings are about the legitimacy of the blues as an expression of his own and other Afro-Americans' lives. Black aesthetic poets like Sonia Sanchez had suggested that blues were just "sounds of oppression," hopeless cries of the pain racism had inflicted on blacks, and, therefore, not a legitimate basis for black liberation or black liberation poetry. In the poem "After Watching B. B. King on T.V. While Locked in No. 8 Cell No. 5 Cage of the Bridgeport, Connecticut, State Jail," the first person speaker who is so close to Knight measures the sounds of B. B. King's blues "that's filled my belly and ears/ for so many many years" against the lines from a "sonia/poem," that says "Blues ain't culture—/they sounds of oppression—/of the game the man's been running/all these years." While Knight is ambivalent and uncertain, he seems to come to some sort of truce with the blues in his "A Poem for Myself (or Blues for a Mississippi Black Boy)" which uses blues rhythms, blues repetitions of lines, blues worrying of a line, and blues phraseology as a way of knowing himself and hardening his determination to be "free in Mississippi/Or dead in the Mississippi mud." Returning home, culturally and geographically, and still being himself, black man Etheridge Knight in the dark heart of white racist Mississippi, is a form of freedom that this collection celebrated and promoted.

Love was also celebrated in the volume, and part of that belly feeling is, of course, the pain of lost love. Using his by now stylistically characteristic repetition, spaced lining, slash marks, and punctuation to indicate how words should sound, Knight's love poems draw upon images from the actual characteristics of sexual love, of water, and of nature to celebrate the fertile life of a man and a woman's coming together. This joy is contrasted to the bleak, barren world of white bone and of stone which is the loss of and the death of love. The effectiveness of the contrast can be seen in "Upon Your Leaving (for Sonia)," in which Knight uses a painful personal experience as the basis for a masterful poem about the loss of love.

Although exploring and celebrating feeling, this collection does not lack poems which thunder for political freedom and freedom from racism and prison. Knight recalls the continuing aftermath of Watts through the hopeless life of a ghetto mother (in a fine variation on Brooks's use of mothers and the poverty of those who must eat beans), and he angrily attacks the politicians performing at Martin Luther King's funeral. Knight's expansion of audience and aesthetic did not mean ignoring social realities that were unjust or leaving commitment to black liberation behind.

Continuing to read his poetry and to conduct poetry workshops, Knight moved toward the 1980s conceiving of himself as a poet. Collecting toasts for publication by the Center for Southern Folklore and incorporating the work, styles, and ideas of a growing range of Afro-American, Anglo-American, African, and European writers, and the attitudes expressed by the audiences to whom he read

Etheridge Knight (right) with poets Don Lee, Dudley Randall, and Sterling Brown.
Etheridge Knight's first book of poetry, **Poems from Prison,** was acclaimed by poet Gwendolyn Brooks with the words "This poetry is a major announcement." Since its publication in 1968, Knight's reputation has grown steadily, and he has read his poetry throughout the nation. He has edited a collection of prison writings, **Black Voices from Prison. Belly Song** has as introduction a moving letter written just before Knight's release from prison. Some of the poems were written in prison, others after his release, but they all show the increasing power and sensitiveness of his often anguished poetry.
Belly Song and Other Poems, by Etheridge Knight
$4.95 cloth, $1.75 paper.
BROADSIDE PRESS
12651 Old Mill Place
Detroit, Mich. 48238

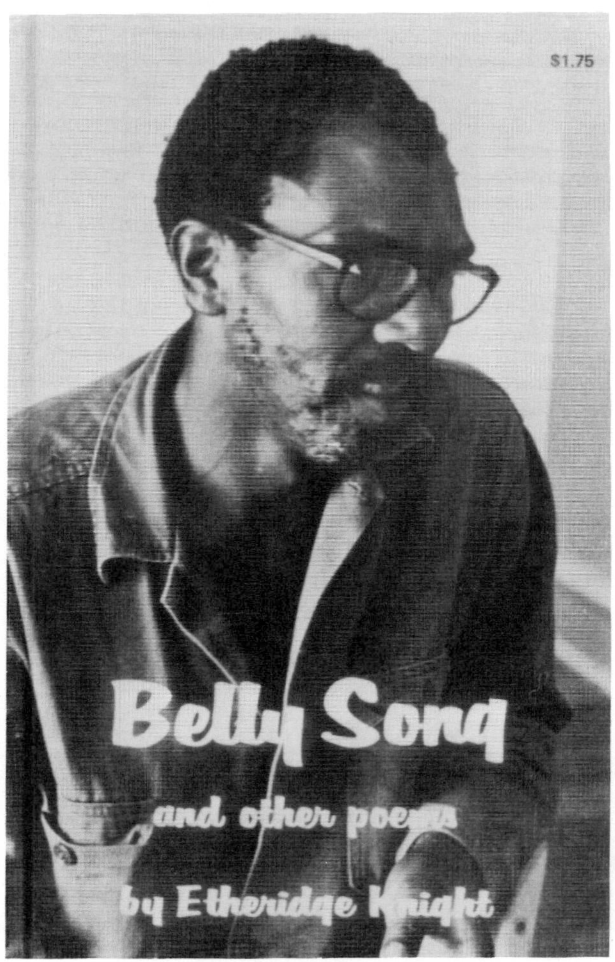

Covers for Knight's 1973 poetry volume, in which he explores traditional black forms like the toast

his own work, Knight concentrated on being a good poet. His life, the ultimate basis for his work, remained problematic, as he and his second wife, Mary Ann McAnally, divorced and the pain, drugs, and drinking continued. Once again, however, vitality was renewed as Knight based himself in Memphis, Tennessee, literally returning to the South, and married a third time to Charlene Blackburn, with whom, according to a poem, he had a son, Isaac Bushie Blackburn-Knight, born in Memphis, Tennessee, in December 1978.

Bringing together all the strands of his personal and poetic life, Knight brought out a volume of poetry which represented what he wished to be considered the fruits of his fifteen or so years of being a poet. Although originally scheduled for publication with Broadside Press in 1977, *Born of a Woman. New and Selected Poems* was published in 1980 by Houghton Mifflin, a large publishing house. The inclusive subject matter and style of the collection are clearly reflected in the prefatory pages in which Knight dedicates the book to his father; cites a passage from the Book of Job (Job 14:1-3), "Man that is born of a woman is of few days, and full of trouble. He cometh forth like a flower, and is cut down: He fleeth also as a shadow and continueth not"; and prints an anonymous poem from the wall of the Bridgeport, Connecticut, Correctional Center:

My friend said—"I'm a junkie."
I said, "You're full of shit!"
  He's dead, he's gone—
  —He's buried now—
I guess his statement was legit.

Following this succinct introduction to the theme of man's brief and painful life which informs the book,

Knight has a long list of acknowledgments of the people who helped him grow, from the negative contribution of politicians like "richard nixon and company" who made him "realize that there are evil forces still alive and incarnate" and "waiting to be unleashed upon the world," to the positive contributions of all the people in his life, including family members like Belzora Knight Taylor and his three wives, Afro-American poets like Audre Lorde, Gwendolyn Brooks, Haki Madhubuti, and Alice Walker, African poets like South African Dennis Brutus and Nigerian Wole Soyinka, Anglo-American poets like Donald Hall, Galway Kinnell, and Robert Bly, Elijah Muhammed for his teachings, and his past fellow inmates, some of whom were back in prison or fugitives whom he hoped would escape. The acknowledgments and the prefatory material suggest Knight's ideas of what a poet writes about and what style of writing he chooses to use. Calling poets "meddlers," Knight puts white New Englander Robert Frost and black poet Henry Dumas, shot in a subway station in New York, twentieth-century Mao Tse-tung, and nineteenth-century American poet Emily Dickinson in the same category because they meddled with "loving concern" for people in human affairs by writing poetry. As a poet or meddler himself, Knight tells the reader that his poems are what he has learned about people in all the places that he has been, from churches and city parks to poolhalls and prison. The reason for his type of writing is his idea of what poetry is: "I see the Art of Poetry as the *logos* ('In the beginning was the WORD') as TRINITY: The Poet, The Poem, and The People. When the three come together, the communion, the communication, the Art happens." His preface warns the reader to expect verbal changes in some of his older poems. Convinced by audiences that his image of the prisoners waiting to see what had happened to Hardrock as "indians at a corral" was racist, he changed the image to sheep. For the same reason he replaced the word "sons" in the original last line of "The Idea of Ancestry," ("and I have no sons/to float in the space between") with "children" because sons had a sexist connotation. The issue was not his popularity with audiences, but his responsibility as a poet, a responsibility he sees as based upon the "authority, the authenticity, the integrity" of his poet's voice. That "integrity" means that his words could not connote, evoke or perpetuate "a lie, an evil," whether "through omission or commission"; and the stereotypes of native Americans as passive and of boy children as more valuable than girl children were both lies and evils which his words could not support.

Awareness of the significance of form governed Knight's arrangement of the poems in the volume as well as his revisions. He chose not to arrange the poems chronologically or by the book in which they appeared. Instead, he put them in clusters or groupings under titles which are musical variations on the book's essential theme—life inside and outside of prison. This structure is a jazz composition mode that Langston Hughes had used in his own arrangement of the body of his poetry in *Selected Poems* in the 1950s.

Knight's book has three sections. The first, "Inside—Out" is an arrangement of the inside or prison poems from his first two books. The second section, "Outside—In," has primarily love and loss poems from his three books and his unprinted or new work. The third section, "All About—And Back Again," is a combination of poems from all stages that constitute a bluesy resolution of the problem presented by living in a world such as his. All the sections have political poems about what the forces of evil are unleashing in the world. The "Inside—Out" section describes the racism of wardens, the second section has a "Love Song to Idi Amin," which attacks the press Amin receives in the West, and the third section has "Welcome, Home Andrew Young—I'm/sho/glad you didn't get Hung," which celebrates Andrew Young's escape alive from white politics.

Despite the pain and evil described and attacked, a celebration and an affirmation of life run through the volume. The affirmation is that of the blues, realistic but not despairing, celebrating the physical, but aware of the death and destruction that attend all physical beings. Ironic humor is particularly evident in the volume, as Knight writes a "Shakespearean Sonnet: To a Woman Liberationist" and an ironic "love song" to himself in "Welcome Back Mr. Knight: Love of My Life." In this love poem, Knight addresses himself wryly, asking himself questions, and intends the pun of saying that he has the "Ol Liver" problem:

Welcome back, Mr. K: Love of My Life—
How's your drinking problem?—your thinking
Problem? you/are/pickling
Your liver—
Gotta/watch/out for the
"Ol Liver": Love of My Life.
How's your dope
problem?—

Knight's unsentimental attitude toward himself, his brutal honesty, takes another turn in many of the new belly songs published in the volume, songs which unsentimentally celebrate human life. In "The Stretching of the Belly," Knight praises the stretch marks a woman obtains from giving birth. In a remarkable use of stripped down language, suggestive concrete images, and musical, rhythmical repetition, Knight sets up a powerful contrast between the beauty of the stretch "markings" of the mother, which represent life, and the ugly "scars" men impose upon one another as the stripes of slavery which represent death:

Marks/of the mother are
Your/self
Stretching
Reaching
For life
For love
. . . .

Scars are/not
Markings scars do/not/come from stars
Or the moon Scars come from wars
From war/men who plunge
Like a bayonet into the gut
Or like a blackjack against the skull
Or prick
Like the end of a safety pin

Scars are stripes of slavery
Like my back
Not your belly
Which/is bright
And bringing forth
Making/music

"The Stretching of the Belly" is dedicated to Knight's third wife, Charlene Blackburn, the mother of Knight's son Isaac Bushie Blackburn-Knight whose birth is celebrated in a poem that is a jazzy blues, full of repeated refrains that detail with tragic irony and joy the pain into which a black boy child is born. In "On the Birth of a Black/Baby/Boy," the speaker sinks inside the belly of his beloved and clings to his son to help him through the bloody fountain of the birth. As he does so he sings of the world the baby will meet, a world not only of the father's and mother's love, but also of the Ku Klux Klan and of the shooting down of San Francisco mayor George Moscone, Martin Luther King, Jr., Malcolm X, and Medgar Evers, and of politicians who would try to stand where King once stood. The poem recreates the coldness, sterility, danger, pain, and racism, which, unfortunately, are the birthright of all black baby boys, but it ends the accumulating lines of blues refrains with a song of welcome:

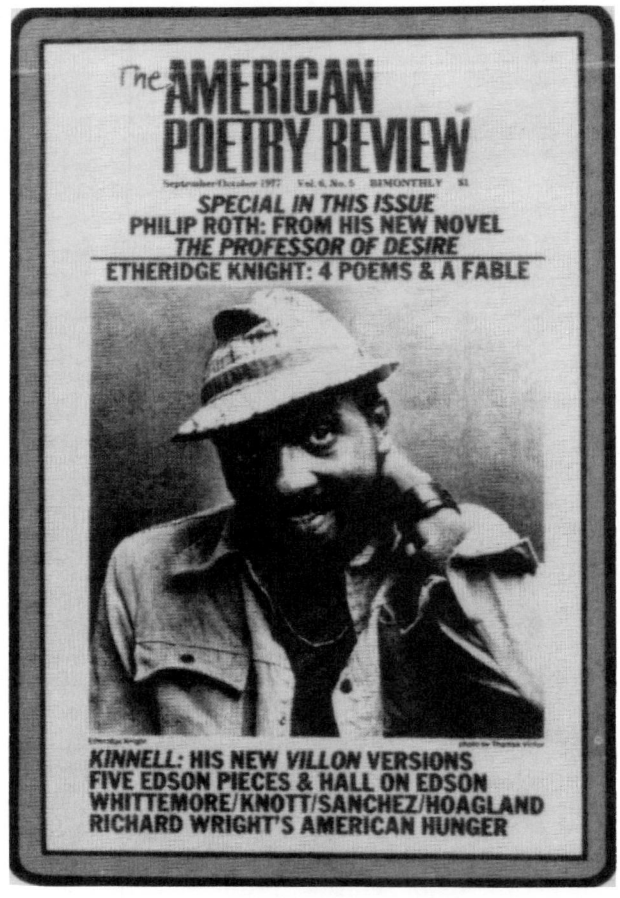

Front cover for a 1977 issue of the critical review that has championed Knight's work

As you lay warming in my arms, son—
all I/can/say is:
You/be a loonngg time coming, boy—
But you're wel/come here.

What is perhaps most Knight's in this collection is his embracing of the blues as the dominant mode of his poetry and his attitude toward life, a choice evident in his title since the blues has always been about trouble and being born of a woman is trouble. The volume is quite deliberately concluded with "Con/tin/u/way/shun Blues," a poem in which the autobiographical "I," Etheridge Knight, becomes the voice of the troubled human community. The speaker is overwhelmed by his own and other people's troubles: his mother tells him he "ain't got nobody else" but himself; a lover says his "nigga" friends are no good; and he says his white friends don't do "the things they should/even if they could." Nonetheless, as soon as he thinks "That our troubles will never end," in typical blues fashion he wakes up in the morning and starts "out all over again." The reason he pushes forward despite all the odds is his faith that someday they will all be free:

They say the blues is just a slave song
But I say that's just a lie
Cause even when we be free, baby—
Lord knows we still have got to die
lovers will still lie
babies will still cry

Like Langston Hughes and other Afro-American writers, Knight found that the tone, the attitude, the structure, and the style of the blues were both specifically Afro-American and specifically human, archetypal expressions of man's pain and spirit. Thus Knight absorbed them into his poetry.

Born of a Woman made the body of Knight's work widely available to critical assessments of his overall achievement. Most of the critical reservations centered around the small amount of work he had produced in fifteen years of writing, his style, and his political astuteness. While some critics point out that producing a large body of work while spending time in prison is unlikely, others maintain that Knight's work is still too slight to make him a major figure. Some critics find Knight's use of street, drug, and prison argot, colloquial and sometimes obscene vocabulary objectionable and unpoetic and think he does not use verse forms well. Others suggest that he does not say anything original or uncommon because he just transcribes Afro-American oral modes. Perhaps the most serious criticism is leveled at the quality of Knight's political judgment. Critics have suggested that he maintains an outmoded, strident black power rhetoric from the 1960s and that he has embarrassingly bad judgment about the worth of African leaders like Idi Amin.

Those with reservations and those who admire his work all agree, however, upon his vital language and the range of his subject matter. They all agree that he brings a needed freshness to poetry, particularly in his extraordinary ability to move an audience. They also all agree about the high quality of "Hard Rock" and "The Idea of Ancestry."

A number of poets, Gwendolyn Brooks, Robert Bly, and Galway Kinnell among them, go further than thinking that Knight has produced a few memorable poems. They consider him a major Afro-American poet because of his human subject matter, his combination of traditional techniques with an expertise in using rhythmic and oral speech patterns, and his ability to feel and to project his feelings into a poetic structure that moves others. Robert Bly goes so far as to suggest that Knight is the best contemporary Afro-American poet.

For the 1980s, Etheridge Knight has settled in Memphis, Tennessee. He expects that the new vital poetry will be coming from the South. He continues to base his poetry upon oral principles derived from the Afro-American culture he grew up in and continues his quest to be a people's poet and make well-crafted words create a living connection between the poet, the poem, and the people. In so doing he has written memorable poems and is traveling, in his own individual fashion, the road trod by one of his heroes, the people's poet par excellence, Langston Hughes.

References:

H. Bruce Franklin, "The Literature of the American Prison," *Massachusetts Review*, 18 (1977): 51-78;

Patricia Liggins Hill, "Blues for a Mississippi Black Boy: Etheridge Knight's Craft in the Black Oral Tradition," *Mississippi Quarterly*, 36 (Winter 1982-1983): 21-33;

Hill, "The New Black Aesthetic as Counterpoetics. The Poetry of Etheridge Knight," Ph.D. dissertation, Stanford University, 1977;

Hill, " 'The Violent Space': The Function of the New Black Aesthetic in Etheridge Knight's Prison Poetry," *Black American Literature Forum*, 14 (Fall 1980): 115-120;

Ken McCullough, "Communication and Excommunication: An Interview with Etheridge Knight," *Callaloo*, 5 (February-May 1982): 2-10;

Howard Nelson, "Belly Songs: The Poetry of Etheridge Knight," *Hollins Critic*, 18 (December 1981): 2-11;

Darryl Pinckney, "You're in the Army Now," *Parnassus*, 9 (Spring-Summer 1981): 306-314.

Pinkie Gordon Lane
(13 January 1923-   )

Marilyn B. Craig
Southern University

BOOKS: *Wind Thoughts* (Fort Smith, Arkansas: South & West, 1972);
The Mystic Female (Fort Smith, Arkansas: South & West, 1978);
I Never Scream: New and Selected Poems (Detroit: Lotus Press, 1985).

OTHER: Patricia L. Brown, Don L. Lee, and Francis Ward, eds., *To Gwen With Love,* includes poems by Lane (Chicago: Johnson Publishing Company, 1971);
Discourses on Poetry, edited, with contributions by Lane (Fort Smith, Arkansas: South & West, 1972);
Sue Abbott Boyd, ed., *Poems by Blacks,* Volumes I and II, include poems by Lane (Fort Smith, Arkansas: South & West, 1973);
Poems by Blacks, Volume III, edited, with contributions by Lane (Fort Smith, Arkansas: South & West, 1973);
Eugene B. Redmond, ed., *Griefs of Joy,* includes poems by Lane (East St. Louis, Illinois: Black River Writers, 1977).

PERIODICAL PUBLICATIONS: "Reaching" and "Rain Ditch," *Journal of Black Poetry,* 1 (Fall-Winter 1971): 38-39;
"On This Louisiana Day," and "Poem Extract," *Louisiana Review,* 1 (Summer 1972): 105-106;
"Portrait," *Negro American Literature Forum* (1972);
"Children" and "For Bill," *Pembroke Magazine,* no. 4 (1973): 26-28;
"Eulogy on the Death of Trees," *Poet: India,* 14 (May 1973): 477;
"Mid-Summer Thoughts," "Telephone Call," *Hoodoo,* 1 (1973);
"A Quiet Poem," Broadside No. 80, *Broadside Press* (February 1974);
"Flight," "Two Poems," and "I Never Scream," *Southern Review,* 10 (Fall 1974): 947-950;
"Survival Poem," "Incident in a Black Ghetto," "Rain Ditch," "Telephone Call," *Confrontation: A Journal of Third World Literature,* 1 (1974): 54-57;

Pinkie Gordon Lane

"Waiting" and "Spring," *New Orleans Review,* 4 (1974): 272-273;
"Message," "Who Is My Brother?," "Nocturne," and "Love Poem," *Obsidian: Black Literature in Review,* 1 (Winter 1975): 87-89;
"While Sitting in the Airport Waiting Room" and "Poem for Lois: An Elegy," *Callaloo,* 1 (December 1976): 15, 18;
"Listenings," "Leaves," and "Opossum," *Obsidian: Black Literature in Review,* 3 (Winter 1977): 54-56;
"Lake Murry," "Baton Rouge # 2," "Southern University," *Southern Review,* 13 (Spring 1977): 351-354;

"Listenings," "Migration," "The Mystic Female," *SouTh aNd WesT: An International Literary Quarterly*, 14 (Fall 1977): 18-21;

"Midnight Song," "When You Read This Poem," "Love Poem: Thoughts Run Wild," *Black Scholar*, 9 (November 1977): 28-29;

"Migration" and "The Mystic Female," *Callaloo* (February 1978): 6, 90;

"Sexual Privacy of Women on Welfare" and "Kaleidoscope," *Nimrod*, 21 (1978): 140-141;

"Renewal" and "Betrayal: On the Loss of a Friend," *Callaloo*, 2 (February 1979): 88, 96;

"The Privacy Report," *Ms.*, 7 (January 1980): 29.

Although her volumes of poetry were published contemporaneously with many of those of the black arts movement poets of the 1960s, Pinkie Gordon Lane differs from them dramatically in style and content. However, she shares with them a general concern for black people across the country and at all levels of society. Her particular concern, though, centers upon the personal, private, quiet moments that have touched her as wife, mother, teacher, and editor. In many ways an occasional poet, she shares with her predecessor Phillis Wheatley the marking of sorrowful and happy events around her. Her poetry includes elegies, eulogies, comments on friends and family, reactions to teaching, tributes to fellow poets, and analyses of her personal growth as a woman and as a poet. Lane is a highly subjective and autobiographical poet whose work constitutes a transcript of the various dimensions of herself.

Representative of one of the quieter strains of poetry over the past two decades, Lane has found a wide audience for her volumes of poems, *Wind Thoughts* (1972), *The Mystic Female* (1978), and *I Never Scream: New and Selected Poems* (1985), and for her editorial and magazine publications. Though she has not yet received critical attention comparable to some of the younger and more politically vocal poets of the 1960s, Lane has been consistently represented in anthologies, and she has consistently been a part of major conferences, festivals, and other gatherings of black poets over the past several years. As a professor of English at Southern University in Baton Rouge, she was instrumental in making the annual Melvin Butler Poetry Festival a national and well-attended event. Her role in keeping black poetry before the public as an editor and festival organizer has added the political dimension to the contributions of a poet who appreciates what others are doing, but who has nevertheless managed to follow her quieter, different drummer.

Born in 1923 in Philadelphia, Pennsylvania, to William Alexander Gordon and Inez Addie West Gordon, Lane was the youngest of four children and the only one to survive beyond infancy. As an only child, Lane found relief from her loneliness by becoming an avid reader and by becoming active in the Methodist Church. She completed grammar school and graduated from Philadelphia School for Girls in 1940, the same year her father died. For the next five years, Lane put her education on hold while she worked in a sewing factory. When her mother became ill and died, she realized what it meant to be alone, to be totally responsible for herself. The loss of both parents, but especially the death of her father, would form the substance of poems she would write later.

Lane sold the family house and goods, and in 1945, enrolled in Spelman College in Atlanta, Georgia, where she had been awarded a four-year academic scholarship. During her senior year in college, she met and married Ulysses Simpson Lane. An apt student, she graduated magna cum laude in 1949 with a bachelor's degree in English and art. She worked as an English teacher in the public schools of Florida and Georgia between 1949 and 1955, before returning to Atlanta in 1955 and working toward a master's degree at Atlanta University. Awarded the degree in 1956, she and her husband left Georgia to make their home in Baton Rouge, Louisiana, where Lane still resides.

By 1956, Lane had become a serious writer of prose, having had some success as a short story writer. After moving to Louisiana, she continued to read and write before securing a teaching position at the now defunct Leland College in Baker, Louisiana. She taught in the English department at Leland from 1957 to 1959, before transferring to Southern University as an instructor of English. Now professor of English at Southern, she has directed the English department there since 1974. In 1963 her only child, Gordon Lane, was born. In 1967, she became the first black woman to receive the Ph.D. degree from Louisiana State University in Baton Rouge.

It was simply by chance in 1960, during the hectic years of working toward the Ph.D., that a colleague, knowing Lane's interest in books, handed her a copy of Gwendolyn Brooks's *A Street in Bronzeville* (1945). Lane was inspired by Brooks's accomplishments, for Brooks was the first contemporary black woman poet that Lane had ever read. A new phase of Lane's life began. Abandoning prose, Lane found that poetry was the medium through which she could best present her own experience. Her first published poem, "This Treasured Book," appeared in *Phylon: The Atlanta University Review of Race and Culture* in the fall of 1961. In this poem, the poet expresses her love of books and escapes momentarily from "bridge and baby talk, and routine wails/about a bill unpaid, or themes to grade. . . ." "This Treasured Book" follows the form of a Shakespearean sonnet, adhering to its controlled rhyme scheme and metrical pattern.

Lane wrote and published prolifically from that point on. Eventually weaned from the use of formal structure, she came to prefer free verse. She began to view poetry as language rather than artifact, and she felt that any subject is suitable for a poem. To her, what makes the difference between poetry and prose is the way in which language is handled; therefore, she began to make greater use of figurative language, relying more on imagery, careful word selection, suggestion, and connotation.

Lane is primarily an imagist whose work falls within the lyric tradition of poetry. Even though she writes about internalized experiences and uses a subjective persona, her subject range has always been expansive and eclectic: she writes about her family ("Poems to My Father"), nature ("Eulogy on the Death of Trees"), people's often unconscious, though no less cruel, insensitivity to the plight of other people ("The Privacy Report"), environment (the Baton Rouge poems), elegies ("Marion" and "Finis"), racism ("Who Is My Brother?"), and her profession ("On Being Head of the English Department").

More recently, Lane has been impressed by Anne Sexton's striking metaphorical style; she now uses the metaphor with uninhibited boldness, although her images are softer, more flowing than Sexton's. Lane familiarized herself with all of Sexton's works, even the collection of letters published posthumously by her daughter, Linda Gray Sexton (*Anne Sexton: A Self Portrait in Letters*), and presented her study, "The Search for Balance in the Poetry of Anne Sexton," to the 1980 Convention of the National Council of Teachers of English.

Saddened by the death of her husband in 1970, Lane plunged into her work, producing her first volume of poems, *Wind Thoughts*, in 1972. In *Wind Thoughts*, she responds to three major poetic worlds: nature, the past, and the inner self—incorporating the themes of love ("Love Considered"), hate ("After the Quarrel"), suffering ("Songs to the Dialysis Machine"), and death ("Finis")—each subject treated almost stoically. The volume also includes the six poems in "Poems to My Father," which depict her father as sometimes so difficult to live with that the poet has tried to "divorce" herself—unsuccessfully—from his memory. Obviously working her way through painful memories, Lane concludes that her father was "a shadow,/a low light,/a lost love/folding into the oval" of his "night." Softer memories guide "Oh You Tender, Lovely Scrubwoman (for my mother)," in which the poet pays tribute to her hardworking mother, laments her untimely death, and wonders if she has returned to a condition comparable to the "paradise" from which she sprang.

Wind Thoughts also pays homage to Sonia Sanchez and Gwendolyn Brooks, who, along with Margaret Danner and numerous others, share in the dedication of the volume. Sanchez is called a "beautiful/black sister, who/knows how to sing about/her/blackness." Lane's recognition that she shares a "common bond" with Sanchez leads her to urge Sanchez to "create beauty out of love" because they possess a "wholeness" that "cannot be destroyed/through oppressive tyranny." Though the poem can perhaps be read as one in which Lane wonders about the value of more vocal protest, it also shows her awareness of the commitments of other poets and her recognition of the differences between herself and them.

"For Gwendolyn Brooks" depicts Brooks as the "Queen of the image" who became Lane's "inspiration," "mentor," "discoverer of songs." While Lane recognizes Brooks's ability to capture the pain often identified with blackness, she chooses finally to celebrate her as woman:

Black woman of Chicago strains
—poet of this age—
poet
Black poet
woman

The many occasional and dedicatory poems in the volume are matched by those from the poet's very private experiences. She writes of her husband, of self-discovery, and of personal achievement. For example, her work toward the terminal degree in English is captured in "While Working Toward the Ph.D. Degree":

Telephone unanswered, parties unserved,
Husband languishing, flat, unnerved,

Friendships neglected, kisses left cold,
Laughter—too much, too sudden, too bold.

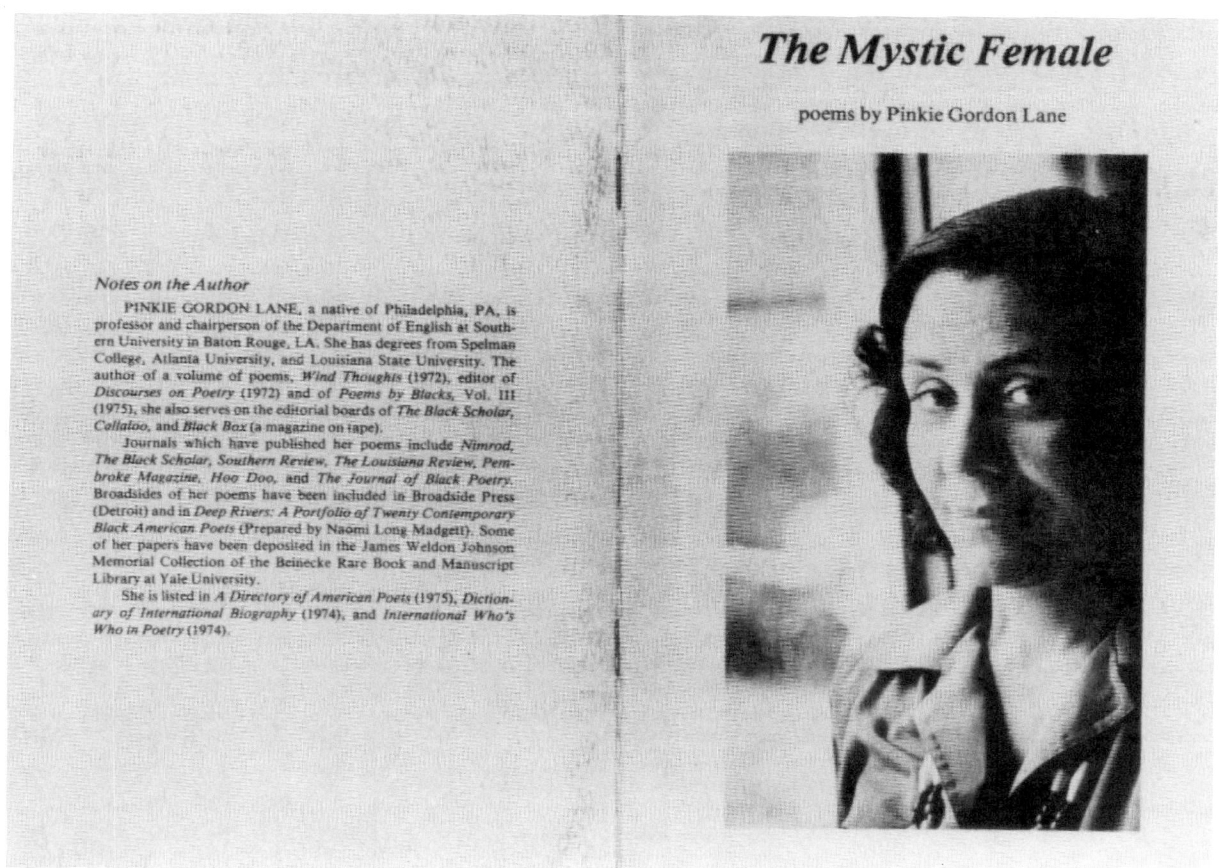

Notes on the Author

PINKIE GORDON LANE, a native of Philadelphia, PA, is professor and chairperson of the Department of English at Southern University in Baton Rouge, LA. She has degrees from Spelman College, Atlanta University, and Louisiana State University. The author of a volume of poems, *Wind Thoughts* (1972), editor of *Discourses on Poetry* (1972) and of *Poems by Blacks*, Vol. III (1975), she also serves on the editorial boards of *The Black Scholar*, *Callaloo*, and *Black Box* (a magazine on tape).

Journals which have published her poems include *Nimrod*, *The Black Scholar*, *Southern Review*, *The Louisiana Review*, *Pembroke Magazine*, *Hoo Doo*, and *The Journal of Black Poetry*. Broadsides of her poems have been included in Broadside Press (Detroit) and in *Deep Rivers: A Portfolio of Twenty Contemporary Black American Poets* (Prepared by Naomi Long Madgett). Some of her papers have been deposited in the James Weldon Johnson Memorial Collection of the Beinecke Rare Book and Manuscript Library at Yale University.

She is listed in *A Directory of American Poets* (1975), *Dictionary of International Biography* (1974), and *International Who's Who in Poetry* (1974).

The Mystic Female

poems by Pinkie Gordon Lane

Covers for Lane's 1978 collection of what critic Jerry Ward calls "quiet poems . . . mysterious, double-edged, supersubtle, a calculated use of verbal juju. . . ."

Tears—much too quickly, as quickly forgot,
A child loved and wanted, but with prudence ungot

Dust on the table, a kitten unmilked,
Love but indulged, flowing loosely like silk,

Ethereally lost in a cold world of print,
A drunken desire, incontinent,

Ideas my only reality,
A slave in pursuit of that damned Ph.D.

While the poem describes the general plight of women who try to manage careers and families, it is designed less with the public, political implications of that predicament in mind than with how the annoyances manifest themselves at the private, domestic level.

The publication of *Wind Thoughts* and the symbolic bonding with black women poets had its counterpart for Lane in the First Annual Black Poetry Festival held at Southern University in 1979. Lane reached out to other black writers in an effort to bring together professional and apprentice poets and to legitimize all forms of black poetic talent. Under Lane's direction, nationally known lecturers, poets, and other writers attended the festival, including such luminaries as May Miller, Naomi Long Madgett, Alice Walker, Julia Fields, Al Young, Stanley Plumly, Dudley Randall, Margaret Danner, Don L. Lee, Nikki Giovanni, and Lance Jeffers. The occasion was also one of personal celebration for Lane; the English department at Southern honored her for her second collection of poetry, *The Mystic Female*, which had been published in 1978.

Nominated for the Pulitzer Prize in 1979, *The Mystic Female* has received wide literary acclaim. It opens with "The Mystic Female," "lingering in the backwaters/of Louisiana bayous," declaring: "I am ghost, spirit, woman/exploring the mirrors of my mind." The volume closes with "Poems to My Father," in which the mystic female, a lovely, sensitive woman, attempts to reconcile herself to her father's death:

> I meant to tell you this, Papa
> I've divorced myself
> from your memory.
> The years never happened . . .
> Only the times when we
> laughed
> And strolled through the York Street Park
>
> . . . while I waited to grow up.

The fact that Lane ends *The Mystic Female* with the same poems that begin *Wind Thoughts* is further indication that the wrestling with the father's influence upon her life and memory continues in spite of her protestations to the contrary. Also in this volume, Lane takes more interest in immediate and daily occurrences as subjects for her poems, for example, "Southern University."

Lane's reaching out to other writers has also been manifested in her editing activities. She is editor-in-chief and vice president of SouTh aNd WesT, which publishes an international journal of the same title, and she has served on the editorial boards of significant black literary publications. She has been advisory and contributing editor to *Callaloo* as well as to the *Black Scholar*.

In February of 1979, Lane was represented in *Callaloo*'s special issue devoted to black women poets. She shared company there with poets such as Mari Evans, Gayl Jones, Sonia Sanchez, and Alice Walker. She received more national attention when one of her poems, "The Privacy Report," appeared in *Ms.* early in 1980.

Since 1970, Lane has traveled widely both in the United States and abroad, visiting, for example, the East African countries of Tanzania, Kenya, Ethiopia, and Zambia; she has also traveled to the Virgin Islands. On a trip to Haiti, she met a number of writers and artists as well as Haitian government officials and business people. In the spring of 1981, she was sponsored by the United States International Communication Agency in a cultural exchange program; she lectured and read her work in Ghana, Cameroon, Zambia, and South Africa.

Over the years, Lane's work has appeared frequently in journals and anthologies. Her third volume of poetry, *I Never Scream: New and Selected Poems*, was published in 1985 by Lotus Press. Lane is a sensitive poet who is able to translate her sensitivity into images with which her readers can identify. Whether writing about the problems of a woman on welfare or a personal reaction to a small event in her life, Lane brings to her poetry creativity and sharp observation of the world around her. In these post-revolutionary years, her work is certain to receive more critical attention.

Reference:

Dorothy W. Newman, "Lane's Mystic Female," *Callaloo*, 2 (February 1979): 153-155.

Papers:

Some of Lane's works are included in the James Weldon Johnson Memorial Collection of Negro Arts and Letters in the Beinecke Rare Book and Manuscript Library at Yale University.

Audre Lorde

(18 February 1934-)

Irma McClaurin-Allen
University of Massachusetts, Amherst

BOOKS: *The First Cities* (New York: Poets Press, 1968);

Cables to Rage (London: Breman, 1970);

From a Land Where Other People Live (Detroit: Broadside, 1973);

New York Head Shop and Museum (Detroit: Broadside, 1974);

Between Our Selves (Point Reyes, Cal.: Eidolon Editions, 1976);

Coal (New York: Norton, 1976);

The Black Unicorn (New York: Norton, 1978);

Uses of the Erotic: The Erotic as Power (New York: Out & Out, 1979);

The Cancer Journals (San Francisco: Spinsters, Ink, 1980);

Chosen Poems, Old and New (New York: Norton, 1982);

Zami: A New Spelling of My Name (Trumansburg, N.Y.: Crossing Press, 1982);

Sister Outsider: Essays and Speeches (Trumansburg, N.Y.: Crossing Press, 1984).

OTHER: Rosey Poole, ed., *Beyond the Blues: New Poems by American Negroes,* includes poems by Lorde (Lympne, Kent: Hand & Flower Press, 1962);

Paul Breman, ed., *Sixes and Sevens,* includes poems by Lorde (London: Breman, 1963);

Langston Hughes, ed., *New Negro Poets, U.S.A.,* includes poems by Lorde (Bloomington: Indiana University Press, 1964);

G. Menarini, ed., *I Negri: Poesie E Canti,* includes poems by Lorde (Rome: Edizioni Academnia, 1969);

Clarence Major, ed., *The New Black Poetry,* includes poems by Lorde (New York: International Press, 1969);

Ted Wilentz and Tom Weatherly, eds., *Natural Process: An Anthology of New Black Poetry,* includes poems by Lorde (New York: Hill & Wang, 1970);

Bernard Bell, ed., *Afro-American Poetry,* includes poems by Lorde (Boston: Allyn & Bacon, 1972);

Erlene Stetson, ed., *Black Sister: Poetry by Black American Women, 1746-1980,* includes poems by Lorde (Bloomington: Indiana University Press, 1981);

Amina Baraka and Amiri Baraka, eds., *Confirmation: An Anthology of African-American Women,* includes poems by Lorde (New York: Quill, 1983).

Audre Lorde (photograph © 1984 by Layle Silbert)

Audre Lorde is probably best known as a feminist poet; yet her contributions to the new black poetry movement cover a wide range of themes.

Audre Lorde

or, to give her full title, Audre Geraldin Lorde Rollins,
was born 18 February 1934 in New York City.
She attended Hunter College there from 1951 to 1959,
with an early year at Mexico University in between,
and followed her BA in English and philosophy
with an MS in library service from Columbia University.

During her college years she worked at all the usual (?) jobs:
medical clerk, arts and crafts supervisor, ghost writer,
social worker, x-ray technician, factory worker.
Later she became young adult librarian in Mount Vernon,
and at present she is back in the city, teaching 'creative
literature' at City College and 'the black experience' at
Lehman: 'neither replaces writing or being black'...

'The second breath I drew was difficult and
(no explanations forthcoming from my elders)
I set out to build my own solutions – or at least
formulate a question. I was a child' – so in the spring
of 1968, as poet-in-residence at Tougaloo College
('a small black college in would you believe it land')
she helped other young people formulate their questions
and eventually edited a collection of their work called Pound:
'poets must teach what they know, if we are all to continue being'.

Audre Lorde's first published poem appeared early in 1949;
she has since had work in various periodicals, including
the Journal of Black Poetry, Negro Digest, Parasite, Venture.
Other poems have appeared in anthologies compiled by
Rosey E. Pool (Beyond the blues; Lympne, England, 1962),
Langston Hughes (New Negro poets: USA; New York 1964) and
Clarence Major (The new black poetry; New York 1969).
Her own first book was published, with an introduction
by the editor, at Diane DiPrima's Poets Press, New York 1968.

Earlier, the only major selection from Audre Lorde's work
had appeared in the Heritage anthology 'Sixes and sevens':
eight poems dating between 1952 and 1962, with a 'statement'
(written especially for the book) which is still being used –
it last reappeared in the Tougaloo anthology – and which begins:

I am Black, Woman, and Poet – all three are facts outside
the realm of choice. My eyes have a part in my seeing;
my breath in my breathing; and all that I am in who I am.
All who I love are of my people; it is not simple.'

'I was not born on a farm or in a forest but in the centre
of the largest city in the world – a member of the human race
hemmed in by stone and away from earth and sunlight.
But what is in my blood and skin of richness, of brown earth
and noon sun and the strength to love them, comes the roundabout
way from Africa through sun islands to a stony coast;
and these are the gifts through which I sing, through which I see.'

Covers for Lorde's second poetry volume, published in London in 1970

Black pride, black love, and black survival in an urban environment are recurring motifs; and the image of the city, in all of its destructive grandeur, dominates many of her poems.

In a statement written especially for the Heritage anthology *Sixes and Sevens* (1963), edited by Paul Breman in London, Lorde wrote: "I am Black, Woman, and Poet—all three are facts outside the realm of choice. My eyes have a part in my seeing; my breath in my breathing; and all that I am in who I am. All who I love are of my people; it is not simple. I was not born on a farm or in a forest but in the centre of the largest city in the world—a member of the human race hemmed in by stone and away from earth and sunlight. But what is in my blood and kin of richness, of brown earth and noon sun and the strength to love them, comes the roundabout way from Africa through sun islands, to a stony coast; and these are the gifts through which I sing, through which I see."

Lorde was born in New York City to laborer Frederic Byron and Linda Belmar Lorde. The youngest of three sisters, Lorde grew up in Manhattan where she attended Catholic school. She loved to read poetry and wrote her first poem when she was in the eighth grade. She attended Hunter College from 1951 to 1959 when she graduated with a bachelor's degree. In 1954 she had spent a year as a student at the National University of Mexico. While she was a student Lorde worked at various odd jobs as a medical clerk, arts and crafts supervisor, ghost writer, social worker, X-ray technician, and factory worker. In 1961 she received a master's in library science from Columbia University and began working as a young adult librarian at Mount Vernon Public Library, where she stayed until 1963. On 31 March 1962 she married attorney Edwin Ashley Rollins. They have two children, Elizabeth and Jonathan. In 1966, Lorde became head librarian at Town School Library in New York City. She worked there until 1968.

The end of her tenure as librarian in 1968 marked a turning point for Lorde. On the book jacket of *Cables to Rage* (1970), she says, "The second breath I drew was difficult and (no explanations forthcoming from my elders) I set out to build my own solutions—or at least formulate a question. I was a child." She received a National Endowment for the Arts grant, and in the spring of 1968 she became poet-in-residence at Tougaloo College, "a small black college in would you believe it land." The result of her search for solutions was the publication of a collection of her students' work called *Pound* (1968), which she edited: "poets must teach what they know, if we are all to continue being."

Lorde's first book, *The First Cities* (1968), was published that same year by the Poets Press. It contained an introduction by Diane DiPrima, who wrote: "Audre Lorde's world is all colors. Its songs move thru large areas of light & darkness. . . . I have known Audre Lorde since we were fifteen, when we read our poems to each other in our Home Room at Hunter High school. And only two months ago she delivered my child." The poems in *The First Cities* differ from the rhetorical style and confrontational stance that prevailed in the black poetry of the time. Dudley Randall, a black critic and poet, wrote in his review of the book that Lorde "does not wave a black flag, but her blackness is there, implicit, in the bone." He went on to note that it was a "quiet, introspective book." "You first notice the striking phrases: 'the crash of the passing sun,' 'a browning laughter,' 'the oyster world.' Then you notice the images, most of them drawn from nature, a source unusual in this age of urban poets who write of concrete and machines. But Audre Lorde is not a nature poet. Her focus is not on nature, but on feelings and relationships. The nature images, many of them pertaining to the season, illustrate inner weather, the changes of love or feelings. . . . Audre Lorde's poems are not strident, and do not grab you by the collar and drag you in, but they attract you by their fresh phrasing, which draws you to return to them and to discover new evocations." Lorde's second book, *Cables to Rage* (1970), was published outside of the United States by Paul Breman, an active supporter of black poetry. The collection was distributed in America by Dudley Randall's Broadside Press. The poems were less introspective and focused on several themes: the transience of human love, the existence of human betrayal, birth, and love.

All of these elements coalesce in the poem "Martha," which one critic called a "virtuoso" piece: "human betrayal, if it exists, is the result of a much larger movement: human mutability. This is the insight that informs the [poem] Martha. . . ." This poem is significant in that it is the first poetic expression of Lorde's homosexuality: "I love you and cannot feel you less than Martha/I love you. . . ."; *"I need you need me/Je suis Martha I do not speak french kissing"*; "we shall love each other here if ever at all"; and "yes Martha we have loved each other and yes I hope we still can/no Martha/I do not know if we shall ever sleep in each other's arms again."

In 1972 Lorde received a Creative Artists Public Service grant, and in 1973 her third book of poetry, *From a Land Where Other People Live,* was published by Broadside Press. The book "reveals the poet's growth as a person and a craftswoman," wrote the reviewer for *Ms.* Lorde's vision is one of global injustice and oppression. Commenting on the death of Malcolm X, she writes: "As I read his words the dark mangled children/came streaming out of the atlas/Hanoi Angola Guinea-Bissau Mozambique Pnam-Phen/merged with Bedford-Stuyvesant and Hazelhurst Mississippi/haunting my New York tenement that terribly bright/summer/while Detroit and Watts and San Francisco were burning." The quiet anger that was beginning to form in *Cables to Rage* is fully developed in this book. But Lorde has other concerns as well: her identity as an Afro-American and as a woman; and her relationships, particularly between mother and daughter. As Joan Larkin writes, "There are other subjects in these poems: her love for her children, the complexities of nurturing, her own growth, tenderness for women seen as sisters and sometimes lovers, the failures and promises of her life as a teacher and a city dweller." *From a Land Where Other People Live* is not limited to Lorde's personal experience, for she makes her vision applicable and understandable to a wide audience. The book was nominated for the National Book Award for poetry in 1973.

Probably her most political and rhetorical work, *New York Head Shop and Museum* (1974), Lorde's fourth book, was published by Broadside Press the following year. Lorde describes her politics as "radical," and we get a glimpse through these poems of her involvement in and feelings about social and political issues.

Having spent all of her life in New York, Lorde shows us her vision of the city. She takes us on an odyssey through the decaying city, and she confronts us with her critical vision of the people living there. She writes, "There is nothing beautiful left in the streets of this city./I have come to believe in death and renewal by fire." Elsewhere she writes, "why it must be mine or my children's time/that will see the grim city quake to be reborn perhaps. . . ."

In *New York Head Shop and Museum,* Lorde

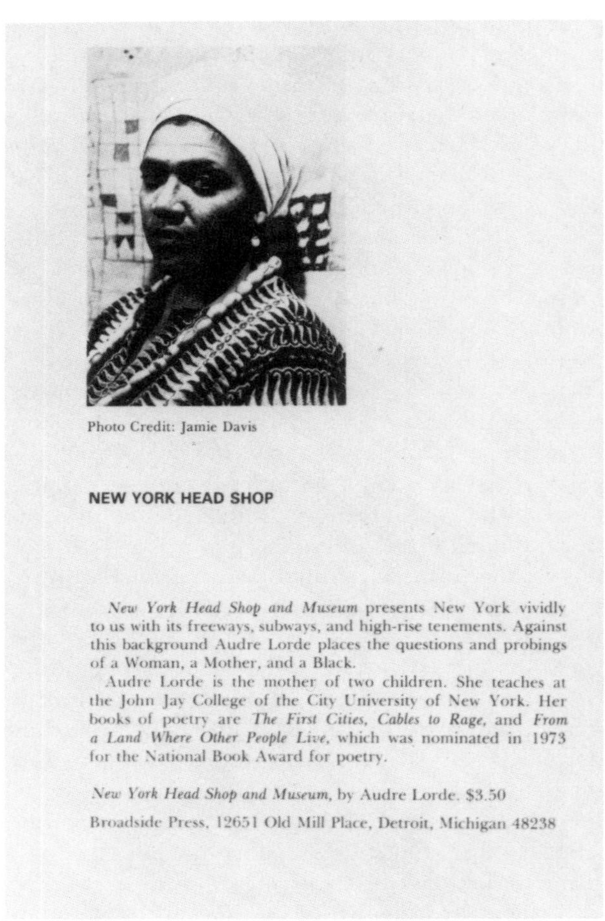

Photo Credit: Jamie Davis
NEW YORK HEAD SHOP
New York Head Shop and Museum presents New York vividly to us with its freeways, subways, and high-rise tenements. Against this background Audre Lorde places the questions and probings of a Woman, a Mother, and a Black.
Audre Lorde is the mother of two children. She teaches at the John Jay College of the City University of New York. Her books of poetry are *The First Cities, Cables to Rage,* and *From a Land Where Other People Live,* which was nominated in 1973 for the National Book Award for poetry.
New York Head Shop and Museum, by Audre Lorde. $3.50
Broadside Press, 12651 Old Mill Place, Detroit, Michigan 48238

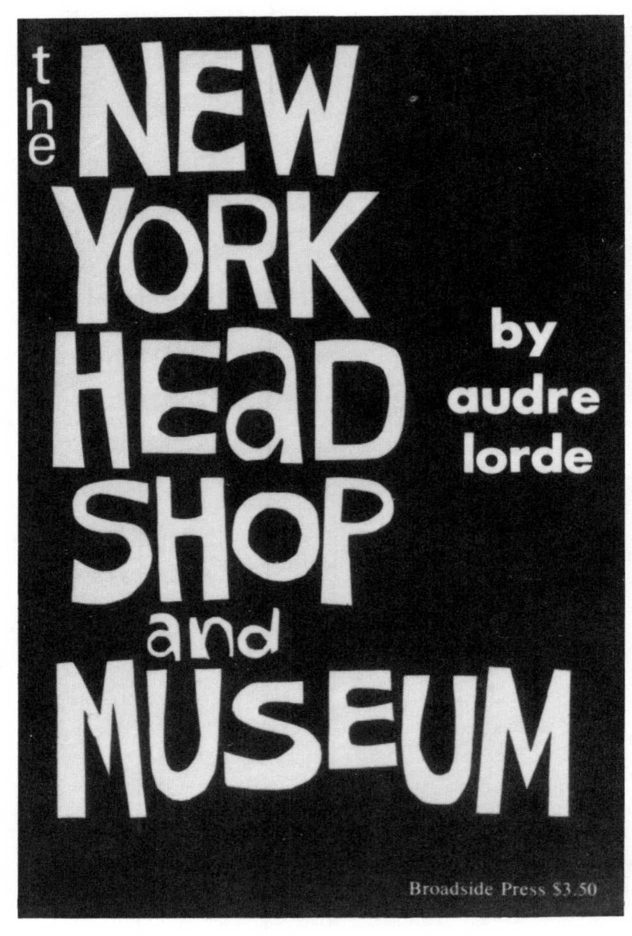

the
NEW
YORK
HEAD
SHOP
and
MUSEUM
by
audre
lorde
Broadside Press $3.50

Covers for Lorde's 1974 collection of poems, which explores her blackness, her roles, and her relationship to her community

sometimes embraces the aggressive yet proud rhetorical style that characterized the new black poetry movement of the 1960s: "Since Naturally Black is Naturally Beautiful/I must be proud/and, naturally,/Black and/Beautiful/who always was a trifle/yellow and plain though proud before." This vision of blackness embodies pride, but also cynicism—". . . and if I die of skin/cancer/oh well—one less/black and beautiful me." The poem ends on an ambiguous note leaving the reader to ponder whether Lorde is affirming the entrepreneurial aspects of cultural nationalism or lamenting the misplaced emphasis on external manifestations of black pride at the expense of basic survival.

The publication of *Coal* by W. W. Norton and Company (1976) was Lorde's first release by a major publisher. The work is a compilation of poems from her first two books, *The First Cities* and *Cables to Rage,* and is significant for introducing Lorde's work to a broader readership than the predominantly black one that supported Broadside Press.

"Coal," the title poem, demonstrates Lorde's facility with metaphor, as well as the tightness and control of her language.

There are many kinds of open.
How a diamond comes into a knot
    of flame
How a sound comes into a word,
    coloured
By who pays what for speaking.

. . . Some words live in my throat
Breeding like adders. Others
    know sun

. . . Love is a word, another kind of
    open—
As a diamond comes into a knot of
    flame
I am black because I come from the

earth's inside
Take my word for jewel in your
open light.

Lorde is a prolific writer. *The Black Unicorn* (1978), also published by Norton, was her seventh book of poetry, and it is at the apex of her poetic and personal vision. In the poems, Lorde has freed herself from the prison of the city and reclaimed her birthright—the land, culture, and people of Africa. The poems are also an assertion of her womanhood and her blackness. She says, "I have been woman/for a long time/beware my smile/I am treacherous with old magic/and the noon's new fury/ . . . I am/woman/and not white." She also asserts her lesbianism—and her politics—"The difference between poetry and rhetoric/is being/ready to kill/yourself/instead of your children/ . . . I have not been able to touch the destruction within me./But unless I learn to use/the difference between poetry and rhetoric/my power too will run corrupt as poisonous mold. . . ."

Poet and critic Adrienne Rich wrote: "Refusing to be circumscribed by any simple identity, Audre Lorde writes as a Black woman, a mother, a daughter, a Lesbian, a feminist, a visionary; poems of elemental wildness and healing, nightmare and lucidity." *The Black Unicorn* is a monumental work that reveals the complexity of Lorde's life and vision.

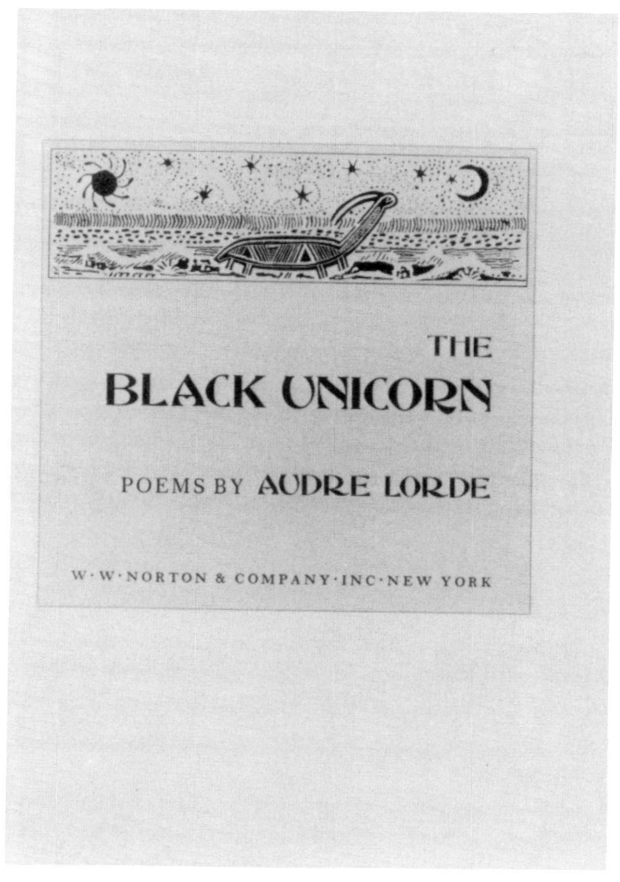

Title page for Lorde's 1978 poetry collection. The black unicorn is, in Lorde's words, "restless" and "unrelenting/the black unicorn is not free."

Lorde's poetic vision has also been shaped by an encounter with cancer, the subject of her first published prose collection, *The Cancer Journals* (1980), although she published the short story "La Llorona" in a 1955 issue of *Venture* magazine under the pseudonym of Rey Domini. *The Cancer Journals* is nonfiction and chronicles her descent into the world of cancer and her recovery from the resulting mastectomy. At times feeling herself on the verge of death or hopelessness, Lorde openly confronts her own fear and anger. In publishing the journals, she openly shares her perspective and philosophy: "This is the work I must do alone. For months now I have been wanting to write a piece of meaning words on cancer as it affects my life and my consciousness as a woman, a black lesbian feminist mother lover poet all I am."

Lorde's book gives us a painful vision of the will to survive and the courage to reject the perfect images of women projected by the media. Alice Walker writes, "Audre Lorde's *The Cancer Journals* has helped me more than I can say. It has taken away some of my fear of cancer, my fear of incompleteness, my fear of difference. This book teaches me that with one breast or none, I am still me." Lorde's book won the American Library Association Gay Caucus Book of the Year Award for 1981.

Lorde is perhaps the best known and most widely published of a small group of black feminists, among them critics Barbara Smith and Gloria Hull, who go beyond the usual in their depictions of Afro-American experiences. Although they share common territory with other black writers, they have also been groundbreaking in insisting that feminism is relevant to black people and that the lesbian experience—different again from feminism per se—should also no longer be considered alien to black women. Placed in a pigeonhole especially because of this latter focus, Lorde has only in recent years begun to enjoy critical attention from scholars. Her many writings on her struggles with cancer perhaps provided one pathway for transcending the labeling, and one of her most recent works, *Zami: A New Spelling of My Name* (1982), in its treatment of the difficult relationship between a mother and her daughter, perhaps exhibited a concern with which more readers could identify and empathize. In 1984, Crossing Press published Lorde's nonfiction collection, *Sister Outsider: Essays and Speeches.* Currently Lorde is active in the promotion of Kitchen Table: Women of Color Press, of which she is a founding member.The press is the first of its kind in this country; it concentrates exclusively upon publishing and distributing works of women of color, from various communities, with a feminist vision. She is also a founding "mother" of Sisters in Support of Sisters in South Africa.

An unusually productive writer, it is quite clear that Lorde will have to be given more critical attention in the future. Through her publishing record and public appearances, she is rapidly influencing a generation of younger writers. She has been a tenured professor of English since 1978, first at John Jay College of Criminal Justice, and since 1981 at Hunter College in New York. She is helping to shape the views of her students who, in turn, will influence others. Her ties to young black feminists who are themselves writers and scholars will be one way of ensuring a continuing discussion of her works, and other scholars who are genuinely committed to literary history will perhaps also be inclined more toward recognizing and treating the unique contributions of this unusual writer.

References:

C. W. E. Bigsby, ed., *The Black American Writer* (Penguin, 1969);

Jerome Brooks, "In the Name of the Father: The Poetry of Audre Lorde," in *Black Women Writers (1950-1980): A Critical Evaluation,* edited by Mari Evans (Garden City: Doubleday, 1984), pp. 269-276;

Joan Martin, "The Unicorn is Black: Audre Lorde in Retrospect," in *Black Women Writers (1950-1980): A Critical Evaluation,* edited by Evans (Garden City: Doubleday, 1984), pp. 277-291;

Claudia Tate, ed., *Black Women Writers at Work* (New York: Continuum, 1983), pp. 100-116;

James Vinson, ed., *Contemporary Poets* (London: St. James Press, 1975).

Haki R. Madhubuti (Don L. Lee)

(23 February 1942-)

Catherine Daniels Hurst
University of South Carolina

See also the Madhubuti entry in *DLB 5, American Poets Since World War II.*

BOOKS: *Think Black* (Detroit: Broadside Press, 1967);

Black Pride (Detroit: Broadside Press, 1968);

Don't Cry, Scream (Detroit: Broadside Press, 1969);

We Walk the Way of the New World (Detroit: Broadside Press, 1970);

Directionscore: Selected and New Poems (Detroit: Broadside Press, 1971);

Dynamite Voices: Black Poets of the 1960's (Detroit: Broadside Press, 1971);

From Plan to Planet; Life-Studies: The Need for Afrikan Minds and Institutions (Detroit: Broadside Press/Chicago: Institute of Positive Education, 1973);

Book of Life (Detroit: Broadside Press, 1973);

Enemies: The Clash of Races (Chicago: Third World Press, 1978);

Earthquakes and Sun Rise Missions: Poetry and Essays of Black Renewal, 1973-1983 (Chicago: Third World Press, 1984).

RECORDINGS: *Rappin' and Readin' by Don L. Lee,* Broadside Press, 1971;

Rise Vision Coming (with the Afrikan Liberation Arts Ensemble).

OTHER: *To Gwen with Love,* edited by Madhubuti as Don L. Lee, Patricia L. Brown, and Francis Ward (Chicago: Johnson, 1971);

A Capsule Course in Black Poetry Writing, includes an essay by Madhubuti (Detroit: Broadside Press, 1975).

Photograph by Karega Kofi Moyo

Haki R Madhubuti

One of the most prominent contemporary black American poets, Haki R. Madhubuti was born Don L. Lee in Little Rock, Arkansas, and reared in the "black bottom" of Detroit, Michigan. Madhubuti's father, James Lee, deserted the family when the boy was very young. His mother, Maxine Graves Lee, became an alcoholic and died when Madhubuti was only sixteen. His fragmented family life, reflected by autobiographical elements in his early poetry, forced the young man into the realities of the working world at an early age. Supplementing the income from his two paper routes, young Madhubuti had a predawn job cleaning up a neighborhood bar.

Madhubuti attended Dunbar Vocational High School in Chicago. He received his associate's degree from Chicago City College in 1966, and he attended Roosevelt University in Chicago (1966 to 1967) and the University of Iowa, where he earned the Masters in Fine Arts in 1984. He served in the United States Army from 1960 to 1963.

Madhubuti's background has been diverse. From 1963 to 1967 he was apprentice curator for Chicago's DuSable Museum of African History, which was directed by Margaret G. Burroughs. During this time, he also worked as a stock clerk for Montgomery Ward (1963 to 1964), a post office clerk (1964 to 1965), and a junior executive for Spiegel's, Chicago (1965 to 1966). All the while, Madhubuti was using poetry as a means of making sense of and bringing order to the fragmented world around him. Having achieved some acclaim with the publication of *Think Black* (1967) and *Black Pride* (1968), he left the world of business to devote his time and entrepreneurial energies to writing, publishing, and teaching others. Since the late 1960s, Madhubuti has been a writer in residence at Cornell University (1968 to 1969), the University of Illinois, Circle Campus (1969 to 1971), Morgan State College (1972 to 1973), Howard University (1971 to 1978), and Central State University (1979 to 1980). He is founder and editor of *Black Books Bulletin* and Third World Press, Chicago-based operations that have provided publishing outlets to many new black voices. He is cofounder and director of the Institute of Positive Education, an organization that actuates many of the ideas of black nation building. And Madhubuti is a founding member of the Organization of Black American Culture, Writers Workshop (OBAC), one of the major collective efforts to broach the 1960s and 1970s American literary scene. (Other OBAC writers include Gwendolyn Brooks, Ebon, Carolyn Rodgers, Johari Amini Kunjufu, and Sterling Plumpp.) Madhubuti is contributing editor to *Black Scholar* and *First World.* In 1969 and 1982, he received grants from the National Endowment for the Humanities; in 1973, the Kuumba Workshop Black Liberation Award; and in 1975, the Broadside Press Outstanding Poet's Award. He has been a member and vice-chairman of the African Liberation Day Support Committee and a member of the Executive Council of the Congress of African People. Rejecting all that his "slave name" (Don L. Lee) implies, the poet began writing under the Swahili name of Haki R. Madhubuti in 1973.

In many ways, Haki R. Madhubuti is one of the most representative voices of his time. Although most significant as a poet, his work as an essayist, critic, publisher, social activist, and educator has enabled him to go beyond the confines of poetry to the establishment of a black press and a school for black children—creations that give substance to his assertions of black awareness. In the introduction to *Think Black,* Madhubuti stresses his belief that "black art will elevate and enlighten" his people and

Don Lee reading from the anthology For Malcolm, at the dedication of Malcolm X Shabazz Park, formerly Washington Park, Chicago. Don Lee is a Chicago Poet and the author of Think Black. His poems have appeared in Negro Digest, the Journal of Black Poetry, Liberator, Muhammad Speaks and other Publications. His latest book is Don't Cry, Scream.

In the introduction to this 1968 collection, Dudley Randall says the poet "writes for the man in the street, and uses the language of the street, and sometimes of the gutter, with wit, inventiveness, and surprise."

"lead them toward an awareness of self "; that it will "show them mirrors, beautiful symbols"; and that it will "aid in the destruction of anything nasty and detrimental" to their advancement as people. For Madhubuti, blackness (Africanness) is the source from which all of his other themes originate and radiate. Consequently, he writes about all facets of black life: black pride, black identity, black beauty, black women, black heroes, black education, black love, as well as black revolution.

Like the other young black revolutionary writers who came on the literary scene in the 1960s and early 1970s, Madhubuti eschews the philosophy of "art for art's sake." He believes that the artist's function is sociopolitical and that he must fulfill his obligations by becoming a "cultural stabilizer," bringing back "old values" and "introducing new ones" in a way that the people can understand and appreciate.

As poet and social critic, Madhubuti believes with Larry Neal that art cannot be separated from life, that everything is political. In the preface to *Don't Cry, Scream* (1969), he asserts that "most, if not all, black poetry will be *political.*" He notes that he has often come across black artists who feel that they and their work should be apolitical, "not realizing that to be apolitical is to *be political in a negative way for black folks.* There is *no* neutral blackart; either it *is* or it *isn't,* period." Madhubuti believes that, by accurate and authentic rendering of the thematic and linguistic features of black life, the poet increases the pride of the black community and reinforces the people's awareness of the vitality and richness of their lives.

Breaking away from Anglo-American poetic tradition in another way, Madhubuti's stylistic form is also free and innovative. Often he uses street language and the dialect of the uneducated black community. He experiments orthographically in an attempt to replicate the sounds and cadences of musical instruments. He uses unconventional abbreviations and strung-together words ("shoeshineblack," "auntjimamablack," "blackisbeautifulblack," "daybeforeyesterday") in a visually rendered dialect designed to convey the stress, pitch, volume, texture, resonance, and intensity of the black speaking voice. By these and other means, Madhubuti intends to engage the active participation of a black audience accustomed to the oral tradition of storytelling and song.

Madhubuti's style is kinetic: quick, explosive, full of movement and high energy. His startling metaphors, variations of refrain, unexpected turns-of-phrase, wordplay, and staccato repetitions combine to produce an impact that keeps audiences spellbound. His magnetic quality has been verified by the masses of college students who have flocked to his readings during his personal appearances on many of the major university campuses of the United States.

Although nontraditional in subject matter and technique, Madhubuti's poetry has generally received favorable critical response. Agreeing with Gwendolyn Brooks that Madhubuti is "at the hub of the new wordway," Ron Welburn proclaims in *Negro Digest* that Madhubuti is a technician, a "poet-linguist continuing the development of a new language for black poetics, the language of familiar experience, the same language black readers have grown up speaking." Similarly, Helen Vendler writes in the *New York Times Book Review* that in Madhubuti "the sardonic and savage turn-of-phrase long present in black speech as a survival tactic finds its best poet." This positive critical attitude is perhaps best summed up by Theodore R. Hudson in *Contemporary Poets:* "Of the strong young black poets of the 'Black arts movement' that began in the United States in the late 1960's Don L. Lee is one of the most powerful and persuasive in content, one of the most creative and influential in technique."

Not all of Madhubuti's critics speak in such superlatives, however. Eugene Ethelbert Miller, for instance, states in his piece for *College English* ("Some Black Thoughts on Don L. Lee's *Think Black!* Thunk by a Frustrated White Academic Thinker") that Madhubuti's poems are "a kind of literary or artistic crime." Miller's assessment, however, seems to reflect not only his more traditional view of the form and function of poetry, but also his Euro-American orientation. In the same vein, but more vitriolic and hysterical, is Jascha Kessler's exhortation in a 1973 issue of *Poetry*: "I've not seen poetry in Don L. Lee. Anger, bombast, raw hatred, strident, aggrieved, perhaps charismatically crude religious and political canting, propaganda and racist nonsense, yes; and utterly unoriginal in form and style; humorless; cruel laughter bordering on the insane. . . . But poetry? Lee is deluded in thinking he has it. What he has is street language, common enough to most of us; the rest is a farago of anybody's W. C. Williams and rehashed and rancid LeRoi Jones. . . . Lee is outside poetry somewhere, exhorting, hectoring, cursing, making a lot of noise. But you don't have to be black for that." A fair and fitting rejoinder to Kessler's highly subjective assessment is David Llorens's observation in *Ebony* that "just possibly, none of us is spared in the face of the wordmaker Don Lee reading his poems. It is not enough that we might consciously identify with the sentiments finding expression in his words. There is the subconscious, where words do not reach but voice is *not* to be denied. And the voice of Don Lee is faithful to its master, resonant, haunting, leaving in the distance all manner of half-truths. Transcending customs. Niceties. Platitudes. Seeking no approval. No applause. No contest. Just making people hear their own silence. A disquieting experience."

Llorens points out that "Lee's sensibility is that of the artist, one who must be vicious as the lion under attack by another beast of the jungle lest he not survive and do his work, but one who knows and makes the distinction between *vicious* and *savage*. . . . And because he believes that black people are . . . under attack, Don Lee is, then, a lion of a poet who . . . gives rhythmic quality to verse that is never savage but often vicious and always reflecting a revolutionary black consciousness."

Madhubuti's first thin volume of poetry, *Think Black,* is unpretentious and down-to-earth. The collection displays the germinal themes which have now been organic to his work for more than a decade and a half: identity and self-determination ("Back Again, Home," "Re-Act for Action," "In a Period of Growth," "Wake-Up Niggers"), prejudice ("Stereo," "Taxes," "UNDERSTANDING BUT NOT FORGETTING," "Mainstream of Society," "The Long Reality"), the beauty of black women ("A Poem for Black Women"), ethnic responsibility for education ("Education"), awareness and unity ("Awareness"). His style in *Think Black* is simple and unformed, vacillating between free verse and rhyme (sometimes employing rough off-rhyme). He uses slang, street rap, and signifying, made-up words, sentence fragments, sounds made of strung-out letters, extended run-on phrases, letters that stand for words, four-letter words, fractured words ("whi-te"), and unexpected abbreviations. While these eccentricities cause some perplexity for readers, the poet's best poems in this volume nonetheless rank with the best of his contemporaries' writing.

"Back Again, Home" is semiautobiographical in its portrayal of the "oreo-schizoid" existence of an aspiring young black junior executive who, for a time, submerges his real self and plays the Euro-American corporate game. Silent, sick, insecure, ostracized in both his professional and his personal life, he suddenly resigns. He has no job and no money, but by rejecting an alien value system he has regained his own identity and self-respect. He is "back again, home," accepting and acknowledging the worth of his own self and the value of his own culture.

While "Back Again, Home" denounces tokenism as it advocates self-acceptance, "America Calling" (included in the introduction to the book) exposes the stereotype of black people being more suited to jobs as domestics and entertainers than to the professions that require intellectual excellence: "America calling./negroes./can you dance?/play foot/baseball?/nanny?/cook?/needed now. negroes/who can entertain/ONLY./others not wanted./& are considered extremely dangerous)."

Madhubuti continues his incisive cataloguing of racial insults in *Think Black* with "Stereo," a conversational prose poem filled with dramatic irony. Paradoxically, the speaker has "BLACK POWER." He can "clear a beach or swimming pool without touching water," clear a lunch counter "in less than an hour," and make property values drop just by "being seen" in a realtor's office. He "ALONE" can make insignificant the work of God to many in "Sunday morning's prayer hour." No cultural institutions are sacred to Madhubuti. Like Langston Hughes, whose Semple character comments on every aspect of the daily experiences and interactions of the ordinary black workingman in America, Madhubuti seeks to expose the evil constraints of

ABOUT THE AUTHOR

Don Lee knows that nothing human is elegant. He is not interested in modes of writing that aspire to elegance. He is well-acquainted with "elegant" literature (what hasn't he read?) but, while certainly respecting the advantages and influence of good workmanship, he is **not** interested in supplying the needs of the English Departments at Harvard and Oxford nor the editors of **Partisan Review**, although he could mightily serve as fact factory for these. He speaks to blacks hungry for what they themselves refer to as "**real** poetry." These blacks find themselves and the stuff of their existence in his healthy, lithe, lusty reaches of free verse. The last thing these people crave is elegance. It is very hard to enchant, with elegant song, the ears of a fellow whose stomach is growling. He can't hear you. The more interesting noise is too loud.

—Gwendolyn Brooks

★

With monk-like singlemindedness and extraordinary passion Don L. Lee casts an unsparing eye on the events of our times. Charlatans of the Black Revolution are buried in a pit of wry humor. The black man-white woman theme is in the grasp of an uncompromising hand. A war that finds black men killing black children inspires the poignant "Nigerian Unity/or little niggers killing little niggers," a poem in which this poet's fury arrives at a new depth. This book's title is well chosen. Don Lee has no energy for crying in appeal to the conscience of the white world. His is a screaming, urgent appeal to the reason of dark victims everywhere. At once he will be hailed and damned for the same reason: because he refuses to write a single line in forgetfulness of his blackness.

—David Llorens, **Ebony**

★

Don L. Lee was born in Detroit and educated in Chicago where he attended college. At present he is black poet in residence at Cornell University. His two previous books are **Think Black** and **Black Pride**.

★

DON'T CRY, SCREAM by Don L. Lee, $4.50 cloth, $1.50 paper.
BROADSIDE PRESS, 12651 Old Mill Place, Detroit, Michigan 48238

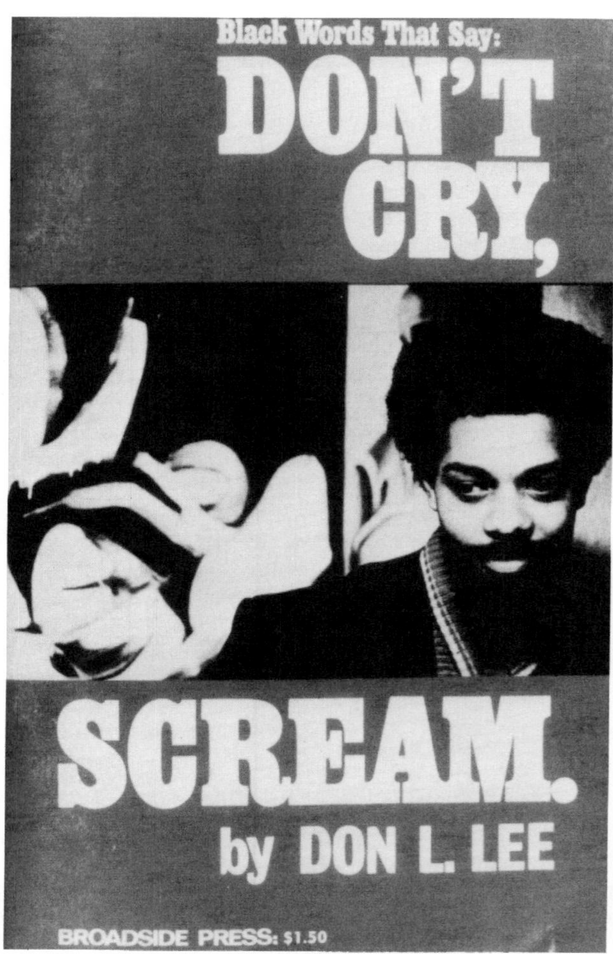

Covers for the 1969 volume in which the poet addresses the concerns of the black revolution

the secular work place, the hypocrisy of the church world, and the greed and insensitivity of the government. A small but telling poem, "Taxes," makes a satirical comment on the fact that the black man pays a high price every day in every way just for the "sin" of being black and alive: "Income taxes,/every year—due,/Sales taxes,/I pay these too./Luxury taxes,/maybe—one or two,/Black taxes,/on everything I do."

Reminiscent of Margaret Walker's "For My People" and "We Have Been Believers," Madhubuti's "Understanding But Not Forgetting" enumerates unforgotten assaults on the black psyche. The most poignant and ironic passages allude to the speaker's sister "with five children before the/age of 22," his mother who "would go out—without money—/to get us something to eat," and "the 'Culturally Deprived'—another way/to say niggers." Madhubuti's images are rife with what Stephen Henderson refers to in *Understanding the New Black Poetry* (1973) as *saturation:* "chiefly the communication of 'Blackness' and fidelity to the observed or intuited truth of the Black Experience in the United States." References to *sisters* and *mothers* and *niggers* need little or no elaboration. The black audience identification is immediate, full of understanding and firsthand knowledge. Neither the black mothers who sacrifice themselves in order to fulfill the basic needs of family sustenance, nor the readership that identifies with them gives thought to the dichotomy between their actions and Western society's expectations.

"Education" underscores the need for blacks to be aware of and take some responsibility for what is being taught their children in the public schools. Traditionally the school system has not included in its curriculum substantial information on black heritage. While Madhubuti bemoans this lack, he also states in the introduction to *We Walk the Way of the New World* (1970) that black people themselves must act to redress this situation. He points out that other ethnic and religious groups (notably Jews and Catholics) have not relied on outsiders to inculcate their youth with essential cultural values and principles: "The most effective weapon used against us has been the educational system. We now understand that if *white nationalism* is our teacher, *white nationalism* will be our philosophy regardless of *all* its contradictory and anti-black implications. The educational process is set up largely to preserve that which *is,* not that which necessarily needs to be created, i.e., black nationalism or black consciousness."

"A Period of Growth," included in the revised

Front cover for the 1970 volume of poetry dedicated "to those/ who helped create a New Consciousness"

edition of *Think Black,* is similar to "Education" and "Awareness" (the final poem in the volume, which also provides the book's title) in urging blacks to self-definition and heightened consciousness. Paralleling the poet's own personal development is the growth of the whole race in taking the hitherto pejorative word "black" and turning it into a concept loaded with pride: "like,/if he had da called me/black seven years ago,/i wd've—/broke his right eye out,/jumped into his chest,/talked about his momma,/lied on his sister/& dared him to say it again/all in one breath—/seven years ago."

Commenting on theme and style in the introduction to Madhubuti's second volume of poetry, *Black Pride,* Dudley Randall observes that Madhubuti's recital of "received pieties" is not what makes him a poet. Instead, Madhubuti is a poet because of his "resourcefulness" with language: "He writes for the man in the street, and uses the language of the

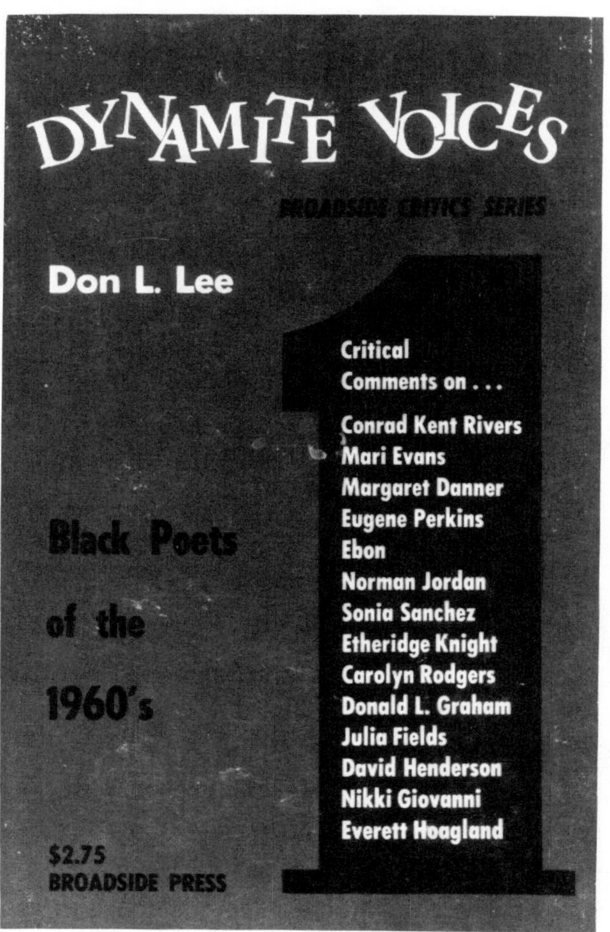

Front cover for Madhubuti/Lee's 1971 critical overview of the black literary scene of the 1960s

street, and sometimes of the gutter, with wit, inventiveness, and surprise." He "joins words together or splits syllables into fractions for greater expressiveness. His shorter lyrics have a sting and his longer poems a force that make him one of the most interesting of the revolutionary young black poets."

The first poem of *Black Pride,* "The New Integrationist," is a succinct eight-word, eight-line thematic continuation of *Think Black:* "I/seek /integration/of/negroes/with/black/people." In "Two Poems," Madhubuti proceeds to phase two of his revolutionary plan (*action* after unity and togetherness): "i ain't seen no poems stop a 38,/i ain't seen no stanzas brake a honkie's head,/i ain't seen no metaphors stop a tank,/i ain't seen no words kill/& if the word was mightier than the sword/pushkin wouldn't be fertilizing russian soil/ & until my similes can protect me from a night stick/i guess i'll keep my razor/& buy me some more bullets."

Celebrating the developing black consciousness broached in *Think Black,* Madhubuti reveals in "The Self-Hatred of Don L. Lee" how he is revolted by his past pride in his light-brown "outer" self that had opened doors of tokenism for him. This false pride has now been replaced by love for his "inner" self, which is "all black." This poem reflects the attitudinal change advocated and spearheaded by Madhubuti and contemporaries such as Amiri Baraka (LeRoi Jones) and Larry Neal, for whom the image of blackness becomes a center of pride instead of shame. Extending this self-admiration to encompass the group, in "The Wall" the poet celebrates the Chicago mural where black artists have painted black heroes such as W. E. B. Du Bois, Marcus Garvey, H. Rap Brown, James Brown, John Coltrane, Ray Charles, James Baldwin, and Muhammad Ali. To the poet, dedicating the wall to black heroes is a revolutionary act.

While Madhubuti honors heroes who have contributed to the cause of blackness, in "The Traitor" he advocates death for black clergy who betray their people by "tomming" and embracing false values such as "honorary degrees" and black Cadillacs. Similarly, in "The Negro" the poet rebukes parents who work and save all year to buy Christmas gifts for their children but ironically give the credit to a white Santa Claus. These Negroes deserve the same scorn as the part-time revolutionist in "Contradiction in Essence," who talks black and sleeps white. The subject of white christianity also makes its way into a broadside published the same year as *Black Pride. For Black People (and Negroes too)* calls into question the viability of a blond, blue-eyed Jesus for a people who have little in common with him.

While Madhubuti's third collection of poetry, *Don't Cry, Scream,* continues the thematic concerns of his first two volumes, the poet here moves beyond the introspection and localism of his earlier work. Although most of Madhubuti's poems contain a didactic dimension, the early poems are relatively more parochial than the later; they deal with personal subjects—his mother, happenings in Chicago, his jobs, his views on politics, religion, and black power. But in *Don't Cry, Scream,* Madhubuti concentrates more on the poetry of revolution, attempting to give meaning to Martin Luther King, Jr.'s and Malcolm X's deaths, to explain Tommie Smith's and John Carlos's actions at the 1968 Olympic Games, and to discuss black politics. The opening section consists of a dedication and preface by

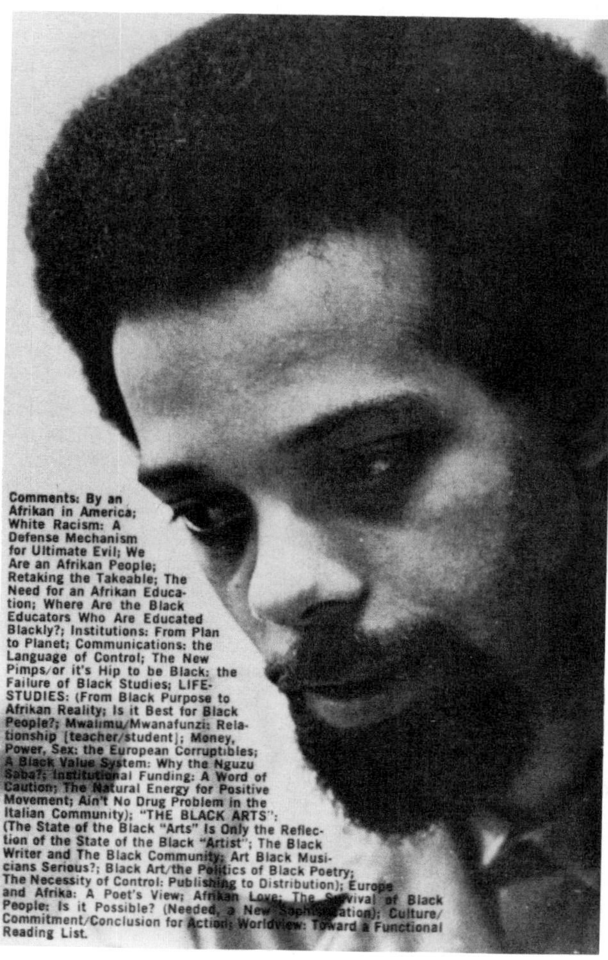

Comments: By an
Afrikan in America;
White Racism: A
Defense Mechanism
for Ultimate Evil; We
Are an Afrikan People;
Retaking the Takeable; The
Need for an Afrikan Educa-
tion; Where Are the Black
Educators Who Are Educated
Blackly?; Institutions: From Plan
to Planet; Communications: the
Language of Control; The New
Pimps/or it's Hip to be Black: the
Failure of Black Studies; LIFE-
STUDIES: (From Black Purpose to
Afrikan Reality; Is it Best for Black
People?; Mwalimu/Mwanafunzi: Rela-
tionship [teacher/student]; Money,
Power, Sex: the European Corruptibles;
A Black Value System: Why the Nguzu
Saba?; Institutional Funding: A Word of
Caution; The Natural Energy for Positive
Movement; Ain't No Drug Problem in the
Italian Community); "THE BLACK ARTS":
(The State of the Black "Arts" Is Only the Reflec-
tion of the State of the Black "Artist"; The Black
Writer and The Black Community; Art Black Musi-
cians Serious?; Black Art/the Politics of Black Poetry;
The Necessity of Control: Publishing to Distribution); Europe
and Afrika: A Poet's View; Afrikan Love; The Survival of Black
People: Is it Possible? (Needed, a New Sophistication); Culture/
Commitment/Conclusion for Action; Worldview: Toward a Functional
Reading List.

Inside front cover for From Plan to Planet, *a collection of essays that Amiri Baraka calls "concrete and directly functional. . . . made for use"*

Madhubuti, an introduction by Gwendolyn Brooks, and quotations from David Diop and Baraka. Typical of Madhubuti's catholic stance, the dedication ranges from honor of "all blackmothers & especially mine" to "my oldman where-ever he is" to "those of u whose names do not appear," ending with the Muslim benediction: "As-Salaam-Alaikum."

Like Du Bois, Baraka, Sterling Brown, and others, Madhubuti sees black music as one of his race's best and most original cultural gifts to the nation. It seems only natural then that the titular poem, "Don't Cry, Scream," should be dedicated to that consummate musician, John Coltrane, whose untimely death left many of his admirers in deep mourning. In this poem (which begs to be read out loud as only the poet himself can do it), Madhubuti strains to duplicate the virtuoso high notes of Coltrane's instrumental sound:

> Trane done went.
> (got his hat & left me one)
> naw brother,
> i didn't cry,
> i just—
> Scream-eeeeeeeeeeeeee-ed   sing loud
> SCREAM-EEEEEEEEEEEEEEE-ED   & high with
> we-eeeeeeeeeeeeeeeeeeeeeee   feeling
> WE-EEEEEEEEEEEEEEEEEEEEE   yr/voice
> WHERE YOU DONE GONE, BROTHER?   breaks

The poem is structured so that the left side of the page echoes sound and meaning while the right side offers directions for the speaker. Praising Coltrane's innovation, his "music that ached," Madhubuti contrasts the life-giving energy of this "soultrane gone on a trip" to the sterile, vacuous lives of Negroes with "split-level homes" and "split-level minds."

In "a poem to complement other poems," Madhubuti does not just castigate "negroes" and "niggers" who have embraced the American way; he urges them to change to a new level of awareness: "nigger wanted a double zero in front of/his name; a license to kill,/niggers are licensed to be killed. change. a negro: something pigs eat." Then, "if u were a match i wd light u into something beautiful. change."

Like the third, Madhubuti's fourth volume of poetry, *We Walk the Way of the New World,* is also dedicated to outstanding blacks and Africans "who helped to create a New Consciousness." The collection is divided into three sections: "Blackwoman Poems," "African Poems," and "New World Poems." Prefaced with epigraphs from Leopold Senghor, Aimé Césaire, Kwame Nkrumah, Malcolm X, and others, the categories are more superficial than real. The poems are inextricably linked by the poet's consciousness of the magnetic and metaphorical quality of the African motherland. Madhubuti uses an apt quotation from Malcolm X which asserts: "Our cultural revolution must be the means of bringing us closer to our African brothers and sisters. It must begin in the community and be based on community participation. Afro-Americans will be free to create only when they can depend on the Afro-American community for support, and the Afro-American artists must realize that they depend on the Afro-American community for inspiration."

In "Change Is Not Always Progress," the poet uses wordplay effectively to entreat Africa not to let

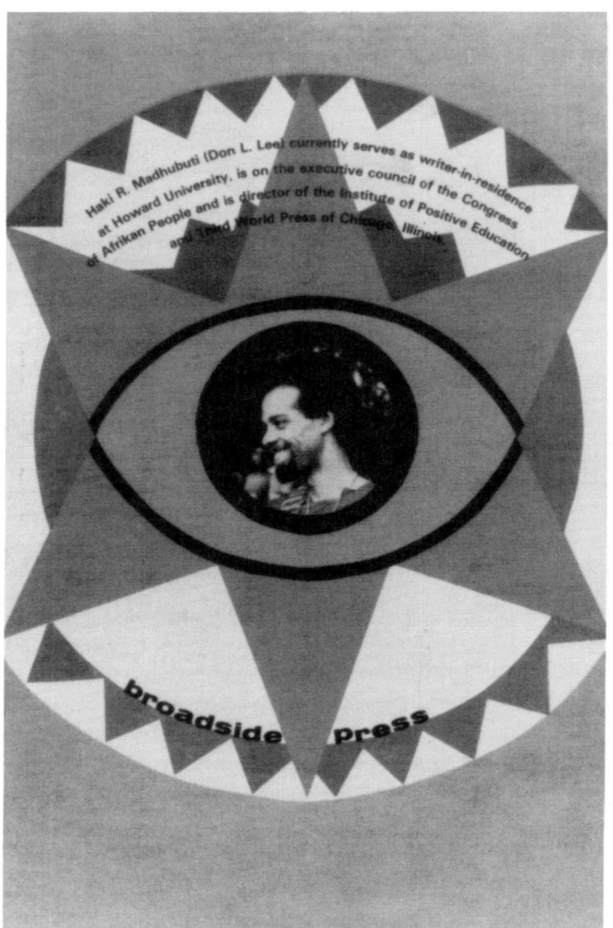

Covers for Madhubuti's 1973 collection of poems, the first book published under his Swahili name, which means precise justice

the Western world corrupt and spoil her primordial beauty: "don't let them/steal/your face/take your circles and make them squares/don't let them/steel/your body as to put/100 stories of concrete on you/so that you/arrogantly/scrape/the/sky." To Madhubuti, the "Blackwoman is African and Africa is Blackwoman and they both represent the *New World.*" Two admirable examples of black womanhood, for Madhubuti, are Miriam Makeba and Nina Simone, singers who are "consistently black and relevant." In contrast is Diana Ross ("On Seeing Diana Go Madddddddd"), who turns her back on her people "to become the new wonderwoman of the dirty-world."

We Walk the Way of the New World represents a movement toward an expanded African/Afro-American view. While the poet continues to explore the concepts and ideas that characterized his early poetry, his work now shows greater maturity as he projects his vision of a new world. Although emotion is still a key element, the style and tone are modified. That this change is the result of conscious effort is noted by the poet himself whose introductory subheading reads: "Louder but Softer." Again, in "Thinking About Woman," the poet observes that his "lines got longer" and his "metaphors softened."

Directionscore: Selected and New Poems (1971) consists of the introductions and representative poems from Madhubuti's first four collections, plus five new poems. This volume can be perceived as a compendium of what the poet himself viewed as his best work up to that time. The introduction is divided into four parts: "Renaissance I to Renaissance III," "Pan-Africanism and Foreign Policy," "Nationalism," and "Black Studies and Black Education." Each title reveals the focus of its subsection. Madhubuti states that "the main difference between renaissance II and renaissance I is that [in the former] people are involved." Whereas the first renaissance, the Harlem Renaissance, made little or no change and left no lasting institutions, the second renaissance has been political, concerned with "change and survival and building." According to Madhubuti, pan-Africanism (reestablishing African roots), nationalism, and education offer the best hope for black survival and achievement.

In 1971, Dudley Randall's Broadside Press published Madhubuti's *Dynamite Voices: Black Poets of the 1960's,* which focuses on the importance of black writers reaching out to the ordinary black community. The critical survey has become one of the major contemporary scholarly resources for black poetry.

In the fall of 1973, under his new Swahili name of Mwalimu (teacher) Haki R. Madhubuti, the poet published his sixth volume of poetry, *Book of Life.* Part I of *Book of Life* consists of six long poems stylistically similar to those in his earlier volumes. Part II, however, reflects a notable shift in technique, though not in substance. It consists of a long prose poem of ninety-two numbered stanzas of varying lengths. Although Madhubuti is not a Muslim, he agrees with and has been influenced by many Muslim precepts, and these "proverbs" in *Book of Life* reflect the life principles characteristic of the philosophy of the Nation of Islam: love and respect for black women and the family unit; clean, drug-free living; establishment of a sound economic base; emphasis on a natural diet of whole-grain foods and fresh fruits and vegetables; respect for the old; reunification with the African homeland; providing a community-based education to ensure perpetuation of the African-American's cultural heritage.

The most notable stylistic advance of *Book of Life* is the poet's use of standard English. Gone are the street language, the misspellings, and other techniques that upset and confused even the most sympathetic critics of earlier volumes. The new

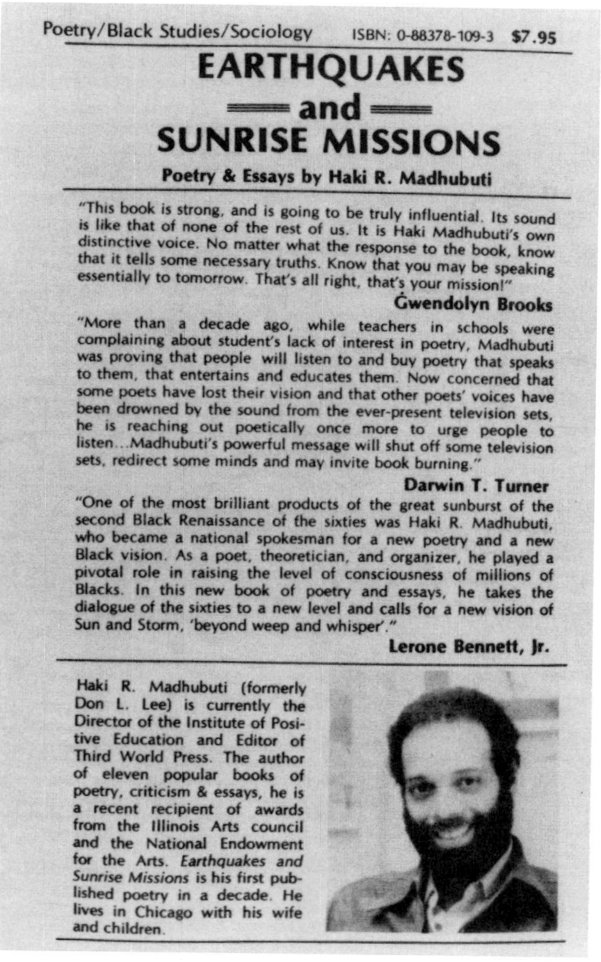
Poetry/Black Studies/Sociology ISBN: 0-88378-109-3 $7.95

EARTHQUAKES
and
SUNRISE MISSIONS

Poetry & Essays by Haki R. Madhubuti

"This book is strong, and is going to be truly influential. Its sound is like that of none of the rest of us. It is Haki Madhubuti's own distinctive voice. No matter what the response to the book, know that it tells some necessary truths. Know that you may be speaking essentially to tomorrow. That's all right, that's your mission!"

Gwendolyn Brooks

"More than a decade ago, while teachers in schools were complaining about student's lack of interest in poetry, Madhubuti was proving that people will listen to and buy poetry that speaks to them, that entertains and educates them. Now concerned that some poets have lost their vision and that other poets' voices have been drowned by the sound from the ever-present television sets, he is reaching out poetically once more to urge people to listen...Madhubuti's powerful message will shut off some television sets, redirect some minds and may invite book burning."

Darwin T. Turner

"One of the most brilliant products of the great sunburst of the second Black Renaissance of the sixties was Haki R. Madhubuti, who became a national spokesman for a new poetry and a new Black vision. As a poet, theoretician, and organizer, he played a pivotal role in raising the level of consciousness of millions of Blacks. In this new book of poetry and essays, he takes the dialogue of the sixties to a new level and calls for a new vision of Sun and Storm, 'beyond weep and whisper'."

Lerone Bennett, Jr.

Haki R. Madhubuti (formerly Don L. Lee) is currently the Director of the Institute of Positive Education and Editor of Third World Press. The author of eleven popular books of poetry, criticism & essays, he is a recent recipient of awards from the Illinois Arts council and the National Endowment for the Arts. *Earthquakes and Sunrise Missions* is his first published poetry in a decade. He lives in Chicago with his wife and children.

Covers for Madhubuti's 1984 book of essays and poetry, published after an eleven-year hiatus in his career. Vivian V. Gordon says that Madhubuti is "tempered by time but . . . writes forcefully about challenge, despair, rebuilding, and . . . love for those of the diaspora."

technique is more polished, showing that the poet has become more settled, more confident of his ability to handle his craft.

Earthquakes and Sun Rise Missions (1984) is Madhubuti's first book of poetry since *Book of Life* (1973). The poet did not cease to write poetry during this eleven-year hiatus (as attested to by the subtitle to the new volume: *Poetry and Essays of Black Renewal, 1973-1983*). He was devoting his creative energy to more directly political writing in two books of essays, *From Plan to Planet; Life Studies: The Need for Afrikan Minds and Institutions* (1973) and *Enemies: The Clash of Races* (1978), as well as to other commitments: marriage in 1974, and children; directorship of the Institute of Positive Education and Third World Press; numerous speaking engagements; and graduate study.

In *Earthquakes and Sun Rise Missions* the poet's voice is still the mature voice of *Book of Life*. As Darwin Turner has observed, Madhubuti is "no less determined than before," but he is "more contemplative, more restrained." Divided into five main sections ("Issues and Killing Time," "The Women," "The Men," "Destiny," and "History, Projections and New Movement") with an Afterword by Turner, the book focuses on the recurring themes of unity, survival, and nation-building. "Destiny" might be seen as a composite of the thought of this volume. The poet urges black people to "take hold," to "put land and selfhood on the minds of our people," to "reverse destruction" and "capture tomorrows."

Black unity is paramount to Madhubuti's philosophy. He believes in collective self-reliance as opposed to the Western concept of individualism and competitiveness. Rejecting assimilationism as a viable means of achieving equity, Madhubuti stresses an egalitarianism to be achieved by the hard work and interdependence of blacks. He castigates whites as well as blacks who embrace white values. He urges blacks to act instead of reacting. Madhubuti follows his own prescription in his own personal, rather ascetic, life, applauding blacks who are *doers*, and dedicating much of his own work to them.

Haki R. Madhubuti's literary career has spanned almost two decades. While some critics have objected to the "sameness" of his ideas, Madhubuti's self-imposed task from the very beginning has been to bring black Americans to a new level of consciousness. Madhubuti's influence and popularity are widespread. His books have sold more than a million copies, without benefit of a national distributor. Perhaps Madhubuti will even succeed in helping to establish some lasting institutions in education and in the publishing world. Whether he does or not, he has already secured a place for himself in American literature. He is among the foremost anthologized contemporary revolutionary poets, and he has played a significant role in stimulating other young black talent. As Stephen Henderson has observed, he is "more widely imitated than any other Black poet with the exception of Imamu Baraka (LeRoi Jones). His unique delivery has given him a popular appeal which is tantamount to stardom. His influence is enormous, and is still growing."

References:

W. Edward Farrison, "Review of *New Directions from Don L. Lee* by Marlene Mosher," *CLA Journal*, 18 (June 1975): 582-584;

Paula Giddings, "From A Black Perspective: The Poetry of Don L. Lee," in *Amistad 2*, edited by John A. Williams and Charles F. Harris (New York: Random House, 1971), pp. 296-318;

Jascha Kessler, "Trial and Error," *Poetry*, 121 (February 1973): 292-293;

Eugene Ethelbert Miller, "Some Black Thoughts on Don L. Lee's *Think Black!* Thunk by a Frustrated White Academic Thinker," *College English*, 34 (May 1973): 1094-1102;

Marlene Mosher, *New Directions from Don L. Lee* (Hicksville, N.Y.: Exposition, 1975);

Roderick R. Palmer, "The Poetry of Three Revolutionists: Don L. Lee, Sonia Sanchez, Nikki Giovanni," *CLA Journal*, 15 (September 1971): 25-36;

Annette Oliver Shands, "The Relevancy of Don L. Lee as a Contemporary Black Poet," *Black World*, 21 (June 1972): 35-48;

Darwin T. Turner, Afterword, in *Earthquakes and Sun Rise Missions*, by Haki R. Madhubuti (Chicago: Third World Press, 1984), pp. 181-189;

Helen Vendler, "Good Black Poems One by One," *New York Times Book Review*, 29 September 1974, pp. 3, 10;

Vendler, *Part of Nature, Part of Us* (Cambridge: Harvard University Press, 1980), pp. 315-318;

Ron Welburn, "Review of *Don't Cry, Scream*," *Negro Digest* (December 1969): 91-94.

E. Ethelbert Miller

(20 November 1950-   )

Priscilla R. Ramsey
Howard University

BOOKS: *Interface*, by Miller and Amma Khalil (N.p., 1972);

Andromeda (Boulder Creek, Cal.: Chiva Publications, 1974);

The Land of Smiles and The Land of No Smiles (Cal.: Miller, 1974);

Migrant Worker (Washington, D.C.: The Washington Writers' Publishing House, 1978);

Season of Hunger/Cry of Rain, Poems: 1975-1980 (Detroit: Lotus Press, 1982).

OTHER: Sue Abbott Boyd, ed., *Poems by Blacks, Volume I*, includes poems by Miller (Fort Smith, Ark.: South and West, 1970);

H. M. Rosenberg, ed., *Patterns: An Anthology of Modern Poetry*, includes poems by Miller (Cal.: Idlewild Publishing Company, 1970);

Noel Alvin Gardner, ed., *And Having Writ*, includes poems by Miller (N.p.: New Dawn, 1973);

Synergy: An Anthology of Washington, D.C. Black Poetry, edited by Miller and Ahmos Zu-Bolton (Washington, D.C.: Energy Blacksouth Press, 1975);

Women Surviving Massacres and Men, edited by Miller (Washington, D.C.: Anemone Press, 1977);

"Creating Traditions," in *Black American Culture and Scholarship: Contemporary Issues*, edited by Bernice Reagon (Washington, D.C.: Smithsonian Institution, 1985), pp. 125-130.

PERIODICAL PUBLICATIONS:

POETRY

"Yesterday's Black Militant," *Black Creation*, 5 (Fall 1973);

"Personal #1975 (in search of an executioner)" and others, *Obsidian*, 2 (Spring 1976);

"The Land of Smiles" and "The Ghostself of the Dead Lecturer," *Blackbox*, 5 (1976);

"Return II" and "Round Midnight," *Painted Bride Quarterly*, 4 (Spring 1977);

"Rhode Island Avenue," *Proteus*, nos. 6-7 (Spring-Summer 1977);

"Who Will Call This Day to Prayer," *New Directions*, 4 (July 1977);

Photograph © 1984 by Julia Jones

"When There Are No More Poems To Be Written," "After The Generals," *LIPS*, no. 5 (1983): 30-31;

"Where Are The Love Poems For Dictators," *Sojourners*, 13 (June/July 1984): 26;

"Elaine Beckford," "The Kid," *Genetic Dancers*, 1 (Second Quarter 1985): 9.

NONFICTION

"Black Poetry of the Sixties," *Third World*, 4 (30 March 1973);

"Something About Jayne Cortez," *Third World*, 4 (13 April 1973);
"The Survival of Black Poetry in D.C.," *Washington Review of the Arts*, 2 (Summer 1976);
"Henderson's New Black Aesthetic," *Washington Review of the Arts*, 3 (Fall 1977).

Hardly a stranger to the Washington, D.C. arts community, E. Ethelbert Miller has helped to shape it through his searches for new talent in the area, his encouragement of other artists, and the contributions of his own gifts as well. Along with serving on the D.C. Community Humanities Council (a fund granting organization), he is former associate editor of *Black Box* magazine (a cassette taped poetry magazine) and senior editor for the *Washington Review of the Arts*. His *Ascension* series reading programs regularly give young and beginning poets an opportunity to read for public audiences in the Washington area. Locally he is popularly referred to as "an aesthetic entrepeneur." More important, he encourages young talent which might otherwise go unnoticed. Miller has read his own poetry in colleges, cultural centers, and galleries across the country. Editors regularly publish his work in journals like the *Painted Bride Quarterly*, *Callaloo*, *Obsidian*, and *Black American Literature Forum*. Following his graduation from Howard University, Miller became an assistant director of Howard's Afro-American Studies Department's Resource Center, an extensive collection of black and third world writing. Today, as the center's director, Miller can reach out to a wider arts community through contacts with internationally-known black writers such as June Jordan, Derek Walcott, and Dennis Brutus. He also provides invaluable resources to research scholars and students. His position at Howard University has also enabled him to encourage new writers within the Howard community. Moreover, the increasingly sophisticated political and psychological development his poetry has undergone suggests the profound influences these relationships have had on him since his graduation from Howard University as an Afro-American Studies major in 1972.

Miller was born in New York City on 20 November 1950 to postal worker Egberto Miller and Enid Miller, a seamstress. His brother Richard, who studied theology, and his sister Marie, a nurse, are both older than he. In a 1985 interview with Patrice Gaines-Carter, Miller explains that his parents did not read writers like James Weldon Johnson to him before he went "to sleep each night. My parents weren't like that, but we went to good schools and read a lot on our own." More "ball player than a poet," Miller attended a predominate Jewish and Italian-American high school in the Bronx.

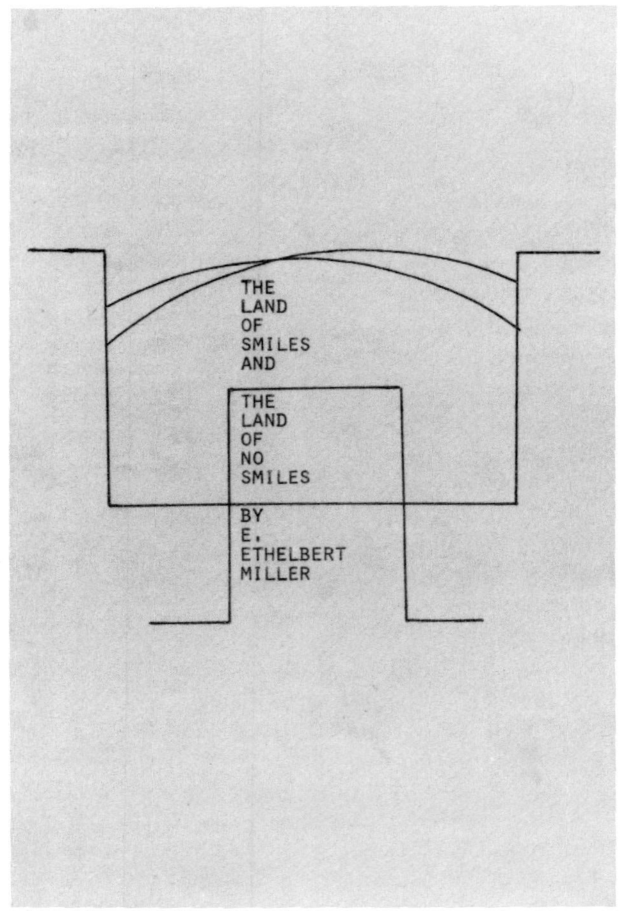

Front cover for Miller's 1974 poetic chronicle of the Western exploitation of African civilization

Writing poetry has intrigued Miller since he was a sophomore at Howard, as he explained in a 1976 issue of the *Washington Review of the Arts*. He was less influenced by Paul Laurence Dunbar than by Paul Simon, Donovan, and other 1960s American folk-rock artists, although readers will find Miller's poetry shares some of the concerns and techniques which predominate in the poetry of the 1960s black arts movement. Despite the exclusively ethnic nature of Miller's social milieu at Howard University in the 1960s, his early diversity of tastes suggests the variety of concerns and issues which characterize his poetry today. He has never veered from the position that poetry should reflect a cultural exchange which takes the poet beyond the limits of race alone; politically, he also embraces a collective notion of humanity which extends beyond his own racial identity. Concomitant with this view is Miller's engagement with black political and social issues. Through his poetry he seeks to internationalize and widen his preoccupation with black concerns in America. Much like a W. E. B. Du Bois writing in his several autobiographies, Miller places his black themes into a wide context from which he draws parallels between the experiences of black Americans and their counterparts in Africa, South America, and even in Europe. The thrust of Miller's argument comes ideologically close to Richard Wright's in his essay "How Bigger Was Born" as Wright describes the factors contributing to Bigger Thomas's creation in *Native Son* (1940). While Bigger's experiences reflected his pain as the black victim of economic and social oppression, Bigger's paradigmatic situation was by no means limited to the fact he was an Afro-American. Wright had seen his models for Bigger not only in the American South, but in the factories of the Soviet Union and throughout much of Europe as well. Similarly, Miller's poetry applies the meaning of the black experience to a setting beyond a specifically black context. His third poetry collection, *Migrant Worker*, published in 1978, particularly reflects this tendency, while his first two books, *Andromeda* (1974) and *The Land of Smiles and The Land of No Smiles* (1974), represent his "poetry as cultural exchange philosophy," but with less emphasis on the extensive and variable nature of that exchange.

In the *Andromeda* collection, Miller's persona voyages through various poetic situations which help define his relationship to his beloved and to his search for spiritual meaning in a secular world. The arrangement of the poem creates a circular movement that allows us to view the parallel developments of both the love and spiritual relationships. As the persona experiences disappointment in love and feelings of isolation, the importance of the spiritual increases. The collection's experiential focus begins with a Muslim call to prayer—certainly a logical beginning for poems which quest toward religious self-definition. In poems that range over a number of subjects, the persona explores his feelings.

In the semiautobiographical, confessional poem "Michelle," the persona discovers the flawed nature of love, and he regrets having loved too humanly and having deluded himself into thinking he was more perfect than he is. The pensive and regretful tone of "Michelle" is offset by the psychic and physical anger expressed in "Liberation":

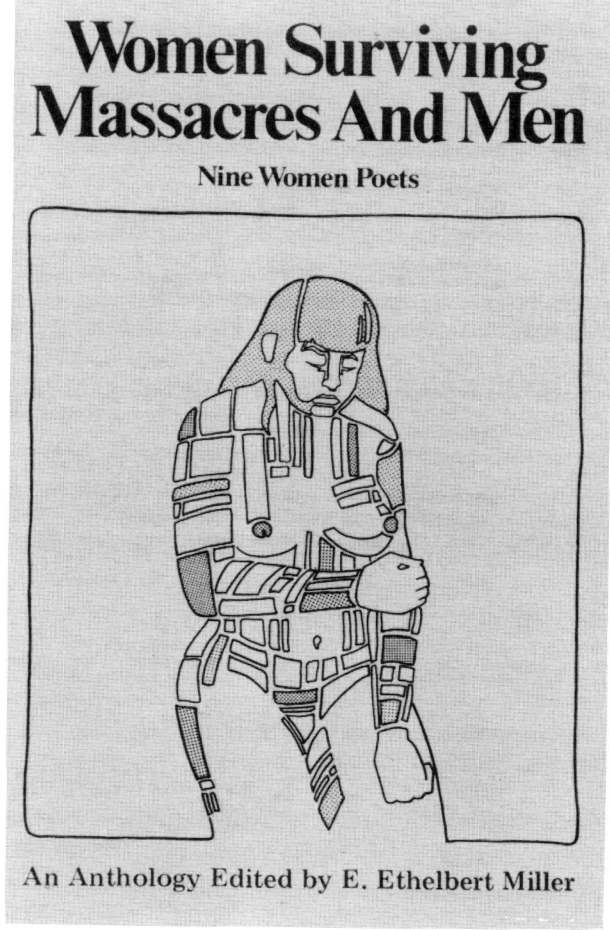

Front cover for the 1977 anthology of poems by women edited by Miller

Liberation

my mouth
opens

I vomit

I am
learning
how to let go

I must
not cling
to people

who say
they love
me

and wish

E. Ethelbert Miller in the 1970s (photograph by Sandra Turner Bond)

to see
me well

The absence of punctuation suggests the unending quality of the poet's pain as well as the loss of "grounding" provided by the love relationship. The narrator notes the ironic significance of his condition: although he is liberated, he is implicitly more alienated than ever. Miller's persona expresses his ambiguous feelings about another human being again. The failed marriage of the poem did not create an idealized potential for positive growth and development. If anything, it had just the opposite effect. The psychic suffering resounds in other poems as well as Miller explores his own vulnerabilities and dependency while searching for a viable means of establishing his masculinity and autonomy. Above all, the premium the poet places upon his emotional life draws the poems of *Andromeda* together.

From *Andromeda* through Miller's later work, we can watch his development of an ironic, self-aware, psychological distancing that is centered on his increasing social and political experience.

Miller says in the opening of *Andromeda*:

> An indication of a good writer is not entirely dependent on his usage of words or even his selection of themes; it is primarily rooted in his capacity to feel and his ability to reach the deepest levels of sensitivity.

Critics, like Jerry Ward, have recognized this sensitivity as the focal point of Miller's work: "Choice of diction and the spirit informing selection of theme are crucial, primal criteria. They are directions to sensibility. The whole configuration of poem (theme plus rhetorical devices plus reader presence) determines whether or not we can share the poet's sensitivity. If pleasure and instruction result from our encounters with the poem, we may say the poet is good. Precisely because in his work there is a judicious sensitivity to human needs, linguistic instinct, and sensibility of the finest order, E. Ethelbert Miller is a good writer."

In *The Land of Smiles and The Land of No Smiles*

(1974), the persona's voice encompasses vaster space and time than did *Andromeda,* published in the same year. In the one long poem that comprises the volume, Miller chronicles Africa's colonial history and the western exploitation of human beings as it separated African people from a cultural identity and sense of place. Jerry Ward said of this collection: "Sign and signified, metaphor and moral history unfold the poet's sensitivity to a chronic problem: the power of history to victimize. The poem restates the problem with cold logic and warm simplicity, and its subtle language and conception make it a poem of rare grace and proportion."

Miller sustains throughout the poem a temporal and spatial division between the concept of Western civilization as experienced through the prism of black human history and the contemporary Western setting in which black people now find themselves in the present. Between the positive African past and the present cultural dismembering, history and cultural identity become the issues which predominate in the work: "in the land of no smiles every soul is trapped," he says, "In the land of no smiles my memory is lynched. . . ." Despite the outlook of devastation, however, the poem is also about "the land of smiles" and hope and creativity: "imagination is a reflection of the past and the future beyond the infinity to come. . . ." Imagination marks the presence of an artist whose vision contributes to the revolutionary reordering of a new world.

Africa's past civilization in *The Land of Smiles and The Land of No Smiles* serves as a symbol for an idyllic simplicity and beauty which Western civilization has annihilated from the memory of black people. This simplicity is represented by Miller throughout an aesthetically pleasing structural symmetry against which he pits the political and psychological chaos of his subject matter. The poem identifies the failure of both Africa and the West to create a new black civilization. The key to Africa's failure lies in the fact that it can only provide a past, not a present. Its cultural past is, by now, merely a disjointed and vague recollection for Afro-Americans. On the other hand, the key to the West's failure lies in its inadequacy to provide for black experience a coherent cultural system which makes human existence meaningful in a contemporary setting divorced from an African past.

Miller's next volume of poetry, *Migrant Worker* (1978), posits a more contemporary perspective. One of the dominant subjects of the collection is the sociopolitical context of life in Washington, D.C., a microcosm of urban life throughout America. Both his "Big Mac: The Columbia Road Connection" and "24 Hours: The All Night Peoples Drugstore/Thomas Circle Washington, D.C." highlight the seediness, false glitter, and decay of a life led by too many people existing in too close a proximity to one another. He capitalizes upon both Christian and Islamic iconography in "Joseph" and "Noah." In "Spanish Conversation," he points up the inherent contradiction in defining one's self as American when one is black.

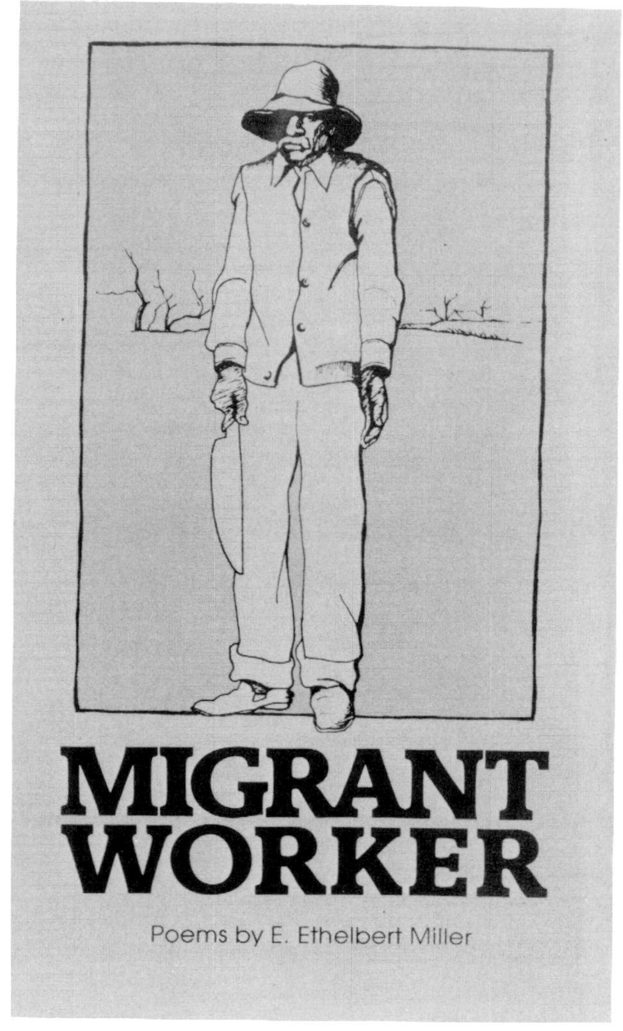

Front cover for Miller's 1978 collection of poems focusing upon the kaleidoscopic range of contemporary urban life

The poem in *Migrant Worker* in which Miller's voice is the least thinly disguised is "Poems to Cathy," a series of brief stanzas that trace the poet's development:

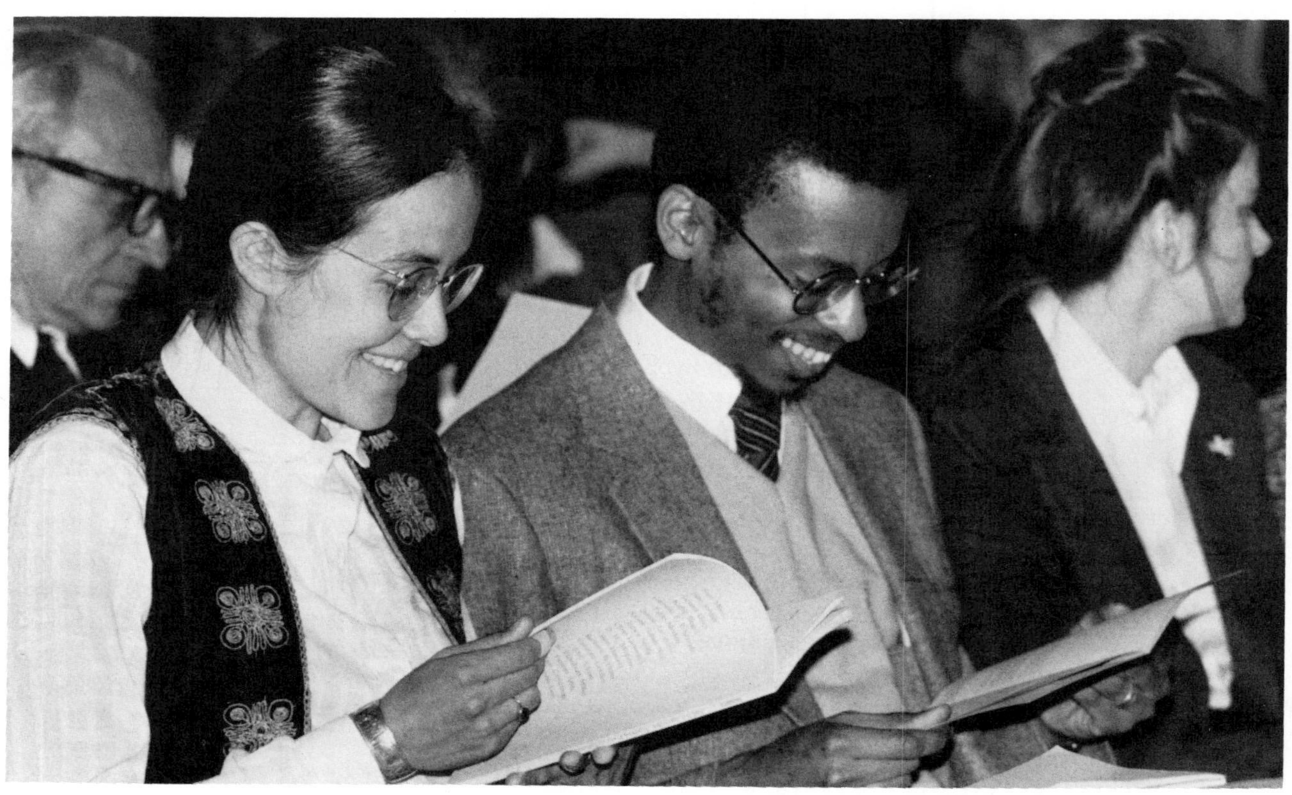

Miller with Naomi Shihab Nye in Washington, D.C., 4 March 1983 (courtesy of the author)

My life in the sixties
unfulfilled
burning on fire inside
the streets of my blood
. . . .
in the seventies
married and separated
somewhere the entire
movement fell apart.

In his typically understated way, he recalls two of the most important decades in his experience and their life-changing events: a marriage and a political movement, both initially offering promise but each one ultimately failing in the end. Miller's enduring optimism helped him to salvage elements from both, which have created new experiences. The 1960s black power political movement manifests itself in Miller's ongoing alliance with writers of the black arts cultural movement which also began in the 1960s.

One of the black cultural arts movement's significant accomplishments during the 1960s occurred in the lowering of barriers between street people and intellectuals. Nikki Giovanni, Haki Madhubuti, Carolyn Rodgers, and many other poets brought to their poems a black idiom that annihilated the previous distinction of poetry as the exclusive domain of intellectual aesthetes.

Miller's "Big Mac: The Columbia Road Connection" reflects this general blurring of class distinctions: "i's cosmopolitan/eatin bo willie's fries." Here it is the poet rather than the intellectual (this is not to imply that poet and intellectual could not be synonymous) who shares a world view with the man on the street. Bo Willie bears a resemblance to Langston Hughes's "Simple," an everyday person whose philosophical positions represent a homespun survival wisdom. The poem's speaker says, "I'm sittin'/here eatin'/got 2 hamburgers/2 fish sandwiches/2 cokes/and a large order of fries." Miller's everyman poet recites the familiar litany of the twentieth-century urban world's staff of life in the language of the man-on-the-street, because the poet shares the common man's concerns; he will not be divorced from his community, and in the poem "poetin' " and "eatin' " are one and the same. Neither act is valued above the other. Class distinctions do not exist between Bo Willie and the speaker-poet.

"Big Mac . . ." appears in a section of *Migrant*

Worker which generally focuses on Bo Willie or the character "zu" "poet ahmos." "Deridder: The Southern Sequence to Southern Spirit" describes "the poet ahmos's" return home (with a friend) to Louisiana. Deridder is a stultifying Southern town in which "there are more churches than pews." So far from being recognized as the true speaker for his people, the poet-survivor is seen by the folks of Deridder as evil. His own mother greets him at the door saying

"I'll tell you right now son
there ain't gonna be no
curses in my home

make sure when you come in
that you leave dem poems
at the door"

With humor and longing "Bo Willie Rides Again?," "The Return of Bo Willie," and "Writer's Conference" chronicle the poet's intimacy with, loss of, and renewed search for Bo Willie, Miller's alter ego, the street poet.

Miller's "24 Hours: The All Night Peoples Drugstore/Thomas Circle Washington, D.C." pictures urban humanity, as did "Big Mac. . . ." The poem's ambiance suggests crowded movement: "prostitutes, junkies, muslim brothers/jack nicholson white boys/easy rider types from Virginia" all create a human mix of tragic souls who "fit" only the roles they have chosen—or rather the roles fate has designed for them. Despite the rhythm of the poem, the subject matter appears tragic. In contrast to "Big Mac," "24 Hours" is missing the tongue-in-cheek snicker at the poet's old lover, C J, who thinks political commitment means fighting for better cafeteria food. A witty portrait of the poet "poetin' " while he eats french fries in the former poem is absent in this one. The absence of a formal climax in the poem points to lack of direction, the meaninglessness of human life. This human collage is uni-

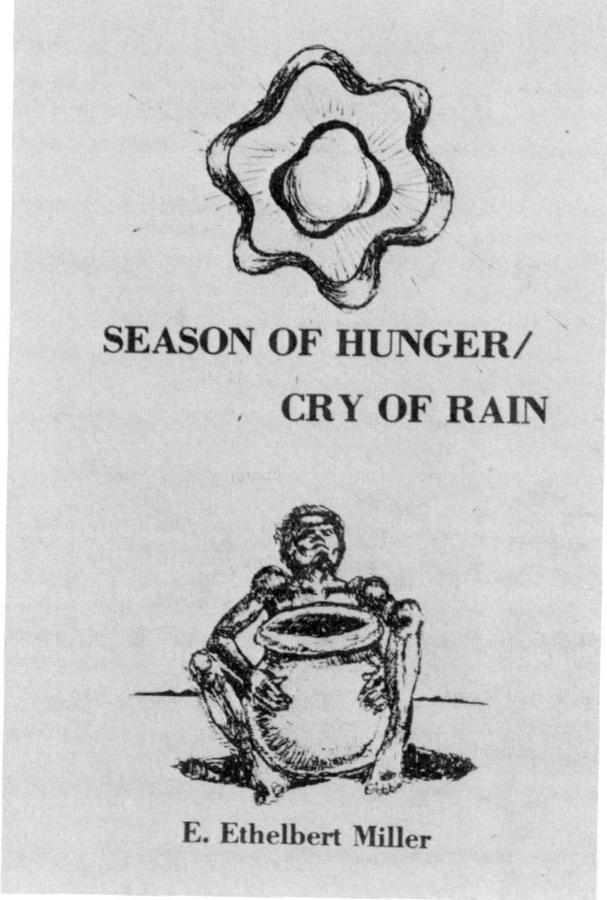

Covers for Miller's 1982 volume of poems, in which, June Jordan says, "you see clearly the dramatic interaction between the poet and his subject in a poem"

Recent flyer advertising a reading for Miller's Ascension series that promotes the work of beginning and unknown writers

versal; only the names change.

Season of Hunger/Cry of Rain, Poems: 1975-1980 was published by Lotus Press in 1982. It marks a maturing political vision, while also reflecting Miller's concern with more personal, immediate, and local issues centering around friendship, love, and loneliness. June Jordan says in her introduction to the volume that Miller's collection is "unerringly personal. . . . There is almost a Talmudic solemnity to these musings: a stern torturing of experience for the sake of utterly definite conclusions." For example, the section of the volume called "Slave Narratives" is comprised largely of poems examining love relationships and the course of love. Happily included in the end section of the volume, "The Last Days of Bowillie," are more poems centered on Miller's streetwise alter ego.

Miller has also finished another collection, "Where are The Love Poems for Dictators," written over a four-year period from 1980 to 1984. Here Miller's political vision comes to fuller realization in poems which encompass his responses to his experiences of study, work, and travel throughout Central America, but especially in Chile, El Salvador, and Nicaragua. The poems also exhibit his ongoing interest in exiles from these countries now living in Washington, D.C. Both collections of Miller's latest poetry illustrate a still-evolving vision and augur well for the coming work of a young and highly prolific poet who has already found his intellectual stride within the comfortable world of complex poetic metaphor.

References:

Patrice Gaines-Carter, "Free Verse: E. Ethelbert Miller is A Poet and A Poem," *Washington Post-Magazine*, 3 February 1985, pp. 10-12;

Priscilla Ramsey, "A '60's Harvest: The Poetic Vision of E. Ethelbert Miller," *Freedomways*, 24 (Fourth quarter 1984).

May Miller

(26 January 1899-   )

Winifred L. Stoelting
North Carolina Central University

BOOKS: *Negro History in Thirteen Plays,* with Willis Richardson (Washington, D.C.: Associated Publishers, 1935);

Into the Clearing (Washington, D.C.: Charioteer Press, 1959);

Poems (Thetford, Vt.: Cricket Press, 1962);

Lyrics of Three Women: Katie Lyle, Maude Rubin, and May Miller (Baltimore: Linden Press, 1964);

Not That Far (San Luis Obispo, Cal.: Solo Press, 1973);

The Clearing and Beyond (Washington, D.C.: Charioteer Press, 1974);

Dust of Uncertain Journey (Detroit: Lotus Press, 1975);

Halfway to the Sun (Washington, D.C.: Washington Writers' Publishing House, 1981);

The Ransomed Wait (Detroit: Lotus Press, 1983).

OTHER: *Green Wind,* edited by Miller (Washington, D.C.: Commission of Arts and Humanities, 1978);

My World, edited by Miller (Bluefield, W.Va.: Fine Arts Commission, 1979).

As a young playwright in the 1920s and 1930s, May Miller early recognized the need to write and produce plays that would break away from the early crude renderings of blacks on stage and portray them with some measure of faithfulness to their daily lives. Encouraged by Carter G. Woodson, Alain Locke, and W. E. B. Du Bois, she is part of the movement of young writers whose literature reawakened racial pride and dignity and created an acceptance and a respect for blacks that had not before been afforded in drama. In the 1940s, she turned her energies to poetry, inspired by the work of the Chicago Imagists and the poetry of Archibald MacLeish. A lyricist of quiet strength, May Miller personifies the same dignity, nobility, and courage found in her dramatic characters. Frequently using nature as a point of reference, she poses the human dilemma of people who must recognize both the ugliness and beauty of life. A disciplined poet, she juxtaposes her images with realistic conclusions.

May Miller, 1976 (photograph by Scurlock)

May Miller was born in Washington, D.C., on 26 January 1899, to Kelly Miller (born in 1863 in Winnsboro, South Carolina; died in 1939) and Annie May Butler (born in 1869 in Baltimore, Maryland; died in 1950), who were married on 17 July 1884. Her father, an eminent Howard University professor and scholar, gained national recognition as an educator and essayist for his work in sociology. In his last year, he founded the Moorland-Spingarn Research Center at Howard. Her mother, raised in a professional family in Baltimore, was a teacher in the Baltimore county schools before her marriage. The five children, Kelly, Newton, May, Irene, and Paul, grew up in the John M. Langston house on the campus where distinguished visitors, W. E. B. Du Bois, Carter G. Woodson, Alain Locke, and Booker T. Washington, among many others, were frequent guests at the Miller home. Moderate in his viewpoint, Professor Miller welcomed all ideas and encouraged scholarly and creative thinking in his children. As a self-taught sociologist, he valued education highly and believed that Washington, in 1926, was "the only city in the country that had a Negro elite of sufficient size to make it a worthwhile entity."

Though the family were members of the Presbyterian Church, Kelly Miller's humanistic, scientific frame of reference emphasized justice, freedom, equality, and reason. Other Miller family members were more conservative in their beliefs. Miller's maternal grandmother, who had been trained in a convent, would stop the play of the active children to have them listen to "the Jesus bell" as it tolled over the row houses in Baltimore. On Sunday mornings in her home the children would meditate in the darkened parlor. Most important in Miller's memories are the joyous times when the five children with Mercer Cook's sister, Marian, gave their "concerts" on Friday nights at the top of the water tank of the Victorian house.

Encouraged by her father, a poet himself, who often challenged his children to remember a line from the piece he was quoting, May Miller was versed in an eclectic literature: Poe and Whitman had been two of her father's favorites. He also recited tales from the folklore of South Carolina: Uncle Remus and Br'er Rabbit, the songs of the frogs, and the story of the man who was put on the moon for burning brush on the seventh day. Through the regimen of studying Greek and Latin, Miller learned the ancient myths. At the age of fourteen, she received twenty-five cents from the publisher of her first poem, "Venus," in the *School Progress* magazine, which in July 1914 printed her first play, "Pandora's Box." Mary Burrill, a playwright, and Angelina Grimké, a recognized poet, were among her teachers at the Paul Laurence Dunbar High School.

Enrolling at Howard University as a student in 1916, she witnessed the pioneering college movement to create black drama at a time when the only plays about blacks deemed worthy were being written by white playwrights. Soon after World War I, Montgomery Gregory and Alain Locke organized the Howard University Dramatic Club to give students sound training in the arts of the theater. One show in which Miller played a part was Clyde Fitch's *The Truth,* staged in the Howard Theater, on 17 May 1919. At her graduation, May Miller won a prize for her play "Within the Shadow." On 29 March 1924, she attended the premiere performance of *Mortgaged,* the folk play by black playwright Willis Richardson.

On 1 May 1925, Charles S. Johnson, editor of *Opportunity* magazine, awarded May Miller a third prize for her play "Bog Guide," one of sixty-five entries in the magazine's first literary contest. The judges were Montgomery Gregory, Alexander Woollcott, Robert Benchley, and Edith Isaacs. At the *Opportunity* dinner to honor the winners, a *New York Herald Tribune* reporter commented upon the novel sight of white critics and black writers meeting on common ground. Among the three hundred guests and contestants were Countee Cullen, Langston Hughes, James Weldon Johnson, Jean Toomer, and many others who, since that memorable occasion, have become part of the American literary heritage; among them was May Miller, then speech, dance, and drama teacher at the Frederick Douglass High School in Baltimore. In 1926 she won an honorable mention in drama, in *Opportunity*'s contest, for "The Cuss'd Thing," also a one-act.

A singular honor for Miller was the publication of her play *Scratches* in the *Carolina Magazine* of the University of North Carolina at Chapel Hill. Lewis Alexander, the editor of the April 1929 Negro Folk Play Number, noted that the Carolina Players, under the leadership of Frederick Koch and Paul Green, had done more for the development of the folk play in America than any other university group. Both men would have a direct influence on Miller's work.

The one-act *Scratches* dramatizes black youth in a ghetto poolhall where poverty becomes respectable in Dan, who plays a game with the dishonest Jeff, now dating Dan's old girl. The play comments on class differences and stereotypes by contrasting the mulatto Abbie and the darker Meldora: "Meldora is clearly a cheap imitation, whereas one indefinably feels that Abbie, in spite of dissipation, is to the manner born." The girl to be won and lavished is Abbie; very little attention is given to Meldora. Darwin Turner in his article "The Dramatist's Image of the Universe, 1920-1960" says that the Negro as an individual did not surface until the plays of the fifties.

The Krigwa Players, founded in 1923 by Du Bois, gave May Miller the opportunity, in the summer of 1927, to act with Frank Horne in Georgia Douglas Johnson's *Blue Blood* at the 135th Street Library in New York City. In 1930, Miller's *Graven Images* and *Ridin' the Goat* were anthologized in Willis Richardson's *Plays and Pageants from the Life of the*

Negro, a collection primarily used in the schools. A special requirement of the contributors was that the dialect, employed in most black plays at that time, was not to be used. Richardson named May Miller "one of the most promising of the Negro playwrights."

Written for eighth grade students, *Graven Images* portrays a classic black hero within a biblical story inspired by the Old Testament verse: "And Miriam and Aaron spake against Moses because of the Ethiopian woman he had married" (Numbers 12:1). The son of Moses faces a hostile environment, but he prevails by using his intelligence. Drama critic Barbara Molette remarked that this play might well have been read to the seven children who integrated the schools in Little Rock; its message has not lost its strength.

On 28 March 1931, the St. Augustine College Players of Raleigh, North Carolina, gave a performance of *Ridin' the Goat* at the Eighth Annual Festival of the Carolina Dramatic Association in the Playmakers Theater of the University of North Carolina, Chapel Hill. Julia Brown Delany was the director of this play which Koch had encouraged May Miller to write when she was a member of his drama workshops at Columbia University in the late 1920s.

Ridin' the Goat gained the recognition of Benjamin Brawley. In *The Negro Genius* (1937) he wrote that Miller's plays come closer to reality than some others in that collection. The play, titled with a term once used for initiation into a lodge, is set in Baltimore. Using the theme of reconciliation between the ideals of an individual and the mores of a community, the comedy shows the mother wit a sensible girl uses in solving the differences in viewpoint between a doctor and his uneducated clients, the townspeople. In the 1920s, when most individuals could not get a college education, the dramatist could raise the question of education as the hope of the race, echoing Du Bois's plea for the educated men and women to serve as spokesmen.

During Negro History Week at Morgan College, Baltimore, in February 1934, Carter Woodson urged Willis Richardson and May Miller to dramatize the lives of black heroes and heroines. A year later *Negro History in Thirteen Plays* was published. In a 1972 interview with Cassandra Willis of the City College of New York, May Miller spoke on the importance of black history plays and how she came to write them:

> In many of the young leaders today I don't find an acknowledgment of the contributions a man like Carter G. Woodson made when he aroused an interest in Negro history when very little interest was being paid. It was he who was responsible for the establishment of the Association for the Study of Negro History, and, in addition, he backed with his own funds the Associated Publishers for the printing of this material. In *Negro History in Thirteen Plays,* Dr. Woodson furnished many of the books which Willis Richardson and I studied before we wrote the plays.
>
> Another important influence was Randolph Edmonds of Morgan College who thought it idle to have children only read history; he believed that productions on stage of those great Negro characters would help the students understand. For a number of years at Morgan College they gave one-act plays, and we wrote for those occasions.
>
> Then, under Du Bois, the great Krigwa Movement was sponsored by the *Crisis* magazine, and it established all over the country little one-act play groups that performed in churches and schools, and all this was a forerunner to what we're doing now. We would have no Lorraine Hansberry if there had not been behind her those people who were slowly leading up to her great productions.

May Miller's plays in the *Negro History in Thirteen Plays* anthology are *Christophe's Daughters,* a story of two Haitian princesses facing their father's inevitable suicide in the tragedy of revolution; *Harriet Tubman,* about the extraordinary trips of this lone black woman who led groups of slaves to freedom through the Underground Railroad; *Samory,* about a fabled leader of the African Sudan and his strategy that outwitted a French general's plan to capture a village; and *Sojourner Truth,* showing one occasion in her militant life when her preaching curbed hostility. *Harriet Tubman* was produced twice, at Morgan College in Baltimore and Dillard University in New Orleans. The Morgan College Dramatic Club presented *Christophe's Daughters* on 14 February 1935.

Miller wrote three other plays at this time. They are unpublished: "Stragglers in the Dust" (1930), a story of the identity of the "unknown soldier"; "Nails and Thorns" (1933), awarded third prize in a writing contest at Southern University; and "Freedom's Children on the March" (1943), a dramatic folk ballad with music by Llewellyn Wilson for the June commencement exercises at the Frederick Douglass High School.

In addition to her work in drama, Miller's prose has won recognition. "Doorstops," a short story, was published by the *Carolina Magazine* in

May 1930. A view of street life ("Willow Street never boasted of virgins"), the plot concerns Irma, a teenaged girl, who seeks the knowledge of physical love, but is repelled by the memory of a fateful night when her mother killed her drink-crazed lover to prevent her daughter from being raped. This drama of deprived lives rings true. A second story, " 'Bidin' Place," appeared in *Arts Quarterly* of Dillard University in April 1937. *Opportunity* published her "One Blue Star" in its summer number of 1945. Here a mother attempts to reconcile herself to the idea of her only son volunteering for service in the armed forces. In the 1930s, May Miller outlined and wrote portions of a novel titled "Fine Market," from the folk saying, "Ain't he brought his brood to a fine market."

In 1944 she retired from the Baltimore schools and with the unflagging support of her husband, John Lewis Sullivan, devoted her time and energy to literary pursuits.

She returned to Washington and enrolled in a poetry workshop directed by Inez Boulton, a participant in the Imagist school originated by Harriet Monroe of Chicago. This experience had considerable influence on the direction of her writing. Among the participants were Owen Dodson, Charles Sebree, and Paul Lawson, who later became her best critic and the founder of the Charioteer Press, the publisher of two of her collections of poetry. An earlier influence had been Alain Locke, who had provided literary guideposts which she describes in her unpublished "Poem to Alain Leroy Locke: Teacher of Aesthetics," written in her twenties. The last of the four stanzas is quoted here.

We dug with him into a store of wisdom
his direction drowned in esoteric phrase.
Clipped words polished Benin bronze
to a glowing heritage.
Responding to new impulse and image
we probed the dark world origin
of the Picasso riddle and romped
in a bacchanal all our own.

Another influence on Miller was Archibald MacLeish whom she had heard read his poems in the 1950s in the Coolidge Auditorium of the Library of Congress. Years later she would acknowledge her debt to him.

Her first major recognition came from Paul Bixler, the editor of *Antioch Review*, then a magazine primarily devoted to serious prose. In its winter number of 1945, he printed "Tally," composed shortly after the bombings of Hiroshima and Nagasaki. Miller voices a deep fear about human reproduction:

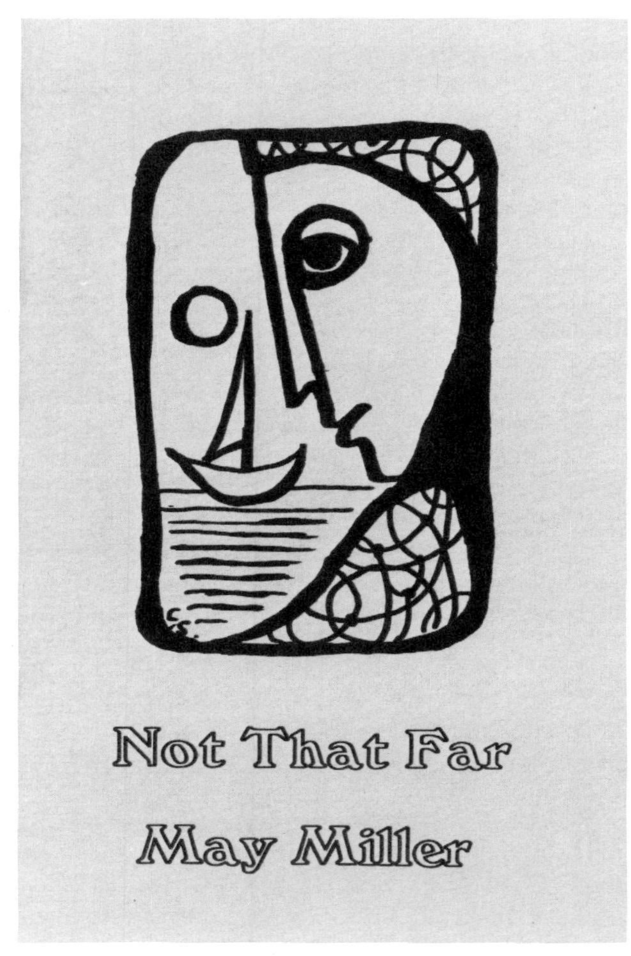

Front cover for Miller's 1973 volume in which each poem is titled for a different country

Fear goads reluctant flesh
Nor stealing lassitude the power
To bind me to the couch.
No seed of mine to sprout
Cork leg, plastic arm, clutching claw.
Better to be lost in muck
And slime of sewer swirl
That yet may run a clearer stream
To lap some lonely lighthouse rock
Or green again the passing plain.

A second poem, "Hierarchy," appeared in *Antioch Review* in December 1950. A sequel, in a sense, to the first, its postwar hope speaks for man who, somehow, stumbles "into the clearing" to witness "the setting/Green again" despite his "wavering faiths and broken laws. . . . " She beseeches man, though "blind with vision," to climb back to sanity, to the instinctive self-preservative knowledge of lower animals "for the privilege of being man."

In December 1948, *Poetry* accepted three poems whose ideas surfaced again in her later poems. "Measurement" places human time on the "unscarred dial" of eternity. "Instant Before Sleep" shows the passage from one state of being to another. "Brief Negro Sermon" reflects her heritage from the anthropomorphic folk sermon with its storytelling and moral giving:

(On the sinking of a great ocean liner)

Thirty turbine boilers;
Thought the Lord couldn't sink it.
It sunk like a lead bob.
    My God, git over.
Babes and grown-ups,
Saints and hell-raisers
Common as fishes in deep dark water.
    God knows his business.
. . . .
    Sweet Jesus, rest 'em.

But if'n they bed in soil or sea weed,
His own raises up at the final trumpet
To smile in His smiling face.
    Amen!

Miller's first poetry collection, *Into The Clearing,* was published by the Charioteer Press in 1959. The opening selection, "Green Leaf," with its reference to Eve and the forbidden fruit of knowledge, sets the scene of the artist "waiting the drop of fruit/to the hungry hand." "When the apple fell," only then could "the word" be heard.

A sequel, "Trail" appraises the cost and the gift:

Bright patterns on a dark bed,
A frieze on splintered wood
Above which no young face looks
Toward morning—

Beneath the hedge
Over a basement sill,
A snail has left
His parable in opal.

"Pond Lament" seems to have been inspired by her father's tales. In the poem the wide-eyed youngsters "leaped in a wind" and heard the frogs dolefully croak: "*Who'll dig my grave when I die? Not I. Not I.*" Like all children, they responded to the call and response with laughter for they were not ready for the somber notes of life:

Not for us that deeper wisdom
Pulsing in a grotesque body:
Even in frolic, seeds of tomorrow sprout
Toward the hour of apprehension.

Who'll pay my debts when I die?
Not I.

She remembers her father again in "My Father":

With springtime my father comes alive again
In the lilac bush he planted
At the kitchen door that we
Might hear the plain voice
Of Walt Whitman burst
Through the bloom.

The relationship of man to a higher power raises questions for Miller. In "Who Gives," man cannot know the answer or even put his trust to questioning "who asks, who gives, who receives,/A wish denied or half-fulfilled." A year later, in her next collection, *Dust of Uncertain Journey* (1975), she asks, "Where is the Guilt?" Seeking absolution, she discovers that "Only the river responds/Promising no unholy footprints."

This volume of poems reflects her continuing concern with questions of morality. "Late Conjecture" questions the value of sacrifice, given the moral history of man since that time of the cross:

Look to the end of the garden
To the scarecrow sticks
Against the stained wall like a cross.
In this tell-tale light
Trace on those limbs nicks and burns
Such as dug by heels in agony
Trying to escape.

Beyond the garden and the hour
Of broken bough and rusted fruit,
Think the legend voice
That must be crying:
What is this thing I do?
Perhaps I'd best climb down.

Her juxtaposed and layered images expose the reality of man's divided condition. The split between knowledge and feeling is the flaw at the heart of civilization. She posits this condition in "The Wrong Side of Morning," where the end may well be a life in a tomb of glass and concrete:

Dust jacket for Miller's 1974 collection, which includes her 1959 volume, Into the Clearing, *and a selection of later poems titled "Beyond"*

We wake on the wrong side of morning
From a nightmare of wings
And mushrooms of huge death.
Weep for us whose lives are caged
In concrete, for our straw images
Seen through glass walls
Are you and you tomorrow.

Three visits to Europe and the Mediterranean left their memories. She had described some of her impressions in *Not That Far* (1973). In *Dust of Uncertain Journey,* she includes "In Venice: First Itinerary." She watches the pigeons "gorge and defecate/ On the saint's strict marble" as "[t]he domes affirm in gold/The brilliance of a shrunken grace,/And the fat birds eat." (This poem was read by Robert Hayden when he was a Fellow of the Academy of American Poets in 1975.)

In addition to her adult literature, Miller has also written for children. *Halfway to the Sun* (1981) contains poems for children which instill curiosity and the joy of discovering a human relationship with all things in this universe—even with the planet itself. In "The Great Gem":

We never knew
the earth is blue
until a fellow called
from outer space

. . . .

Hey! look what I see
huge and curved—
a sapphire globe.
Honest, it's a picture
of our earth I'm sending
back to you.
It's your world you're
too close to see.

May Miller did not stop teaching. She was Poet-in-Residence at Monmouth College (1963), at

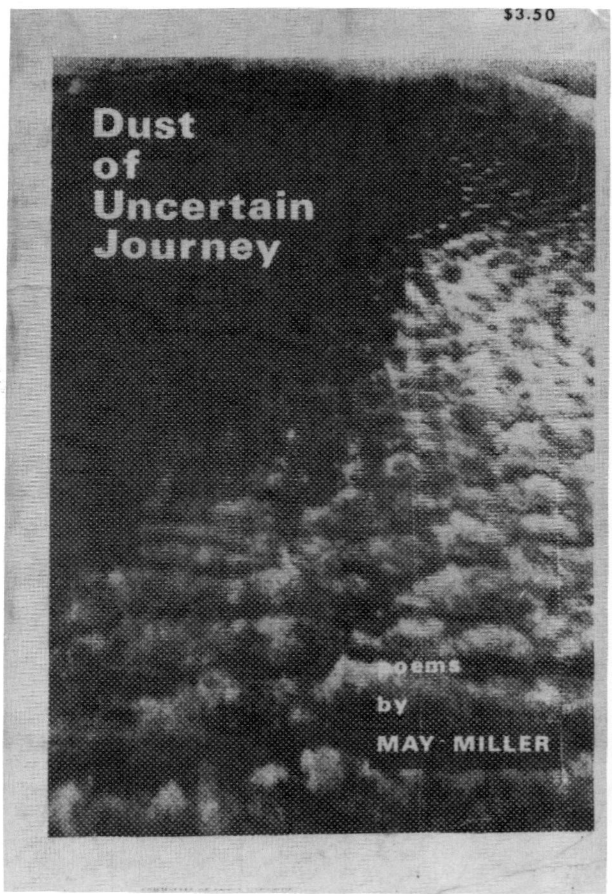

Front cover for Miller's 1975 poetry collection. Robert Hayden says she "writes with quiet strength, lyric intensity. She is . . . a poet of humane vision."

the University of Wisconsin (1972), at Bluefield, West Virginia State College (1974), with the Bluefield Arts Commission (1975), at the Southern University Poetry Festival (1975), and at Exeter Academy (1973, 1976). She has read her poetry at national celebrations, including the Washington, D.C., Bicentennials of 1973 and 1974 and the inaugurals of Walter Washington, first black mayor of Washington, D.C., and President Jimmy Carter. Her last presentation was a three-day Folger Library Celebration (17-20 January 1977) at which occasion such prominent, yet diverse, poets as James Dickey and Robert Hayden also read their poetry. In 1972, she recorded for "Poets Reading Their Own Work," an archival collection at the Library of Congress. She has participated in radio broadcasting at American University. Under Dorothy Goldberg, she served as coordinator for performing poets for the Friends of Arts in the Public Schools of Washington, D.C., in 1964 and 1965. From 1970 to 1978, she was a member of the District of Columbia Commission of the Arts and served as chairperson of the literature panel. In 1979 she became a member of the Folger Library Poetry Advisory committee.

Her creative work has been published in twenty-nine periodicals and magazines and in nineteen anthologies, among them *Cavalcade* by Arthur Davis and Saunders Redding (1970). Two studies for schools, *A Student's Guide to Creative Writing* (1980) by Naomi Long Madgett and *Reading Counts* (1982), the Rochester Secondary Reading Program, include her poems.

Pinkie Gordon Lane, editor of *Poems by Blacks* (1973), wrote that Miller is an author "of deep personal insight, of unquestioning moral courage" and one who has "suffered the imbalances of our society," yet retained "a grace and wholeness of spirit." Robert Hayden, who knew the poet as a friend and critic from 1962, wrote, "May Miller writes with quiet strength, lyric intensity. She is perceptive and compassionate, a poet of humane vision. I am grateful for her poems." To these comments, poet and editor Naomi Long Madgett added: "At a time when the gentle murmur of love is often drowned out by the scream of wrath, we believe that it is most necessary that our quiet voices be heard."

References:

Benjamin Brawley, *The Negro Genius* (New York: Dodd, Mead, 1937);

Arthur P. Davis, *From the Dark Tower* (Washington, D.C.: Howard University Press, 1974);

Davis and Saunders Redding, *Cavalcade* (New York: Houghton Mifflin, 1971);

Montgomery Gregory, "The Drama of Negro Life," in *The New Negro,* by Alain Locke (New York: Albert & Charles Boni, 1925);

James V. Hatch, *Black American Playwrights, 1823-1977: Annotated Bibliography of Plays* (New York: R. R. Bowker, 1977);

Hatch and Ted Shine, *Black Theater U.S.A. 1847-1974* (New York: Free Press, 1974);

Robert Hayden, "Preface," in *The New Negro,* by Alain Locke (New York: Atheneum, 1970), pp. ix-xiv;

Archibald MacLeish, *Poems: 1924-1933* (Boston & New York: Houghton Mifflin, 1933);

Kelly Miller, "Howard: The National Negro University," in *The New Negro,* by Alain Locke (New York: Albert & Charles Boni, 1925), pp. 312-322;

Miller, "Where is Negro Heaven?," *Opportunity,* 4 (December 1926): 370-373;

Barbara Molette, "Black Women Playwrights," *Black World,* 25 (April 1976): 28-34;

Julia Boublitz Morgan, "Son of a Slave," *Johns Hopkins Magazine,* 32 (June 1981): 20-26;

"The *Opportunity* Dinner," *Opportunity,* 3 (June 1925): 176;

Eugene Redmond, *Drumvoices: The Mission of Afro-American Poetry, A Critical History* (Garden City: Anchor/Doubleday, 1976);

Erlene Stetson, ed., *Black Sister: Poetry by Black American Women, 1746-1980* (Bloomington: Indiana University Press, 1981);

Darwin T. Turner, "The Negro Dramatist's Image of the Universe, 1920-1960," *College Language Association Journal,* 5 (December 1961): 106-120.

Pauli Murray

(20 November 1910-1 July 1985)

Nellie McKay
University of Wisconsin-Madison

BOOKS: *Proud Shoes: The Story of An American Family* (New York: Harper & Row, 1956);
Dark Testament and Other Poems (Norwalk, Conn.: Silvermine Publishers, 1970).

OTHER: Arna Bontemps, ed., *American Negro Poetry,* includes poems by Murray (New York: Hill and Wang, 1963);
Arnold Adoff, ed., *The Poetry of Black America,* includes poems by Murray (New York: Macmillan, 1968);
Langston Hughes and Bontemps, eds., *The Poetry of the Negro 1746-1970,* includes poems by Murray (Garden City: Doubleday, 1970);
Lindsay Patterson, ed., *A Rock Against the Wind: Black Love Poems,* includes poems by Murray (New York: Dodd, Mead, 1973).

In 1956, twenty years before Alex Haley's *Roots* (1976) fired the imagination of black and white Americans as never before, to the importance of tracing genealogical heritage, Pauli Murray published *Proud Shoes: The Story of An American Family,* a book that demonstrated her awareness of how vital the past is as a means of understanding the present and for devising criteria to guide the future. Nor was the concept new to black Americans, for the headnote to Murray's book comes from the diary of her grandfather, Robert G. Fitzgerald, and reveals his consciousness of it almost a full century before her book. On 26 July 1867 he wrote: "The past is the key to the present and the mirror of the future, therefore, let us adopt as a rule, to judge the future by the history of the past, and having the key to past experience, let us open the door to present success and future happiness." *Proud Shoes,* like Haley's *Roots,* was the resolution of an individual's search for identity, but it also serves as microcosm for a collective goal of black Americans to take positive meaning out of the black American experience in white America. Murray was unable to ferret out her African roots, but her portrayal of the entanglement of her black and white American heritage provides us with a dramatic metaphor of what it is to be an American.

Pauli Murray (courtesy Schomburg Center for Research in Black Culture, The New York Public Library, Astor, Lenox and Tilden Foundations)

Pauli Murray was born in Baltimore, Maryland, in 1910, and she grew up in Durham, North Carolina, in the home of her maternal grandparents, the Fitzgeralds, both of whom impressed a fierce sense of pride of self and independence of spirit on their granddaughter. As a black veteran of the Civil War and one who suffered disabilities as a result, Robert Fitzgerald had no doubts concerning his relationship to America; and Cornelia, his wife, the mulatto offspring of a prominent Chapel Hill, North Carolina, white family, closely connected to the establishment of the university there, was no less secure in her identity than her husband. Murray attended public schools in Durham, after which she went to Hunter College in New York City, where she majored in English, and took a minor in history. She graduated in 1933. The years in which Murray attended college in New York were, culturally and artistically, the most exciting ones for black people in that city until then. This was the time of the Harlem Renaissance, and Murray had an opportunity to meet and know writers such as Dorothy West, Wallace Thurman, Sterling Brown, Robert Hayden, Countee Cullen, and Langston Hughes. The first poem that she published, "The Song of the Highway," appeared in Nancy Cunard's anthology *Color* in 1934, through the efforts of Langston Hughes.

In her last year in college Murray took a course in poetry reading. One of the poems assigned, and which had long-lasting effects on her, was Stephen Vincent Benét's "John Brown's Body." What struck her most was Benét's challenge to black poets to express their feelings about Brown and their honest thoughts concerning their relationship to America. He had noted that he could understand Brown's actions and share the inner sentiments of black Americans only so far as his "too white heart" allowed him. It was his conviction that an authentic rendition in honor of Brown's sacrifice, and an expression of the soul of blackness, was then still to come from black bards. Some seven years after she had taken the course Murray sent Benét a draft of some of her poems, including one called "Dark Anger," which later became "Dark Testament," the title poem of her collection by that name, which was published in 1970. Thus began a warm friendship between Murray and the Pulitzer Prize-winning poet. He gave generously of the constructive criticism that she needed during those years until his death in 1943.

Although she has said that writing was her first love, Murray's life has been spent in a variety of other professions that have kept her from pursuing the muse full-time. She was active in the civil rights movement, beginning in the 1940s, as an advocate of Gandhi's passive resistance. She holds law degrees from Howard University, the University of California, Berkeley, and Yale University and has practiced the legal profession in New York and California and was admitted to practice before the Supreme Court in those states; she has also written books on the law. She has been a college professor in America and Africa. In 1977 Murray became the nation's first black woman to be ordained an Episcopalian priest, among the ten first American women to be ordained that year. Even with a limited output in creative writing—*Proud Shoes* and *Dark Testament and Other Poems* (1970)—she is a significant figure in black letters.

Proud Shoes: The Story of An American Family had its genesis in ideas for a children's story that would educate the young descendants of the Fitzgerald clan about their ancestors. Murray changed her mind about the limits of this perspective as she experienced the social and political climate of the country undergoing conflict and change in the early 1950s. On one hand, she was active in the civil rights movement which was gaining tremendous momentum then, and on the other hand, McCarthyism and an irrational fear of communism were spreading across the nation. Her book, in which history and literature intersect, is the product of a lively imagination and four years of devoted research in oral and documented history. She points out that it is the biography of her grandparents, the story of three generations of a family "involved in a crucial turning point in our nation's history." Much of the saga centers around the racial conflicts through which the family worked out its destiny, focusing on the courage, strength, and fearlessness in the face of danger that all members of the group exhibited. The women, both white and black, are noteworthy in their independence and recognition of moral duty, and the men are stalwart, and refuse to accept any status less than that of honorable men. Race and sex are the explosive elements of suffering and shame that Murray exorcises through her honest confrontation of them, while education and tenacious survival are the foundations on which she builds a strong and positive identity.

Murray's grandfather, Robert George Fitzgerald, a free black man in the slave South, was the epitome of the nineteenth-century romanticized version of the American. Slender in build, and delicate in health, he nevertheless displayed phenomenal physical endurance. At age twenty-three he was a soldier in the Union Army; at age seventy-five, and by then blind, everything in his bearing and behavior was still that of a soldier's. Self-reliance, discipline, trustworthiness, and confidence in his own worth were the governing forces in his long life. To Pauli Murray, even in his old age he seemed "solid and indestructible." Fitzgerald, born in Delaware in 1840, was the son of a mulatto father who claimed aristocratic Irish heritage through several generations, and a white mother who was not afraid to accept the burdens of the racial conflicts inherent in her marriage to a nonwhite man and the task of raising mulatto children. The Fitzgeralds moved to Pennsylvania in 1855, and to

North Carolina in 1869, where Robert married Cornelia Smith, the daughter of a slave woman and Sidney Smith, son of a prominent Chapel Hill family. As a small farmer, brick maker, and teacher, vocations he followed sometimes separately and sometimes simultaneously, he spent his life in a morally successful struggle against social, political, and economic forces that were relentless in their efforts to destroy his will.

As black and American biography, *Proud Shoes* embodies the most important elements in the evolution of the contemporary black family, and Murray achieved this at a time when it was still too psychologically painful for many black Americans to explore their personal hurt as deeply as this book does. At the center of its meaning is the author's recognition that "true emancipation lies in the acceptance of the whole past, in devising strength from all of [her] roots, in facing up to the degradation as well as the dignity of [her] ancestors." She does not hesitate to examine the brutality of the rape of her great-grandmother by her great-grandfather, or her grandmother's uncritical admiration for the perpetrator of that heinous crime; she addresses the victimization of black women slaves and the powerlessness of black men to protect their families from such assaults; she looks at the delicate balance on which black psychological dignity rests; and she sees and praises the triumph of human decency regardless of the racial or sexual group to which those worthy of commendation belong.

Proud Shoes is a realistic and convincing representation of the black experience. The story is told in a language that is without rhetoric or bombast, and which evokes the reader's sympathy and empathy without resorting to sentimentality. One of the most powerful images in this work is that of her grandparents' home in Durham, where she grew up. When Robert Fitzgerald built the house in the 1890s, on a broad shelf of land between two hills, to its rear there were meadows and wheat fields, and beyond, and to its front, a forest of oaks, pines, cedars, and sassafras bushes. Surrounded by the beauty of the natural environment, it was a peaceful, if modest, haven for a black family that had previously endured many trials. Metaphorically, the location represented the promise of a better life which has always been the hope of black Americans. Within a short time, however, all that changed as Durham became a bustling factory center. In an expansion of the town's white cemetery, the land behind the house, on the hill above it, became a graveyard, and the forest in front, a community of shacks in which factory workers lived. Murray's descriptions of the effects of these changes on that house, particularly those of the cemetery, with its confederate gun at the top of the hill, are memorable. The house seemed dwarfed by death, which was like an ever-present enemy; the drainage from the hill forced the Fitzgeralds to abandon their well; and in rainy weather, the stench that pervaded all around was almost unbearable. Nor did the city fathers recompense the family for these hardships. Again, as a metaphor, this situation represented the broken promise which has been white America's way of frustrating the dreams of black Americans for a better life. But the story does not end there. When Pauli Murray was young, she found the cemetery frightening at nights, when "dancing ghoulish arms and legs and the indefinable shapes made of wind and shadow would move slowly across the faces of the tombstones," yet, in the daytime, she found it a "beautiful park of birds" and small animals where "in summer, flowers were blooming everywhere." Her fantasies of dark and light in the white graveyard which overshadowed her childhood, in relationship to her experiences of race and segregation in white America and the ways in which she transcended them through mammoth achievements, make her life another paradigm for black survival and success. *Proud Shoes* is the biography of the Fitzgeralds and Murray's search for her identity in her past, but it is also the story of the struggles of all black Americans, and of all people who seek dignity in a world that would deny them full humanity.

Dark Testament and Other Poems contains verses composed between 1933 and 1969. The book is a poetic mirror of Murray's life and career, and a testament to the enormous breadth of her interests as a person. Verses range from racial poems and the bitter tragedies of the lives of the poor and the powerless, to more general contemplations on nature, human life, and philosophical questions of being. The title poem was begun in the 1930s and completed during the Harlem riot of 1943, the year of Benét's death. Divided into twelve sections, it recounts the history of the relationship between black and white Americans and the psychological struggle of blacks to hold on to their humanity. Using the dream as the symbol of the imagination's ability to transcend oppression, it addresses the nature of the human will and the creative powers of the mind. The dream of freedom is beyond price and without boundaries, Murray says, and has been the guiding principle in the lives of black Americans, as well as the hope of the universe to which all people cling when all else fails. Citing America's history of violence and oppression toward black people, the poet calls on white Americans to restore the original promise of their land—freedom for all. The poem praises America's high ideals, even as it expresses feelings of sadness at the nation's failure to fulfill its promises. It calls on white America, in a reasoned way, to open its eyes to the reality of its responsibility to its black citizens. From recognition of past injustices there can be reconciliation and the restoration of the dream of America for all humanity.

Other poems in the volume address specific problems in the nation or pay tribute to special people. In the latter group, there is one on "The Passing of F. D. R.," which follows a line that is interesting and imaginative. It neutralizes the fears of death and the incomprehensibility of the unknown by presenting an image of the dead Roosevelt, in a state of physical health, in the new "life" he has entered. On the other hand, "Mr. Roosevelt Regrets" is a scathing work that attacks the President's insensitivity to the tragic causes of violence in the black ghetto. Written as an angry response to a Presidential statement made to the newspapers after the Detroit riots of 1943, the poet speaks to the double victimization of blacks.

The nonracial poems in the volume fit into the tradition of the American imagists. They reveal many of Murray's interests and concerns outside of race and oppression. Among them are a number of poems about love and friendship. We observe her genius in the carefulness with which her lines are sculptured, and in the seriousness she invests in the art of writing. In her racial poetry, where either she is angry and lashes out, or when feelings of powerlessness inform the verse, the results are poignant, and her voice is resonant. Both *Proud Shoes* and *Dark Testament* are in the best tradition of the creative imagination in American letters.

Reference:

Barbaralee Diamonstein, *Open Secrets* (New York: Viking, 1972).

Eugene Perkins

(13 September 1932-   )

Michael Greene
North Carolina A & T State University

BOOKS: *An Apology to My African Brother and Other Poems* (Chicago: Adams Press, 1965);
Black is Beautiful (Chicago: Free Black Press, 1968);
West Wall (Chicago: Free Black Press, 1969);
Silhouette (Chicago: Free Black Press, 1970);
Home Is a Dirty Street: The Social Oppression of Black Children (Chicago: Third World Press, 1975);
When You Grow Up: Poems for Children (Chicago: Black Child Journal, 1982);
Midnight Blues in the Afternoon and Other Poems (Chicago: INESU Production, 1984).

PLAY PRODUCTIONS: *The Image Makers,* Chicago, Kuumba Theater, 1975;
Professor J. B., Chicago, Parkway Community House, 1976;
The Black Fairy, Chicago, LaMont Zeno Community Theater, 1976;
Pride of Race, Chicago, Regis Theater, 1984.

OTHER: Don Arthur Torgersen, ed., *Port Chicago Poets: A New Voice in Anthology,* includes poems by Perkins (Chicago: Chicago International Manuscripts, 1966), pp. 136-141;
Black Expressions: An Anthology of New Black Poets, edited by Perkins (Chicago: YMCA, 1967);
Ahmed Alhamisi and Harun Kofi Wangara, "Heart of Black Ghetto," in *Black Arts: An Anthology of Black Creations* (Detroit: Black Arts Publications, 1969), p. 99;
"The Black Arts Movement: Its Challenge and Responsibility," in *The Black Seventies,* edited by Floyd B. Barbour (Boston: Porter Sargent, 1970): 85-97;
"Bronzeville Poet," in *To Gwen with Love,* edited by Patricia L. Brown, et al. (Chicago: Johnson, 1971), p. 78;
Dark Meditations: A Collection of Poems, edited by Perkins (Chicago: Free Black Press, 1971);

Eugene Perkins

Poetry of Prison: Poems by Black Prisoners, edited by Perkins (Chicago: DuSable Museum of African-American History, 1972);

"Diary of a Bronzeville Boy," in *You Better Believe It: Black Verse in English from Africa, the West Indies and the United States*, edited by Paul Breman (Harmondsworth: Penguin, 1973), pp. 300-302.

PERIODICAL PUBLICATIONS: "The New Voices Sing of Black Cultural Power," *Panorama, Chicago Daily News*, 7 December 1968, pp. 4-5;

"The Changing Status of Black Writers," *Black World*, 19, no. 8 (1970): 18-23, 95-98;

"Black Theater as Image Maker," *Black Books Bulletin*, 1 (Spring/Summer 1972): 24-29;

"Literature of Combat: Poetry of Afrikan Liberation Movements," *Journal of Black Studies*, 7 (December 1976): 225-240.

Had Eugene Perkins never published a volume of poetry, or staged a single play, his contribution as a sociologist, particularly as a leader who improved the lot of disadvantaged young people, would still have given him stature as an important force in Chicago culture. Despite the fact that his creative work has not been his livelihood, he has been a prolific poet, essayist, and playwright. The impulse behind his creative work cannot be separated from the energy that has driven him as a sociologist; the same compassion, the same strong sense of social commitment, of having a responsibility to the urban ghetto, appears in his poetry.

Eugene Perkins was born in Chicago on 13 September 1932, the son of sculptor Marion Perkins and Eva Perkins. Despite his wide recognition as an artist, Marion Perkins had to work as a porter and dishwasher at times. Although the children did not grow up with wealth, they nevertheless acquired a strong sense of pride in their culture and a strong dedication to the arts. "My father was an inspiration to me," Perkins recalled in a 1985 interview in the *Chicago Defender*; "I was ten years old when he took me to see Paul Robeson star in Shakespeare's 'Othello'. . . . It was the turning point in my life. I knew then that I wanted to write." His first publication was a poem in the Chicago *Tribune* when he was eleven. Perkins wrote poetry and essays, and even detective plays, while attending Wendell Phillips High School, where he was editor of the school newspaper. He attended colleges in Knoxville, Tennessee, and Winston-Salem, North Carolina, but graduated in 1961 from George Williams College in Chicago with a degree in group work. He received a masters from the same school in 1964.

His formal professional career since then has been as a sociologist specializing in helping the young and disadvantaged. From 1965 to 1982, he was Executive Director of the Better Boys Foundation Family Center, a large social agency involved with community, social, educational, and cultural development. His 1975 book, *Home Is a Dirty Street: The Social Oppression of Black Children*, is a major contribution to urban sociology and has been praised by Lerone Bennett, Jr., as "a profound and deeply disturbing book which should be read by every person in this troubled land." Perkins has also taught at several universities and has served on numerous civic and educational boards and task forces. Most currently, Perkins has been active in his consulting firm, INESU Consultants, and he is engaged in further graduate work at DePaul University under a 1985 Community Service Fellowship. He has been married since 1969 to Janis Perkins and has three children.

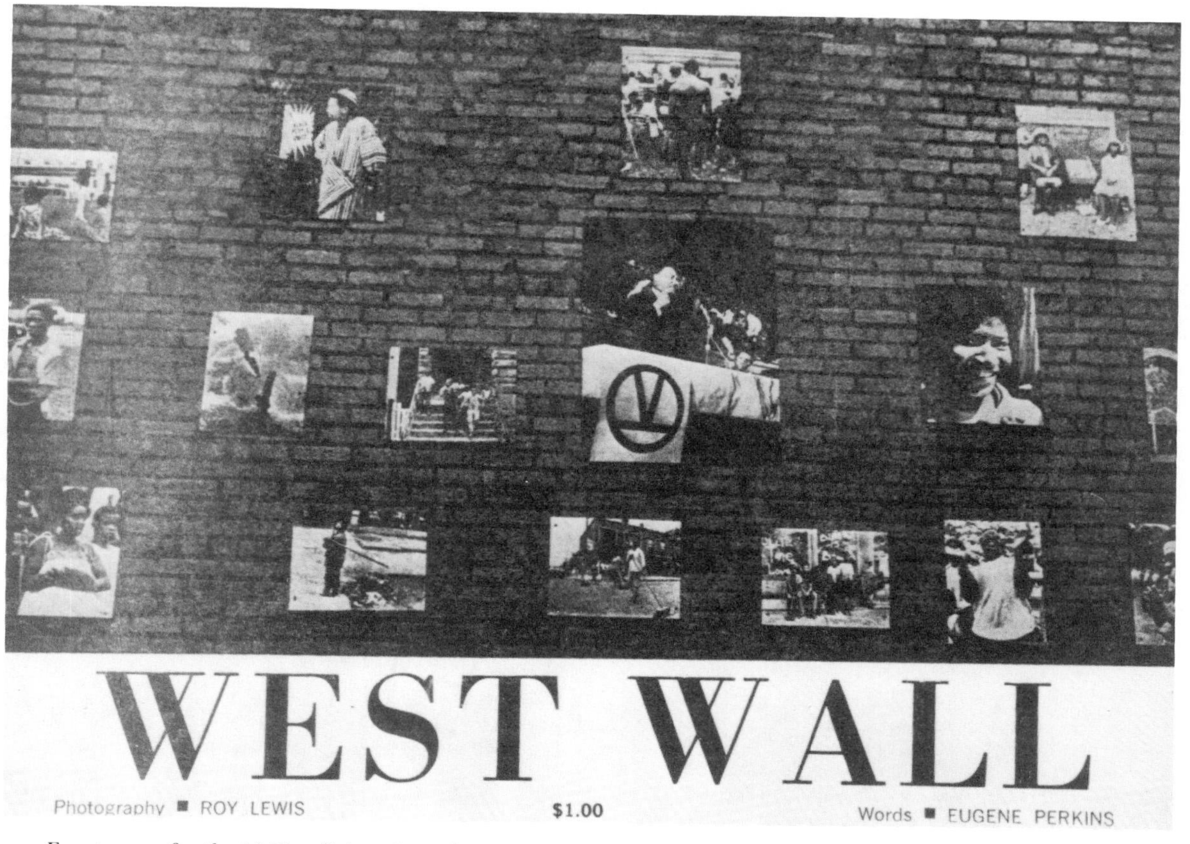

Front cover for the 1969 collaborative volume of poems and photographs by Perkins and photographer Roy Lewis

Perkins's work as a creative writer has frequently been a response to the problems he saw as a sociologist. His strong social conscience led him not only to social and political activism but also to encouraging other blacks to find their creative identities. He has published volumes of poetry by young people and others who participated in workshops he conducted, for example, *Black Expressions: An Anthology of New Black Poets* (1967) and *Poetry of Prison: Poems by Black Prisoners* (1972).

Perkins's first volume of his own poetry, *An Apology to My African Brother* (1965), contains some poems which are proudly conscious of his heritage, some which reflect the pain of seeing poverty and discouragement, and others which find poignant beauty in the blues and jazz that grew from that heritage. In the title poem, the speaker apologizes for being Americanized ("in my urbane apartment hangs/A reproduction of the Mona Lisa/And a painting by Grandma Moses"), and he ends with an exalted prayer for reunification with his African roots:

O, if I could only build a bridge!
Over the sea which has diluted our blood.
And recapture some of the lost treasures
Long buried by European customs.
Help me black brother!

All of the poems in this volume address aspects of what blackness means in America. Some poems are political, such as "Who'll Sound the Requiem," in memory of the three murdered civil rights workers in Mississippi, and the poem that commemorates black heroes such as Toussaint Louverture, W. E. B. Du Bois, and Malcolm X. The more overtly political poems tend to be too portentous. The most effective poems in the volume use lyrical images and the rhythms of music to create disturbing portraits of urban distress. In "Jazz on a Hot Summer Night," "Tenements creak/At the timbre of mellifluous music" at the beginning of the poem, but by the end, "A siren sounds/To intrude on the melodic darkness/A helpless man lay groping/In a stream of torrid blood." The poem quietly flashes image after image to create a disturbing harmony of sounds: "The pulse of jazz," the poem concludes, "Has befallen a city/Filled with tene-

Karega Kofi Moyo

"Eugene Perkins has written a profound and deeply disturbing book which should be read by every person in this troubled land. A poet, a social analyst and a counsellor of street people, he approaches his subject with compassion and an arsenal of new and revealing concepts. Because he has a primary relationship with oppressed black children and because his subject with compassion and an arsenal of new and the social commentator, he reveals nuances and subtleties which are beyond the range of the traditional social scientists. His book, in my opinion, is one of the most important on the sociology of the streets since publication of BLACK METROPOLIS."

Lerone Bennet, Jr.
April 14, 1974

Third World Press **•Chicago•**

7524 South Cottage Grove Avenue 60619 [312] 651-6121

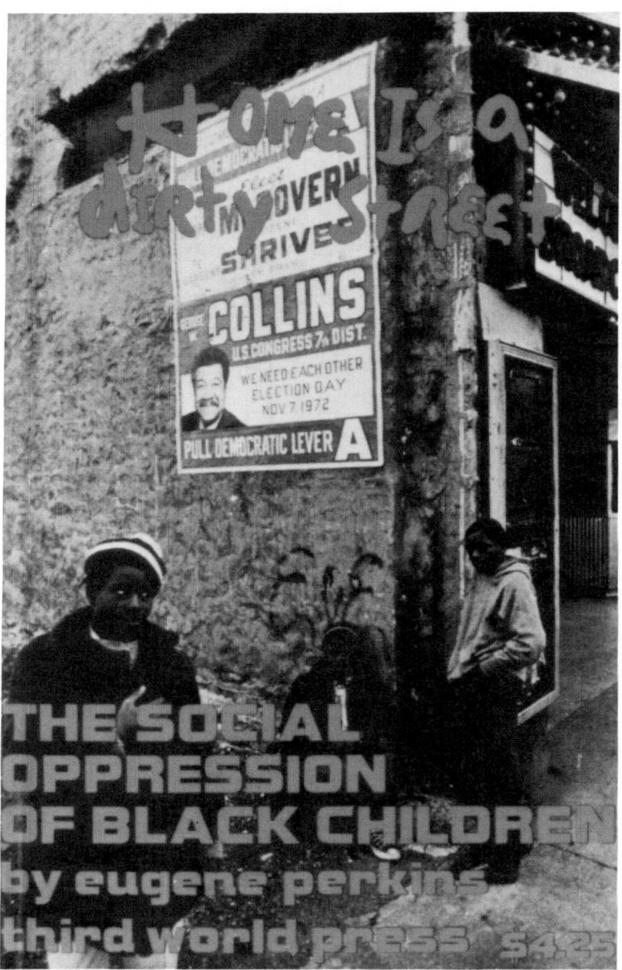

Covers for Perkins's 1975 sociological study of the black urban community, which he calls the "ghetcolony"—derived from "ghetto" and "colonialism"—and which he says is "an extension of the old plantation system"

brous omens." Perkins has a gift for the compassionately observed detail. Here he describes the poor artist at a fair: "The lines embedded/On his taut face/Had more expression/Than the paintings/Which hung, like/Soggy gaudery/On a dirty clothesline." The poems in the volume are uneven, but the sad lyricism of pieces like "Shadows" and "Last Night Blues," the intensity of "A Derelict on a Skidrow Corner," and the dignity of the volume's last poem, a tribute "For Father," make the book auspicious.

A silhouette, Perkins says in his 1970 volume of that name, is "a BLACK image/reflection of something." He goes on to explain that "poems should paint two, three, and even four dimensional pictures which can capture the totality of a concept/vision instead of merely a fragmented expression. But even more important, poems must be real poems. I mean real in the sense that one can almost FEEL/HEAR/SEE/SMELL that which the poem is attempting to project." The "silhouettes" in this volume are varied and ambitious and present a wide-ranging political and social canvas. Several poems develop the notion that white culture has attempted to copy black cultural styles, particularly in music, but has failed. There are other poems which present vigorous and closely detailed pictures of Chicago life: "The Gladiators OR The Name of the Game is Sandlot Basketball" captures the excitement, the imagery, the rhythm of a city game, and even recreates a series of moves by the players:

> then a muscular hand
> palms the ball
> and swiftly hurls

it to a jitterbugging gladiator
GO BABY GO
GO/GO/GO
who
begins to weave
downcourt like an angry
alley cat
his ebony torso brushing
past outstretched arms
that lunge at him with
fierce claws

The variety and scope of the volume are impressive. There is considerably more discipline, more crafted control of the language, than in Perkins's earlier work.

Perkins's work with troubled and disadvantaged youth has been central to his career, and he has voiced his love of the young by encouraging and publishing young people's work, as well as by writing poetry and plays for and about them. One of his plays, *The Black Fairy* (produced in 1976), is a musical about Black Fairy who lacks pride and is rescued by Black Bird and Queen Mother, who escorts her through a series of meetings with characters central to Afro-American culture, thus giving the Black Fairy an exciting vision of her new mission to black children. Perkins also published a book of poetry, *When You Grow Up* (1982), dedicated to his three children, Julia, Russell, and Jamila, "And to all Children of Afrikan Descent." The poetry is simple without being condescending, and it is strongly rhythmical without being singsong. Much of it is designed to reinforce the child's individual and racial sense of worth; and several of the poems celebrate heroes as different as Deadwood Dick, Josh Gipson, Leadbelly, Nat Turner, Patrice Lumumba, and Martin Luther King, Jr.

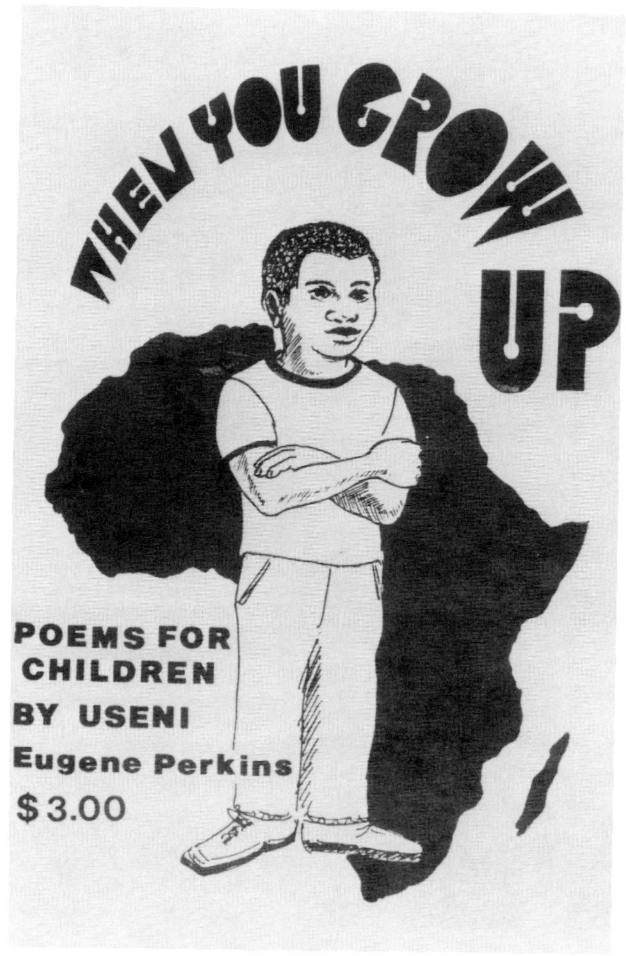

Front cover for the 1982 book in which Perkins presents poems about black role models, children's games, and African heritage

The title poem of Perkins's most recent volume of poetry, *Midnight Blues in the Afternoon and Other Poems* (1984), describes an old woman in a rocking chair "humming the legends/of jelly roll morton," vaguely aware of the rich inheritance of black music. As in some of the poems in his earlier volumes, Perkins hears music everywhere, but the music of

life in the urban renaissance
is an endless chorus of
shouts and screams and blares
and rapid paces of feet keeping
in time with the quick
inventions of ibm machines

Perhaps the point is that "the logic of all music/is misunderstood by most people/except those who give it form" and that if modern blacks want any music other than "ibm machines," they need to turn to the heartfelt artistry of the many black musicians whose works are celebrated, one by one, in this volume.

Perkins has said that the poetry of Langston Hughes has influenced him more than any other work; that debt is obvious in *Midnight Blues*, but the poems are, nevertheless, innovative and experimental. Perkins demonstrates, for example, virtuoso skill in his imitation of the rhythms of various styles: blues or bop, slow soul, pulsing drumbeat. A few of the poems suggest quiet, but haunting music: for example, in "Last Night Blues," the line "Last night the blues came to bed" and the erotic encounter described also recreate the speaker's mood, until the poem concludes with union, and some consolation for the speaker, as "the blues/hung her/dress/

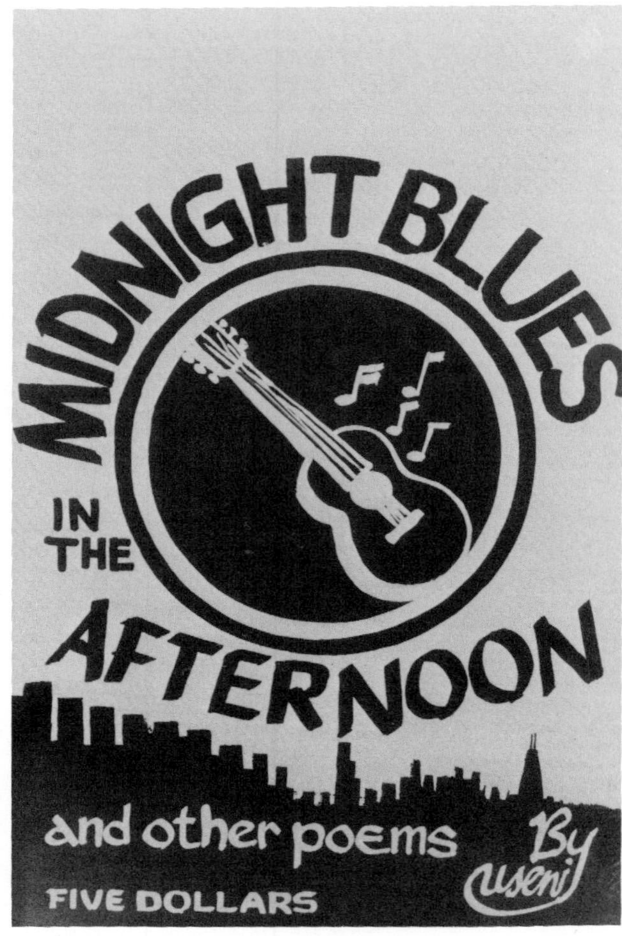

Covers for Perkins's 1984 book of poetry. Perkins is pictured here with his youngest daughter, Jamila Saran.

on a/lamppost,/as night/encroached/upon her/privacy." Among poems celebrating individual musicians, "Lady Day" captures the spirit of Billie Holiday:

>   her voice
> became the
> essence of
> our existence
>   soft
>   deep
> the transmitter
> of our most
> basic life style
>   not always
> what we wanted
> but what life gave us

The range of moods in *Midnight Blues* is extraordinary, from the quiet praise of Nina Simone to the strident "Tribute to Rahsaan Kirk." The poems shift in time from the early blues singers to young trumpeter Wynton Marsalis, "who plays Monk and Mozart/with a deftly touch/that shakes memories." In all these diverse poems one major theme keeps being reinforced: the music of black America is one of many proud heritages, to be nourished and protected from dilution, and to be used as a source of joy and reinforcement. Tonally, thematically, and stylistically, this volume is Perkins's best poetry to date.

Critical recognition of Perkins as a playwright has been primarily local, and the plays are not available in published form, but many of them were given warm reception by Chicago audiences and reviewers. "The mission of Black drama," Perkins said in the Chicago *Courier* in 1972, "is to politicize the Black community and raise the consciousness of Black people to better cope with their oppression, and, in addition, create a means for liberation." One way of effecting this liberation, he explained in an essay in *Black Books Bulletin* in 1972, is for the black playwright to see himself as an "image maker"—not "creating new stereotypes," such as "the super nigger," the "puritanical revolutionary," the "oratorical militant," or the "ghetto prince," but instead consciously developing "his characters so that during some place in their lives they offer us something which is positive and directed toward raising our level of consciousness."

One of Perkins's plays, *The Image Makers*, staged by the Chicago Kuumba Theatrical Workshop in 1975, is an attack precisely on the stereotypical images reinforced by black exploitation films of the *Super Fly* and *Shaft* sort. John Lanahan, in the *Reader*, praised the play for using "satiric form to attack the general commercialization and McDonaldization of blacks in the U.S.," but added that the play has "more to it than a message" by demonstrating "a basic faith in humanity in its refusal to accept the Hollywood definitions of a people." Another, more somber play, *Professor J. B.*, staged in 1976 by Chicago's "X-Bag" experimental players, deals with the tragedy of a community leader whose political ambitions are threatened by his son's political activism; the play ends tragically, but reinforces the son's espousal of Pan-Africanism. One review, by Ellis Cose, faulted the play's acting but praised its power and brilliance. Perkins's most recent plays have been biographical: one about the founder of Chicago, Jean Baptiste Point du Sable; and one, *Pride of Race* (produced in 1984), about W. E. B. Du Bois. Perkins is currently writing a play about Paul Robeson.

Widely respected in the Chicago area, and recognized chiefly in the Midwest, Perkins has not had a wide national audience for his poetry. His plays have often been performed and praised but not published. He has been more active as a playwright over the last five years, primarily because the drama offers him a more readily available forum than poetry does. Nevertheless, his first love is poetry, the language of which, he says, is basic to other types of writing; the form of which, he believes, is the most difficult. He sees himself still as a developing poet.

Considering the dignity and beauty of poems like those in *Midnight Blues in the Afternoon*, Perkins's stature as an important poetic voice should increase as his work becomes better known. The faults of his earlier poetry, an occasional awkward phrase or failed image, are largely absent from his later work, which possesses discipline and variety and reflects Perkins's sense of caring.

Reference:

James V. Hatch and Omanu Abdullah, eds., *Black Playwrights, 1823-1977* (New York: R. R. Bowker, 1977).

Sterling D. Plumpp

(30 January 1940-)

James Cunningham
Daytona Beach Community College

BOOKS: *Portable Soul* (Chicago: Third World Press, 1969);

Half Black, Half Blacker (Chicago: Third World Press, 1970);

Black Rituals (Chicago: Third World Press, 1972);

Steps to Break the Circle (Chicago: Third World Press, 1974);

Clinton (Detroit: Broadside Press, 1976);

The Mojo Hands Call, I Must Go (New York: Thunder's Mouth Press, 1982).

OTHER: "Black Angel Child," in *To Gwen With Love*, edited by Patricia L. Brown, Don L. Lee, and Francis Ward (Chicago: Johnson, 1971);

Joyce Jones, Mary McTaggart, and Maria Mootry, eds., *The Otherwise Room*, includes poems by Plumpp (Carbondale: The Poetry Factory Press, 1981);

Somehow We Survive: An Anthology of South African Writing, edited by Plumpp (New York: Thunder's Mouth Press, 1982).

PERIODICAL PUBLICATIONS:

POETRY

"Metamorphosis (for Bro Yakie)," *Black World*, 20 (June 1971): 17;

courtesy of the author

"A Poem for Poets," *Black World,* 20 (September 1971): 72;

"Miss Jane (for Cicely Tyson)," *Black World,* 23 (September 1974): 65;

"Seasons (for Keorapetse, Hoyt & Ayi Kwei)," *Black World,* 24 (March 1975): 45-48;

"Decade (for Dudley Randall)," *Black World,* 25, no. 3 (Jan. 1976): 82-83;

"Fractured Dreams," *Another Chicago Magazine,* 3 (1978): 53-62;

"The Mojo Hands Call/I Must Go," *Another Chicago Magazine,* no. 4 (1979): 57-69;

"Time," *Black American Literature Forum,* 14 (Winter 1980): 172;

"In Remembrance of Fire (for Hoyt W. Fuller)," *Black American Literature Forum,* 15 (Summer 1981): 47;

"Split Skirt Blues," "The Coda's Last Breath," "Three Mile Island," *Another Chicago Magazine,* no. 7 (1982): 39-43;

"Quilomban," *AFRODIASPORA,* 1 (May-September 1983): 13-14.

FICTION

"Mighty Long Time," *Black Scholar,* 12 (July/August 1981): 47-51.

NONFICTION

"A Requiem For a Blindfolded Statue," *Black Books Bulletin* (Fall 1971): 16-17;

"Blueprint for Developing Young People's Workshops," *Black Books Bulletin* (Spring-Summer 1972): 38-40;

"Sweetblood Call: The Blues Purity of Louisiana Red," *Black World,* 24 (September 1975): 17, 53.

The profoundly introspective and retrospective poetry of Chicago writer Sterling D. Plumpp represents an important development in post-black arts writing: a return to earlier notions of literary blackness. Thus it is to writers like W. E. B. Du Bois, Richard Wright, Ralph Ellison, and James Baldwin that one must look for major sources of influence.

Plumpp's work is remarkably free of the restrictions imposed by the black aesthetic movement on such matters as subject matter, diction, and aesthetic stance. In his poetry, for instance, and in his limited forays into fiction, the Southern rural experience is on an equal footing with that of the urban Midwest. Although the swiftness of his extraordinary phrasing owes much to the example of the jazz musician, the blues and the spiritual are probably more central to his work—especially as sources of situation, character delineation, tone, and diction. Indeed, the range and complexity of statement, so characteristic of his poetry, can be viewed as significant correctives to the arbitrary biases of the black arts writer of the 1960s and early 1970s.

Above all, much of Plumpp's uniqueness stems from the uses to which he has put James Baldwin's influence. His "Baldwinism" can be seen in his pursuit of writing as essentially an exploration of his own past. It can be seen equally in Plumpp's dedication to art as a medium of expression with its own exacting demands to be taken seriously.

That synonyms for words like "legacy" and "heritage" reverberate throughout Plumpp's poetry is an index to how thoroughly he has come to view his art as an instrument for excavating his past. And what he constantly returns to in his work is indicated by an expression which he frequently applies to himself—a "displaced peasant." In fact, it was his decision to recover his origins as a tenant farmer—at the height of a crisis he experienced in the army during his early twenties—that ultimately set him on the course to becoming a writer.

Plumpp was born on 30 January 1940 to Cyrus Hampton and Mary Emmanuel Plumpp. His upbringing as a member of a sharecropper's household in the Clinton, Mississippi, of the 1940s and early 1950s is reflected throughout his work, but nowhere more compellingly than in the tough, spir-

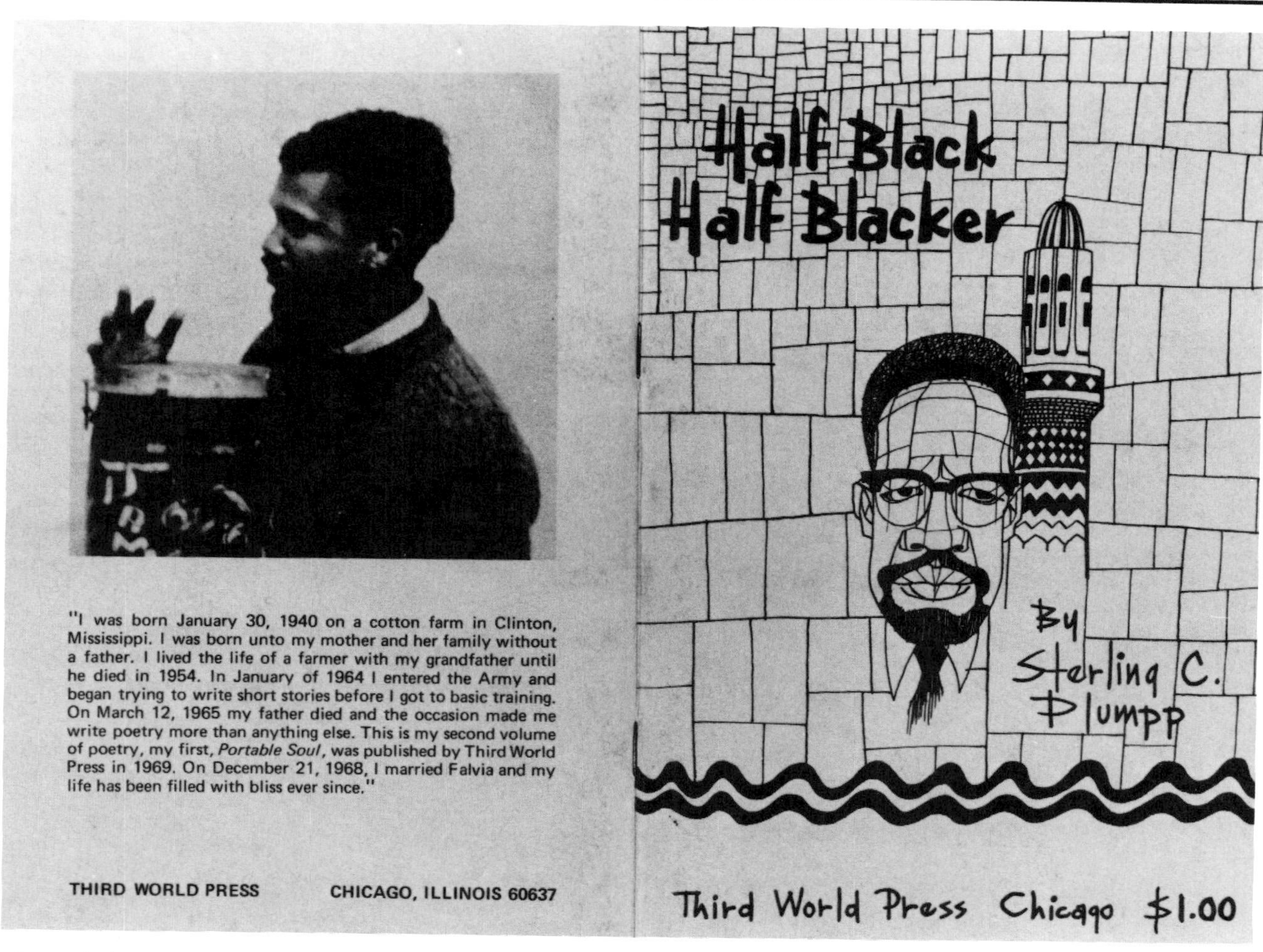

"I was born January 30, 1940 on a cotton farm in Clinton, Mississippi. I was born unto my mother and her family without a father. I lived the life of a farmer with my grandfather until he died in 1954. In January of 1964 I entered the Army and began trying to write short stories before I got to basic training. On March 12, 1965 my father died and the occasion made me write poetry more than anything else. This is my second volume of poetry, my first, *Portable Soul*, was published by Third World Press in 1969. On December 21, 1968, I married Falvia and my life has been filled with bliss ever since."
THIRD WORLD PRESS
CHICAGO, ILLINOIS 60637
Half Black Half Blacker
By Sterling C. Plumpp
Third World Press Chicago $1.00

Covers for Plumpp's 1970 poetry volume which frequently employs unceremonious black vernacular. Yet, "this is the same brother," Haki Madhubuti (Don L. Lee) says in the introduction, "that can take Freud, Jung, or Carl Rogers and interpret them in a black perspective."

itually serene, and seasoned figures of old men modeled on the grandfather who raised him. His move to Jackson in 1956, following the death of his grandfather, began the disastrously ambivalent process of flight and rupture from the folk and church-centered black culture he had confused with the oppressive tenant system. He reacted to the black powerlessness which that system institutionalized by converting to the Catholic church. In the church schools, however, he experienced intense pressure to compete with a large body of aggressive middle-class students. In fact, members of his seventh grade class later rose to prominence as Mississippi's first black post-Reconstruction judges and state legislators. Plumpp, the former sharecropper, felt especially challenged to strive for distinction. In his book on black psychology, *Black Rituals* (1972), he says somewhat jokingly of this period: "In High School I became an honor student because the Black Bourgeoisie had the money and popularity and I couldn't let them have everything."

The further the poet moved away from the emotional and intellectual moorings of his Clinton years, the more disoriented and isolated he felt. His college years at St. Benedict's College (now Benedictine College) in Atchinson, Kansas, from 1960 to 1962; his years as a clerk in Chicago's Main Post Office, from 1962 to 1964, and from 1966 to 1969; and the years he served as a draftee at the Aberdeen Proving Ground in Maryland from 1964 to 1966 were a series of brutal lessons in how institutions work to turn people, Plumpp felt, into robots and zombies. Consequently, the varieties of tyranny that menaced Plumpp taught him what rare and endangered species individual voices and individual points of view truly are. And it was especially due to his army experiences that he made his important gesture in recovering his voice and vision through

Sterling Plumpp (photograph by Nancy Ortenberg)

the attempt to write. When he returned to civilian life, the fledgling writer had hundreds of poems to testify to the seriousness of his effort.

Pursuing both undergraduate and graduate studies at Roosevelt University in Chicago, Plumpp received his Bachelor of Arts in psychology in 1968. His studies laid the groundwork for his analysis of Afro-American cultural behavior in his only book-length prose work, *Black Rituals,* published four years later. In 1969, he left the post office and worked as a counselor at Chicago's North Park College. In 1971, he became an instructor at the University of Illinois, Chicago Circle, in its Black Studies program. He is currently an associate professor there. In the 1970s, he became increasingly interested in editorial work. For instance, in association with poet and educator Haki R. Madhubuti (Don L. Lee), Plumpp served as an editor for the Institute of Positive Education. He was especially instrumental in helping to launch the widely read *Black Books Bulletin* for the Institute. At the same time, his work was beginning to appear regularly in *Black World,* edited by Hoyt Fuller—one of the most important and energetic exponents of black aesthetics throughout the 1960s and 1970s.

Sterling Plumpp's first book-length published work of poetry, *Portable Soul* (1969), is more of an announcement of his intentions than of his arrival as a poet. The individual pieces are clearly products of a divided mind and spirit; and even the more promising of these are often plagued by Plumpp's then uncertain sense of form. Yet, however dimly, some of his basic strengths are foreshadowed in this initial work: simplicity of structure and freedom of diction, graphic and evocative imagery.

The poems of *Portable Soul* are a procession of psychological states which range from anguish to rejoicing, and the roles of the poet range from that of denouncer to celebrant. What is lamented and deplored are loss, outrage, rupture, and death, and what is admired and honored are the efforts to reclaim the fallen and to rejuvenate the spiritually defeated and dead. In fact, there is much of the familiar diction and unsettling concerns of the revivalist minister.

There are more memorable titles, phrases, passages, and stanzas in this book than there are memorable poems, largely because Plumpp's powers of phrasing were more mature at this stage than his structural control of the whole poem. His formidable descriptions are all but hidden under abstract diction, hurried elliptical expressions bordering on the telegraphic, and a denseness of words that suggests a kind of rambling, verbal clutter. Nonetheless, *Portable Soul* contains some fine work, for example, "I'll Find Our Way" and "You Made Them Walk," which, although typical black arts tribute poems honoring Amiri Baraka (LeRoi Jones) and the late Elijah Muhammad as intellectual and spiritual rebuilders of the black community, also exhibit the elegant, tapering structure characteristic of the poet's mature work. Moreover, the mild tension between the private and the public view suggested by the title "I'll Find Our Way" augurs Plumpp's ultimate mastery of the lyric and epic blend of voice associated with the blues and the spirituals. "Sugar Woman" represents one of Plumpp's few attempts to work with private memory in this volume. The two most accomplished pieces in *Portable Soul* signal what will be the poet's progressive mastery of format and voice. "Sez My Mind" is a short, tapering poem, composed of a single sentence that recalls Madhubuti's "The New Integrationist" in succinctness and ironic thrust. The poem's combative speaker speeds to stunning battle with himself in a psychological posture that will become typical of Plumpp's work. The poet's descriptive and evocative powers of portraiture are given their only distinctive and full-scale play in "Traveling." Its brilliance does not appear again until the long pieces, *Steps to Break the Circle* (1974) and *Clinton* (1976). What emerges from "Traveling," written in the second person, is the experience-loaded figure of the black Southern refugee. The figure seems to be a woman who has witnessed and fled from the most harrowing loss and death, only to be exposed, in the end, to the impersonal menace of the North where she is closed up, far from the fields she has known, in vaults that shut out the light and blueness of the sky. The life of rupture and disorientation mirrored here is one of the author's major recurrent themes, which Plumpp handles in different works in profoundly distinct manners in terms of structure, length, and voice.

Sterling Plumpp's second book, *Half Black, Half Blacker,* is separated from the first by only one year, but it is quite a triumph on several levels. Published in 1970 and dedicated to the poet's wife, its advances over the earlier book include a greater concentration of focus and a wealth of ironically titled, vividly worded poems and, more important, lively, witty personae to deliver their thematic burdens. His tributes to prominent blacks are at once more indirect and more dramatic than before. "Flight" presents Richard Wright's most famous character, Bigger Thomas, as a larger-than-life folk figure on the order of John the Conqueror or Staggerlee. In "The Living Truth," the scholar and writer W. E. B. Du Bois is depicted as a recruiter who goes about arming refugees and restoring fallen dreamers to their former historical stature. The refrain from this poem reveals the poet to be a great phrasemaker: "black history/is a banned epic." Plumpp's effort to show in endless ways how and

Somehow We Survive

An Anthology of South African Writing

edited by Sterling Plumpp

illustrations by Dumile Feni

Thunder's Mouth Press • New York • Chicago

Frontispiece and title page for Plumpp's 1982 anthology of South African poetry, "Dedicated to/Nelson Mandela/confined to imprisonment on/Robben Island for his/activities against Apartheid."

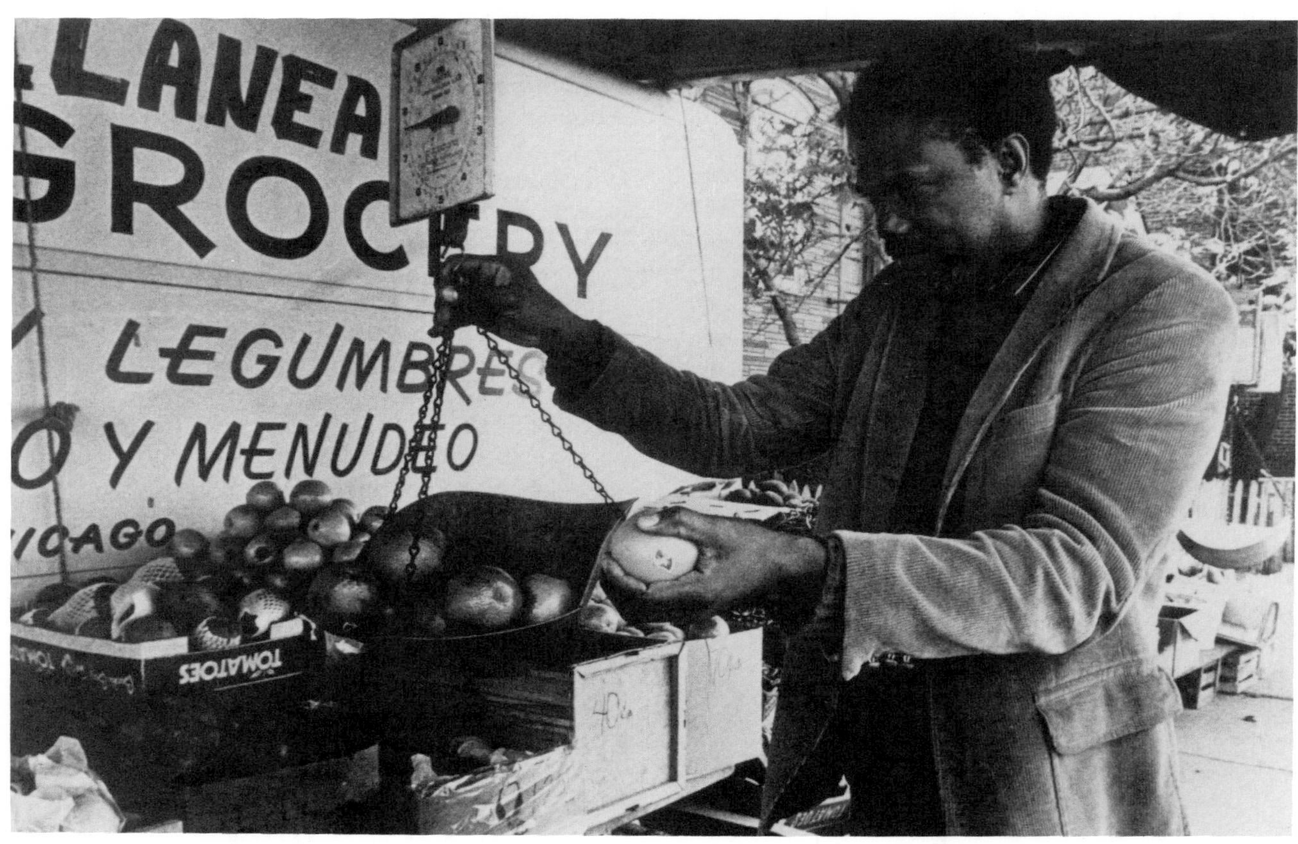

Sterling Plumpp (photograph by Nancy Ortenberg)

why this is so accounts for much of what makes his work so unique and memorable.

Humor is a significant part of Plumpp's appeal. The poet as soldier—a staple of black arts writing—is poked fun at by the collective voice of black women in "From Manless Sisters to Big Bad Black Rappers": "whom can we follow?/when u soldiers/are firing/only blank verses?" The humor here is checked, however, by the urgent refrain which asks for someone to follow. This poem is representative of Plumpp's work, for abandoned black women, long-awaited leaders, and black manhood are givens in his poetry.

Sharp characterization, narrative format, and verbal economy make "Last Ride" one of the most trenchant and masterful of the poet's short pieces, and one of the earliest and most formidable demonstrations of his satiric power. The Vietnam veteran returns "to where his killings/were paid for," and he is shot in the head for coming "back alive." "I See the Blues" retains the swift, cinematic dissection of the psychological plight of the transplanted Southern refugee thwarted in his or her bid for life in a Chicago seen fitfully from the perspective of frosted windows and el trains. The three main elements of Plumpp's poetic imagination are here fully at work: a graphic landscape that shifts from past to present, the complicated and lively victims who people it, and a passionate, ironic observer-commentator with the gifts of swift narration and musical phrasing. With this second book then, Plumpp staked out much of his literary territory and technical resources, and he was ready to embark on his major work.

His next significant work, and one of the most important for understanding his thought, is not a book of poetry, but a prose work. In fact, he is writing as a social psychologist. While partly autobiographical, *Black Rituals* is an analysis of the historical and psychological patterns of thought and behavior which explain why the oppressed state of the black community persists. In this 1972 work, the author attempts to present what he calls the Afro-American's developmental history. Here he can be seen laying the foundation for the long narrative poem *Steps to Break the Circle* (1974), which attempts to translate the developmental history described in *Black Rituals* by reducing it to lively and conflicting patterns of advice offered to a young, naive refugee from Mississippi who sets out in the mid-1960s for Chicago in search of freedom and prosperity. Going back and forth between Chicago and his home town in the deep South, he finds himself trapped in a circular journey. But the trip is not altogether a fool's errand, for he eventually comes to view liberation as a struggle for self-discovery and self-assertion.

Steps to Break the Circle singles out some of the major philosophical and psychological stances examined in *Black Rituals*. For instance, there is the grandfather figure who embodies the personal wisdom of the survivor whose toughness has withstood long and repeated exposure to the most brutal expressions of racism. There is also the Reverend who initially embodies conventional religion, only to emerge at the end of the poem as a spokesman for the most unorthodox notions of spiritual and intellectual independence. An old woman carries the predictable banner of the pastoral ideal of returning to the ancestral soil of the South. There are young people to argue for both a street-wise brand of defeatism and eager, hedonistic expediency. Tossed about by the conflicting counsels of these fellow travelers, Plumpp's naive and picaresque hero is made to reflect the larger historical dilemma of black society.

Most significantly, behind all these figures is the clear, analytical voice of the author-commentator whose overview operates as the book's major metaphor. His perspective underscores, by its very presence, the importance of mastering a broad spectrum of knowledge if one is to gain a clear sense of the historical alternatives Afro-American leaders have had at their disposal. Not surprisingly, the juggling of different perspectives on how the problem of oppression is to be solved leaves the hero in the same position with which *Black Rituals* concluded. After the clamor of rival programs and formulas for liberation is brought under control by the critical effort to weigh and assess their individual merits and limitations, Plumpp leaves us with the *individual* thinker whose first duty is to come to terms with himself.

An account of a person actually coming to terms with himself through a reconstruction of his own developmental history is precisely what Plumpp offers in his fourth book of poetry, *Clinton*. Originally, *Clinton* appeared in excerpt in the winter 1974 issue of *Savage* magazine, and Plumpp received the Illinois Arts Council Literary Award for it in 1975. Published in its entirety in 1976, this long poem resembles *Steps* in its cinematic tech-

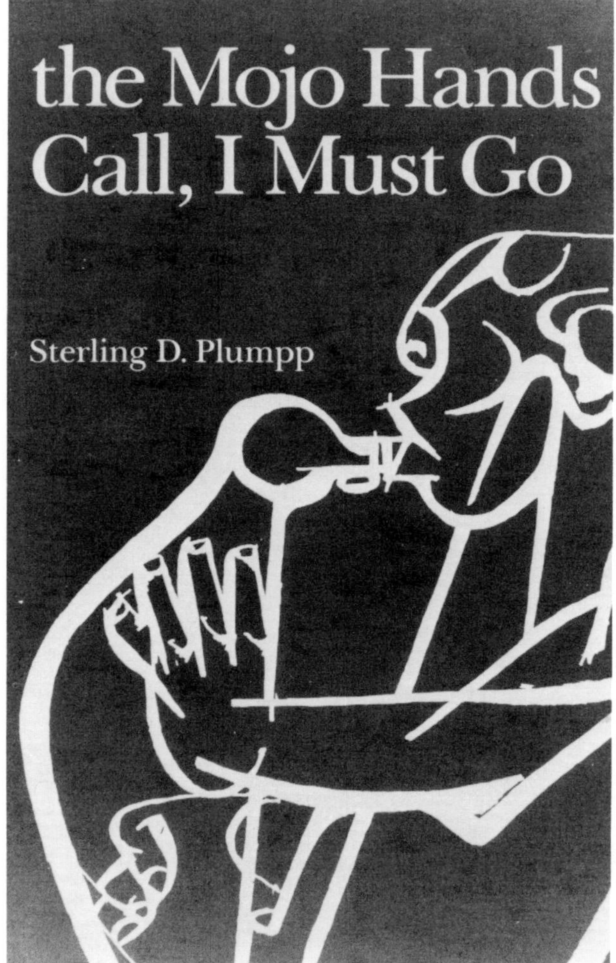

Front cover for the poet's 1982 collection. Hugh Masakela says "Plumpp rips open the city's wounds with horns, blues, riffs, worksongs, gospel hollers, doo-wops, shuffles, and splits. A lyrical and deeply poetic outcry."

nique, lyrical and panoramic sweep, and in its psychological probing, but its structure is strictly chronological since it is concerned with tracing the precise steps by which the author eventually arrived at his basic outlook as a black artist. Nor are the people, places, or events at the center of the poem's recollections meant to function within the symbolic framework of a circular journey. Moreover, since *Clinton* is not meant to be taken strictly as a fable, as was the previous work, Plumpp is free to exploit to the fullest his flair for descriptive and evocative detail and ambiguous statement. The result of this expressive prowess is a network of shifting moods and emphases. What never changes is the pervasive sense of menace in the environments in which the

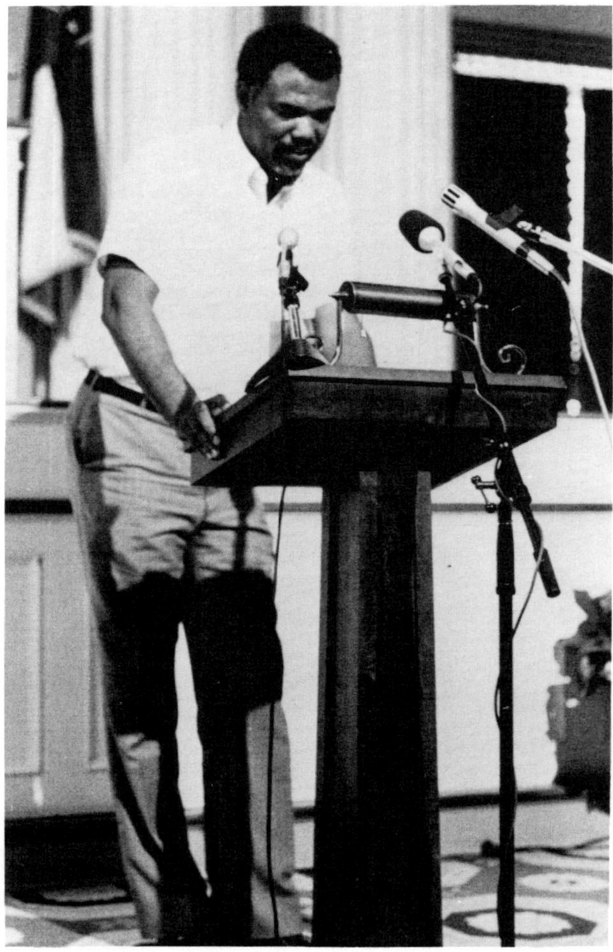

Plumpp, reading from his work on 27 April 1985 at Mississippi Writers Day in Jackson

picaresque protagonist chances to be.

As readers follow the poet from one period, from one part of the country, from one area of experience to another, they witness a great deal of psychological maiming. With the exception of the black Southern church, the chief violators are seen to be the major institutions in the hero's life: the tenant farming system, the educational system, the federal government in the civilian and military guises of post office employer and army trainer. Their main violence against the protagonist is their concerted effort to have him trade in his own vision for theirs. The spectres who inhabit the nightmarish *Clinton,* and other of Plumpp's works, are nothing more than the self-serving versions of reality offered by society, in general, and they are a significant part of the compulsion that has driven the autobiographical protagonist to become a writer out of self-defense. For the business of becoming a writer, as sketched here, and its appeal for the besieged hero, are equivalent to achieving two forms of mastery: a personal point of view and the skill to express and preserve this vision through the medium of words.

The remainder of the 1970s after *Clinton* was marked by steady gains for Plumpp in terms of both visibility and professional stature. Reflecting the increased clarity and technical confidence he gained from writing *Steps* and *Clinton,* he made the conscious decision not to restrict the publishing of his individual poems to *Black World.* His work began to surface in a variety of publications such as *Black Scholar, Obsidian, Callaloo,* and *Another Chicago Magazine.*

The 1980s seem to promise more of the same for Sterling Plumpp: greatly enhanced professional visibility and stature. In 1981, for example, the poet won an Illinois Art Council award for his long poem "The Mojo Hands Call/I Must Go." It first appeared in 1979 in *Another Chicago Magazine (ACM).* "Mojo" also received the 1983 Carl Sandburg Literary Award for Poetry. The 1982 collection of Plumpp's major long poems, *The Mojo Hands Call, I Must Go,* is his most comprehensive volume. Of its seven selections, "Clinton" and "Steps to Break the Circle" appeared earlier as book-length poems. "Sugar Woman," a short lyric, derives from Plumpp's first volume, *Portable Soul.* The strongly anticolonialist "Zimbabwe" is a powerful evocation of the history of anguish and fortitude of black mothers. "I Hear the Shuffle of the People's Feet" makes twin figures of the African exile and the itinerant blues singer. By blending the voices and the sensibilities of these two archetypical witnesses, Plumpp provides complexity and continuity of perspective for the poem's historical survey of the black experience in America.

"Fractured Dreams" dramatizes the effort of a self-doubting and self-denouncing protagonist to keep faith with that reservoir of collective identity best articulated by the blues tradition. In short, the work expresses the disjointed, unsettling testimony of a visionary whose narcissistic self-scrutiny has paralyzed him by reinforcing his sense of powerlessness. In contrast to the fractured dreamer's spiritual dislocation, the protagonist of "The Mojo Hands Call/I Must Go" embodies apocalyptic salvation. Although the confessional tone of the self-indicting champion is common to both poems, the Mojo speaker's testifying includes hopeful prophetic revelations based on a strong, compassionate sense of history. He is, therefore, the embodiment of Sterling Plumpp's attempts to explore the complicated psychology of the struggling black liberator. The poet has edited *Somehow We Survive,* an anthology of South African writing published by Thunder's Mouth Press (1982), the same press that publishes *ACM.*

Plumpp's more recent work for the magazine—"Split Skirt Blues," "The Coda's Last Breath," and "Three Mile Island"—indicate respectively a surrealistic turn of mind, great originality in the handling of the Afro-American music poem, and an intensified preoccupation with improving the quality of life in America, especially for families. Of equal importance for the poet's creative and editorial work is *Black American Literature Forum (BALF),* for which he became one of its poetry editors in 1982. Plumpp's most ambitious recent efforts, in *ACM* and *BALF,* have revealed not only a writer at the height of his current powers of illumination and eloquence but one who is intent on stretching himself to the utmost as an artist. Plumpp is currently working on a novel that is to focus on a blues singer. This is no great surprise, for it was the recordings of singers like Ray Charles and Odetta that saved Plumpp's sanity when, as a young man in college, the formal education he was trying to pursue worked to alienate him from the most vital and accessible sources of himself—his black Southern cultural roots.

The question of roots is a reminder of how important a place reconciling differences in point of view occupies in the poet's work as a whole. The resourcefulness with which he has exploited differences in how the rural Southerner looks at the world and how the urban Midwesterner looks at the world has provided a rich source of both verbal and psychological tension for his art. But one of Plumpp's most original, and often neglected, contributions as a writer lies in his emphasis on the very nature and importance of perspectives themselves—how they are acquired and what their limitations and strong points are. Much of the symbolic force of the journeys undertaken by his vivid and restless travelers derives from their roles as witnesses bearing testimony through stories. Their testimony is as important as their mobility. Finally, the self-scrutiny of Sterling Plumpp simply reinforces his originality by serving as a point of departure for asking hard questions of himself and of others in order to see the world more clearly.

Reference:

Eugene B. Redmond, *Drumvoices: The Mission of Afro-American Poetry, A Critical History* (Garden City: Anchor/Doubleday, 1976).

Dudley Randall

(14 January 1914-)

R. Baxter Miller

University of Tennessee

BOOKS: *Poem Counterpoem,* by Randall and Margaret Danner (Detroit: Broadside Press, 1966);

Cities Burning (Detroit: Broadside Press, 1968);

Love You (London: Paul Breman, 1970);

More to Remember: Poems of Four Decades (Chicago: Third World Press, 1971);

After the Killing (Chicago: Third World Press, 1973);

Broadside Memories: Poets I Have Known (Detroit: Broadside Press, 1975);

A Litany of Friends: New and Selected Poems (Detroit: Lotus Press, 1981).

OTHER: *For Malcolm: Poems on the Life and the Death of Malcolm X,* edited by Randall and Margaret G. Burroughs (Detroit: Broadside Press, 1967);

Black Poetry: A Supplement to Anthologies Which Exclude Black Poets, edited by Randall (Detroit: Broadside Press, 1969);

Black Poets, edited by Randall (New York: Bantam, 1971);

"The Black Aesthetic in the Thirties, Forties and Fifties," *The Black Aesthetic,* edited by Addison Gayle, Jr. (Garden City: Doubleday, 1971).

PERIODICAL PUBLICATIONS:

POETRY

"To An Old Man," *Obsidian*, 6, nos. 1, 2 (1980): 38;

"Poems," *Black American Literature Forum*, 17 (Winter 1983): 168-170.

NONFICTION

"White Poet, Black Critic," *Negro Digest*, 14 (February 1965): 46-48;

"Ubi Sunt and Hic Sum," *Negro Digest*, 14 (September 1965): 73-76;

"A Poet is Not a Jukebox," *Obsidian*, 6, nos. 1, 2 (1980): 172-181.

Dudley Randall (photograph © 1984 by Layle Silbert)

Writer, librarian, and publisher, Dudley Randall has made significant contributions to twentieth-century American literature. A child during the Harlem Renaissance of the 1920s, he became a poet of the next generation, and later, he helped to pioneer a third poetic era during the 1960s. Exploring racial and historical themes, introspective and self-critical, his work combines ideas and forms from Western traditional poetry as well as from the Harlem Renaissance movement. Often incisive humor and cryptic satire inform his work. Beyond Randall's contributions as a poet, his roles as editor and publisher have proven invaluable to the Afro-American community. Since he founded the major black enterprise Broadside Press in 1965, Randall has published numerous important works of black writers who have helped to shape the contemporary American literary scene.

Dudley Felker Randall was born in Washington, D.C., on 14 January 1914, to Arthur George Clyde and Ada Viola Bradley Randall. He showed an early interest in poetry; when he was four he composed lyrics for "Maryland, My Maryland," a song played at a band concert in Towson, a suburb of Baltimore. At thirteen he won the one dollar first prize for a sonnet he submitted to the poet's page of the *Detroit Free Press*. His father encouraged Randall's intellectual curiosity and took him to hear lectures by black intellectuals such as James Weldon Johnson and W. E. B. Du Bois.

Later, Randall learned about other writers, such as the postbellum black poet Paul Laurence Dunbar, as well as the Harlem Renaissance group; immediately he liked the work of Countee Cullen and Jean Toomer. These early influences helped to mold Randall's own later work.

Randall worked in the foundry of the Ford Motor Company from 1932 to 1937. From 1943 to 1946 he served in the United States Army signal corps in the South Pacific. In 1949 he earned a bachelor's degree in English at Wayne State University. He also completed all requirements for a master's degree in the humanities, except for his thesis, a translation of Chopin's music into words. In Randall's first year of study at Wayne State, he won the Tompkins Award for fiction (he won a second one for poetry in 1966, after he founded Broadside). In 1951 he earned a master's degree in Library Science from the University of Michigan. Randall worked at the United States Post Office, where he stayed until 1951 when he became a librarian at Lincoln University (1951 to 1954). He moved to Morgan State College (now Morgan State University) as a librarian from 1954 to 1956, and then to the Wayne County Federated Library System from 1956 to 1969. From the 1960s through the 1970s, as a collaborator and mentor during the black arts movement, he helped to deepen the technical breadth and authenticity of American black poetry.

In 1962 Randall became interested in Boone House, a black cultural center which had been founded by Margaret Danner in Detroit. Every Sunday Randall and Danner would read their own work to audiences at Boone House. Over the years the two authors collected a group of poems which became the first major publication of Broadside Press, *Poem Counterpoem* (1966).

Perhaps the first of its kind, the volume contains ten poems each by Danner and Randall. The poems are alternated to form a kind of double commentary on the subjects they address in common. Replete with allusions to social and intellectual history, the verses stress nurture and growth. In "The Ballad of Birmingham" Randall establishes racial progress as a kind of blossoming, as he recounts the incident, based on a historical event of the bombing in 1963 of Martin Luther King, Jr.'s church by white terrorists. Eight quatrains portray one girl's life and death. (Four girls actually died in the real bombing.) When the daughter in the poem asks permission to attend a civil rights rally, the loving and fearful mother refuses to let her go. Allowed to go to church instead, the daughter dies anyway. Thus, there is no sanctuary in an evil world, Randall seems to say, and one may face horror in the street as well as in the church. After folk singer Jerry Moore read the poem in a newspaper, he set it to music, and Randall granted him permission to publish the tune with the lyrics.

The next of Randall's poems in *Poem Counterpoem* is "Memorial Wreath," a lyric of celebration structured on a series of analogues that address the processes of resurrection, love and blossoming, ancestry, suffering, and sacrifice. Likening the blues to racial continuity, the inseparability of pain, beauty, and art, and to the irony of racial experience, the speaker addresses his spiritual ancestors through images that come from the American nineteenth century. More dramatically conceived, the frequently anthologized ballad "Booker T. and W. E. B." presents one voice's call and another's response. In alternating stanzas, the two black leaders express opposite views. While Washington (who lived from 1856 to 1915) favors agriculture and domestic service, Du Bois (1868 to 1963) emphasizes the human quest to learn in an atmosphere of freedom. Following Washington's focus upon attaining property while keeping silent about abrogated civil rights, Du Bois proposes dignity and justice. Randall, who tries to present each man realistically, seems to favor Du Bois, to whom the poet intentionally gives the last word. Another piece in *Poem Counterpoem* is a work in free verse, "For Margaret Danner / In establishing Boone House." It fuses quest and rebirth into benediction: "May your crocuses rise up through winter snow." And the speaker in "Belle Isle," the last lyric, addresses the poet's calling, "the inner principle . . . endowing/ the world and time . . . joy and delight, for ever." Randall's central position in the black artistic and literary community was quickly becoming established as his network of contacts burgeoned.

At Boone House, where Randall attended art exhibits, jazz sessions, and monthly readings of poetry, he befriended poets Betty Ford, Harold Lawrence, and Naomi Long Madgett, as well as Edward Simpkins and James Thompson, whom he heard read from such works as the then-new anthology *Beyond the Blues* (1962) and from a special issue of *Negro History Bulletin* (October 1962). Later, in 1966, he met the celebrated poet Gwendolyn Brooks. When a reading club in Detroit invited her to read at Oakland University, he had asked about the escort arrangements. Told that none existed, he requested that several English teachers meet her at the train station. When he himself finally greeted her after the reading, she was surprised. From what she had read of him in book reviews in *Negro Digest*, she had thought him fierce, but he had proved pleasantly mild. "I thought you were terrible, but you're all right." While the two poets took snapshots together, she threw her arms happily around her new friend's shoulders. Asked later to submit a poem for the new Broadside series, Brooks granted permission to republish "We Real Cool." Randall would later bring out her pamphlets *Riot* (1969), *Family Pictures* (1971), and *Aloneness* (1971). At first he declined to issue her autobiography, *Report from Part One* (1972), because he believed that Harper and Row, her original publisher, could better promote the volume. When Brooks disagreed, he finally accepted the privilege. Toni Cade Bambara responded enthusiastically to the edition on the first page of the *New York Times Book Review*.

During the first writer's conference at Fisk University, Randall strengthened the professional associations that would insure his publishing the verses of established poets Robert Hayden, Melvin B. Tolson, and Margaret Walker in the Broadside series. After having secured Brooks's permission to use the colloquial "We Real Cool," he had published the first group of Broadsides, "Poems of the Negro Revolt." The collection was distinguished. Though Randall had intended at first to issue famous poems for popular dissemination, a reviewer in *Small Press* suggested he might serve contemporary writing better by printing unpublished verse.

At the Fisk conference, Randall had met Margaret Burroughs, the founder and director of the DuSable Museum of African-American History in Chicago. He had first seen Burroughs with Margaret Walker sitting near the front of one of the school's dormitories. While Burroughs sketched portraits, Walker rehearsed for an afternoon reading of a piece about Malcolm X. Randall observed to them the fact that most black poets then were writing about Malcolm X. When Burroughs responded by proposing that Randall edit a collection of those works, he invited her to coedit the volume. Shortly thereafter, David Llorens promised to announce the anthology in *Negro Digest* (later *Black World*), and Randall received the first submission a few days later.

For Malcolm: Poems on the Life and the Death of Malcolm X (1967) brought together the poets Robert Hayden, Margaret Walker, and Gwendolyn Brooks with the younger writers Amiri Baraka (LeRoi Jones), Larry Neal, Sonia Sanchez, and Etheridge Knight. (Through this collaboration Randall learned about the magazines *Soulbook* and *Black Dialogue.)* At Fisk Randall had seen a slim girl with David Llorens. When he returned to Detroit, he received a letter from the young woman, Nikki Giovanni, who requested a copy of *For Malcolm* to review in the college publication edited by her. Problems with printers delayed publication of *For Malcolm* until June 1967, when Giovanni had already graduated from Fisk. She reviewed the book anyway for a Cincinnati newspaper.

During the book-signing party for contributors at Margaret Burroughs's museum, Randall met Haki Madhubuti (then Don L. Lee). Madhubuti sent Randall a copy of his *Think Black,* which he had published himself in an edition of 700 copies that had sold out in a week. A short time later, Madhubuti and Randall were reading together for a memorial program at a Chicago high school. Randall advised his new friend, "Now Don, read slowly, and pronounce each word distinctly." Because Madhubuti, who read first, earned a standing ovation, Randall humorously promised himself to read thereafter "before, not after Don." When he went to Detroit, Madhubuti usually visited Randall. Their social and professional relationships flourished. All agreements between the two poets were oral: "It was only with later poets that I had to have written contracts," Randall said. Madhubuti had refused an offer to sign with the prestigious "white" firm Random House. When Madhubuti's second book, *Black Pride* (1968), was ready for issue, the author asked Randall to introduce and print the book, which he did. In 1969 Randall brought out Madhubuti's *Don't Cry, Scream* in both paperback and cloth editions (the latter a first for Broadside, although Randall would publish later a similar edition of *For Malcolm*). Working on the volume, Randall became familiar with Sonia Sanchez, a contributor. She visited his poetry class at the University of Detroit and was faced with the happy dilemma of choosing to have her work published by Third World Press, Madhubuti's firm, or Broadside, which she finally chose. She maintained close contact with Randall; for example, when she learned that he had a heart murmur, she sent him various teas; in New York, she chauffeured him to various bookstores, chiding him all the while for smoking. When he flew to Africa in 1970, she and Nikki Giovanni went to the motel to see him off.

Randall had followed the progress of Audre Lorde's work from her first book, *The First Cities* (1966), to *Cables of Rage* (1970) published by Paul Breman. Asked to publish her third book, *From a Land Where Other People Live* (1973), he hesitated, fearing he would be overextending the capabilities of Broadside. Though he started to decline the request, Brooks intervened on Lorde's behalf. Randall relented, and the volume was nominated for a National Book Award in New York. Following the ceremonies there ("enlivened by a streaker"), he and Lorde went to meet poet Adrienne Rich backstage. As he paused at the breast-high platform and wondered how to mount it, Lorde gave him a hand. "How's that," she asked, "for a fat old lady?" A representative for Rich's publisher drove the two in a limousine to a cocktail party at the Biltmore Hotel, and Randall secretly wondered when Broadside might afford the luxury. Though Randall says in *Broadside Memories* (1975) that Lorde had promised to take him on the Staten Island ferry and to show him her house in the area, they had celebrated too late and had no time left the next morning.

Despite his extensive publishing activities Dudley Randall remained a poet in his own right. *Cities Burning* (1968) captures his zeitgeist. Here the visionary lyrics and apocalyptic revelations concern subjects such as urban riot, generational opposition, and black image-making. When he avoids clichés and hackneyed rhymes, he excels at his craft. "Roses and Revolutions," which had been written in 1948, is a prophetic lyric in free verse that addresses both the civil rights movement and the personal conscience. From a vision of total annihilation the speaker advances to the hope of a communal confirmation of life.

Two poems, "The Rite" and "Black Poet, White Critic," clarify Randall's theory of art. In two brief quatrains, "The Rite" presents the conflict between the old artist and the young one. The young writer, by virtue of his youth, is condemned to relive the human ritual of rebelling against his predecessor. In the poem, the youth literally internalizes his elder by drinking his blood and eating his heart. In a paradoxical act suggestive of transubstantiation and cannibalism, the artist who wants to be innovative can only do so by assimilating the art that has come before his own. Because rebellious youth relives the old lessons, change is necessarily incomplete. In "Black Poet, White Critic" the poet's drama becomes more racially focused as the distanced narrator humorously works through to an interrogative punch line. Advising the poet to write "safely," the critic cautions against writing about the subjects of freedom and murder. Moved by "universal themes and timeless symbols," he proposes a verbal portrait of the "white unicorn." Through quipping back ("a *white* unicorn?"), the narrator underscores the subjectivity of beauty.

Two other poems, "The Idiot" and "The Melting Pot," reveal Randall's technical range. The first blends violence with humor and psychological depth with colloquial speech to portray police brutality. Having called the speaker a black "boy," the police officer punches him in the face and drags him to the wall, where the officer searches and handcuffs him. Sufficiently angry to chastise the officer, the narrator relents because, "I didn't want to hurt his feelings,/and lose the good will/of the good white folks downtown,/who hired him." The irony is complex. Though the speaker feigns courage, the rationalization signifies his true cowardice. Why did the "good" people downtown hire the demonstrably bad policeman? Rather than see others truly, the persona chooses doubly to blind himself. Almost hopelessly naive to white hypocrisy, he misinterprets direct racism as well. Later in eight rhymed quatrains, "The Melting Pot" illustrates the irony of the American mainstream myth. The comic ballad leads to the persona's ultimate epiphany: survival comes with individuality. Thrown out of the American crucible a thousand times, the protagonist reconfirms, "I don't give a da . . ./Shove your old pot. You can like it or not,/but I'll be just what I am." Randall's poetry is shaped frequently by the writings of others. Through poems such as "A Different Image," for example, he acknowledges the influence of African and Caribbean poets on his own work.

In 1968 he brought out James Emanuel's first book of poetry, *The Treehouse and Other Poems,* and he issued Nikki Giovanni's second book, *Black Judgement.* Reprinting Margaret Danner's *Impressions of African Art Forms,* a facsimile of the 1960 original, he redistributed the only known volume devoted entirely to the subject. During 1969 he published books by poets Jon Eckels, Beatrice Murphy, Nancy Arnez, and Sonia Sanchez, as well as those by Marvin X, Keorapetse Kgositsile, and Stephany. He served as instructor at the University of Michigan in 1969 and from then until 1974 as poet-in-residence at the University of Detroit. For awhile at the University of Ghana, he studied African arts, and then he visited Togo and Dahomey. From 1970 through 1976 he completed a tenure on the advisory panel of the Michigan Council for the Arts.

In the meantime, his literary career prospered. The poems in *Love You* (1970) achieve more thematic and formal focus than did the previous poetry. He writes poems of celebration, monologues, and short visionary lyrics. His subjects range from the transitory nature of lovemaking to the discrepancy between appearance and reality; he observes the tension between the tangible and the intangible. Sometimes he employs wordplay that is reminiscent of Gertrude Stein's work. Through structured dramatic situations, he delivers personal advice and consolation. "The Profile on the Pillow," a well-crafted verse set against the race riots of the late 1960s, links the narrator's memory of the lover to the mature poet's commitment to humanity: "We may be consumed in the holocaust,/but I keep, against the ice and the fire,/the memory of your profile on the pillow." Though love is intangible, the persona holds onto it as a mental anchor in a time of insanity. The final poem of *Love You,* "Sanctuary," has a similar theme. Retreating from chaotic history, one person asks the other to "step into the circle of my arms." One must withdraw from the metaphorical whirlwind and fire.

For Dudley Randall the early 1970s meant balance and personal retreat. Written between the 1930s and the 1960s, the poems in *More to Remember* (1971) comprise his first comprehensive collection. Though the individual verses are not arranged chronologically, they are grouped to represent a particular decade of his work. While times changed, Randall's biting irony and humor developed. *Poem Counterpoem* had contained only the verses appropriately paired with Danner's, and *Cities Burning* had collected only those which treated the theme of a disintegrating era. *More to Remember* revealed Randall's range, and the new book contributed to his growing reputation. Addressing topics like kindness and cruelty, bounteous harvests, diversely classical forms, and natural beauty, Randall explored contradictions in human psychology and in the black arts movement. A thinking and skillful poet, he displays artistic breadth. Although sometimes

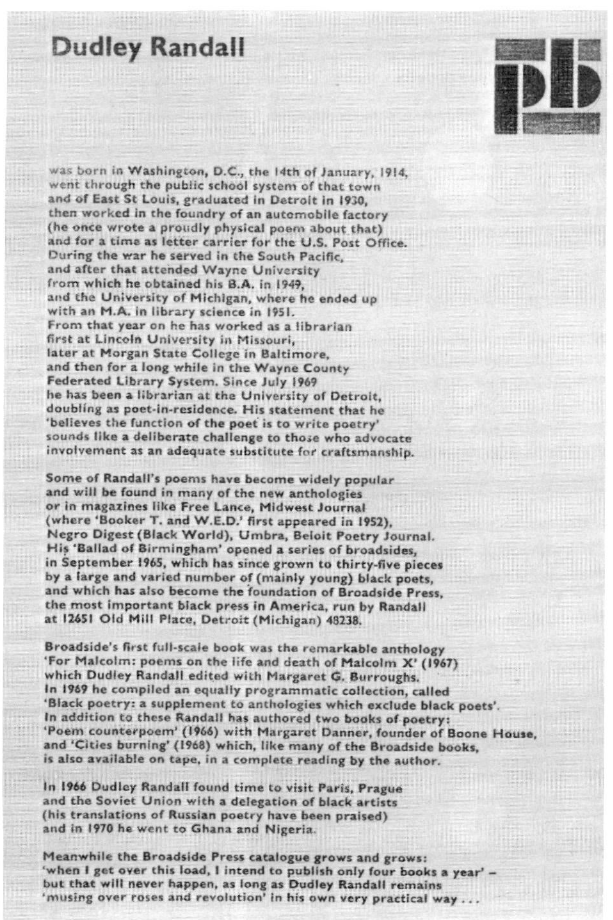

Dudley Randall

pb

was born in Washington, D.C., the 14th of January, 1914, went through the public school system of that town and of East St Louis, graduated in Detroit in 1930, then worked in the foundry of an automobile factory (he once wrote a proudly physical poem about that) and for a time as letter carrier for the U.S. Post Office. During the war he served in the South Pacific, and after that attended Wayne University from which he obtained his B.A. in 1949, and the University of Michigan, where he ended up with an M.A. in library science in 1951. From that year on he has worked as a librarian first at Lincoln University in Missouri, later at Morgan State College in Baltimore, and then for a long while in the Wayne County Federated Library System. Since July 1969 he has been a librarian at the University of Detroit, doubling as poet-in-residence. His statement that he 'believes the function of the poet is to write poetry' sounds like a deliberate challenge to those who advocate involvement as an adequate substitute for craftsmanship.

Some of Randall's poems have become widely popular and will be found in many of the new anthologies or in magazines like Free Lance, Midwest Journal (where 'Booker T. and W.E.D.' first appeared in 1952), Negro Digest (Black World), Umbra, Beloit Poetry Journal. His 'Ballad of Birmingham' opened a series of broadsides, in September 1965, which has since grown to thirty-five pieces by a large and varied number of (mainly young) black poets, and which has also become the foundation of Broadside Press, the most important black press in America, run by Randall at 12651 Old Mill Place, Detroit (Michigan) 48238.

Broadside's first full-scale book was the remarkable anthology 'For Malcolm: poems on the life and death of Malcolm X' (1967) which Dudley Randall edited with Margaret G. Burroughs. In 1969 he compiled an equally programmatic collection, called 'Black poetry: a supplement to anthologies which exclude black poets'. In addition to these Randall has authored two books of poetry: 'Poem counterpoem' (1966) with Margaret Danner, founder of Boone House, and 'Cities burning' (1968) which, like many of the Broadside books, is also available on tape, in a complete reading by the author.

In 1966 Dudley Randall found time to visit Paris, Prague and the Soviet Union with a delegation of black artists (his translations of Russian poetry have been praised) and in 1970 he went to Ghana and Nigeria.

Meanwhile the Broadside Press catalogue grows and grows: 'when I get over this load, I intend to publish only four books a year' – but that will never happen, as long as Dudley Randall remains 'musing over roses and revolution' in his own very practical way . . .

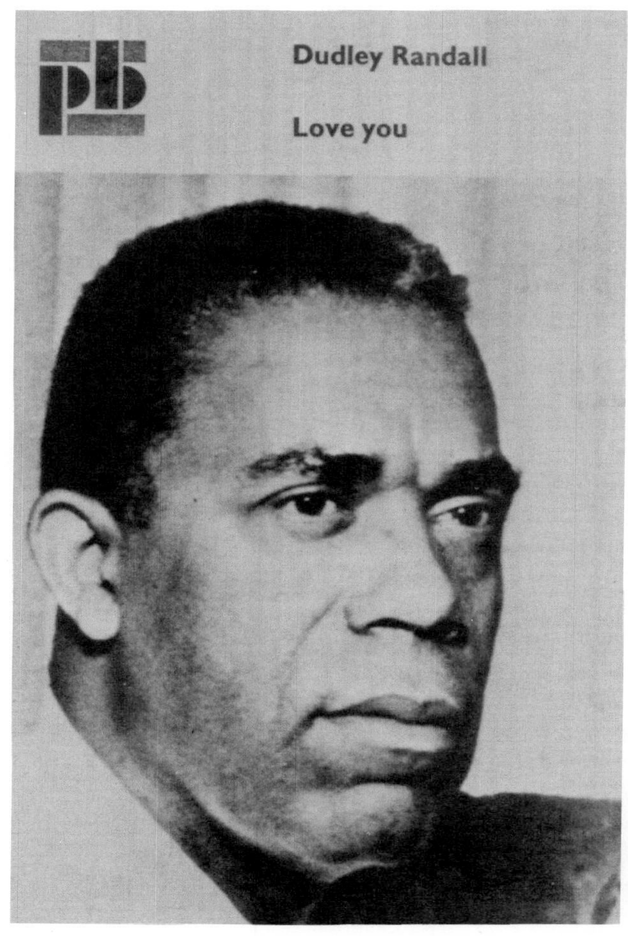

Covers for Randall's 1970 selection of celebratory love poems and visionary lyrics

guilty of overstatement, he deftly manipulates point of view; he writes the lyric and the parable equally well. In "The Line Up," a poem in four quatrains, a police inquiry becomes an extended metaphor for literary values. One hears the common speech of the accused criminals, the murderer, the young pimp, and the dirty old man, but one sympathizes with them through the narrator. For him the investigators ask the wrong questions. Though the police indict the people and "objectively" record the crimes, the officers hardly address the underlying motives. Such people bequeath more fact than wisdom to posterity.

"Interview," possibly the most sustained and brilliant of the generational poems, pictures an entrepreneur turned philanthropist. The old man explains his principles to an intruding young reporter who has crossed a protective moat and scaled a barbed wire fence. The youngster is the mirror image of the philanthropist, the older man who repudiates the cynicism of youth: "Not snivel . . . prove to those/Who could not take the world just as they found it/And therefore lack the power to change it at all/That one old, greedy and predacious villain/Can do more good . . . than . . . their years of whining and complaining." "On A Name for Black Americans," a political, angry sermon, stresses self-reliance as well. "The spirit informs the name, not the name the spirit." While Randall prefers Du Bois, by temperament as well as ideal, he understands the pragmatism of men like Benjamin Franklin and Booker T. Washington. From childhood he remembers that blacks worked hard once to have *Negro* capitalized. He never considered the word derogatory. Though some blacks, he feels, demean the term by decapitalizing it or by applying it only to submissive people, Randall still asserts that "what you are is more important than what you are called . . . that if you yourself, by your life and actions, are great . . . something of your greatness will rub off . . . dignity . . actions affect words. . . ."

The distinctions between appearances and reality pervade *More to Remember*. "Put Your Muzzle Where Your Mouth Is (or shut up)" is a sarcastic aside to a theoretical black revolutionary. Loudly telling others to kill, he has murdered no one. The protagonist who shouts "Black Power" in the poem "Informer" similarly deludes the listeners, who overlook his whispers to the FBI. "Abu" reveals the contradictions between reality and appearance through low burlesque. Apparently having decided to blow up City Hall, the activist advertises in the *New York Times*. Right in front of the FBI infiltrators, he promises to assassinate a white liberal who gave "only" half a million dollars to the NAACP. Asked to comment later, however, he "Says nothing 'bout that Southern sheriff/killed three black prisoner/'cept he admired him/for his sin/cerity." Consumed with self-hatred, Abu is a self-acknowledged coward. His posture and rhetoric are less dangerous than foolishly deceiving. Readily criticizing some white liberals who pose no obvious threat, he rationalizes away the need to confront the extremely threatening racist sheriff. He is as hypocritical as is the protagonist in "Militant Black, Poet," who hangs himself after a white suburbanite downplays the militant's bitterness. Finally, the poem "Ancestors" exposes the revolutionary's own elitist tendencies. While fantasizing about royal heritage, he demeans his humble origins. In "On Getting a Natural (for Gwendolyn Brooks)," the volume's final poem, Randall's speaker celebrates the humanist. At first too humble to admit her own charisma ("beauty is as beauty does"), Brooks develops racial awareness and self-acceptance.

More to Remember clearly displays Randall's aesthetic theory. In "The Ascent" he has represented the poet as visionary, and in "The Dilemma (My poems are not sufficiently obscure? To please the critics—Ray Durem)," he portrays the artist as a modifier of both literary tradition and classical form. Whether traditional or revolutionary, the artist asserts intellectual independence. The appropriately titled nineteen-line poem "The Poet" illuminates Randall's notion. Sloppily dressed and bearded, the writer reads when he should work, converts to "outlandish religions," consorts with blacks and Jews, often disturbs the peace, as "foe of the established order," and mingles with revolutionaries. Satirically addressing the poet, the narrator temporarily plays the bigot's part: "When will you slough off/This preposterous posture/And behave like a normal/Solid responsible/White Anglo Saxon Protestant." Randall's artist feels deeply ("Mainly By Music"), but he philosophizes more than he lives ("The Trouble with Intellectuals").

Nineteen seventy-two through 1974 were especially rewarding years for Randall. With Woodie King, Jr., he codirected a poetry festival called The Forerunners at Howard University in 1972. He bolstered, indirectly, the early success of the Howard University Press, which would issue the proceedings. In Washington he heard Owen Dodson, who read from a wheelchair, and he heard Sterling Brown present "Strong Men." As a recipient of the Kuumba Liberation Award in 1973, Randall participated in a seminar about socio-literature in the East West Culture Learning Institute at the University of Hawaii. He had established himself, says Addison Gayle, as one "who came to prominence, mainly, after the Renaissance years, who bridged the gap between poets of the twenties and those of the sixties and seventies . . . began the intensive questioning of the impossible dream, the final assault upon illusion that produced the confrontation with reality, the search for paradigms, images, metaphors, and symbols from the varied experiences of a people whose history stretches back beyond the Nile."

Randall's next pamphlet, *After the Killing* (1973), often assumes the style and voice of the younger poets. Although some of the poems are older, most of the verses had been recently written. Here Randall experiments with typography and sharpens his satire, as he exposes prejudice and semantic deceptions. In "Words Words Words" he criticizes black activists who seem to prefer white or light-skinned over black women, noting that their words belie their deeds. The narrator concludes that "maybe black/doesn't mean black,/but white." A graphic double space printed between "black" and "but white" underscores the pause as well as the insight.

Killing is a subject central to many of the poems in the collection. Through a reversal of meaning the poem "Beasts" reassigns the values we normally place upon men and the "lower animals." Men kill for sport, but animals kill to live, and the narrator observes the switch in morality: "To praise a man/call him bestial./To slander beast/cry, Human!" The title poem, "After the Killing," is a parable about murder and the power of literary creation to transmute experience. Suggestive of the return to "normal" life after a war, the poem focuses on the bloodthirster, a character who is supposedly dedicated to ultimate peace: however, the protagonist kills other people, whose children in turn kill his own. Three generations later, another blood-

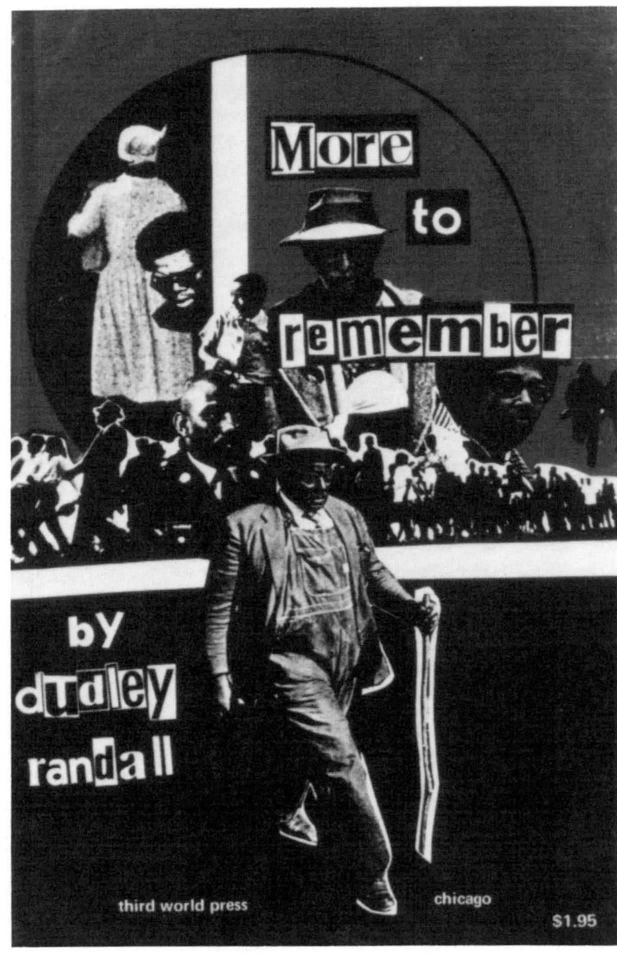

Front cover for Randall's 1971 collection of poems written between the 1930s and the 1960s. "Here are the ways I was," Randall says of the volume, "Warts and all."

thirster echoes the original one's words. "To The Mercy Killers," grouped with poems written in the 1960s and 1970s, presents another view of killing. Randall's narrator states: "There are degrees of courage./One man is not afraid to die./A second is not afraid to kill./A third is not afraid to be merciful."

In "Detroit Renaissance (For Mayor Coleman A. Young)," Randall moves beyond themes of modern violence to a vision of communal rebirth in six sestets of iambic pentameter. In the face of contemporary mechanization, he asserts the value of wisdom. Calling not only for racial, but human consciousness, Randall spans 3,000 years of social and literary history—from Dante through Shakespeare, Cervantes, and Goethe, to Frederick Douglass, Yeats, King, and Malcolm X—replacing black contributors in the story of humanity. The final lines allude at once to Langston Hughes's *Montage* and Shakespeare's *Tempest:*

> Together we will build
> a city that will yield
> to all their hopes and dreams so long deferred.
> New faces will appear
> too long neglected here;
> new minds, new means will build a brave new world.

Randall's book *A Litany of Friends* (1981) contains twenty-four reprints and forty-eight new poems. Six appeared first in *Poem Counterpoem* (1966), four in *Cities Burning* (1968), and one in *Love You* (1970). Fourteen others appeared first in *More to Remember* (1971), and nine came out in *After the Killing* (1973). Grouped by topics such as friends, eros, war, Africa, and self, the verses demonstrate Randall's technical skill.

Imaginatively rereading and reshaping traditional literature, Randall enlarges the humanity of poetry written in English. He invokes Robert Hayden as easily as he invokes Alfred Lord Tennyson. He alludes equally well to Thomas Gray's graveyard school or to the blues tradition of Langston Hughes and Sterling Brown. Responsive to romance and tragedy, he achieves both the lyric as well as the dramatic. Creating a private persona and a detached narrator, he reveals the landscapes of human consciousness.

In the volume's title poem of forty lines, Randall celebrates the family members and fellow artists who helped him through a severe personal depression in the mid-1970s. Leading back from black America to Africa, images of kinship, journey, and communal ritual contribute to the poem's ceremonial tone. Without the mention of last names, the speaker thanks Gwendolyn Brooks for remembering him and sending gifts. He praises the late Hoyt Fuller for respecting him as a man rather than as a hero. Reminded of the blues aesthetic, he hears Etheridge Knight tell him to confront the pain and to transcend it. While he thanks Audre Lorde for writing and sending donations, the writer praises Sonia Sanchez, who phones him and sends herbs. Friendship, Randall seems to say, inspires personal restoration. Cultural renewal follows personal resolve, and in the seven stanzas of "My Muse" Randall restores the African muse to her place beside the muses of Greece and Rome, beside Shakespeare's dark lady and Poe's Annabel Lee. Restored to her rightful niche in human mythology, the African muse appears as, "My Zasha/Who will live for ever in my poems,/Who in my poems will be forever beautiful." Randall echoes the same idea in "Maiden, Open" when he says, "who ever tastes the poet's lips/Will never grow old, will never die. . . ."

Litany also contains political poems, such as "A Leader of the People (for Roy Wilkins)" and "A Poet Is Not a Jukebox." Wilkins, a NAACP leader, was alive when Randall wrote "A Leader of the People," now an appropriate threnody. The poem is a dramatic dialogue between what may be Wilkins and the skeptical narrator, or Wilkins's two selves, the one visionary and the other pragmatic. Wilkins acknowledges a commitment to self-respect and independence, but the negative voice assures him that sacrifice earns the enduring hatred of men and women. When Wilkins answers that he will risk hatred for love, the counterpart argues that others will rebuke him. Wilkins agrees to bear scorn and pride for the sake of blacks, and he reaffirms his mission to withstand the attacks of enemies and to save the people. The pessimistic voice warns at the end, "It is not your enemies who will do these things to you,/but your people."

"A Poet Is Not A Jukebox" reaffirms artistic independence and endurance. After writing a love poem, the speaker must defend the choice of subject to a militant inquirer. Why, she asks, does he not portray a Miami riot? But the poet, removed from social upheaval, has worked mainly for the census lately and has listened to music. He has not watched the news or read the papers. The poet's right to political neutrality is questioned. But, out of love and the commitment to happiness and joy, he "writes about what he feels, what agitates his heart."

With remarkable energy and commitment, Randall has supported the modern black movement for self-determination. His work at Broadside has created an alternative press. Through his efforts, established writers as well as young black poets are largely free to choose a small publisher if they wish to do so. To achieve editorial freedom and flexibility, Randall has declined partnerships as well as incorporations. Having devoted Broadside Press to poetry, he fears that stockholders would demand profits and lower quality or go mercenarily into prose. While his income from the Press goes into publishing new volumes, he pays royalties to other poets. He confesses, "I am not well qualified to operate in a capitalistic society. I came of age during the Great Depression, and my attitude toward business is one of dislike and suspicion. Writers who send me manuscripts and speak of 'making a buck' turn me off." Dedicated to ideals, he remembers well the pragmatic lessons of the black Renaissance. When the Depression came in the 1930s, white publishers dropped blacks, who only a few years earlier were exotically popular. He recommends therefore that Afro-Americans "build a stable base in their own communities," and he has devoted most of his professional life to providing the foundation.

References:

Richard K. Barksdale and Keneth Kinnamon, "Part VI: Since 1945," in *Black Writers of America: A Comprehensive Anthology,* edited by Barksdale and Kinnamon (New York: Macmillan, 1972), pp. 808-809;

Woodie King, Jr., ed., *The Forerunners: Black Poets in America* (Washington, D.C.: Howard University Press, 1981);

D. H. Melhem, "Dudley Randall: A Humanist View," *Black American Literature Forum,* 17, no. 4 (1983): 157-167;

Charles H. Rowell, "In Conversation with Dudley Randall," *Obsidian,* 2, no. 1 (1976): 32-44;

Marilyn Nelson Waniek, "Black Silence, Black Songs," *Callaloo,* 6, no. 1 (1983): 156-165.

Eugene B. Redmond

(1 December 1937-   )

Joyce Pettis
East Carolina University

BOOKS: *A Tale of Two Toms, or Tom-Tom (Uncle Toms of East St. Louis & St. Louis)* (East St. Louis, Ill.: Privately printed, 1968);

A Tale of Time & Toilet Tissue (East St. Louis, Ill.: Privately printed, 1969);

Sentry of the Four Golden Pillars (East St. Louis, Ill.: House of Truth, 1970);

River of Bones and Flesh and Blood (East St. Louis, Ill.: Black River Writers, 1971);

Songs from an Afro/Phone: New Poems (East St. Louis, Ill.: Black River Writers, 1972);

Consider Loneliness as These Things (Rome, Italy: Centro Studi E Scambi Internazionali, 1973);

In a Time of Rain & Desire: New Love Poems (East St. Louis, Ill.: Black River Writers, 1973);

Drumvoices: The Mission of Afro-American Poetry, A Critical History (New York: Anchor , 1976).

PLAY PRODUCTIONS: *The Ode to Taylor Jones,* East St. Louis, Illinois, Southern Illinois University Performing Arts Training Center, 1968;

9 Poets With the Blues, Sacramento, California State University Little Theatre, 1971;

The Face of the Deep, Sacramento, California State University, 1971;

River of Bones, Sacramento, California State University, 1971;

The Night John Henry Was Born, Baton Rouge, Louisiana, Southern University, Little Theatre, 1972;

Will I Still Be Here Tomorrow?, Sacramento, California State University; New York, Martinique Theatre, 1972;

Kwaanza: A Ritual in 7 Movements, Sacramento, California State University, 25-31 December 1973;

Music And I Have Come at Last!, Sacramento, California State University Outdoor Theatre, 1974;

There's a Wiretap in My Soup, Sacramento, California State University, 1974;

Drumvoices: The Mission of Afro-American Poetry, adapted from Redmond's book of critical essays, Sacramento, California State University Center Theatre, 1976.

photograph ©1984 by Layle Silbert

RECORDING: *Bloodlinks and Sacred Places,* Black River Writers, 1973.

TELEVISION: *Cry-Cry, Wind, Through the Throats of Horns and Drums: A Jazz Ballet,* KXTV, 1977;

If You Love Me Why Don't You Know It: A Blues Ballet, KXTV, 1977.

OTHER: Clarence Major, ed., *The New Black Poetry,*

includes poems by Redmond (New York: International, 1969);

Sides of the River: A Mini-Anthology of Black Writings, edited by Redmond (East St. Louis, Ill.: Black River Writers, 1969);

Henry Dumas, *Ark of Bones and Other Stories*, edited by Redmond and Hale Chatfield (Carbondale: Southern Illinois University Press, 1970);

Dumas, *Poetry for My People*, edited by Redmond and Chatfield (Carbondale: Southern Illinois University Press, 1970);

Arnold Adoff, ed., *The Poetry of Black America*, includes poems by Redmond (New York: Harper & Row, 1972);

Abraham Chapman, ed., *New Black Voices*, includes poems by Redmond (New York: New American Library, 1972);

Negro American Literature Forum, Black Poetry Issue, edited by Redmond, 6 (Spring 1972);

Dumas, *Play Ebony: Play Ivory*, edited by Redmond (New York: Random House, 1974);

"Into the Canaan of the Self," in *Giant Talk: An Anthology of Third World Writings*, edited by Quincy Troupe and Rainer Schulte (New York: Random House, 1975);

Griefs of Joy: An Anthology of Afro-American Poetry, edited by Redmond (East St. Louis, Ill.: Black River Writers, 1976);

Theodore Gross, ed., *Open Poetry*, includes poems by Redmond (New York: Random House, 1976);

Dumas, *Jonoah and the Green Stone*, edited by Redmond (New York: Random House, 1976);

Dumas, *Rope of Wind and Other Stories*, edited by Redmond (New York: Random House, 1979);

Ishmael Reed, et al., eds., *Califía*, includes poems by Redmond (Berkeley, Cal.: Yardbird, 1979);

"Racism or Regalism? Poetic License or Literary Apartheid? Conrad's Burden in *The Nigger of the Narcissus*," in *Nigger of the Narcissus: Norton Critical Edition* (New York: Norton, 1980).

PERIODICAL PUBLICATIONS: "What the Poet Is," *Sou'Wester* (Spring 1964): 33-35;

"Indigenous Struggle Pays Off," *Focus/Midwest* (Fall 1968): 40-45;

"Today's Black Woman: Is She Scurrying from Sun to Sun?," *National Beauticians Directory* (Summer 1969): 12-13;

"Olanjunji: Controlled Center in a Rhythmic and Ritualistic Deluge," *Fine Arts* (February 1970): 8-9;

"It Is, Again, About Respect and Hard Work," *Nickel Review*, 4 (6 February 1970): 8;

"The Black American Epic: Its Roots, Its Writers," *Black Scholar*, 2 (January 1971): 15-22;

"How Many Poets Scrub the River's Back?," *Confrontation: A Journal of Third World Literature* (Spring 1971);

"Five Black Poets: Book Reviews," *Parnassus: Poetry in Review* (Spring-Summer 1974);

"Black Poetry: Views, Visions, Conflicts," *Yardbird Reader*, 4 (1975): 65-72;

"Stridency and the Sword: Literary and Cultural Emphasis in Afro-American Magazines," *TriQuarterly*, 43 (1978): 538-573.

A poet, critic, journalist, playwright, and educator, Eugene B. Redmond is counted among the number of significant black literary figures who shaped the black arts movement of the late 1960s.

Born on 1 December 1937 in St. Louis, Missouri, to John Henry and Emma Jean Hutchinson Redmond, the young Redmond was raised in East St. Louis, Illinois. Redmond told *Contemporary Authors:* "Motherless and fatherless at age [nine], I was raised in part by a grandmother and a group of neighborhood fathers—friends of my older brother and members of the Seventh Day Adventist Church I attended. . . ." Redmond's interest in writing stems partly from his activities on the Lincoln Senior High School newspaper and yearbook projects, and partly from composing songs for several neighborhood "doo-waa" groups. His fascination with the oral delivery of words, which is evident in his mature work, began with his performances in high school and church plays.

After a stint in the United States Marine Corps from 1958 to 1961, he completed his formal education and received a bachelor's degree in English literature from Southern Illinois University in 1964. In 1966 he earned a master's degree in English literature from Washington University. During his college years Redmond pursued his interest in journalism through various writing positions with the Southern Illinois University student newspaper, where he became the first black student editor. In 1963 he cofounded *The Monitor*, an East St. Louis weekly, and at various times over a seven-year period he worked on the paper as associate editor, editor of the editorial page, and executive editor.

Since those college years, he has engaged in a diverse career in literature and the arts. He has been poet-in-residence at several universities—Southern Illinois University, Oberlin College, California State University, Southern University (Baton Rouge), and the University of Wisconsin (Madison).

He has been a senior consultant to Katherine Dunham at Southern Illinois University's Performing Arts Training Center (1967 to 1969) for which he wrote, acted, directed, and supervised the writing and drama departments. Redmond has had several plays performed; his mythic ritual drama, *The Face of the Deep*, was performed in 1971 at California State University, Sacramento, and also at Southern University, Baton Rouge, Louisiana. Two one-act plays, *There's a Wiretap in My Soup* (produced in 1974) and *Will I Still Be Here Tomorrow?* (produced in 1972), have been performed locally in California on television and at California State University at Sacramento. The latter play was also produced at New York's Martinique Theater with the assistance of Pulitzer Prize-winning playwright Charles Gordone. A number of Redmond's other works have been performed as choral dramas: a musical adapted from the prose and poetry of Henry Dumas; and a ballet (coauthored by Katherine Dunham) in memory of Taylor Jones, a midwestern black community leader. Redmond himself narrated the ballet and managed the road company on a national tour.

Redmond has also recorded two albums of his poetry. With poets Sherman Fowler and Dumas, he founded Black River Writers Publishing Company, which has published most of his poetry. He is also literary executor for the estate of the late poet and fiction writer Henry Dumas, and he has edited much of Dumas's work. After Dumas's death in 1968, Redmond succeeded him as director of language workshops and as poet-in-residence at Southern Illinois University's Experiment in Higher Education in East St. Louis. Dumas, who Redmond credits for helping to reshape and expand his own approach to poetry and criticism, enthusiastically and unselfishly gave his time and energies to local cultural projects in East St. Louis. The almost daily conversations between the two poets, along with their efforts to sponsor student literary publications and readings in area taverns and homes, produced reciprocal influences and broadened local audiences for poetry readings and cultural festivals.

It is clear from Redmond's poems that he is a poet of black consciousness, and his work is stylistically linked with the distinctive black poetry that was written during the 1960s, the most important decade for black poetry since the 1920s. On one hand, many poems express pride in the cultural heritage and history of Afro-Americans and in the endurance of a people stymied by racism. A small number of poems voice the bleakness and despair of ghetto life. On the other hand, some poems exhibit little emotional kinship with other 1960s poets because the speaker focuses upon private thoughts and emotions in an introspective posture generally absent from the poetry of that decade. Other poems are quiet lyrics, more romantic and traditional than the works of some of Redmond's contemporaries.

A TALE OF TIME
&
25 cents **TOILET TISSUE**

(A hipsofical, gritical, symbolical,
coplogical, allegorical rip-Rap--
"on all the contemporary shit that's
going down.")

By Eugene Redmond

For Larry Becham,
"Moody"--"Bird"--
"Red"--"Sherm"--
and all those
Professors "Nigger-Know."

PRO-RAP
Dig!
How the Grim Rapper
Raps on kin
Of
Robinhood,
Redd Fox
&Rumpelstillskin.

In this year of Damballa, Haitian Serpent God

Copyright, May 1969 by Eugene Redmond

Front cover for Redmond's 1969 pamphlet poem, written for oral performance

In keeping with the style of the 1960s, Redmond, characteristically, does not use traditional rhyme schemes and forms. The pamphlet poem *A Tale of Time & Toilet Tissue* (1969), for example, obviously intended for performance, is a rhythmic "Rap," where strong end-rhyme is only necessary for oral delivery to punctuate the ends of lines. Rather than a block of print denoting a unit, some poems resemble sentences arranged vertically down the page; other poems begin with emphatic or startling sentences, a practice not only prevalent in the black poetry of the 1960s but also generally highly visible in modern poetry.

Perhaps the strongest characteristic of Redmond's poetry is a marked historical and cultural perspective. Like many black poets of the 1960s and 1970s, Redmond is very conscious of choosing his allusions, images, and symbols from the black cultural context. For Redmond, music is an inseparable element of the cultural heritage. Thus his poetry abounds with direct allusions to spirituals, blues, jazz, soul music, and black musicians. His poetry also shows an indebtedness to folk songs and expressions, the great "folkloristic trunk" from which Redmond believes black literature stems.

Although the order of poems in each of Redmond's volumes of poetry seems to follow no perceptible thematic arrangement, certain allusions, themes, and subjects are recurrent throughout the volumes. For example, allusions to the African culture are frequently used to link the present-day black American with the African heritage. In *Sentry of the Four Golden Pillars* (1970), Redmond uses "Smoke and Fire," subtitled "For 'Smokey' Bill Robinson," to link Robinson's sound to Africa:

Medicine man from Motown
Mixing multi-phonic brown
Rhythmic Sun Ra on the ground
Tonal Bridge to Africa!

In another poem the speaker thinks of his beloved while standing beneath a street light being drenched by rain. He is mentally transported to Africa and becomes "Chaka, Zulu-zealous,/Dancing/Through jungle traffic lights. . . ." "There are few persons in the United States who have not been touched or influenced (in one way or another) by the folk expression of Black America," Redmond has written in *Drumvoices: The Mission of Afro-American Poetry, A Critical History* (1976). In the tradition of the folk portraits in Margaret Walker's *For My People* (1942) and Sterling Brown's *Southern Road* (1932), Redmond constructs an urban equivalent of Walker's "Poppa Chicken." In the poem "Invasion of the Nose," from *River of Bones and Flesh and Blood* (1971), the character is a "cool daddy"—a lover, a fashionable dresser, rapper, and crooner like Smokey Bill; he is informed about jazz musicians and life.

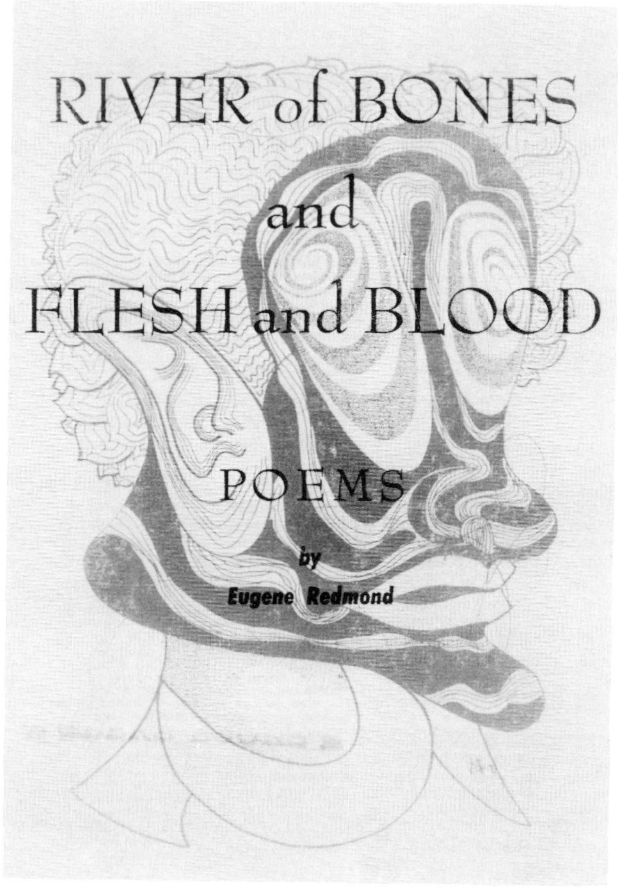

Front cover for Redmond's 1971 poetry collection. The river of the title poem is the Mississippi, which carried black slaves, he says, "Crouched and huddled / . . . in the bellies / Of steamships."

He stood / hung / laid / dealt
On the corner,
Bent in a 20-degree angle,
One hand clutching the wrist
Of the opposite arm behind his back.
. . . .
He was an acknowledged action eater
Who was hip to *Trane,*
Bird. . . .

Unlike Poppa Chicken who retained the respect engendered by his stance with the ladies, Redmond's character is ironically netted by one of his women. He falls irredeemably in love.

In "Epigrams For My Father," also from *River*

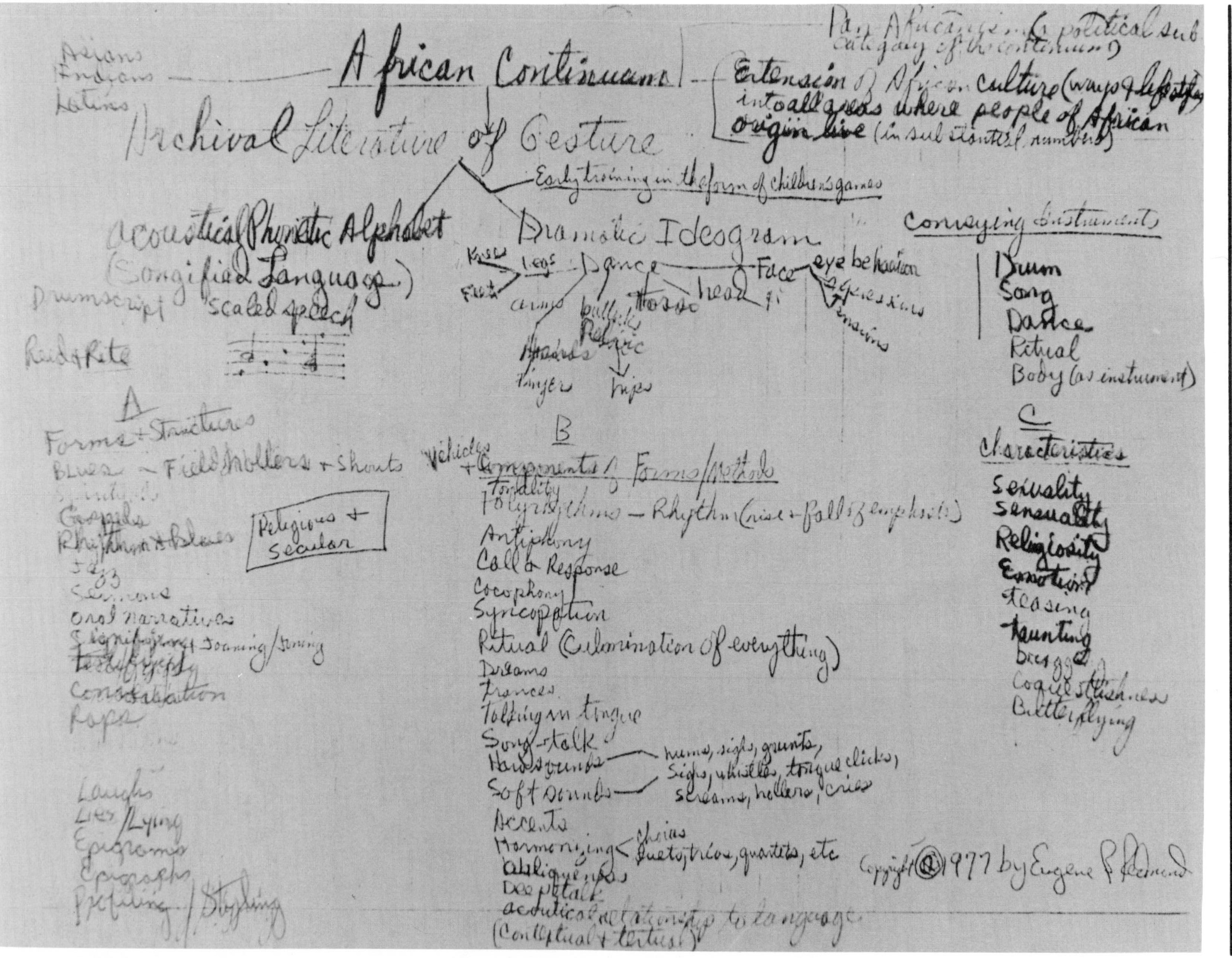

Redmond's notes on the African continuum (courtesy of the author)

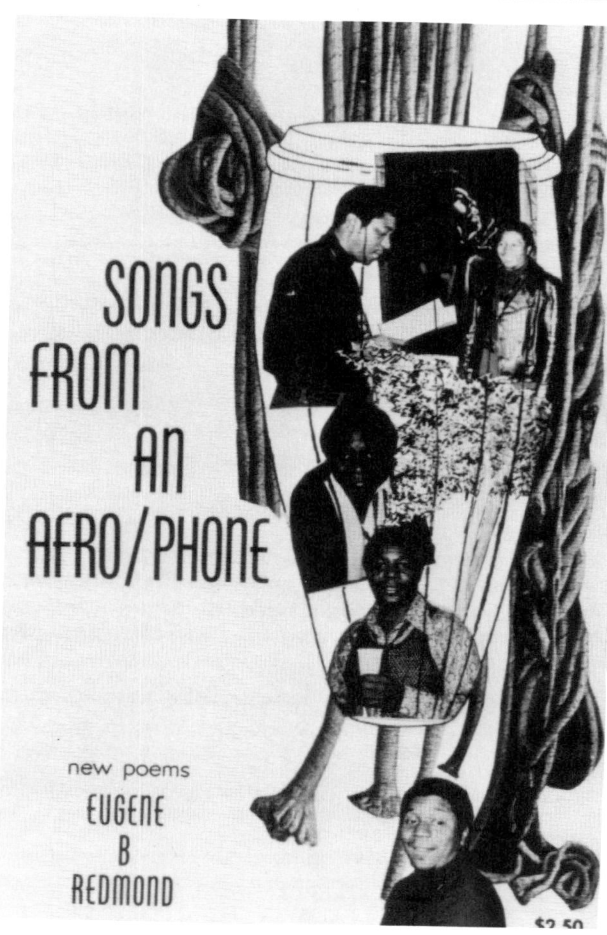

Front cover for Redmond's 1972 poetry volume. The epigraph comes from Léopold Senghor: "take the sculptor who carves a mask . . . while this sculptor carves, he sings a song, he sings a poem and he weaves a poem. . . . artists must have the gift of . . . rhythm."

of Bones, the stance Redmond attributes to the father is easily that of a tough, but respected folk hero:

Fatherlore: Papa-rites, daddyhood;
  Run & trapsong: Search & dodgesong.
Steelhammeringman.
Gunbouter; whiskeywarrior.
Nightgod!
Moonballer/brawler grown old.
Slaughterhouse/river mackman:
Hightale teller & totempoleman.
. . . .
45 degree hat, Bulldurham butt bailing from lips;
Garbardine shining shining shining
Above white silk socks—
    satin man
    satin man
    silksure & steelstrong
    hammerhold on life
    hammerhold on life

The father, as a character in the poem, has adjusted to what the culture demands of him; he has progressed through an initiation to full fatherhood and adulthood, from tenuous searching to the cold certainty that toughness is necessary for survival. Redmond tells us that survival depends on "folkbrilliance & Geniusgrit," that the struggle to survive is difficult. The stressed primary syllables, single-word descriptions, and strong alliterative phrases underscore the tough stance that dominates the poem.

Unlike "Epigrams for my Father," some of Redmond's poems in the same volume do not convey a positive adjustment to the stresses of modern black culture. A few are quiet evocations of despair and hopelessness, such as "Dragons at Noon," in which, after a solar eclipse, children play hide-and-seek, but men take rings from fingers of the dead. In another poem, "The Bastard," the black-faced

Redmond pours a libation to begin one of his performances of poetry (photograph © Charles Behnke, courtesy of the author).

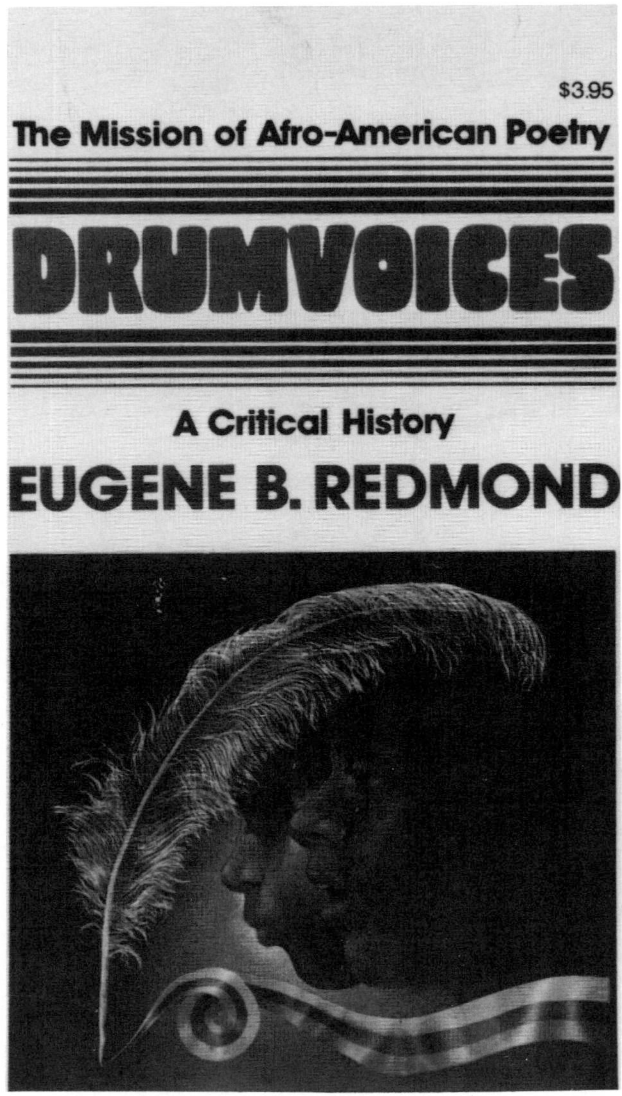

Front cover for Redmond's 1976 critical history of black American poetry

persona moves across the white desert, clearly a metaphor for America; "on his brow/lie stillborn the hopes/of 3 centuries":

Beside the oasis,
Mother offers a
Sword
To his burning
Tongue
While orphans cast
Lots
For his inheritance.

"Disneyland" contrasts life in the suburbs, where "the dead—and animals—live better than the *living*," with existence in the ghetto, where "skinny rats and roaches are scarce."

Family unity is also important in Redmond's poetry. Several of his poems about his grandmothers are particularly entertaining. In one, titled "Grandmother," the grandmother is no longer the person to "fathom rough lies/on a little black face," but now "relishes the taste of peppermint/and the somber hum of spirituals." In "Love Necessitates," the grandmother's love was "stern and firm/precise preparation (mercy!)/for the Academy of Hard Knocks."

Some of Redmond's most successful poems are lyrics that demonstrate a variety of themes and subjects. "The Bum," for example, from *Sentry of the Four Golden Pillars,* views the solitary existence of a wino. In *River of Bones and Flesh and Blood,* "September in March," constructed around the wind as an extended metaphor, depicts a persona who achieves clarity of vision in spite of obstructions; "The Edge of Myself" shows a persona who acknowledges the seamy destructive side of his life and runs from it, "vomiting shallow/bubbles of hope down the highway of time." "Spring in the Jungle" is a quiet love poem that communicates the stunned reaction of the speaker to falling in love." "Time . . . Love," a love poem from *In a Time of Rain & Desire* (1973), relies on African allusions. The clock propels the lovers three centuries backward:

Where I was mojo-man, juju-led,
Karate-king in a Bantu-chariot;
Your lips bowstrings, harp-held
Your eyes Kikuyu-arrows
Your forehead a temple
Leaning against the Godvoice in my throat;
And we became hardthings
And we became soft-things,
Swelling to what *we were*
And what we would *become.*

When Redmond's poems are not fully successful, it is frequently because he allows his metaphors to overpower the poem, or he mixes metaphors and the result neutralizes the desired effect of the poem. Sometimes the metaphors are trite expressions, rather than startling creative comparisons a reader expects from an experienced poet. Too often when Redmond writes about sex, his inclusion of slang and vulgar terminology is inappropriate and distracting. "POSTCRIPT," from *In a Time of Rain & Desire,* is not an isolated example of metaphors out of control. The sexual reference here, however, is not an example of the poet's vulgar usage.

At 2 a m this morning
        I awoke
2 a m webbed in a wrinkled geography of sheets
        I awoke
To see your hands ploughing your hair
Your body an incompleted S
In fetus-like tranquility,
Cocooned in the port of our last orgasm;

With throttle open, I thought;
        You always swell so-quickly
        And I grow to contain, refrain you:
        Yet like a tree, you branch and branch
        In the forest of my expanding hungers;
        Like a balloon in puberty, you multiply
        And burst—multiply and burst:

At 2 a m your rage is a timid whir: otherwise, othering:
And I wonder what voodoo vassal shrank you so?
What manner of God forested your fruits and,
At 2 a m, shrinks & calms your fire into the
                crook of my arm?

Sometimes the mixed metaphors and dense language lack clarity.

"... Morning so Soon, too Soon ...," intended to capture the moment of reluctant awakening, when one remembers the activities of the previous night, is rife with faulty metaphors and uninhibited references to sex. Examples of other poems, like "All a-Thighed in Black" and "Main Man Blues," sometimes fail because Redmond's attempt to create a "hip-rap" quality is transparent.

Nonetheless, Redmond is dedicated to his craft, and the best evidence of his commitment is found in his book-length study of Afro-American poetry, *Drumvoices: The Mission of Afro-American Poetry, A Critical History* (1976), the result of eight years of exhaustive research, travel, interviews, and writing. The volume, which surveys black American poetry from 1746 through 1976, is important for students and teachers of Afro-American poetry because it follows a historical perspective, and links the eclipsed African culture with the American culture of the earliest black writers. One of the most informative chapters is the 123-page "Black Poetry of the 1960s and 1970s." It includes information about many minor poets of those decades, as well as stimulating discussion about major figures. Redmond also includes an extensive and helpful bibliography.

The intellectual principle underlying *Drumvoices* is the paradigm of the African continuum, which Redmond characterizes as "a complex web of beliefs, customs, traditions and significant practices that tie diasporan black cultures to their African origins." This anthropological and multidisciplinary approach to history had been shaped, Redmond says, under the influences of Katherine Dunham and team teaching for the Experiment in Higher Education with painter Oliver Jackson, sociologist Joyce Ladner, and Dumas. The result was complete reorientation of Redmond's critical vision from an academic one to a cultural, ritualistic, and experiential one.

Currently, Redmond is Cultural Arts consultant and poet-in-residence for public school district 189 in East St. Louis, Illinois, and a visiting professor at the University of Missouri. He trains teachers and makes Afro-American literature and culture accessible to schoolchildren and other students from diverse backgrounds. He tours, giving readings, performances, and lectures which focus upon "central cultural literacy" as the "nervous system" of human understanding and self-awareness. He seems settled in his roles as poet, critic, playwright, editor, and educator. Although he has met with success in all his related endeavors, his critical and creative efforts have hardly been exhausted.

Papers:

Redmond's plays are collected at Hatch-Billops archives in New York.

Conrad Kent Rivers

(15 October 1933-24 March 1968)

Edwin L. Coleman II
University of Oregon

BOOKS: *Perchance to Dream, Othello* (Wilberforce, Ohio: Wilberforce University Press, 1959);
These Black Bodies and This Sunburnt Face (Cleveland, Ohio: Free Lance Press, 1962);
Dusk at Selma (Cleveland, Ohio: Free Lance Press, 1965);
The Still Voice of Harlem (London: Paul Breman, 1968);
The Wright Poems (London: Paul Breman, 1972).

OTHER: Paul Breman, ed., *Sixes and Sevens: An Anthology of New Poetry,* includes poems by Rivers (London: Breman, 1962);
Arna Bontemps, ed., *American Negro Poetry,* includes poems by Rivers (New York: Hill & Wang, 1963);
Arnold Adoff, ed., *I am the Darker Brother: An Anthology of Modern Poems by Black Americans,* includes poems by Rivers (New York: Macmillan, 1968);
Dudley Randall, ed., *The Black Poets,* includes poems by Rivers (New York: Bantam Books, 1971);
Richard K. Barksdale and Keneth Kinnamon, eds., *Black Writers of America: A Comprehensive Anthology,* includes poems by Rivers (New York: Macmillan, 1972);
Bernard W. Bell, ed., *Modern and Contemporary Afro-American Poetry,* includes poems by Rivers (Boston: Allyn & Bacon, 1972).

PERIODICAL PUBLICATIONS: "Letter from Paris to Gwendolyn Brooks," *Negro Digest,* 13 (February 1964): 60-66;
"Goodbye, Baby Boy," *Negro Digest,* 13 (April 1964): 55-58;
"The Poet's Song: Langston Hughes and the Fantasy of Harlem," *Negro Digest,* 13 (September 1964): 72-76;
"The Day King Marched in Chicago," *Negro Digest,* 15 (March 1966): 54-58;
"Chinese Food," *Negro Digest,* 15 (October 1966): 53-56.

The lasting significance of Conrad Kent Rivers's poetry lies in the fact that he spoke for a generation of young blacks forced to make the transition from the helpless, often hopeless 1950s to the chaotic, rage-filled 1960s. Young blacks, taught in the fifties to contain their individuality for safety's sake, could well understand Rivers's overwhelming concern with loneliness, alienation, and rejection and his responding to the new possibilities of the 1960s with only tentative energy. For Rivers, freedom could be realized only through death, and his poetry expresses that deeply sad helplessness with both intensity and dignity. In the poem "In Defense of Black Poets," he wrote, "A black poet must remember the horrors." Rivers's horrors were those of the sensitive introspective examining the injustices of black pain, sadness, and isolation.

He was born in the North—Atlantic City, New Jersey—to Cora McIver and William Dixon Rivers. There was one brother, named after his father, and apparently little money. He spent most of his formative years in Philadelphia but also attended public school in Georgia for a time. In 1951, while attending high school in Savannah, Georgia, his poem "Poor Peon" won the Savannah State Poetry Prize. His mother's brother, Ray McIver, was a poet and a favored relative, and "Uncle Mack" undoubtedly contributed to Rivers's early interest in poetry.

Rivers served in the army in Georgia, Maryland, and Kentucky from 1953 to 1955. He wrote that he experienced in Georgia, on his first day off-post, an unexpected and overwhelming sense of dehumanization—not so much because he was black as because he was a soldier among too many soldiers. His narration of the experience underlines the importance of recognition and respect for the individual. "I remember my first day off-post, proud of my uniform, wanting to be noticed because in my pockets I had several white certificates telling me that I had completed, without injury or disgrace, boot training," he wrote in a piece for *Negro Digest* in 1964. "I knew something about the Southland; I'd been there before. Never like then, a man, just a guy in uniform without any serious qualms. No racial bugaboos cluttered my mind. I felt neither Northern or biggety, black nor white. Needless, I suppose, to say . . . I returned a whimpering, naked, dehumanized speck of a man."

Rivers's army benefits enabled him to go to college, and he entered Wilberforce University in Ohio in 1956, where he majored in history and English and received a bachelor of arts degree in 1960. He was to find at Wilberforce three important mentors: Yvonne Walker-Taylor, now provost of Wilberforce, then his remedial English teacher; Geraldine E. Jackson, then head of the English department; and Caspar L. Jordan, the Wilberforce librarian, who published Rivers's first three volumes of poems through the Free Lance Press. Walker-Taylor recalls that Rivers arrived in her remedial English class after failing freshman English. In spite of his difficulties with spelling—he used to "draw" words phonetically—she was impressed with his unusual maturity and advanced technique in poetry. For months he had left poetry anonymously at her door until she began reading the poems in all her classes in an attempt to discover their author. (The "anon." to whom *Dusk at Selma* is partially dedicated is Walker-Taylor.) Rivers worked hard at Wilberforce, planned to go on to law school, was popular, involved, liked putting on plays and pageants with his best friend Byron Kigh (who died even earlier than Rivers), and read his poetry at nearby universities such as Cincinnati State and the University of Ohio. He also met Langston Hughes there, whom he names, along with Carl Sandburg, as a principal influence.

While Rivers was at Wilberforce, his poetry was selected three times for inclusion in *America Sings*, an anthology of American college verse, and his first collection of poems, *Perchance to Dream, Othello*, was published in 1959, his senior year.

Conrad Kent Rivers

was born in Atlantic City, New Jersey, on 15 October 1933.
He went to school in Pennsylvania, Georgia, Ohio
(he graduated from Wilberforce University), Illinois
(Chicago Teachers College) and Indiana (University),
then served in the army in Maryland and Kentucky.
While in high school he won the Savannah State poetry prize
for 1951, and afterwards he was three times included
in the 'America sings' college verse annuals.
Casper LeRoy Jordan, who was the Wilberforce librarian
when Conrad studied there, acted as godfather to his career.
Under the auspices of The Free Lance (a 'little magazine'
which is 'the oldest black-bossed literary journal' going)
he brought out three mimeographed pamphlets of poetry:
Perchance to dream, Othello, in 1959,
These black bodies and this sunburnt face, in 1962,
Dusk at Selma, in 1965.
The Heritage anthology 'Sixes and sevens' featured
a strong group of Conrad's poems in August 1962,
prefaced by a 'statement' on his reasons for writing
and on the place of 'race' in his work – this preface
has since been reprinted as often as some of the poems.

In the middle 'sixties, living in Chicago and teaching
in its industrial suburb Gary (across the Indiana state line)
Rivers and other aspiring young black writers and journalists
like Ronald Fair, David Llorens and Gerald McWorter
formed an active and lively discussion group out of which,
through tortuous byways, was born the Organization of
Black American Culture (OBAC) which has remained
an active force in Chicago's black arts scene ever since.
Conrad Rivers, however, would see but little of its realization:
he died a senseless and completely avoidable death
on 24 March 1968, just three weeks before publication
of his fourth book of poetry, 'The still voice of Harlem',
which appeared as volume 5 in the Heritage series.

Rivers was a writer with a great deal to say,
on an interesting quest for ways in which to say it.
One of the recurring themes in his work is the question
of the black writer's position and responsibility,
and his ambiguous relations with his dual audience.
Much of this particular motif found expression
in the present series of poems addressed to or occasioned by
Richard Wright – the most important figure in the trinity
which influenced Conrad's literary development:
the others were Langston Hughes, whom he adored,
and his uncle Ray McIver, the family's hidden genius
who burst on the scene with a marvellous black comedy
called 'God is a (guess what?)' too late for Conrad to see.

Conrad's stories and other fiction, and his dramatic work
which includes a play on the life of Paul Laurence Dunbar,
still await the hand of a sympathetic publisher or producer.

Covers for the 1972 selection of Rivers's poems published posthumously. In the introduction, Ronald Fair explains that Rivers believed Richard Wright "was a god," who should have returned to America from his Parisian sanctuary "to lead young Black writers to Wright's own level of consciousness."

Postscript To A Poem

I

This poem reached the hands of Richard Wright shortly before his untimely death; it is a poem that should not have been published. Strangely enough, it was not only published, but read. Jud Jerome and Nolan Miller of the Antioch Review, found a place for it; and, I might honestly admit, here and now and never again; I wanted to withdraw it immediately after I re-read it a dozen times or more.

Langston Hughes sent Richard a copy. "He liked it," my idol wrote. So, I took a pat on my back by my own hands and decided to let the cup pass. A few weeks passed and I began to feel dishonest about the whole damn mess. "Is it really a poem," I asked. Does it say anything worthwhile? What is the poetry of? (Spirits) How much of my consciousness dominates it? Who am I? Where am I going? What am I doing here? What is my name?

The next morning I wrote the editors a foggy letter; in fact, many foggy letters followed. And in time (Jud was on a junket to the olde world) the editor in charge made it very clear to me that they no longer understood what I was trying to accomplish by storming their quarters with foggy comments about a poem which had been accepted several millenniums ago. "If you wish to withdraw it, much to our---- So. I ended my foggy letters and with the courage of a Bison I faced my writing pad with renewed faith in the best failure I had ~~ever~~ penned. I thought.

II

Karl Shapiro is the finest critic-poet around, I thought. I'll send him a copy and get the truth. Of course I never got his copy in the mail. Oh. I read the poem to Mrs. Tucker; we were friends "employed" by the same organization. She was a former English teacher and knew her stuff. I was living and dying and dreaming in Harlem at the time. Two days after I gave her a copy to study and read— she lost it. I gave her another worn copy. I can't recall her exact words to me, but I do recall her mentioning e.e. cummings or someone in that umbra.

I gave my Aunt Lucille a copy to read; I think it embarrassed her. My mother shouted "Oh, Conrad!" My brother wasn't around, I am sure he would have called it as he felt, saw, and heard, assuming of course, that these senses functioned during his analyses.

I never found the borderline between prose and poetry. Richard never found it either. Therefore, it must not exist. His works centered on Race. The people of our streets, and the critics of any race, dislike the use of the ugly. I found no insincerity in Richard's work. Freud, yes! Richard's positivistic stand bordered on fanaticism. Some of his critics and to my knowledge, many of his friends, labeled him a fanatic.

III

And like all great men who dare to prognosticate; his vision foreshadowed his prophecy, and he was without honor in his land. To my mind Richard was the first American author to examine the Negro psyche in such easy and unoccupied language that all who read him in earnest, knew exactly what he was writing about, perhaps many had lived through the ugly and beautiful found in his words. Certainly, every symbol carried a different interpretation for every individual set (pair) of eyes. But if the reader caught a glimpse of the "neurosis," if the neglect of our American society towards its black brothers was visualized and just briefly conceptualized, something was gained. Richard wrote the truth. The truth shall write about him. It shall do him honor when you and I are blank pages. His mystique shall live on. And all who dare to follow— cannot. It is no longer possible to blaze his trails (own). It is one thing to place a pen in your hands, move through Harlem— on to Chicago— alas! Paris.... the soft lights of Rome; but try letting the place of occupancy live in the pen. Richard was not a magician; his feat remains to be duplicated.

I only met Richard Wright the poet.---- I never knew Richard Wright the man. His language took me on a journey. His truth showed me how ignorant and ugly and beautiful I AM: His prophecy warned me that soon I would be dead---- unless? His truth told me that the American Negro did not buy the biggest car nor wear the bright colored ornaments to be seen or heard —— no!.... it was something else altogether different. Our SANITY was involved. To be hated is not to be loved by those who dare to hate.

IV

The absence of love indicates the presence of hate. We hate ~~what~~ what we fear and do not understand. We teach our children to hate. They teach it in turn---- hate can become amoral. We are going crazy and no one really cares and few honestly know. Look at our streets! Look! I dare you! Look into our average homes— not lower middle. Look! Look! Listen! Forget about your front page heroes. All the men are dead. Forget about your century of progress! All the men are dead— and what is fairer to the dead, than for the living to be unalive. Walk into an alley near a bar in an all Non-integrated neighborhood— tell me what you hear. If you have any culture don't expect to believe what you see. And don't give me that snow job about Lena Horne and the rest---- nice people! But they DON'T live around here anymore. ~~I do~~ We do----

I never knew Richard Wright the MAN. I mourn for the poet. It was too soon. God! Jehovah! Whatever name you use— it was too soon. Where shall we find another poet? We've only lost two: Dunbar and Richard.

I dislike this poem very much! I shall not re-publish it again. There's little truth in it——. The language does not take us on a journey; it does not allow us to see, to hear, to feel, to know, to believe. I like the title though. Naturally, I liked the man it fails to honor. I struggled with this piece— searching, pleading alone; all for FORM. Richard's FORM. His language. His spirit. Of course I failed. Only three small changes occurred, maybe four. It is not a poem. I am not a poet. But I adored the craftsmanship of the poet I wrote it for.

Facsimile of a manuscript written by Rivers on 22 February 1962 and published for the first time in The Wright Poems

Othello's voice, Rivers says in his introduction, "is an echo from what I like to call 'a new generation.' A generation tired of apologies and colored or Negro 'fogieisms,' which have no place in a world of Sputniks. Culture is the key, cultivation of the dangerous curve."

Though the introduction seems to herald the dawn of a new age of American artistic awareness, the echo of a proud, determined "new generation," most of the poetry in this tiny volume is sad and muted. It is more a lament for a societal condition in which black is black and white is white and the twain have yet to meet, than it is an echo of anything new. In it, the poet carries on a series of dreamy dialogues with Othello, with Harlem, with America. "Perchance to dream," he says, "of a colorless morning void of hate and petty fears . . . of lustless worlds . . . of strength . . . of truth. . . . of life not black, not white." And then "Wake to behold a tabooless world, colorless and Tom tired." *Perchance to Dream, Othello* is a wistful little book. Yet it is important to remember that it was one of only ten or so easily traceable volumes of black poetry published in that decade. It has always been an act of courage for black artists to articulate black feelings. And one of the poems, "On James Weldon Johnson's Creation," has genuine power; it is, as well, a sort of paradigm of Rivers's view of the world. It is the story of God's creation of man, and his subsequent rejection because of a broken promise.

> man found out
> How to cry, he discovered his hopelessness and hurt
> tearfully real
> . . . .
> But God did not answer, and man was left
> to cry alone with
> His strange winds and in all his mornings after, until
> . . . then.

Rivers went on to graduate school at Chicago Teachers' College, Indiana University, and Temple University and taught high school in Chicago and in Gary, Indiana, while living just over the state line in Chicago, for most of the rest of his life, from 1961 to 1967. During these years a number of his articles, stories, and poems were published by *Negro Digest, Kenyon Review, Antioch Review, Umbra,* and other periodicals.

In 1962, his second volume of poems, *These Black Bodies and This Sunburnt Face* (titled after a quotation from William Blake), had appeared. The structures of his poems remained traditional, but the poems in this volume are less abstract, more concrete, and have more passion and energy than those in the earlier volume. Yet for all their increased intensity, they still express an essential hopelessness. Rivers reaches out, but, as in his earlier version of the creation myth, he really does not believe anything is there.

For example, "The Last Song the Colored Jazz Man Played" is a genuine innovation for Rivers. He leaves his rather formal philosophizing for black dialect and jazz rhythms and ends with a strong (and Blakeian) affirmation of human vitality:

> Walk the river baby gal
> Ain't nothing right or wrong,
> Cause every human emotion
> Done purified our song.

In "Four Sheets to the Wind" he imagines France as a place where he is no longer alien, a place where he might belong and "die an old Parisian, with much honor." The same hope is expressed in "A Letter to Parris My Unborn Son." Yet, in "On a Mystic Summer Night" he writes,

> Each night a new moon.
>
> Yet the distance between all things
> Becomes a universal syndrome of blue ice.
> Sparkling cinders. Blazing hues.
>
> Two things we can never do:
> Go home.
> Get happy.

In the middle 1960s, Rivers formed a discussion group with novelist Ronald Fair, journalist David Llorens, and organizer Gerald McWorter that was later to lead to the formation of the Organization of Black American Culture (OBAC), long important to Chicago's black arts. He was also a participant in the Seven Arts Guild, the American Society of Writers, the Poetry Guild of America, the Art Guild of Chicago, and, shortly before his death, began booking artists through his newly formed public relations company, Kent Conrad Associates. This period of his life, like his college years, was active, social, and productive.

Rivers spent the summer of 1963 in Europe, mostly in Paris, a city long of symbolic importance to him. His teacher, Walker-Taylor, remembers his walking the floor "like a caged animal," restlessly expressing his need to expand, travel, see the imaginary Paris where he might at last be at home. Yet the actual experience, as he describes it in a letter to Gwendolyn Brooks published in 1964 in *Negro*

Digest, was a failure. He was still alone.

His third collection of poems, *Dusk at Selma,* published in 1965, is arguably his best work. In it Rivers is technically more facile and innovative—the poems are concrete, tight, dramatic, even witty—but the old helpless rage is still there. He writes in the title poem,

Let our querulous dream explode;
Wipe black blood on America's Constitution.
Let us die early and get to death.
. . . .
We are dumb driven cattle
Marching as early forgotten Spring
Freezes our nerve near Selma's courthouse.

Rivers died on 24 March 1968, a few weeks before his final volume of poetry, *The Still Voice of Harlem,* was published in London. He was thirty-four. That volume, the first really professionally and carefully produced, stands as the major representation of his work. About half the poems were drawn from previous volumes; the other half were new. Of the new ones, "The Death of a Negro Poet" seems both prophetic and pivotal:

In a few moments
the song will set me free
but the yearning returns.

Rivers said in the introduction to his first volume that he wrote "to examine the world around me." In fact, his poems are far more concerned with his inner world, one in which "worlds crumble, kings die, pain reigns." Though he gained steadily in technical power, he primarily used traditional forms; though he struggled with admirable perseverance and dignity to come to terms with that inner world, his preoccupation with death, and equation of death with freedom, foreshadowed the likelihood of his losing the struggle. His poetry expresses a gentle and sensitive man's pain and courage in a fearsome time. As such it will always be of value. As he wrote in his poem for Nat King Cole,

I disagree with a death that strikes down the makers
of songs. There are so many things waiting for silence like
the bombs waiting for doors to open.

In 1972, Paul Breman published *The Wright Poems,* a short collection of work by Rivers that was dedicated to or inspired by the author Richard Wright.

References:

Nancy L. Arnez, "Black Poetry: A Necessary Ingredient for Survival and Liberation," *Journal of Black Studies,* 11 (1980): 3-22;

C. W. E. Bigsby, *The Second Black Renaissance: Essays in Black Literature* (Westport, Conn.: Greenwood Press, 1980);

Paul Breman, "Poetry into the Sixties," in *The Black American Writer, Volume 2: Poetry and Drama,* edited by C. W. E. Bigsby (De Land, Fla.: Edwards, 1969);

Breman, *You Better Believe It* (New York: Penguin Books, 1973);

Mercer Cook, *The Militant Black Writer in Africa and the United States* (Madison: University of Wisconsin Press, 1969);

James A. Emanuel and Theodore L. Gross, eds., *Dark Symphony: Negro Literature in America* (New York: Free Press, 1968);

Robert Hayden, *Kaleidoscope* (New York: Harcourt, Brace & World, 1967);

Langston Hughes, *New Negro Poets U.S.A.* (Bloomington: Indiana University Press, 1964);

Blyden Jackson and Louis D. Rubin, Jr., *Black Poetry in America: Two Essays in Historical Interpretation* (Baton Rouge: Louisiana State University Press, 1974);

Abby Arthur Johnson, *Propaganda and Aesthetics: The Literary Politics of Afro-American Magazines in the Twentieth Century* (Amherst: University of Massachusetts Press, 1979);

Don L. Lee, *Dynamite Voices: Black Poets of the 1960s* (Detroit: Broadside Press, 1971);

Clarence Major, *The Dark and Feeling: Black American Writers and Their Work* (New York: Third Press, 1974);

Dudley Randall, *For Malcolm: Poems on the Life and Death of Malcolm X* (Detroit: Broadside Press, 1967);

Eugene B. Redmond, "The Black American Epic: Its Roots, Its Writers," *Black Scholar,* 2 (January 1971): 15-22.

Carolyn M. Rodgers

(14 December 1945-   )

Jean Davis
Wayne State University

SELECTED BOOKS: *Paper Soul* (Chicago: Third World Press, 1968);
Songs of a Blackbird (Chicago: Third World Press, 1969);
2 Love Raps (Chicago: Third World Press, 1969);
how i got ovah: New and Selected Poems (Garden City: Anchor/Doubleday, 1975);
The Heart As Ever Green (Garden City: Anchor/Doubleday, 1978).

OTHER: *For Love of Our Brothers,* edited by Rodgers (Chicago: Third World Press, 1970);
Tom Weatherly and Ted Wilentz, eds., *Natural Process: An Anthology of New Black Poetry,* includes poems by Rodgers (New York: Hill & Wang, 1970);
Gwendolyn Brooks, ed., *Jump Bad. A New Chicago Anthology,* includes poems by Rodgers (Detroit: Broadside, 1971);
Dudley Randall, ed., *The Black Poets,* includes poems by Rodgers (New York: Bantam, 1971);
Arnold Adoff, ed., *The Poetry of Black America,* includes poems by Rodgers (New York: Harper & Row, 1972);
Stephen Henderson, ed., *Understanding the New Black Poetry: Black Speech and Black Music as Poetic References,* includes poems by Rodgers (New York: Morrow, 1973);
Roots, edited by Rodgers (Bloomington: Indiana University Press, 1973);
Erlene Stetson, ed., *Black Sister: Poetry by Black American Women, 1746-1980,* includes poems by Rodgers (Bloomington: Indiana University Press, 1981).

PERIODICAL PUBLICATIONS:
FICTION
"Blackbird in a Cage," *Negro Digest,* 16 (August 1967): 66-71;
"A Statistic, Trying to Make it Home," *Negro Digest,* 18 (June 1969): 68-71;
"One Time," *Essence,* 6 (November 1975).
POETRY
"New Poems by Carolyn Rodgers," *Black World,* 24 (June 1975): 82-83.

Carolyn M. Rodgers (photograph by John Tweeple)

Carolyn Marie Rodgers is best known as one of the new black poets to emerge from the Chicago Organization of Black American Culture during the 1960s. A Chicago native, she has spent most of her career as a poet in that city; however, she has achieved a national reputation, largely since the mid-1970s, because of her thematic concerns with feminist issues, particularly those affecting the black woman in a changing society. Her earliest poems, collected in *Paper Soul* (1968) and *Songs of a Blackbird* (1969), repeat the tenets of black revolutionary thought characteristic of the new black poetry, but they also contain the seeds of ideas about women's roles, female identity, and mother-daughter relationships that mark her mature accomplishment in *how i got ovah* (1975) and *The Heart As Ever Green* (1978). With these two volumes, Carolyn Rodgers has become one of the strongest voices among contemporary poets and one of the most effective black women poets writing today.

The daughter of Clarence and Bazella Rodgers, she attended public schools in Chicago, where she enrolled in the University of Illinois in 1960. She began writing while a college freshman as a means of coping with the pressures of academic life. Rodgers has recalled that she wrote "quasi seriously" during her first year at the university because "it seemed to be a natural, enjoyable, effective outlet." Her writing was not enough, however, to sustain her at Illinois, so she enrolled in Chicago's Roosevelt University in 1961. She received a bachelor's degree from Roosevelt in 1965 and is currently working on a master's degree there.

It was her association with other Chicago writers, rather than her formal educational experiences, that led to her career as a poet. While working as a social worker at the YMCA (1963-1966) and in the poverty program (1965-1968), Rodgers began to meet with the OBAC Writers Workshop and with Gwendolyn Brooks's Writers Workshop. Through these workshops, she met both young, aspiring writers, such as Don L. Lee (Haki Madhubuti), Johari Amini, and Sterling Plumpp, and more established authors, such as poet Brooks and editor Hoyt Fuller, who became one of her mentors. Rodgers recalls the now deceased Fuller as her "good literary father figure," who would push her when she needed to be pushed and who encouraged her to complete her first volume of poems. Gwendolyn Brooks, her teacher and mentor, inspired Rodgers to undertake her first book while attending Brooks's workshop. It was Brooks with whom she consulted about the title *Paper Soul* and it was Fuller whom she asked to write the introduction.

Paper Soul was published in 1968 by Third World Press, which Rodgers had cofounded earlier that year with Madhubuti and Johari Amini. In the introduction, Fuller remarked that Rodgers's "perspective, both sharp and sweeping, encompasses the broad regions of what is and also the clear image of what might be. . . ." He also observed what was to become the most characteristic aspect of her poetry, her mediation between traditional black life and its institutions and black cultural revolution: "Carolyn Rodgers is a child of double worlds. She is an inhabitant of that construct most of us still recognize as middle-class America, an entity of special certainties and institutions; and, at the same time, she dwells among the spiritual and cultural revolutionaries who would shatter the weighty irrelevancies of that world, leaving stand only the soldier outposts and bastions onto which a more humane edifice might be joined."

Paper Soul reflects the duality of an individual struggling to reconcile complex realities, dilemmas, and contradictions. The themes address identity, religion, revolution, and love, or more accurately a woman's need for love. The poetry is vivid and forceful; the language is, as Fuller observes, "spare and angular." Three poems, in particular, reveal Rodgers's concerns and style: "Now Ain't That Love," "FOR SOME BLACK MEN," and "TESTIMONY." "Now Ain't That Love," one of the more frequently anthologized poems from *Paper Soul,* portrays the poet's concern with her own identity as it is shaped by a lover:

who would
who could
    understand that
when i'm near him
i am a skinny, dumb, knock-kneed
lackey, drooling on the words of
my maharajah (or what/ever they call them
        in those jive textbooks). . . .

Representing an adolescent self in less than flattering terms, Rodgers projects a hip style, but her subtext shows her vulnerability. The reality is that the female responds to love with her whole self, as in "FOR SOME BLACK MEN":

A woman finds it hard
to/give for/give, a man
whose calling card's
a hardness.
Woman is softness,
warm of warmth
need from need.

In this poem, "Woman is child/hold[ing] a hurt or lip up to be kissed," and in childlike innocence, she exposes her emotional needs. The powerful and indifferent black males are not unlike the image of God that Rodgers creates in "TESTIMONY." This God, who "run[s] wild in [her] soul," has turned blacks into bowing and scraping people unable to stand up to whites and exploited by preachers:

God—
they fear you, they hold you so
tight they squeeze the truth in you
out, . . . I

know you are not the whip they
dream of, you do not tell them to
scrape their hearts and knees, moaning
while whitey kicks pockets in their
asses, they make you a gauze puppet, a
dumb parrot for their whims and darky-time
whispers.

Though all of the poems in her first volume suggest cultural revolution in spirit or act, "TESTIMONY" stands out because Rodgers reserves her harshest criticisms of institutions and relationships for organized religion and its detrimental effect on black life.

After the publication of *Paper Soul,* Rodgers won the first Conrad Kent Rivers Memorial Fund Award (1968) and began *Songs of a Blackbird,* which consists of poems that deal with survival, street life, mother-daughter conflict, and love. Published in 1969, *Songs of a Blackbird* shows Rodgers's increasing concern with the black woman poet as a major theme in her work. "Breakthrough" conveys the difficult inner reality of being black, female, and a poet. Rodgers voices the complex problem of being an artist and of defining self:

I've had tangled feelings lately
about ev'rything
bout writing poetry, and otha forms
bout talkin and dreamin with a
special man (who says he needs me)
uh huh
and my mouth has been open
most of the time but
I ain't been saying nothin but
thinking about ev'rthing
and the partial pain has been
how do I put my self on paper
the way I want to be or am and be
not like any one else in this
Black world but me

Questions of identity for the poet remain connected with relationships between black men and women but become more centrally located in the woman's ability to express herself. The rhetoric of black nationalism is not a solution: "I am very tired of and trying/and want Blackness which is my life, want this to be/easier on me, want it not to suck me in and/out so much leavin me a balloon with no air, want it not to puff me up so much sometimes. . . ." The poet asks the question, "how do I put my self on paper/the way I want to be or am and be/not like any other else in this/Black world but me." Her search is for her own voice and her own self projected in its uniqueness into her own poetry. She both longs for and rejects the expected roles for black women:

I want to take long bus rides and cop sunsets
for the soul I'm not sure I have/would want it, and
sometimes I want to hibernate in the summer
and hang out in the winter and nurse babies
and get fat and lay around and be pinched by my man
and just love and laugh all the time. . . .

Whether as mother or lover, she knows that roles are not enough for her, because she has a special need: "I want to write a POEM, a poem poem, a/poem's poem poem on a poem that ev'ry u could/dig, just if only a littl bit." She unmasks her own ambiguous emotions, reveals her sensitivity to the reality of her own life and meaning, and she concludes:

if u read this u
will dig where I'm at
and feel that i mean/that/where
i am
and could very possibly
be
real
at this lopsided crystal sweet moment. . . .

The poet's "tangled feelings" find resolution in a "lopsided crystal sweet moment," which is not a permanent solution to the problems faced by the woman who wants to write a poem, but who also wants to be fully female.

The most dynamic poem in *Songs of a Blackbird* is a tribute to Hoyt Fuller:

a man, standing in the shadows of a
white marble building
chipping at the stones earnestly, tirelessly,
moving with the changes of the hours,
the days,
the seasons and years,
using the shadows to shield him
such a man,
can go un noticed. . . .

Less prose-like than some of the other poems in the volume, the poem is finely crafted without rhetorical excesses. Its imagery is memorable and wedded to the idea of the poem:

but the man who grows inside the shadows,
chipping at the foundation, long after
windows and doors have been replaced,
the man, who becomes the dark shadow of a

white marble building, will
pick the foundation to pieces,
chip by chip, and

the
building
will
fall.

This poem effectively demonstrates Carolyn Rodgers's stylistic and technical development in her second volume, and it has rightly been one of her more acclaimed works, about which Don L. Lee has stated: "There is the touch of the inner self here. Her images are effective and new, tell much about an obviously complicated, yet simple man. There is growth in this poem. There is commitment to craft and serious subject matter."

Carolyn Rodgers's first two volumes of poetry, however, did not receive unanimous praise. Nor did the young poet win unqualified acceptance as a significant new voice among black poets. Fellow poets and critics, Dudley Randall and Haki Madhubuti for instance, had reservations about her language and her rendering of black speech. Randall found her use of too many unfamiliar spellings in *Songs of a Blackbird* distracting; Madhubuti questioned her mixing of standard English forms and black idiomatic constructions. Indeed, Rodgers was not very strong in either of her early books in rendering black speech, and she was unconventional, even for a revolutionary black woman poet, in her use of obscenities. Nonetheless, Madhubuti, Hoyt Fuller, Stephen Henderson, David Llorens, Gwendolyn Brooks, and other poets and critics recognized her genuine talent and remarked her development. In 1970, the year after the publication of *Songs of a Blackbird,* she received the Poet Laureate Award of the Society of Midland Authors and an award from the National Endowment of the Arts. As Bettye Parker-Smith has concluded, "Certainly, there never was a gap between the world of Rodgers's vision which she glorifies and the authentic Black community. She simply lacked understanding of some of its components at the beginning."

Though inconsistent in her language in her earliest volumes, Rodgers nonetheless had an eye for the contradictions of black experience, particularly the revolutionary or militant experience of the 1960s. Her use of speech patterns and of lengthened prose-like lines was an attempt at breaking away from the restrictions of conventional forms and modes, and most especially from those considered appropriate for women poets. While never an accurate recorder of street talk, as is clear from the poem "The Revolution is Resting," which is a dialogue between two street-wise people, Joe and Little Willie, Rodgers is perceptive in rendering the ideas that ordinary black individuals might have about the larger world, and she intuits well the possible ways in which they understand their relationship to that world. She acknowledges that she is concerned with form and style in her work but that ultimately she puts "the poem on paper by sense and touch, much like a blind person fumbling in the dark for light."

She may not have demonstrated a careful use of language in her early works, yet Carolyn Rodgers has exhibited a clarity of expression and a respect for well-crafted language in her next book, *how i got ovah: New and Selected Poems,* which was published in 1975 by Anchor/Doubleday. The poems in this collection are mainly autobiographical, and they "reveal Rodgers's transformation from a . . . militant Black woman to a woman intensely concerned with God, traditional values, and her private self," as a reviewer for *Library Journal* has observed. Many of the poems are written in black English primarily for communicating with the black community, but a substantial number of others are written in standard English. Rodgers writes with humor, sincerity, and love in the poems of this volume that treat black revolution, feminism, religion, God, the black church, and the black family, especially the mother. Although her messages often explore social conflict, they usually conclude with a sense of peace, hope, and a desire to search for life's real treasure—inner beauty.

Rodgers's messages and concerns all seem to come together in her poems involving her mother, whom she has called one of the staunch rocks of the AME church. In poems such as "for muh' dear," "It Must Be Deep," "It is Deep," and "Jesus Was Crucified," she brings to life the generational conflict between a militant daughter with "wild free knotty and nappy/hair" and a "religious-negro" mother, but she also records the daughter's growing appreciation for her mother and her way of living and surviving. "for muh' dear" suggests a coming to terms with her mother and an understanding of her religion: "Grace has brought me safe this far, and grace will lead me on." In the companion poems, "It Must Be Deep" and "It Is Deep," the poet is initially uncertain about her mother's postures in life, primarily her dependence on God and religion. But

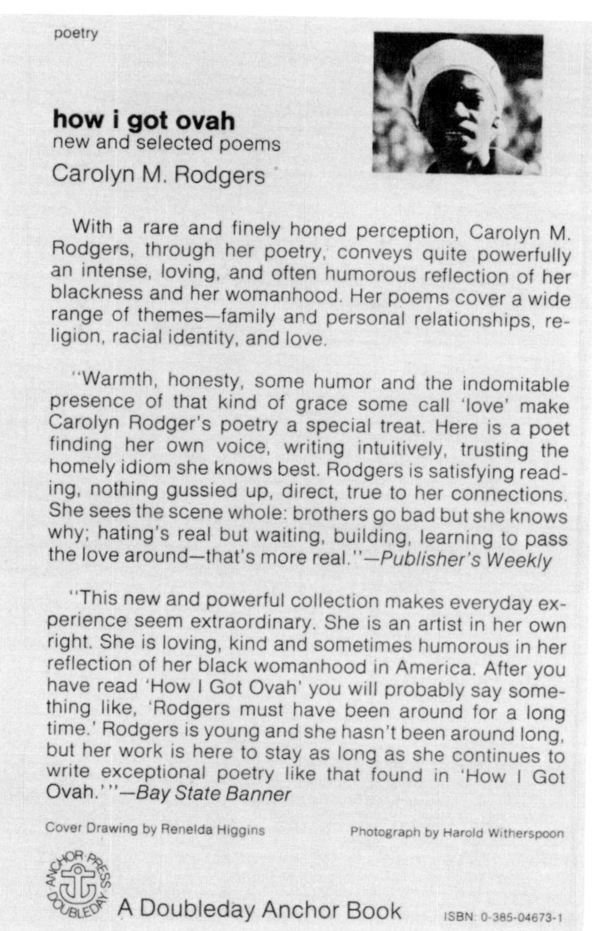

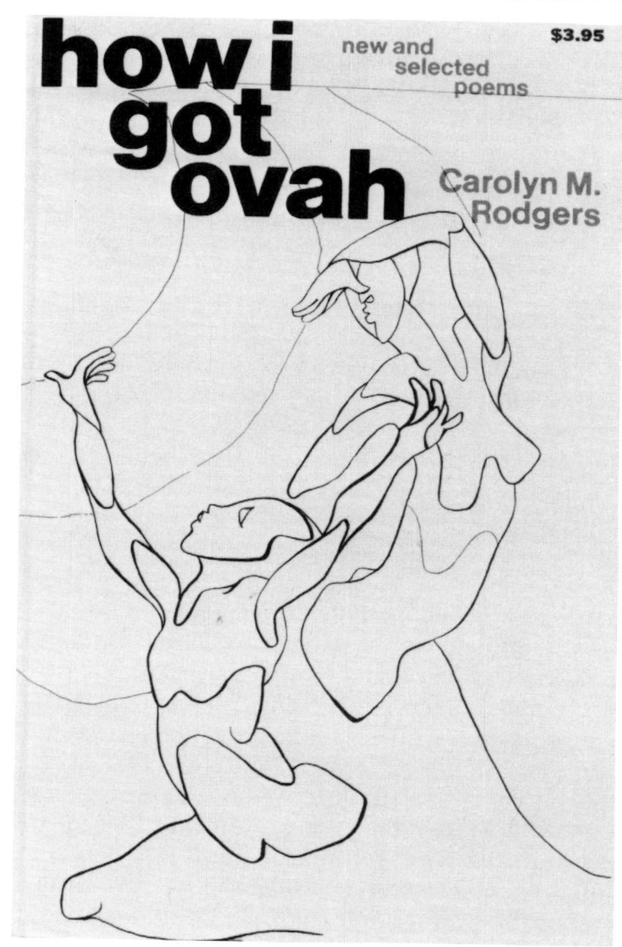

Covers for Rodgers's 1975 book. Angela Jackson calls Rodgers "a choir in herself" and a "singer of sass and blues."

the revolutionary daughter, sick and in need, soon understands the necessity of being sustained and cared for:

My mother, religiously girdled in
her god, slipped on some love, and
laid on my bell like a truck,
blew through my door warm wind from the south
concern making her gruff and tight-lipped
    and scared
that her "baby" was starving.

The ideological differences may be great between daughter and mother who "did not/recognize the poster of the/grand le-roi (al) cat on the wall/had never even seen the books of/Black poems that I have written," but so are their bonds to each other. The mother does recognize a vast gap between herself and her daughter ("U DON'T BELIEVE IN GOD NO MO DO U???/u wudn't raised that way!"), but she loves her child ("i mon pray fuh y tuh be saved . . . if yuh need me call me/i hope we don't have tuh straighten the truth out no mo"). At the same time, the mother realizes that her daughter needs more than spiritual nurturing, a point that her daughter does not overlook: "[she] pressed fifty/bills in my hand saying 'pay the talk bill and buy/some food; you got folks who care about you. . . .' " Her mother's practical, almost overwhelming presence forces the daughter to concede: "My mother, religious-negro proud of/having waded through a storm is very obviously/a sturdy Black bridge that I/crossed over, on."

The complexity of the mother-daughter relationship in the poems is one main source of their power, just as the mother, despite her strong will to control and determine her daughter's fate, is the source of her daughter's strength. Mother and God merge when the daughter makes the slip: "Catch yuh later on jesus, i mean motha!" She may struggle against her mother's values, but she is comforted by her mother's love and caring. The healing power suggested by the mother makes it possible for the daughter to remain simultaneously detached from and engaged with her mother and possibly to reconcile the various divergent threads of her existence. Rodgers's poems are especially effective in rendering the staunch, old-fashioned, religious mothers who sacrifice for their children, particularly for their daughters. Her concern is similar to Alice Walker's in poems such as "The Women." In her poems, Rodgers acknowledges a major part of the history of black women, who, like the mother in "Portrait," "saved pennies/fuh four babies/college educashuns" but who could not anticipate the changes in their children's worlds that would move them away from the values and beliefs of their parents. The dilemma of both generations is realistic and moving in *how i got ovah.* In identifying Rodgers's "wide range of topics as revolution, love, black male-female relationships, religion, and the complexities of Black womanhood," Angelene Jamison also points to the way Rodgers "convincingly reinterprets the love, pain, longings, struggles, victories, the day-to-day routines of Black people from the point of view of the Black woman." Jamison notices that Rodgers is "gracefully courageous enough to explore long-hidden truths . . . [with] honesty, warmth, and love for Black people."

In her foreword to *how i got ovah,* poet Angela Jackson calls attention to Rodgers as "a choir in herself," as a "singer of sass and blues" who has a "sanctified soul." Jackson makes clear that with the poems of this volume, Rodgers is no longer the "skinny, . . . knock-kneed lackey" of her self-portrait in *Paper Soul;* instead "she is all grown up . . ./she reminds u of church,/her eye is seeing holy . . ./she is a witness. will glorify you . . ./Carolyn is a poet/. . . . humming her people/to the promised land." Jackson quite correctly celebrated Rodgers's coming of age in her third book, whose poetry demonstrates a mature talent with musical gifts and penetrating insights.

In looking back at her work, Rodgers observes that her "focus is on life, love, eternity, pain, and joy," but she is quick to add that "something *is* expected of women that is not expected of men. . . ." The evolving feminism in her poems of the 1970s is a natural extension of her reflections on herself and her world. One reviewer for *Booklist* noticed that in *how i got ovah,* she brings to her work "the doubts and uncertainties of being true to herself and her Black heritage, the search for a meaningful voice in her poems." Works such as "Trilogy—Untitled," "No Such Thing as a Witch/Just a Woman, Needing Some Love," "For Women (Amazing Grace)," and "Masquerade" all treat the special lot of the black woman in relationships with men, men who are the dreams but not the realities of women who are sometimes neglected and unloved. Often Rodgers portrays the loneliness of these women as lessened by the church and God, and she shows how as they go about the business of "praising, singing and praying," these women maintain hope and stability in their lives. Much of this poetry bears Rodgers's own social history, and by extension, it also carries the dilemma of other contemporary black women, who in "Poem for Some Black Women" are presented as "talented, dedicated, well-read/BLACK COMMITTED," but who are also alone and attempting to cope with "the music of silence" and with emptiness, but whose recognition is "we need ourselves sick, we need, we need/ . . . we grow tired of fear/we grow tired but we must al-ways be soft and not too serious . . . not too smart not too bitchy not too sapphire/ . . . a little less a little more/add here detract there. . . ." Rodgers emphasizes the various pressures on the black woman and her sense of self and identity; nonetheless, she does not relinquish the possibility for the black woman's definition of self. In "I Have Been Hungry" she states that she is "no longer a simple girl/bringing lemonade and cookies/begging favor"; she is a "saved/sighing/singular thing. a woman. . . ." And in "Some Me of Beauty" she is content with the essential "me" of her own identity: "I woke up one mornin/and looked at my self/and what i saw was/Carolyn. . . ." She sees in herself "more than a 'sister' "; she recognizes a "woman. human./and black." The experience is "a spiritual transformation/a root revival of love/and i knew that many things/were over. and some me of—beauty—was about to begin. . . ."

The acts of defining self and of becoming are central to the feminist themes that have grown more prominent in Rodgers's poetry. She has observed the changes in herself and in her work. In the beginning of her career, she reveals, "I was just a writer out here just writing. Then I went to an orientation of Black (Negro) work and then I wrote with a message, a sociological orientation. Actually, I've come full circle to a certain extent. I don't write the same message." Even more revealingly, she has observed more of the specific changes in her thought and poetry: "I think I write more as a woman than . . . as a person, but then I think I write more as a human as opposed to a person or a personality, perhaps, more than anything I write as a human, a woman, who is Brown. I am questioning the use of the word Black, i.e., Blacks. I now prefer the word Brown, i.e., Brown people, and with this change goes an ideology and a new set of ideas." What is apparent is that Carolyn Rodgers continues to struggle with words and meaning all the while she persists in evolving her own selfhood.

Rodgers's most recent volume of poetry, *The Heart As Ever Green,* was published by Anchor/Doubleday in 1978. The themes of human dignity, feminism, love, black consciousness, and Christianity are repeated throughout the book; however, the overarching theme is expressed metaphorically by the title poem "The Black Heart As Ever Green":

> My heart is
> ever green. green
> like a season of emeralds
> green as in tender & like buds or shoots,
> determined to grow
> determined to be
> . . . .
> green
> like a light
> in the world, for freedom
> for
> what is to come
> what we must know
> what we must be

Determination to grow and to be is the most prevalent idea in the volume. While Rodgers takes advantage of the opportunity to express concern for truth, knowledge, and conflicts in life, she insists in poems such as "Earth Is Not the World, Nor All Its Beauty," "Black Licorice," "Feminism," and "Translation" that creation, becoming, renewal, and growth are not only potentialities, but accessible realities, if one but looks at the larger picture of the world and nature and then reads its truths. The result for the individual, in particular the woman and the poet, will be peace, inner harmony, and beauty. "Translation," the final poem in *The Heart As Ever Green,* renders her message with clarity and simplicity: "I say,/we will, live./no death is a/singular unregenerating/event." The poem, along with the others in the volume, shows why one reviewer, Antar Sudan Katara Mberi, writing for *Freedomways,* has praised Rodgers's new work for its search for "truth, meaning, peace with equality, love and human compassion."

One major stylistic development in *The Heart As Ever Green* seems especially appropriate for the themes. Rodgers relies upon images and metaphors, often drawn from the natural world, in order to paint her ideas. For example, in "Earth Is Not the World, Nor All Its Beauty," she uses the spring flowering, yellow forsythia bush as a metaphor for the process of annual renewal and for the sudden, bright appearance of hope and positive creation:

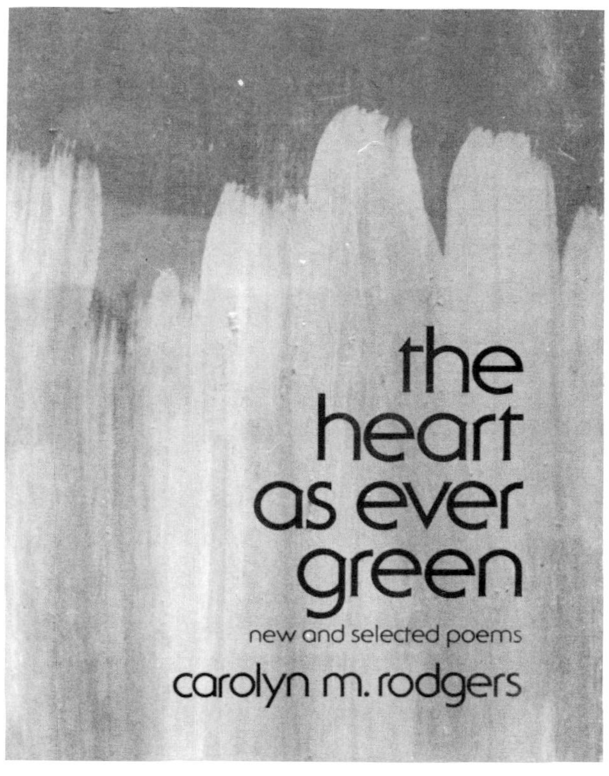

Dust jacket for Rodgers's 1978 collection of poetry. The title comes from her lines " . . . and when we spoke of freedom/we spoke of our hearts/as/ever green."

> here comes
> the forsythia, opening
> all golden
> like a low down
> weeping willow.
> the arms not so sorry but
> arched slightly, stiffened &
> down proud, blooming blooming
> all golden and petals belled—
> contrasted against stark air
> showcased against blue sky
> against the blackkneed bronzed Benin
> of trees
> against the stencil green of April—
> ah look,

here comes
the forsythia.

By employing a reference to "the blackkneed bronzed Benin," Rodgers suggests the connection between the natural process portrayed in the poem and the condition of people of African descent. This subtle poem shows the distance Rodgers has traveled since the publication of her first strident works.

In addition to poetry, Rodgers has also published short stories. "Blackbird in a Cage," which appeared in the August 1967 issue of *Negro Digest*, is about a little girl trapped both in a bad neighborhood and by her mother's dictates. Her mother would not let her cross the street to play with the other children, even though she was allowed outside. The girl accepted her mother's rationale for treating her so strictly:

> since I was lefthanded, I owed the
> devil a day's work, and he was not
> going to collect it if she had anything
> to do with it. So to church I went so I
> could get saved and cheat the devil
> out of his due.

This story parallels Rodgers's own life, as she has stated: "My mother was like toll the line until we get out of here. You can't do this, you can't do that, you can't go here, you can't go there because this is a bad neighborhood." To the little girl, not only was the neighborhood a cage, her mother was as well.

In June of 1969, one of Rodgers's favorite stories, "A Statistic, Trying to Make It Home," appeared in *Negro Digest*. Benny Loman, the main character, tries to decide whether to buy two reefers or two pills so he can get high. After deciding on the pills, he gets caught by the police for being out past curfew. The story is based on a reality familiar to Rodgers who was working in a school dropout program when she wrote the story. "I just could pinpoint something that was tragic. They didn't know where home was," she remembers of the boys and girls who would get high. Benny Loman was trying to get home. But home was not a high, as he discovers in the story and avoids becoming a statistic.

Another short story, "One Time," was published in the November 1975 issue of *Essence*. The dominant theme is the black woman's survival. Marlene, the main character, is pregnant and attending a training program for dropout girls. When she does not submit a note from her doctor verifying that she had been ill on a day she was absent, she is afraid her check will be short. Not only is Marlene's check short, but she also gets dropped from the program. She becomes highly frustrated because she cannot be recycled back into high school, nor can she get a job because she is pregnant, which is the result of her "first time," just as her being dropped from the training program is the result of just one time. Her aunt does not give her any money and Spider, the man who fathered the baby, cannot find a job. Marlene has only one alternative left—public assistance, which Rodgers depicts as robbing the individual of human spirit.

In her stories as in her poetry, the dominating theme is survival, though she interweaves the idea of adaptability and conveys the concomitant message of life's ever-changing avenues for black people whom she sees as her special audience. Rodgers says that her writing "is for whoever wants to read it . . . one poem doesn't do that. But I try to put as many as I can in a book. A poem for somebody young, religious people, the church people. Just people. Specifically, Black people. I would like for them to like me."

Although she has been writing poetry for over twenty years, Carolyn Rodgers still sees herself as "becoming": "I am a has-been, would perhaps, going to be. Underneath, I'm a dot. With no i's." During her career as a writer, she has also been a teacher: Columbia College (1968-1969); University of Washington (Summer 1970); Malcolm X Community College (1972); Albany State College (1972); Indiana University (Summer 1973). She has also been a book reviewer for the *Chicago Daily News*, as well as a columnist for the *Milwaukee Courier*. Throughout the years of different positions and interests, she has been sustained by her poetry and by music.

She admits that she has always loved music. Her father "was a musician of a sort in that he loved to sing and so he introduced it in the house in a traditional way—quartet (Negro quartet)," and her mother was also so fond of music that she required all of her children to take piano lessons. Rodgers is a master of the guitar and for a time sang folk songs. Although she once considered becoming a musician, she decided against it because she did not appreciate the musician's night life. In terms of her poetry, Rodgers's future appears to be very bright, but music is certain to play a role of increasing importance, as she has said:

> I also hope to really stretch out in music because I already have, but I haven't introduced

> it to the world. I compose and I really hope to become a musician . . . tying up some things in this field [writing]. I don't think that I will put it down but music is where I'm headed. I really do love music. I always have, but I never could get to it. I put it off and I could never get to it like I wanted to. . . . I finally was able to really get to it . . . and now I'm really beginning to open up.

Because she is so talented a poet, it is fortunate that Carolyn Rodgers plans to continue with her writing while developing her musical gifts and composing music. However, her four already published volumes of poetry have assured her a place among the best of the new black poets.

References:

Mari Evans, ed., *Black Women Writers (1950-1980): A Critical Evaluation* (Garden City: Anchor/ Doubleday, 1984);

Don L. Lee, *Dynamite Voices: Black Poets of the 1960's* (Detroit: Broadside Press, 1971);

Antar Sudan Katara Mberi, "Reaching for Unity and Harmony," *Freedomways*, 20 (First Quarter 1980): 48-49.

Sonia Sanchez

(9 September 1934-)

Kalamu ya Salaam

BOOKS: *Homecoming* (Detroit: Broadside, 1969);

Liberation Poem (Detroit: Broadside, 1970);

We A BaddDDD People (Detroit: Broadside, 1970);

It's A New Day (poems for young brothas and sistuhs) (Detroit: Broadside, 1971);

Ima Talken bout the Nation of Islam (Astoria, N.Y.: TruthDel., 1972);

A Blues Book for Blue Black Magical Women (Detroit: Broadside, 1973);

The Adventures of Fathead, Smallhead, and Squarehead (New York: Third Press, 1973);

Love Poems (New York: Third Press, 1973);

A Sound Investment (Chicago: Third World Press, 1980);

I've Been A Woman: New and Selected Poems (Sausalito, Cal.: Black Scholar Press, 1981);

Crisis In Culture–Two Speeches By Sonia Sanchez (New York: Black Liberation Press, 1983);

homegirls & handgrenades (New York: Thunder's Mouth Press, 1984).

PLAY PRODUCTIONS: *The Bronx is Next*, New York, Theatre Black, University of the Streets, 3 October 1970;

Sister Son/ji, in *Black Visions* (includes Neil Harris's *Cop and Blow* and *Players Inn* and Richard Wesley's *Gettin' It Together*), New York, Shakespeare Festival Public Theatre, 1972;

Uh, Huh; But How Do It Free Us?, Chicago, Northwestern University Theatre, 1975?;

Malcolm/Man Don't Live Here No Mo', Philadelphia, ASCOM Community Center, 1979;

I'm Black When I'm Singing, I'm Blue When I Ain't, Atlanta, OIC Theatre, 23 April 1982.

RECORDINGS: *Sonia Sanchez*, Pacifica Tape Library, 1968?;

We A BaddDDD People, Broadside, 1969;

Homecoming, Broadside, 1969;

A Sun Woman for All Seasons Reads Her Poetry, Folkways, 1971;

Sonia Sanchez and Robert Bly, Blackbox, 1971;

Sonia Sanchez: Selected Poems, 1974, Watershed Intermedia, 1975;

IDKT: Captivating Facts About the Heritage of Black Americans, Ujima, 1982.

OTHER: Dudley Randall and Margaret Burroughs, eds., *For Malcolm: Poems on the Life and the Death of Malcolm X*, includes poems by Sanchez (Detroit: Broadside, 1967);

LeRoi Jones and Larry Neal, eds., *Black Fire: An Anthology of Afro-American Writing*, includes poems by Sanchez (New York: Morrow, 1968);

Sister Son/ji, in *New Plays From the Black Theatre*, edited by Ed Bullins (New York: Bantam, 1969);

Arnold Adoff, ed., *Black Out Loud: An Anthology of Modern Poems by Black Americans*, includes poems by Sanchez (New York: Macmillan, 1970);

Arthur Davis and Saunders Redding, eds., *Cavalcade: Negro American Writing from 1760 to the Present,* includes poems by Sanchez (Boston: Houghton Mifflin, 1971);

Randall, ed., *The Black Poets,* includes poems by Sanchez (New York: Bantam, 1971);

Bernard W. Bell, ed., *Modern and Contemporary Afro-American Poetry,* includes poems by Sanchez (Boston: Allyn & Bacon, 1972);

Three Hundred and Sixty Degrees of Blackness Comin' At You, edited by Sanchez (New York: 5X Publishing Company, 1972);

Donald Gibson, ed., *Modern Black Poets,* includes poems by Sanchez (Englewood Cliffs, N.J.: Prentice-Hall, 1973);

Stephen Henderson, ed., *Understanding the New Black Poetry: Black Speech and Black Music as Poetic References,* includes poems by Sanchez (New York: Morrow, 1973);

J. Paul Hunter, ed., *Norton Introduction to Literature; Poetry,* includes poems by Sanchez (New York: Norton, 1973);

James Schevill, ed., *Breakout: In Search of New Theatrical Environments,* includes play by Sanchez (Chicago: Swallow Press, 1973);

We Be Word Sorcerers: 25 Stories by Black Americans, edited by Sanchez (New York: Bantam, 1973);

Uh, Huh; But How Do It Free Us?, in *The New Lafayette Theatre Presents: Plays with Aesthetic Comments by 6 Black Playwrights,* edited by Ed Bullins (Garden City: Anchor/Doubleday, 1974);

Lucille Iverson and Kathryn Ruby, eds., *We Become New: Poems by Contemporary Women,* includes poems by Sanchez (New York: Bantam, 1975);

Quincy Troupe and Rainer Schulte, eds., *Giant Talk: An Anthology of Third World Writings,* includes poems by Sanchez (New York: Random House, 1975);

Ann Reit, ed., *Alone Amid All This Noise,* includes poems by Sanchez (New York: Four Winds/Scholastic, 1976);

Erlene Stetson, ed., *Black Sister: Poetry by Black American Women, 1746-1980,* includes poems by Sanchez (Bloomington: Indiana University Press, 1981);

Amiri and Amina Baraka, eds., *Confirmation: An Anthology of African-American Women,* includes poems by Sanchez (New York: Morrow, 1983);

"Ruminations/Reflections," in *Black Women Writers (1950-1980),* edited by Mari Evans (Garden City: Anchor/Doubleday, 1984);

Sonia Sanchez (courtesy of Lordly & Dame)

"The Poet as Creator of Social Values," in *Swords Upon this Hill,* edited by Burney Hollis (Baltimore: Morgan State University Press, 1984);

Jerome Rothenberg, ed., *Technicians of the Sacred: A Range of Poetries from Africa, America, Asia, Europe and Oceania,* includes a poem by Sanchez (Berkeley: University of California Press, 1985).

PERIODICAL PUBLICATIONS:

POETRY

"Life is Not a Dream," "The Inmate," *Minnesota Review,* 2 (Summer 1962): 460-461;

"I Want to Know; I Needs to Know," *Black World,* 19 (September 1970): 53.

DRAMA

The Bronx is Next, Drama Review, 12 (Summer 1968): 78-83;

Dirty Hearts, Scripts, 1 (November 1971): 46-50;

Malcolm/Man Don't Live Here No Mo', Black Theatre, no. 6 (1972): 24-27.

NONFICTION

"Nefertiti: Queen to a Sacred Mission," *Journal of African Civilizations,* 6 (April 1984).

Poet, activist, playwright, editor, teacher, scholar, and nurturer of Afro-American creativity, Sonia Sanchez holds a respected place in American letters of the past two decades. Her commitment to black communities throughout the country is apparent from the many roles she has played, and her untiring perpetuation of Afro-American literature is enviable. Shaped by the creativity of the 1960s, coming to maturity in the 1970s, and thriving as a scholar and teacher in the 1980s, Sanchez is one of the few creative artists who have significantly influenced the course of black American literature and culture. Consistently giving of her time, energy, and resources to a variety of causes in the black community, Sanchez provides the example for what she preaches, and she "lives the life that she sings about in her songs."

Sanchez was born Wilsonia Driver on 9 September 1934 in Birmingham, Alabama. Her mother, Lena Driver, died when Sonia was one, and as a consequence, Sonia and her sister Pat spent their early years living with different relatives of the Driver extended family. As a child she stuttered and often describes herself as being "shy" during that phase of her development. To those familiar with the outspoken, articulate, and assertive Sanchez of the post-1960s, such a beginning may seem incredible. When Sonia was nine years old, her father, Wilson L. Driver, moved the family to Harlem, New York, although a stepbrother remained in the South.

In 1955 Sanchez received a B.A. degree in political science from Hunter College in New York City. She did graduate work in poetry with Louise Bogan at New York University for one year following her graduation from Hunter.

In the 1960s Sanchez emerged as a writer as well as a political activist. In the early part of the decade, she began publishing in Dan Watts's magazine, the *Liberator,* as well as in the *Journal of Black Poetry,* edited by Joe Goncalves. Her work also appeared in Hoyt Fuller's *Negro Digest* and in *Black Dialogue,* the editorial board of which included Ed Spriggs. Sanchez's first book, *Homecoming* (1969), was brought out by Broadside Press, the publishing house started by Dudley Randall, which had published a number of influential poets. Although numbering less than thirty individuals, the poets published by Randall had an emotional and intellectual impact on America which had not been felt since the heady days of the Harlem Renaissance. Indeed, some referred to the black arts movement of the 1960s as a new "Renaissance" in the black arts.

Sanchez's early voice was one of militant blackness. Her poetic style was brief, razor sharp, and full of scorn and invective for "white America." Recalling that period, she credits Malcolm X, specifically, and popular street culture, generally, as the inspirational matrix for much of her poetic technique. "A lot of our words and language came from Malcolm," she says. "He was always messing with the language and messing with people, and sometimes in a very sly kind of way demanding things of people and also cursing people out." "For Unborn Malcolms," from *Homecoming,* typifies both the inspiration from Malcolm X and the militant stance of retaliation for white violence:

its time
    an eye for an eye
    a tooth for a tooth
    don't worry bout his balls
they al
        ready gone.
            git the word
out that us blk/niggers
            are out to lunch
and the main course
is gonna be his white meat.
            yeah.

In her early work, Sanchez skillfully wields a word arsenal that includes hyperbole, name calling (wolfing, the dozens), double entendre (she aptly applied the phrase "a badddd people" to blacks in the 1960s—meant as the highest compliment), and the profanity that characterized so many of her contemporaries. She has commented upon what she saw herself and others doing:

> A lot of the Black poetry that we wrote during the sixties was playing the dozens on a very interesting level and also playing with words on a very interesting level. On some levels, you had to know Black culture in order to deal with it. . . . Lightly tapping people and sometimes slapping them, and saying "deal with this" and this is what it really be about. Going back and reading some of that poetry, you have to really understand the time and what the politics were about.

Sanchez developed techniques for reading her poetry that were unique in their use of traditional chants and near-screams drawn out to an almost earsplitting level. The sound elements, which give a musical quality to the intellectual statements in the poetry, are akin to West African languages; Sanchez has tried to recapture a style of delivery that she felt had been muted by the experience of slavery. In her successful experimentation with such techniques, she joined Haki Madhubuti (Don L. Lee) and others in being innovative enough to bring black poetry to black people at a level that was accessible to the masses, as well as enjoyable for them.

Sanchez's militancy with words was carried over into her political activity. During part of the 1960s, she was in California and actively involved in the movement to bring black studies programs into college curricula. Known informally as the "Black Studies Movement," the activities Sanchez became involved in challenged the basic assumptions of America's higher educational system. Sanchez was joined by other writers and activists, including Amiri Baraka, Marvin X, Ed Bullins, Huey Newton, Eldridge Cleaver, Maulana Ron Karenga, and Nathan Hare, in working to bring about change. The efforts to change the system that she herself was a part of were only the beginning of Sanchez's political fervor. To this day, she continues to speak out as a lecturer and as an organizer. She has lectured and read her poetry at over five hundred universities and colleges in the United States and has traveled extensively to such places as Cuba, England, the People's Republic of China, Norway, and the West Indies. Each occasion has provided her with an opportunity to share her convictions about the ways in which human beings should live with and among each other.

Sanchez continues to offer support for causes that can easily bring retribution; for example, she wrote an introduction to a volume by Assata Shakur, a member of the Black Liberation Army who was put on the FBI's most wanted list. After she had been involved in a shootout during which a state trooper was killed, Shakur was convicted of murder and sentenced to prison, but she effected a daring escape. Sanchez's support for her occasioned an explicitly unfriendly visit from the FBI. Never faltering in her determination to stand up and be counted, Sanchez is consistent in her advocacy of revolutionary elements in this country and abroad. She is a frequent agitator on behalf of the liberation struggles of African peoples in their homeland and throughout the Diaspora. In addition to being an avid supporter of the Plowshares (direct action antinuclear activists) and the Brandywine Peace Community, Sanchez is a member of MADRE (an international organization in solidarity with the mothers of Nicaragua), and she supports numerous grassroots/local political organizations, such as MOMS in Alabama and the National Black United Front. "Reflections After the June 12th March for Disarmament" serves as an affirmative credo of Sanchez's internationalist view of humanity:

> I am here because I shall not give the
> earth up to non-dreamers and earth molesters.

In the mid-1960s, Sanchez began the long teaching career that has lent support to her work as a writer and an activist. She taught at the Downtown Community School in San Francisco from 1965 until 1967; at San Francisco State College (now University) from 1967 until 1969; and at the University of Pittsburgh from 1969 until 1970. She has also taught at Rutgers University (1970-1971), Manhattan Community College (1971-1973), and Amherst College (1972-1975), and the University of Pennsylvania (1976-1977). Currently, she is professor of English at Temple University, where she teaches black American literature and creative writing.

Teaching provided Sanchez with the opportunity to put her politics into effect in two very specific ways. In 1972, she edited *Three Hundred and Sixty Degrees of Blackness Comin' At You,* a collection of writings by her students in a creative writing class she conducted in Harlem. Her concern for young minds also manifested itself during this period in her publication of several books for children. Beginning with *It's A New Day* (1971) and including *The Adventures of Fathead, Smallhead, and Squarehead* (1973) and *A Sound Investment* (1980), Sanchez has written children's books the intent of which is to orient and teach through fable, fantasy, and figurative lessons. Of her intentions, Sanchez comments:

> In my head those stories always came out of a conscious reason for dealing with something. When the children were little, I heard a comment about someone being slow one day when a bunch of children were playing in the house. That pushed me to do a story that seemingly was absurd in terms of Fat Head, Small Head and Square Head but it was meant to involve children in that fantasy land in which they live. Children like and laugh at that fantasy, but they also get to the part about the slow. So the movement from fantasy to a lesson, that is concrete and real, that happens.
>
> Another example is the fable "How the Rain Was Made." It grew out of a need to

explain fully and scientifically how rain was made. So you do the whole cloud bit and pull out the encyclopedia, but then you also try to hit upon the spiritual. I've always attempted, and not always successfully, to balance the scientific and the spiritual. From my guts, I see the need for that. I think that's what a lot of African things were about: the balancing of that which is scientific with that which is spiritual and creative in order to let people see that there must be a balance in the world. That is very important to me.

In her general concern for children, Sanchez perhaps paralleled what was happening in her own life. In the late 1960s, her political activism led her to befriend Etheridge Knight, who was in prison at that time on drug charges. They were married and divorced. She is the mother of a daughter, Anita, and twin sons, Mungu and Morani.

The 1970s saw Sanchez expanding her writing into drama, and the decade anticipated her later expansion into autobiographical writings. Her most popular play, *Sister Son/ji* (produced in 1972), a one-character drama, grapples with the contradiction of a revolutionary movement weakened and rendered almost ineffective by the antiblack-woman actions of the men who dominated that movement. In *Uh Huh; But How Do It Free Us?* (1975?), Sanchez depicts a black male character who beats a black woman into submission after she confronts and challenges him about lying to her. In direct contrast to a similar scene in Amiri Baraka's *Madheart,* produced in the same period, Sanchez does not idealize the woman's submission as "revolutionary," nor does she suggest that the woman is happy in that position. Hindsight obviously renders Sanchez's position as the correct one, but she was voicing an unpopular sentiment at the time; her position was in opposition to the perceived and publicly acknowledged ideas of the leaders of the movement.

Sanchez incorporated into *Uh Huh* a scene that she had drawn from her own life and included in a poem written in 1967. In the play, Sister, one of the characters, recounts: "And you were at the airport with a rose, one lone red rose. And I thought, man, that's beautiful. I'm going to press that rose in the first book you sent me. Do you remember?" Brother responds: "Yeah. It was Fanon's *Studies in a Dying Colonialism,* wasn't it?" "After the Fifth Day," in *Love Poems* (1973), depicts the same scene:

After the fifth day

Front cover for Sanchez's 1971 book for young people

with you
i pressed the
rose you brought me
into one of fanon's books.
it has no odor now.
but
i see you. handing me a red
rose and i remember
my birth.

Although the poem was published later than the play, it is just one example of the many instances in which Sanchez worked and reworked her life experiences into her art.

Her autobiographical writings, which may be called "neo-slave narratives," share a similar purpose to the originals in that genre. In slave narratives, the life of an individual or family was used to comment on the evils of slavery and the necessity of abolition; they ultimately aimed for psychological and physical freedom. In like manner, Sanchez comments upon the social condition of contemporary Afro-Americans in an effort to accomplish their psychological freedom and, where necessary, their physical freedom. In her most recent and powerful book, *homegirls & handgrenades* (1984), she builds the neo-slave narrative to a stunning artistic summit in prose poems that reflect on a lifetime of struggle. This volume contains Sanchez's best-known prose piece, "After Saturday Nite Comes Sunday." Based on her life and delivered in tattered, yet vivid images, the work concentrates upon a woman whose love is being abused by a man strung out on dope. Images of dope—the debilitating practice first noticed in her childhood in a New York tenement—pervade Sanchez's work as a metaphor for ultimate evil; it is a living death, a snuffing out of the will to live. From such debilitations, Sanchez would make her people free.

During all of her ventures into other genres, Sanchez continued her publication of poetry, and it is primarily as a poet that she has earned a place for her literary contributions since the mid-1960s. She has perhaps made her sharpest observations on the theme of alienation and its myriad manifestations. Oppression and discrimination unavoidably produce alienation from the oppressive society. Another kind of alienation can develop within the self: the warrior self despises the victim self, hence an active self-love/self-hate dialectic. Those who attempt to escape the psychological death of the ghetto by adhering to middle-class American values also become alienated, as do the artists whose very work makes them distinct from the masses of blacks. Sanchez unsentimentally examines these various levels of alienation.

In the prose poem "Bubba," about a childhood male friend, she writes:

> One summer day, I remember Bubba and I banging the ball against the filling station. Handball champs we were. The king and queen of handball we were. And we talked as we played. He asked me if I ever talked to trees or rivers or things like that. And I who walked with voices for years denied the different tongues populating my mouth. I stood still denying the commonplace things of my private childhood. And his eyes pinned me against the filling station wall and my eyes became small and lost their color.

Years later, "after graduation," Sanchez attempts to "return to the source." She wants to bridge the alienation and vows: "As long as I have hands that write; as long as I have eyes that see; as long as I can bear your name against silence; I shall never forget our last talk Bubba." But it is a last talk that ends with Bubba moving away from Sanchez after asking her for twenty dollars to support a drug habit: "He finally pulled himsef up off the bench. He stood up with the last breath of a dying man."

In another prose piece, "Traveling on an Amtrak Train Could Humanize You," Sanchez opens by observing the arrival of a "different" kind of commuter on the train. "I saw him enter the train. His walk announced a hipster for all seasons; his clothing said doorways, hunger and brawls. A lifetime of insults." In the 1960s, such an opening would be a set-up for instant identification with the "brother" getting on the train whose presence upsets the white order of things. But Sanchez understands and does not flinch from the realization that part of her is part of the order of things on this Amtrak train. Painfully, she tells us: "I immediately put my large brown bag on the seat next to mine, lowered my eyes, turned my head to peer out at the figures rushing to catch the train to NYC." The stranger/brother sits behind her, next to a white man, and engages the man in conversation about their respective conditions in society. At the end of the ride, pulling into New York City and coming out of the train station, Sanchez continues the identification with those who have ignored the stranger/brother. In the process she confronts herself: "Here we are, people, I wanted to cry out. Here we are in NYC without the slightest idea of why and who when we ignore the men and women keloiding before us with pain." The scene in the 1980s is dramatically different from that in the 1960s.

In putting forth her themes, Sanchez is, above all, a sound poet; she loves words not just for their meaning in an intellectual sense but also for their sounds. To hear her read is to know this instantly, particularly when she "speaks in tongues": using the voice of a child searching for parents on a slave ship or in a South American village under attack by fascist forces, or the voice of a slave moving from crying submission to an angry war chant. She makes new music, not just simple melodies borrowed from popular songs or traditional hymns and blues but improvised music that reaches beyond the tempered scale. At times, Sanchez literally cries, screams, pleads, and moans. Although this is a part of her poetry that is difficult to convey on the printed page, from time to time she provides instruction to the reader in the form of annotations that are also part of the poem. The following excerpt from one of her poems illustrates this point:

> (to be rise up blk/people
> sung de dum da da da da
> slowly move straight in yo/blackness
> to tune da dum da da da da

of my favorite things.) step over the wite/ness
that is yesssss terrrrrr day
weeeeeeee are toooooooday.

"When I write," Sanchez says, "I always read my poems aloud, even as I construct the poem and also at the end of the poem. I've always told people that on some levels every poem is threefold. One is the private self when you read a poem silently. The other is when you hear a poet read her or his poem, which brings another self. And then of course there's the point of you reading it aloud yourself, which brings a whole other dimension to it." Although Sanchez has recorded her work, the recordings fall short of the power of her in-person performances.

A master technician, she is equally at home in the long, praise poem format and in the brevity of the haiku and tanka. In her work from the 1960s, she restructured traditional English grammar to suit her interest in black speech patterns. *We A BaddDDD People* (1970) best exemplifies her sound experiments and her restructuring of grammar. The latter is evident in lines such as "if mothas programmed/sistuhs to/good feelings bout they blk/men/and i/mean if blk/fathas proved/they man/hood by fighten the enemy. . . ." In one poem, she played on the sound of the popular four-syllable curse word to diminish its effectiveness, then asserted that it was time to move on to other things. In shorter, denser poetic forms, she described her personal movement; especially is this true of some of the poems in *Love Poems*, which includes work between 1964 and 1973.

The collection opens with two poems that prefigure Sanchez's literal move into a new life of militancy and social activism. In "Poem No. 1," written in 1964—the pivotal year of the black power movement—she augurs her separation:

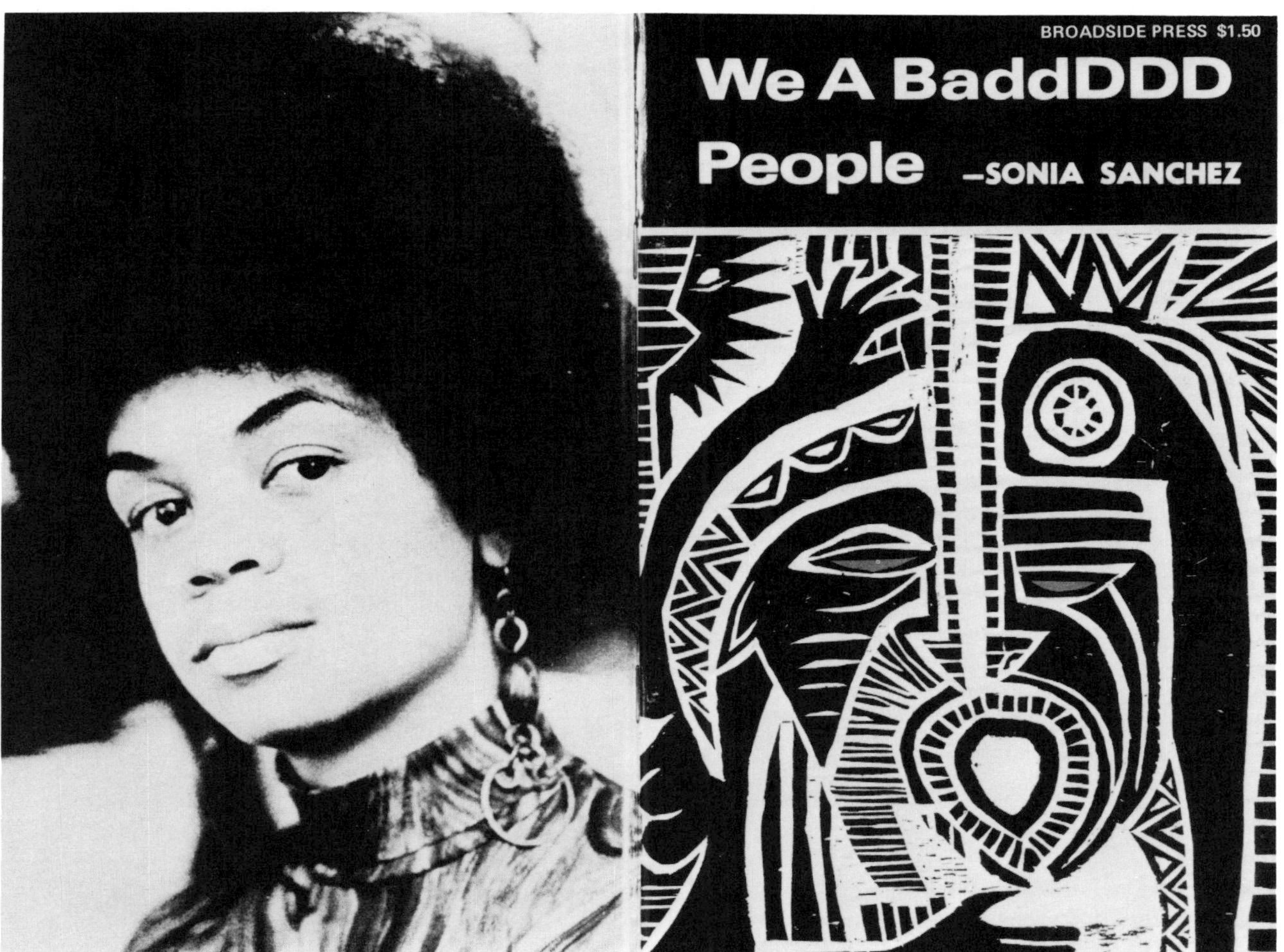

Covers for Sanchez's 1970 volume of poems. Dudley Randall, speaking of Sanchez's bare written style in this book, and of her oral delivery, says, "It is a case of Sarah Bernhardt's moving an audience to tears by declaiming the telephone directory."

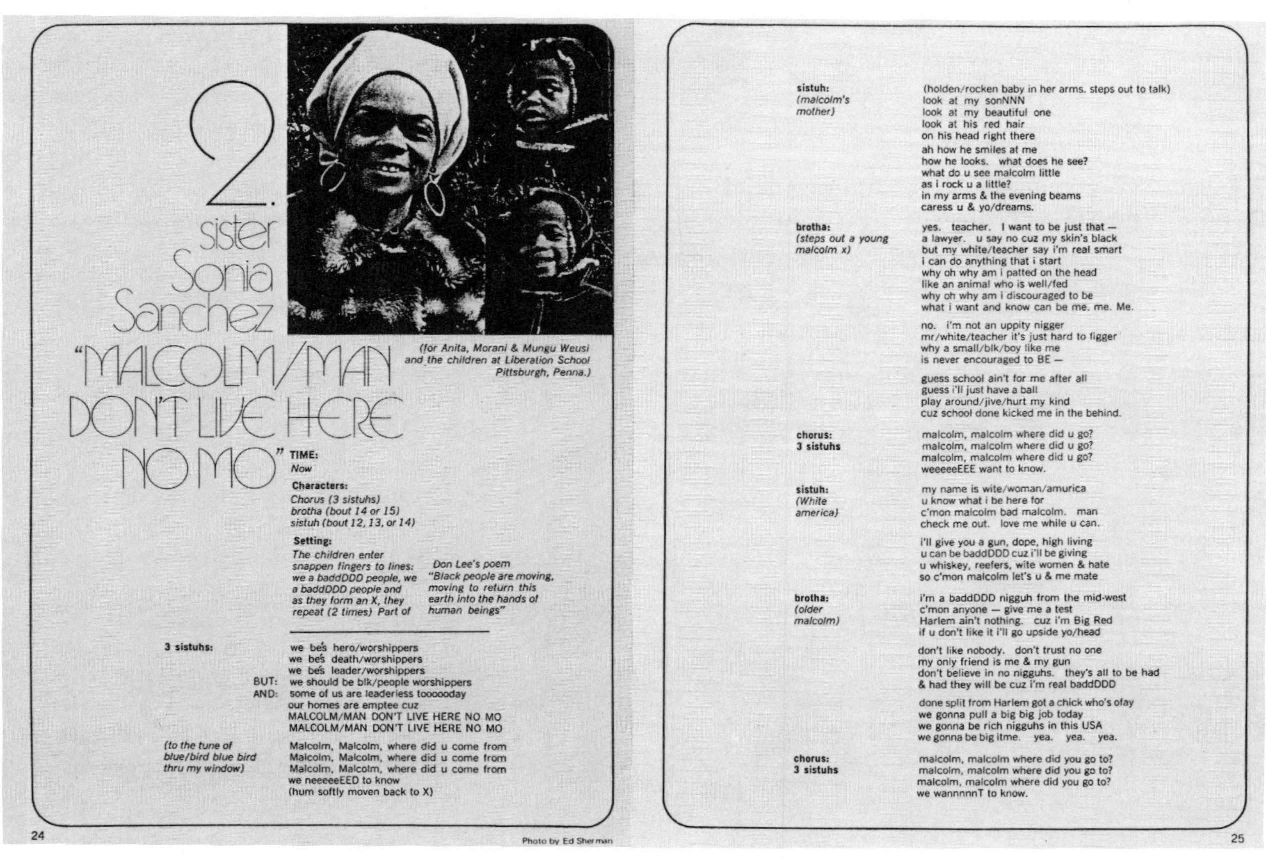

2.
sister
Sonia
Sanchez
"MALCOLM/MAN DON'T LIVE HERE NO MO"

(for Anita, Morani & Mungu Weusi and the children at Liberation School Pittsburgh, Penna.)

TIME:
Now

Characters:
Chorus (3 sistuhs)
brotha (bout 14 or 15)
sistuh (bout 12, 13, or 14)

Setting:
The children enter snappen fingers to lines: we a baddDDD people, we a baddDDD people and as they form an X, they repeat (2 times) Part of Don Lee's poem "Black people are moving, moving to return this earth into the hands of human beings"

3 sistuhs:
we bes hero/worshippers
we bes death/worshippers
we bes leader/worshippers
BUT: we should be blk/people worshippers
AND: some of us are leaderless toooooday
our homes are emptee cuz
MALCOLM/MAN DON'T LIVE HERE NO MO
MALCOLM/MAN DON'T LIVE HERE NO MO

(to the tune of blue/bird blue bird thru my window)
Malcolm, Malcolm, where did u come from
Malcolm, Malcolm, where did u come from
Malcolm, Malcolm, where did u come from
we neeeeeEED to know
(hum softly moven back to X)

24

Photo by Ed Sherman

sistuh:
(malcolm's mother)
(holden/rocken baby in her arms. steps out to talk)
look at my sonNNN
look at my beautiful one
look at his red hair
on his head right there
ah how he smiles at me
how he looks. what does he see?
what do u see malcolm little
as i rock u a little?
in my arms & the evening beams
caress u & yo/dreams.

brotha:
(steps out a young malcolm x)
yes. teacher. I want to be just that —
a lawyer. u say no cuz my skin's black
but my white/teacher say i'm real smart
i can do anything that i start
why oh why am i patted on the head
like an animal who is well/fed
why oh why am i discouraged to be
what i want and know can be me. me. Me.

no. i'm not an uppity nigger
mr/white/teacher it's just hard to figger
why a small/blk/boy like me
is never encouraged to BE —

guess school ain't for me after all
guess i'll just have a ball
play around/jive/hurt my kind
cuz school done kicked me in the behind.

chorus:
3 sistuhs
malcolm, malcolm where did u go?
malcolm, malcolm where did u go?
malcolm, malcolm where did u go?
weeeeeEEE want to know.

sistuh:
(White america)
my name is wite/woman/amurica
u know what i be here for
c'mon malcolm bad malcolm. man
check me out. love me while u can.

i'll give you a gun, dope, high living
u can be baddDDD cuz i'll be giving
u whiskey, reefers, wite women & hate
so c'mon malcolm let's u & me mate

brotha:
(older malcolm)
i'm a baddDDD nigguh from the mid-west
c'mon anyone — give me a test
Harlem ain't nothing. cuz i'm Big Red
if u don't like it i'll go upside yo/head

don't like nobody. don't trust no one
my only friend is me & my gun
don't believe in no nigguhs. they's all to be had
& had they will be cuz i'm real baddDDD

done split from Harlem got a chick who's ofay
we gonna pull a big big job today
we gonna be rich nigguhs in this USA
we gonna be big itme. yea. yea. yea.

chorus:
3 sistuhs
malcolm, malcolm where did you go to?
malcolm, malcolm where did you go to?
malcolm, malcolm where did you go to?
we wannnnnT to know.

25

Opening pages of Sanchez's 1972 play as it appeared in Black Theatre

my husband sits
buddha like
watching me weave my
self among the sad
young men of my time.
he thinks i am going
to run away.
maybe i will.

"Poem No. 2" is a kind of explanation:

my puertorican
husband who feeds me
cares for me and loves me
is trying to under
stand my Blackness.
so he is taking up
watercolors.

What is clear is that Sanchez has moved "away," and that although there is love and concern in their relationship, her husband cannot adequately deal with her new birth into "Blackness." The futility of her husband's attempts to understand are touchingly expressed in the image of him taking up "watercolors," for her blackness was not simply about skin color but about consciousness and culture as well.

Love Poems reads like a slide show of Sanchez's emotional life. Rather than chronicle names, dates, and places, the poetry delineates the emotions and attitudes, the hopes and consequences, the temperature and temperament of her life as she moved into "Blackness" and away from one kind of love and into another.

In 1966 Sanchez wrote a love poem which celebrates both public and private shows of affection common to lovers. "Magic" gives voice to a more lyrical Sanchez:

short magic
is a kiss
in the street
with hangers
on hoping
for more
action.
long magic

is days
wrapped
in your
Black
juice

But in the following year love is gone and Sanchez turns to the structured brevity of the haiku to express her emotions. It is an exceptional dichotomy not only of moods but also of poetic forms. "Was it yesterday/love we shifted the air and/made it blossom Black?"

Almost as if to answer the implications of her own question, Sonia Sanchez wrote this haiku in 1967:

O i am so sad, i
go from day to day like an
ordained stutterer.

"Ordained stutterer" is a striking image particularly when we understand Sonia Sanchez's childhood and her impulse for writing. In a 1971 edition of the *Black Collegian* Sanchez wrote in an interview article titled "It Bees Tuff":

> I used to write a lot in my head. I used to like always to write poetry when I was little. And I would hide it cuz my sister would find it and go around and say, "Look at this stuff. This stupid stuff. She writes poetry." One of the first poems I wrote was around February, around George Washington's birthday, talking about George Washington crossing the Delaware. And she took it and read it. She cracked up and everybody in the family cracked up cuz here I was writing poetry. I love it but I did it mainly because as a child I stuttered. It was one of the ways I could communicate. Like I would write down to myself that I didn't want to stutter.

In response to a question about why she began using the haiku, she candidly acknowledged,

> I think it had a lot to do with a movement in my life, how I felt I had to compress a lot of emotion . . . to stay sane. In *Love Poems* I began to experiment with the haiku. I do a lot of haiku in *I've Been A Woman* which is about '75/'76. That was a time when I had moved to Philadelphia and was very much, in a sense, by myself with the children again. Understanding the kind of resistance I had been involved with, the situation threatened to make us all go under as a family. We came to Philly from Chicago with, I guess, with like thirty-five dollars. Haiku seemingly was a form that allowed me to put a lot of emotion into three lines and allowed it to be finished in a sense. It allowed me also to reflect on it, smile and gain some insight. I wasn't at that point writing long pieces, I was doing a lot of prose, but in my poetry it was haiku and tanka.
>
> At that same time I was very much involved with dealing with a very bad health situation with myself. I was very much involved in trying to reconstruct me in health ways in order to survive. I had to say a lot in three lines and I did not have a long time to do it. I could not have written a novel at that point because I didn't think that there was a lot of time there. There was a brevity to everything at that point. Not a lack of emotion nor a lack of discipline but a brevity to everything, so therefore I gravitated toward the haiku. It was not something I had planned to do. It was just a response to everything I had viewed and experienced. Later in 1977 I began to write longer poems just as I had done in 1973.

In haiku after haiku, Sanchez becomes a cartographer of her heart and graphs with chilling candor her emotional landscape. Comparing her haiku to the other poems she was writing in her hot period, it might seem that there are two poets at work. Rather, this is one of Sanchez's distinguishing hallmarks; she remains the fiery, poetic advocate of revolutionary change, but she also gives full voice to the individual human being struggling to survive sanely and to find joy and love in life.

While remaining committed to social consciousness in her writings, Sanchez has been, simultaneously, prolific and intimate in writing poems which detail her personal life experiences, especially her affairs of the heart. No other poet of the 1960s and 1970s managed so masterfully to chronicle both their public and personal development with poetry of such thoroughgoing honesty and relevant and revelatory depth. The personal poetry is almost embarrassingly precise, albeit unsentimental, in rendering her emotional development. In 1968 she asks a quiet question that implies many, many lonely hours: "did ya ever cry/Black man, did ya ever cry/til you knocked all over?" Trying again in 1968 she composed: "o i was wide and/open unto him and he/moved in me like rain." But in 1969 she forlornly intones: "if i had known, if/i had known you, i would have/left my love at home."

Essentially an optimist, Sanchez writes with guarded hopefulness in 1972, the year she joined the Nation of Islam:

this heart conditioned
on severity trembles
among promised release.

In 1973, Sanchez published the long praise poem *A Blues Book for Blue Black Magical Women;* it chronicles her growth into womanhood. *Blues Book* is a summoning of all of Sanchez's poetic prowess to make a statement on the past, present, and future condition of black womanhood; Sanchez uses many of the particulars of her own life as illustrations of a general condition. Although openly an advocate of the philosophy of the Nation of Islam (she resigned in 1975), *Blues Book* is not a propaganda tract—it stands on its own merits as a graceful, poetic work of uncommon vision.

David Williams calls the poems in the volume both "ritualistic and religious" and asserts that they take us "back to an awareness of beginnings, a green world whose innocence can redeem our sense of sin." Sanchez is viewed as a "shaman" whose words guide her readers to a sense of communal worship; from the specific focus on black women, she presents truths relevant to all black people. In "Rebirth," her identification with black women of all the ages becomes clear:

whatever is truth becomes known. nine
months passed touching a bottomless sea.
nine months i wandered amid waves
that washed away thirty years of denial . . .
nine months passed and my body
heavy with the knowledge of the gods
turned landward. came to rest . . .
i became the mother of sun. moon. star children.

In "Present," she focuses on current and previous conditions in painting the peculiar heritage that is black women's:

there is no place

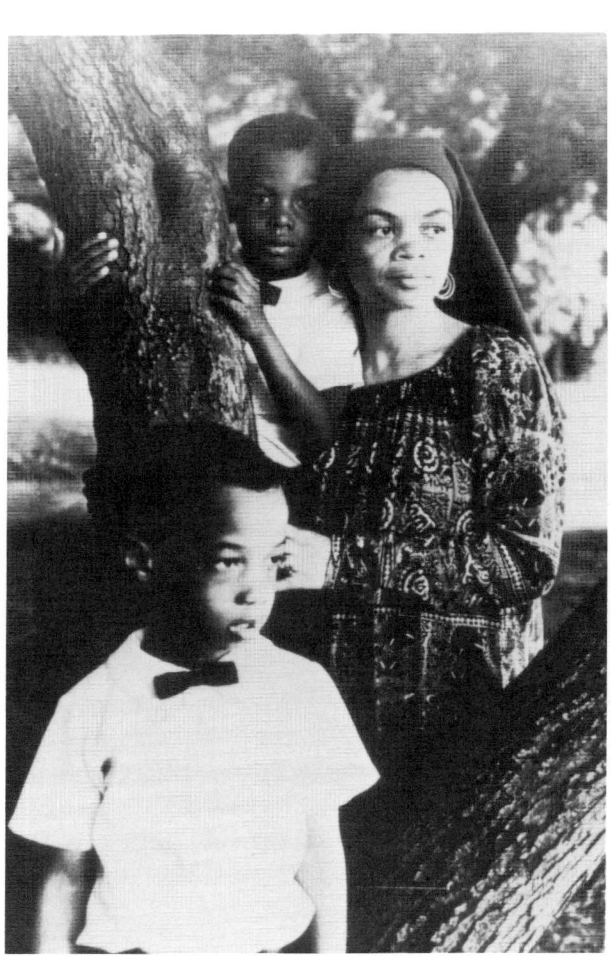

Covers for Sanchez's 1973 poetry volume. David Williams says the poems take us "back to . . . a green world whose innocence can redeem our sense of sin."

for a soft/black/woman.
there is no smile green enough or
summertime words warm enough to allow my growth.
and in my head
i see my history
standing like a shy child
and i chant lullabies
as i ride my past on horseback
tasting the thirst of yesterday tribes
hearing the ancient/black/woman
me, singing hay-hay-hay-hay-ya-ya-ya.
hay-hay-hay-hay-ya-ya-ya.
like a slow scent
beneath the sun. . . .

The blue black magical woman recounts her literal and metaphoric history and affirms a plethora of racial truths.

In 1981, Black Scholar Press published *I've Been A Woman,* Sanchez's new and selected poems. The volume is a definitive statement of the various phases of Sanchez's life; it offers an exciting panorama of her technical brilliance in both the short and long poetic forms. Such a sustained and lengthy production of quality poetry is testimony to the discipline and time Sanchez has successfully invested in developing her skills and talent as a writer.

Sanchez is unflinching in her willingness to confront the chaos of black, female life in modern America from the vantage point of an activist who has been a black nationalist nearly all of her adult life. Matured in techniques as well as vision, Sanchez writes in "Personal Letter no. 3":

nothing will keep
us young you know
not young men or
women who spin
their youth on
cool playing sounds.
we are what we
are what we never
think we are.
no more wild geo
graphies of the
flesh. echoes. that
we move in tune
to slower smells.
it is a hard thing
to admit that
sometimes after midnight
i am tired
of it all

And yet, when morning comes, Sanchez always rises

Sonia Sanchez (photograph ©1978 by Layle Silbert)

and works, fueled by an inner strength directly descended from the black slave women who witnessed death, who had seen health and everything that was good ground into the dust, who had seen their gods fail them, and who had suffered unnamed agonies, but who somehow emerged from the shadow of slavery on the strength of their will to survive. Sanchez endures because she refuses to die, not because America has not tried to kill her, not because men have not tried to maim her, not because she has inherited economic well-being. She refuses to die, and in that refusal she finds a way to live, or, as Sweet Honey in the Rock sings, to make "a way out of no way."

The greatness of Sonia Sanchez is not simply that she has survived, but that she has not been a mute survivor. She is also a witness, a very important witness to the history of and hope contained within the struggle for a better world. In "Reflections After the June 12th March for Disarmament," included in *homegirls & handgrenades,* she gives stirring images of her steel-willed determination. In a form comparable to a Coltrane piece, Sanchez establishes a rhythmic pattern and reiterates key phrases as she develops her poem. Short and sharp images are strung together within each stanza; they collectively build to the conclusion. The following stanza captures Sanchez's delineation of how people should live together on various levels: the sensual ("walk, talk"); the mental ("plan"); the spiritual ("hope"); and the cultural ("sing"):

> I have come to you tonite because no people
> have been asked to be modern day people
> with the history of slavery, and still
> we walk, and still we talk, and
> still we plan, and still we hope and
> still we sing;

The greatness of Sonia Sanchez is that she is an inspiration.

The inspiring nature of her contributions to Afro-American life and culture is reflected in some of the awards she has received. She has an honorary Ph.D. in fine arts from Wilberforce University, and in 1984 she won the Lucretia Mott Award. She has also been the recipient of an Academy of Arts and Letters award to support her writing. In 1969, she received the P.E.N. Writing Award, and a National Endowment for the Arts Award in 1978-1979, and in 1985, an American Book Award for *homegirls & handgrenades*.

Perhaps Sanchez's greatest award has been the continuing recognition of her works and the continuing requests for readings of her poetry. Still, her tasks go on, and she is ever ready to share her vision with the world:

> I have a notebook full of poems and observations that probably mean nothing to anyone other than myself. Maybe, at some point, there would be things that I would consider in terms of publishing a diary, which might be interesting kinds of observations. But I think that because much of our work is tied up with the idea of change in this country, much needed change—and certainly change must come in the next five or ten years just for the survival of the earth at this stage in the game, if you really see the kind of fools and madmen who are now getting in control all over this planet—if we understand that, then we can see that although the need for some of the private notes and observations might still be there and might still be of interest to some people perhaps who might want to buy a book and read the diary of someone to check what they were thinking, . . . there is a greater need.
>
> The need to put work out that will help people want to hold on and survive, and to make people see a "win" or a hope, or a movement toward something, or even just some lines which say that "yes, the idea of freedom is still possible," or "I'm still moving toward that," or that struggle is a viable way of living—I think those are much more important kinds of things that need to be said.

References:

Sebastian Clarke, "Sonia Sanchez and Her Work," *Black World*, 20 (June 1971): 44-48, 96-98;

Mari Evans, ed., *Black Women Writers (1950-1980): A Critical Evaluation* (Garden City: Anchor/ Doubleday, 1984);

Joyce Joyce, "The Development of Sonia Sanchez: A Continuing Journey," *Indian Journal of American Studies*, 13 (July 1983): 37-71;

George E. Kent, "Notes on the 1974 Black Literary Scene," *Phylon*, 36 (June 1975): 197-199;

R. Roderick Palmer, "The Poetry of Three Revolutionists: Don L. Lee, Sonia Sanchez, and Nikki Giovanni," *CLA Journal*, 15 (September 1971): 25-36;

Raymond Patterson, "What's Happening in Black Poetry?," *Poetry Review*, 2 (April 1985): 7-11;

Claudia Tate, ed., *Black Women Writers at Work* (New York: Continuum, 1983);

Barbara Walker, "Sonia Sanchez Creates Poetry for the Stage," *Black Creation*, 5 (Fall 1973): 12-14.

Gil Scott-Heron

(1 April 1949-   )

Jon Woodson
University of Rhode Island

BOOKS: *The Vulture* (New York: World Publishing, 1970);

Small Talk at 125th & Lenox (New York: World Publishing, 1970);

The Nigger Factory (New York: Dial Press, 1972).

RECORDINGS: *Small Talk at 125th & Lenox,* Flying Dutchman, 1970;

Free Will, Flying Dutchman, 1972;

The Revolution Will Not Be Televised, Flying Dutchman, 1972;

Pieces of a Man, Flying Dutchman, 1973;

Winter in America, Strata East, 1973;

The First Minute of a New Day, Arista, 1975;

From South Africa to South Carolina, Arista, 1975;

It's Your World, Arista, 1976;

Bridges, Arista, 1977;

The Mind of Gil Scott-Heron, Arista, 1978;

Moving Target, Arista, 1978;

1980, Arista, 1980;

Real Eyes, Arista, 1980;

Gil Scott-Heron and Brian Jackson, Arista, 1980;

Reflections, Arista, 1981.

Though his publications include only two novels and a single volume of poems, composer, pianist, vocalist, lyricist Gil Scott-Heron has established himself in the literary world and in the field of popular music. His trend-setting production of almost two dozen record albums has overshadowed his writings to such a degree that, in the main, his audience is not aware of his early literary creations. It is typical that only after long acquaintance with his live performances, record albums, and television concert series do his followers come upon his novels. His poems are the more familiar of his written works, since a selection of his poems has been printed in a booklet included with the 1978 album *The Mind of Gil Scott-Heron.* As a rule, Americans do not read poetry; but many do listen to records.

Scott-Heron's choice of the record album as his chief medium has placed him solidly within the oral American tradition. Disseminating his work this way has given him an audience that cuts across racial, social, and intellectual groupings. His songs and poems of biting and topically relevant social commentary receive radio airplay on such national holidays as the Fourth of July and Martin Luther King, Jr.'s birthday, and several of his jazz-inspired songs of social protest brought him recognition as a committed spokesman for social change. This wide exposure has given Scott-Heron an audience that includes black and white college students, young professionals, leftist intellectuals, and many contemporary musicians.

While his early published writings address the problems of urban blacks, Scott-Heron's songs and later poems, or street-raps, range into such diverse areas as the apartheid policy of South Africa, alcoholism, drug abuse, and governmental corruption in the United States. Because he is a popular recording artist and a dynamic live performer, Scott-Heron's novels have attained a status that they would never have achieved on their own merits; the novels have taken on importance simply by being the literary outpourings of a figure better known as a public voice speaking out against oppression in the world.

The son of a Jamaican professional soccer player and a librarian, Scott-Heron was born 1 April 1949 in Chicago, Illinois. As a small child, he played the piano, and he was writing detective stories by the time he was in the fifth grade. This early interest in crime fiction shows up again in his first novel, *The Vulture* (1970), which is, despite its disjointed handling of time, very much a conventional crime story. Scott-Heron's early years were spent with his grandmother in Jackson, Tennessee. He later rejoined his mother in the Bronx, New York, but he did not meet his father until becoming an adult. While a high school student at the prestigious Fieldston School in the Bronx, he began to absorb modern black poetry by men like Langston Hughes.

As a self-described "semi-student" at Lincoln University, a small, private, black college in rural southeastern Pennsylvania, Scott-Heron's career began in earnest. He attended Lincoln University for three years, working as a stock clerk, gardener, referee, and a remedial reading tutor to earn money for his tuition. For one year he played on the school's basketball team. Scott-Heron was recognized for his creative work and was awarded Lincoln University's Langston Hughes Creative Writing Award in 1968. Lincoln University proved to be helpful to the young writer in allowing him to associate with poet Gylan Kain and novelist Steve Cannon who were, at times, on the faculty. Other writers who visited the campus for readings and lectures during this period, and who influenced Scott-Heron, were Ishmael Reed and Larry Neal. It was also during the years at Lincoln University that Scott-Heron began to collaborate with Brian Jackson and to formulate the beginnings of his oral style of poetry backed up by jazz.

Scott-Heron was twenty when he began to publish; his first record album was released that same year. With the success of his first efforts behind him, Scott-Heron was able to continue his education at Johns Hopkins University, where he earned a master's degree in creative writing in one year on a teaching fellowship. From 1972 to 1976 he taught creative writing at Federal City College in Washington, D.C.

The tumultuous and crisis-ridden character of life in America during the late 1960s was a major influence on the early writings of Gil Scott-Heron. While visiting New York's black neighborhoods, the young writer absorbed the current attitudes and styles of speech and put them directly into his poems and novels. While on the campus of Lincoln University, he worked with other creative students to find the means to express the influences that he had absorbed. He formed his first band while still a student, but political unrest broke in upon the aesthetic work, and the history of campus discord is recorded in his angry novel *The Nigger Factory* (1972).

The new poetry that reflected the militant posture of many blacks in the late 1960s was popular with the students of Lincoln University, and the selections by New York's Last Poets (David Nelson, Felipe Luciano, Gylan Kain) were often heard on the jukebox in the student union. This influential group was easily the most sophisticated political-literary association of the time: they combined the medium of film with oral and written poems in order to disseminate their black and third-world revolutionary ideas. The poems produced by the Last Poets were jazz-influenced, free-verse expressions that embodied the revolutionary message of the ghettos of New York's black and Hispanic populations. Building on the foundation laid by the Last Poets, Scott-Heron's derivative first album, *Small Talk at 125th & Lenox* (produced in 1970), took up where the Last Poets left off. In the years that followed, his musical sophistication and widening social concerns culminated in the creation of a satisfactory, expressive vehicle that is emotionally complex, aesthetically rich, and international in scope.

The theme of the inescapable hypocrisy of American life dominates the poetry in *Small Talk at 125th & Lenox*; it was also the theme of his first novel, *The Vulture*. His early writings advocated the then-popular view that a revolution was necessary if the ills present in American society were to be cured. But the twenty-year-old poet was, even then, more of an intellectual than a street fighter; his militance has, in his recent albums, moderated to the point where "Third World Revolution" anthems can be balanced by such optimistic statements as "Better Days Ahead" and "A Prayer for Everybody." Songs on recent albums have spoken against judicial discrimination against blacks in the South, unsafe coal mines, and the power and influence of both Madison Avenue and show business.

In *Small Talk* Scott-Heron touched upon the frustration and fury of urban blacks, using an approximation of their own idioms to depict their unrest:

> Do this:
> Show the man you call Uncle Tom
> where he's wrong.
> Show that woman that you're
> a sincere Black man.
> Shut up and be Black.
> Help that woman!
> Help that man!
>
> That's what brothers are for, brothers.

The poems in *Small Talk* are accompanied by photographs taken on Harlem streets. The implication is that, like the photographs, the poems are reportage, directly revealing the feelings of the residents of Harlem. Scott-Heron's strategy is to assume the voice of a street-wise hipster who sermonizes to his audience much like a traditional preacher. Where this voice is most insightful, the poems work best, as in "the future as I see it," where Scott-Heron confides:

> Well, since I know your type so well
> I guess I may as well sit a spell

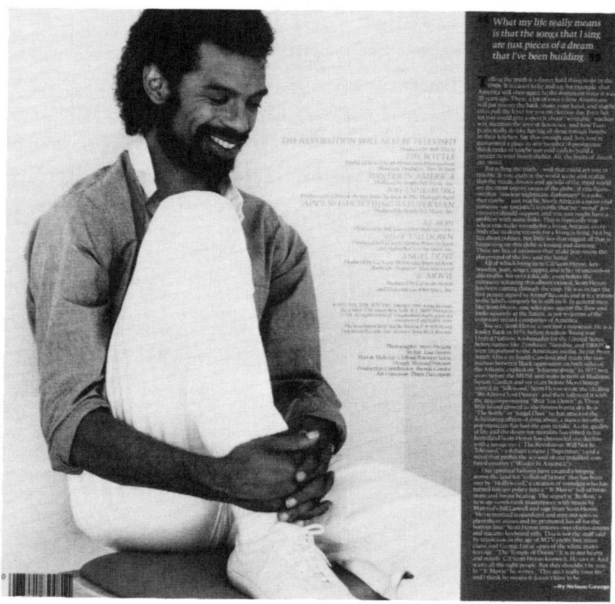

Front and back covers for a 1984 record album, which highlights a decade of Scott-Heron's work

and unravel the truth 'bout what's
comin'.
some blood who is a prince of the
blood
will be talkin' 'bout the flood
of tears he's shed
for years
'cause he couldn't find you
an' he'll like to boogaloo
an' you mama's gonna dig 'im
an yo poppa too.
yawl goin' to Africa on his
yacht.
Howzat? Still no?

Despite the rage in his poems, the effect is one of optimism: things can be changed. In "enough" Scott-Heron depicts the revolution:

There is
no promised land! There is only
the promise!
the promise is my vow that until
we have been nerve-
gassed, shot down, and murdered—
or done some of the
same ourselves—look over your
shoulder motherfucker,
I AM COMING!

The poems in *Small Talk* show the influence of Langston Hughes in their closeness to black speech patterns and choice of subject matter. However, Scott-Heron's poems, in contrast to the Imagist-inspired free verse of Hughes, use rhyme, as in "paint it black":

Picture a man of nearly thirty
who seems twice as old with clothes torn
and dirty.
Give him a job shining shoes
or cleaning out toilets with bus
station crews.

Where Scott-Heron does employ free verse, it is in a random, open, and patternless handling of lines, as in "omen":

a giant eye zapped across the screen
with
tentacle type
feeler type thin roots
reaching for someone, maybe me.

The poems in *Small Talk* fall into two types: the free verse street-rap, and the shorter rhymed poems which are close to the blues in their familiar and folksy tones.

Gil Scott-Heron's concern with the street culture of Harlem was carried over to his first novel.

The Vulture, published in 1970, is a story about teenage street gangs in Harlem. *The Vulture* ostensibly portrays the destructive impact of drugs on black neighborhoods, but reveals a corruption so basic to American society that even revolutionary groups that attempt to wrest power from their oppressors are finally included in the same destructive and parasitical patterns that drive the majority culture.

In *The Vulture,* the Harlem youths move from the breaking up of street gangs into careers as drug dealers. The novel is essentially a murder mystery with a complicated chronological scheme of "phases" that slice up events and scramble time in order to deliver a surprise ending when it is revealed that John Lee, one of the principal characters, has been murdered in an unexpected way. Structurally the novel consists of character sketches, each more or less complete unto itself, that depict one of the major characters in detail. The events narrated by each of the characters overlap in time and content. The characters are not clearly differentiated, and much of the action is stiff and conventional. The language is flat and unconvincing, and at times Scott-Heron strains for effects that do not succeed.

The Nigger Factory was Scott-Heron's second novel, and was based on his own experiences as a student at Lincoln University in the late 1960s. His fictionalized account is an indictment of the American system of higher education. He says in the introduction to *The Nigger Factory* that "The main trouble in higher education lies in the fact that while the times have changed radically, educators and administrators have continued to plod along through the bureaucratizing red tape that stalls so much American progress."

The Nigger Factory narrates the events of a student strike that Scott-Heron was instrumental in organizing. In the novel, Lincoln University becomes Sutton College; however, the novel fictionalizes the violence of the confrontations between students and the authorities, and it provides new motives for the student strike. The novel does portray the atmosphere of that period, in its deft capturing of the revolutionary rhetoric of the MJUMBE activists, the confusion of the campus factions, and the refusal of campus authorities to resolve the issues that were tearing apart their institution.

Both of Scott-Heron's novels share a concern with black revolutionary groups. They were written at a time when the Black Panthers were media stars and served as models for black youths. In *The Vulture,* BAMBU, a group of urban guerrillas, assigns Tommy Hall, a would-be revolutionist, to murder Siddy, a major drug peddler, in a campaign to "get rid of the pushers and sellers of the various narcotics." BAMBU is revealed as having the intention of controlling "all drug traffic in New York City." In *The Nigger Factory* MJUMBE falls apart as one member takes it upon himself to escalate the level of violence by planting a bomb on the campus. Though the militants arm themselves, they are stunned when the bomb goes off, and they are not prepared for the scene of destruction and violent confrontation with a National Guard unit that ends the novel.

Both of Scott-Heron's novels describe the difficulty of bringing about social change. According to his dark view of American society, good intentions are not enough. There is a constant subversion of positive plans by individuals who are misguided, duped, selfish, or corrupt. In the world of these novels, there is seemingly no escape from these conditions.

The numerous record albums that Scott-Heron has released indicate his development as an artist. Beginning with poems and songs of bitterness and rage, his relaxed, resonant baritone still urges sociopolitical awareness, but the voice is soothing, persuasive, and a little bit funky. Scott-Heron's Midnight Band, co-led by Brian Jackson, plays in a warm jazz groove with gentle congas underpinning Jackson's keyboards and horns. Scott-Heron plays electric piano or concentrates on lead vocals. The formats of the albums vary. *The Mind of Gil Scott-Heron* is all poetry. It presents live readings with language that sometimes gets hardcore, backed up by jazz instrumentation. "I try to do something different with each successive album," Scott-Heron has said.

Perhaps because of his success as an oral performer and recording artist, Scott-Heron's novels and poems have not been taken seriously by literary critics. For instance, Eugene Redmond, in *Drumvoices,* referred to Scott-Heron's "combination of blues, jazz, and street conversation," the very basis of his poetry, as "an impressive ritualistic vehicle of protest and exhortation." The comment seems more dismissing than evaluative. Scott-Heron's records have received uniformly favorable reviews, and the record sales have been impressive. The *Village Voice* said that he "has taken risks with the idea that messages about modern disasters could be popular music." Scott-Heron's career soared when his song about alcoholism, "The Bottle," became his first hit on the popular charts. Other hits have been his "Winter in America" and "Johannesburg." Scott-Heron's influence continues to grow as new political bands such as Steel Pulse acknowledge him as a role model.

Reference:

Eugene B. Redmond, *Drumvoices: The Mission of Afro-American Poetry, A Critical History* (Garden City: Anchor/Doubleday, 1976).

A. B. Spellman

(7 August 1935-)

Carmen Subryan
Howard University

BOOKS: *The Beautiful Days* (New York: Poets Press, 1965);

Four Lives in the Bebop Business (New York: Pantheon, 1966); republished as *Black Music: Four Lives* (New York: Schocken, 1970).

OTHER: Rosey E. Pool, ed., *Beyond the Blues: New Poems by American Negroes,* includes poems by Spellman (Lympne, Kent: Hand & Flower Press, 1962);

Anselm Hollo, ed., *Negro Verse,* includes poems by Spellman (London: Vista Books, 1964);

Langston Hughes, ed., *New Negro Poets: U.S.A.,* includes poems by Spellman (Bloomington: Indiana University Press, 1964);

LeRoi Jones (Amiri Baraka) and Larry Neal, eds., *Black Fire: An Anthology of Afro-American Writing,* includes poems by Spellman (New York: Morrow, 1968);

Clarence Major, ed., *The New Black Poetry,* includes poems by Spellman (New York: International Publishers, 1969);

Dudley Randall, ed., *The Black Poets,* includes poems by Spellman (New York: Bantam Books, 1971);

Arnold Adoff, ed., *The Poetry of Black America,* includes poems by Spellman (New York: Harper & Row, 1972).

Alfred B. Spellman has been hailed as one of the new black poets of the 1960s whom Gwendolyn Brooks describes as "prevailing stars of an early tomorrow" and whose themes she assesses as encompassing "passion, or a desperate comedy, an adult anger which may be intellectual or intestinal, or a wishful joy." According to Stephen Henderson, the poetry of these new black artists is motivated by "an interior dynamism which underlies much of the best of contemporary Black poetry." It is poetry which attempts "to speak directly *to* Black people *about themselves* in order to move them toward self-knowledge and collective freedom. It is therefore not 'protest' art but essentially an art of liberating vision."

Spellman was born on 7 August 1935, in Nixonton, North Carolina, to Alfred and Rosa Bailey Spellman, both schoolteachers. Young A. B. was influenced by his parents' academic background and by his father's avocational interest in painting. Spellman and his brother Roland, who is eight years younger, grew up in Elizabeth City, North Carolina, at a time when racial segregation there was simply accepted as the social norm. He attended public schools, which, he says, presented no challenge, until 1952 when he entered Howard University in Washington, D.C.

Spellman's interest in writing began at Howard when he began to read poetry extensively. His schoolmates included dramatist Joseph Walker, poet and children's writer Lucille Clifton, and LeRoi Jones (Amiri Baraka), who were members of a small, informal writing and discussion group that gave Spellman peer support and feedback on his poetry. He was further encouraged in his interest in writing by the model provided by many of his teachers at Howard. He took a playwriting course with Owen Dodson, a theater course with Arthur Davis, and several literature courses with Sterling Brown. Apart from writing activities, Spellman says he took advantage of all the artistic outlets available to him at Howard; for example, he was an active member in the Howard Players theater group. The other major influence in Spellman's developing commitment to art and his dawning sociopolitical awareness was the Brown versus the Board of Education desegregation decision that occurred in Spellman's junior year.

Having decided to devote himself to writing, Spellman toyed with the idea for awhile of supporting himself some other way. He went to law school for a year and a half and took some graduate courses in literature. He finally left Howard in 1958 after six years, graduating with a bachelor's degree "in political science and history, ½ a law degree, and ¼ of a masters." At the suggestion of Baraka, whom Spellman calls the "pathfinder," he went to New York to join its thriving artistic community. The latter part of the Beat movement was in full swing; "abstract, expressionist art was hot, jazz was going into a new avant-garde," Spellman said, and poetry was at its most popular point. "Then Malcolm X appeared on the scene; the civil rights movement heated up; and black consciousness swept down from Harlem." The aesthetic atmosphere at the time, his commitment to the cause of human rights and to the anti-Vietnam war movement "affected how I wrote, lived, and what I did with my time," Spellman said.

During his time in New York from 1958 until 1967, Spellman wrote poetry and supported himself mostly by working in bookstores. He disc jockeyed a morning show for one year on the then-radical WBAI radio station. In 1967 he moved to Atlanta, Georgia, and became involved in college life. He taught courses in poetry, writing, black literature, Afro-American culture, and jazz at several universities, including Emory University, Atlanta University Center, and Rutgers University. In 1973 Spellman left Atlanta to teach at Harvard University, an experience about which he has mixed emotions. After several years, he left Boston to begin working on a policy study for the National Endowment for the Arts and Education. He also served on a Rockefeller Foundation panel studying the arts. In 1978 he joined the NEA Expansion Program, directing funding for projects in the arts for minority and rural populations.

At present he resides in Washington, D.C., where he continues in his position at the NEA. Although Spellman has authored only one book of poetry, *The Beautiful Days* (1965), his poetry has appeared in literary journals, newspapers, and anthologies such as *The Poetry of Black America, New Negro Poets: U.S.A, The New Black Poetry,* and the *Norton Anthology of American Literature.*

Apart from his poetry, Spellman's writings about jazz artists have caused him to be recognized as one of the foremost jazz critics of all time. *Four Lives in the Bebop Business* (1966), his book which profiles the lives of Herbie Nichols, Jackie McLean, Ornette Coleman, and Cecil Taylor, has won critical acclaim and so have his numerous articles on jazz which have appeared in magazines such as *Ebony, Nation, Liberator,* and *Metronome.* Spellman has also edited the *Cricket,* a critical journal of black music, and in 1969 he founded the Atlanta Center for the Black Arts, which published *Rhythm.* In the early 1960s he helped to found *Umbra,* a New York based tabloid newspaper which included unpublished works by black poets, such as Langston Hughes, LeRoi Jones (Amiri Baraka), and Ishmael Reed. More recently, he has written a booklet to accompany the Giants of Jazz series of albums produced by Time-Life publishers.

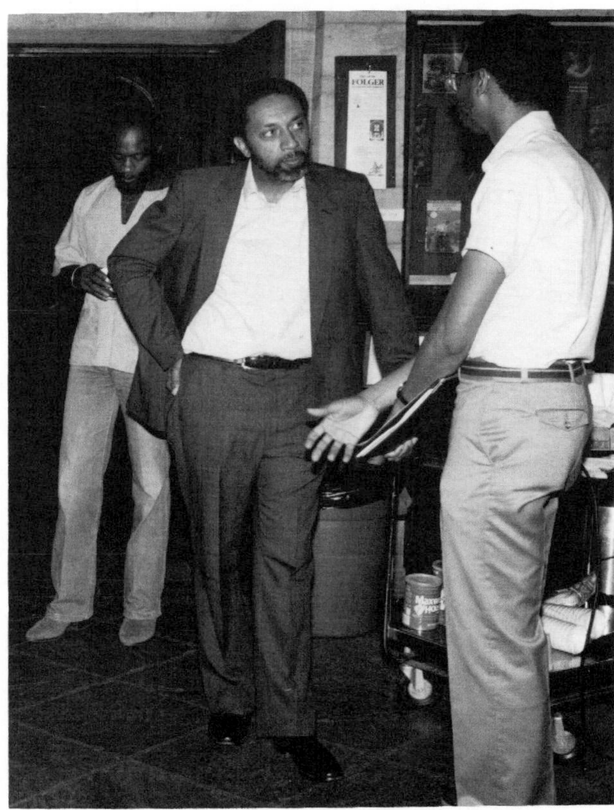

A. B. Spellman (center) talking to poet E. Ethelbert Miller (right) at the Larry Neal Writers Conference at Folger Shakespeare Library (photograph ©1983 by Julia Jones)

Spellman's poetry, which is intensely personal, has been described by poet Frank O'Hara, who wrote the introduction to *The Beautiful Days,* as "lean, strong, sexy poems." O'Hara continues, "he cuts through a lot of contemporary nonsense to what is actually happening to him, and that actuality reveals his real voice sounding above the inspired or willed (in the moral sense) technical choices."

The Beautiful Days, a slim volume with unnumbered pages, consists of approximately twenty-seven poems, some untitled, which can be grouped by the broad themes of music, nature, love, and sorrow. The work is held together loosely by eight poems entitled "the beautiful day." Most of these poems show the influence of the Beat poets and of the black arts movement in poetry. Spellman embraces modern, sometimes surrealistic techniques, such as an almost incongruous juxtaposing of images and the dispensing of traditional elements like end rhymes. He often uses lower case letters to begin words, including the word *I;* the ampersand (&) for the word *and;* and an almost indiscriminate amount of italics. Some of these techniques make for great economy of language, but mostly Spellman gains poetic effect through the images he creates and the symbols he uses. His images, which are vivid, sensual, real, and believable, stimulate the imagination, as these lines taken from Spellman's poem "the beautiful day, V" demonstrate:

he went
to the window
it folded & shrank.

quietly, & without warning
them, night leaked into the
room, into the 'idea' of the group.

Similar images appear in Spellman's later poetry, as in these stanzas from his poem on John Coltrane, "Did John's Music Kill Him?"

then john. *little old lady*
had a nasty mouth. *summertime*
when war is. *africa* . . . ululating
a line bunched up like itself
into knots paints beauty black.
. . . .
kill me john my life eats
life.   the thing that beats out of
me happens in a vat enclosed
& fermenting & wanting to explode
like your song.

These forceful images are recreated again in several poems which demonstrate not only Spellman's love of jazz, but also his love of dance. In "14 pirouettes & 9 entrechats," emblems of classical ballet are interwoven with a powerful image of cottonmouths mating in a swamp in North Carolina, and in "the twist," rhythm is described as "god's last breath," "the last beating/of his heart." Another poem, "the joel blues," which depicts the influence of music on Spellman's life, is, in reality, a song lyric, complete with refrain, as this stanza demonstrates:

i know your door baby
better than i know my own.
i know your door baby
better than i know my own.
    it's been so long since i seen you
    i'm sure you done up and gone.

It is in Spellman's love poems, however, that the personal passions which move the artist erupt. Poems such as "the beautiful day," "daniele's poem," "the beautiful day, III," and "the beautiful day #8" express raw and honest sexuality which is often juxtaposed to images of nature. Spellman displays tremendous preoccupation in *The Beautiful Days* with the image of snow, which he often pairs with death, as the following excerpts from this untitled poem demonstrate:

my face
is in it, & yours, we
are freezing together, a whole year's rot
is burning our faces
blacker than any ne
groes sun.

and in the following:

those eyes, those frozen
eyes, turn them inside
or outside & they lay down that
same icy blankness.
    & even that tongue
    warm as it floats turns out
    to be a snowcloud.

In "1½ seasons" Spellman repeats the image of winter as stifling to the soul, as he does in "the beautiful day, IV," where he writes:

from the window
i watch you turn
& go.   it is snowing

you are so white
you vanish
into the ground

up & down.   the
softest ice in town.

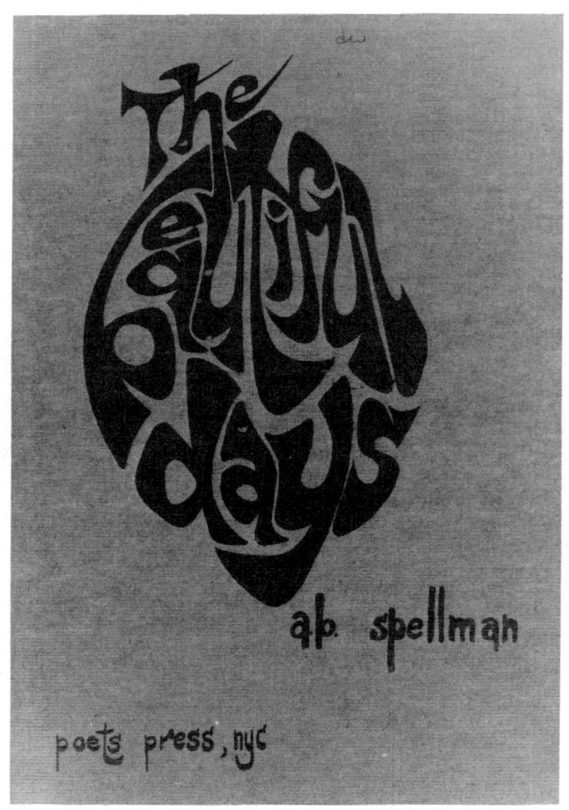

Front cover for Spellman's 1965 collection. Frank O'Hara says, "His poems speak about an existence happening between extreme heat and extreme cold . . . and what a poet's sensibility must ask of him."

In "the beautiful day VI," the image of snow predominates again.

came down from the sky &
settled
    on my eye.   this
is what snow
        does.   there
you go, an object
            of snow
the day
melts into water.

The cycle of death and life in nature is also portrayed in completely different imagery, for example, in Spellman's poem, "*john coltrane* an impartial review": "may he have new life like the fall/fallen tree, wet moist rotten enough/to see shoots stalks branches & green/leaves (& may the roots) grow into his side."

Themes of the despair of modern life in the black community and the world community pervade Spellman's poetry. In "the beautiful day #2," Spellman recounts the concrete images which assail the white man's conscience. These include "P.R.s playing/dominoes, chinese waiters, black southerners/just sent for, all the old jews, have those dead/junky forces in their faces, set as with old brick." In "*after reading tu fu,*" Spellman invokes the universal leveler, death:

& my hopeless poor who live for only death
& children & a superior music fashioned
from filth
make as many mountains on the mind's horizon
as those nicely murdered irish politicians
handsome in profile, murderous in deed
invisible in death, coequal in death
with europe's horny image
with harlem's greasiest junky
with dead fish rotting on nagasaki beaches

In "for white" the poet notes the hopelessness experienced by his artist friend who drinks as he paints the day away. The new year's poem, " *'64 like a mirror in a darkroom. '63 like a mirror in a house afire,*" is a touching elegy for Spellman's dead friends with whom he still identifies closely. He writes:

the newly dead silly
my best sentiments by an absence
more vital than memory, how
write for them except say the difference
in potency between a.b. & the newly
dead is barely measurable.

a.b. & the newly dead. we could sing together.
a quartet of my own familiar, with a.b. singing
bass. we'd sing for people like us.

This theme of despair and identification with the dead is manifested again in "a theft of wishes," where the poet describes himself as living in "eternal dusk," apart from the world around him. He even chooses not to go home, even though he knows that "home they say, repairs/the spirit. home is/where i never go."

More recently Spellman's poetry voices a restrained protest. His later poems, submitted to anthologies such as *Black Fire* and *The Poetry of Black America*—poems like "the beautiful day #9," "tomorrow the heroes," "friends i am like you tied," "when black people are," and "in orangeburg my brothers did"—present a more universal vision than the mainly personal ones found in *The Beautiful Days*. Most of these later political poems signal Spellman's maturing social conscience, as the subjects are drawn from the realm of contemporary affairs. For instance, "the beautiful day #9," which is addressed to former Secretary of Defense, "rob't mcnamara," outlines the persona's dilemma. Fighting within the system he is fighting for, he tells "mcnamara":

& when alone i sometimes walk
from wall to wall fighting visions
of white men fighting me
& black men fighting white men
& fighting me & i lose my
self between walls &
ricocheting shots & can't say
for certain who i have killed
or been killed by.

The image of collective death is crystalized again in another more recently published poem, "in orangeburg my brothers did." The slaughter of Africans is climaxed in the refrain, "black death/ black death black death black/brothers black sisters black me with no white blood on my hands." Spellman's message of strife and death as the only means of reclaiming racial dignity and heritage is clear: "we are so beautiful/we study our history backwards/& that must be the beast's most fatal message/that we die to learn it well."

In the introduction to *The Beautiful Days,* Frank O'Hara sums up Spellman's poetry in the following manner: "His poems speak about an existence happening between extreme heat and extreme cold, between black and white, fire and snow, and what a poet's sensibility must ask of him. He's honest, so naturally a lot of them are perfect." However, it is in the later poems that Spellman's perfection as an artist is manifested. Spellman is a product of his day, a poet of the 1960s who wrote at a time when black art was coming of age and black writers were concerned not only with their personal struggles, but also with the struggles of their brothers universally. Spellman now devotes his creative energies to his administrative responsibilities. Limelight Publishers will shortly reprint *Four Lives in the Bebop Business.*

References:

Stephen Henderson, ed., *Understanding the New Black Poetry* (New York: William Morrow, 1973), p. 16;

Langston Hughes, ed., *New Negro Poets: USA* (Bloomington: Indiana University Press, 1964), pp. 13-14.

Lorenzo Thomas

(31 August 1944-   )

Tom Dent

BOOKS: *A Visible Island* (Brooklyn: Adlib Press, 1967);

Fit Music (New York: Angel Hair Books, 1972);

Dracula (New York: Angel Hair Books, 1973);

Framing the Sunrise (Houston: Sun Be/Am Associates, 1975);

Chances are Few (Berkeley: Blue Wind Press, 1979);

The Bathers (New York: I. Reed Books, 1981);

Blues Music in Arkansas, with Louis Guida and Cheryl Cohen (Philadelphia: Portfolio Associates, 1982).

OTHER: *Ankh: Getting It Together,* edited by Thomas (Houston: Hope Development, 1974);

Steve Cannon, ed., *Jambalaya,* contributions by Thomas (New York: Reed, Cannon & Johnson, 1974).

PERIODICAL PUBLICATIONS: "Askia Muhammad Touré: Crying Out the Goodness," *Obsidian,* 1 (Spring 1975);

"Two Crowns of Thoth: A Study of Ishmael Reed's *The Last Days of Louisiana Red,*" *Obsidian,* 2 (Winter 1976);

"A Change Is Gonna Come: Black Voices of Louisiana," *New Black Writing, Nimrod,* 21/22 (double issue 1977): 262-283;

"The Shadow World: New York's Umbra Workshop and Origins of the Black Arts Movement," *Callaloo,* no. 4 (1978);

"Finders, Losers: Frank Standford's Song of the South," *Sun & Moon: A Journal of Literature and Art,* no. 8 (Fall 1979): 8-23;

"Juke Boy Bonner Sang the Blues," *Callaloo,* 2, no. 3 (1979);

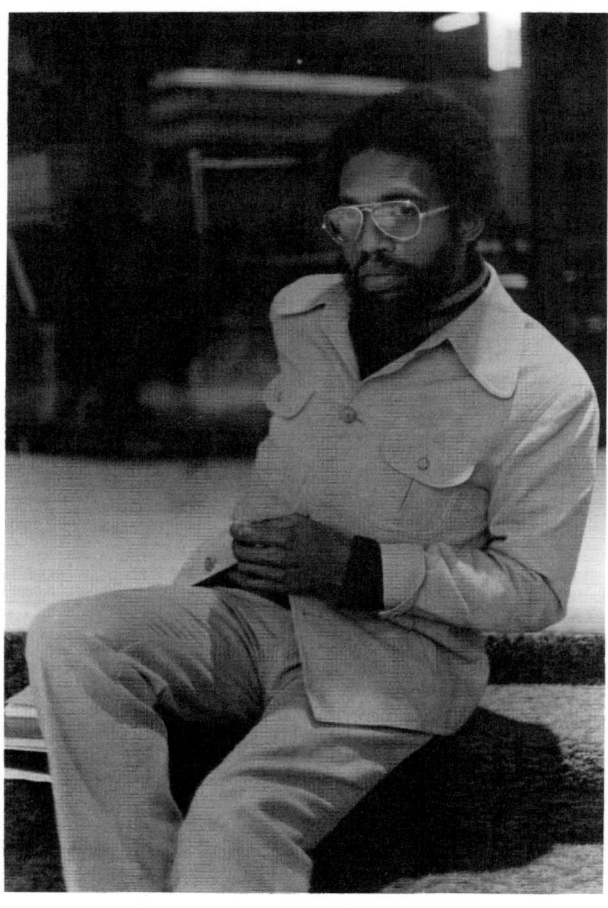

Lorenzo Thomas (photograph ©1984 by Layle Silbert)

"Bill Brett," *Pawn Review,* 4, no. 1 (1980-1981): 36-43;

"Texas Tradition," *Houston City Magazine,* 5 (June 1981): 103-105.

The life and literary interests of Lorenzo Thomas span vast distances, ranging from Central America to New York City to the American Southwest, underscoring his stature as one of the most broadly based and multifaceted writers of African descent in America today. Thomas's most extensive work has been in poetry, though his few critical essays are remarkable for their vision and comprehension. His poetry is noteworthy for its extraordinary, imaginative depiction of popular American culture and for his unique intermixture of apparently unrelated frames of reference.

Born in the Republic of Panama on 31 August 1944, Lorenzo Thomas came to the United States in 1948 when his parents immigrated to New York. His mother, Luzmilda Gilling Thomas, born in 1914 in Costa Rica to Jamaican parents, has been a community organizer and has been active in local New York politics. Thomas's father, Herbert Hamilton Thomas, was born in St. Vincent, West Indies, in 1906. The son of a stonemason, he was educated to be a pharmacist, worked as a chemist in the oilfields of Venezuela, Aruba, and Curacao, emigrated to Panama, and then to the United States, where he was chief dietary purchasing agent for St. Luke's Hospital in New York City until his retirement. Thomas's brother Cecilio (Cess) is a commercial artist and book designer who frequently illustrates the poet's work. Thomas was raised as part of a closely knit family in the Bronx and Queens. Having spoken Spanish as a child, Thomas refers to his childhood interest in reading and writing English as an attempt to master his new language, and thus, to make himself more acceptable to his schoolmates. This attempt, in turn, led to his early interest in creative writing. His strivings for literacy were abetted, he has said, by "the whole business of being Black and from a home full of race conscious people, and the idea that if you are Black you had to be more qualified than necessary."

While still a teenager attending Queens College, Lorenzo Thomas sought out and became a member of the influential Umbra workshop, which was meeting on the Lower East Side of New York from 1962 to 1964. In intense, highly charged weekly group sessions, he was exposed to the beginning work of young black writers like Ishmael Reed, Calvin Hernton, Joe Johnson, David Henderson (himself only nineteen years old), Askia Muhammad Touré (then Rolland Snellings), Tom Dent, Lloyd Addison, James Thompson, Oliver Pitcher, Norman Pritchard, Art Berger (not black, but nevertheless a faithful member), Steve Cannon, Brenda Walcott, and Lennox Raphael, among others. All of these writers were struggling to find their artistic voices; in 1962 only one or two had published. By 1982, the combined artistic output of the Umbra workshop writers comprised some forty published volumes of prose and poetry.

Lorenzo Thomas's earliest literary influences, as with other Umbra writers, were shaped by all the salient social and artistic forces of the 1960s: the civil rights movement and the concomitant drive toward black pride and consciousness, the emergence of Africa as a world force, and a new, positive cultural identification with their African heritage by many members from the African diaspora. The multi-ethnic matrix of New York itself was also influential, especially the atmosphere of the Lower East Side, with its strong European, Caribbean, and

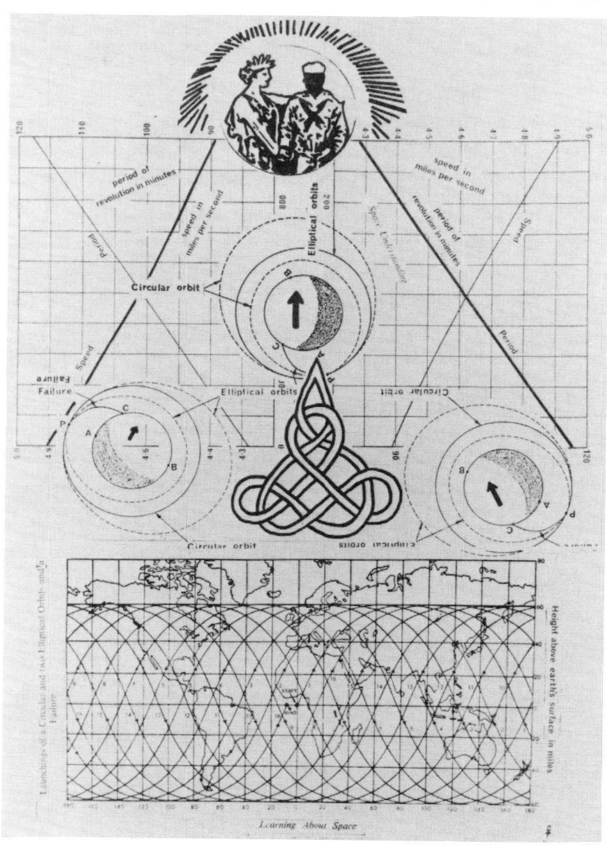

Front cover and artwork for Thomas's 1972 poetry collection, which takes its title from Ezra Pound's "Canto XIII": "And Kung said, 'Without character you will/be unable to play on that instrument/or to execute the music fit for the Odes'" (art by Cess Thomas).

Chinese communities. The Lower East Side was also then the newly found domicile of avant-garde, beat, antiestablishment artists—an avant-garde set amidst a nineteenth-century cultural milieu: poetry readings in new coffee houses adjacent to bodegas, open food and clothing markets, and Eastern European saloons. The Lower East Side was not only the crucible for much of the antiestablishment art emerging during that time, it was the first setting for what soon came to be known as the black arts movement—Umbra, LeRoi Jones (Amiri Baraka) and his movements, and the Negro Ensemble Company all developed out of that section of New York.

Lorenzo Thomas, looking back on those years in his 1978 *Callaloo* essay, "The Shadow World: New York's Umbra Workshop and Origins of the Black Arts Movement," observes that this avant-garde 1960s movement had strong historical roots in the black community: "cultural black nationalism of our moment did not spring forth from inspiration of the *New York Times* or the Late News; it is the result of a continuing tradition transmitted as naturally as possible under the circumstance of a specially malicious and aggressive white American culture which expediently implemented its hostility with the integrationish ideologies of the NAACP and the Urban League." He asserts that in the black folk tradition, *griots* of the Harlem street, "bedraggled saints from southern communities . . . somehow (by a process still incompletely documented) managed to transmit to the young writers of the 1960s an entirely alternative approach to doing art that has made contemporary black literature of the United States one of the most vibrant and beautiful human flowerings on the planet."

A sense of new black consciousness and activism, along with a national mood of artistic change, experimentation, and social relevancy made strong impact upon the budding literary ideas of Lorenzo Thomas by the time he was twenty years old. Despite influences, however, the task of discovering an individual voice is one each writer has to struggle alone with in order to emerge as a distinct literary presence. Lorenzo Thomas's poetry and prose matured in the 1970s and 1980s after his initial Umbra period.

Leaving New York for the first time in 1968, Thomas joined the United States Navy in which he served as Petty Officer 2nd Class (Radioman). In 1971 he served as a military advisor in Vietnam. He returned to the States in 1972, worked as a librarian at Pace College in New York, and in 1973 was invited to serve as writer in residence at Texas Southern University in Houston, Texas, a section of the United States he had never before visited. At Texas Southern, Thomas helped edit the literary journal *Roots*. After completing his year there he decided to remain in Houston where he conducted writing workshops at the newly formed community Black Arts Center from 1974 to 1976. Sinking roots and deciding to remain in Texas, Thomas cemented ties with other black writers in the South, published his poems widely in national journals, gave regular readings of his work, and became active with the Texas Commission of Arts and Humanities. He was among the first black writers to work in artists-in-the-schools programs in Texas, Oklahoma, and Arkansas. Thomas also served during the mid-1970s as a member of the board of directors of the Coordinating Council of Literary Magazines. Recently, Lorenzo Thomas has given expression to his broad interests in black and American indigenous musics through his work as an organizer of the successful Juneteenth Blues Festivals in Houston and other Texas cities.

By 1983 he had published a number of broadsides and pamphlet poems as well as three volumes of poetry: *Jambalaya* (1974, an anthology of Thomas's works and the poetry of Cyn Zarco, Thulani Davis, and Ibn Mukhtarr Mustapha), *Chances are Few* (1979), and *The Bathers* (1981). His poems and other writings have been anthologized in *New Black Voices, Nimrod (New Black Writing: Africa, West Indies, the Americas), Another World,* the *Poetry of Black America,* and *Black Fire: An Anthology of Afro-American Writing.* He is a winner of two Poets Foundation awards and the Lucille Medwick Prize. In 1983 he was the recipient of a National Endowment for the Arts Creative Writing Fellowship, and in 1984 he received the Houston Festival Foundation Arts Award.

The poetic style of Lorenzo Thomas gives the reader the feel of a camera gliding through a maze of sensual impressions and memories. It is primarily a cultural world he contracts out of. Though Thomas employs grammatical devices designed to evoke "black English," his approach is not similar to the familiar styles developed in the 1920s and 1930s by Langston Hughes and Sterling Brown, or in the 1960s by Sonia Sanchez or Haki R. Madhubuti.

Lorenzo Thomas has said that one of his earlier influences was the great Martinican poet, Aimé Césaire, the first Afro-Caribbean surrealist and one of the leading proponents of the francophone Negritude movement, with Léopold Sédar Senghor and Léon Damas. It is said that Césaire adopted his surrealist style under the influence of French poet André Breton as a way of discovering more imaginative devices to portray the complex realities of the Caribbean than was possible through the limited forms of folk verse.

There is no question that Thomas's style reflects many of the elements contained in the work of Césaire: surrealism, or magic realism, strong identification with Africa and the African past as a symbol of home and ancestry, strong identification with the conditions and struggles of the masses against the oppression of their rulers, identification with a folk culture, particularly black culture, not officially recognized by European cultural czars, and extreme skepticism toward the technological, scientific/rational overemphasis of contemporary Western society. This technological bias is counterposed against African and Afro-American spirituality, exemplified in its most assertive form for Thomas through the genius of black music. Like Césaire's work, Thomas's poems are composed of disparate and widely varied elements: song, criticism, erudite allusions, sharp description, memory—all flow along rather evenly in his versification. And like Césaire, the quest for identity is a major theme, though Thomas has experienced increasing assurance and rootedness in his identification as a black American.

Finally, Lorenzo Thomas shares with Aimé Césaire a belief in the powers of imagination and spirituality to overcome the more tangible problems of powerlessness, along with a belief in poetry as a protector of truth that cannot be bought, sold, or tailored by commerce. It is almost as if he accepts as credo Césaire's assertion: "In this climate of flame and fury that is the climate of poetry money has no currency, courts pass no judgements, judges do not convict, juries do not acquit."

The Bathers, an ironically titled collection of poems published in 1981, contains a fine chronological presentation of the poet's work—ranging from his earliest poems in New York, his poems about and around his Vietnam experience to a very representative collection of his best work emanating from Houston and the Southwest. Sections of *The Bathers* were originally published as broadsides or pamphlet poems. The cover for the book is an imitation drawing of European Rubens-like paintings of lazing bathers at the seashore. The book's inside cover is a collage of black demonstrators being attacked with high pressure water hoses, as in Birmingham during civil rights demonstrations in the 1960s. The collage is by Cecilio Thomas, the poet's brother.

Among his early New York works, "The Unnatural Life" is a characteristically surreal portrait of the New York scene. There is, however, a personal, almost private voice in this rather abstract love poem, possibly an allusion to what might have been love devoid of conclusion or consummation. Here we see early evidence of Thomas's powers of sharp observation and his gnawing discomfort with cosmetic or domestic tranquility, a recurring theme in his later work, first projected as a theme in itself in "Domestic Horror." Thomas has the gift of spotting inner turmoil hiding behind the seemingly mundane—an inner turmoil born of tragedy, passion, memory:

> who is this dread child, bounding through our home
> devouring the furniture?

The theme of hidden or masked malaise is given heavy treatment in "Dracula," written in 1966, published separately in 1973, and collected in *The Bathers*. A lengthy, philosophical poem, "Dracula" in substance and style anticipates Thomas's finest and most fully realized work. Difficult as it is to summarize "Dracula" in rational, linear, narrative terms, it may be said that Thomas juxtaposes the popularity of the Dracula films, which he believes is firmly rooted in American boredom, with the insatiable Western appetite for conquest without coming to terms with consequences, which include the spiritual and moral impact of conquest on the conquerors. Like Dracula, the appetite for conquest is an appetite for blood, a desire to destroy life by always going for the jugular vein of the victim. No matter how much bloodsucking has occurred in American history, there is always the suppressed, but irresistible appetite for more and more. Possibly, Thomas suggests, a failure to face historical truth lies at the heart of so much of the irrational, unexplained violence and horror that have always been so deeply embedded just below the plastic surface of American culture—thus, the American subconscious attraction to the Dracula myth and films: "only such emotion could complete us/When we are tired of our thoughtful survival and/Cry to be married to a cringing darkness and capture/It in our souls."

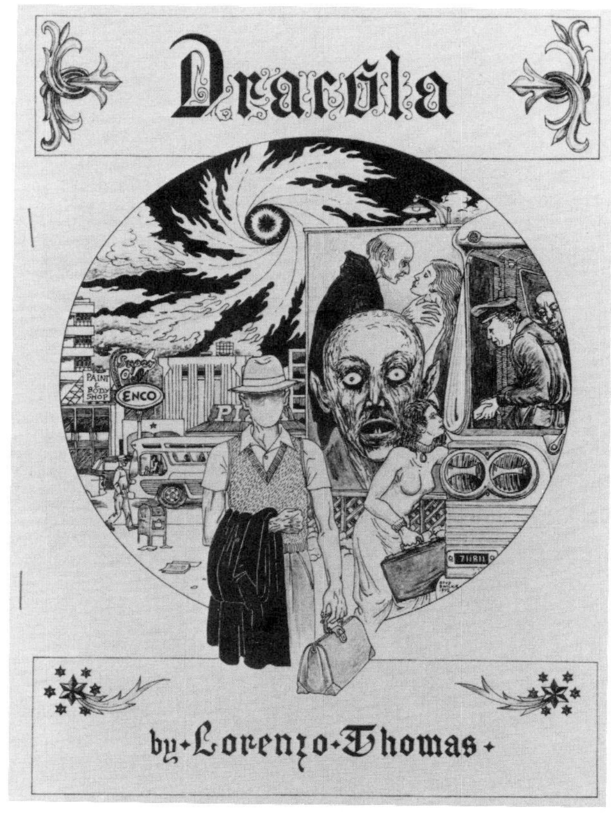

Front cover for 1973 publication of Thomas's poem written in 1966

All of Thomas's poems reflect an extraordinary sensitivity to contemporary American culture, particularly the suggestive and image-laden world of cinema. He uses cinematic imagery in an effort to come to terms with the African heritage, an identity framed first by his West Indian upbringing, and by his experiences as a black youth in New York.

One of Thomas's earliest poetic references to black identity is contained in his *Umbra II* poem "South St. Blues." Here Thomas presents his vague black persona as possibly frighteningly limited and depressing but undeniably real. However, in the full-length 1970 poem "The Bathers," the title poem of his 1981 collection, Thomas addresses the Southern civil rights struggle and racial reality in his own, very personal terms. "The Bathers" is a series of refractions off the indelible photographic image of black demonstrators being attacked with police fire hoses during the Birmingham demonstrations of April 1963. Thomas employs several images to depict the conversion of black people via

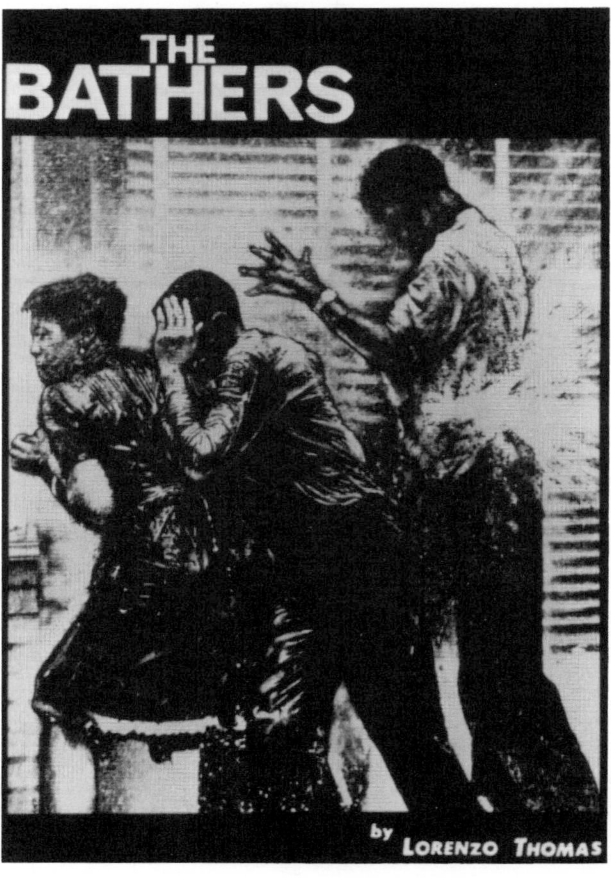

Front cover and title page for Thomas's 1981 collection. "We turned to fire when the water hit / Us," Thomas says in the ironic title poem. "Some threw the water / On their heads," he continues, "They was Baptists."

this brutalization, which he views as a magically transforming ritual: when hosed, the demonstrators "Turn to fire," becoming akin to a "sun" people, newly endowed with the age-old strength of ancient Egypt, through the poet's evocation of the regenerative legend of Horus. There is also the image of baptism:

Some threw the water
On their heads.
They was Baptists

And that day Horus bathed him in the water
Again
. . . .
And Orisha walked amid the waters with hatchets
Where Allah's useful white men
Came there bearing the water
And made our street Jordan
And we stepped into our new land.

Here, for the first time in Thomas's published work, he deals directly with the struggle for civil rights and black equality so much in the news and consciousness of black America in the 1960s. Thomas weaves an identification with ancient African culture into the contemporary American struggle. He views the ritualistic freeing, wrought by the Southern struggle, as a spiritual descendent of the mythical emergence of ancient Egyptian, national consciousness wrought by the imaginative reconstitution of Horus's body. Thomas is suggesting that for the Afro-American emergence into national consequence to be most meaningful, there must be a sense of return to ancestral and mythical "home," even if the sense of home, or fatherland, lies buried deep in layers of subconscious, and even if there is little evidence of such memory in the day-to-day rhetoric of the civil rights struggle. This black American regeneration is also symbolized, as was common with several black poets of the period, by the metaphor of Afro-Americans emerging spiritually into a "new land," that is, a new, more positive concept of self as a people distinct from territorial identity as Americans, thus helping to shed the psychological shackles of slavery.

Nineteen seventy to 1976 was an extremely creative period for Thomas; it was a time when his powers of imagination and observation were at their height. It was during this period that he was adjusting to moves from Vietnam to New York, and then to the Southwest. "Envoy," for instance, is a fine short poem, humorous and introspective; the poet returning to America from duty in Vietnam notes the landmarks of the San Francisco Bay Area while descending in an airplane:

The first sight was McDonald's
Neon yellow arc

A beckoning out the cold, windy night

A rainbow promising nothing
And warning that that nothing
Is serious business
. . . .
How did you like being the envoy of a monstrous epic
Or saga of Western corruption
When the white guys blacked their mugs
Before the ambush, what did you do kid?

In "Wonders" the persona is stuck in the delta swamps of Vietnam. He discovers he longs for New York and the pleasurable times in the city he had known as home. In a gush of nostalgia, he says, "I feel so simple to be thinking of Harlem/New York the apple/Where we had our own Adam/And damn near all/The wonders of the world."

But it was in the post-Vietnam period that Lorenzo Thomas achieved a new synthesis of experience and belief. Never losing his sharp sense of irony or his feel for the absurd, the poet became more at ease with elements of black culture and history, particularly black music. His succinct portrayals of the Southwestern terrain add a new dimension to his poetry, contrasting, or rather, adding to his heretofore almost exclusively New York frame of reference. The creative genius of black music becomes a frequent theme, as in his 1972 piece for Charlie Parker, "Historiography":

There was space

And the sun and the stars he saw in his head
In the sky on the street and the ceilings
Of nightclubs and lounges as we sought to
Actually lounge trapped in the dull asylum

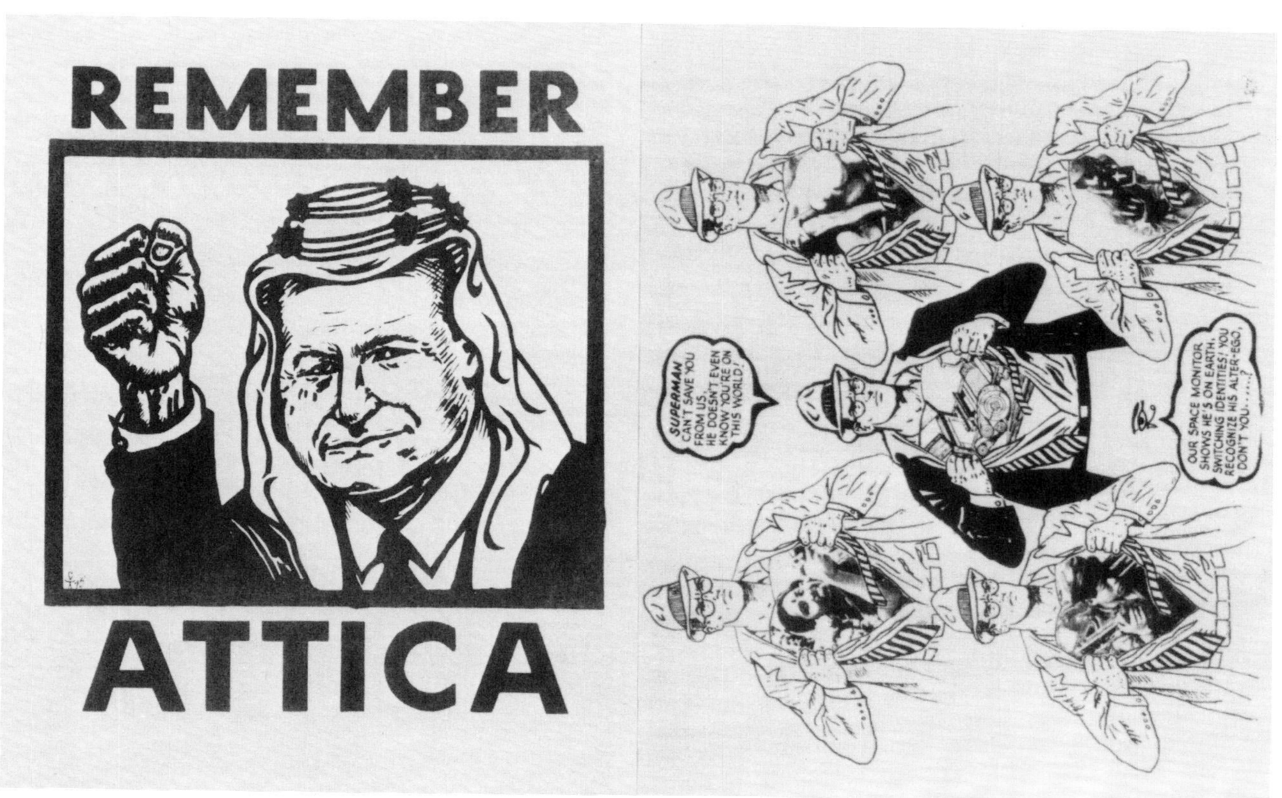

Covers for Thomas's 1975 pamphlet poem, Framing the Sunrise, *which addresses the horror of war being televised*

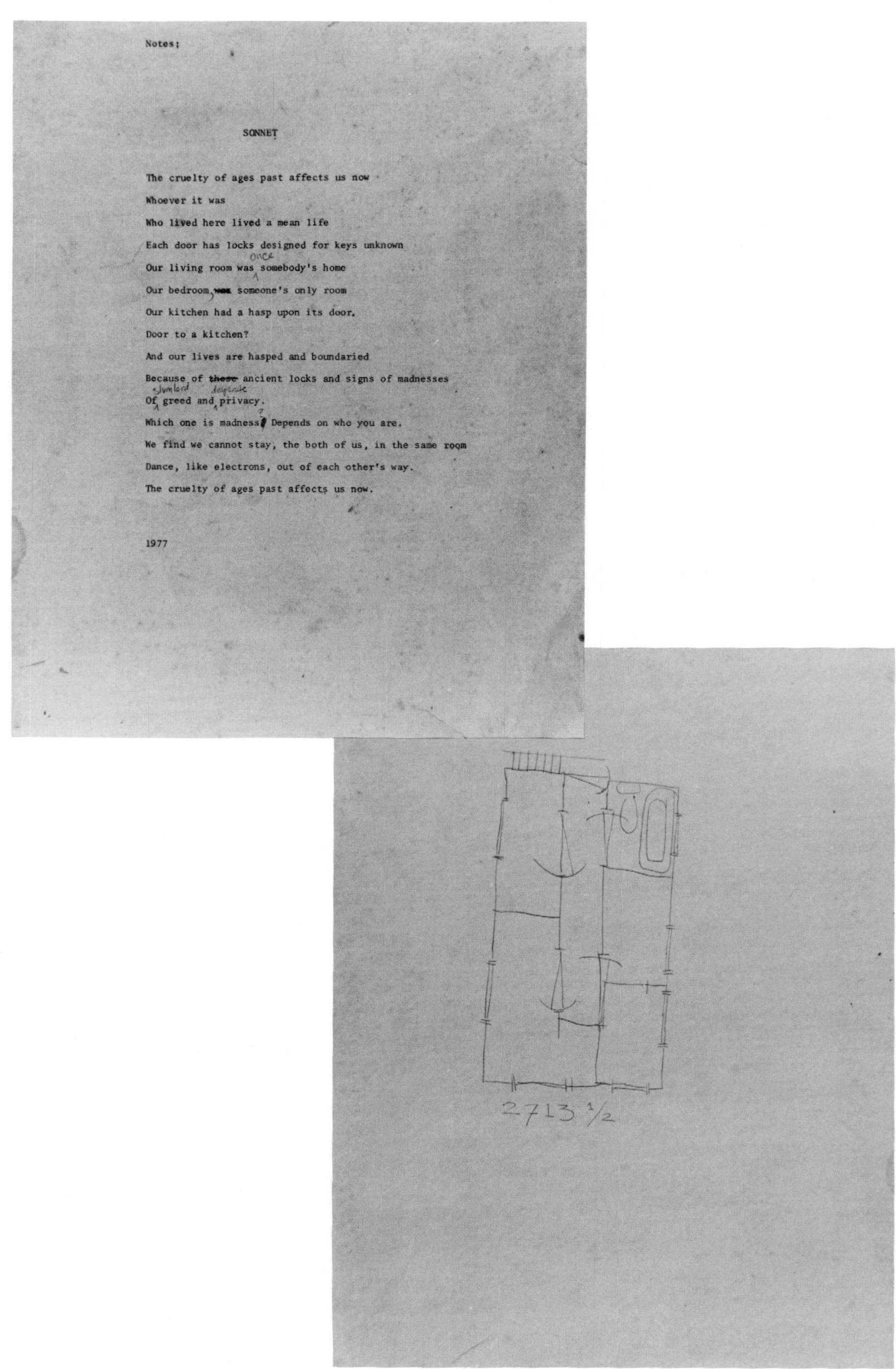

Notes:

SONNET

The cruelty of ages past affects us now
Whoever it was
Who lived here lived a mean life
Each door has locks designed for keys unknown
Our living room was once somebody's home
Our bedroom, ~~was~~ someone's only room
Our kitchen had a hasp upon its door.
Door to a kitchen?
And our lives are hasped and boundaried
Because of ~~these~~ ancient locks and signs of madnesses
Of symbols greed and desperate privacy.
Which one is madness? Depends on who you are.
We find we cannot stay, the both of us, in the same room
Dance, like electrons, out of each other's way.
The cruelty of ages past affects us now.

1977

Front and back of a page from the second draft of a poem which was published in Chances are Few *as "MMDCCXIII½"* *(courtesy of the author)*

What we see, then, is that the Rukus Song is a mirror image of the Church's Jubilee Shout; the eulogistic Mournin' Blues, an outward mode of Moanin' for one's personal sorrows. We see that wishing retributive punishment upon one's enemy modulates to a higher desire for one's own redemption and, once the fact of redemption seems assured, premature joy in the expected reward. ~~We see also that~~ Suffering always commissions defiant expression which, in its own term, leads to boasting self-affirmation and, for those who are fortunate, genuine praise from others or one's own praise for the powers beyond the self that strengthen us. Similarly, in all love songs, there is a modulated progression from despair to delight that depends almost wholly upon the response of the one that the lover desires. In the European courtly tradition, the loved one was often so fickle, ~~the~~ that sonneteers incorporated both modalities in the same poem. "I freeze," says Petrarch, "and I burn." "John Henry," the most incredibly extreme version of a praise song, full of displaced aggression, defiance, and prideful boast, is also in its rhythms a work song for those who, in their menial situation as convicts or common laborers would catch hell to utter aloud their own names in such terms. ~~And~~ All ~~of~~ this should be obvious to those who listen. The lyrics of "John Henry" or "Take This Hammer" by mocking the boss, almost turn labor into entertainment for the workers, while the rhythms make their exertions a dance.

the Lady oscillated so trifling,

Educated white folks call 'em sonnets; I call em Afro-folksongs stolen away into Arabic poetry, and borrowed into English from Italian.

Page from a working draft for an unpublished essay about blues song forms (courtesy of the author)

Of our own enslavements. . . .

The phoniness of society also becomes a recurring theme as in "Fly Society," which comments on the language of a woman friend who, in conversation, "mentions nineteen high priced islands." The complex, but smoothly flowing "While Madness Reigns" tackles the theme of the present nature of nature in America, where:

Things perish, begging
The sky for rebirth

Mountains demand RSVP and
Poisons flood the clouds
The fishes ignore everyone
In their portable ocean

Echoing the theme of "Dracula," Thomas sees us "Destroying life to make a living. . . .": the Western compulsion to destroy raging out of control.

"Work Song," written in 1972, makes strong social and economic comment on the state of the poor and oppressed in America, reflecting on Victor Hugo's nineteenth-century *Les Miserables*. Of all Thomas's poems, this is the most in keeping with the traditions of social realism in style and militancy, as he depicts the fate of twentieth-century masses, whom he views as guileless, voiceless, and endlessly victimized by their rulers.

We work all day. With or without pay.
They spread the pyramids we build
To crucify us. We soldier well and they
Return us frozen hearts and fallen stars
And etch taps into our circle of sound.

Nothing much has changed since Hugo's time to better conditions for the poor. A hundred years of technological advances have hardly advanced the quality of our lives.

Victor Hugo was happier in Paris
Than I am now in New York never hearing the stars
Singing their worksongs or chansons of space joy
Because the news keeps blunting the starwaves.

The poem ends with a declaration of the necessity for revolution, for the "masters" of the world have failed the people of the world:

We shall surely unpower these criminal lords.
May the Creator be pleased with our songs. . . .

"Framing the Sunrise," dated 1975, is representative of Thomas's most accomplished and imaginative work. The poem literally springs forth from the American family television set and offers several fascinating comments on the influence of television in blurring images of reality. The poem presents a parade of television images/icons from our recent national past: Ike (Dwight D. Eisenhower), FDR (Franklin Delano Roosevelt), supermarkets, Eddie Fisher, the Selma (Alabama) Bridge, the Kent State killings, and especially Vietnam, that peculiarly American war, the war within the American soul experienced by the American populace through the television evening news, the unpleasant, dirty war seeping into safe American living rooms like a putrid gas. Thomas focuses on the distortion inherent in commercial television, in the way events are programmed in America—the incapacity of our new electronic media to capture the full impact of reality—especially war, evil, and tragedy.

Throughout the poem, images of events and faces flow from the omnipresent screen, filtered through the poet's memory as they have penetrated the living rooms of our collective consciousness, at the same time deadening our consciousness and our capacity to feel. Thomas repeats the phrase "the state of the art has improved," meaning technological advances, an advance paradoxically concomitant with our diffusion of the impact of reality, a theme Thomas developed earlier in "Work Song." Harry Truman on his morning constitutional, White Sands test planes, the late night movies, "each became monsters/lazy unfeeling/brutally corrupted by our senses."

Lorenzo Thomas's sense of irony, absurdity, and his social awareness are very much a part of the shared concerns of contemporary black literature, despite his surreal influences. He is not, however, a racial protest poet, but a critic of the Western world writing from the perspective of Afro-America, with inherited and acquired attitudes of an Afro-Caribbean. His sympathies are with "the people," the folk, the poor, the oppressed, of which people of African descent happen to be card-carrying members in the Western world.

Lorenzo Thomas has said that his appreciation of folk culture was enhanced in the Southwest through his growing knowledge of Southern blues singers. He mentions as influences the legendary Robert Johnson, the late Lightnin' Hopkins, a native of Houston, Clifton Chenier, the western Louisiana Zydeco blues singer who sings in French and English, and the late Juke Boy Bonner, a poet-singer of the Houston streets, eulogized by Thomas in *Callaloo,* no. 7. Thomas's knowledge of music is extremely catholic; he seems to be on intimate terms with every form of American popular music. In terms of poetic concept, he has observed: "I write poems because I can't sing." We assume he means even though his poems are not written in song form, or that his language is not the language of the blues, the poet should play an artistic role akin to that of blues singers. The poet is like a blues singer with the same migratory tendencies, the same qualities of street prophet and historian, and the same fate of being held in low esteem by the ruling classes.

Several of Thomas's short poems pull all of these ideas and concerns together. Especially noteworthy is "Suicide Administration," a political satire in the form of a letter from the inner depths of the Central Intelligence Agency to those it plans to destroy:

Gentlemen:
Please forward your last letters
Then we can close these files.

"Hiccups," based on the famous Léon Damas poem, addresses the problem of Caribbean identity by referring to a "proper" European upbringing, mulattoness, religious orthodoxy, and so forth. However,

There's no MULATTO water-fountain south of here
. . . .
So
Let me drink the BLACK water!

"Collective Poems" is a kind of anthem for the communally-oriented black poet and his role of reclaiming his culture:

I made bards of my excluded brothers
When the bigots refused me my name.

Been so poor, but a magnet with my shamed English
I have relived the legends.

"Class Action" is a major effort in which Thomas assimilates his earliest, childhood, and youthful impressions, the black consciousness of the 1960s, and his new Southern experiences. Lengthy and difficult to summarize, it addresses racism in American culture as it is represented primarily in old Hollywood cinema and music, a process of examination from which Thomas extracts an unusually well-defined sense of personal values. As for blacks and the neglected masses he terms the "wallpaper" of American culture, those never depicted in the grand Hollywood film, those relegated to the balconies of the theaters of the silver screen, he sees them as a basic spiritual force that can counter the power and control of the ruling classes, the makers of the silver screen, the creators of official American art. There is and has been a deeper logic to the life of black people:

Lorenzo Thomas (photograph ©1985 by Wayne Duffer)

Unlettered Negroes called this logic Jazz
Relating thought to life, love to projection
Spirit entertained by spirit
as in life . . .

The powerful, on the other hand, produce: "Self-serving histories of the self-serving"; they have used American cinema to project false histories. The power to do this has come from what Thomas calls "the force of circumstance":

The force of circumstance
Is stronger than one thinks
It draws on everything and riddles hope
Circles the future on our calendars
Claims all the past as its own
as memory's "I told you so"

And the poet notes that the first speaking movie was "The Jazz Singer," a violation of black spirituality:

Projected through the fantasy of aberration
For which the blame accrues to those who thought
That anyone was free to choose among spirits
Like segregating folks
or seating suckers at the picture show.

Blacks can only counteract the forces of American circumstance by adhering to and believing in the wisdom of their own spirituality, which is fundamentally African:

the juju spirits shout through us
Our screams speak rapture of their presence
Not our pain. . . .
Without them, we will live in silent movies.

"Us," singularly and plurally, as blacks, as "wallpaper people," must speak out, for:

If I should speak, the wallpaper would break
Its silence too.

. . . we must speak or be patterns on a wall,
Moving or pasted still; it doesn't matter which.

The poem ends with a jest, a mild tone of self-deprecation which beautifully heightens his "we" concept:

You don't have to take my word
For "it."

"Class Action" is a profound and complex long poem, shifting in mood, allusion, suggestion, and meaning. Satire and irony are fundamental to Thomas's style; an oral reading of the poem brings that out.

"Class Action" integrates Thomas's social and political concerns, folk values, and criticisms of the fairy-tale world of grand Hollywood cinema with his counterposition of the strength of black music, spirituality, and culture. Although "Class Action" does not really represent new elements in the poetry of Lorenzo Thomas, in no other poem are all his major themes so well blended and so brilliantly conveyed in metaphor and image.

"Class Action," like "Framing the Sunrise" and "Dracula," deals with the projection of popular American film images and the unrelatedness of these images to the life of not only black Americans, but to most of the people in America. Underlying these poems is a call for a more meaningful truth, a more lasting and useful art.

One can conclude, particularly after his move southward, that Thomas believes Afro-Americans, guided by the light of the star of African culture and life principles, have the potential to lead the way in a freeing from the destructive, capitalistic, money-obsessed American value system, and such an act of liberation must be at its core cultural and spiritual. This is the pervasive logic behind the fascinating and challenging poems and essays of Lorenzo Thomas.

References:

Tom Dent, "Two Collections of Unusual Strength," *Freedomways,* 20 (Second Quarter 1980): 104-107;

Michel Leiris, "Who is Aimé Césaire?," *Sulfur 5* (1982);

Michel Oren, "A 60s Saga: The Life and Death of *Umbra,*" *Freedomways,* 24, nos. 3 and 4 (1985): 167-181, 237-254;

Charles Rowell, "Between the Comedy of Matters and the Ritual Workings of Man: An Interview with Lorenzo Thomas," *Callaloo,* 4 (February-October 1981): 19-35.

Askia Muhammad Touré
(Rolland Snellings)

(13 October 1938-   )

Joanne V. Gabbin
Lincoln University

BOOKS: *Samory Touré,* by Touré, Tom Feelings, and Elombe Brath (New York, 1963);

Earth: For Mrs. Mary Bethune and the African and Afro-American Women (Detroit: Broadside Press, 1968);

JuJu: Magic Songs for the Black Nation, by Touré and Ben Caldwell (Chicago: Third World Press, 1970);

Songhai! (New York: Songhai Press, 1973).

Since the early 1960s Askia Muhammad Touré has been a leading architect of the black arts movement. As poet, essayist, and editor, he has responded on many levels to the culture of black liberation. His poems and essays, widely published in the *Black Scholar, Soulbook, Black Theatre, Black World, Freedomways,* and *Essence,* embody the ideology of a people seeking to reclaim their images and history from the arbiters of Western culture. Touré, known as a poet whose vision is as expansive as is his love for black people, represents the determination of contemporary black writers to shed "the white plaster" of their "negroness" in exchange for a deeper sense of blackness and a new world view. Touré has also been a moving spirit behind the emergence of several revolutionary journals, including *Black Dialogue, Liberator Magazine,* and the *Journal of Black Poetry* (now known as *Kitabu Cha Jua*). Through these journals Touré and the other editors have punctuated their ideological break with the West and have influenced an entire generation to reject decadent values and myths for values consistent with political and cultural liberation. Above all, he, along with Amiri Baraka, Larry Neal, and others, raised the national consciousness and gave shape, direction, and vision to the black arts movement.

Askia Muhammad Touré

Touré was born Rolland Snellings in Raleigh, North Carolina, to Clifford R. Snellings and Nancy Bullock Snellings on 13 October 1938. The eldest of two sons, he spent his first five years with his paternal grandmother in La Grange, Georgia. When he was six years old, he moved to Dayton, Ohio, with his family and attended the public schools there. His early years in Dayton were sprinkled with frequent trips to North Carolina, his mother's home, and back to Georgia, where his romance with the South began. On one such trip, Touré noticed the red clay banks of the Georgia landscape as his train lumbered down the tracks. The red clay stuck in his mind. Like the other vivid images of rural life, it urged from him a lyrical response that many years later found its way into an unpublished poem:

Red clay, red clay
Warm, sticky, blood clay
Moonlight on a Georgia pine.
Red clay, red clay
Rank, fertile, wet clay
Night rain on the Georgia hills.

The poem also includes his fond reminiscences of simple joys shared with a childhood friend: "chinaberry trees," "church supper," and "shadow monsters on kerosene lit walls." For Touré, "these were the young years, the fun years." And his Southern experience provided the anlage for his development as a poet.

Touré's first attempt at writing poetry came in grade school in Dayton. When he was in the seventh grade, he wrote a poem about snow. His teacher refused to believe that he had written the poem, and the teacher's insistence that he had not written the poem was enough to convince him to stop writing. However, during his years at Roosevelt High School, 1952 to 1956, his poetic nature emerged in another form. In this period dominated by the music of rhythm and blues, Touré and others of his age imitated the cool "doo-whops" of the Orioles, the Ravens, the Platters, and Frankie Lyman and the Teenagers. At the age of seventeen, he began singing in nightclubs and was about to cut a record on the King label when he decided to join the Air Force. In the service he sang with blues singer Little Willie John, Robert Green of the Flamingos, and Herman Dunham from the Solitaires. His talent for creating lyrical, rhythmic lines was realized, for a while, as he crooned with Herald Upshaw and the Swans. He later wrote: "In those years of Martin Luther King, bus boycotts and other evidence of our growing struggle, we grew up, developed, expanded our souls, our minds churning to the beat of our people's only music, Rhythm and Blues."

When Touré completed his military service in 1959, he went to New York where his career as an artist and a writer was launched. From 1960 to 1962 Touré studied visual arts at the Art Students League of New York. During this time he met illustrator Tom Feelings and artist Elombe Brath. Out of their close association came the illustrated biography of Samory Touré, the fiery grandfather of Sékou Touré, who courageously resisted the domination of Guinea by France in the 1800s. Jointly authored and published by Touré, Feelings, and Brath in 1963, the book was one of the first of the period to reclaim the heroes and heritage of the African past.

A year earlier Touré and Tom Feelings were invited to illustrate *Umbra* magazine by members of its staff. In 1962 the staff included Tom Dent, one of the founders of the Free Southern Theatre; poet Calvin C. Hernton; David Henderson, poet and editor of *Umbra;* artist-poet Albert E. Haynes; and novelist Ishmael Reed. It was in their company that Touré ventured to read some of his fledgling poems. The *Umbra* organization, with its dynamic blend of integrationists and nationalists, also provided Touré with fertile ground for his maturing political philosophies.

As a young poet, Touré struggled to develop an appropriate style. Choosing first to study the technique of a master, he gave himself a crash course in W. E. B. Du Bois. He read *Dusk of Dawn, Dark Water, Souls of Black Folk,* and most of Du Bois's poems and cultivated what amounted to a nineteenth-century epic style of writing. "Sunrise," which is anthologized in *Black Fire: An Anthology of Afro-American Writing* (1968), perhaps best illustrates his early style:

In the Void, in the Storm, in the Wastelands of our hearts—
a cry is heard.
In our dreams, in the wind, in the sweatpangs of the night—
a call is heard.
This Cry, this Call is the Song of the Race—through the years,
through the Veil, from the lash that captured our humanity,
from the Mark that's slashed upon our bosoms in this land:
the Mark of Cain.

Touré found, however, that his message and this outdated style were contradictory. Therefore, he turned to other writers like Langston Hughes and the Negritude poets, Leopold Senghor, Aimé Césaire, and Léon Damas. In fact, Senghor's poem "Congo" and Paul Laurence Dunbar's "Corn Song" influenced greatly the structure and tone of one of Touré's most beautiful lyrical poems, "Floodtide." Written in a natural, spontaneous, musical style, "Floodtide" reflects his deep respect for the tenacity and endurance of black tenant farmers as they confront capricious, often relentless natural forces and racism:

They carry on
though sorrows completely
bend them down
they carry on
though butchered

and maimed
by nature and whitefolks
they carry on
and sing their songs.

However, nothing influenced the sound, rhythm, and form of Touré's poems more than black music. Touré first experimented with the new black music as a referent for his poetry in 1967 when he was involved in the Uptown Poetry Movement. After he left *Umbra* in 1963, he joined South African poet Keorapestse Willie Kgositsile and poet-activist Larry Neal and began reading in the lofts with the young jazz musicians. Larry Neal introduced Touré to the music of John Coltrane, Pharaoh Sanders, Sun Ra, and others. Communicating his enthusiasm for this music as the primary cultural contribution of blacks, Neal saw the new black music influencing the very style and structure of the literature. Encouraged to experiment with these forms, Touré developed a style characterized by polyrhythms, long lines, sharp, staccato phrasing, and the vibrant lyricism of the saxophone solo. With the example of Neal, who studied the structure of black classical music and used it to inform such outstanding poems as "Don't Say Good-bye to the Pork-Pie Hat," Touré achieved a similarly skillful synthesis in "JuJu."

One of Touré's finest poems, "JuJu" is a lyrical masterpiece that captures the syncopation, the polyrhythms, the tone, and the riffs of a John Coltrane solo. It is a praise song to the priest-prophet Coltrane who intones the essence of the black man's pain and joy. For Touré, Coltrane's matchless sounds have magic to conjure up the silent years of endless despair and disappointment, the suffering, the want, and the often unspeakable heartache. Yet Coltrane is also the joy-bringer—"the magic piper of Vision of Now," "with Eternity upon his horn cascading diamonds of Destiny to our blues-ridden hearts." He is the gift the ancestors sent to affirm racial strength and continuity.

Solo Solo Solo for Africanic joys: rhythms thrilling
from
the mobile hips of choclit mamas Bird-of-Paradise
pagan colors
Joy vibrating from the rat-nests of the West.
And greens and cornbread sweet potatoes booga-
looing
in the brilliance of his smile.

Ultimately Touré gives homage to Coltrane: his spiritual inspiration, his message, and his life. And "JuJu" is a good example of Touré's developing style: a fusion of the lyric and the epic presented in the rhythms of classical black music.

In 1965 Touré wrote "Keep on Pushing" for *Liberator Magazine.* Borrowing his theme from David Henderson's epic poem "Keep on Pushing," and paying tribute to the Impressions, whom he considered nationalistic black artists, Touré focused on black music as a social and spiritual force behind the black struggle.

During this period Touré was most actively involved with what critic Carolyn Fowler calls "the revolutionary journals." From 1963 to 1965 Touré was a member of the editorial board of *Black America,* the theoretical journal of the Revolutionary Action Movement (RAM). From 1965 to 1966, he was a staff member of *Liberator Magazine,* along with Neal, playwright Charles Russell, Carlos Russell, Harold Cruse, and journalist Eddie Ellis. Later Touré became an associate editor of *Black Dialogue* which first appeared in the Spring of 1965. When the *Journal of Black Poetry* grew out of *Black Dialogue,* Touré became editor-at-large of the publication, a position he has held since then. The emergence of these journals, according to Fowler, "was the literary enactment of the crisis of the sixties: The Break with the West." Providing sociopolitical analysis, documentation of oppression, and an acceptable world view, the pages of these journals dispel the notion that the movement was haphazard and without guidance and direction.

During the mid-1960s, Touré was also actively involved in the politics of the black liberation struggle. Perhaps no single event affected his political activism more than the murder of Malcolm X on 21 February 1965 in Harlem. His death caused a flurry of activity. Touré and Larry Neal came out with a newspaper patterned after Marcus Garvey's *Negro World,* called *Afro World.* Distributed nationally only one week after Malcolm's death, it helped to shore up the black community. Two months later Touré and Neal held a Harlem Uptown Youth Conference which introduced Amiri Baraka (LeRoi Jones) and the artists of the Black Arts Repertoire Theatre School to the cultural and activist Harlem community. It was after this conference that the Black Arts Theatre opened in Harlem. Developing their own audience, Baraka, Charles Patterson, William Patterson, and Clarence Reed were among the black artists who joined Touré, Neal, Kgositsile and other Harlem-based poets and took their programs into the streets of Harlem. They would block off streets, and masses of people would gather to hear Sun Ra, Milford Graves, and other musicians or to see one of Baraka's revolutionary plays. Touré and the other poets would recite their poems. Recalling these days, he said: "We would serenade the people on the streets of Harlem, and it made the authorities nervous as hell. We went all over Harlem and brought to its neglected, colonized masses the messages of Black power, dignity, and beauty."

At the closing of the Black Arts Theatre School in Harlem, the artists inspired and linked up with a number of peoples' theaters throughout the country. Black House and Black Arts West sprang up in San Francisco; Free Southern Theatre in New Orleans; Freedom Theatre in Philadelphia; Karamu House in Cleveland; OBAC poets theater in Chicago; and Spirit House in Newark. The Harlem artists encouraged the spread of the movement on college campuses where student activism gave it further momentum. Political activists joined the artists in raising consciousness and in seeking support for black institutions, journals, and newspapers.

During this time when the black liberation movement was creating a massive cultural movement nationwide, Touré's life changed substantially as he responded to personal, political, and religious demands. In 1965 Touré met Dona Humphrey; they were married in June 1966. Soon after their marriage, Touré and his wife moved to San Francisco, where he participated in RAM, a revolutionary black nationalist, scientific socialist organization. In response to the urban rebellions of 1967 through 1968, RAM allied itself with SNCC, the Nation of Islam, and independent nationalist and black Marxist-Leninist groups. These coalitions brought Touré in direct contact with activists who had differing ideologies and methods for dealing with what they saw as their mutual struggle against repression. However, Touré came under the direct influence of the Nation of Islam and converted to the Islamic faith. With this conversion, he changed his name from Rolland Snellings to Askia Muhammad Touré and ultimately changed the way he thought about the world. In his poem "Extension,"

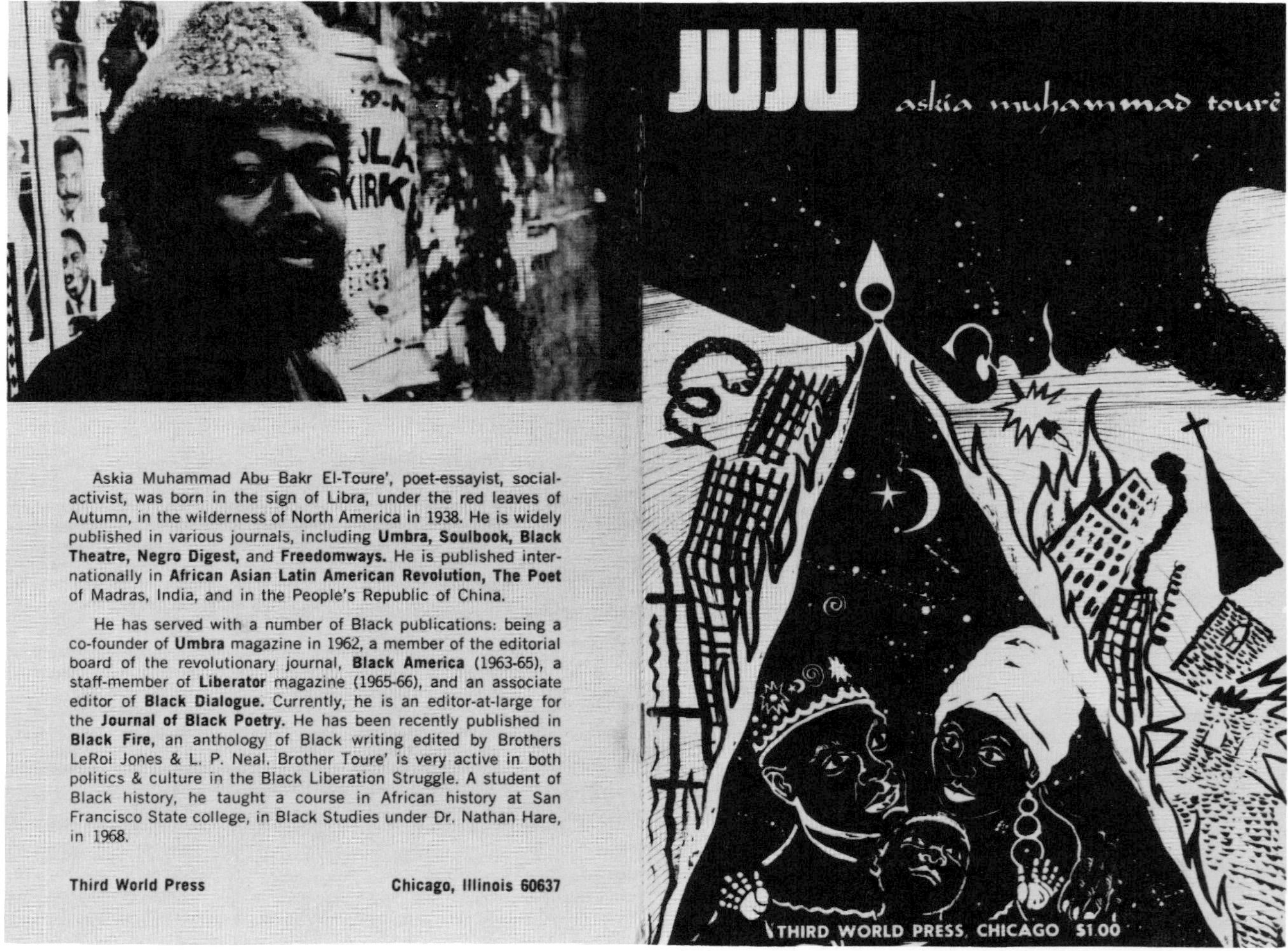

Askia Muhammad Abu Bakr El-Toure', poet-essayist, social-activist, was born in the sign of Libra, under the red leaves of Autumn, in the wilderness of North America in 1938. He is widely published in various journals, including **Umbra, Soulbook, Black Theatre, Negro Digest,** and **Freedomways.** He is published internationally in **African Asian Latin American Revolution, The Poet** of Madras, India, and in the People's Republic of China.

He has served with a number of Black publications: being a co-founder of **Umbra** magazine in 1962, a member of the editorial board of the revolutionary journal, **Black America** (1963-65), a staff-member of **Liberator** magazine (1965-66), and an associate editor of **Black Dialogue.** Currently, he is an editor-at-large for the **Journal of Black Poetry.** He has been recently published in **Black Fire,** an anthology of Black writing edited by Brothers LeRoi Jones & L. P. Neal. Brother Toure' is very active in both politics & culture in the Black Liberation Struggle. A student of Black history, he taught a course in African history at San Francisco State college, in Black Studies under Dr. Nathan Hare, in 1968.

Third World Press **Chicago, Illinois 60637**

Covers for Touré's 1970 book of prose and poetry. "Juju is a West African word for a magical charm."

published in *JuJu: Magic Songs for the Black Nation* (1970), Touré enthusiastically embraces the Islamic vision:

The TRUTH THE TRUTH: Islam in our women's
  eyes,
in their sweet souls, flowing robes—and the Earth
one large community with open doors open minds
  open
hearts: Souls stretching forth into the Universe.
ISLAM:
This is my vision, my song of Man;
. . . .
(A Nation rising in Midnight Robes; let it rise, *Let the Black Nation Rise!*) EXTENSION let the music flow
EXTENSION and ten thousand Muslim Angels shall
light our way through the burning bloody Night until
the Trumpets of the Fiery Dawn. ALLHUMDULIL-
  LAH!

At the time of his conversion Touré was teaching a course in African history at San Francisco State College in its black studies department. Touré worked under Nathan Hare, who for several years was the editor of the *Black Scholar*. There, too, he began his long-term friendship with poet Sonia Sanchez, who was also teaching in the black studies department.

Convinced that black writers must produce more literary journals in every region of the country, Touré continued his involvement with *Black Dialogue* as an associate editor. He began his association with *Black Dialogue* when he urged Abdul Karin (Gerald Labrie) to include his "Letter to Ed Springgs: Concerning LeRoi Jones and Others." In this open letter Touré leveled a caustic attack at Baraka for what he called "Reactionary Super-Blackism, a dogmatic nihilism—in Black literature as well as politics. . . ." The letter caused much dissension among the members of the editorial board; however, it was printed. Touré, aware of the need for serious internal self-criticism, continued to stress this need when he moved to California and became one of the magazine's associate editors. The article was also the first of several which directed criticism at Baraka, Ron Karenga, and others whom he believed had weakened the movement by destructive iconoclasm and cultural nationalism.

Touré's years in San Francisco were tumultuous. His first years of marriage, the birth of his son Tariq Abdullah bin Touré, his conversion to Islam, and his first teaching experience took place on political and cultural battlefields. It is, therefore, not surprising that his activities put strains on his marriage and that the marriage was dissolved by the time he returned to New York.

In New York Touré became immersed in the religion of the Sunni Muslims. His spiritual leader, Imam Tawfiq, whom Touré describes as "moving with youthful strength towards fulfillment of prophecy," taught Touré about Islamic theology and encouraged his spiritual evolution. Believing devoutly that religion would free him, he absorbed this theology with enthusiastic fervor.

In 1970 Touré married Helen Morton Hobbs, a writer and editor. Called by her Muslim name, Halima, she inspired Touré toward further self-actualization in his writing and in his commitment to Islam. She appears to be the inspiration for the poem "Al Fajr: The Daybreak," which was published in *Songhai!* (1973):

Who is this woman before me now with sparkling eyes?
This woman panther-lithe and tawny, a princess come
back to haunt me with ghosts of splendor rising from
my epic past?

They appeared, for a time, to grow together spiritually, "turning 180 degrees in harmony with pyramids and holy mosques." A son, Jamil Abdus-Salam bin Touré, was born to them, and Jamil, like Tariq, became a symbol of the Islamic world community and its new birth. However, despite their mutual interests in writing and editing and their strong commitment to Muslim family life, Touré admitted that their marriage was turbulent and had no chance of survival. His continued involvement in political activities and the growing dissension and dissaffection within his mosque also contributed to the ultimate dissolution of his second marriage.

During the period from 1971 until 1974, Touré participated in the John Oliver Killens Writers Workshop at Columbia University. Killens emerged as Touré's principal mentor in literature and significantly influenced the strengthening of his craft, his experimentation with different literary forms, and his deepening appreciation of the Southern experience and the epic quality of black life.

It was fitting, therefore, that John O. Killens was chosen to write the introduction to Touré's second volume of poetry and sketches, *Songhai!* Killens almost "unqualifiedly" praised the book. Though Killens was uncomfortable with Touré's caustic criticism of Roy Wilkins, Jim Brown, and other black leaders and entertainers, he enthusiastically praised the book's "flowing undulating rhythms," "its images and metaphors," "love for humanity," "religious fervor," and "its cosmic and its epic view of the world and its people." Killens described Touré as "a man and a writer who loves his black brothers and sisters with a revolutionary fervor." The poet's optimism, hope for mankind, expansive vision, and unabashed confidence in their ultimate victory were for Killens consequences of his love.

In the preface to *Songhai!*, entitled "Tomorrow's Jihad," Touré describes the volume as "a living vector composed of the rare triumphs and costly failures of a grizzled warrior treading upon the Sacred path." The "grizzled warrior" is at once griot-historian, singer-musician, and priest-prophet. He is the griot, chronicling the triumphs and failures of his people, conjuring up a "Glorious Future" and the spirits of departed ancestors who recall the horrors of the Middle Passage, "castrated warriors, raped mothers, lynch-rape victims of liberty." Touré is the singer of black love, tenderly touching the "secret regions of the heart" and exposing love's flourishing promise. In his poem "Green Edens Flourish After Storms," Touré makes the unbeliever believe in the possibility of love:

> Melodies harmonizing with other hearts/minds/souls
> all as One, One as all—a symphony of ecstasy,
> the loving cosmic harmonies of earth
> Yes, make it summer. It would be summer:
> golden sunlight, incense, flowers nourishing butter-
> flies
> azure skies breathing love; my ebony darling laughing
> softly beneath my touch. I veteran
> older wiser greying at the temples
> lounging on a persian rug, stroking my reward
> for wading through sewers of bloody death
> to come back whole and laughing in an Age
> of possibility and love.

Addison Gayle, Jr., perhaps the most sensitive and sympathetic critic of Touré's work, responded to the power of Touré's poetry in his review of *Songhai!* and in his autobiography, *Wayward Child:* "Askia, like few others of my contemporaries, had retained the vision of yesteryear, the faith and hope engendered in the sixties and early seventies. . . . The book had captured a great deal of the meaning of the Black aesthetic movement. The poetry of Askia was the poetry of love and faith . . . it was hewn out of a faith in human possibilities—in the ability of people to transcend their own mundanity."

Touré is also the priest-prophet. In this role he becomes his metaphorical "eagle-soul soaring upwards through seven layers of the Cosmos to reach the Living Truth." Urging his followers to gain strength from their past, reclaim their heritage, and pay homage to their heroes, he gives them a deep sense of their heroic presence in the history of mankind. He encourages them to walk the difficult, purifying path of Jihad, to battle the forces that would keep men and women "starving in the streets of Calcutta, dying on the reservations, nodding in the Harlems, napalmed in Vietnam." Touré inspires in them a courage and righteous rage. And as prophet he opens before his followers the visions of a new world coming to birth, Songhai.

The poetic timbre of *Songhai!* was greatly influenced by the Nobel laureate of Chile, Pablo Neruda. Neruda's character—his sincerity, his optimism, his faith in the future of mankind, his exuberance, and his prophetic vision—are mirrored in Touré's vision. Like Neruda, Touré sees himself as the people's poet, "devoid of pessimism, dynamic and joyful in the expression of a new world." In his poem "A Hymn to the People," Touré eulogizes Comrade Neruda, revealing his philosophical and political affinity with the Chilean poet:

> Rest Now, Don Pablo; dream with the
> martyrs in your island grave, brave fighter
> Heroes arrive to pick up your rifle.
> We will fulfill your legacy with a
> New Age rising from the ashes of
> imperial greed.
> We move now to implement your
> vision of a socialistic planet;
> we will sing your sacred songs
> in the coming Age of Light!

In matters of craft, too, Touré shared with Neruda a talent for painting rather than describing scenes, a virtuoso handling of rhythms, and a mature lyrical voice.

Touré, by virtue of these talents, has thrilled audiences on college campuses and in conference settings with his renditions of his poetry. Lecturing at such schools as the University of California at Berkeley, Stanford University, the University of Tennessee, Yale University, Tufts University, Howard University, and others, Touré found his most receptive audiences.

In 1974 Touré went to Philadelphia, leaving behind him the remnants of his second marriage, a bitter confrontation and break with the members of his mosque, and some unsold copies of *Songhai!* Before leaving New York he taught at the Community College of New York. A few months after his arrival in Philadelphia, he began teaching at the Community College of Philadelphia.

Since 1975 Touré has been working on a new volume of poetry, "Sunrise: A New Afrikan Anthem." The book documents Touré's philosophical turning away from religion as a vehicle of social and political change and his turning toward scientific socialism. It explores the tenacity of the New Afrikan extended family, again raises the issue of the role of black music in the overall ethos of urban blacks. It celebrates the eternal beauty and endurance of African people, as in the poem "Cornrow 3":

Queen Mother of the
salt & pepper Cornrow,
Queen Mother of the honey-suckle
springtime.
Dark goddess of the river,
crossing over.
Red clay which feeds the roots
of our survival
Continue on this earth
for evermore!

And most significantly "Sunrise: A New Afrikan Anthem" attests to Toure's continued revolutionary vision, a vision that transcends aesthetic movements and political and religious ideologies. In his poem "Scarifications 4 (War Chant of Avatars)," Touré again embraces the bright vision of liberation in a triumphant eulogy to his spiritual brother, Larry Neal:

O Poet/
Drum-master; open Griot realms
of Racial Memory: Speak!
to these multitudes—
on the corners, in the churches, in the bars—
resurrect the memories;
reconnect the Centuries:
finger-blaze the
Drums of their
rebirth
into revolutionary Self (Blackhearts
pumping passion
in your lives) people; become the Midnight Warriors,
. . . .
creating a liberated universe. . . .

For Touré, Larry Neal's untimely death robbed black people of a superb warrior as well as a poet/critic. Neal was to be the major critic of the black arts movement. He and Amiri Baraka had not only pioneered in the new writing, but had also produced its most perceptive criticism. Touré regrets the fact that some critics have ignored the literature, dismissed it as the screaming polemics of deranged militants, or have been alienated from it because they were alienated from the music that inspired it. He said, "If we had the kind of critics of our literature who had the stature of the poets, our literature would be widely known." To assure against the critical neglect that left Neal's *Black Boogaloo* unreviewed, he is looking to critics like Addison Gayle, Stephen Henderson, Houston Baker, and others to project such writers as Mari Evans, Sonia Sanchez, and Jayne Cortez, who are sturdy in their craft, mature of vision, and faithful to the speech and life-style of black people.

Most recently, Askia Touré has turned his attention to play writing. Disturbed by the lack of the sense of the epic in modern black writing, he has begun to mime the rich heritage of resistance and revolt in American history. More than a decade after Touré outlined the tasks of the New Poetry in *JuJu* (1970), he continues to personify his credo: "The New Black Poet must cast himself into the role of priest & ritual master, the living vessel of the myths and legends of his people, as well as a community teacher, cultural historian, raiser of Collective Consciousness, the living link of connection to the Racial Ancestors."

Quincy Thomas Troupe, Jr.

(23 July 1943-)

Horace Coleman
Wilberforce University

BOOKS: *Embryo Poems 1967-1971* (New York: Barlenmir House, 1972);

The Inside Story of TV's Roots, by Troupe and David L. Wolper (New York: Warner Books, 1978);

Snake-back Solos: Selected Poems, 1969-1977 (Berkeley & New York: I. Reed Books, 1978).

OTHER: *Watts Poets: A Book of New Poetry and Essays,* edited by Troupe (Los Angeles: House of Respect, 1968);

Giant Talk: An Anthology of Third World Writings, edited by Troupe and Rainer Schulte (New York: Random House/Vintage, 1975);

Arnold Adoff, ed., *Celebrations: A New Anthology of Black American Poetry,* includes Foreword by Troupe (Chicago: Follett, 1977).

PERIODICAL PUBLICATIONS: "For Wes: an elegy," "Exquisite," "Flies on Shit," "A day in the life of a poet," "To a cat I know," and "poem for friends," *New Directions,* 22 (1970): 170-181;

"Birds fly without motion to the summit," "Distance," "After the Holocaust," and "Snapshot," *Mundus Artium,* 4 (Winter 1970): 28-31;

"On a New York Street Corner: Canvas Number 14," *Iowa Review,* 6 (Spring 1975): 38-39;

"The Old People Speak of Death," *Black World,* 24 (September 1975): 62;

"These Crossings, These Words" and "Snake-back Solos," *Callaloo,* 1 (October 1978): 87-91;

"My poems have holes sewn into them," *Essence,* 10 (January 1980): 17.

Quincy Troupe, a multi-talented writer, has made contributions to literature as a poet, performer, editor, publisher, teacher, and scholar. He has published two volumes of poetry, coauthored a book of nonfiction, and edited two anthologies and several magazines. He has also made use of the popular media; his recent article on Harlem, which appeared in the *Village Voice,* and his book about the television production of *Roots* have assured him a wider audience than previously available to him through his poetry volumes. Contemporary with, but more academically based than most of the younger poets of the 1960s and 1970s, Troupe's works have been equally well anthologized—appearing in more than twenty-five volumes—and he has been equally effective as a lecturer and reader of his own poetry. A productive writer and scholar/teacher, Troupe is a maturing artist with a promising future for the 1980s.

Quincy Thomas Troupe, Jr., was born 23 July 1943 to Dorothy Marshall and Quincy Troupe, Sr., of New York City; he was raised in St. Louis, Missouri. From St. Louis, he went to Louisiana, where he received a bachelor's degree in history and political science from Grambling College (now State University) in 1963. He then earned an Associate of Arts degree in journalism from Los Angeles City College in 1967. Troupe was a part of the group of young black writers in the Los Angeles area during the latter 1960s; he taught creative writing for the Watts Writers' Movement from 1966 to 1968 and served as director of the Malcolm X Center in Los Angeles during the summers of 1969 and 1970. During the same summers, he was also director of the John Coltrane Summer Festivals in Los Angeles.

The earliest poetic influences upon him, Troupe says, were Pablo Neruda, John Joseph Rabearivello, Aimé Césaire, Cesar Vallejo, Jean Toomer, and Sterling Brown. The Toomer and Brown influences are immediately obvious; following in their paths, Troupe has made one of his dominant themes the intense life of black people in America, "the daily kinds of feelings" and "the innumerable daily insults" that people encounter "for trying to think and live." To depict such life-styles and incidents, Troupe sees his primary objective as follows: "To write as well as I can and to write as continuously as I can. I write because I have to communicate with my self—a chronicle of thoughtful insanity . . . to leave a record for whatever it will do and to whoever it will help and to get on with the business of living."

Troupe's first published poem appeared in *Paris Match* in 1964. Titled "What Is A Black Man?," the poem answers the question by simply asserting the truth: he is a man who is black, though politics and economics frequently make it otherwise.

Troupe's early writing experiences were nurtured in a responsive environment. He was a member of the Watts Writers' Movement for several years and participated in workshops where Budd Schulberg gave instruction. He had constant contact with writers Jayne Cortez, Stanley Crouch, K. Curtis Lyle, Ojenke, and Johnny Scott and with musicians Sly Stone and Maurice White, founder of Earth, Wind and Fire. Troupe's interest in music as content and as technique is reflected in several of his later poems, and he dedicates many of his works to musicians and prominent figures in the music world. "South African Bloodstone—For Hugh Masekela," "Chicago—For Howlin Wolf," and an elegy for Wes Montgomery all appear in *Embryo,* and he has also penned "Ode to John Coltrane."

In 1968, still connected to the group of writers on the West Coast, Troupe began the first of an extended series of editing experiences. He served as associate editor of *Shrewd* magazine in Los Angeles and, in the same year, edited an anthology entitled *Watts Poets;* it was published in Los Angeles by House of Respect. His editing continued in 1975 with the massive *Giant Talk: An Anthology of Third World Writings.* Designed to be as broadly based in Third World peoples and cultures as possible, the volume includes many of the young black American writers of the revolutionary 1960s, along with a sampling of African, Caribbean, and Latin American authors. With its extensive representation of authors who have earned critical acclaim in their own right, it is surprising that the volume was not widely reviewed or accepted; perhaps a part of the problem occurred when the title appeared without the subtitle, thereby giving prospective readers no clear indication of the contents of the volume. Rainer Schulte, editor of the internationally known *Mundus Artium,* assisted Troupe in the editing of *Giant Talk.* Troupe also guest-edited two issues of *Mundus Artium* in 1973, one on black poetry and one on black fiction. He culminated his editing experiences in 1979 with the founding of *American Rag,* a magazine with two clearly defined objectives: "to represent American Literature and to comment on it from a position of power" and "to publish the very best . . . in North and South America and the Caribbean."

It was also in 1968 that Troupe began his long series of academic appointments. During that year, he taught creative writing and black literature at UCLA and at the University of Southern California. From 1969 until 1972, he taught creative writing and Third World literature at Ohio University, where, in the summer of 1970, he founded and began editing *Confrontation: A Journal of Third World Literature.* At its peak in 1974, the journal published such well-known writers as Chinua

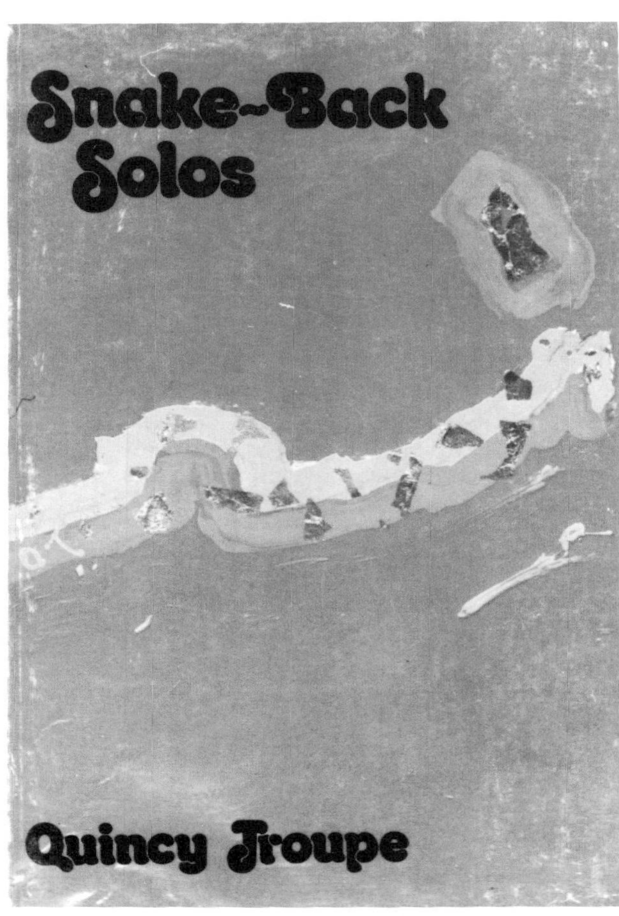

Covers for Troupe's 1978 volume of poems which takes its title from a local name for the Mississippi river

Achebe, Toni Cade Bambara, Julius Lester, Audre Lorde, Herberto Padilla, Amos Tutuola, and Alice Walker; it also included an interview with Nina Simone.

Troupe has also taught at Richmond College, the University of California at Berkeley, California State University at Sacramento, and the University of Ghana at Legon. He is currently associate professor of American and Third World Literatures at the College of Staten Island, CUNY, and director of its Poetry Center.

Embryo Poems 1967-1971, Troupe's first volume of poetry, was published by Barlenmir House of New York in 1972. A compilation of personal, communal, folk, and musical impressions, the volume illustrates an array of influences upon Troupe's work, and it contains several dedicatory poems. The collection went through three printings of five thousand copies each.

One of the poems in the volume is especially vivid in tying Troupe to the experimentation with dialect that was so characteristic of the poets of the 1960s. "Profilin, A Rap/Poem—For Leon Damas" evokes in its title the rhetoric of Stokely Carmichael and H. Rap Brown and in its style the evaluative criticisms of Nikki Giovanni.

People be profilin like
slick stylin pimps leanin bent
at forty-five degree angles
behind mink covered steerin wheels
of cold-gold lamed el dorados
with golden brown velvet roofs for tops
wide brimmed apple hats
pulled rakishly down
slashes their scowling mugs

People be profilin.
People be profilin everyday
of their lives

The musical influences upon Troupe are reflected in titles such as "The Scag Ballet," which

Quincy Troupe (photograph ©1980 by Layle Silbert)

describes the peculiar dance of junkies; "Midtown Traffic," which compares the sounds of traffic to a "black jazz piano"; and "Woke Up Crying the Blues," which describes the death of Martin Luther King as bringing on a state of the blues in the speaker:

> Woke up crying the blues:
> bore witness to the sadness of the day;
> the peaceful man from Atlanta
> was slaughtered yester/day.

The bad news of King's death and a generally unsatisfactory day lead to the poet's late afternoon discovery of a poem having been accepted for publication, his "good news during a bad news' weekend," which reflects the mixture of emotion so typical of the blues and "another day in the life" of a black human being.

Several dedicatory poems in *Embryo* pay tribute to individuals Troupe respects and comment on worldwide or communal events. "The Earthquake of Peru; 1970; In 49 Seconds—For Cesar Vallejo, Great Peruvian Poet" emphasizes the suddenness of death in the face of those teeming with life. "In the Manner of Rabearivello" celebrates the Madagascan surrealistic poet who committed suicide at thirty-six; in like manner of creating unusual images, Troupe conjures up "a black head that has no color" and "at the bottom of white volcanos 1000 sharks" struggling "to swim free of the grip/of a hundred boneless skeletons." "Poem from the Third-Eye—For Eugene Redmond" describes a kind of futuristic poetry in which the words of the poems will have the power to grant freedom.

At the time of the publication of *Embryo,* Troupe was reported living in New York with his wife Karen ("Black Star, Black Woman" in that volume is dedicated to her). He has three children, Antoinette, Tymme, and Quincy Brandon.

Also in 1972, Troupe won an International Institute of Education travel grant for $10,000. He used the funds to travel to Senegal, Ivory Coast, Guinea, Ghana, and Nigeria. In 1978, he won a National Endowment for the Arts award in poetry. In 1979, he received a $6,000 grant from the New York State Council of the Arts, and, in 1980, he won an American Book Award for *Snake-back Solos,* a collection of poetry.

In 1978, Troupe completed, with David L. Wolper, *The Inside Story of TV's Roots;* Warner Books sold over one million copies of the volume. Also in 1978 Troupe's volume of poetry *Snake-back Solos* was published by I. Reed Books. Among Troupe's personal favorites in the volume are "Springtime Ritual," "The Day Duke Raised," "La Marqueta," and "For Miles Davis." He appropriated the title of his volume from the local name he had learned for the Mississippi during his youth in St. Louis—"Snakeback." The "Solos" of the title refer to the significance of the river in American history and music, and to the praise poems included in the volume for St. Louis poet Eugene Redmond, writer Steve Cannon, and Louis "Satchmo" Armstrong.

Musical cadences, rhythms, and phrases continue to strongly influence Troupe's work. His reading/performance of his work is reminiscent of a horn player, a good sax man, working his way through theme and variation. Troupe has made the following comment on the intertwining of music and poetics: "I don't believe so much in writing schools. American speech idiom—blues and jazz forms—is a viable poetic form. At the base of American creativity is language . . . what black people can do with the rhythms and the words and musicians with the sounds coupled with the words is extraordinary. A modest goal is to continue the work of Dunbar, Sterling Brown, Hughes and James Weldon Johnson and to meld the forms."

Troupe is taking his critical efforts to a new

medium with a series of interviews with Sterling Brown and Gwendolyn Brooks scheduled for airing on National Educational Television. Since 1973, he has worked to present "Life Forces: A Festival of Black Roots," a series of lectures and readings held at the Church of St. John the Divine in Manhattan under the auspices of the Frederick Douglass Creative Arts Center. To date, Toni Morrison, Gwendolyn Brooks, Derek Walcott, Ishmael Reed, Amiri Baraka, Audre Lorde, and Alice Walker are among those who have participated.

Along with his other projects, Troupe continues to read his own poetry to diverse audiences. He has read at Harvard, UCLA, New York University, Howard, Yale, Princeton, Louisiana State University, Dartmouth, Oberlin, Ohio State, Michigan, and Michigan State, among others. He continues, as well, to be his own exacting critic; he greets each new poem with enthusiasm but hopes, too, to "get better." With the contributions he has made thus far, it is certain that his solos will get longer and stronger.

References:

Tom Dent, "*Snake-back Solos*," *Freedomways*, 20 (Second Quarter 1980): 104-107;

Michael Harper, "*Snake-back Solos*," *New York Times Book Review*, 21 October 1979, pp. 18-21;

Debbie Meyer, "Is there a poetry mafia?," *Coda*, 8 (April-May 1981): 10-14;

Mel Watkins, "Hard Times for Black Writers," *New York Times Book Review*, 21 February 1981, pp. 3, 26.

Papers:

Some of the manuscripts and correspondence of Quincy Thomas Troupe, Jr., are held in the Archives of Ohio University.

Tom Weatherly

(3 November 1942-)

Evelyn Hoard Roberts
St. Louis Community College at Meramec

BOOKS: *Maumau American Cantos* (New York: Corinth Books, 1970);

Thumbprint (Philadelphia: Telegraph Books, 1971);

Climate, published with *Stream*, by Ken Bluford (Philadelphia: Middle Earth Books, 1972).

OTHER: *Natural Process; An Anthology of New Black Poetry*, edited by Weatherly and Ted Wilentz (New York: Hill & Wang, 1971);

Arnold Adoff, ed., *The Poetry of Black America: An Anthology of the 20th Century*, includes poems by Weatherly (New York: Harper & Row, 1973);

George Quasha and Jerome Rothenberg, eds., *America A Prophecy; A New Reading of American Poetry from Pre-Columbian Times to the Present*, includes poems by Weatherly (New York: Vintage Books, 1973).

Thomas Elias Weatherly, Jr., forged and purified by the white heat of nonconformity, has responded to the external, fragmented reality of the black-white world that he has engaged and sought to conquer through mythmaking. Although his poetry has not commanded wide critical acclaim, his diverse roles as poet-in-residence, teacher of poetry in elementary and secondary schools, and conductor of workshops have helped him reach a wide range of audiences. Seeking to interpret the human condition by particularizing the black experience, he has recognized African culture as the heritage of American blacks who have been brought to the Western world via the indentured servants and slaves who struggled through emancipation, reconstruction, and the American industrial revolution, and who are now engaged in a social revolution. Weatherly, like poets Countee Cullen, Langston Hughes, and Amiri Baraka (LeRoi Jones), has made a dynamic contribution to Afro-American literature.

Weatherly was born on 3 November 1942 in Scottsboro, Alabama, where his father, Thomas Elias Weatherly, Sr., was born in 1917. His mother, Lucy Belle Golson Weatherly, was born in Huntsville in 1918. His sister, Yvonne Delores Weatherly, born in 1944, teaches mathematics in Philadelphia, Pennsylvania. Scottsboro gained nationwide attention in the 1930s for a contrived race conflict involving nine black youths and two white girls (the Scottsboro Case). Tom (as he prefers to be called) grew up heavily influenced by the strong black Southern culture that has been dominated for centuries by the white majority. It is doubtful that any black youth could develop in such a racist atmosphere and escape the negative impact of sociopolitical and economic injustices. Later Weatherly would compose several poems addressing the theme of black subservience: "first monday scottsboro alabama," "southern accent," and "to old elm, in cemetery for confederate dead."

Weatherly's intellectual, political, and ethical development was nurtured, primarily, by his parents, schoolteachers, and other contacts at the George Washington Carver High School where he completed the eleventh grade. He admits that his early country school gave him a general education, but he says his true education derived from his warm, loving, home environment that emphasized "learning and, sometimes, openness to new ideas." He remarks that he and his mother argued "loudly." Mary Emily Hunter, his paternal grandmother, required him to memorize poems (two of her favorite poets were Langston Hughes and Alfred Lord Tennyson). Others who influenced his thinking and nurtured his spirit by listening to his fantasies were Alfred Morris, a high school teacher; James Vinson, a college English teacher, who encouraged him to major in English; and Muriel Michal Hollander, a continuing source of encouragement and inspiration, who became his third wife.

As a child, Weatherly collected stamps, coins, matchbooks, and facts, storing in his mind the data that would provide the basis for his later fiction. Being a "nosy child," he vowed that he would know the universe. He comments: "Probably the motions of the heavenly bodies and basketballs occurred to me at the same period." He bought a telescope—perceived and pondered everything. He says that when he realized that he was too young to be a philosopher, he knew he must become a poet. At an early age he had a vision, a "call" that he believed came from God: "feel that i was called . . . years ago at eight" to make poems. The call took the form of a dream about Homer in which the ancient poet gave Weatherly his advice to become a "wekwom teks," a weaver of words. Written at eight years old, his first poem chronicles his dream: "Homer spoke/I awoke/Into dream/That I'd try/Poetry./It did seem/That he said/Sing until dead." Throughout his life, Weatherly has responded to this call. He does not remember the title of his first published poem, but he recalls that it appeared in the Carver High School newspaper. His first poem published outside of high school was a koan (a nonsense question, asked of a student of Zen, to force him to a greater awareness of reality) in the *Buddhist World Philosophy Magazine*.

Weatherly attended Morehouse College from 1958 to 1961. He originally enrolled as a psychology major, but switched to English, and while at Morehouse, he wrote for the *Maroon Tiger*. He also attended Alabama A & M College (now University) in 1961, in Normal, Alabama, but was suspended for having published *The Saint*, an unauthorized periodical featuring poetry, satire, humor, and essays. In 1974, having relocated in New York, he registered at the City College of New York as a special student. That same year he enrolled in the Master of Fine Arts program at Columbia University but subsequently withdrew, "because of boredom," he said.

A prolific reader, Weatherly says he has been influenced by John Dos Passos, Edgar Rice Burroughs, E. E. "Doc" Smith, Ralph Waldo Emerson, Cordwainer Smith, Saki, E. B. White, Ezra Pound, William Butler Yeats, Wilfred Owen, Emily Dickinson, Samuel Coleridge, Percy Bysshe Shelley, Ogden Nash, John Donne, Jerry Leiber, Mike Stoller, H. D., and Marianne Moore, among others. Not surprisingly, Weatherly calls himself a poet from an "eclectic tradition," and he has blended the tradition of formalists and nonformalists in his own poetry.

A different call in the mid-1960s led Weatherly to enter the African Methodist Episcopal ministry, and he was appointed assistant pastor of Saint Paul's in Scottsboro, where he served as an associate of the Reverend J. C. Coleman. In the second year of Weatherly's ministry, Bishop I. H. Bonner, respecting tradition, assigned Weatherly to be pastor of the church that his paternal ancestor (his great-grandfather Elias Donegan) had pastored. Like Ralph Waldo Emerson, whose ministry imposed so many restrictions that he resigned his pastorate, Weatherly withdrew from his ministry in Alabama and returned to his vocation as poet; and, along with other black Americans, he participated in the second great migration from the South to the North.

Weatherly moved to New York and lived in both Harlem and Greenwich Village, charting a nomadic trail, oddjobbing as a dishwasher at a Happy Bagel restaurant, a waiter in the mountains, a

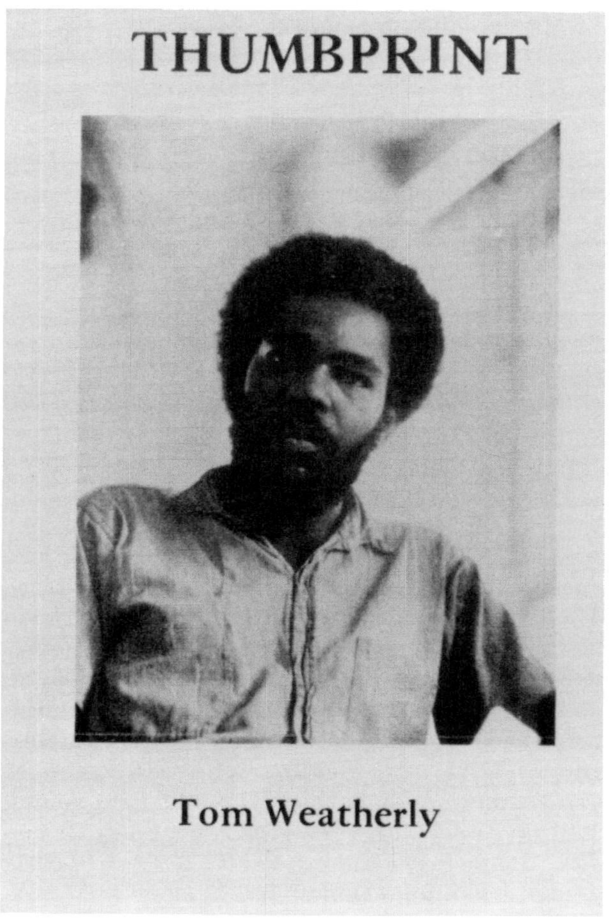

Front cover for Weatherly's 1971 book of poems about women, which is dedicated "to the souls & flesh / these mamas, real & fancy"

cook at Lion's Head, a bellhop, a camp counselor, a proofreader, and a copy editor. These varied experiences enlarged his mind and stimulated his imagination and sensitized him to a world plagued with racism, civil discrimination, economic injustices, international distrust, and conflicting ideologies.

Weatherly's diverse professional pursuits and art engagements in formal and informal settings have appealed to both youth and adults. He conducted the Afro-Hispanic Poets' Workshop in East Harlem, at Our Lady of Esperanza in Washington Heights, from 1967 to 1968. With the New York Parks Department, under a grant from the State Council on Arts and the National Endowment for the Arts (1968 to 1969), he advanced the Natural Process Workshop, East Harlem for Teachers' and Writers' Collaborative. The name was chosen because it reflected Weatherly's desire for "something not racist, but racial." As his audience grew and changed, his ethnic and human perspectives were modified.

In 1970, Weatherly became adjunct instructor in the Art Department at Rutgers University. From 1970 to 1971 he was poet-in-residence at Bishop College, and he conducted a seminar, "Criticism of Black Poetry," at Grand Valley State College where the National Poetry Festival was held in 1971. In *Climate* (1972), Weatherly's poem "#18" for Bishop College reflects this experience.

From 1971 to 1972 he assumed several professional commitments. He merged the Natural Process Workshop with the Saint Mark's Poetry Project at Saint Mark's Church-on-the Bowery in New York City, and he became poet-in-residence at Morgan State College. That spring he taught poetry at the Web School in Westchester, New York. He directed the Natural Process Poetry Workshop, from 1973 to 1974, as the Brooklyn Poetry Project. At the same time he taught in a "Poetry in the Schools" program at the Richmond School District in Richmond, Virginia, and at the Sampson G. Smith Intermediate School, Somerset, New Jersey.

From 1975 to 1977, Weatherly conducted a workshop, "Poetry Teacher for Free Space in the Women's House of Detention," at the New York Department of Corrections on Riker's Island. He effectively demonstrated that the Natural Process could stimulate the creativity of those separated from the community. He concedes that in departing the South he had pursued a course leading to vastly changed religious, philosophical, and political views. Guided by the religion of his A.M.E. ministry and from his playful, political position as "oxymoronic conservative," Weatherly came to embrace the practice of Taoism and politics of libertarianism. He now advocates simplicity and selflessness in his occupational pursuits, human relationships, and art.

Weatherly's art theory is complex. He affirms that he creates because of his inner forces. Like many black writers before him, he has drawn from oral tradition as a foundation for his art. Weatherly perceives mythmaking as a justification for the act of creating; he grants the poet power to achieve unity and to interpret the past for the young. For Weatherly, poetry is an art whose rhythms, sounds, pitch, and images aid the young to comprehend their culture and to gain an identity; the poet himself has pursued these identical goals: ways of knowing the self and appreciating the dignity of all men.

Maumau American Cantos (1970), his first pub-

entered a.m.e. ministry
assistant pastor of saint pauls scottsboro
disciple of saint/j.c.coleman
+ next year pastor of church great granddad
pastored (bishop i.h. bonner had feel for tradition).

had a division: left god mother hooded youth +
the country for new york, lived on streets,
parks, hitchd the states. dishwasher at hip bagel,
waiter in the mountains, cook at lion's head,
proofreading, copyediting, baking, bellhopping,
camp counselor, dealing, fuckd up in the head.
rantd in the saint marks poetry project, ranting
now in afro-hispanic poets workshop east harlem.

HOLDER OF THE DOUBLE MOJO HAND
+ 13TH DEGREE GRIS-GRIS BLACK BELT.

CORINTH BOOKS
$1.75

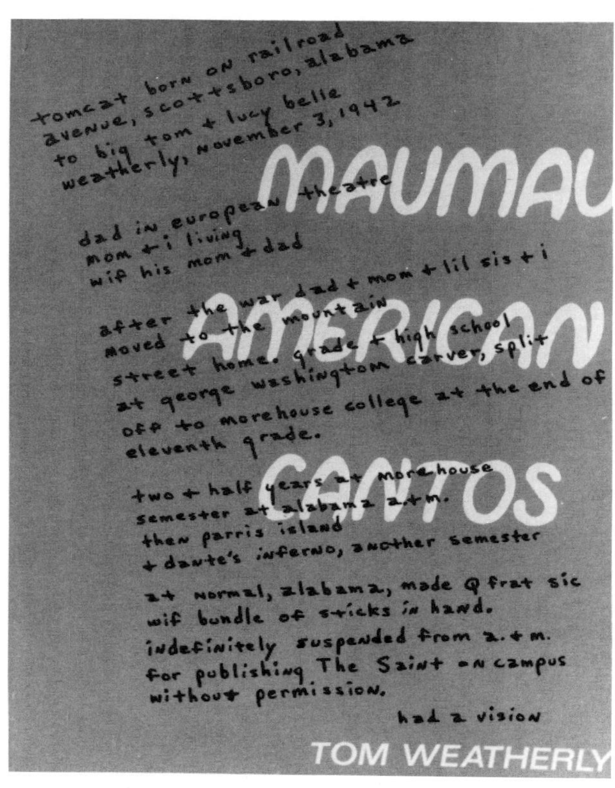

tomcat born on railroad
avenue, scottsboro, alabama
to big tom + lucy belle
weatherly, november 3, 1942
MAUMAU
dad in european theatre
mom + i living
wif his mom + dad
AMERICAN
after the war dad + mom + lil sis + i
moved to the mountain
street home. grade + high school
at george washingtom carver, split
off to morehouse college at the end of
eleventh grade.
CANTOS
two + half years at morehouse
semester at alabama a+m.
then parris island
+ dante's inferno, another semester
at normal, alabama, made Q frat sic
wif bundle of sticks in hand.
indefinitely suspended from a.+m.
for publishing The Saint on campus
without permission.
had a vision
TOM WEATHERLY

Covers for Weatherly's 1970 poetry volume which compares the uprisings of the African mau maus with the conflicts of modern American life

lished volume of poetry, and *Thumbprint* (1971), his second, constitute a mosaic of ancestral, historical, environmental, and communal forces (noticeably paradoxical and ambiguous) that disclose Weatherly's profuse, sometimes profane and unorthodox, nevertheless genuine and profound viewpoints. His vehement protest against the dehumanization of blacks represents his determined defiance of authority and the needless constraints of society.

Through the title, *Maumau American Cantos,* Weatherly invokes a comparison between the African mau mau movement associated with the Kenyan insurrections of the 1950s and the turbulent sociopolitical movements of the 1960s in the United States when blacks demonstrated against racism throughout the nation. Mau mau insurrectionists, on the one hand, sought to achieve land reforms that would alleviate African hunger and would secure effective African participation in the British-ruled Kenyan government. Blacks in the United States, on the other hand, pressed for full voting rights, equality in employment, housing, and education to attain justice. The poet addresses other concerns in the volume, for example, in "southern accent," where he examines the controversy between environmentalists and the government regarding the use and condition of the Tennessee Valley. In the central poem, "imperial thumbprint," Weatherly presents the white/black dichotomy, but proclaims that relationships are ever changing and, thus, "outside where there is white/tomorrow is today the black."

The remainder of the poems in *Maumau* and the poems in *Thumbprint* center around the idea of "Natural Process." The eleven cantos specifically titled "Maumau American Cantos" are a kaleidoscope of microcosmic portraits and scenes which blend history and fantasy, local and universal events and ideas to create a song of the American black experience. He shifts from describing Malcolm X as a wootem (a Harlem cat) to creating a time capsule protesting the human condition by describing the decadent environment. "Canto 7" characterizes the misery, hopelessness, and despair that contributed to the unconsolable grief blacks experienced when "m. l. k., jr." was assassinated.

In *Thumbprint,* Weatherly affirms the roles of woman, as the dedication page indicates: "to the

Carolyn Weatherly's portrait of Tom Weatherly in Maumau American Cantos

souls & flesh/these mamas, real & fancy." He then lists ninety-four names of women he has loved, respected, admired, and revered in numerous ways. With such an inclusive dedication, Weatherly acknowledges that each and all have become a part of his world and he, in turn, has imposed a stamp upon them. He uses the ancient Sumerian symbol for woman △, and the symbol for man ⌂.to express mutual allegiance.

In some pieces, Weatherly becomes the scribe, recording events for posterity. In one poem, young demonstrators clashing with "law and order" agents scream "we'll teach lil tomcat/the magic we learn/burning our soul flesh." Elsewhere, the poet evokes vital images of sexual urgency and social unrest that vivify the explosive 1960s when he writes: "her shoulders rust/in the sun where mine/burst fire/ran. the molotov cocktail/red explode."

In the introduction to Arnold Adoff's anthology of black poetry (1973), Gwendolyn Brooks writes: "Black poets can write hauntingly out of the well-springs of their despair, despondency, and troubled indignities—such provide an inspirited authoritative tone of protest. . . ." Through his unique style, Weatherly voices such a protest. In poetry pregnant with vigorous rhythms, strident protests, subtle Afro-American slang, numerous foreign phrases, and various mythological allusions, Tom Weatherly underscores a new commitment to the wholeness of blackness which mirrors significant social change and heralds a great future. He has become an ally of black poets who have aided in shaping a new value structure and enhanced political awareness. Weatherly's message to his readers is: through art the human spirit and mind can achieve self-esteem and freedom.

References:

Lerone Bennett, Jr., *The Shaping of Black America* (Chicago: Johnson Publishing Company, 1975);

Stephen H. Bronz, *Roots of Negro Racial Consciousness; The 1920s: Three Harlem Renaissance Authors* (New York: Libra Publishers, 1964);

Gwendolyn Brooks, Introduction to *The Poetry of Black America,* edited by Arnold Adoff (New York: Harper & Row, 1973);

Harold Cruse, *The Crisis of the Negro Intellectual; From Its Origins to the Present* (New York: Morrow, 1967);

J. D. Fage, *A History of Africa* (New York: Knopf, 1978);

William M. Gibson and George Arms, eds., *Twelve American Writers* (New York: Macmillan, 1962);

Stephen Henderson, *Understanding the New Black Poetry: Black Speech and Black Music as Poetic References* (New York: Morrow, 1973);

Mildred A. Hill-Lubin, "And the Beat Goes On . . .: A Continuation of the African Heritage in African-American Literature," *CLA Journal,* 23 (December 1979): 172-187;

Langston Hughes, *I Wonder as I Wander: An Autobiographical Journey* (New York: Rhinehart, 1956);

Arnold Rampersad, "The Universal and the Particular in Afro-American Poetry," *CLA Journal,* 25 (September 1981): 1-17.

Sherley Anne Williams

(25 August 1944-)

Lillie P. Howard
Wright State University

BOOKS: *Give Birth to Brightness: A Thematic Study in Neo-Black Literature* (New York: Dial Press, 1972);

The Peacock Poems (Middletown, Conn.: Wesleyan University Press, 1975);

Someone Sweet Angel Chile (New York: Morrow, 1982).

OTHER: "Meditations on History," in *Midnight Birds*, edited by Mary Helen Washington (Garden City: Anchor Press, 1980);

Dexter Fisher, ed., *The Third Woman: Minority Women Writers of the United States*, includes poems by Williams (Boston: Houghton Mifflin, 1980);

Erlene Stetson, ed., *Black Sister: Poetry by Black American Women, 1746-1980*, includes poems by Williams (Bloomington: Indiana University Press, 1981).

PERIODICAL PUBLICATION: "The Blues Roots of Contemporary Afro-American Poetry," *Massachusetts Review*, 18 (Autumn 1977): 542-554.

Sherley Anne Williams (photograph by Margaret Ysuada)

Poet and critic, Sherley Anne Williams uses her poignantly lyrical voice to speak for and to the reader, often singing a blues so real that when one reads her poems, one unconsciously supplies the music and begins a foot-stomping, down-home rhythm of one's own. That Williams can render the cadence of the blues so accurately attests to her skill; that she uses the blues to reach back and bring the past to the present attests to her role as a tradition bearer and puts her firmly in that long line of artists that stretches all the way back to the beginnings of black folk culture. In her writings, Williams mentions Alice Walker, Sterling Brown, Langston Hughes, James Baldwin, Zora Neale Hurston, Ernest Gaines, Amiri Baraka (LeRoi Jones), and Toni Morrison as black artists who make a conscious effort to carry on the past of their ancestors in their writing. If one hears echoes of these writers when reading Williams's work, then that is because Williams has consciously and deliberately added her voice to those who sing the songs of the past.

Williams has published three books, two of them volumes of poetry, *The Peacock Poems* (1975) and *Someone Sweet Angel Chile* (1982). *Give Birth to Brightness* (1972) is a volume of literary criticism. In all three, Williams "creates new images of Blackness and explores relatively untouched areas of Black experiences." Her aim is to recreate "a new tradition built on a synthesis of black oral traditions and Western literate forms."

Sherley Anne Williams (also Shirley Williams) was born the third of four girls on 25 August 1944 in Bakersfield, California, to Jessee Winson and Lena Silver Williams. In an interview in *Black Women Writers at Work,* Williams describes her background as somewhere between the North that Langston Hughes wrote about and the farmers and sharecroppers found in the works of Sterling Brown. From what we can glean from a section of *Someone Sweet Angel Chile* called "The Iconography of Childhood," Williams's childhood was filled with sadness—"Two bedrooms in the Project," a father who suffered from and was hospitalized for tuberculosis, a mother, now Lelia, a withdrawn "shadow of some former self, her down-home ways worn down to nubs"—and "middle-class aspirations in [an] obviously underclass body." Williams writes in *Midnight Birds:*

> We danced crystal
> sidewalks thrilled in the
> arms of neighborhood
> boys and beheld our
> selves as we could be
> beyond the Projects:
> the nine and ten year
> old stars of stage and
> screen and black men's hearts.

Williams enjoyed a close relationship with her sisters, "Ruise" (Ruby), Jesmarie, and Baby Lois, until the older sisters married and left home, leaving Sherley to face the turbulent adolescent years alone.

While she was attending Edison Junior High School in Fresno, California, she began her search for books about black people, a search which, though she did not know it at the time, would inevitably lead her to herself. Early on she discovered an interest in and appreciation for black women. When sister Ruise's marriage broke up, Ruise returned home and provided emotional support for Sherley. When their mother died when Sherley was sixteen, Ruise became Sherley's guardian, and with her friends, she provided Sherley "with a community, with models, both real-life and literary."

Since she did not begin to write seriously until after she had received her B.A. degree in history from California State University, Fresno, in 1966, one might see Williams's stint in college as an incubation period which provided just enough geographical and emotional distance from home for her to begin to see how she might turn everyday experiences into literature.

According to the interview in *Black Women Writers at Work,* Williams began writing short stories around 1966, always writing "with the idea of being published, not just to slip it away in a shoebox somewhere." Her topics, she says, "select me. Then I just go ahead and try to work with them. I really try not to push things. If it's going to come, it'll come. . . . Writing for me is really a process of saying, 'Here, read this.' It reinforces the fact that I'm in touch with somebody other than my own mind."

She began her first story because she "wanted specifically to write about lower-income black women," whom she felt had been significant forces in her own life. In "Driving Wheel: Myth, story and life," which appears in *The Peacock Poems,* Williams describes her debt to them in this way:

> Like my mother before me and my
> sisters around me. We share the same
> legacy are women to the same
> degree . . .
> we do not tell ourselves all the things we
> know or admit, except perhaps in dreams,
> oblique reminiscence, in sly yearnings, all
> the people we feel ourselves to be.

Williams's first published short story, "Tell Martha Not to Moan," appeared in *Massachusetts Review* in 1967. The story is Williams's tribute to all those women whose "courage and humor helped each other and me thru some very difficult years."

As she wrote, Williams continued her formal education at Howard University in Washington, D.C., where, between 1966 and 1967, she pursued a graduate degree. From 1970 to 1972, she worked as a community educator at D.C.'s Federal City College. In 1972, she earned an M.A. degree from Brown University in Providence, Rhode Island, where she was also teaching in the Black Studies Program. She did not pursue a Ph.D. at Brown because, while graduate school had been necessary for her career as a college teacher of Afro-American literature, she says in *Midnight Birds,* "I didn't want to spend the rest of my life poring over other people's work and trying to explain the world thru their eyes. Rather, what I gain from books . . . must be melded with, refracted through my experiences and what I know of my contemporaries, my ancestors, my hopes for my descendants (and the 'my' is used in the collective sense, implying *we,* implying our)." Between her graduate work at Howard and her studies at Brown, Williams wrote the manuscript that was published by Dial Press in 1972 as *Give Birth to Brightness: A Thematic Study in Neo-Black Literature.*

As a first major publication, *Give Birth to Brightness* is impressive. The book is, for Williams, "a public statement of how I feel about and treasure one small aspect of Blackness in America." Using Baraka's plays *Dutchman* and *The Slave*, James Baldwin's *Blues for Mister Charlie*, and Ernest Gaines's *Of Love and Dust*, Williams repeatedly makes the point that she would later make in "The Blues Roots of Contemporary Afro-American Poetry": that there has emerged from the literature of brilliant black writers "a vision of Black life" which explores "Black existence and life from the inside as life experiences which have significance in and of themselves rather than as a culturally deprived heritage which takes its significance and meaning from the fact that it has been a source of irritation and embarrassment for white America." The participants in this "Neo-Black" movement look at "Black as person, history, tradition and culture . . . with new eyes which attempt to discover and retrieve those things which may prove useful as Black people create a present which gives them dignity, positive self-images and economic strength." This, of course, sounds very similar to what black writers were attempting to do in the 1920s during the Harlem Renaissance. As Stephen Henderson points out in *Understanding the New Black Poetry*, however, the neo-black movement of which Williams is a part "is different from the Harlem Renaissance in the extent of its attempt to speak directly *to* Black people *about themselves* in order to move them toward self-knowledge and collective freedom. It is therefore not 'protest' art but essentially an art of liberating vision." The new black writers of the 1960s and 1970s, then, were eschewing the literature of their immediate predecessors, coming inevitably to share in the opinion of Julian Mayfield that there is a black aesthetic which grows from a shared racial memory and common future.

In *Give Birth to Brightness*, Williams quoting James Baldwin points out that heretofore "the main current in Black literature had always been political . . . an expression of a limited aspect of the lives of Black people [which] led readers 'to believe that in Negro life there exists no tradition, no field of manners, no possibility of ritual intercourse such as may, for example, sustain the Jew even after he has left his father's house.' "

Williams's view is shared by other black writers. Most black literature of the past and present has used the white world as a prominent and often

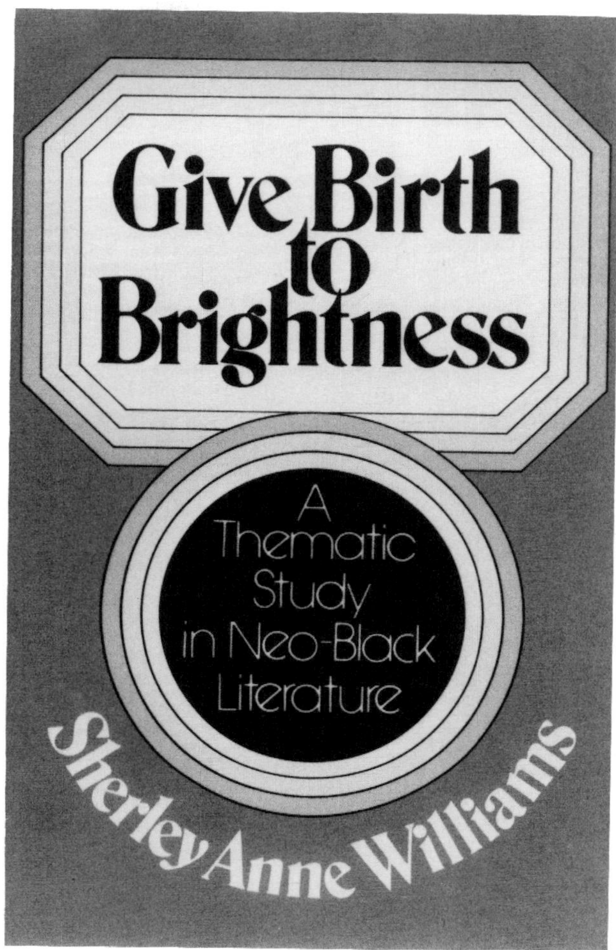

Dust jacket for Williams's 1972 critical volume, which presents the modern black writer as articulator of "a black aesthetic which grows from a shared racial memory and common future"

intrusive backdrop against which the drama of black life is enacted. In such works, Williams points out—as Alice Walker has pointed out and as Zora Neale Hurston pointed out before her—"Black life is made to seem unimportant except as it interacts with or comes up against the white world." There is much more to black life than that, and because there is, she asserts, there can be much more to black literature as well.

In *Give Birth to Brightness*, Williams pitches Baraka's *Dutchman* and *The Slave*, which represent one extreme in black literature, against Baldwin's play and Gaines's novel, which represent another extreme. Baraka's characters are very much a part of the Western literary tradition where the hero falls because of a tragic flaw in his own nature, while the central characters in *Blues for Mister Charlie* and *Of Love and Dust* are heroic antiheroes, drawn from the life of the collective black community, answering to such names as "streetman," "rebel," "warrior," and even "my man." When one tries to couch black characters in what is essentially a white context, the characters are doomed to frustration, self-denial, failure (witness Clay and Walker of *Dutchman* and *The Slave*). Black characters must be placed in a black context where they can "learn to deal with whites, with the western world, as incidentals," where they can repeatedly touch base with and be nurtured by their blackness.

Though there is little in *Give Birth to Brightness* that has not been said before by other gifted writers, still, no one has said it better than Williams. Her writing is clear, composed with an eye toward drawing the reader in, making him see, with new eyes, what has always been there. Whereas writers such as Robert Stepto, who addresses the same ideas in his writings, step outside of the black experience to use critics such as Northrop Frye to confuse and mystify, Williams lets the writings of well-known black artists speak for themselves, to illuminate a particular aspect of blackness. In "Listen to the Drum," from *The Peacock Poems*, she writes, "Much as you learn from the old ones/What they know is from their days;/it's some things you have to learn for yourself/and you take that and add it to their ways."

When *Give Birth to Brightness* was published in 1972, Williams was an associate professor of English at her alma mater, California State University at Fresno. In 1975, she moved to the University of California, San Diego, where she is currently a professor of literature.

While, like Nikki Giovanni, Williams began her career by writing short stories, she is better known as a poet. Some of the things Williams learned for herself she includes in *The Peacock Poems* (volume 79 of the Wesleyan Poetry series), which was nominated in 1976 for the National Book Award in Poetry. In an autobiographical piece in *Midnight Birds*, Williams explains that *The Peacock Poems* "contains something of that early, early life when my father and mother were alive and we followed the crops."

In *The Peacock Poems*, Williams annotates her poems with her own prose and with definitions of key terms and concepts that will be exemplified in the poems that follow. The definitions and the prose narratives set the scene, form the backdrop for the thoughts and emotions that follow.

Williams admits in *Midnight Birds* and records in *The Peacock Poems* that she traveled extensively "wandering from coast to coast, Nashville, Fresno, San Francisco, D.C., Birmingham, back to Fresno, L.A., back to Fresno, Providence, R.I., Fresno and finally San Diego." In the narrative that begins *The Peacock Poems*, Williams examines her ambivalent relationship to the San Joaquin Valley which, no matter how far she wanders, lures her back: "I had hated this, hated all the squat Valley towns; had left, returned, left: The memory of the sun on the dirt and grass graves, on the shiny black skins of my family and friends draws me back." Says the speaker in "For Ronald King Our Brother":

> Poems are crafted thought, channelled feeling
> and now . . . Now. Yes, and living
> set in one moment of timeless
> time   Always and love.

The San Joaquin Valley, then, is the rich incubator of the raw feelings that are channeled through the poems.

Because of Williams's own fondness for prefatory poems and definitions, one is encouraged to pursue the same course with the title she selected for these poems. Thus—

> Peacock: n. 1. The Male Peafowl, distinguished by its crested head, brilliant blue or green feathers, and long tail feathers that are marked with eyelike, iridescent spots, and that can be spread in a fanlike form. 2. A vain person given to self-display; a dandy. To strut about like a peacock; exhibit oneself vainly.

While Williams has admitted that *The Peacock Poems* is autobiographical, that "I am the women I speak of in my stories, my poems," the poems in this volume are mostly about Williams's son, John Malcolm, whom Williams struts about, rather vainly, in various poses before the reader.

The first poem of the volume, "Say Hello to John," records the birth of "Shel's" son. In other poems and in some of the narratives, we get glimpses of John's childhood, see him on the road, with his mother, to knowledge, to being:

> We been a long time on the road, all his birthdays, always looking for the next with him sittin', then standing right behind me, right between the bucket seats, laughin', sleepin', singin', pointin' out the signs along the road.

In "Time," we see how much he means to his mother: "He/hold me to this world not just/one spot. People don't belong/to you. You belong to

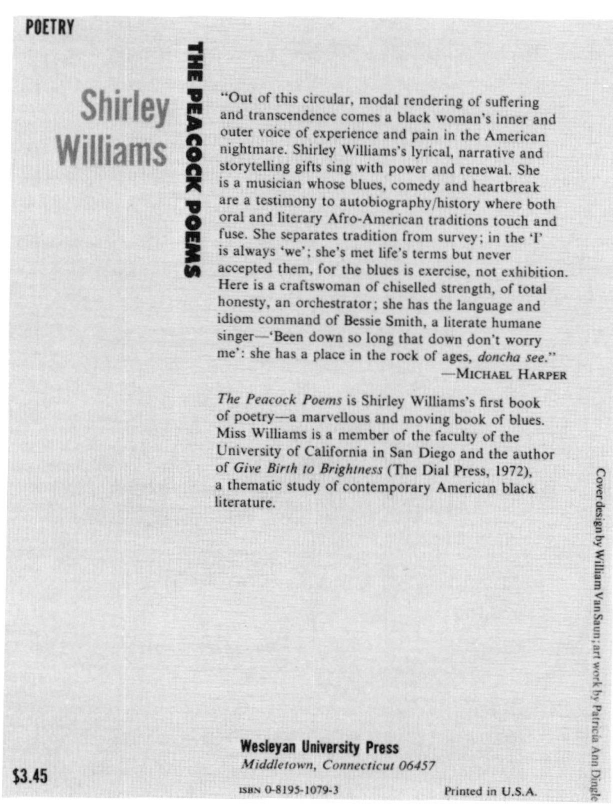

Covers for Williams's 1975 book of poems, the central image for which is best expressed in "The Peacock Song": "They don't like to see you with/yo tail draggin low so I try to hold mines up high. . . ."

them—/but only if they let you." And in "Quartet" he shares in and bears his mother's history as he becomes himself:

> I piece together my child
> hood for my son and this is
> more than reminiscence more
> than who said or what happened
> or what I have done. I weave
> the word ritual where time
> and pace are meaning, weave it
> best in anger and love: You
> don't believe fat-meat greasy,
> huh? as I wield the belt; grunt
> behind his good night kiss, say
> Yo suga almos mo'n one
> mamma can stand; giving him
> sounds to link what's gone with what
> we renew in our coming.

The last poem of the volume, "I see my life . . . ," is also devoted to John. Whereas in "Say Hello to John," the son is literally emerging from his mother, this last poem records another kind of emergence, a second kind of birth in which John is letting go of his mother to become himself. In the first of the three sections that make up this poem, the poet acknowledges what she has given her son and his inalienable right to make himself:

> I see my life by my son's
> eye know his mind is in some
> part my own   that he carries
> me as he moves through the world.
> I am some percent of the
> sum of my mother and my
> father   of the grandparents
> the old ones . . . I don't
> know all that comes through them to
> me and him who are now their
> factors in the world. Yet I
> am me; he is he.

In the third section of the same poem, John

> springs up from the bottom
> of the pool head
> back   eyes closed

water sheeting his body
with light and caught like stars in
the dark burrs of his hair.

John has "named himself." He is still John Malcolm, "Shel's" son, but he is also himself, beginning to learn for himself and to add his own ways to what he has taken from his mother. In *The Peacock Poems,* then, we literally see John Malcolm grow up and begin to spread his feathers.

The glimpses of John Malcolm caught in the act of becoming are broken up with personal bits about Williams's mother, father, sisters, and friends. Much of what is here is about the hurts of life, which Williams expresses through blues poetry, for example, in "Time":

trying to find the father
to tell him we had made a son
Be my stomach that tenses
Keeping back the bitter words
I try not to speak
before my son.
It is my cheeks that are ridged with rage.

In "A Pavonine Truth," Williams captures the therapeutic regenerative powers of the blues:

Life put a hurt on you
only one thing you can do.
When life put the hurt on you
not but one thing a po chile can do.
I just stand on my hind legs and holla
just let the sound carry me on through.

This power of the blues to heal even as it recalls the most excruciating of pains is best explained by Ralph Ellison in "Richard Wright's Blues." In explaining that Richard Wright is singing the blues in his autobiography *Black Boy,* Ellison points out that in the culture into which Wright was born, "the specific folk-art form which helped shape the writer's attitude toward his life and which embodied the impulse that contributes much to the quality and tone of his autobiography was the Negro blues." Ellison continues: "The blues is an impulse to keep the painful details and episodes of a brutal experience alive in one's aching consciousness, to finger its jagged grain, and to transcend it, not by the consolation of philosophy but by squeezing from it a near-tragic, near-comic lyricism. As a form, the blues is an autobiographical chronicle of personal catastrophe expressed lyrically."

In *The Peacock Poems,* Williams fingers the "jagged" edges of a pain that is both hers and ours. Perhaps anticipating her own poetry, Williams says in "The Blues Roots of Contemporary Afro-American Poetry" that "In some contemporary Afro-American poetry, the devices and structures of the classic blues form are transformed, thus allowing the poetry to function in much the same way as blues forms once functioned within the black communities across the country." Williams's own poetry in *The Peacock Poems* perfectly exemplifies this point. She writes in "Any Woman's Blues":

My bed one-sided
from me sleepin alone so mucha the time.
My bed one-sided, now,
cause I'm alone so mucha the time.
But the fact that it's empty
show how this man is messin with my mind.

The poems in *Someone Sweet Angel Chile* continue the blues of *The Peacock Poems.* They are told from a woman's point of view and feature people and experiences from the past. The first section, "Letters from a New England Negro," is set in the nineteenth century around the time of the reconstruction and recalls the slave narratives of sojourners such as Frederick Douglass. The language of the letters rings true to the period, true to the people, and they feature a young black New England schoolmarm, freeborn, who has gone to the South to teach newly freed slaves. The letters address events that occur between 25 August 1867 and 3 March 1868 and record a subtle growth on the part of the schoolteacher who comes to know herself through her pupils. In one letter to "Miss Nettie," her white benefactress back in the East, the speaker, Hannah, admits that though there continues to be some distance between herself and her students, "yet, in unguarded moments,/I speak as they do, softly/a little down in the throat/muting the harsh gutterals and/strident dipthongs on my tongue." In a later letter, she marvels that "The men play their bodies like/drums, their mouths and noses like/wind instruments, creating/syncopated rhythms, wild/melodies that move the people/to wordless cries as they dance." These "natural" musicians are better than the "true" musicians who play the banjo or the fiddle: "yet it is the music of/those who play themselves, that tone/half voice, half instrument that/echoes in my head. Tonight at/Stokes' wedding I was moved by/this to moan and dance myself."

In "Regular Reefer," the second section of *Someone Sweet Angel Chile,* Williams pays homage to the "Empress of Blues," Bessie Smith. Bessie is the

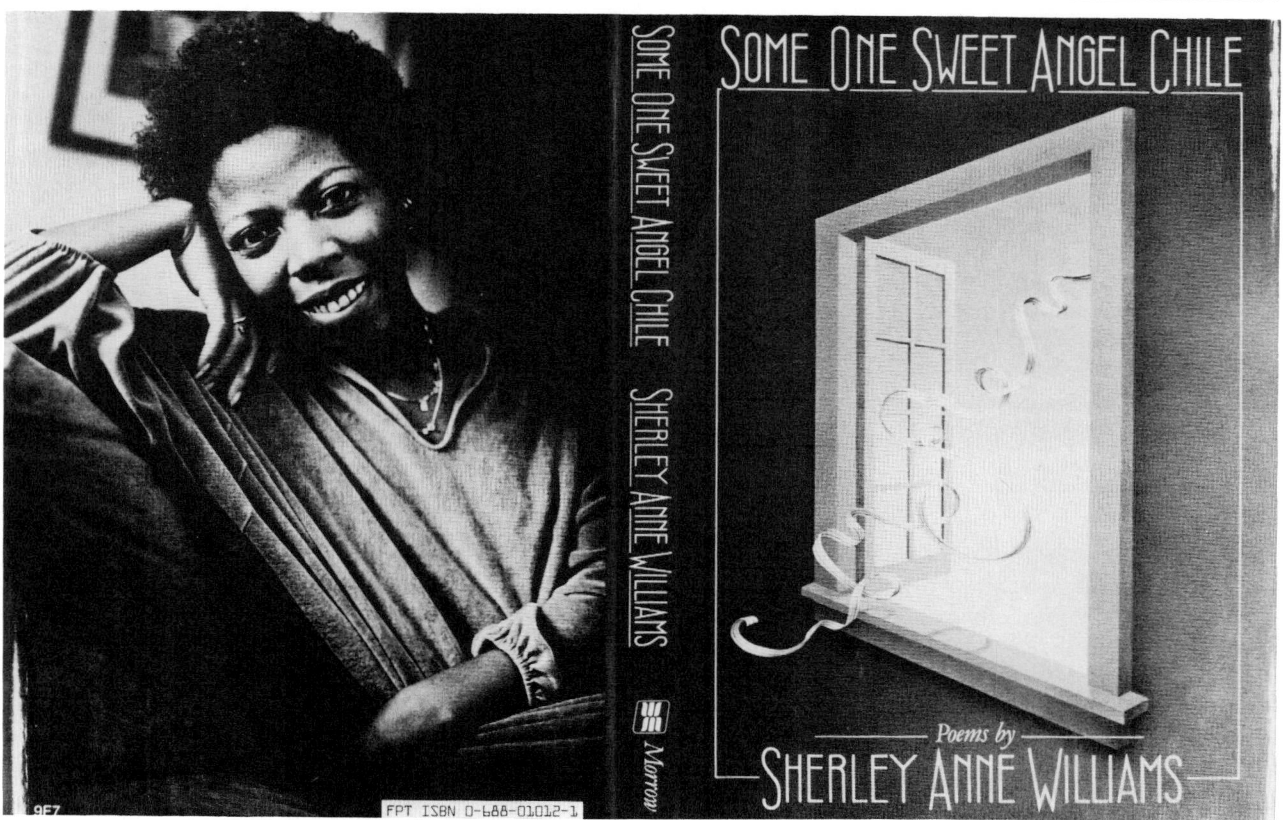

Dust jacket for Williams's 1982 poetry collection, which centers on what she calls the " 'knee baby,' the child next to the youngest waiting at the mother's knee" for the attention and love given to the oldest and the youngest

"sweet angel chile," and many of the poems in this section incorporate real occurrences in the life of Bessie Smith. The blues here, like the blues in *The Peacock Poems,* sing of hard times, money troubles, man/woman troubles, brown-versus-black-versus-yellow skin colors. Singing the blues gave Smith a temporary lifeline which sustained her through all her sufferings until she was fatally injured in an automobile accident in 1937. Williams resurrects her, perpetuating her through the blues.

The fourth section, "The Iconography of Childhood," defines the relationship between the children in this section and the "grown," the adults, particularly the women, in the preceding section, "The Songs of the Grown." In "You were never Miss Brown to me," the speaker points out the loving respect the children felt for certain adults who contributed to and enriched their lives:

> I call you Miss in tribute
> to the women of that time,
> the mothers of friends, the friends
> of my mother, Mamma
> herself . . .
>
> I call
> you Daisy and acknowledge
> my place in this line. I am
> the women of my childhood
> just as I was the women of
> my youth, one with these women
> of silence who lived on the
> cusp of their time and knew it;
> who taught what it is to be grown.

There are more poems about Williams's early life in *Someone Sweet Angel Chile* than in *The Peacock Poems.* She documents many journeys from squat town to squat town, as she followed the crops with her family. Williams pays tribute to this uncertain period of her life in a number of poems in "The Iconography of Childhood," doing so because, "I think that our migrations are an archetype of those of the dispossessed and I want somehow to tell the story of how the dispossessed become possessed of their own history without losing sight, without forgetting the meaning or the nature of their journey."

One might say that *Someone Sweet Angel Chile,* like Jean Toomer's *Cane,* is "a swan's song to a dying era." Yet in the very act of recalling the era, the poet resurrects the times and the people, ensuring them a long-running place in her heart and in the hearts of her readers.

Though Williams limits her discussion in *Give Birth to Brightness* almost exclusively to the works of black male writers, her poetry is a sensitive history of black women, their loves and triumphs, pains and defeats. Through the black women of her past and present, Sherley Anne Williams stands bright, tall, and strong.

Williams has been called a brilliant critic, a moving poet. She is both brilliant and moving in all of her writings, sometimes not so much in what she says as how she says it. She works with language in such a way that the old becomes new, the stale becomes refreshing, the dull illuminating. Her formal schooling has stood her well, freeing her to see and use the beauty of the speech cultivated and perpetuated by blacks. Like Zora Neale Hurston, Williams moves between the two languages with ease, even in her most learned discussion pleasantly surprising those saturated in the black experience with allusions to "Lit." She has said that her responsibility as a writer is "basically, to be as good as I can be and to say as much of the truth as I can see at any given time."

Although critical attention to Williams's work has been sparse, she is beginning to be recognized as an important voice in the literary community. She is well known among the "Neo-Black" writers, and her work has been anthologized in special collections such as Dexter Fisher's *The Third Woman,* and in a special edition of *Callaloo* devoted to black poets.

References:

Ralph Ellison, *Shadow and Act* (New York: Random House, 1964);

Dexter Fisher and Robert B. Stepto, eds., *Afro-American Literature: The Reconstruction of Instruction* (New York: The Modern Language Association of America, 1979);

Stephen Henderson, *Understanding the New Black Poetry* (New York: Morrow, 1973);

Langston Hughes, "The Negro Artist and the Racial Mountain," *Nation,* 122 (23 June 1926): 692-694;

Alain Locke, ed., *The New Negro: An Interpretation* (New York: Boni Press, 1925), pp. 3-16;

Julian Mayfield, "You Touch My Black Aesthetic and I'll Touch Yours," in *The Black Aesthetic,* edited by Addison Gayle, Jr. (New York: Doubleday, 1972);

Claudia Tate, ed., *Black Women Writers at Work* (New York: Continuum Press, 1983);

Alice Walker, in *Interviews with Black Writers,* edited by John O'Brien (New York: Harcourt Brace Jovanovich, 1973).

Jay Wright

(25 May 1935-)

Phillip M. Richard
Arkansas State University

BOOKS: *Death as History* (Milbrook, N.Y.: Kriya Press, 1967);

Balloons, A Comedy in One Act (Boston: Baker's Plays, 1968);

The Homecoming Singer (New York: Corinth Books, 1971);

Soothsayers and Omens (New York: Seven Woods Press, 1976);

Dimensions of History (Santa Cruz, Cal.: Kayak, 1976);

The Double Invention of Komo (Austin: University of Texas Press, 1980).

OTHER: Henry Dumas, *Poetry for My People,* edited by Hale Chatfield and Eugene Redmond, includes introduction by Wright (Carbondale: Southern Illinois University Press, 1970);

"Love's Dozen," in *Chant of Saints: A Gathering of Afro-American Literature, Arts and Scholarship,* edited by Michael S. Harper and Robert Stepto (Urbana: University of Illinois Press, 1979).

Jay Wright's work focuses largely on personal biography, Afro-American historical experience, and spiritual quest. Within his writing, these subjects are assimilated into mythological and ritual forms derived from his studies in the history of religions, literature, and anthropology. Although Jay Wright is typical of his generation of black poets in his attempt to create a vision of what might be called black culture, his poetry is distinguished by the systematic use of African and native American cosmologies and his attempt to incorporate early Christian and Renaissance writers, such as Augustine and Dante, into the fabric of his vision. Wright's most recent work shows increasing sensitivity to the continuities between Western and African traditions in the themes of spiritual quest for redemption and creativity.

Jay Wright was born in Albuquerque, New Mexico, in 1935 to Leona Dailey and Mercer Murphy Wright. His father, a mechanic and jitney driver, was born in Santa Rosa, New Mexico, and his mother in Virginia. Wright grew up in New Mexico where he started school in Albuquerque. He completed high school in San Pedro, California.

Before entering college, Wright played semiprofessional baseball and served in the Army. In 1961 he earned a bachelor's degree, after three years of study at the University of California at Berkeley. Wright attended Union Theological Seminary in New York for a brief period following college. In 1962 he enrolled in graduate school at Rutgers University from which he received an M.A. degree. At Rutgers, Wright completed all the requirements for a doctorate except the dissertation. In addition to his formal graduate training, Wright has been a Hodder Fellow at Princeton University and a Fellow in Creative Writing at Dundee University in Scotland. Wright taught at Tougaloo and Talladega colleges for brief periods between 1968 and 1970. He taught at Yale University from 1975 to 1979.

Wright's poetry demonstrates his acquaintance with European literature as well as with the religions and folklore of the Americas and Africa. His researches, as they are described in the "Afterword" of *The Double Invention of Komo* (1980), have focused on the studies of African literature carried out by Marcel Griaule and the group of French anthropologists connected with him, including Michel Leiris, Solange de Ganay, Genevieve Calame-Griaule, and Deborah Lifchitz, among others. In the work of these writers, Wright has studied the religions of the Dogon and Bambara along with those of the Akan and Nuer. His researches into primitive religions have taken him also into the study of Navajo poetry. Conversant in anthropology, the philosophy of science, and the European literatures of the Renaissance and the Middle Ages, Wright's poetry is, in large measure, the fruit of this extensive scholarly enterprise. His dedications to Francis Fergusson in *Dimensions of History* (1976) and Marcel Griaule in *The Double Invention of Komo* are typical of his sense of scholarly indebtedness.

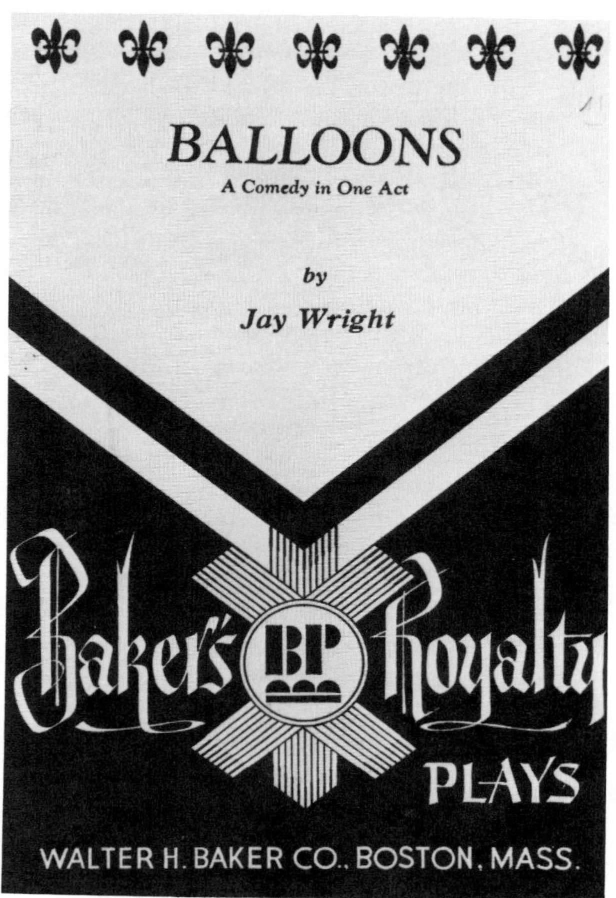

Front cover for Wright's 1968 play, which he calls "A Participatory and/or Non-Participatory Comedy," although it ends with a senseless death

Wright's poetic development has been deeply influenced by his synthesis of a variety of disparate sources into an intricate historical vision that rests on two controlling ideas: all historical, artistic, and mythical thought have the same ground, and the intellectual and spiritual content of a culture is inseparable from its material being. As a people moves from place to place, it brings its spirit embodied in its material culture. Rejecting dualisms of mind and matter, Wright asserts what he takes to be an African sense of unity between spirit and the physical world.

Within Wright's poetry, this idea bears fruit in a number of ways. The notion of the existence of an African spirit borne to America by blacks allows Wright to find the roots of Afro-American culture in African ritual and art. Contrasting the firmly articulated, traditional, African religious beliefs with the cultural habits acquired in the American setting, Wright is able to create powerful images of alienation and inauthenticity which derive from the denial of that African spiritual ground which is the special heritage of Afro-Americans. In the exposition of his central theme of the reappropriation of a once-dispossessed spiritual life, Wright delineates the growth of the understanding of one's traditional identity from a shadowy sense to a full sense of the authentic cultural heritage.

Another major focus in Wright's work, which he articulates in his introduction to Henry Dumas's *Poetry for My People* (edited in 1970 by Hale Chatfield and Eugene Redmond after Dumas's tragic death), is the central precept that a poem ought to expound the vital rhythm of the culture which it portrays. Wright sympathizes with Dumas's appropriation of the vital Afro-American rhythms most evident in gospel and jazz. Like Dumas, Wright is fully committed to a search for poetic forms which embody the rhythms of black culture. This artistic focus links the poetic method of Wright and Dumas with both the black, poetic, folk tradition of Langston Hughes and the "projective verse" tradition, represented by Charles Olson, which stresses the nature of the poem as a spoken action whose rhythms reflect the being of the speaker.

Wright uses ritual, material culture, and speech as natural embodiments of and metaphors for the spiritual and intellectual themes which he wishes to pursue. For Wright, ideas reside primarily in things; thus his poetry frequently focuses on the ritual objects and acts of the native American and African cultures which he finds to be the wellsprings of those spiritual traditions. Wright's stress on the material and ritualistic base of tradition leads in *Dimensions of History* to the use of collages to bring together historical quotations, Hispanic-American art forms, and even geographical descriptions to show the continuities of feeling and spirit which traverse various Afro-American cultures as Wright perceives them.

The Homecoming Singer (1971) is Wright's first major book. It was preceded by a 1967 chapbook, *Death as History,* from which many poems were reprinted in *The Homecoming Singer.* The 1971 collection draws heavily on autobiographical sources which are shaped in the book into a record of artistic and spiritual development. *The Homecoming Singer* shows some evidence of Wright's interest in the history of religions and his evolving thought on the nature of Afro-American culture, although the poetry does not make explicit use of this material as do his later three books. Instead, in individual poems that are firmly grounded in well-defined geographical settings and fully evoked states of mind, Wright explores the social and psychological experiences of his autobiographical persona.

With the exception of poems on Crispus Attucks and W. E. B. Du Bois, the verse of the book's first section draws heavily upon Wright's early experiences in the Southwest and on the West Coast. These settings serve as backdrops for developing the persona's sense of exclusion from white society, in poems such as "The Fisherman's Fiesta," and his deep ambivalence toward the failures of the religious rituals of the black church, in "Wednesday Night Prayer Meeting." The writing here shows Wright's sympathy with the dreams, postures, and pride of older male figures in poems such as "Jason's One Command." Other poems explore the persona's disillusionment with the conventional postures of bohemian black artists. And finally, in the best poem of the book, "The Homecoming Singer," Wright takes the occasion of a homecoming celebration at a black college to project his persona's dream of what might be a true homecoming to traditional black values.

In the second section of *The Homecoming Singer,* there are several poems which portray the persona's sense of displacement in Mexico, a geographical scene to which Wright will return in *Soothsayers and Omens* (1976). In this section, an important shift takes place from the social experience which forms the subject matter of the earlier section to psychological states of alienation and displacement.

In the third section, a tightly developed series of poems, Wright's persona moves from diffidence about his vocation as an artist to confidence in his creative ability. The poems here are meditative and focused, for the most part, on the persona's spiritual, artistic, and emotional growth. The settings are not precisely described places that lend atmosphere to the poem, but instead serve as symbolic renderings of the persona's inner state.

The fourth and final section of the book develops a black folk vision, describes religious rituals,

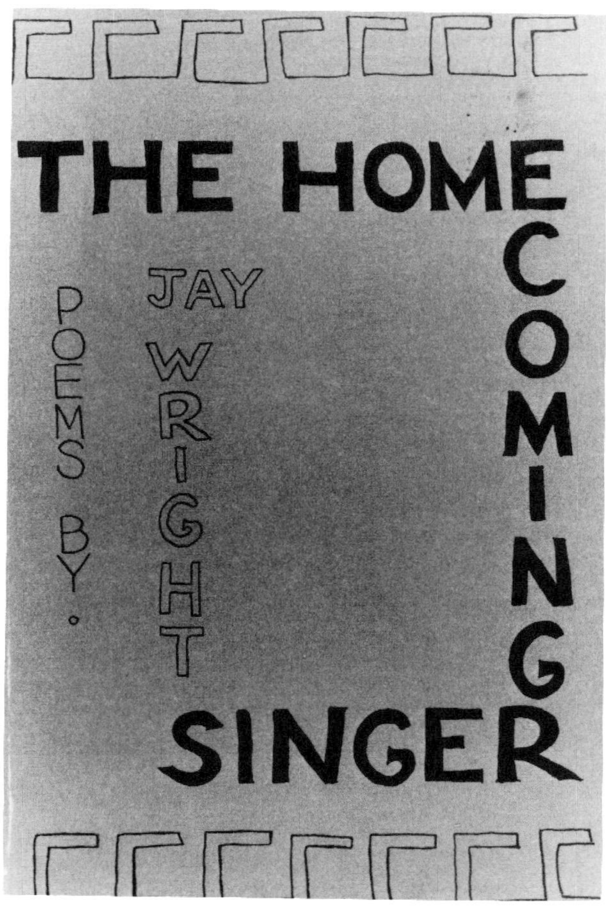

Front cover for Wright's 1971 book of poems which dramatizes the discovery of African culture as a point of reference in black American life

and continues the concern with art developed in previous sections. However, these familiar subjects are revived with a new sense of the persona's intellectual and spiritual growth. The persistent undersong of these poems is an undefined yet imminent sense of life and tradition to which the persona is now attuned.

Appearing in 1971 at the height of interest in contemporary black writing, *The Homecoming Singer* attracted critical notice. In a 1975 omnibus review of several black poets, "Five Black Poets: History, Consciousness, Love, & Harshness," Eugene B. Redmond notes Wright's handling of his erudition, his fine portraits of black folk life, and the historical thrust of much of his poetry. Redmond, editor of Henry Dumas's poetry and short stories, has insisted for some time on Wright's importance, calling the writer "a major poet of this era" in *Drumvoices: The Mission of Afro-American Poetry, A Critical History* (1976).

In the period between the publication of *The Homecoming Singer* and the two books published in 1976, *Dimensions of History* and *Soothsayers and Omens,* Wright traveled to Mexico and to Scotland, where he stayed for two years between 1971 and 1973. From 1973 to 1978, Wright spent extensive time in New Hampshire. In 1975 he assumed teaching duties at Yale, where he continued until 1979. In a 1974 Howard University interview, the poet spoke of his intention of writing three books which would assemble the results of his studies in African, Hispanic, and Native American sources. The appearance of the two 1976 books and *The Double Invention of Komo* (1980) points to the period after the writing of the poems of *The Homecoming Singer* as one of deliberate articulation and refinement of his poetic mythology which appeared at mid-decade.

Soothsayers and Omens and *Dimensions of History* are also concerned with the autobiographical development of an individual Afro-American persona of the Afro-American and with an examination of ritual, history, and material culture of Afro-Americans. *Soothsayers and Omens* assimilates the themes of the individual quest into the larger context of the African-American tradition. *Dimensions of History* creates a cultural history of Afro-Americans with a view to the achievement of what the poem's voice calls "our life among ourselves."

In each section of *Soothsayers and Omens* Wright relates his persona to a religious and historical context which extends away from him in time and place. The individual poems within the four sections of the book function in groups which contrast with and allude to each other. If there is a central continuity in the book, it is the effort of the persona who seeks to understand his experience in the context of broad cultural knowledge. And if there are dominant motifs in the work, they are the soothsayer and omen which suggest, albeit in piecemeal fashion, the underlying mythology which gives the work thematic unity and finally appears full-fledged in the Nani's account of Dogon cosmology with which the book concludes.

The predominant theme of the opening section of *Soothsayers and Omens* is engagement with the past. Upon the birth of his son, the persona confronts his father in "The Charge." He struggles to understand a number of mythologies in the series of poems named "Sources." The engagement with the past is again dramatized in the encounter between the persona and Benjamin Banneker in

"Benjamin Banneker Helps to Build a City" and in the meditation on Banneker's letter to Thomas Jefferson in "Benjamin Banneker Sends His *'Almanac'* to Thomas Jefferson." Often Wright's best poetry comes from the use of poetic mythology. This is true of "Benjamin Banneker Sends His *'Almanac'* to Thomas Jefferson" in which the theme of the loss of harmony between Banneker and the white world is explored with great penetration.

> Uneasy, at night,
> you follow stars and lines to their limits,
> sure of yourself, sure of the harmony
> of everything, and yet you moan
> for the lost harmony, the crack in the universe,
> your twin, I search it out,

Here, the speaker enters Banneker's point of view directly, and invoking the Dogon concepts of the divine twins and the water spirit, Nommo, the persona evokes a sense of his common origin with Banneker through African comsology. Employing a number of sources drawn from African religion and American history, Wright is, paradoxically, working in the wholly American tradition of writers such as T. S. Eliot, Ezra Pound, and Charles Olson. His contribution, in this regard, is to locate in the New World a continuity of feeling stretching back to Africa and to show the interplay of that tradition with its American context.

In his third book, *Soothsayers and Omens,* Wright reappropriates the Mexican setting from its function in *The Homecoming Singer,* as a scene in which to explore the protagonist's sense of alienation, to a new use as a place for an encounter between the speaker and tradition. From this experience, the persona is able to move on, in the section, to be a series of poems in which he confronts his relatives and his own American experience with a better defined sense of identity. In the post-Mexican poems in the third section, he comes to an understanding of himself as engaged in a serious intellectual and spiritual quest, a search which will culminate in the book's fourth section in the persona's contact with his Nani, a teacher of Dogon mythology, who instructs him in the creation lore of the Dogon religion. This section, which parallels in content and form the account of the contact between Marcel Griaule and his Dogon informant in Griaule's *Dieu d'eau,* takes the shape not only of an account of the Nani's teaching but also of an initiation into a new world view. Through the process of the ritualistic instruction described in the poems "Binu," "Altars and Sacrifice," and the "Dead," the initiate gains a sense of participation in the universe of the Dogon which links him with that African tradition and firmly establishes his sense of place in an African past which he has heretofore perceived only in individual dispersed points of time. This conversion process completes the account of spiritual development begun at the start of *Soothsayers and Omens* and in many ways fulfills the sense of participation in a darker, primeval, spiritual order.

Haunting and evocative, *Soothsayers and Omens* powerfully reveals the Afro-American sense of participation in a tradition and world view other than that in which blacks live in America, and most successfully of all Wright's books, it assimilates a mythological world view to personal experience. Its experiments with religious mythology, however, do foreshadow problems in the combination of myth and history which occur within the later books.

Dimensions of History and *Soothsayers and Omens,* in many respects, represent two strands of Wright's artistic vision. Whereas *Soothsayers* illustrates the theme of personal quest, *Dimensions of History* embodies the search for collective self-understanding. The narrative voice of the book is a spokesman for his people. At one point, he refers to himself as a dyeli, the historical archivist of his tribe. The search for collective values is accomplished through introspection, individual quest, and the evocation of the spiritual values implicit in Afro-American culture in both of the Americas.

The first of the three sections of *Dimensions of History,* entitled "The Second Eye of the World: The Dimensions of Rites and Acts," situates the speaker in his historical predicament. Confronting a land from which the gods, who represent the traditional African spiritual presence, have withdrawn, the poem's persona takes up the quest for an account of the original act of God which can explain the divine withdrawal, resolve the predicament of his people, and justify the persona's vocation as historian and interpreter of his people's experience.

In search of an answer to these questions, the speaker addresses a blind religious sage akin to the figure of the Nani at the end of *Soothsayers and Omens.* From this encounter, the speaker learns that in withdrawing God gives man self-knowledge by throwing him back on his own resources. From the sage, moreover, the persona learns the paradox that this withdrawal is a means of instruction.

Thrown back upon himself, the persona turns

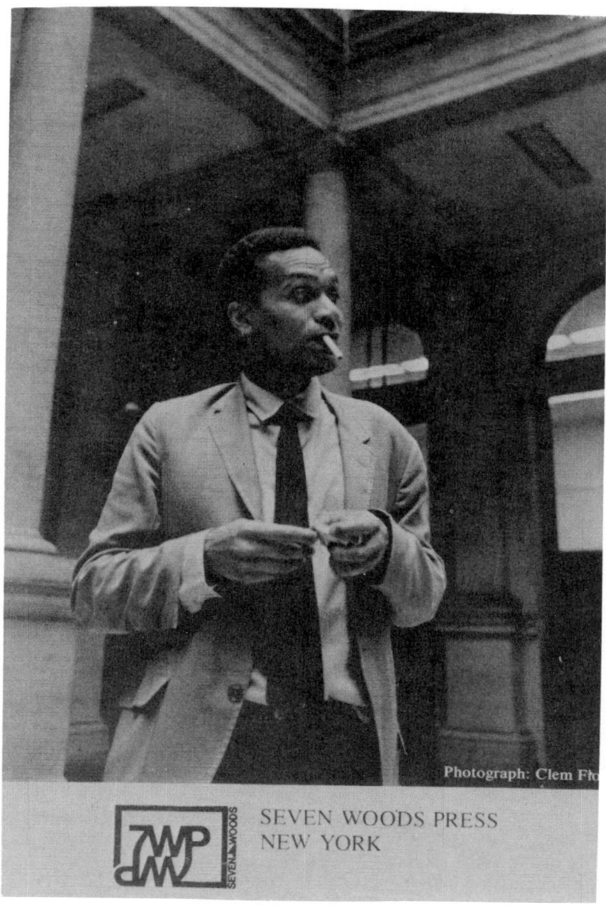

Covers for Wright's 1976 poetry volume in which a mythological world view becomes integrated with the persona's quest for individual identity

to an examination of his collective racial memory. Moving through a series of dreamlike visions, the process of the soul's ascension, through dances and rituals in Cuba, Lima, and Guinea, the poem's speaker comes to the conclusion that men may find "the dwelling-place of the act, / the spirit holding the understanding / of our life among ourselves." Midway in this section, the persona learns from his sage that the first act of God (which he has sought before to explain his predicament) is embodied in the rising and the recreation of the spirit.

What is the first act
if not the body rising from itself,
becoming itself again,
            spirit, shadow, spirit,
heart of its own bones,
the name of the wise one?

He has found that man's regeneration of himself through recreative introspection is itself an embodiment of God's creative act in forming the universe. The soul, the persona has learned, is a synecdoche for the entire universe. Thus, he describes it as "an All in All." In a universe created through a divine initial act by the deity identical to that evoked in the Benjamin Banneker poem, Wright prepares both reader and speaker for an exploration of the aesthetic dimensions of history as creative acts of the race and, thus, parts of the process of divine creation.

The second section of the poem, "Modulations: The Aesthetic Dimension," traces the central character's quest for an understanding of the creative acts in his culture in their material and ritualistic form. This section is divided into a number of parts: "Rhythm, Charts and Changes" is a collection of poems based on musical instruments and dances; "The Body Adorned and Bare" presents poems which are meditations on clothes and jewelry; "Retablose" contains meditations on Hispanic interpretations of Christ and the saints in pictures; "The Log Book of Judgments" portrays images of the mother and the beloved as aesthetic and erotic ideals.

The second section of *Dimensions of History* is a tour de force which provides Wright the opportunity for some of his best poems. A number of vivid poems in this section dramatize the playing of drums as an artistic process providing a gateway to surreal ecstasies and a spiritual experience of the triumph of life over death. In the poem "d," a meditation on the musical sound produced by the strings of a bandola, the poet explores the ways in which the string's resonance represents the heavenly joy which follows death. The poem begins with an evocative description of the sound of the instrument as heavenly, yet derived from the winding sheet, a cloth in which a corpse is wrapped.

Dolorosa,
what is heaven
but the breath
of that string
taken from the gaffer's
winding sheet?

From this paradox, the poet conceives of the musical note as part of the persona's spiritual nature brought down to earth in the form of music.

Trio of clarity,
in the darkness of your pitch,
I hear my absent voice
absent itself from angels
and the air they ride
to flesh the bones that here
my doves will dance upon.

In its stress on the earthly shaping of spiritual transcendence, the density and haunting quality of its imagery, striking metaphor, and paradoxical statement, this poem is typical of the section "Aesthetic Modulations."

"Landscapes: The Physical Dimension" is the next and final section of *Dimensions of History*. It is structured around a collage of geographical descriptions of landscapes in North and South America. The introduction of the section and the geographic descriptions of Venezuela and Panama contain meditations on Christian ritual and art. However, following the section on Colombia, the poetic voice again takes up the theme of the withdrawal of the gods and shifts his vision to a wasteland where "My cattle settle in the dust, and die." Here he invokes a "bird god" whom he asks for relief. The description of Panama is followed by the persona's observation that the Virgin Mary has supplanted his "goddess" and taken over her temple. Wright concludes with an account of a people (in imagery evoking the tribes of Israel) led by a star. This procession continues after a geographical description of North America and ends with the persona's return to Mexico which he designates as "A Star land, a golden land" and declares to be "our dark and true light,/the image of our life among ourselves."

The final section of the poem thematically resolves the issues tackled by *Dimensions of History* in a number of ways. It fulfills the stipulation of the early sections that the persona, who represents the collective values of his people, must understand the spiritual ideals of his culture through introspection and meditation. It is Wright's most systematic treatment of the theme of inauthenticity and the quest for redemption in tradition of an African people cut off from their origins.

Dimensions of History is strongest in the second section in which it presents poems that dramatize the musical, artistic, or ritualistic acts which the persona wishes to present as the embodiments of spiritual tradition. It is weakest in its meditations on geographical places at the end. The first section is flawed by a problem that will become even more significant in *The Double Invention of Komo*. Here many of the historical voices which the persona of the poem confronts lack a clear sense of identity and personality. Without clear dramatic situations and well-defined poetic voices, the collages of the first section tend to become a hodgepodge lacking enough individual definition to create the vital contrasts and similarities on which this historical pastiche must depend for its effect.

Taken as an attempt at the understanding of the collective experience of Afro-Americans, *Dimensions of History* is revealing in its achievement. Although the persona takes on the form of a seeker searching the meaning of the social life of his community, there is very little evocation of social life in the poem. For the most part, the persona is concerned with his own aesthetic perception of rites, history, and art. In spite of his explicitly stated intention, Wright's primary concern in this poem is the formulation of a mythological understanding of the persona's imaginative and introspective experience. Yet, although *Dimensions of History* is a poem on the development of personal sensibility, one cannot say that it is any worse for being so. It marks Wright's movement to a personal, hermetic, and reflective poetry in which the exposition of his historical and cultural vision is a goal in itself rather than a scaffolding in which to frame the representation of experience of "our life among ourselves." Wright's ambivalence about seeking a collective versus a purely personal understanding deepens in *The Double Invention of Komo*.

Dimensions of History has generated few, but significant critical responses. Praising the poem "What is True" as "one of the finest meditations I have read in years," Harold Bloom has described Jay Wright as "a very much neglected and superb black poet." He said the book was the best volume of poetry from a small press in 1976. Robert Stepto, in a brief look at the first section of *Dimensions* in the *Chant of Saints*, entitled "After Modernism, After Hibernation: Michael Harper, Robert Hayden, and Jay Wright," stresses the universal and "macrocosmic" nature of the imagery by which Wright articulates his historical vision.

The personal and freewheeling synthetic quality of *Dimensions of History* in many respects sets the stage for *The Double Invention of Komo*, Jay Wright's fourth and most ambitious book. It is structured largely along the lines of the cosmology and the initiation ceremony of the Komo society which exists in the Bambara tribe and other African tribes. A major source for the work, Wright indicates in the book's afterword, is *Les Fondements de la sociéte d'initiation du Komo* by Germaine Dieterlen and Youssouf Tata Cissé. The Komo are an all-male society within the Bambara. This society sees itself as the conservator of the central intellectual, spiritual, and social values of its culture. Its aim is the creation of self-knowledge on the part of the initiate within the framework of the values of the group. The ritualistic symbols and acts described in Wright's poem symbolically represent the dominant values of the Bambara culture. And to a large extent Wright has, in this book, chosen a scheme of character development which follows a well-defined formulature. In this respect the book differs markedly from previous volumes.

Wright's use of the concepts derived from the Komo ritual and cosmology requires some explanation. One important feature of the Komo cosmology is a system of 266 signs which represent the particular names of the god, Komo, and which are associated with certain material substances. The signs are, moreover, represented by 266 altars. The signs are also connected with individual stars and parts of the body in a wide range of symbolic links between the central sacred values of the Komo and their daily lives.

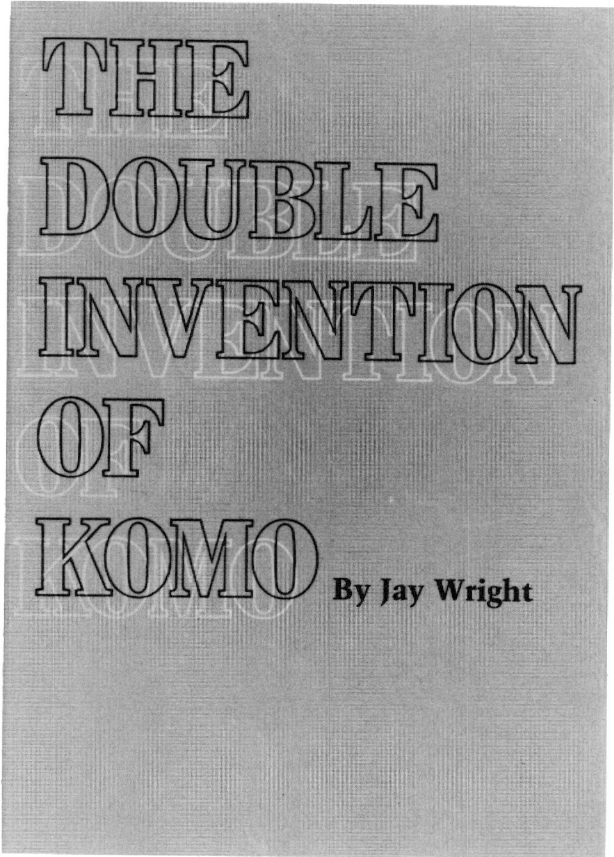

Front cover for paperback edition of Wright's 1980 poem of initiation. In the afterword Wright says, "Komo's end, like history's, is to permit man to know himself."

A second concept dealing with the ritual of initation is the concept of the double. Each initiate in the ritual is said to have a double who corresponds to the initiate's future development after the initiation process has been completed. This double is spoken of as a female twin of the initiate in a reflection of the Komo religious belief that the creative act is a feminine one, or as Cissé and Dieterlen put it, the universe is feminine in its regenerative function.

Wright explains the title and function of the poem in terms of this concept of the double. The poem is to be perceived as written by the initiate's double from the perspective of the autobiographical subject who has passed through the initiation process. The poem's "double invention" is the process of maturation which leads to the creation of the initiate's double and the process of writing which creates the poem itself. Through the initiation process the subject is brought to self-knowledge, and this knowledge is the central theme of the poem.

The Double Invention of Komo can be divided into two sections. The first part of the book, which takes up about three-fifths of the poem, details the preparation for the ceremony of Komo; the ceremony itself takes up the remainder. The preparation includes an invocation in which the ritual celebrant defines the manner of initiation and introduces himself as a religious adept, a professor of those values by which the initiate will be fulfilled. The initiate, in turn, states that he takes the celebrant's "woman's heart" within himself and feels himself already doubled. Other sections of the poem involve a dance in which the celebrant dramatizes the creation of the world and tells the initiate that he must define his identity from the stars of the constellation (the system of 266 signs of sacred values). The ritual altars representing the signs are presented before the initiate.

Fully acquainted with the values steadily inculcated in him in the first third of the poem, the initiate in the "Opening of the Cycle of Redemption" entreats the ritual celebrant to give him knowledge. He struggles with his desire for self-knowledge. In the next section, "The Abstract of Knowledge/The First Test," the initiate seeks knowledge of the first creative act of God and later concludes that it is his very desire for knowledge which is an embodiment of the first creative act. These two sections are the crucial ones of the poem in their dramatization of the central theme of the coming into self-knowledge.

The second part of the poem, "The Opening of the Ceremony/the Coming Out of Komo," involves the passage through the actual ritual itself. This ritual is defined by four signs which detail the important qualities to be cultivated in the initiation. And the book details many more stages in what amounts to a process of conversion. Creation myths, monologues addressed to important thinkers, or dialogues between different voices are all brought together by Wright within this section to dramatize the teaching of the values achieved during the initiation process. The symbols and values remain abstract, however. Despite the suggestion of the theme of socialization, the book is not primarily devoted to the concrete description of the crucial cultural and social symbols and values of the Komo.

However, the strategy of the initiation ceremony is an effective scheme for the description of the cultural education of the autobiographical subject. And as the detailed account of the poet's reading at the end of the poem suggests, *The Double Invention of Komo* is largely an intellectual biography. Wright uses the dialogue between ritual celebrant and initiate as a means of situating speeches by or addresses to writers and thinkers central to the poet's development. In a confident assertion of the breadth of the African world view which he has created, Wright shapes his wide reading in the traditions of the West into an assertion of the inclusiveness of an essentially African educative and socialization process.

The most important Western references in the poem include addresses by or to Augustine, Dante, a German poet, and a philosopher in Paris. In the context of the poem, these thinkers affect the development of the subject in the ritual process in different ways. Augustine appears in the section "The Abstracts of Knowledge/The First Test" as an exemplary Christian pilgrim, speaking in a voice paralleling that of the ritual celebrant. Here the Christian saint offers his own quest as a paradigm for the attempt to return to God through the means of understanding.

> Strap holiness and renunciation
> to your feet, buckle the desire
> to walk to God to your loins,
> walk on the wave of God's mercy,
> step down here and sail away
> to God in his boat of grace.

It is Augustine, again speaking as a kind of celebrant, who defines the first act of creation as the act of God moving through the initiate, creating the desire for salvation.

> The act grows from delight,
> prepared by the hidden,
> quivering arrow of a god's hand.
> The act is in the longing for God's hand,
> or your own hand, in the act.

Similarly, in a moving homage to Dante, Wright praises *The Divine Comedy* as an exposition of its writer's "spirit's truth," that is as a record of the author's self-knowledge. Wright invokes Dante's work in a play upon the symbolic forest which appears in both books.

> Your art is a second creation,
> a true bleeding of the world.
> You have entered the wood;
> you turn, out of the holy waves,
> born again,
> even as trees renewed,
> pure and ready to mount to the stars.

Coming near the end of *The Double Invention of*

Komo, this passage dramatizes the writer's sense of kinship.

In its intricate and detailed schematization of the persona's intellectual and spiritual development, *The Double Invention of Komo* is extremely complex. The evocation of the German poet in the "Opening of the Cycle of Redemption" contains Wright's poignant statement of the plight of the artist who cannot bring his spiritual truth into the world. Near the end of "The Initiate Takes His First Six Signs, the Design of His Name," in a moving address to a philosopher, the speaker gives a lyrical defense of artistic creation as an expression of freedom.

Despite its difficulties, *The Double Invention of Komo* is an important book in terms of its artistic and cultural ambition. Its difficulties, however, diminish somewhat as the book is reread, and the reader is assimilated into the world of the poem. Indeed as the work is viewed in relation to Wright's other works, it is clear that *The Double Invention of Komo* has much to tell us about the interplay of the traditions of Africa and the West in the sensibility of a cosmopolitan thinker.

Wright, as is evident to anyone who comes to his last book fresh from a reading of the first three, is a careful craftsman. And both *The Double Invention of Komo* and *Dimensions of History* demonstrate, in the face of an increasingly abstract and hermetic corpus, great concern for the reader setting about these difficult works. In both cases, Wright furnishes help in the form of notes and references to sources needed to explicate the works. He cites a number of sources which bear directly on his other works, for example, *Le Renard Pâle* by Griaule and Dieterlen is important for understanding parts of *Dimensions of History* and the first of the two Benjamin Banneker poems in *Soothsayers and Omens* where Dogon mythology comes into play.

Yet, despite its many literary virtues, Wright's assistance, and the justifiability of some of its difficulty, *The Double Invention of Komo* has certain flaws. Wright's statement that the initiate is the author of the poem does not solve all problems of interpretation. This explanation does not completely clarify the identity of the ritual celebrant in the poem. At times, this celebrant seems to function as an alter ego of the subject. In the book's second half, voices from the initiate's past and his reading are absorbed into the dialogue between initiate and ritual celebrant which make the two voices part of a larger cultural process. More than the initiate, the celebrant becomes protean in character and difficult to perceive as a unified voice.

Significantly, Wright has dealt with this criticism in the context of his introduction to Dumas's *Poetry for My People.* Speaking of Dumas's refusal to maintain in his poetry a specific tone or voice, Wright points to the other writer's desire "to be everything, to participate intensely in whatever was human and good. . . ." This desire permeates both voices in *The Double Invention of Komo,* often with debilitating effect. At too many places the poet simply fails to sustain developed characters. And as a consequence, in the course of the poem, continuity, dramatic force, and clarity are lost. Wright's many voices simply lack the sharp distinctiveness which characterizes the many voices of Eliot's *The Wasteland,* a successful, long poem with which Wright's later works have a number of affinities.

In one way or another, the critics who have praised or blamed *The Double Invention of Komo* have had to confront its complexity. Darryl Pinckney, writing in *Parnassus: Poetry in Review,* has called it pretentious, attacked it as a "private journey," and berated its monotony and obscurity. Other reviewers have attacked the poem for its lack of clearly defined structure. One reviewer who has praised the book has compared its language to Pound's "Pisan Cantos."

John Hollander, in a review of Wright's book in the *Times Literary Supplement,* has praised Wright as "the most intellectual and the most imaginatively serious and ambitious black American poet I know of" and characterized *The Double Invention of Komo* as Wright's attempt to liberate his writing from the level of merely good verse. His review points trenchantly to the patently experimental quality of the book. For despite its function as a summation "of many of the literary influences upon Wright as a writer, *The Double Invention of Komo* is clearly a transitional book, and the passage it marks is fraught with trends which from *Dimensions of History* are increasingly apparent. Increasingly, Wright's poetry has become private in its refusal to dramatize some of its symbolism, schematic in its plotting which relies increasingly on ritual and patterns of redemption, and weak in its articulation of individual voices within the poem. Moreover, Wright has relied increasingly on notes to guide his reader."

Perhaps the most problematic element in assessing Wright as a poet is his singleness of theme. All four of his books have been shaped in some way around the themes of personal development through spiritual or intellectual quest. Whether developed through traditional narrative autobiography, ritual, or patterns of redemption taken from

Dogon or Bambara cosmology, Wright's autobiographical theme has stayed largely the same. It may be that this singlemindedness is not a limitation, however. Certainly few poets have so much to tell us about the complexities of the relationship between the Afro-American present and the past.

References:

Germaine Dieterlen and Youssouf Tata Cissé, *Les Fondements de la sociéte d'initiation du Komo* (Paris: Mouton, 1972);

Marcel Griaule, *Dieu D'Eau: entretiens avec Ogotemmeli* (Paris: Fayard, 1966);

Griaule and Dieterlen, *Le Renard Pâle* (Paris: Institut D'Ethnologie, Musee de L'Homme, 1965);

Robert B. Stepto, "After Modernism, After Hibernation: Michael Harper, Robert Hayden, and Jay Wright," in *Chant of Saints: A Gathering of Afro-American Literature, Arts and Scholarship,* edited by Michael S. Harper and Robert B. Stepto (Urbana: University of Illinois Press, 1979).

Ahmos Zu-Bolton II

(21 October 1935-)

Lorenzo Thomas

University of Houston/Downtown College

BOOK: *A Niggered Amen* (San Luis Obispo, Cal.: Solo Press, 1975).

OTHER: "Homeless," "Martha of the Adult Crowd," "The Poem," in *Poems by Blacks,* volume 3 (1975), edited by Pinkie Gordon Lane (Fort Smith, Ark.: South & West, 1975), pp. 107-109;

Quincy Troupe and Rainer Schulte, eds., *Giant Talk: An Anthology of Third World Writings,* includes poem by Zu-Bolton (New York: Random House, 1975);

Synergy: An Anthology of Washington D.C. Blackpoetry, edited by Zu-Bolton and E. Ethelbert Miller (Houston: Energy BlackSouth Press, 1975);

"Taxi Cab Blues," in *Yardbird Lives!,* edited by Ishmael Reed and Al Young (New York: Grove Press, 1978), pp. 26-27.

PERIODICAL PUBLICATIONS: "Sunset Beach/ L.A.," *Ideas,* 3, no. 1 (1971): 69;

"The Crown," *Alternative* (Winter 1972): 24;

"Livewire and Company," *The Spirit That Moves Us,* 3 (Winter 1977): 16;

"StruggleRoad Dance," *First World,* 1, no. 1 (1977);

"In Peking," "Some Space Lore," "Ritual Workings," "Quicktales of a Blind Painter," *A,* 4 (Spring 1979): 18-24;

"A Neo-Folklore," "Ain't No Spring Chicken," "A Galveston Rock of Ages," "A Crucifix for DeRidder, or the Governor of Ollie Street Returns," "Beachhead Preachment," *Open Places,* no. 29 (Spring 1980): 3-9.

Ahmos Zu-Bolton II, one of the most dynamic poets and energetic literary organizers of the 1970s and 1980s, is an artist who applies much of his talent to the community while issuing his own compositions sparingly. His work as a literary publisher and book distributor in the South served as a practical exercise of ideas put forward by the black arts movement developed in the nation's large cities in the 1960s. In some ways, Zu-Bolton's work and career also present the fulfillment of both integrationist and black nationalist ideas current since the late 1940s. A poet could scarcely find a more richly diverse historical tradition, and Zu-Bolton, as both writer and publisher, has attempted to reconcile the contradictions presented by this heritage.

Born 21 October 1935 in Poplarville, Mississippi, Ahmos Zu-Bolton II grew up in the rural community of DeRidder, Louisiana, near the Texas border. He is the eldest of thirteen children born to Annie Lou McGee Bolton and Ahmos Bolton, a career soldier who rose to the rank of sergeant major in the United States Army. Zu-Bolton attended public schools in DeRidder and later, during the 1950s, he had a wide range of experiences. He left high school in 1953 to help support the family. "I cut sugarcane and did farm work," he says, "and I bummed around a little bit, too." When his father was stationed overseas and permitted to bring his family, Ahmos—though too old to be listed as a military dependent—sometimes traveled with the family to bases in Europe. He also traveled through the South from 1954 to 1957 as shortstop for the Shreveport Twins of the American Negro Baseball League. "I *guess* we *were* professional ballplayers," he says. "We got $25 a game and all expenses paid for the season. It supported me during the summer and, since we all knew about Jackie Robinson, it was a possible option of being so-called 'discovered' and getting into the major leagues . . . sort of how Columbus 'discovered' people who were already here."

Zu-Bolton returned to George Washington Carver High School in DeRidder in 1962 and when he graduated was among seventeen black students chosen to integrate Louisiana State University in 1965. He was sponsored by scholarships from the NAACP and the American Legion. After Louisiana State University, Zu-Bolton was drafted into the Army and served overseas as a medic in Germany and Vietnam. After his discharge from the Army, he attended Los Angeles City College and graduated with a bachelor's degree in English literature and journalism from California State Polytechnic University in 1971. He was one of many talented and socially committed black Vietnam veterans who sought to employ their skills and education for the betterment of their communities.

Zu-Bolton's launching of *HooDoo* magazine in 1972 is a fair indication of the impact the black arts movement and aesthetic ideas inspired by the civil rights struggle had accomplished nationwide over two active decades. If the Harlem Renaissance of the 1920s adhered to the nation's great metropolitan areas as the focus of black cultural innovation, the civil rights movement of the 1950s and 1960s localized that struggle in the rural South. So it was that Zu-Bolton could quite readily envision founding an important literary magazine in his hometown, DeRidder, Louisiana, a nondescript, rural Southern town—comprised of a piece of highway, a railroad track with a few factories, a feed store—rather than in a large urban center. Certainly the feasibility of such a project was encouraged by the hearty acceptance of black arts movement ideas on college campuses (the Southern Black Cultural Alliance based at Tougaloo College in Mississippi, *Roots* magazine at Texas Southern University) and significant responses from inner city cultural groups in Houston (Black Arts Center, Urban Theater, and Thomas Meloncon's Sudan Arts/Southwest), New Orleans (BLKARTSOUTH, John O'Neal's Free Southern Theatre), and elsewhere in the region.

In some ways, perhaps, *HooDoo* went against the grain of traditional literary magazines more than its editors might have intended. While many of the contributors were not local (though the magazine's nucleus was Zu-Bolton's Witchdoctor Theater featuring Russell and Carolyn Chew), *HooDoo* served to carry the message of black arts poetry to a grassroots audience the movement may not have previously reached. Zu-Bolton enterprisingly placed copies of his publication in local barbershops and liquor stores and happily noted enthusiastic responses from the public as well as from other poets.

Later, beginning in 1977, Zu-Bolton augmented the publication of the magazine by producing a series of HooDoo Festivals in New Orleans, Galveston, Austin, and Houston. The festivals featured writers and musicians performing their works at colleges, churches, and popular restaurants, and the performances were taped for radio broadcast. For several years Zu-Bolton also attempted to expand the audience for black literature by directing a regional book distribution company and, most recently, a bookstore in New Orleans. He also was coeditor (with Alan Austin and Etheridge Knight) of *Blackbox,* a poetry magazine issued on tape-recorded cassettes. He served as poet-in-residence in artists-in-the-schools programs in Virginia, Georgia, and Texas. From 1973 to 1976, he was associate director of the Afro-American Resource Center at Howard University. Zu-Bolton has also been honored with an editor's fellowship from the Coordinating Council of Literary Magazines and a creative writing fellowship from the National Endowment for the Arts.

Zu-Bolton's interest in literature began during his teens. The poet cites the influence of his father, who "taught me to be self-sufficient. Daddy thought that he could do anything." He was also influenced by "a mathematician named Lonnie Machen who taught me math in high school, introduced me to certain books, and played chess with me. I got interested in literature through him by reading and discussing books such as *The Fountainhead* by Ayn Rand and Richard Wright's *Native Son.*"

In some ways, Zu-Bolton's poetry draws on the early influences of his mentors and depends upon his ability to recognize important aspects of human character. His poems are often portraits of people known in DeRidder, a cast of characters that includes Blackjack Moses, Sister Blues, "the governor of Ollie Street," and Livewire Davis, a basketball scholar who looks forward to a sensational professional sports career. The poet sketches Livewire with deft economy:

except for the terrible puzzle of books
he was free

Zu-Bolton's early poems are full of such fine touches. A work entitled "The Crown" comments upon a black Vietnam veteran, a recipient of the Medal of Honor, who is shot to death in a holdup while on leave from the mental hospital:

& you wore your crown with pride i hear,
back to the dark side you brought your spoils,
wearing it like a ph.d.
from a northern white school

But this man's life and honors become a cruel joke:

(and perhaps the man in washington
didnot realize
that he had placed the crown
lopsided on your head,
then again
perhaps he did realize,
& perhaps bro
you didn't.

"Homeless," a fine lyric written in California in 1972 when Zu-Bolton coedited a little magazine called *The Last Cookie* (with Jack Schifflett and David Arnold), is a spiritual from a liberated generation, a "sorrow song" from one who has experienced the lopsided benefits of racial integration:

i am a stranger
in this new year, i rub
the psychedelic hangover
from my eyes, i rise
a foreigner in an old place,
an alien in a new time

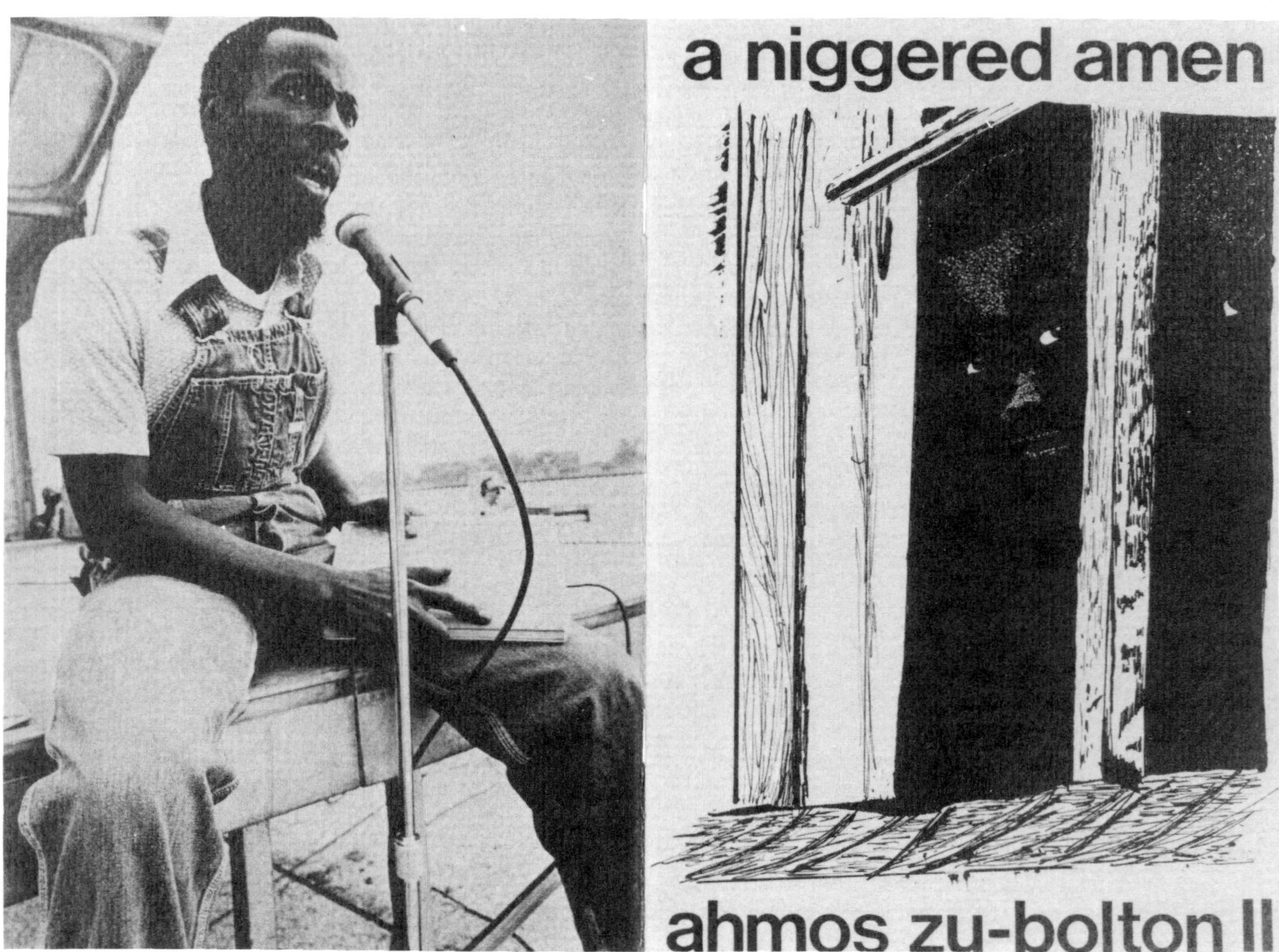

Covers for Zu-Bolton's 1975 collection of poems, intended to be the first book of his darktrilogy

The poem ends on a tone of melancholy resignation:

i linger here
for the mountains, the waves,
& the shadows only,

this tribe ain't mine

A poem like "Homeless" expresses the frightening dilemma faced by most black people concerning the question of integration. Thirty years after the Supreme Court decision that opened the way to desegregation of education, housing, and the workplace, it is not easily recalled that there was a party of cynical black men who saw Jackie Robinson's acceptance by Branch Rickey's Brooklyn Dodgers as the death of the Negro professional baseball leagues, school integration as the means to demote black educators, and the lowering of the color bar at nationwide chain hotels and restaurants as the final destruction of local black businesses that catered to the black community.

The cynics, of course, were both correct and extreme in their assessment. Many of Zu-Bolton's poems express the feeling of confronting such crucial contradictions.

Zu-Bolton approaches the question with several techniques. "Taxicab Blues" is typical of his effectively communicative dramatic monologues which turn on the problem of overrated European cultural values opposed to a finely honed appreciation of Afro-American "mother wit." In the poem, a white cabbie tells the speaker "ain't never been no/great/colored/poets." The speaker responds:

and i think to myself:
man this cat is hip/smooth,
there's truth in his meter,
so i sez to him i say, hey man
how come a professor like you is
driving a cab?

The line break in the last two lines shows Zu-Bolton's clever manipulation of "proper" grammatical structure to create black English: it is not "a professor like you," but "a professor like you is," and "driving," by itself, becomes the verb. Later in the poem, the speaker (abandoning academicians down on their luck) prefers to cast his lot with young, unemployed black men on the street, those with "eyes educated by the tales of restless/ancestors."

"Ain't No Spring Chicken" and "A Galveston Rock of Ages" present other aspects of Zu-Bolton's individualistic diction. In his gallery of portraits modeled on people of DeRidder and the inner cities, the poet has chosen to carefully explore the natural, and often brilliant imagery in everyday black speech, while adapting and recasting traditional poetic formulas found in Afro-American folklore and liturgy. "Ain't No Spring Chicken" blends the oral tradition form of a boast with a science fiction sense of an endless time continuum. The singer, who claims to be "as old as sin," tells us:

I used to turn my eyes inside-out
and cure a headache,
in a time before color 3D TV
in a time before footprints on the moon
in a time before the wheel
. . . .
Even then there was more to the world
than meets the eye

Loosely inspired by oral history interviews Zu-Bolton and poet Harryette Mullen conducted with senior citizens in the late 1970s, "A Galveston Rock of Ages" describes one of the venerable ancestral figures so often celebrated in Zu-Bolton's work:

longball george, texas leaguer,
known from el paso to lampasas,
known for the big grin and the open heart,
known from prairie view to deridder,
from dugout to press box

longball who said:

"if i can't hit it out of the park
i won't hit it"

longball who said:

"i live
in the second game
of a rained-out doubleheader"

Again, it is Ahmos Zu-Bolton's wonderfully evocative economy that captures the reader's attention and illumines both the meaning and the moment of a character's life. This effect is as much a result of the poet's own gregarious curiosity and personal insight into human nature, as of his mastery of technique.

Ahmos Zu-Bolton's deceptively simple (or surrealistically complex) poetry and his untiring advocacy of Afro-American folklore and culture have enlivened the American literary scene for more than a decade. If limited edition volumes of his own works such as *A Niggered Amen* (1975) and "Stumbling Thru: earthpoems" (collected in 1977) have not reached a wide audience, his editorship of seven numbers of *HooDoo* magazine and numerous other small press projects has made an impact on writers who enjoy much greater circulation. A man of unique experience, Zu-Bolton expressed his agenda for literature in an introductory essay to the anthology *Synergy*, coedited with poet E. Ethelbert Miller. "For me," wrote Ahmos Zu-Bolton, "*Synergy* has come to mean the bringing together of many energies. When I say energies, I also mean experiences. Experiences which generate poetry from our people."

Ahmos Zu-Bolton II, in his concern for the energies and life experiences of others, is generous. In his reluctance to publish his own poems more widely Zu-Bolton might be stinting on the pleasure and recovered insight of future readers. His work to date, however, is important and deserves much more critical attention.

Reference:

Lorenzo Thomas, "A Change Is Gonna Come: Black Voices of Louisiana," *New Black Writing, Nimrod*, 21/22 (double issue 1977): 262-283.

Contributors

June M. Aldridge .... *Spelman College*
Enid Bogle .... *Howard University*
Ruth L. Brittin .... *Auburn University*
Fahamisha Patricia Brown .... *Boston College*
Mary Williams Burger .... *Tennessee State University*
Norris B. Clark .... *Colgate University*
Terry Joseph Cole .... *Fiorello H. LaGuardia Community College*
Edwin L. Coleman II .... *University of Oregon*
Horace Coleman .... *Wilberforce University*
Robert A. Coles .... *Fordham University*
Marilyn B. Craig .... *Southern University*
James Cunningham .... *Daytona Beach Community College*
Jean Davis .... *Wayne State University*
Tom Dent .... *New Orleans, Louisiana*
Mary Jane Dickerson .... *University of Vermont*
David F. Dorsey, Jr. .... *Atlanta University*
Joanne V. Gabbin .... *Lincoln University*
Michael Greene .... *North Carolina A & T State University*
Norman Harris .... *Wayne State University*
Lucy K. Hayden .... *Winston-Salem State University*
Ronald Henry High .... *Chicago, Illinois*
Lillie P. Howard .... *Wright State University*
Catherine Daniels Hurst .... *University of South Carolina*
Pamela Masingale Lewis .... *Ohio State University*
Shirley Lumpkin .... *Marshall University*
Irma McClaurin-Allen .... *University of Massachusetts, Amherst*
Nellie McKay .... *University of Wisconsin-Madison*
R. Baxter Miller .... *University of Tennessee*
Carolyn A. Mitchell .... *University of Santa Clara*
Mozella G. Mitchell .... *University of South Florida*
Wallace R. Peppers .... *University of North Carolina at Chapel Hill*
Joyce Pettis .... *East Carolina University*
Priscilla R. Ramsey .... *Howard University*
Phillip M. Richard .... *Arkansas State University*
Evelyn Hoard Roberts .... *St. Louis Community College at Meramec*
Kalamu ya Salaam .... *New Orleans, Louisiana*
Linda E. Scott .... *Washington, D.C.*
D. L. Smith .... *Williams College*
Winifred L. Stoelting .... *North Carolina Central University*
Carmen Subryan .... *Howard University*
Lorenzo Thomas .... *University of Houston/Downtown College*
Edward T. Washington .... *Boston University*
Douglas Watson .... *Oklahoma Baptist University*
Rhonda V. Wilcox .... *DeKalb Community College*
Clara R. Williams .... *Mercer University*
Jon Woodson .... *University of Rhode Island*